Citizenship Today

International Migration Publications from the Carnegie Endowment for International Peace

From Migrants to Citizens: Membership in a Changing World (2000)
T. Alexander Aleinikoff and Douglas Klusmeyer, Editors

Monograph Series

Reinventing Japan: Immigration's Role in Shaping Japan's Future (2000)
Demetrios G. Papademetriou, Kimberly A. Hamilton

Balancing Acts: Toward a Fair Bargain on Seasonal Agricultural Workers (1999)
Demetrios G. Papademetriou, Monica L. Heppel

Between Principles and Politics: The Direction of U.S. Citizenship Policy (1998)
T. Alexander Aleinikoff

Reorganizing the Immigration Function: Toward a New Framework for Accountability (1998)
Demetrios G. Papademetriou, T. Alexander Aleinikoff, Deborah Waller Meyers

Between Consent & Descent: Conceptions of Democratic Citizenship (1996)
Douglas B. Klusmeyer

Coming Together or Pulling Apart? The European Union's Struggle with Immigration and Asylum (1996)
Demetrios G. Papademetriou

Balancing Interests: Rethinking the U.S. Selection of Skilled Immigrants (1996)
Demetrios G. Papademetriou, Stephen Yale-Loehr

Converging Paths to Restriction: French, Italian, and British Responses to Immigration (1995)
Demetrios G. Papademetriou, Kimberly A. Hamilton

U.S. Refugee Policy: Dilemmas and Directions (1995)
Kathleen Newland

Managing Uncertainty: Regulating Immigration Flows in Advanced Industrial Countries (1995)
Demetrios G. Papademetriou, Kimberly A. Hamilton

Citizenship Today

Global Perspectives and Practices

T. Alexander Aleinikoff
Douglas Klusmeyer
Editors

CARNEGIE ENDOWMENT FOR INTERNATIONAL PEACE
Washington, D.C.

Citizenship Today: Global Perspectives and Practices
may be ordered from the Carnegie Endowment's distributor:
Brookings Institution Press
1775 Massachusetts Avenue, N.W.
Washington, D.C. 20036
Tel. 1-800/275-1447 or 202/797-6258
Fax: 202/797-6004
www.brookings.edu

Library of Congress Cataloging-in-Publication data

Citizenship today: global perspectives and practices / T. Alexander Aleinikoff,
    Douglas Klusmeyer, editors.
        p.   cm.
Includes bibliographical references and index.
    ISBN 0-87003-184-8 (pbk.: alk. paper)
    1. Citizenship. 2. Citizenship (International law). I. Aleinikoff, Thomas
Alexander, 1952– II. Klusmeyer, Douglas B., 1957– III. Carnegie Endowment
for International Peace.
K3224.C568 2000
342'.083—dc21   00-012778

9 8 7 6 5 4 3 2 1

The paper used in this publication meets minimum requirements of the American National
Standard for Information Sciences—Permanence of Paper for Printed Library Materials:
ANSI Z39.48-1984.

Typeset in Times Roman

Composition by AlphaWebTech
Mechanicsville, Maryland

Printed by R. R. Donnelley and Sons
Harrisonburg, Virginia

Contents

Foreword vii
    Jessica T. Mathews

Acknowledgments ix

Abbreviations and Acronyms x

Introduction 1
    Douglas Klusmeyer

Part One. National Policies in Comparative Perspective

1.   Access to Citizenship: A Comparison of Twenty-Five
    Nationality Laws 17
    Patrick Weil

2.   The Evolution of Alien Rights in the United States,
    Germany, and the European Union 36
    Christian Joppke

3.   Plural Nationality: Facing the Future in a Migratory World 63
    T. Alexander Aleinikoff and Douglas Klusmeyer

4.   Relational Nationality: On Gender and Nationality in
    International Law 89
    Karen Knop

Part Two. Locations of Citizenship

5.   Citizenship and Federalism............................... 127
     Vicki C. Jackson

6.   Ethnic Marginalization as Statelessness: Lessons from
     the Great Lakes Region of Africa.......................... 183
     Francis M. Deng

7.   City-States and Citizenship.............................. 209
     Richard T. Ford

Part Three. Redefining Citizenship: Concepts and Practices

8.   Denationalizing Citizenship 237
     Linda Bosniak

9.   The Emergence of Transnational Citizenship among Mexican
     Immigrants in California................................. 253
     Paul Johnston

10. Immigrant and Minority Representations of Citizenship
     in Quebec 278
     Micheline Labelle and Daniel Salée

Part Four. Concluding Reflections

11. Cultural Citizenship, Minority Rights, and Self-Government 319
     Rainer Bauböck

12   Integration Policy and Integration Research in Europe:
     A Review and Critique 349
     Adrian Favell

About the Authors 401

Index... 405

Carnegie Endowment for International Peace 411

Foreword

CITIZENSHIP IS COMMONLY understood as membership in a nation-state. If nation-states today find themselves under pressure from the cross-cutting forces of globalization and devolution, is citizenship becoming an out-dated concept? Hardly. Interest in the practice and promise of citizenship is strong and growing—perhaps because citizenship is seen as providing a status and a tradition that can unite members of a polity under challenge from above and below. Citizenship also fosters a form of social cooperation and identification that, in most developed states, avoids the divisiveness of racial, religious, and ethnic affiliations.

Citizenship is taking on added significance because of another worldwide phenomenon: the mass movement of people. Virtually all developed states today are multicultural and multiracial, and much of this diversity is the product of migration. In most states migrants were initially welcomed as temporary workers. But many chose to remain, family members joined them, and new—frequently large—communities were formed. The integration of these immigrant communities now presents significant domestic and foreign policy issues for both receiving and sending states.

The essays collected in this volume are directed at aiding policy making on these issues in two ways. First, several of the essays provide a comparative perspective on citizenship policy in developed states—considering issues such as acquisition of citizenship, naturalization policy, dual nationality, and the political and social rights of immigrants. Second, the essays seek to describe and analyze larger themes that influence citizenship debates. These include concepts of federalism, integration, gender equality, and immigrant political mobilization.

This collection is the second published by the Comparative Citizenship Project of the Endowment's International Migration Policy Program. The first, *Migrants to Citizens: Membership in a Changing World* (2000), examined the citizenship law and policy of eleven states and the European Union and provided a rich source of information for the comparative and contextual work of the present volume. In a final publication, the Project will propose specific recommendations on citizenship policy. Together these three volumes will provide the background, conceptualization, and analysis necessary for a full and informed discussion of citizenship.

We thank the Ford Foundation and the Luso-American Development Foundation for their generous support of this work.

JESSICA T. MATHEWS
President
Carnegie Endowment for
International Peace

Acknowledgments

THE INTERNATIONAL MIGRATION POLICY PROGRAM originally commissioned the essays collected here for a conference held June 1999 in Lisbon, Portugal, as part of a larger three-year study of citizenship policies in advanced industrial democracies. Unless otherwise noted, the authors have translated extracts from their original languages into English. As we prepared this volume, Ana K. Carrión and Jennifer McElhinny provided valuable research assistance. We would also like to express our appreciation to Yasmin Santiago and Paula Vicente, who coordinated planning for the conference and have contributed considerably to the overall success of the project. Completion of the work has owed much to Sherry Pettie, who carefully supervised all preparations for publication, and Lorraine Alexson, who skillfully copy edited the entire manuscript. Jon Michael Thompson performed the indispensable task of preparing the volume's index. Finally, we are pleased to acknowledge our debt to the Ford Foundation for its generous support of this project from its inception, and to the Fundação Luso-Americana para o Desenvolvimento for hosting the conference and supporting this volume's publication.

Abbreviations and Acronyms

CEDAW	Committee on the Elimination of Discrimination against Women
CEPIC	Centre d'Étude des Politiques de'Immigration, de l'Intégration, et de la Citoyenneté
CIS	Commonwealth of Independent States
CRE	Commission for Racial Equalty
CRER	Centre for Research in Ethnic Relations
CRISP	Centre de Recherche et d'Information Socio-Politiques
ECJ	European Court of Justice
ECOSOC	Economic and Social Council (UN)
ECOWAS	Economic Community of West African States
ECT	European Community Treaty
EEC	European Economic Community
ERCOMER	European Research Centre on Migration and Ethnic Relations
ERISA	Employee Retirement Income Security Act
ESRC	Economic and Social Research Council (U.K.)
ETS	European Treaty Series
EU	European Union
GATT	General Agreement on Tariffs and Trade
HCI	Haut Conseil à l'Intégration
IGAD	Inter-Governmental Authority for Development
ILA	International Law Association
ILO	International Labour Organization

ILC	International Law Commission
IMF	International Monetary Fund
INED	Institut National d'Études Démographiques
INS	Immigration and Naturalization Service
IO	international organization
INSEE	Institut National de la Statistique et des Études Economique
IRCA	Immigration Reform and Control Act
IRIN	Integrated Regional Information Network (UN)
LPR	legal permanent resident
NGO	nongovernmental organization
MOST	Management of Social Transformations (UNESCO program)
MPG	Migration Policy Group
NAFTA	North American Free Trade Agreement
NRA	National Resistance Army (Uganda)
OECD	Organization for Economic Cooperation and Development
OSCE	Organization for Security and Cooperation in Europe
PRC	People's Republic of China
PRI	Policy Research Initiative
PSI	Policy Studies Institute (U.K.)
QUANGO	quasi autonomous nongovernmental organization
RPF	Rwandan Patriotic Front
RSFSR	Russian Soviet Federative Socialist Republic
SADC	Southern Africa Development Community
SOPEMI	Système d'Observation Permanente des Migrations (OECD)
TEU	Treaty of European Union
TSER	Targeted Social Economic Research
UFW	United Farm Workers
USSR	Union of Soviet Socialist Republics
UNTS	United Nations Treaty Series

Introduction

DOUGLAS KLUSMEYER

CITIZENSHIP HAS EMERGED as a major thematic link connecting policy domains that range from welfare, education, and labor markets to international relations and migration. Citizenship provides this link because it brings within its orbit three fundamental issues: how the boundaries of membership within a polity and between polities should be defined; how the benefits and burdens of membership should be allocated; and how the identities of members should be comprehended and accommodated. As a simple matter of law, citizenship, or nationality, is the primary category by which peoples are classified and distributed in polities across the globe. In political theory, citizenship, understood as active participation in governing, has been the benchmark of models of democracy since Aristotle. Over the past several decades, the sheer mass of the academic literature on citizenship each year attests not only to the breadth of scholarly interest in it, but also to the extent that citizenship themes have become interwoven across academic disciplines. Finally, the continuing rise of new forms of identity politics has challenged traditional understandings of belonging and membership and has contributed to rethinking the meaning of citizenship.

Although citizenship has traditionally been conceived as primarily a domestic concern of states, the reality of immigration and emigration, the formation

The author is grateful to T. Alexander Aleinikoff and Dilek Çinar for the benefit of their comments on an earlier draft of this introduction.

of such supranational bodies as the European Union (EU), the formation of new successor states, the movement of refugee populations, and the codification of international human rights norms has prompted increasing recognition of citizenship as a transnational matter. The growing incidence of plural nationality exemplifies the transnational dimension of citizenship not only as an object of policy but also increasingly as a source and marker of social identity. The paradox in this growing incidence is that it has arisen through the interaction of citizenship rules that states, acting independently as sovereign agents, have adopted, but whose effects reach into the domestic jurisdictions of other states and invest individuals with binding affiliations to two or more states. This paradox is compounded for liberal-democratic states because their normative self-understandings are grounded in affirmations of the universal rights of individuals as human beings and the practical reality that these rights are most effectively exercised by the citizens of particular states.

This volume is the second of three that the International Migration Policy Program of the Carnegie Endowment is publishing as part of its comparative citizenship project.[1] This project has been designed to investigate citizenship policies in advanced industrial liberal-democracies. The International Migration Policy Program commissioned the articles in the first two volumes to provide background material in developing policy recommendations that address central issues of citizenship policy. Those proposals will be published in the third volume.

The current volume presents articles on citizenship from different comparative perspectives and is organized in four parts. Part one examines the leading trends in national citizenship policy regarding the rules that govern access to citizenship, the rights of aliens, and plural nationality. In investigating these national policies, citizenship is approached largely as a bundle of rights and duties. Part two expands this approach to explore how forms of citizenship and their practice are, can, and should be located within broader institutional structures. These structures range in scale and type from supranational bodies like the European Union and federal polities like the United States to "global cities." These structures create multiple levels of citizenship both within nation-states and beyond them.

Part three builds on these themes to examine various conceptions of citizenship as developed in the official policies of government bodies, the scholarly

---

1. The first volume provided a series of case studies on citizenship policy in Australia, the Baltic States, Canada, the European Union, Israel, Japan, Mexico, the Russian Federation, South Africa, and the United States (Aleinikoff and Klusmeyer, 2000). As a preliminary step in the project, see also Klusmeyer (1996).

literature of the academy, and the understandings of immigrants. These different conceptions indicate not only how our understanding of citizenship is being expanded and revised, but also the concrete stakes involved in struggles over definitions. Part four addresses normative-political questions of citizenship policy and research. It challenges traditional concepts of integration that have framed much of this policy and research as a means of charting new directions for both.

Part One

That anyone has found credible a fanciful world organized into a collection of independent, self-enclosed political units that exercise complete jurisdiction over a sovereign territory is a testament to the power of state image making.[2] The citizenship rules of states inevitably reflect a far more complex and entangled reality, where the historical, cultural, social, and political bonds that define relations between persons and groups cross the formal borders of states and also intersect within them. States experiencing high levels of emigration, for example, have routinely exercised the right to preserve membership links with their departed nationals long after they have become the permanent residents, if not citizens, of other states. They have even maintained such links with the descendants of those residents and citizens. Thus, the movement of persons and groups across borders connects states in a global migration system. States interact in this system as both conduits and (often contentious) partners who must manage with interpenetrating, multilayered spheres of membership.

In his contribution to this volume, Patrick Weil emphasizes the importance of congruence between the definition of a state's people and their residence within its territorial boundaries in understanding differences between the acquisition rules for citizenship of various states. His survey of twenty-five state nationality laws shows that, despite often markedly different national legal traditions, a remarkable trend toward convergence is now evident among advanced industrial, liberal-democratic states around a relatively permissive combination of birthright (jus soli) and descent-based (jus sanguinis) citizenship acquisition rules.

He identifies three main factors that have encouraged states toward this convergence in their citizenship policies: (1) the influence of democratic values,

---

2. Thus, e.g., a leading liberal political theorist like John Rawls (1993, 12) displays no hesitation in proceeding from the postulate of a wholly bounded polity: "I assume that the basic structure is that of a closed society; that is, we are to regard it as self-contained and as having no relations with other societies. Its members enter it only by birth and leave it only by death."

(2) the stabilization of borders, and (3) a shared experience with immigration. The perpetuation of a separate subclass of aliens over generations has been recognized as incompatible with modern democratic norms and potentially dangerous to the social cohesion of states. A commitment to democratic values has forced states with restrictive acquisition rules to modify them in order to facilitate (particularly) the integration of second- and third-generation immigrants. The stabilization of borders has reduced the "disconnection" between the unitary aspirations of peoples and their division by territory, as in the case of Germany. Those states that have allowed relatively open access to residence by newcomers have moved to restrict their citizenship rules, as has the United Kingdom. Likewise, states with highly restrictive rules, such as Germany, have had to liberalize them.

In highlighting these three factors, Weil seeks to rebut arguments that attribute differences between the regimes of citizenship acquisition rules of states to expressions of particular national characters. Such arguments, as put forward in Rogers Brubaker's (1992) influential study of modern French and German citizenship laws, have sought to draw out correspondences between features in a state's national self-understanding and the level of restrictiveness and principles of acquisition in its citizenship policies. Instead of relying on the notoriously amorphous category of national character to explain differences in policy regimes, Weil pinpoints three concrete variables whose interplay as general causal factors may be tested and refined through further comparative research.

Complementing Weil's approach, Christian Joppke also challenges the explanatory significance of national character through his examination of policies on the rights of aliens in Germany, the European Union, and the United States. Like Weil with respect to citizenship acquisition rules, Joppke discerns an underlying trend toward convergence around stronger guarantees of the rights of aliens irrespective of fundamental differences in the officially pronounced national self-conception of the United States as an immigration country and Germany as a "nonimmigration country." Joppke attributes this convergence to the role that the judiciary has played since the end of World War II as the guardian of minority rights in liberal-democratic states but emphasizes the sensitivity of courts to active controversies between public opinion and resolute policy stances by other branches of government. Courts have acted most boldly in securing or expanding the rights of aliens when their decisions have been least subject to close scrutiny or to anticipated opposition.

Joppke's analysis of the judiciary's role in advancing the trend toward broader guarantees of the rights of aliens emphasizes the importance of domestic constitutions rather than international instruments of human rights as the foundation for this trend. He contends that the courts have relied almost exclusively on the authority and rights provisions of domestic constitutions to justify their work. He directs this thesis against postnational scholars, such as Yasemin Soysal, who have argued that the development of international human rights instruments that guarantee the rights of "person(s)" is gradually displacing the importance of national citizenship that protects the rights of individuals by virtue of their state nationality. Joppke points out that Soysal and other postnational scholars have been too quick to read tangible results from the symbolic promise of these instruments and have not been sufficiently attentive to the institutional contexts that the effective enforcement of rights require.

Just as Weil and Joppke have found an international trend toward the convergence around the rules governing the acquisition of citizenship and the rights of aliens, Aleinikoff and Klusmeyer observe that an increasing number of states are relaxing their formal opposition to plural nationality and are supporting more permissive attitudes. Such supranational bodies as the Council of Europe and the European Parliament have also endorsed this more permissive policy stance. Aleinikoff and Klusmeyer review many of the traditional policy objections to plural nationality and argue that these objections are based more on conjecture than on actual, demonstrable evidence. Indeed, it is striking how little empirical documentation opponents of plural nationality (as a formal legal status) have offered to support their concerns over the threats they see it posing to the security and social cohesion of states or to the stability of international order.

The core objection to plural nationality has always turned on the issue of *divided loyalties* that this status may imply, but discussing this status has almost always involved imputing meanings to it that may or may not be held by its bearers or may be held by them incidental to this status. (This is one of those empirical questions that are routinely passed over in the debate.) Although it is not difficult, for example, to imagine that a nationality group residing in one state and feeling strong loyalties toward another could well create a highly destabilizing situation, it is quite another to ascribe this threat to the formal legal status of that minority and rather naive to assume that this status is itself the source of the tension. Moreover, whatever policy purposes are served by reducing the incidence of plural nationality may be outweighed by other important policy considerations, such as upholding the norms of gender equality. In fact, the rising incidence of plural nationality is (in part) attributable to the fact that an increasing number of states have modified their citizenship rules to reflect those norms. In light of this rising incidence, Aleinikoff and Klusmeyer conclude that states should concentrate their efforts not on reducing it, but on effectively managing it so as to minimize potentially disruptive effects.

In her contribution, Karen Knop examines plural nationality from the standpoint of gender equality. Focusing on developments in international legal conventions, she traces a two-stage process by which demands of equality have been articulated and accommodated. In the first stage, the main issue concerns establishing the right of married women to an independent nationality that is not automatically forfeited upon marriage to a foreigner and that can be retained separately over the life of the marriage. In the second stage, broader challenges of inequality facing married women have been addressed, most notably inequalities involving the right of mothers to pass their nationality to their children. Knop's analysis demonstrates clear progress in reducing the more blatant forms of discrimination that married women have encountered historically, but she also emphasizes throughout her discussion the abundant work that remains to be done in these areas.

Although this work continues, Knop sees a third stage emerging, in which the issues of gender equality will and should be approached from a more "relational," rather than individualistic, perspective. Such an approach recognizes that persons define their identities through their closest relationships with others and not as atomistic selves in abstraction from the everyday, concrete realities of their lives. One of the most fundamental relational contexts for individuals is as members of families, and the value of family unity needs now to be reintroduced, Knop argues, into a consideration of issues of gender equality. In families of plural nationals, she observes, individuals often suffer significant disadvantages or restrictions by virtue of their different nationalities, and this harm can have serious consequences for their families as a collective unit. When restrictions on a foreign national's access to the labor market impair a spouse's earning power, the effect may be felt by all family members. Gender equality requires that spouses enjoy full and equal rights to their own nationality. The interest of family unity argues for minimizing the discriminatory effects of differences in nationality among family members. Taken together, these considerations support a broadly tolerant policy toward plural nationality or citizenship.

Part Two

The European Union's recent formal recognition of a "European citizenship" that supplements the national citizenships of its member states illustrates not only the importance often attached to citizenship, at least as a symbolic marker of a polity's collective identity, but also how distinct forms of citizenship may coexist, denoting the membership affiliation of different types and reflecting different levels on which the forms are practiced. In the EU, European and national citizenships constitute two of these possible levels because some EU member states, such as Germany, are themselves federal bodies comprising subordinate member states. Relations between various levels are often highly dynamic as lines of authority are redefined, competition between interest groups gravitates, and jurisdictional spheres of influence are contested. The allocation of power and resources across levels can offer a flexible means by which social, political, and cultural differences may be mediated and accommodated. They can also serve to frustrate the implementation of resolute policy, reinforce divisions between contending interests, and create barriers to cooperation.

Vicki Jackson analyzes these potential strengths and weaknesses by examining how levels of citizenship are formally arranged in different models of federalism. Drawing upon a rich array of concrete examples from Europe and North America, Jackson carefully delineates the structural characteristics of different models as they bear on citizenship. She identifies three main types: (1) where the national government determines national citizenship policy and subnational governments determine the subnational policy, (2) where the national government exercises exclusive authority to make all citizenship policy, and (3) where the subnational governments hold this authority. She does not argue from normative or theoretical grounds that one of these models is preferable, but rather emphasizes the importance of particular contexts in assessing a model's suitability and of empirical criteria in measuring its success.

The principal common element of any successful model appears to be a provision for clear "rule(s) of priority" that facilitate dispute resolution between levels of government. In their structural dispersal of authority, federal systems, she observes, create multiple sites of conflict that can become intractable without an established hierarchy of rules binding on all parties. Where such rules of priority have been developed, she argues, federal models offer promising examples of how various claims and entitlements arising from multiple citizenships can be managed. The coexistence of forms of citizenship can give particular classes of individuals decided advantages in terms of available rights and benefits. Such differences may offend the fundamental norms of equality that liberal-democratic citizenship is designed to promote. Nevertheless, Jackson concludes that these differences have proved manageable when contained within a general framework that upholds norms of equality.

If multiple forms of citizenship can be a source of tension and division within a polity, the absence of effective citizenship can have still graver consequences. In his chapter, Francis Deng demonstrates the importance of citizenship as an institution by showing the consequences that occur when the formal guarantees of protection and rights that citizenship claims are grossly ignored. His contribution focuses on the situation of the Banyarwanda, "a collective term for the people of Rwandan origin," in the Great Lakes region of central Africa. The chronic manipulation of citizenship rules by states in this region in favor of one ethnic group over others has deepened the marginalization of large numbers of persons and reduced many to a status of de facto statelessness in states where they hold legal nationality. The combined effects of exploitation and marginalization have at times escalated to genocide.

In exploring the roots of these conflicts, Deng emphasizes the difficulties that exclusive notions of tribal and ethnic identity pose in building a broadly inclusive sense of collective nationhood. A democratic model of citizenship, he argues, can offer an important basis for promoting this progressive sense of nationhood by relying on universal membership criteria, such as common territorial residence, which can be defined independently of tribal and ethnic affiliations. He cautions that in practice such models have always displayed their own, strongly exclusionionary, dimensions.

Tensions between exclusivist notions of ethnic identity and inclusivist understandings of political nationhood are hardly unique to Africa, but the legacy of colonial rule has compounded the challenges there by imposing state borders with little account for existing tribal and ethnic boundaries of affiliation. These challenges, Deng observes, have intensified as states have repeatedly failed to manage effectively their diverse peoples through an equitable sharing of power and resources.

In searching for feasible solutions, Deng suggests looking beyond membership models conceived narrowly around the unit of the nation-state and toward developing broader, regionally based institutional structures, possibly (in the future) along federal or confederal lines. Emerging in response to a half century marked by war, genocide, and ethnic conflict, the EU, he observes, may offer an example of the constructive role that supranational institutional arrangements might play in regional solutions. It also illustrates the limitations of such arrangements.

Just as significant as considerations of regionally based supranational and federal models are to discussions of citizenship is the new attention to the role of large urban centers, what Richard Ford describes as global cities. In his chapter, Ford observes that the confluence of trends known under the rubric globalization has been accompanied by countertrends toward intensive localism and subnational fragmentation. The hallmark of the former has been the internationalization of a growing wcb of commercial, travel, knowledge, and communication links that have radically compressed distances in time and space. The hallmark of the latter has been the revival of local attachments as a source of identity understood in terms of ethnicity, language, religion, and history.

Both these trends come together directly to shape the dynamic of global cities, as these cities typically combine extensive international connections as central sites of global commerce with ethnically diverse local populations multiplied through immigration. Because of the increasing strength of their international links, these cities, Ford observes, can exercise important, strategic roles in influencing patterns of change extending far beyond their own geographical borders and in ways vastly disproportionate to their physical size. Because the scale of civic relations and institutions within cities are locally bounded, these cities can provide effective forums wherein diverse interests can meet to find common ground for cooperation while offering room to accommodate the practice of different forms of identity. These twin features, Ford argues, make global cities promising settings for the promotion of an active, inclusive politics of democratic citizenship situated locally but linked internationally. This form of urban citizenship will certainly not replace national citizenships but can supplement and be accommodated by it.

Part Three

No single definition can adequately capture the complex, multidimensional character of citizenship as a general legal status, unitary institution, or fixed, delimited sets of practices. The forms and meanings of citizenship vary broadly according to their context; their social, political, and cultural links; and the interests and identities of those engaged with them. The definition of citizenship is not simply an analytical or empirical matter; it is also a deeply normative and political matter. Any definition of citizenship always involves choosing between rival conceptual alternatives, each carrying its own particular merits and limitations. Struggles that contest the meaning and substance of citizenship are central to its history and essential to its continued relevance.

In this book Linda Bosniak examines the contested meanings of citizenship that inform recent debates over "postnational interpretations" of citizenship. Advocates of this view have challenged traditional assumptions that locate citizenship within the framework of the nation-state. They call attention to the emergence of increasingly nonnational forms and practices of citizenship that extend beyond the immediate institutional contexts of states. To assess the merits of these challenges, Bosniak tests the plausibility of the claims supporting them against different criteria for understanding citizenship. Using these criteria enables her to clarify the main issues of dispute in the debate over citizenship.

When conceived as primarily a legal status of affiliation with a political community, this form of citizenship, she observes, is most directly located in the context of the nation-state. If it is more broadly understood as the "enjoyment of rights," then citizenship has a more expansive context because these rights are grounded not solely on the nation-state, but also on regional and international systems of human rights. The transnational dimension of citizenship is even more strongly evident, she finds, when it is viewed as a form of political activity. From many perspectives, she points out, increasing numbers of individuals and groups are working together across state boundaries to advance particular causes they believe transcend the interests of particular states. When it is approached in psychological or cultural terms as a form of collective experience or a shared source of identity, the transnational dimension of citizenship, she contends, is most immediately apparent in the ways by which migrants and members of diaspora communities understand their relationships.

Drawing from his experience as a political organizer and scholar, Paul Johnston emphasizes in his chapter the transnational aspects of the Mexican immigrant struggle for citizenship in California. He shows how that struggle is inextricably linked to a longer struggle for labor rights, and how a broad span of rights—ranging from the right to permanent residence to the right to vote to the right to an education—becomes mutually interdependent in this struggle. The California labor market, he observes, is deeply embedded in a transnational migration system, and the struggle for labor rights shapes and is shaped by the structure of employer-employee relations in this market. Family ties across the California-Mexico border strengthen transnational links and significantly influence perceptions of identity and interest.

Johnston argues for a conception of citizenship that is understood as "participation in public institutions" of many types. Since its earliest strikes in the 1970s, the Mexican immigrant labor movement, he observes, has been expanding its access to various public institutions and has thereby changed the orientations of labor unions, school boards, political parties, and municipal, state, and federal agencies. It has created the conditions for new political coalitions and influenced the calculus of electoral politics. All the activities involved in this process, Johnston contends, are aptly described as practices of citizenship, and the immigrant labor movement is itself a form of citizenship movement.

In their chapter, Micheline Labelle and Daniel Salée highlight the gap between the official discourses on citizenship promoted by the Canadian and Quebec governments and the understandings of citizenship expressed by Montreal immigrants. The federal citizenship policy of Canada, Labelle and Salée observe, reflects a tension between a commitment to maintain multiculturalism that respects the diverse origins and identities of Canada's peoples and an increasing concern with promoting cohesion and a primary attachment to Canada. Quebec has developed its citizenship policy in the context of its effort to build a "distinct society" around the French language and heritage while recognizing the distinct identities of its minorities. In contrast to the ideals espoused in these official discourses, the Montreal immigrants interviewed by the authors approach citizenship with an instrumental attitude toward its value and with skepticism toward the terms of inclusion that have been offered.

This skepticism suggests the limitations that states may face in using citizenship as a tool of integration. The immigrants expressed wariness about official definitions of collective national identity and about top-down attempts to inculcate prescribed values and beliefs. Rather, they expressed a desire to define the terms of their belonging for themselves, fashioned from their own experiences and cultural understandings. They appear to view the coexistence of diverse loyalties and multidimensional identities as far less problematic than either the Canadian or the Quebec governments have. From the perspective of these immigrants, the greatest barriers to civic inclusion, Labelle and Salée conclude, are the perceived patterns of discrimination and differentiated modes of integration encountered in their everyday lives. Perhaps, as a means to encourage civic allegiance and a fuller sense of belonging, it would be more effective for states to focus policy efforts here rather than on formal loyalty requirements in their citizenship rules.

Part Four

One of the main reasons for current debates about citizenship is a growing concern over finding new frameworks for integration amid our increasingly ethnically and racially diverse societies. *Integration* is a highly problematic concept, which, like the term *citizenship,* connotes several meanings and values to those who use it. The concept of integration is ambiguous and amorphous. Such qualities invite us to project rather uncritically our own assumptions and preferences about social cohesion, political justice, national solidarity, cultural pluralism, and economic fairness. The concept of integration, then, often carries an entire set of (at least partially hidden) normative understandings and aspirations that are seldom clearly elucidated. We are prone to think that we are "for" integration without asking specifically what that advocacy entails.

When applied to the immigration context, the concept of integration has traditionally meant the assimilation of migrants into the social and cultural environments of their host states. In recent decades, expectations that assimilation should precede the recognition of citizenship have been increasingly contested and modified in official policies. As ideas about citizenship have expanded, focus has turned to cultural rights as a distinct entitlement of citizenship for both national minorities and ethnic groups newly immigrated. Rainer Bauböck points out in this volume that citizenship in liberal democracies has a universalist dimension that is inclusive and a particularist dimension that is often exclusionary. The former provides the basis for the incorporation of immigrants as equal citizens under the law. The latter refers to membership in a nation as a collective self-governing polity and is, as such, a primary source of exclusionary barriers to membership.

Bauböck argues that modern citizenship, as a bundle of civil, social, and political rights, needs to be supplemented by cultural minority rights. Concentrating here on the issue of the right to speak one's language, he argues that cultural rights should apply generally and include the freedom to use minority languages in both public and private for personal, commercial, political, and cultural purposes. In certain respects, he observes, the same grounds that have been invoked traditionally to defend the toleration of religious liberty apply in making a case for the toleration of different languages. Still, any attempt to draw an analogy between religious liberty and the liberty to speak one's native tongue must acknowledge the important practical difference that states cannot be neutral about language. A state must promote the use of one (or more) language(s) over others in order to conduct its internal affairs and to foster a common public culture. This promotion may place special burdens on minorities that are not adequately comprehended by similar rights designed to protect religious liberties.

To appreciate the character of these burdens, Bauböck contends that we need to understand that language not only operates as an instrument of communication, but also serves as a constituent feature of social identity and as a marker of political boundaries. Language often plays a "strategic" role in the assertion of claims to collective self-government, and Bauböck uses this political dimension of language to distinguish between the rights of national minorities to speak their native language and those of immigrant minorities. National minorities, he argues, are entitled to stronger protection of such freedom than are immigrant minorities, where the former have some claim to autonomous self-government on the basis of their historical incorporation into the polity.

In the final contribution to this book, Adrian Favell offers a broad critical review of the research on integration in Europe. He argues that, despite differences in approaches, the common assumption guiding this research has been to frame the problem of integration narrowly within the context of the nation-state model. This focus too readily accepts the categories and structures of state institutions as the organizational terms for understanding the challenges of ethnic and racial diversity. These terms obscure the complex, multilayered patterns of relations that characterize the migration experience, give it dynamics of its own within the nation-state, and extend in innumerable directions outside this context. These terms presuppose a simplistic dichotomy between "state" and "society" that reduces the interaction of groups and persons in society to one-dimensional objects of policy management by state administrative agencies.

The guiding assumption of this research strongly reflects, Favell contends, the material conditions that have shaped its production and most especially the state sponsorship of academic work on issues that governments find useful for their purposes. Academic scholars have been attracted by the combined lures of generous financial support and the (often illusionary) expectation of influence in policy making. Although much of the work produced under these circumstances has been of high quality, policy intellectuals have failed to appreciate how much state-approved research agendas influence the types of questions posed, the methods used in gathering data, and the results obtained.

In the process, the criteria by which "integration" is measured have become imprinted by the norms of the state's bureaucratic management perspective. Rather than challenge this perspective by investigating how the bureaucratic apparatus of the state itself is implicated in the systematic causes of inequality, modes of racial and ethnic exploitation, and social marginalization, policy intellectuals have focused on devising reforms within the established political-legal framework of the state. This focus is most directly evident in their choice of citizenship policy as the primary object of their research.

In fashioning this critique, Favell aims not only to contest the dominant paradigm shaping integration research, but also to open new lines of inquiry for conducting comparative studies that might be both more sensitive to concrete differences of particular contexts and less state-centered in approach. He proposes a set of guiding elements for future research that uses the city as the common unit of comparison. This unit, Favell concludes, offers an excellent vantage point from which to view the interaction of local, national, and transnational influences on the challenges of integration in our increasingly diverse societies.

The chapters in this volume amply demonstrate the value of comparative perspectives in the consideration of citizenship policy. Comparisons across states offer a kind of laboratory for testing the causal significance of particular variables and for identifying broader patterns. Comparisons across different locations of membership provide a basis for analyzing the myriad ways by which citizenship is exercised and structured. Comparisons of definitions or forms of citizenship help to clarify normative and political issues in the formulation of policy.

Like *alien, citizen* is one of the primary categories by which states define membership. States attach important rights and duties to such formal categories, so their definition has both practical and material significance. Struggles over the definition of citizenship, then, are not mere semantical or rhetorical games, but rather, as Bosniak argues, they involve serious questions about the allocation of status, power, and resources in a society.

The attribution of formal citizenship has always been as much an act of exclusion as of inclusion. In both theory and practice, the history of citizenship demonstrates how narrow and contingent those criteria have been and that those criteria are constantly subject to challenge, revision, and compromise. Citizenship, then, is a powerful instrument of selection that allocates finite membership in particular polities across a universe of persons and peoples.

Even when understood as solely a formal category of law, citizenship can also be a potent source and marker of social identity. States do not readily comprehend individuals and groups as human beings, but rather recognize them by their status within such categories. As Hannah Arendt observed,[3] the Nazis were able to rob the Jews of their perceived common humanity under the Third Reich by first stripping them of their legal status as citizens, thereby effectively rendering them "nonpersons" in the eyes of their "German" neighbors, and, in the view of other states, outside the protection of law.

This book brings together a collection of articles from a rich variety of comparative perspectives. The collection is designed to provide a foundation for developing new answers to difficult policy questions involving citizenship. Such questions, as well as any answers to them, must by nature have a provisional character, but the authors in this volume show how far we have come over the past two decades in improving our ability to do both.

Works Cited

Aleinikoff, T. Alexander, and Douglas Klusmeyer (eds.). 2000. *From Migrants to Citizens: Membership in a Changing World*. Washington, D.C.: Carnegie Endowment for International Peace.

Brubaker, Rogers. 1992. *Citizenship and Nationhood in France and Germany*. Cambridge: Harvard University Press.

Klusmeyer, Douglas. 1996. *Between Consent and Descent: Conceptions of Democratic Citizenship*. Washington, D.C.: Carnegie Endowment for International Peace.

Rawls, John. 1993. *Political Liberalism*. New York: Columbia University Press.

Soysal, Yasemin N. 1994. *Limits of Citizenship: Migrants and Postnational Membershipin Europe*. Chicago: University of Chicago Press.

3. See discussion in Klusmeyer (1996), 69–76.

PART ONE

National Policies in
Comparative Perspective

Access to Citizenship: A Comparison of Twenty-Five Nationality Laws

PATRICK WEIL

NATIONALITY RESTS with territory at the heart of the definition of *nation-state*. If territory determines the geographical limits of state sovereignty, nationality determines its population. Beyond these limits one finds foreign land, foreign sovereignty, and foreigners. Drawing the boundary within which some human beings are included and others excluded as foreigners, permitting some of them to acquire citizenship with certain conditions and some citizens to lose citizenship are all state prerogatives that require legal tools. Nationality law is made up of these tools. They can be compared to different colors that are subsequently mixed to achieve a desired effect. Two of these colors are always mentioned in nationality laws:

—Birthplace, or *jus soli:* the fact of being born in a territory over which the state maintains, has maintained, or wishes to extend its sovereignty.

—Bloodline, or *jus sanguinis:* citizenship as the result of the nationality of one parent or other more distant ancestors.
Two other "colors" are often forgotten or neglected.

—Marital status, such as marriage to a citizen of another country, which can lead to the acquisition of the spouse's citizenship.

—Past, present, or future residence within the country's past, future, or intended borders (including colonial borders).

The mixture of these features determines the conditions under which nationality is granted in any country in the world. It also determines techniques through which citizenship is either attributed or acquired. Both features and techniques constitute the particular legislation of one country, its national "configuration." Nationality law is legally constituted at the boundary of public and private law. As a matter of public policy, determination of nationality is an inherent element of a sovereign state's power to decide who is a citizen. With regard to private law, nationality determines the way national law regulates one's life in such diverse matters as property rights, travel rights, equality of gender within marriage, and the right to inheritance. Nationality law also stands on the boundary between domestic and international law. Since the attribution of nationality is inherently part of a state's sovereignty, legal conflicts are likely to emerge when citizens from one country develop a relationship either with the territory of another country or with one of its citizens. Sometimes these relations lead to an intermingling of laws, as seen in the growing recognition of dual citizenship, and at other times they may lead to the disappearance of one's legal link to a state: statelessness.

Consider the complexity of nationality law. Each state's law is simultaneously influenced by its juridical traditions, nation-state building, examples from abroad, and the role played by migration (emigration and immigration) or the presence of minorities. Divergence between the nationality laws of different countries has been sometimes been presented as reflecting varying essential or dominant conceptions of the nation (Brubaker, 1992) which they are not.

The most commonly adopted classification posits a divergence between regimes based predominantly on the principle of jus soli and those based on jus sanguinis. Regimes associated with the former principle are presumed to be more inclusive and less ascriptive than regimes based on the latter principle, which relies on blood-based descent as a fundamental criterion for nationality acquisition. This reliance has led many academic and popular observers to attribute a jus sanguinis regime to the ethnic character of its framer's conception of nationhood and to serve as a general expression of the state's national self-understanding. But such generic explanations prove highly problematic when tested against the historical record of twenty-five states: Australia, the Baltic states (Estonia, Latvia, and Lithuania), Canada, the European Union (Austria, Belgium, Denmark, Finland, France, Germany, Greece, Ireland, Italy, Luxembourg, the Netherlands, Portugal, Spain, Sweden, and the United Kingdom), Israel, Mexico, the Russian Federation, South Africa, and the United States.

To take two European examples, France is frequently portrayed as having a strong integrative national identity forged through its revolutionary experience; in fact, the principle of jus sanguinis (with no ethnic overtones) dominated its national legislation throughout most of the nineteenth century (1803–1889). By contrast, the modern German national self-understanding has often been depicted as almost paradigmatically ethnic in character—but since 1998 the

German government has been moving toward making its nationality law more inclusive in ways that combine a mixture of jus sanguinis and soli elements. In the aftermath of the 1870 Franco-Prussian war, French and German philosophers and politicians battled over two very different conceptions of the nation, while at that time both France and Germany kept nationality laws based on jus sanguinis (Weil, 1996). On the other hand, under nazism, both Germany and France implemented racist and anti-Semitic legislation while keeping opposite criteria (jus sanguinis and jus soli, respectively) as the basis of their nationality laws. Differences in nationality laws cannot therefore be explained by the differences in the philosophical conception of nationhood. But what *can* explain the convergence between nationality laws? This convergence is illustrated by the recent changes that have occurred in many of them, reflected by the four tables below, drawn according to the mode of access to citizenship: nationality of origin, naturalization, marriage, and the specific provisions for second- and third-generation migrants.

To understand the differences and similarities between different legislation, one must take into account two main factors: legal tradition and the disconnection between territory and constituted population (e.g., the phenomena of emigration and immigration). I will attempt to show that, even across different legal traditions and different historical patterns of immigration, emigration, and minorities, convergence in nationality laws occurs. They converge through different paths and national political agendas because, in the context of the stabilization of borders and of the incorporation of democratic values, many of these countries have faced similar problems of immigration. In this model, jus soli states became slightly more restrictive and jus sanguinis ones moved toward jus soli.

The Different Legal Traditions

Were a population and territory to match one another exactly, attributing citizenship on the basis of jus sanguinis or jus soli would not make any difference. Nationality law would concern the same population and would have the same juridical effects. In eighteenth-century Europe, jus soli was the dominant criterion of nationality law in the two most powerful kingdoms: France and the United Kingdom. The state simply inherited feudal tradition: human beings were linked to the lord who held the land where they were born. The French Revolution broke with this feudal tradition. Because jus soli connoted feudal allegiance, it was decided, against Napoleon Bonaparte's wish, that the new civil code of 1804 would grant French nationality at birth only to a child born to a French father, either in France or abroad. This decision was not ethnically

Table 1-1.   *Nationality of Origin*

Country	Jus Soli (Date of Inclusion)	Jus Sanguinis (Date of Inclusion)
Australia	Yes (one parent citizen or permanent resident or child herself if permanent resident for 10 years from birth)	Yes (one parent citizen and registration at a consulate within 18 years of birth)
Austria	No	Yes (1811)
Belgium	Yes (for third generation)	Yes (1831)
Canada	Yes	Yes (loss of citizenship in third generation unless residency in or special connection with Canada before age 28)
Denmark	No	Yes (1898)
Estonia	No	Yes (1992)
Finland	No	Yes (1941)
France	Yes (for third generation, 1889)	Yes (1803)
Germany	Yes (with condition: dual citizenship, 1999)	Yes (Prussia, 1842)
Greece	No	Yes (1856)
Ireland	Yes (1935)	Yes (1935)
Israel	No	Yes (1950 Law of Return)
Italy	No	Yes (1865)
Latvia	No	Yes (1919)
Lithuania	Yes (with condition: dual citizenship)	Yes (1991)
Luxembourg	No	Yes (1804)
Mexico	Yes	Yes (not beyond second generation)
The Netherlands	Yes (for third generation)	Yes (1888)
Portugal	Yes (with condition of residence)	Yes, first rank (if alone, obligation for applicant to declare his or her will)
Russia	Yes (under condition)	Yes (1864)
South Africa	Yes (both parents permanent residents)	Yes (notification of birth to South African authorities)
Spain	No	Yes (1837)
Sweden	No	Yes (1894)
United Kingdom	Yes (with condition of residence)	Yes (no transmission to third generation unless residency established in U.K. before birth of child)
United States	Yes (by Constitution, 1868)	Yes (no transmission to third generation unless residency established in U.S. before birth of child)

motivated; it meant only that family links transmitted by the pater familias had become more important than subjecthood. This marked the reintroduction of Roman Law into modern nationality law. This French innovation, through codification and imitation, progressively spread and became the dominant law of continental European countries. In the aftermath of this French reform, the following states adopted jus sanguinis in their civil codes: Austria (1811), Belgium (1831), Spain (1837), Prussia (1842), Italy (1865), Russia (1864), the Netherlands (1888), Norway (1892), and Sweden (1894) (Weiss, 1907).

The British tradition of jus soli, on the contrary, was transplanted, unamended and unbroken, to its colonies in North America (the United States and Canada), Europe (Ireland), Africa (South Africa), and Australia (Watson, 1974). It also influenced Portugal and Denmark until the Nordic countries adopted a common nationality regime in the 1920s.

The Disconnection between Territory and Constituted Population

When disconnection occurs between a territory and its constituted population, one can distinguish between countries of immigrants, of immigration, of emigrants, and of emigration.

—In "countries of immigrants," the majority of citizens are immigrants or descendants of immigrants. The United States, Canada, Australia, and, until recently, South Africa can be included in this list.

—"Countries of immigration" are those where foreign populations have settled as permanent residents. In these countries, there is a dominant sense that a core, majority population has existed since time immemorial and is not descended from immigrants. Immigrant populations are seen to have joined this "native" core. In western Europe, France has been in that situation since the midnineteenth century. Since World War II, all western European countries have gone from being predominantly countries of emigration to being countries of immigration. South Africa is also now a country of immigration, a characteristic that developed only after the abolition of apartheid. In a different manner but with the same consequences, the Baltic states can be considered countries of immigration where a strong Russian minority happens to reside.

—"Countries of emigrants" are countries where part of the core population resides outside the national boundaries. These expatriates are perceived to retain a link with their country of origin, as was the case with Germany between 1913 and 1933 and between 1949 and 1989 and Russia since 1989, and Israel, as we will see later, can also be placed in this category.

—Finally, there are "countries of emigration," where segments of the population emigrated so as to build a new life in another country. This applies to the majority of European countries before World War II (with the exception of France) and Mexico since the 1930s.

When a legal tradition is perceived to fulfill the interest of the state in terms of migration, or at least does not oppose it, the core of national legislation is maintained. In countries of immigrants such as Australia, Canada, and the United

Table 1-2. *Naturalization*

Country	Residence	Knowledge of History	Knowledge of Language	Loyalty Oath	Sufficient Income	Good Character	Absence of Conviction	Renunciation of Prior Citizenship
Australia	Permanent no less than 1 of 2 years before application; no less 2 of 5 years before application	—	Yes	—	—	Yes	—	—
Austria	10 years	—	Yes	Yes	Yes	—	Yes	Yes
Belgium	3 years	—	—	—	—	—	—	—
Canada	Permanent 3 of 4 years before application	Yes	Yes	Yes	—	—	Yes	—
Denmark	7 years	—	Yes	—	Yes	Yes	Yes	—
Estonia	5 years	Yes	Yes	Yes	Yes	—	—	—
Finland	5 years	—	—	—	Yes	Yes	Yes	—
France	5 years	—	Yes	—	Yes	Yes	Yes	—
Germany	Permanent 8 years	—	Yes	—	Yes	—	—	Yes
Greece	5 years after application or 10 of 12 years before	—	—	Yes	—	—	Yes	—
Ireland	1 year continuous residency before application + 4 of 8 years before application	—	—	Yes	—	Yes	—	—
Israel	Permanent 3 of 5 years before application	—	Yes	—	—	—	—	Yes

Country	Residency requirement							
Italy	10 years	—	—	—	—	—	—	—
Latvia	5 years before 1990	Yes	Yes	Yes	Yes	—	—	—
Lithuania	Permanent previous 10 years	—	Yes w/test	Yes	Yes	—	—	Yes
Luxembourg	10 years continuous residency, including past 5 years	—	Yes	—	Yes	Yes	Yes	Yes
Mexico	5 years	Yes	Yes	—	—	—	—	Yes
The Netherlands	Permanent or habitual for 5 consecutive years before application	—	Yes	—	—	—	—	—
Portugal	10 years	—	Yes	—	Yes	Yes	—	—
Russia	5 years	—	—	—	—	—	—	—
South Africa	Permanent, cont. for 1 year before application; resident for 4 of 8 years before application	—	Yes	—	Yes	Yes	—	—
Spain	10 years	—	—	—	—	—	—	—
Sweden	5 years	—	—	—	Yes	Yes	Yes	—
United Kingdom	Main residence or Crown service; 5 years residency	—	Yes	Yes	Yes	Yes	—	—
United States	5 years permanent settling	Yes	Yes	Yes	Yes	Yes	Possibly	Yes

Table 1-3. *Marriage*

Country	Existence of a Specific Provision	Residence	Delay	Other Requirements
Australia	No	—	—	—
Austria	Yes	1 + 4 years or 2 + 3 years	1 year	—
Belgium	Yes	3 years	—	—
Canada	No	—	—	—
Denmark	No	—	—	—
Estonia	No	—	—	—
Finland	Yes	3 years	2 years	—
France	Yes	—	1 year	Facilitated naturalization (by declaration)
Germany	Yes	5 years	—	—
Greece	No	—	—	—
Ireland	Yes	—	3 years	—
Israel	Yes	—	—	At discretion of Minister of Interior, no commission of certain crimes
Italy	Yes	6 months in Italy or total 3 years abroad	—	—
Latvia	No	—	—	—
Lithuania	No	—	—	—
Luxembourg	Yes	3 years	—	Proof of life in common
Mexico	Yes	2 years	—	—
The Netherlands	Yes	3 years	—	—
Portugal	Yes	3 years	—	—
Russia	Yes	—	—	Facilitated naturalization
South Africa	Yes	—	2 years	—
Spain	Yes	—	1 year	—
Sweden	Yes	Permanent (3 years)	2 years	—
United Kingdom	Yes	3 years	—	—
United States	Yes	3 years	—	Same as for other aliens

States, jus soli allows the children of immigrants to acquire Australian, Canadian, and U.S. citizenship automatically. For continental European countries that were once countries of emigration, jus sanguinis allowed citizens abroad to maintain links until their descendants lost touch. The United Kingdom and Ireland were countries of emigration. To keep links with their nationals abroad, both countries added jus sanguinis provisions to their existing tradition of jus soli. Jus soli could remain in effect as long as the countries did not become countries of large-scale immigration.

Since World War II, however, nationality laws have converged across these four state types. First, countries with nationality laws predicated upon jus soli attracted a number of immigrants into their territories that greatly exceeded public policy choices, which forced the countries to become more restrictive. For instance, the United Kingdom's imperial and expansive conception of territory, combined with jus soli, involuntarily encouraged immigration to the United Kingdom. Before World War II, all subjects of the British Empire were equal in allegiance to the monarch and had access to British citizenship simply by residing in the territory of the United Kingdom proper. Following the Canadian example, the 1948 legislation on nationality created six separate forms of citizenship. The sum of these constituted the concept of British nationality. This extensive approach to jus soli led to the arrival of an unexpected number of colonial immigrants to the United Kingdom who soon became citizens. In response, British legislation on nationality underwent a swift and silent revolution away from the extended and pure jus soli. From the mid-1950s on, the United Kingdom modified its legislation to restrict further immigration from Commonwealth countries. The passing of the Commonwealth Immigrants Act of 1962 and of the Immigration Act of 1971 placed limits to their freedom of entry into the United Kingdom and created an intermediate, distinct category that was between nationals and aliens for patrials, or those benefiting from a right of abode. This right was attributed to citizens of the United Kingdom or to those of the colonies, provided that they were born, adopted or registered in the territory of the United Kingdom, or that they had been residents in the United Kingdom for at least five years. The 1981 legislation created British citizenship. It automatically attributed jus soli to children born in the United Kingdom to a British citizen or to a non-British permanent resident born in the United Kingdom; otherwise, a minor could acquire British citizenship if resident in the United Kingdom for ten continuous years before applying. In addition, British citizenship is automatically attributed through jus sanguinis to the first generation born abroad. In the next generation, the descendant of the British citizen has to settle in the United Kingdom; otherwise he or she loses British citizenship (Hansen, 2001).

Table 1-4. Second-Generation Immigrants

Country	Entitlement to Citizenship	Existence of a Specific Provision	Residence	Age	Other Information
Australia	Yes	Automatic	None	—	—
Austria	No	Yes	6 or 4 years instead of 10	—	Naturalization
Belgium	Yes	Yes	Parents resident for 10 years	Before 12; between 18 and 30	Registration
Canada	Yes	Automatic	None	—	—
Denmark	Yes	Yes	10 years continuous	21–23	Declaration
Estonia	Yes (Dec. 1998)	Yes	—	Before 15	Birth after 1992 and application by parents
Finland	Yes	Yes	10 years	21–23	Declaration
France	Yes	Yes	5 years noncontinuous	After 13	With parents' consent at 13; by request at 16; automatic at 18
Germany					
Born in Germany	Yes	Yes	Parents permanent residents	At birth	At 23 dual citizenship
Not born in Germany	Yes	Yes	8 years, incl. 6 in primary education and 4 in secondary	16–23	Dual citizenship; registration and absence of criminal conviction
Greece	No	No	None	—	—
Ireland	Yes	Automatic	—	—	—
Israel	No	No	—	—	—
Italy	Yes	Yes	Continuous since birth	Majority	—

Latvia	Yes (June 1998)	Yes		—	Birth after 1990 and application by parents
Lithuania	Yes	Yes	None	—	—
Luxembourg	No	No	—	—	—
Mexico	Yes	Automatic	None	—	Declaration
The Netherlands	Yes	Yes	Continuous since birth	18–25	
Portugal	Yes	Yes	None	Any time	Parents residents 10 or 6 years if from Portuguese-speaking country
Russia	No	No	—	—	—
South Africa	Yes	Yes	—	—	Parents are permanent residents
Spain	Yes	Yes	1 year	18–20	Declaration
Sweden	Yes	Yes	10 years	21–23	Declaration
United Kingdom	Yes	Yes	None (1981)	—	Parents are permanent residents
United States	Yes	Automatic	None	—	—

Note: For EU countries, information is taken mainly from Hansen (1998).

The evolution of the United Kingdom might soon find its way to the agenda of the Irish Parliament, since Ireland has recently become a country of immigration. Ireland, which until the past decade was the only remaining country of emigration in western Europe, has recently received increasing numbers of immigrants. The migratory balance shifted in favor of immigration beginning in 1995 (in 1998, 45,000 v. 20,000) and the number of asylum seekers has risen (from 39 in 1992 to 4,626 in 1998).

In the United States, jus soli opens access to citizenship to the children of illegal aliens (Schuck and Smith, 1985). But it would not be easy to restrict U.S. citizenship, since the adoption of the Fourteenth Amendment enshrined the jus soli provision in the U.S. Constitution. It grants U.S. citizenship to all persons born in the jurisdiction of the federal state (Aleinikoff, 1998). Schuck and Smith have argued that the Fourteenth Amendment was never intended to apply so broadly.

On the same restrictive ground, I must mention one other development. Each of the twenty-five countries that had a provision for the automatic acquisition of citizenship through marriage in its legislation has repealed it within the past forty years. Such was the case in Sweden in 1950, Denmark in 1951, Portugal in 1959, Italy in 1983, Belgium in 1984, Greece in 1984, and Israel in 1996. Moreover, the delays required before a foreign spouse can apply for citizenship have been lengthened. In all cases, the repeal of the automatic nature and timely consideration of citizenship found its origin in the desire to ensure the equal treatment of men and women and the progress of the desacralization of marriage. In many cases, however, there were also justified worries about fraudulent marriages with illegal aliens. Another development, however, occurred in the continental European states. After following a legal tradition of jus sanguinis, they evolved as they became countries of permanent immigration.

France, at the end of the nineteenth century, was the first country to face a contradiction between legal tradition and migration. Frequently thought to have an open conception of nationhood based on the integration of immigrants, France's nationality legislation was dominated by jus sanguinis without an ethnic understanding for the larger part of the nineteenth century (1804–1889). In the years after the adoption of the 1804 civil code, with its jus sanguinis provisions, unanticipated and undesired social consequences of this law emerged. The majority of individuals born on French territory to foreign parents, even though they belonged to families that had lived on French territory for an extended period, were in no hurry to claim their French citizenship. This was a way of avoiding the military draft that accompanied citizenship. Therefore, on February 7, 1851, a law introduced optional double jus soli: an individual born in France to an alien father born in France was a French citizen at birth. He or she could renounce his or her French citizenship at the age of majority. This option was withdrawn with the 1889 law: to fulfill the principle of equality of public responsibilities and duties, third-generation "immigrants" were automatically granted French citizenship and were drafted. Since then, double jus soli has been at the heart of French nationality law. It is both a mechanism for granting French nationality automatically to third-generation immigrants born in France and the simplest means by which French citizens prove their nationality.[1] In addition to double jus soli, a child born in France to foreign parents born abroad becomes French not at birth but at the age of majority, unless he or she expresses the wish to remain a foreigner (Weil, 2001).

Meanwhile, until World War II, the other continental European states remained countries of emigration and maintained jus sanguinis as the prevalent criterion of attribution of citizenship at birth. With large-scale postwar immigration, however, increasingly large parts of the population born in their territory, namely, second- and third-generation immigrants, were unable to access citizenship easily.

Large-scale permanent immigration created a pressure in favor of provisions that guaranteed permanent residence to long-term immigrants and opened the way for their right to accede to citizenship. In the 1970s, the French and German supreme courts recognized the right of permanent residence for foreigners living in their territories. In one of its decisions, the French administrative supreme court contested the attempt by the French government to forcibly repatriate the majority of legal North African immigrants in 1978–1980. The government was forced to back down because of public and judiciary pressure. Furthermore, in June 1984, a law was passed guaranteeing permanent residence to 95 percent of foreign workers in France and their families. The same process had been under way in Germany. In 1972, the German constitutional court confirmed that a foreign worker's stay in Germany of more than five years was sufficient ground "to deny further residency (authorization) as each extended residency (authorization) would tend towards settlement" (quoted in Weil, 1998, 7). This right of integration was then extended by the right to citizenship (through jus soli or facilitated naturalization) for second- and third-generation immigrants.

To secure access to citizenship for third-generation immigrants, double jus soli has been formally included in the nationality laws of Belgium (Art. 10) since 1992,[2] in France since 1889, in Spain (Art. 17) since 1990, and in the Netherlands since 1953.[3] There is de facto access in Ireland in all cases and in

---

1. For that purpose they just need to produce their birth certificate and the birth certificate of one parent.

2. Under the conditions of five years of residence of the parent in the ten years preceding the birth.

3. Exclusively through maternal descent in Netherlands.

almost all cases in the United Kingdom and Portugal. Access to citizenship at the second-generation level occurs automatically at birth in Ireland, and under conditions of legal residence in the United Kingdom and Portugal.[4] Yet in the majority of European countries access to citizenship occurs not only automatically at birth, but also under conditions of residency or through voluntary acquisition, both of which are presumed to entail socialization (Hansen and Weil, 2001). In Belgium, Denmark, Finland, Italy, the Netherlands, and Sweden, a person born in the country to foreign parents can acquire citizenship at the age of majority after fulfilling certain residency requirements. In Belgium, it is acquired between the ages of 18 and 30;[5] in Denmark, Finland, and Sweden, between 21 and 23;[6] in the Netherlands between 18 and 25,[7] and in Italy, in the year following age 21, the age of majority.[8] In Spain, naturalization can be requested by the parents one year after the child's birth. Finally, throughout the European Union, with the exception of Austria, Greece,[9] and Luxembourg, access for second or third generations is facilitated, often as a result of recent reforms. In the case of Austria, the most recent amendment to the 1985 Nationality Act (Nascimbene, 1996), which was adopted in June 1998, identifies two further "privileged" groups of foreign citizens who may be naturalized after at least four or six years of residence, respectively: applicants who can prove "durable personal and occupational integration" in Austria and applicants who were born there. The latter category is significant because, for the first time, birth in Austria has been introduced as a relevant factor in the acquisition of citizenship. Foreign citizens born in Austria, however, still do not have an individual entitlement to naturalization.

There remains the case of Germany. When in 1842 Prussia adopted jus sanguinis, it adopted the dominant principle of French nationality law. The Prussian law, moreover, was not ethnically motivated: it included Polish and Jewish Prussians, and it excluded Germans from other German states (Fahrmeir, 1997). Jus sanguinis was reinforced in 1913 in a context in which Germany had become a country of emigration and of emigrants. Yet, the German Empire was perceived in France as being built on an ethnic logic because of the annexation

---

4. If the parents have resided in Portugal six or ten years before the birth.

5. Under Art. 12 bis and Arts. 13 and 14, nationality can be claimed by the parents before the age of twelve if they have ten years' residence in Belgium and if the child has lived in Belgium since its birth (Art. 11 bis, 1991).

6. Under conditions of continuous residence since sixteen or residence of five years before sixteen.

7. Under condition of residence since the birth (Art. 6 of the law), established in 1984.

8. Under condition of residence since the birth (Art. 4 of the law).

9. In Greece, it is taken into account in the naturalization process.

of Alsace-Lorraine in 1871. This perception was created in the United States by the German 1913 law and in all the allied countries during World War I. Jus sanguinis, however, became ethnic and racist only under the Nazi regime. It was maintained after 1949 as a way of maintaining legal ties with East Germans and the millions of "ethnic Germans" expelled from the Soviet-occupied territories in Central and Eastern Europe. As in France at the end of the nineteenth century, the shift to jus soli could only occur with the coexistence of three factors: stable borders that included the majority of nationals; immigrants who had acquired the right of permanent settlement; and the consolidation of democratic values. Since the beginning of the 1970s Germany has become a country of permanent immigration, and since 1990 most Germans are reunited within the same borders and form a democratic citizenry. Conditions are therefore fulfilled for a convergence of European nationality laws.

This convergent guarantee of residency for foreign residents, linked with the idea of territorial nationality, belongs to the new paradigm of international law identified by Diane Orentlicher (1998). Western European states have converged through internal debate and along a parallel path (Hansen and Weil, 2000). Convergence has occurred in the Baltic states through another means, that is, through the pressure of international organizations that emphasize the rights of foreign residents.

The cases of Estonia and Latvia are most relevant in this respect. The study of these cases first requires an examination of the situation of the citizenship legislation of the three Baltic states at the time of their independence. When this took place in 1991, it seemed that the three states would follow different paths. Whereas Lithuania and Estonia passed new citizenship laws within the next two years (Lithuania in 1991 and Estonia in 1992), Latvia did not do so, restoring Latvian citizenship only to those who had it before the Soviet period and to their descendants. Because officials stated that such a law would have to wait until the election of a new Parliament, the Latvian citizenship law was adopted only on June 21, 1994. The three laws of the Baltic states can be classified along an inclusive-exclusive line. Lithuania, combining jus soli and jus sanguinis provisions, is the most inclusive. Latvia, with no jus soli, is the most exclusive: it has established a "window" system, which provides for the examination of applications from certain categories of persons each year. In 1996, those born in Latvia who were 16 to 20 years old; in 1997, those who were up to twenty-five years old, and so on. Under the original law, those born outside Latvia must wait until 2001–2003 even to apply (Barrington, 1999, 17–18).

Latvian and Estonian postindependence nationality laws were criticized by intergovernmental organizations on the grounds of human rights, for they excluded from nationality entire portions of the population, especially long-term residents of Russian origin. Both Latvia and Estonia were potential applicants for entry into the Council of Europe and the European Union, and there was an explicit link between a serious and hopeful application and the applicant countries' respect for the policies supported by these intergovernmental organizations. In that respect, specific provisions regarding nationality and human rights in general were part of these conditions, and they conformed almost exactly to the recent developments in international law of territorial nationality. In Europe, not only did the European Union and the Council of Europe push these countries toward inclusiveness, but the Organization for Security and Cooperation in Europe (OSCE) did as well. The OSCE has undoubtedly been a significant actor in the recent changes in the nationality laws of both Estonia and Latvia. In the latter case, the OSCE High Commissioner on National Minorities had recommended the inclusion of several provisions: among them, the right of citizenship for noncitizens; the acceleration of the naturalization process; the abolition of the windows system; the granting of citizenship to stateless children born in Latvia; the limitation of the residency requirement to no more than five years; the reduction of the fee for naturalization; and the simplification of citizenship tests on the history and constitution of Latvia. Through several amendments to the law on June 22, 1998, the Latvian Parliament fulfilled these recommendations, as the high commissioner noted the following day.[10]

Moving from an approach chiefly based on jus sanguinis and the restriction of naturalization toward a more inclusive one, the Baltic examples show that the process of convergence is not over yet. In December 1998, Estonia modified its legislative provisions on the attribution of citizenship to second-generation immigrants, but those provisions became effective only on July 12, 1999. Nationality law is always a work in progress.

This process of convergence extends far beyond Europe. It concerns almost all advanced industrial democracies insofar as they share certain basic characteristics of European states: democratic values, stable borders, and a self-perception as countries of immigration rather than of emigrants or emigration.[11] When these three conditions are achieved, two distinct lines of convergence appear. First, access to nationality was restricted when the law was perceived as permitting easy access to residence without having respected immigration

10. Statement of the High Commissioner on National Minorities, 23 June 1998, document provided by the Latvian Embassy in France.

11. As countries of immigration also have some citizens living abroad, all laws have some provisions permitting the transmission of citizenship to children born abroad. That kind of jus sanguinis is often restricted at the third generation unless a special connection is established by the applicant with his/her country of origin (United States, 1978; United Kingdom, 1981; Canada, 1999).

laws. Second, all provisions that did not provide for the facilitated integration of second- and third-generation immigrants were progressively overturned: access to citizenship was thus opened to long-term residents and their children. Convergence has been illustrated in the numerous changes that have occurred in many nationality laws. The techniques vary but they usually come as amendments to existing laws concerning the granting of nationality of origin, the status of second- and third-generation migrants, or the status of married people.

Those countries not following this pattern of convergence are the countries that fail to fulfill one of the three conditions mentioned above; in fact, the number of determining factors is reduced to only two, since all case countries are democratic or in the process of democratization. Self-perception and stable borders are what differ.

The first missing condition can be related to the migration situation: even if all countries in the study have a foreign residence population and citizens living abroad, the presence of immigrants in a territory is not sufficient in itself to cause convergence. When the interests and the attention of the state are focused on maintaining links with potential nationals residing abroad, when there is a dominant feeling that a large part of the population lives abroad, and when the state grants more importance to them than to foreign residents living in its territory, legislative convergence will not take place. Such is the case of Israel. Despite the common perception of Israel as a country of immigrants, the famous Law of Return is a law that permits a returning person *(oléh)* or the descendant of an émigré to be reintegrated into his or her country of origin. In other words, from the viewpoint of nationality law, Israel is much like a country of emigration and not a country of immigration.

Russia, which feels that many of its citizens are outside its borders in the territories of former soviet republics, is another good example of this. The provisions on Russian citizenship are contained in the Citizenship Act of November 28, 1991 (in effect from February 6, 1992, amended on June 17, 1993, and February 6, 1995). According to this legislation, any child born to Russian citizens is a Russian citizen regardless of where he or she is born (Art. 14). Thus, jus sanguinis is the main way in which Russian citizenship is acquired.

The second main factor in divergence is unstable boundaries. Territorial disputes or diasporas tend to make the passage to more inclusiveness impossible, and even unthinkable. Unstable borders favor jus sanguinis, which provides a more secure way to keep control of the citizenry than jus soli. In many such cases, citizens reside across borders or large and irredentist minorities reside within them. The most obvious case of the importance of this issue is Germany. Only after reunification was it possible for Germany to seriously examine the issue of the integration of the children of immigrants, an issue that had long been absent from the political agenda. The Israeli case is also significant in that respect. The interests of the state of Israel are in large part determined by the instability of its frontiers and by political conflicts linked to the Palestinian presence. These circumstances may explain why access to Israeli citizenship is not given to children born to non-Israeli parents.

In conclusion, a comparison of countries with very different geographical and historical situations demonstrates the weight of legal tradition in the establishment of rules for citizenship. Substantive convergence takes place within preexisting legal frames and occurs only when states are subjected to important contradictions. Historical traditions in the matter of citizenship were in fact modified when disjunctures appeared between the consequences of traditional law and either the interest of the state itself or that of individuals who could legitimately claim a right to become citizens. All stable, democratic nation-states with immigrant populations have moved in the same legislative direction. Despite much academic writing to the contrary, there is no causal link between national identity and nationality laws.

Works Cited

Aleinikoff, T. Alexander. 1998. *Between Principles and Politics: The Direction of U.S. Citizenship Policy.* Washington International Migration Policy Program. Washington, D.C.: Carnegie Endowment for International Peace.

Barrington, Lowell W. 1999. "The Making of Citizenship Policy in the Baltic States." Paper presented at meeting of the Carnegie Comparative Citizenship Project, Virginia, June. Revised.

Brubaker, Rogers. 1992. *Citizenship and Nationhood in France and Germany.* Cambridge: Harvard University Press.

Fahrmeir, Andreas K. 1997. "Nineteenth-Century German Citizenships: A Reconsideration." *Historical Journal* 40(3): 721–52.

Hansen, Randall. 1998. "A European Citizenship or a Europe of Citizens? Third Country Nationals in the EU." *Journal of Ethnic and Migration Studies* 24(4): 751–68.

———. 2001. "From Subjects to Citizens: Immigration and Nationality Law in the United Kingdom." In Randall Hansen and Patrick Weil, *Nationality Law in Europe.* London: Macmillan.

Nascimbene, Bruno (ed.). 1996. *Nationality Laws in the European Union.* Milan: Giuffrè Editore.

Orentlicher, Diane F. 1998. "Citizenship and National Identity." In David Wippman (ed.), *International Law and Ethnic Conflict,* pp. 296–325. Ithaca: Cornell University Press.

Schuck, P. H., and R. M. Smith. 1985. *Citizenship without Consent: The Illegal Alien in American Polity.* New Haven: Yale University Press.

Watson, Alan. 1974. *Legal Transplants.* Edinburgh: Scottish Academic Press; Charlottesville: University Press of Virginia.

Weil, Patrick. 1996. "Nationalities and Citizenships: The Lessons of the French Experience for Germany and Europe." In D. Cesarani and Mary Fulbrook (eds.), *Citizenship, Nationality, and Migration in Europe,* pp. 74–87. London: Routledge.

———. 1998. *The State Matters. Immigration Control in Developed Countries.* New York: United Nations.

———. 2001. "The History of French Nationality: A Lesson for Europe." In Randall Hansen and Patrick Weil (eds.), *Nationality Law in Europe.* London: Macmillan.

Weiss, André, 1907. *Traité théorique et pratique de droit international privé. Tome premier: La nationalité.* Paris: Larose et Tenin.

CHAPTER TWO

The Evolution of Alien Rights
in the United States, Germany,
and the European Union

CHRISTIAN JOPPKE

THE EVOLUTION OF alien rights, which Virginie Guiraudon (1998) characterized as the development of "citizenship rights for non-citizens," marks a significant change in liberal postwar states.[1] How can we explain it? A recent
prominent theory argues that nation-states have become permeable to the norms
and discourses of global human rights, which protect people as universal persons rather than as national citizens (Jacobson, 1996; Soysal, 1994). This theory
is undeniably attractive because it helps explain the convergence of similarly
expansive schemes of alien rights across countries. It gives, however, an incomplete and in important ways misleading account of the origins and dynamics of alien rights in the United States, Germany, and the European Union (EU).
First, the response from Singapore and China to the concept of "universal"
human rights is that these are really "Western" human rights, with limited validity and application elsewhere. In fact, the forced rotation and denial of elementary residence and family rights to labor migrants is disturbingly vital
outside the Western hemisphere (see Weiner, 1995, 80–83). This suggests that
global human rights cannot be as "global" as they are proclaimed to be by the
globalists.

---

1. "Alien rights" pertain to the residence, employment, and welfare interests of immigrants.
Their logic is to approximate immigrant to citizenship status, and to remove discrimination on
the basis of one's immigrant status. This definition of alien rights excludes the right of asylum,
the rights of temporary visitors, the right to citizenship, and ethnic minority rights.

Second, even Germany, since World War II clearly a "Western" country, is currently experimenting with second-generation guest-worker schemes whose legal provisions are to ensure that the recruited contract workers will not stay this time (Rudolph, 1996). This suggests that even in a Western stronghold of human rights different legal regimes apply to different categories of migrants, each endowed with different sets of rights. Those migrants who have come to enjoy quasi-citizen rights are a limited and distinct group of people, who are either set apart from the start as legal immigrants (as in the United States) or who acquired a similar status over time through the failure of the state to set clear time limits for work and residence (as was the case with Germany's guest workers). The reference to universal human rights, which indiscriminately apply to all persons and groups, cannot explain the internal differentiation of alien rights even in those countries where those universal norms and discourses originated.

Finally, globalists have exaggerated the force of inter- or supranational regimes in legitimizing and diffusing human rights norms. In turn, they have underestimated, if not ignored entirely, the role of domestic legal orders and legitimizing principles in alien rights. As John Herz (1957) argued provocatively, international law boils down to enshrining the principle of state sovereignty and deducing some of the consequences. This position, formulated at the height of the Cold War, may appear extreme today. But the entry of the individual into the exclusive sphere of interstate relations, which occurred with UN conventions on universal human rights protection, has still remained declaratory and inconclusive (see Henkin, 1990). The real constraints to state sovereignty are to be found in domestic legal orders, particularly in constitutional law, which has been key to the development of alien rights.

In this chapter I compare the development of alien rights in the United States, Germany, and the EU. Why compare these cases? The United States and Germany are the world's foremost immigrant-receiving countries. Although both are liberal states, each has responded to postwar immigration in opposite ways: the United States has endorsed immigration as compatible with its recovered national self-description as "a nation of immigrants"; (West) Germany has rejected immigration as incompatible with its newfound self-description as not being "a country of immigration." These are extreme versions of the general coincidence of immigration and nation building in the transoceanic new settler nations and of the extraneousness of immigration to nation building in Europe. If the United States and Germany now have similarly expansive schemes of alien rights, one would have to conclude that their opposing national self-descriptions could not be responsible. In fact, the opposite cases of the United States and Germany show that the weakening, if not the absence, of nationalist semantics has been a prerequisite for expansive alien rights in liberal postwar states. Nonnationalism, however, is not postnationalism, because both states have incorporated their immigrants on the basis not of global norms or regimes, but of nationally distinct domestic legal orders.

Adding the European Union to this comparison seems odd. Unlike the United States and Germany, the European Union is not a state. Moreover, Germany is part of the European Union, and comparing the whole with one of its parts may appear nonsensical. These reservations notwithstanding, the comparison still makes sense. While its origins are functional, not territorial, the European Union is increasingly evolving into a statelike entity with its own currency, supremacy in expanding policy domains, and a membership as "citizenship." The Amsterdam Treaty has supranationalized the immigration function and thus created the prospect of a "European" immigration policy. If the Union is serious about its proclaimed human rights identity, its alien rights provisions will have to be measured against the world's most advanced alien rights regimes, such as that of the United States. At the same time, the EU is unlikely to evolve into a full-blown federal state; it is better conceived of as a multitiered polity whose constitutive units will remain sovereign nation-states, not people. This implies that European alien rights have to be measured and evaluated in the context of the alien rights already instituted by the member states—such as Germany. Comparing the European Union with other federal states, such as Germany and the United States, has a long tradition.[2] While the federal control of immigration and immigrant policies is an increasingly contested issue, particularly in the United States (see Schuck, 1998; Spiro, 1994), it is not the main focus here. Instead, my purpose is to point out peculiarities of the European Union's treatment of alien rights in light of some of the world's most elaborate alien rights regimes.

Two questions will structure the comparison. First, is there a convergence across states in the development of alien rights or is there systematic variation? Second, is there a linear development of alien rights or are these rights reversible?

The United States

An alien, according to the Immigration and Naturalization Act, is "any person not a citizen or national of the United States." United States immigration

---

2. Next to the obvious literature (Cappelletti et al., 1986; Scharpf, 1994; Leibfried and Pierson, 1995), see the interesting comparison of state resistance to federal authority in early America and the European Community by Friedman Goldstein (1997).

law further distinguishes, on the one hand, between immigrant and resident aliens, who are permitted permanent residence and who are expected to proceed to citizenship, and, on the other hand, nonimmigrant aliens, who—like students, tourists, diplomats, and temporary workers—are admitted only for temporary periods and are expected to return to their countries of origin. This distinction is crucial because different regimes of alien rights apply to both, with significant movements of rights expansion (and contraction) limited to the category of resident aliens. Consider also that the easy access to citizenship in the United States limits the practical relevance of more or less developed resident alien rights.

The rights of resident aliens, which is my focus here, are shaped by two opposite legal-constitutional principles. One principle, which has been labeled the "plenary power" principle, endows the political branches of the federal government (the presidency and Congress) with unconstrained, judicially nonreviewable authority over the entry, stay, exclusion, and naturalization of immigrant aliens: "Over no conceivable subject is the legislative power of Congress more complete," the U.S. Supreme Court first declared in 1909, reaffirming this view in numerous decisions late into the twentieth century (see Aleinikoff et al., 1995). A second, opposite principle, which one could call the "personhood" principle, puts resident aliens on a par with citizens as protected by a constitution whose key provisions revolve around personhood and are thus indifferent to formal citizenship status. Neither the plenary power principle nor the personhood principle as applied to aliens can be found explicitly in the U.S. Constitution; instead, they have been judicially constructed by courts and legal scholars. The development of alien rights is thus largely one of case law, which is conditioned by changing views of the Constitution.

As opposite as they are, the plenary power and personhood principles first appeared almost simultaneously in the 1880s, which was the germinating period of federal immigration law. Plenary power was infamously expounded in the Chinese Exclusion Case of 1889, in which the Supreme Court upheld the racially motivated exclusion of Chinese workers from the United States, arguing that "[if Congress] considers the presence of foreigners of a different race in this country . . . to be dangerous to its peace and security, . . . its determination is conclusive upon the judiciary" (quoted in Schuck, 1984, 14). Personhood as applied to aliens appeared first in *Yick Wo v. Hopkins* (1886), in which the same court argued that the equal protection clause of the Fourteenth Amendment was "not confined to the protection of citizens," but was "universal in [its] application . . . to all persons within the territorial jurisdiction" (quoted in

Bosniak, 1994, 1098).[3] While the two principles appeared almost simultaneously, plenary power prevailed over personhood well into the 1960s, when under the influence of the civil rights revolution activist courts began to defend the rights of aliens more aggressively. But this reversal has remained incomplete, and an unrepealed plenary power principle has been the constitutional gateway to the massive federal restrictions of the welfare rights of immigrants in the late 1990s.

Reflecting its origins in the late-nineteenth-century world of imperialism and state nationalism, the plenary power doctrine depicts the alien as a member of a competing state unit, and the federal government as entrusted with the defense of the national community against outside threats. In its expansive (yet judicially contested) reading, plenary power covers not only the entry and departure of the alien, but also his or her rights and obligations while on the territory of the United States. To be sure, plenary power can cut both ways: the federal government is free not to discriminate against resident aliens, for instance, in the provision of federal welfare programs, as it usually did until the recent welfare backlash; but it is also free to discriminate against aliens in the most blatant and capricious ways, since immigration law remains one of the few domains in public law (along with foreign affairs and war powers) that is not subject to judicial review. This has implied the exclusion and deportation of homosexuals (who were labeled psychopathic personalities) until the Immigration Act of 1990 ruled them out statutorily, and of political radicals (most often communists). The only moderation of plenary power has occurred regarding deportation procedures, in which aliens (through the countervailing personhood principle) have come to enjoy constitutional due process rights, and regarding "exclusion" procedures against returning resident aliens, which are now processed under the more lenient deportation rules.[4] While the plenary power principle has never been officially rescinded by the Supreme Court, its legitimacy has grown thin over time. Recent case law refrained from defending

3. Note, however, that *Yick Wo* was a state (not federal) case, which renders the contradiction between the (predominantly state-related) personhood and (always federal) "plenary power" principles less extreme.

4. "Deportations" are directed against aliens (regardless of their legal status) within the territory of the United States, so that constitutional due process protection applies. "Exclusions" are directed against entering aliens, who are considered outside the territory of the United States, so that the Constitution does not apply. Until *Landon v. Plasencia* (1982) put an end to it, this meant that returning legal resident aliens enjoyed lesser constitutional protection than illegal aliens within the territory. The benchmark case is *Shaughnessy v. Mezei* (1953), where the Supreme Court upheld the permanent exclusion, without a hearing and on the basis of undisclosed information, of a permanent resident who had lived in the United States for twenty-five years (see Motomura, 1990, 558). In *Landon v. Plasencia,* the Supreme Court extended constitutional due process protection to a returning permanent resident, thus acknowledging that returning resident aliens had higher level membership rights than first-time entrants.

it positively, pointing instead to the accumulated weight of past practice (stare decisis), according to which, desirable as constitutional checks on federal immigration power may be, "the slate is not clean" and plenary power had become "firmly imbedded in the legislative and judicial tissues of our body politic" (quoted in Rubio-Marín, 2000, 141).

Having been little used for eight decades, the personhood principle of alien rights reappeared with a vengeance in the early 1970s. In *Graham v. Richardson* (1971), the Supreme Court invoked the equal protection clause of the Fourteenth Amendment to strike down state statutes that withheld welfare benefits from resident aliens. Seen from the vantage point of personhood, resident aliens were not first aliens, that is, members of competing state units, but residents, that is, members of the societal community, who deserved equal treatment. As the Court argued in *Graham,* "aliens, like citizens, pay taxes and may be called into the armed forces. . . . [A]liens may live within a state for many years, work in the state and contribute to the economic growth of the state" (*Graham v. Richardson,* 403 U.S. 365 [1971], cited in Rubio-Marín, 2000, 145). Furthermore, the Court characterized aliens as constituting a "discrete and insular minority," which the state was not allowed to discriminate against. Following *Graham,* the Supreme Court and lower courts struck down most existing state restrictions against resident aliens regarding professional licenses, civil service employment, welfare programs, and scholarships.

However, *Graham's* turning of alienage into a suspect classification, which states were not allowed to discriminate against, was riddled with ambiguity. Looking at aliens through the minority lens, the Court was evidently influenced by the civil rights revolution of the time. Yet, if alienage classification was as suspect as race classification was, it should follow that aliens had to be allowed to vote (to remedy their "political powerlessness," which was offered in *Graham* as justification of their suspect class status); that nonimmigrant aliens and illegal aliens were even more than resident aliens an "insular minority" entitled to constitutional protection; and that aliens had to be every bit a minority for the federal government as for state governments, which would derail plenary power. Later case law attests to the unwillingness of the Supreme Court to consider alienage a "garden-variety suspect classification" (Rosberg, 1983, 400) First, in *Sugarman v. Dougall* (1973), the Court introduced the so-called political function exception, which reserved to citizens state jobs that were closely tied to the "formulation, execution, or review of broad public policy" (quoted in Levi, 1979, 1079). Invoking this doctrine, subsequent court decisions upheld state statutes that made citizenship a condition for being a police officer, a public school teacher, or a deputy probation officer. From the point of view of *Graham,* which had made aliens a suspect class because of their political powerlessness, the political function exception was paradoxical because it relegitimized the political exclusion of aliens. Second, in *De Canas v. Bica* (1976) and *Elkins v. Moreno* (1978), the Court affirmed that states could regulate illegal immigrants and nonimmigrant aliens, respectively, in upholding a California statute that outlawed the knowing employment of illegal aliens *(De Canas)* and allowing the state of Maryland to charge higher college fees for nonimmigrant aliens *(Elkins)*. Finally, in *Mathews v. Diaz* (1976), the Supreme Court reaffirmed that the personhood protection at the state level was not available at the federal level, where it was within the immigration power (that is, plenary power) of the federal government to exclude resident aliens from Medicare benefits if it so wished.

An influential legal comment pointed out that in its *Graham* and post-*Graham* decisions, the Court had relied on an "unarticulated theory of preemption" (Levi, 1979), which would obliterate the resort to the equal protection standard of judicial review and do away with the ambiguity of *Graham*'s alienage as suspect classification theory. The federal preemption alternative to equal protection rests on the Constitution's supremacy clause, which ensures the hierarchy of federal over state laws. This hierarchy is violated whenever states take positions on aliens that deviate from those of the federal government, and in which states arrogate to themselves immigration powers that are the exclusive domain of the federal government. The federal preemption standard was first applied in *Takahashi v. Fish and Game Commission* (1948), where the Supreme Court argued that California could not deny fishing licenses to certain resident aliens, because the federal government had admitted resident aliens "on an equality of legal privileges" that states were not entitled to overstep. Preemption is consistent with *Graham,* because it had struck down alien restrictions at the state level that had no parallel at the federal level; and it was consistent with post-*Graham* decisions, some of which simply applied existing federal restrictions to the state level.

The debate on preemption or equal protection as an adequate standard of review in alien cases is not merely academic, but has enormous practical consequences. In fair weather, when the federal government decides to be generous to aliens, preemption is an effective tool to prevent states from discriminating against aliens. Yet in tempestuous times, when the federal government may switch to discrimination, preemption will force the states to do the same (but see n.6). This is undeniably the situation today, after the exclusion of aliens from most federal welfare programs, and it is an open question as to whether the Supreme Court will soon allow the states to do the same.

Plyler v. Doe (1982) was still decided on equal protection grounds. In this most famous of all alien cases in the United States, the Supreme Court invalidated a Texas statute that withheld a free public school education from the children of illegal immigrants. Protecting those people that the federal government wanted out by definition, *Plyler* is the apogee of constitutionally sanctioned alien rights: "the most powerful rejection to date of classical immigration law's notion of plenary national sovereignty over our borders," as one author put it darkly (Schuck, 1984, 58). The Court refused to consider illegal aliens a "suspect class" as resident aliens were considered in *Graham,* because it was dealing with people who had entered the country without the consent of the government. Subjecting the state policy to the more lenient legal test of "intermediate scrutiny," the Court still argued that the state's interest in saving money and deterring illegal immigrants was not important enough to justify withholding a vital public function, education, from "innocent children" who could not be held responsible for the lawbreaking of their parents. Before *Plyler*, illegal aliens had enjoyed formal due process rights under the Constitution, which, for instance, protected them in deportation proceedings; the novelty of *Plyler* was to extend to them substantive equal protection rights, which entitled them to a share of the state bounty.

Against the fears of conservative commentators at the time, however, *Plyler* did not open up a new round of alien rights expansion. Rather, it was a high point, after which any further movement had to be in retreat. After *Plyler*, the fear of uncontrolled illegal immigration became a highly charged public issue, which was eagerly picked up by political entrepreneurs, especially in such immigrant-dense states as California. Attacking alien rights, particularly to social services, was seen as a way of relieving states of fiscal pressure and deterring new immigration. In the dual context of plenary power and constitutionally sanctioned equal protection rights for aliens, an attack on alien rights had to occur in a two-stage "bottom-up top-down" movement: state pressure moving the immigration issue to national level, with Congress passing restrictive alienage legislation; and the Supreme Court taking Congress's restriction of alien rights as justification for overturning *Plyler* and retroactively validating restrictive state laws on aliens. If there ever was such a "strategy," it has paid off so far, with the exception of a final Supreme Court verdict, which is still awaited.

The kickoff in the political crusade against alien rights was Proposition 187, California's highly successful state initiative of November 1994 that barred illegal aliens from most state-provided services, including nonemergency health care and school education. An open violation of *Plyler* and an intrusion into the federal immigration domain, Proposition 187 was immediately stalled in the federal courts. Yet, the most conservative Congress in half a century, which was installed in the same November 1994 elections, proceeded quickly toward similar legislation at the national level. The Personal Responsibility and Work Opportunity Reconciliation (Welfare Reform) Act of 1996 broadens the anti-illegal immigrant impulse of Proposition 187 into a generic exclusion of aliens from virtually all federal cash assistance programs. At the same time, most public welfare responsibilities are devolved to the states, and the latter are either required or permitted to discriminate against aliens (legal and illegal) in their welfare laws (see Schuck, 1998, 218–21).[5] The federal offensive threatens to reverse the evolution of alien rights from *Graham* to *Plyler*, unless the Supreme Court finds it in violation of the Constitution.[6]

Germany

The German Alien Law defines as aliens *(Ausländer)* "everyone who is not German according to Article 116(1) of the Basic Law." This points to a phenomenon unknown in the United States and in most other Western countries: ethnic priority immigration. Article 116(1) defines as Germans not only the nominal holders of German citizenship, but—in combination with the Federal Expellee Law *(Bundesvertriebenengesetz)*—the descendants of German settlers in eastern Europe and Russia who are German not by citizenship but by ethnicity. On the assumption of being subject to persecution and discrimination by the former communist regimes of the region, the ethnic Germans were the only foreign nationals whom postwar Germany accepted as "immigrants," that is, as entrants set on a path for permanent settlement and citizenship. At the same time, these de facto immigrants, who in the 1990s were subjected to numerical quotas and formal application procedures similar to those in classic immigration countries, were never officially considered immigrants. Rather, they were treated as "resettlers" *(Aussiedler)* who acted on their constitutional right to return to their country of origin.[7]

---

5. The 1996 federal welfare law thus preempts California's Proposition 187. This has facilitated the mediated settlement between opponents and proponents of Proposition 187 on July 29, 1999. In this settlement, California dropped its appeal of a federal court ruling that Proposition 187 was unconstitutional, and proposition opponents agreed to make it a state crime to manufacture and distribute false identity documents. The only proposition-turned-welfare-law provision that California refuses to follow is the denial of public school (K–12) education to the children of illegal immigrants, which the state's lawyers find unconstitutional. See *Migration News* 6(8), August 1999.

6. Permitting states to withhold certain benefits from noncitizens directly contradicts the Supreme Court verdict in *Graham* that "Congress does not have the power to authorize the individual States to violate the Equal Protection Clause" (see Needelman, 1997, 352, n.18).

7. Germany is not the only country with ethnic priority immigration. Other prominent examples are Great Britain (until 1981), Greece, Israel, Portugal, Spain, and Russia.

The rejection of the immigration label also applied, and now explicitly, to the other source of de facto immigration after World War II: the recruited labor migrants *(Gastarbeiter)* of southern Europe. In response to this labor migration, the (West) German political elite waged one of its few attempts at national self-description: "not a country of immigration." This notoriously misunderstood term, which "articulates not a social or demographic fact but a political-cultural norm" (Brubaker, 1992, 174), still stands for the failure of the government to steer the incorporation of labor migrants. The result was drift, a shying away from forcibly rotating labor migrants once they were no longer needed, but also refusing to accept the consequence of nonrotation, which was permanent settlement. The self-abdication of the political process is expressed in the fact that an austere and rudimentary Alien Law passed in 1965, which grants no rights whatsoever to the labor migrant and puts him or her at the mercy of a benign state, went unreformed for twenty-five years. If in this period the labor migrants achieved a secure permanent resident status, akin to the legal immigrant status in the United States, we have to look to the legal process for an explanation.

As in the United States, aliens in Germany enjoy extensive constitutional rights. In the absence of a political process giving clear signals toward either terminating or consolidating the presence of labor migrants in Germany, an aggressive federal constitutional court stepped in to secure the residence and family rights of labor migrants, thus in effect crossing out the "not a country of immigration" label of the political elite. Two differences to the U.S. situation stand out. First, the German constitutionalization of alien rights started at a lower level, that is, for aliens admitted only for temporary work, not for permanent settlement. It then moved toward creating a "resident alien" status whose existence could be taken for granted and was the starting point for further rights expansion in the United States. Second, there is no parallel in German constitutional law to the plenary power principle, which exempted the federal immigration powers in the United States from constitutional constraints. In a conscious departure from the legal positivism of the Weimar Constitution, and from the German state tradition more generally, the Basic Law establishes the ontological primacy of the individual over the state in all policy domains (see Kommers, 1997, 41). This is expressed in the opening article of the Basic Law: "The dignity of the human being is untouchable. Its recognition and protection is the obligation of all statal power." The absence of a plenary power principle has allowed the constitutional court not just to enter the immigration domain, which remained largely closed to the U.S. Supreme Court, but to work actively against and stall the government's (no) immigration policy.

In contrast to the U.S. Constitution, the German Basic Law distinguishes more explicitly between universal human rights *(Jedermannrechte)* and rights reserved to Germans *(Deutschenrechte)*. Among the *Deutschenrechte* are the right to free assembly and to form associations; free movement *(Freizügigkeit);* and the right to choose a profession *(Berufsfreiheit)*, the last two being crucial for a secure residence status. However, the constitutional court has established in its case law that, over time, aliens are due even *Deutschenrechte,* the rights reserved for Germans. The key to this is Article 2(1) of the Basic Law, which guarantees the "free development of personality." The court has expansively interpreted this article as a "residuary" fundamental right *(Auffanggrundrecht),* which guarantees long-settled aliens access to the *Deutschenrechte*. Note that whereas in the United States the constitutional incorporation of aliens occurred in the name of equality, in Germany it occurred in the name of freedom.

If the general freedom clause of the Basic Law is the "how" of constitutional protection for aliens, the question remains as to "when" it applies. If it applied indiscriminately to all aliens who happen to put their feet on German territory, the German state would be a small world state, which it obviously is not. Here the court, in line with constitutional scholarship, has argued that with the alien's increasing length of stay in the territory, the extent of constitutional protection increases. The underlying idea, formulated by Gunther Schwerdtfeger (1980) as *Rechtsschicksal der Unentrinnbarkeit* (the legal fate of inescapability), is that with the alien's increasing stay in Germany the return option becomes ever more fictional, so that he or she has to rely on the German state for existential protection. The constitutional court most succinctly applied this logic in its so-called Indian Case decision of 1978, which concerned the renewal of residence permits (Decision of 26 Sept. 1978 [2 BvR 525/77]). According to the alien law, residence permits were valid for only one year, after which the alien could ask for renewal. Crucially, there was no legal difference between a first and a renewed permit. A renewal could be denied as though it were a first-time application. Yet, in practice, with each renewal the legal situation of the alien did not improve; it grew even worse because continued residence could be seen by the *Land* authority granting residence permits as contradicting the official policy of no immigration of the federal government after the recruitment stop of 1973. In the Indian Case, the constitutional court reversed this logic, arguing that the routine renewal of residence permits in the past created a "reliance interest" on the part of the alien in continued residence, according to the constitutional principle of *Vertrauensschutz* (the protection of legitimate expectations), which the court derived from Article 19 of the Basic Law (the so-called *Rechtsstaatsprinzip*). The court famously added that this individual reliance interest outweighed the state's interest in implementing its no-immigration policy.

The constitutional court's Indian Case decision reveals two distinct features of constitutional alien rights in Germany. First, constitutional protection is incremental. It increases with the length of residence until a threshold is reached that makes even the *Deutschenrechte* available to the alien. This differs from the logic of alien rights in the United States, which started with constitutional equality as a general rule (at least at the subfederal level), and required special justification if differential treatment was introduced (see Rubio-Marín, 2000, 208). Second, this incrementalism is conditional upon a lack of resolve on the part of the state. Temporary guest workers did not turn into permanent settlers because of the automatism of constitutional law; rather, constitutional law was activated only because the state had failed to be explicit about limits and deadlines. Accordingly, the court argued in the Indian Case: "If the residence permit had been issued . . . with a clear indication of its . . . nonrenewability, the plaintiff could not have relied on a renewal and derived claims from his integration [in German society]" (Decision of 26 Sept. 1978 [2 BvR 525/77] p. 188). In other words, Germany's guest worker immigration was a historical accident. It could have been avoided if the state had shown more determination to stop it at an early stage.

This is why, in the early 1990s, Germany was able to embark on a second round of guest worker recruitment, this time with the countries of eastern and central Europe (see Rudolph, 1996, 1998). These programs, which in 1996 accounted for 10 percent of the 2.14 million legally employed foreigners in Germany, have a variety of motivations, such as resolving temporary labor shortages in certain sectors (agriculture, hotels and restaurants, and the construction industry); legalizing existing illegal employment patterns; and reducing migration pressure at the vulnerable eastern EU border. This time, individual work and residence permits, which are framed by bilateral agreements with the sending states, stipulate maximum periods that cannot be extended (with a threat of forced rotations); they preclude the possibility of family reunification; and they do not allow the "upgrading" of a worker's legal status over time. To implement these provisions, the German state authorities have introduced a tight internal control system with frequent checks at work sites and substantial employer fines in cases of violations of work contract conditions and illegal employment. If the state maintains its resolve, there will be no Basic Law to protect the new labor migrants from eastern and central Europe.

Germany's two guest worker programs, both of which were processed under rather different legal regimes, should caution against making blanket statements about alien rights without specifying the distinct category or group of aliens in question. Matters are further complicated by the existence of "privileged" categories of foreigners, such as the nationals of member states of the European Union, who are exempt from Germany's Foreigner Law altogether and who enjoy equal work and residence rights according to European Community (EC) law. Accordingly, guest workers from Italy, Spain, and Greece have never had to rely on constitutional law; they were already protected by EC law. The alien groups around which the system of constitutional rights protection has been built are all from non-EU states, especially from Turkey and the former Yugoslavia, which together provided more than half the classic guest workers in Germany. Constitutional law has helped them to avoid deportation, stabilize their residence, reunify with their families,[8] and ultimately to enjoy equal civil and social rights.

Equally important, however, has been the development within the political elite of a moral compact with Germany's guest workers, who had been brought into the country and could not then be disposed of at will. The new Foreigner Law of 1990, which put into the form of statutory law the positions hammered out by earlier constitutional court decisions, also contains some extra concessions that transcend the constitutional minimum, such as waiving a one-year waiting period for the spouses of settled foreigners and granting the right of (re)return to second-generation guest workers who had temporarily returned to their country of citizenship. This was perhaps a moral calculation, according to which being generous to old guest workers was the best way of being decidedly less generous to the new ones.

The European Union

The European Union is not a state, but a treaty-based, functional regime established by a number of European states to create and supervise a common economic market, that is, "an area without internal frontiers in which the free movement of goods, persons, services, and capital is ensured" (European Community Treaty, Article 7a). However, adding human beings to the list of free movement entities helped to unleash a dynamic that brought the EU to the brink of state building, which is acknowledged in the Maastricht Treaty's creation of an EU "citizenship."[9] Human beings were originally conceived of as functionally specific factors of production ("workers," according to Article 48 of the European Community Treaty), but in having bodies, souls, and social needs attached to them, they eventually matured into functionally diffuse "citizens," which in common understanding are state-constituting units. The spillover from worker to citizen repeats at the supranational level a dialectic that Karl

8. For a discussion of the constitutional court's three "classic" alien cases, dealing with deportation, residence, and family reunification, see Joppke (1999, chap. 3).

9. Originally reluctant to include free movement rights for workers, the founding states of the European Community were pushed in this direction by Italy, which sought a European solution to its domestic unemployment problem (see Romero, 1993).

Polanyi (1944) identified in the national development of welfare capitalism. However, a legal dynamic, not class struggle, is what is responsible for this outcome. This dynamic consists of the transmutation of the European Community from a treaty-based international organization into a lawmaking sovereign in specified domains. A key element in this transmutation is the "constitutionalization" of the European Community Treaty, which refers to the process in which the European Court of Justice (ECJ) (created as the guardian of EC law) came to interpret the European Community Treaty as though it were the constitution of a federal state, conferring rights on individuals and trumping the national laws of the member states (see Weiler, 1991). This was a process fiercely resisted by the member states and, regarding the work- and settlement-oriented movement of people across borders (that is, immigration), it showed a conflict constellation similar to the one in nation-states: courts defending the rights of immigrants against the restrictionist leanings of governments.

There is one crucial difference, however, between the legal empowerment of immigrants in Europe and in nation-states. The formal constitutions of nation-states guarantee elementary human rights irrespective of citizenship, which courts may use to protect (settled) aliens. In contrast, the informal constitution of Europe applies only to nationals of the member states, over whose definition Europe also has no competence. The legal empowerment of immigrants in Europe is thus limited to exogenously defined "privileged" immigrants who are citizens of one of the member states of the European Union. In the early literature these privileged cross-border movers were referred to as migrant workers, which one author characterized as "a legal status somewhere between immigrant [and] citizen" (Garth, 1986, 89). The notion of a migrant worker has, in the meantime, disappeared, which attests to the successful integration of internal cross-border movers into the fabric of Europe.

States may have created the European Community to further their economic and political interests, but their creation, like the fabled sorcerer's apprentice, in turn took on a life of its own, one that conflicted with the interests of its creators. In few domains is the clash between state interests and emergent supranational interests as visible as it is in the free movement of workers, and in few domains has the victory of supranational over state interests been more marked. The hero in this play has been the European Court of Justice, about which one of its former members remarked: "If it can be said to be a good thing that our Europe is not merely a Europe of commercial interests, it is the judges who must take much of the credit" (Mancini, 1992, 67). In its case law, the ECJ first established "a hermeneutic monopoly" over the concept of worker and the rights attached to it, and then interpreted both as broadly as possible (p. 67).

Articles 48 to 51 of the EC Treaty, which establish "freedom of movement for workers," do not define who is a worker. As the ECJ determined in *Hoekstra* (1964), "worker" had to be an EC term because otherwise "each Member State [could] modify the meaning of the concept of 'migrant worker' and . . . eliminate at will the protection afforded by the Treaty to certain categories of persons" (quoted in Craig and DeBurca, 1995, 662). In subsequent case law, the court has used its hermeneutic monopoly in a liberal way, defining as work every "effective and genuine economic activity" (*Levin* case of 1982), which included part-time work, work below the minimum wage, and unpaid work. In *Antonissen* (1989), the court ruled that "freedom of movement for workers" included even the right to look for work in other member states. This was plainly against the meaning of Article 48, which allowed only demand-induced migration, that is, free movement "to accept offers of employment already made." This wording was not accidental but betrayed the intention of member states to reduce the migratory implications of the Community (see Romero, 1993). With *Antonissen,* the court single-handedly turned demand-induced into supply-induced migration, thus increasing potential migration within the Community, in direct contradiction of state interests.

Not only did the ECJ interpret the notion of "worker" as broadly as possible, it also defined the two remaining weapons of member states—the "public service" and "public interest" derogations of Article 48—as narrowly as possible. Article 48(4) states that free movement rights "shall not apply to employment in the public service." In dealing with this "public service" derogation, the court followed the same strategy as above: establish that public service is an EC concept and then interpret it in the "spirit" of the EC Treaty, which is about eroding the barriers to the "free movement of goods, persons, services and capital." In the two *Commission v. Belgium* cases (1980 and 1982), whose importance to the member states is evidenced by the fact that Belgium was supported by the governments of France, Germany, and the United Kingdom, the member states claimed an institutional interpretation of "public service," according to which the site of employment mattered. This meant that states had the right—in the case of France and Belgium, even the constitutional obligation— to restrict railway, hospital, and postal jobs to their nationals. The court did not follow this reasoning, arguing that for the sake of the "unity and efficacy" of EC law, public service had to be an EC concept, and it then prescribed a narrower, functional understanding of this term to denote the actual exercise of state authority by, for instance, police officers, soldiers, and tax assessors (see Craig and DeBurca, 1995, 677).

The court applied a similarly narrow interpretation to the "public interest" derogation, the second state defense against free movement rights, according to which the latter were "subject to limitations justified on grounds of public policy, public security or public health" (Article 48[3]). In the early days, member states used this derogation expansively to expel unwanted pocket thieves, prostitutes, members of religious sects, and trade union activists. In successive case law, the court narrowed the grounds for deportation to exceptional cases of individually proved "personal conduct" that threatened "the fundamental interests of society," which was a difficult threshold for member-state governments to meet (*Boucherau* case of 1977, quoted in Mancini, 1992, 76).

It is important to visualize the context of all these court decisions: the denial of residence permits or deportation orders against EU aliens by member states, which were invalidated by the court's creative interpretation of "migrant worker." While the court could not sever the functional nexus between "worker" and the entitlement to free movement, it made it nearly meaningless.

ECJ activism thus destroyed the capacity of sovereign nation-states to control the conditions of entry and residence of a large class of noncitizens, which in each case by far exceeded the number of its own citizens. This fact alone qualifies as a novelty in the history of the international state system. The enormity of this intervention is further magnified if one considers not only the scope, but the substance of the free movement right. Applying the general nondiscrimination clause of the European Community Treaty (Article 6) to the free movement of workers, Article 48(2) prescribes "the abolition of any discrimination based on nationality between workers of the Member States as regards employment, remuneration, and other conditions of work and employment." This sounds harmless and does not go much beyond the bilateral agreements that have framed the recruitment of guest workers in postwar Europe. "Judicial acrobatics" (Mancini, 1992) of the European Court of Justice, however, have turned the nondiscrimination guarantee into a massive, workplace-transcending encroachment on national education and welfare systems, which dwarfs even the EU-induced loss of state control over entry and residence.

The lack of a European social policy is proverbial and much deplored (see, e.g., Streeck, 1996). However, most authors have overlooked the "negative" social policy reforms forced upon member states by the imperative of unhindered labor mobility (see Leibfried and Pierson, 1995). Among other adaptive changes, European welfare states have lost control over their beneficiaries since they were forced by EC law to include EU aliens on equal terms. Of particular importance for the "low politics" of ECJ-driven social policy coordination has been Regulation 1612/68, a secondary legislation that explicates the substantive rights of workers and their families (who are not mentioned in the EC Treaty). An extensive list of migrant rights already, it has been even more extensively interpreted by the court. Article 12 of this regulation guarantees "equal access" for the children of migrant workers to the host state's educational system. In *Michael S.* (1973), the court ruled that the list of educational arrangements enumerated in the article was not exhaustive and could cover also disability benefits, which is in contravention to a Belgian law that granted disability benefits only to those foreigners who had been diagnosed as disabled *after* their entry in Belgium. This ruling amounted to an invitation for "welfare shopping" (see Garth, 1986, 102). In *Casagrande* (1974), the court determined that "equal access" to the educational system included the entitlement to state-paid educational grants for secondary school in Germany (which had been confined to nationals). This controversial rule construed a link between European free labor mobility and educational and cultural policy, over which the EC usually has no competence, and which in Germany is even the prerogative of the subfederal *Länder*.

But the most far-reaching provision for migrant workers and their families has been Article 7(2) of Regulation 1612/68, which states that migrant workers "shall enjoy the same social and tax advantages as national workers." In its case law, the ECJ detached the notion of social advantage from employment, so that it came to justify, for instance, the right to a minimum wage for the parent of a migrant worker, university grants for the benefit of a migrant worker's child, and reduced railway fares for large families (see Mancini, 1992, 74). In *Reina* (1982), even an interest-free "childbirth loan" issued by a German state bank to German nationals in order to boost the country's low birthrate was considered a "social advantage" within Article 7(2), so that it could not be withheld from an Italian couple living in Germany. This meant that the free mobility imperative incapacitated a member state's demographic policy and its attempt to tie a small benefit to citizenship. "Are there limits to the rights which may be claimed by a worker under Article 7(2)?" two authors (Craig and DeBurca, 1995, 693) have asked, apparently rhetorically because, short of the political right to vote in national elections, the court's liberal interpretation of this clause has erased all limits to substantive rights accruing from free movement.[10]

The friendly picture for EU aliens is counterpointed by a decidedly less friendly picture for non-EU aliens (commonly labeled third-state nationals). These "immigrants" proper, who form more than 60 percent of all noncitizen

---

10. The violation of fundamental state interests by the ECJ decisions on migrant workers raises the general question why the member states did not resist. This is one of the most fascinating chapters in the history of de facto European state building, which also sets the EC sharply apart from pre-Reconstruction America (where subfederal states were much more prone to ignore or even explicitly reject federal Supreme Court ruling; see Friedman Goldstein, 1997). One part of the answer is the "preliminary rulings" procedure under Article 177 of the EC Treaty, which enlisted the authority of national courts in the European Court's imposition of European over national law. See the interesting reflections by a participant (Mancini, 1991).

residents in the EU,[11] are definitionally excluded from the reach of EC law. The free movement clauses of the treaty (Article 48 to 51) do not specify the nationality of "workers," so that it is possible to construe residence, rather than nationality, as the activating condition (see Plender, 1988, 197). However, secondary legislation and ECJ rules have left no measure of doubt that only member-state nationals are covered by these clauses.

The contradiction of expansive rights for third-state resident aliens at the member-state level and their niggardly exclusion from the European project has been the target of endless polemics, but it still awaits a convincing scholarly explanation. Such an explanation would certainly identify the grounding of free movement rights in nationality rather than residence as a "political choice" by member states that wished to minimize the migratory implications of an integrated Europe (O'Leary, 1992, 66).[12] If one applies a state analogy to the EU, the exclusion of third-state nationals from free movement rights amounts to a state reserving civil and social rights to its citizens only, which is a deviation from the practice of liberal states to grant such rights also to its resident aliens. The successful inclusion of third-state nationals at member-state level notwithstanding, it is questionable whether such a gross violation of a liberal state principle by the EU can be stable over time.

The sharp distinction between privileged EU aliens and nonprivileged third-state aliens shows that even at the supranational level it is bounded quasi-citizen norms rather than unbounded human rights norms that have helped (or hindered!) the integration of immigrants. At the EU level, third-state nationals enjoy only indirect rights, which accrue from family ties to EU citizens or employment ties to EU service providers.[13] Second, third-state nationals have rights flowing from international agreements, such as the "association treaties" between the EU and Turkey and a number of Maghreb countries.[14] Finally, third-

11. Of the approximately 13 million noncitizen residents in the EU, more than 8 million are from third states, the rest being from other member states.

12. Considering that only 5 million of more than 300 million member state citizens have chosen to reside in another member state, the migratory implications of granting free movement rights to the 8 million third-state nationals in the EU are believed to be small (see Muus, 1997).

13. There are some exceptions, such as the equality of treatment for men and women prescribed in Article 119 of the EC Treaty and a few EC directives on worker protection, which apply irrespective of nationality (Hailbronner and Polakiewicz, 1992, 65).

14. The rights flowing from association treaties include the free choice of employer after prescribed periods of lawful residence and employment in a member state, and equal treatment in the area of social security. In a series of controversial rules, the ECJ sought to bring association law under the scope of European Community law, thus approximating the rights of (Turkish or North African) third-state nationals to those of European Union citizens (see critically Hailbronner and Polakiewicz, 1992, 55–59).

state nationals have resort to the non-EU, nationality-blind European Convention of Human Rights.[15] Taken together, these European sources of immigrant rights are inferior to (and sometimes imitative of) the protections that settled third-state aliens enjoy at the member-state level (see Guiraudon, 1998b).

Since the mid-1970s, the European Commission (the executive organ of the European Union) has waged repeated initiatives to bring third-state nationals under the umbrella of EC law—to no avail (see Cholewinski, 1997, 233–37). Control over external immigration has turned out to be one of the most jealously guarded prerogatives of member states. When the Commission, in 1985, wanted to bind the member states into a notification and consultation procedure regarding their external immigration and immigrant policies, the member states successfully appealed through the ECJ, and they added to the Single European Act of 1987 that "nothing in these provisions shall affect the right of Member States to . . . [control] immigration from third countries" (quoted in Papademetriou, 1997, 24). In the wake of the Maastricht Treaty, which invited member states to at least coordinate their external immigration policies within the so-called Third Pillar, a second Commission attempt to launch a comprehensive European approach to immigration was all but ignored (Papademetriou, 1997, 83–88). The Amsterdam Treaty's move of the immigration function from the intergovernmental Third Pillar into the supranational First Pillar, however, will make a European policy on third-state nationals inevitable. The sheer fact that borderless free movement will remain unavailable to member-state nationals if third-state nationals continue to be controlled by states suggests upward pressure on the rights of the European Union's remaining "immigrants."

Conclusion

The preceding comparison demonstrates the central role of courts and domestic legal orders (especially constitutions) in the development of alien rights while suggesting that the migrant group and polity under investigation be differentiated carefully. It is now time to link the generalizing and particularizing strands of my analysis. The case of alien rights is part of a larger trend in postwar societies, in which activist courts have aggressively defended the rights of individuals against intrusive states. Next to policing the complex division of powers within an expanding state machinery, the protection of fundamental rights and liberties has been one justification for courts to take on the role of active policy maker, and thus to intrude into a domain that had previously been

15. For overviews of the rights of third-state nationals in the EU, see Alexander (1992), Hailbronner and Polakiewicz (1992), and Peers (1996).

reserved for parliament and the state executive (Shapiro and Stone, 1994, 414). A long-standing feature of American political life, the judicialization of politics, is a novelty in Europe, where reference to the democratic deficit of the judiciary and a traditional view of the state as the sole originator of rights, against whom individuals could not have rights, had kept the courts and the legal system in low profile. The legal empowerment of immigrants, which we observe in all three polities considered here, is thus part of a larger story of an expanding judicial domain and the proliferation of "rights" that goes along with it.

Yet the picture of an adversarial relation between courts as rights defenders and executive states as rights bashers conveyed by this comparison needs to be qualified. In functionally differentiated societies, legal systems are autonomous, and they operate according to system-specific codes and principles, which are different from those that govern the political system (see Luhmann, 1993). But courts are also dependent parts of political regimes, endowed with the tasks of conflict resolution and social control (see Shapiro, 1981). Immigrants—always vulnerable individuals in need of protection from vindictive states—are tailor-made targets for the courts to assert (in important respects citizenship-blind) individual rights against the whims of majoritarian governments. If one defines individual rights as "trumps" over the preferences of the government-represented majority in society (Dworkin, cited in Waldron, 1991, 364f), one could argue that immigrants—by definition excluded from this majority—are the most dramatic test case of rights in general. Yet there is also a line, differently drawn in different polities and varying over time, that prudent and self-limiting courts will not transgress. The German constitutional court has championed the rights of guest workers, but it did so in the context of an undecided government that hesitated to rotate the guest workers. By contrast, when the government was firm in its intention to close down unwanted asylum seeking, the court refused to get in its way, rubberstamping an unprecedented restriction of a fundamental right guaranteed by the Basic Law. The court's approval, in May 1996, of the so-called asylum compromise between government and the opposition, which ratified a contraction of the Basic Law's asylum guarantee, has accordingly been interpreted as an unwillingness to undo by legal means a hard-won solution of a major conflict in society. One critic (Leicht, 1996) denounced this as "morality losing out against reality." The U.S. Supreme Court has largely defended the rights of permanent resident aliens (legal immigrants) against state governments, which arrogated to themselves unconstitutional immigration powers. When it tackled the politically more sensitive case of illegal immigrants in *Plyler v. Doe* (1982), the Court clarified that its immigrant-friendly decision was premised on the absence of a countervailing federal policy. Further, the

Court has never dared to question the plenary power doctrine, which gives the federal government the upper hand in all immigration matters. Finally, the European Court of Justice has single-handedly transformed migrant workers into Euro-citizens, which was not the least daring of its many factual state-building exercises. However, it has abstained from venturing the possibility that the "workers" or "persons" granted free movement rights by the European Community Treaty could be defined by residence rather than nationality.

A critical variable in the readiness of courts to champion alien rights is the level of political and societal conflict surrounding immigration. If conflict is low, the courts are likely to take a more daring stance, and vice versa. This has been the case in Germany, where the constitutional court's crucial guest worker rulings happened during the 1970s and early 1980s, which was (except for the first national debate on mass asylum seeking in 1980) a period of low conflict. Similarly, the U.S. Supreme Court's landmark rulings on immigrant rights, culminating in *Plyler v. Doe*, were issued at least a decade before a massive anti-immigrant movement would spread eastward from California. This resonates with Virginie Guiraudon's (1998) interesting findings, based on the cases of Germany, the Netherlands, and France, that episodes of rights expansion for immigrants were conditional upon keeping the public out and containing the issue behind the "closed doors" of bureaucracy and judiciary. In her view, under conditions of low conflict, the state executive and judiciary are even more like accomplices, rather than adversaries, in an "enlightened" treatment of immigrants. Danger arises when the public becomes involved and when democratically accountable governments are pushed into defending the rights of "their" people—who are by definition not immigrants. These are moments of potential reversal of alien rights.

I have touched on one example of "high conflict" surrounding immigration: welfare reform in the United States. It has worked to the detriment of immigrants and has been characterized by little judicial interference. The Republican-dominated Congress deemed itself protected by its plenary power in immigration matters. A conservative Supreme Court that in a string of recent decisions against affirmative action has proved susceptible to the current backlash against immigrants and minorities is unlikely to seize this opportunity to question the (however antique) plenary power doctrine.

Next to stressing the legal sources of alien rights, I have also shown that a thoroughly transnational phenomenon, migration, has found a thoroughly national treatment, perhaps most extreme in the European Union case, which left non-EU migrants entirely outside its legal grid. This goes against the grain of a recent postnational approach that sees migrants as being protected by international human rights norms and discourses. A legal version of the postnational approach has been presented by David Jacobson (1996), who claims that international human rights norms, as embodied in customary law, treaties, and conventions, have become the central legitimizing principle of Western states.[16] "Midwives" of the postnational state, according to Jacobson, are domestic courts, which are said to "pay increasing attention to international—indeed, transnational—laws and norms" (p. 106). Unfortunately, Jacobson cannot provide much empirical evidence for these bold propositions.[17] Not only is international law a "soft" law that lacks implementation force, there is also no need for domestic courts in western Europe and North America to invoke international norms, because the scope of protection provided by domestic constitutions is by far superior (see Guiraudon, 1998b).[18]

A more sociological version of the postnational approach comes from Yasemin Soysal (1994). Whereas Jacobson was at least concrete enough to focus on one presumed carrier of international human rights norms (the courts and international law), Soysal conceives of international human rights as a more diffuse and discursive "institutionalized script" that shapes actor identities and provides states with clues on how to treat foreigners in their territories (p. 7). She claims that on the basis of global human rights norms, a "postnational model of membership" has come into existence that has relativized the importance of traditional citizenship. As evidence of the effectiveness of global-level norms, she adduces that similar schemes of postnational membership can be found across (European) states. Not unlike Jacobson, Soysal sees states as mere transmission belts of global human rights norms.[19]

Because of its vagueness, the "discursive" version of the postnational approach is more difficult to counter. Its strongest point is certainly to offer a parsimonious explanation for the convergent trend of expansive alien rights across liberal postwar states. A purely domestic approach fails in this respect, unless it incorporates diffusion and demonstration effects, whereby similar ideas and institutions find sedimentation in different societies. Yet this is no novelty

16. "[I]n North America and Western Europe, the basis of state legitimacy is shifting from principles of sovereignty and national self-determination to international human rights" (Jacobson, 1996, 2).

17. Jacobson (1996) identifies only one U.S. lower-court ruling that invoked international law in an asylum case, and this was quickly overturned by the court of appeals (pp. 98–100). Regarding Western Europe, he cannot cite a single domestic court ruling using international law in a migration case.

18. By the same token, the impact of international human rights norms is more likely to be found in non-Western states with a thin or even absent liberal infrastructure (see Risse, Ropp, and Sikkink, 1999).

19. Unlike Jacobson, however, Soysal (p. 157) admits that the principle of national sovereignty remains a strong contender to that of universal human rights.

resulting from globalization, as Soysal assumes. Reinhard Bendix (1978) has famously shown that systematic international borrowing and emulation through print-based "intellectual mobilization" dates back to the Reformation era and overseas exploration: "Once the church was challenged, a king beheaded, or a parliament supreme; once industrialization was initiated and the ideal of equality proclaimed, no country could remain unaffected. Everywhere people were made aware of events and 'advances' which served as reference points for the assessment of developments at home" (p. 265). States have never been monads but are mutually imitative of each other's ideas and institutions—after all, they are all "nation-states" displaying homologous principles and structures. Discursive postnationalists, however, go one step further in stating that the concept of "human rights" is not just an invention of one state spreading to other states, but a reality existing outside and separate from states, constraining these states from the outside. Applied to immigrant rights, the onus of this approach is to show that the latter derive from this extra-state, "transnational" reality. This forces Soysal, much like Jacobson, into a mechanical listing of "explicit" international human rights codes and conventions (pp. 145ff), conveying rather than demonstrating their effectiveness at the domestic level. If my analysis is correct, however, the latter are plainly irrelevant. Not international norms and conventions, but domestic constitutions have been the spring of immigrant rights.

Even more modestly conceived diffusion and demonstration effects have played a marginal role in the evolution of alien rights, at least in the cases I consider. The European Union, as I have shown, does not recognize the concept of (non-EU) alien rights. In the United States, the triggering factor in mobilizing the personhood clause of the Constitution has been the domestic civil rights revolution of the 1960s, which suggested a perception of aliens as a race-analogous "discrete and insular minority" not to be discriminated against. In Germany the trauma of nazism, where the state carved out a "racial" group only to annihilate it, incapacitated the state from rotating unwanted guest workers and emboldened the constitutional court to put life into the Basic Law's celebration of universal human rights, which no state was allowed to interfere with. In both cases, the legitimation (not just implementation) of expansive alien rights after World War II thus has exclusively domestic roots.[20] The temporal marker "after World War II" points to the only communality between both, which is the moral outlawing of all that smacked of ethnic, national, or racial discrimination after the West's victory over a regime that had carried such discrimination to its murderous extreme.

20. This is in contrast to Soysal's claim (1994, 143) that only the implementation of alien rights is domestic, whereas their legitimation is based on a "transnational order."

Postnationalists have misjudged not only the locus of alien rights, but also their logic. In a postnational reading, alien rights are universal human rights, which protect abstract personhood irrespective of an individual's communal boundedness and involvements. Regarding migrants, however, the only such personhood right is probably the right of asylum. For all other migrants, a different, communitarian logic is at work: the scope of rights increases with the length of residence and the development of ties to the receiving society. This was most clearly expressed in the German legal doctrine *Rechtsschicksal der Unentrinnbarkeit,* according to which over time even constitutional citizen rights (except the right to vote) could not be denied to long-settled foreigners. Tempered by a stronger constitutional equality norm, a similar "affiliation model" (Motomura, 1998) has also undergirded the rights of legal permanent residents in the United States. It was formulated most explicitly in the Supreme Court's *Mathews v. Diaz* (1976) decision, which allowed the federal government to deny Medicare benefits to permanent residents who had been in the country for less than five years: "Congress may decide that as the alien's tie [with this country] grows stronger, so does the strength of his claim to an equal share of that munificence" (quoted in Motomura, 1998, 205).

According to the logic of affiliation and *Unentrinnbarkeit,* alien rights are not abstract human rights but are bounded protocitizen rights that reflect the involvement of individuals in the rights-granting community.

What are the implications of this comparison of alien rights for citizenship, the subject of this volume? One way of drawing a connection is on the normative plane: if liberal-democratic states are faithful to their own principles, they must either approximate the status of legal permanent resident alien to that of citizen, or they can continue to discriminate against settled aliens, but they must then make citizenship easily accessible to them (see Rubio-Marín, 2000). However, this normative either-or has generally not been followed in the real world. Before the welfare onslaught in the 1990s, the United States granted alien rights that were nearly equal to citizen rights, while citizenship was easily accessible. This was the backdrop to the "devaluation of citizenship" (Schuck, 1989) complaint of, by now, earlier days. The most one can say about the U.S. case is that the compromising of alien rights, which was always structurally possible because of the plenary power doctrine, looks much less dramatic if held against a (now as before) liberal nationality law. By contrast, Germany once did come close to an either-or constellation in which one of the most expansive systems of alien rights stood against one of the most restrictive citizenship regimes in the Western world. For reasons that cannot be further explored here, this constellation proved to be untenable. It was documented by Germany's liberalization of nationality law in the spring of 1999. The recent

U.S.-German citizenship experience combined—in which a restrictionist attack on a liberal citizenship regime could be deflected (United States) and a liberalizing attack on a restrictive citizenship regime prevailed (Germany)—supports the thesis of a general liberalization of nationality law in liberal-democratic states (see Weil in this volume; Joppke, 2000). The impact of liberalized citizenship regimes on alien rights remains to be seen. In the case of Germany, it is safe to say that for constitutional reasons alone a rollback of alien rights is not in the cards.

Works Cited

Aleinikoff, T. Alexander, et al. 1995. *Immigration: Process and Policy.* St. Paul, Minn.: West.

Alexander, Willy. 1992. "Free Movement of Non-EC Nationals." *European Journal of International Law* 3: 53–64.

Bendix, Reinhard. 1978. *Kings or People?* Berkeley: University of California Press.

Bosniak, Linda S. 1994. "Membership, Equality, and the Difference that Alienage Makes." *New York University Law Review* 69(6): 1047–1149.

Brubaker, Rogers. 1992. *Citizenship and Nationhood in France and Germany.* Cambridge: Harvard University Press.

Cappelletti, Mauro, Monica Seccombe, and Joseph Weiler (eds.). 1986. *Integration through Law: Europe and the American Federal Experience.* Berlin: de Gruyter. (Multiple volumes)

Cholewinski, Ryszard. 1997. *Migrant Workers in International Human Rights Law.* Oxford: Clarendon Press.

Craig, Paul, and Grainne de Burca. 1995. *EC Law.* Oxford: Clarendon Press.

Friedman Goldstein, Leslie. 1997. "State Resistance to Authority in Federal Unions." *Studies in American Political Development* 11: 149–89.

Garth, Bryant G. 1986. *Migrant Workers and Rights of Mobility in the EC and the US.* In Cappelletti et al. (1986).

Guiraudon, Virginie. 1998a. "Citizenship Rights for Non-Citizens." In C. Joppke, *Challenge to the Nation-State: Immigration in Western Europe and the United States.* Oxford: Oxford University Press.

———. 1998b. *Sovereign After All? International Norms, Nation-States, and Aliens.* Unpublished manuscript.

Hailbronner, Kay, and Jörg Polakiewicz. 1992. "Non-EC Nationals in the European Community." *Duke Journal of Comparative and International Law* 3: 49–88.

Henkin, Louis. 1990. *The Age of Rights.* New York: Columbia University Press.

Herz, John. 1957. "The Rise and Demise of the Territorial State," *World Politics* 9: 473–93.

Jacobson, David. 1996. *Rights Across Borders.* Baltimore, Md.: Johns Hopkins University Press.

Joppke, Christian. 1999. *Immigration and the Nation-State: The United States, Germany, and Great Britain.* Oxford: Oxford University Press.

————. 2000. "Mobilization of Culture and the Reform of Citizenship Law: Germany and the United States." In Ruud Koopmans and Paul Statham (eds.), *Challenging Immigration and Ethnic Relations Politics*. Oxford: Oxford University Press.

Kommers, Donald P. 1997. *The Constitutional Jurisprudence of the Federal Republic of Germany*. 2nd ed. Durham, N.C.: Duke University Press.

Leibfried, Stephan, and Paul Pierson (eds.). 1995. *European Social Policy*. Washington, D.C.: Brookings Institution.

Leicht, Robert. 1996. "Adieu Asyl." *Die Zeit*, May 17, p. 1.

Luhmann, Niklas. 1993. *Das Recht der Gesellschaft*. Frankfurt a.M.: Suhrkamp.

Mancini, Federico. 1991. "The Making of a Constitution for Europe." In Robert O. Keohane and Stanley Hoffmann (eds.), *The New European Community: Decisionmaking and Institutional Change*. Boulder, Colo.: Westview.

————. 1992. "The Free Movement of Workers in the Case-Law of the European Court of Justice." In D. Curtin and D. O'Keefe, *Constitutional Adjudication in European Community and National Law*. Dublin: Butterworth.

Motomura, Hiroshi. 1990. "Immigration Law after a Century of Plenary Power." *Yale Law Journal* 100(3): 545–613.

————. 1998. "Alienage Classifications in a Nation of Immigrants." In Noah Pickus (ed.), *Immigration and Citizenship in the Twenty-first Century*. Lanham, Md.: Rowman and Littlefield.

Muus, Philip. 1997. "A Study on the Expected Effects of Free Movement for Legally Residing Workers from Third Countries within the European Community." In Philip Muus et al., *Free Movement for Non-EC Workers within the European Community*. Utrecht: Nederlands Centrum Buitenlanders.

Needelman, Jeffrey. 1997. "Attacking Federal Restrictions on Noncitizens' Access to Public Benefits on Constitutional Grounds." *Georgetown Immigration Law Journal* 11: 330–87.

Levi, David F. 1979. "Notes. The Equal Treatment of Aliens: Preemption or Equal Protection?" *Stanford Law Review* 31:1069–91.

O'Leary, Siofra. 1992. "Nationality Law and Community Citizenship." *Yearbook of European Law* 12.

Papademetriou, Demetrios. 1997. *Coming Together or Pulling Apart: The EU's Struggle with Immigration and Asylum*. Washington, D.C.: Carnegie Endowment for International Peace.

Peers, Steve. 1996. "Towards Equality: Actual and Potential Rights of Third-Country Nationals in the European Union." *Common Market Law Review* 33: 7–50.

Plender, Richard. 1988. *International Migration Law*. 2nd ed. Dordrecht: Nijhoff.

Polanyi, Karl. 1944. *The Great Transformation*. Boston: Beacon Press.

Risse, Thomas, Stephen Ropp, and Kathryn Sikkink (eds.). 1999. *The Power of Human Rights*. Cambridge: Cambridge University Press.

Romero, Federico. 1993. "Migration as an Issue in European Interdependence and Integration: The Case of Italy." In Alan Milward et al., *The Frontier of National Sovereignty*. London: Routledge.

Rosberg, Gerald. 1983. "Discrimination against the 'Nonresident' Alien." *University of Pittsburgh Law Review* 44: 399–407.

Rubio-Marín, Ruth. 2000. *Immigration as a Democratic Challenge*. Cambridge: Cambridge University Press.

Rudolph, Hedwig. 1996. "The New Gastarbeiter System in Germany." *New Community* 22(2): 287–300.

———. 1998. *The New German Guest-Worker Schemes and Their Implementation*. Paper presented at the European Forum conference "Dilemmas of Immigration Control in a Globalizing World," European University Institute, June 11–12, Florence.

Scharpf, Fritz. 1994. *Optionen des Föderalismus in Deutschland und Europa*. Frankfurt a.M.: Campus.

Schuck, Peter. 1984. "The Transformation of Immigration Law." *Columbia Law Review* 84(1): 1–90.

———. 1989. "Membership in the Liberal Polity." In Rogers Brubaker (ed.), *Immigration and the Politics of Citizenship in Europe and North America*. Lanham, Md.: University Press of America.

———.1998. "The Re-Evaluation of American Citizenship." In C. Joppke (ed.), *Challenge to the Nation-State: Immigration in Western Europe and the United States*. Oxford: Oxford University Press.

Schwerdtfeger, Gunther. 1980. *Welche rechtlichen Vorkehrungen empfehlen sich, um die Rechtsstellung von Ausländern in der Bundesrepublik Deutschland angemessen zu gestalten?* Gutachten A zum 53. Deutschen Juristentag Berlin 1980. Munich: Beck.

Shapiro, Martin. 1981. *Courts*. Chicago: University of Chicago Press.

Shapiro, Martin, and Alec Stone. 1994. "The New Constitutional Politics of Europe." *Comparative Political Studies* 26(4): 397–420.

Soysal, Yasemin Nuhoğlu. 1994. *Limits of Citizenship: Migrants and Postnational Membership in Europe*. Chicago: University of Chicago Press.

Spiro, Peter J. 1994. "The States and Immigration in an Era of Demi-Sovereignties." *Virginia Journal of International Law* 35: 121–78.

Streeck, Wolfgang. 1996. "Neo-Voluntarism." In Gary Marks et al., *Governance in the European Union*. London: Sage.

Waldron, Jeremy. 1991. *Liberal Rights*. Cambridge: Cambridge University Press.

Weiler, Joseph. 1991. "The Transformation of Europe." *Yale Law Journal* 100(3): 2403–83.

Weiner, Myron. 1995. *The Global Migration Crisis*. New York: HarperCollins.

CHAPTER THREE

Plural Nationality: Facing the Future in a Migratory World

T. ALEXANDER ALEINIKOFF
DOUGLAS KLUSMEYER

IN A PERFECTLY symmetrical world each individual citizen or national is a member of one and only one state. In the past, many political theorists and legal scholars have imagined such a world. They denounced the very idea of dual nationality as unnatural and likened it to a bigamous marriage. Today, defenders of postnational and transnational understandings of political membership see in the phenomenon of dual nationality the harbinger of a new world, one no longer dominated by the nation-state. Whether one sees the rising trend of plural nationality as positive or negative, there is no denying that its incidence is widespread and growing. One recent study, for example, has estimated that more than a half million children born each year in the United States have at least one additional nationality (Aleinikoff, 1998, 28). Another study reports that 60 percent of Swiss nationals who live abroad do so as dual nationals (Schuck, 1998, 223).

How should the rising incidence of plural nationals be understood? In this chapter we address this question by first examining the concept of nationality under domestic and international law. Then we focus on the issue of plural nationality itself and on state responses to it. We group state responses to dual nationality as *open, tolerant,* or *restrictive* according to a range of factors. With this background, we conclude by assessing traditional objections to the phenomenon of plural nationality, arguing that the threats that plural nationals seemingly pose have historically proved to be more hypothetical than real.

Part I: The Concept of Nationality under Domestic and International Law

Nationality is a legal-political category that constitutes the most basic legal nexus between an individual and a state. It involves a reciprocal relationship, obligating the state to protect an individual and investing an individual with duties to that state.

The right of a state to determine its nationality policy has long been considered an essential attribute of sovereignty, although emerging international legal norms have somewhat qualified this authority. Accordingly, nationality has traditionally been determined under municipal law, and states have wide latitude in setting their rules for its acquisition and loss. While under the direct province of municipal law, nationality has important functions under international law. The first concerns a state's right to protect its nationals in relation to other states. Nationality provides the basis under international law for one state to protect persons or property in another. A second function is the right that nationality confers on an individual to be admitted to and to reside in the territory of the state of nationality. This right rests on the premise that the international order requires a territorial allocation of persons according to membership in states. These twin functions establish a link between the individual and international law, whose primary subjects are states.

Nationality can be acquired by several means. The most common are: (1) by birth on the sovereign's territory (jus soli), (2) by descent from one or both parents who are nationals (jus sanguinis), (3) by marriage, (4) through adoption or legitimation, (5) upon naturalization, and (6) by territorial transfer from one state to another. Because there is no international uniformity among states in their application of these criteria, their overlap affords multiple opportunities for the acquisition of multiple nationalities. Children can acquire them from parents having different nationalities. Children may also obtain multiple nationalities when they are born in states that recognize the principle of jus soli and whose parents are nationals of states that base acquisition on the principle of jus sanguinis. Spouses of different nationalities may acquire their partners' nationalities without having to renounce their own. States that have experienced large-scale emigration may offer their emigrants the right to retain their nationality even when acquiring a new nationality and may facilitate the descent of nationality to future expatriate generations.[1] (Table 3-1 summarizes the key citizenship rules for twenty states.)

1. Determining the criteria of acquisition can be especially complex when one state succeeds another as sovereign of a territory. Under international law, successor states cannot impose na-

The limitations that international legal norms impose on a state's authority over nationality policy are unclear but remain decidedly modest. The Universal Declaration of Human Rights, adopted by the General Assembly of the United Nations in 1948, sets forth two general principles with direct bearing on nationality (Brownlie, 1992, 21–27). Article 13(2) recognizes that "[e]veryone has the right to leave any country, including his own, and to return to his or her country." Article 15 proclaims the right of everyone to a nationality. It further stipulates that "no one shall be arbitrarily deprived of his nationality nor denied the right to change his nationality." As the preamble makes clear, the Universal Declaration was not intended to be legally binding, but its provisions (along with other indications of state practice) are often invoked as evidence of customary international human rights law.[2]

Later human rights convenants that implicate different aspects of nationality *are* legally binding on contracting states. Article 1 of the 1957 Convention on the Nationality of Married Women, for example, stipulates that "neither the celebration nor the dissolution of a marriage between one of its nationals and an alien, nor change of nationality by the husband, shall automatically affect the nationality of the wife" (Plender, 1997, 119–23). Article 2 provides further: "Each Contracting State agrees that neither the voluntary acquisition of the

---

tionality on their new territorial inhabitants, and any conferment must be construed as an offer that must be accepted to be valid. An offer is never automatic and is governed by the municipal law of the successor state, if not by treaty. Nevertheless, the presumption in international law is that the municipal law of the successor state will result in the conferral of nationality on the persons residing in the transferred territory. For nationals residing outside the transferred territory, the municipal law of the transferring state (presuming the state has not lost its sovereignty through conquest or other means) determines whether the nationals retain their nationality. If the predecessor state does withdraw nationality from such persons, the successor state cannot confer nationality without the permission of the state of residence. In cases of territorial cession, the ceding state is obligated to remove its nationality from those persons who receive the nationality of the acquiring state and to respect the municipal law of the acquiring state. (This obligation is grounded on the premise that a ceding state's refusal to withdraw nationality is tantamount to a state imposing nationality on a foreign national residing outside its territory. By this refusal, the ceding state has an *extraterritorial effect* on persons outside its territorial jurisdiction. This effect can be binding only if the state of residence has given its consent, since it has supreme authority in its own jurisdiction.) Should the ceding state not fulfill this obligation, third-party states have a duty to recognize only the nationality of the acquiring state.

Art. 10 of the 1961 United Nations Convention on the Reduction of Statelessness imposes a duty on contracting parties to include provisions in every treaty involving territorial transfer "designed to secure that no person shall become stateless as a result of the transfer. A Contracting State shall use its best endeavours to secure that any such treaty made by it with a State which is not a party to this convention includes such provisions" (Plender, 1997, 127).

2. The preamble describes the declaration as setting forth "a common standard of achievement for all peoples and nations" that will "promote a common understanding of these rights and freedoms."

Table 3-1. *Rules of Citizenship in Selected Countries*

Country	Jus Soli[1]	Jus Sanguinis (1st generation)[2]	Jus Sanguinis (2nd generation)[3]	Renunciation Requirement at Naturalization[4]	Foreign Naturalization/ Retain Citizenship
Australia	Yes, if parent is a citizen or resident alien	Yes, if child registers by age 18 or after if good reason is shown	Yes, if parent has been resident in Australia for a total of two years	No	No, unless naturalization is automatic (i.e., through marriage)
Austria	No	Yes	Yes	Yes	No
Canada	Yes	Yes	Yes, if registers before age 28 and establishes one-year residency or "substantial connection"	No	Yes
Denmark	No	Yes	Yes, with residency requirement or petition	Yes	No
Estonia	Yes, for children born after restoration	Yes	Yes	Yes, except for ethnic Estonians	Yes, but naturalized citizens will lose their Estonian citizenship
Finland	No	Yes	Yes, with residency requirement or petition	Yes	No
France	Yes, with conditions	Yes	Yes	No	Yes

Germany	Yes, for children born after Jan. 1, 2000, if parent is a citizen or permanent resident with a minimum of eight years' legal residence[5]	Yes, with registration if parent is born abroad after Jan. 1, 2000	Yes	No, with exceptions for national interest
Israel	No	No	Yes, but does not apply to Jews	Yes
Italy	No	Yes	No. The law is currently blocked by ministerial decree to prohibit dual citizenship	Yes
Japan	No	Yes, with registration	Yes	Yes
Latvia	Yes	Yes	Yes	No, unless naturalization occurred before restoration
Lithuania	Yes, if parent is a citizen	Yes	Yes	No
Mexico	Yes	No	Yes	Yes, retain nationality
Portugal	Yes, if parent is a citizen or resident alien	Yes	No	No
Russian Federation	No	No	No	Yes

(table continues)

Table 3-1. *continued*

Country	Jus Soli	Jus Sanguinis (1st generation)	Jus Sanguinis (2nd generation)	Renunciation Requirement at Naturalization	Foreign Naturalization/ Retain Citizenship
South Africa	Yes, if parent is a citizen or permanent resident	Yes	Yes	No	Yes, unless other citizenship is activated
Sweden	No	Yes	Yes, with residency requirement or petition	Yes, unless citizenship is acquired by right of declaration	No
United Kingdom	Yes, if parent is a citizen or permanent resident	Yes, if at least one parent is a British citizen other than by descent	No, except when one grandparent is a British citizen otherwise than by descent and at least one parent has resided for three years in U.K. before the birth of the child	No	Yes
United States	Yes	Yes	Yes, with residency requirement of parent	Yes	Yes

1. Territorial right to citizenship.
2. Children of citizens.
3. Children of parent whose citizenship derives from descent.
4. Some countries make exceptions in cases of hardship (such as for refugees).
5. To retain German citizenship, must renounce any foreign citizenship by age 23.

nationality of another State nor the renunciation of its nationality by one of its nationals shall prevent the retention of its nationality by the wife of such national." Article 1 of the 1961 Convention on the Reduction of Statelessness obligates a "contracting state" to "grant its nationality to a person born in its territory who would otherwise be stateless," while Article 7 stipulates limitations on a contracting state's discretion to revoke nationality. For example, it provides: "A national of a Contracting State who seeks naturalization in a foreign country shall not lose his nationality unless he acquires or has been accorded assurance of acquiring the nationality of that foreign country."

Article 5 of the 1966 International Convention on the Elimination of All Forms of Racial Discrimination guarantees "the right of everyone, without the distinction as to race, color, or national or ethnic origin, to equality before the law, notably in the enjoyment of the following rights" (Brownlie, 1992, 148–68). These rights expressly include the right to leave any country, including one's own, and to return to one's country, and the right to nationality. This convention does not directly guarantee an individual's right to nationality but does mandate observance in the nationality area of the principles of equality and freedom from discrimination.[3] The 1979 Convention on the Elimination of All Forms of Discrimination against Women promotes these principles in the context of gender equality (Brownlie, 1992, 169–81). Article 9(1) of the convention stipulates: "States Parties shall grant women equal rights with men to acquire, change or retain their nationality. They shall ensure in particular that neither marriage to an alien nor change of nationality by the husband during marriage shall automatically change the nationality of the wife, render her stateless or force upon her the nationality of the husband." Article 9(2) provides further: "States Parties shall grant women equal rights with men with respect to the nationality of their children."[4]

Despite the steady growth in adherence to these human rights instruments, commentators who have studied nationality law most closely in both its domestic and international contexts have emphasized the decisive role, and relative autonomy, of states in regulating nationality policy (see, e.g., Weis, 1979, 248–49). Instruments like the UN Convention on the Nationality of Married

---

3. The convention reiterates and expands on the principle enunciated in the 1961 Convention on the Reduction of Statelessness: "A Contracting State may not deprive any person or group of persons of their nationality on racial, ethnic, religious or political grounds" (Art. 9).

4. The 1989 Rights of the Child Convention recognizes a child's independent right to nationality. Art. 7(1) provides: "The child shall be registered immediately after birth and shall have the right from birth to a name [and] the right to acquire a nationality." Art. 8(1) provides further: "State Parties undertake further to respect the right of the child to preserve his or her identity, including nationality . . . without lawful interference" (Brownlie, 1992, 182–202).

Women have probably had their greatest effect in influencing the development of domestic legislation in particular states rather than as binding international legal norms. Nonetheless, these instruments do provide a body of international standards and lay the foundation for the emergence of an international customary law of nationality (Donner, 1994, 389).

Part II: The Issue of Plural Nationality

Traditional theories of the modern state posited that subjects of a state owed an exclusive duty of loyalty and obedience to their sovereign (Spiro, 1997). By this view, multiple ties of loyalty were unthinkable, and an individual could not transfer obligations of allegiance from one sovereign to another without the sovereign's agreement. The old common law doctrine of "perpetual allegiance," for example, denied an individual the right to renounce obligations to his sovereign. The bonds of subjecthood were conceived in principle to be both singular and immutable. In the early nineteenth century, England invoked this doctrine to justify impressing into the British navy naturalized Americans who had been born in the United Kingdom. This policy helped to precipitate the War of 1812.

Yet immutability did not prove a sustainable legal principle in a world of liberal democracies and high levels of immigration. The refusal of many states to recognize expatriation posed a chronic problem for a country like the United States, with its large immigrant population. Naturalized U.S. citizens visiting their native homelands remained liable for duties of citizenship imposed there. To address this problem, the U.S. Congress adopted legislation in 1868 declaring expatriation "a natural and inherent right" of all people. In the same year, George Bancroft, the U.S. ambassador to the North German Confederation, concluded a treaty that recognized the naturalized status of German-born Americans. Similar treaties soon followed with Austria-Hungary, Belgium, Denmark, Norway, Sweden, and the United Kingdom.

Traditional international suspicions toward plural nationality continued well into the twentieth century. The constitutional court of the Federal Republic of Germany, for example, made one of the most sweeping contemporary statements against plural nationality in an opinion delivered in 1974:

> It is accurate to say that dual or multiple nationality is regarded, both domestically and internationally, as an evil that should be avoided or eliminated in the interests of states as well as in the interests of the affected citizen. . . . States seek to achieve exclusivity of their respective nationalities in order to set clear boundaries for their sovereignty over

persons; they want to be secure in the duty of loyalty of their citizens—
which extends if necessary as far as risking one's life—and do not want
to see it endangered by possible conflicts with a loyalty to a foreign state.[5]

The statement captures well the core traditional objections to plural nationality,
and the strong declarative tone of the court's language suggests that the described "evil" needs little qualification.

Despite international efforts to discourage it, the incidence of plural nationality continued to rise throughout the past century. The most important factor
behind this rising incidence has been the lack of agreement between states over
the rules governing the acquisition and loss of nationality in a world witnessing
significant movement of people over state borders (Goldstein and Piazza, 1996).[6]
If all states practiced a pure form of jus soli or jus sanguinis, then the issue of
plural nationality would be minor, except perhaps in cases of mixed marriages.
Conversely, the conflicting combinations of these forms among states almost
ensure that the incidence of plural nationality will continue to grow. Additional
causes also foster this growth, such as changes in gender policies behind the
rules governing the acquisition and loss of nationality. Until recent decades,
women of a different nationality were expected to assume the nationality of
their husbands at marriage. Now women increasingly have the option (the right)
to retain their own nationality irrespective of marital status, which increases the
likelihood that parents within such a marriage will pass on different nationalities to their children. Finally, advances in travel technology and the globalization of commerce have made the movement of people across states much faster,
easier, and more common. The incidence of plural nationality is growing because people increasingly have the means to live with concrete connections to
multiple states.

One of the most important international agreements regulating plural nationalities, the Convention concerning Certain Questions relating to the Con-

5. Opinion of German federal constitutional court, May 21, 1974, 254–55. The court did not
consider whether permitting plural nationality will in the long run facilitate the integration of
minorities into German society and thereby promote a deeper attachment to the German Federal
Republic. Despite liberalization of its naturalization rules in the early 1990s, naturalization rates
in Germany remain low when compared with many other European states (Clarke, van Dam, and
Gooster, 1998). Critics of the German naturalization policy point out that liberalization will not
be effective until prohibition against plural nationality is eliminated. See, e.g., Brubaker (1992,
173).

6. Goldstein and Piazza (1996) published the results of a survey on dual citizenship. One
hundred and twenty-eight countries responded to the survey question, "If a citizen of (the country
in question) acquires U.S. citizenship, does he or she retain or lose (the country in question's)
citizenship?" Of that figure, sixty-two countries answered that their citizens would retain their
citizenship, although a procedure might need to be followed to do so.

flict of Nationality (opened for signature at The Hague on April 12, 1930), constitutes a modest attempt to ameliorate the problems occasioned by dual citizenship.[7] Based on the central (restrictive) premise that "every person should have a nationality and should have one nationality only" (Preamble, 179 L.N.T.S. 89, 93 [1937–1938]), the convention actually does little to help bring it about: it establishes no norms regarding the loss or acquisition of nationality nor regarding the function of nationality in international law. Rather, it leaves nationality rules primarily in the hands of states. Articles 1 and 2 recognize that each state has the right "to determine under its own law who are its nationals" and the right to decide "[a]ny question as to whether a person possesses the nationality" of that state. Article 3 provides that "a person having two or more nationalities may be regarded as a national by each of the States whose nationality such person also possesses." The convention seeks to prevent statelessness, providing rules for the acquisition and retention of nationality for out-of-wedlock children, foundlings, adopted children, and children born to parents of unknown nationality (Arts. 14–17). It also protects against the statelessness of women who marry foreigners by declaring that they should not lose their citizenship in their native country unless they acquire the nationality of their husbands (Arts. 8, 9).

The convention significantly impaired progress toward its aim of ensuring that each person has but one nationality by its failure to set forth at the outset a uniform principle for the acquisition of nationality at birth, given the multiple ways in which the principles of jus soli and jus sanguinis intersect to produce dual nationals. Indeed, the protocol to the convention acknowledged the impossibility of reaching its goal under existing circumstances.

The continuing international aversion to plural nationality was reflected in the 1963 Convention on Reduction of Cases of Multiple Nationality (Plender, 1997, 131–42). The convention provides for contracting parties that nationals who acquire the nationality (by their own free will) of another contracting party state shall lose their former nationality. However, this convention also recognized the inevitability of plural nationality. For persons possessing two or more nationalities of contracting party states, it provides that individuals will be required to perform military service only for one state.[8]

---

7. One of the primary objectives of The Hague convention involved limiting statelessness. Many of its provisions therefore condition any loss of nationality upon the acquisition of another nationality. The broader aim of The Hague convention, which was sponsored by the League of Nations, was to promote the codification of international legal rules.

8. A similar provision was included in The Hague convention's 1930 Protocol relating to Military Obligations in Certain Cases of Double Nationality.

Efforts under international law to reduce the incidence of dual nationality have been largely ineffective. This result was predictable because international instruments regulating dual nationality have lacked enforcement mechanisms. If the increase of dual nationals does pose a significant threat, states have not acknowledged it, in that they have not taken concrete steps to cooperate in reducing its incidence through such means as sharing naturalization information. The time has come, then, to consider whether this threat has been overstated.

The traditional posture of states against plural nationality is now changing. The Second Protocol amending the 1963 Convention on the Reduction of Cases of Multiple Nationality, for example, expands the discretion of Contracting Party States to tolerate plural nationality (Plender, 1997, 140–42). The 1997 European Convention on Nationality reflects this trend toward the recognition that plural nationality is not a short-term abnormality to be eliminated, but rather a growing reality that must be accommodated.[9] Article 14, for example, provides: "A State Party shall allow: children having different nationalities acquired automatically at birth to retain these nationalities; its nationals to possess another nationality where this other nationality is automatically acquired by marriage." Article 16 provides: "A State Party shall not make the renunciation or loss of another nationality a condition for the acquisition or retention of its nationality where such renunciation or loss is not possible or cannot reasonably be required."

States have also sought to deal with the conflict that can arise when nationals of one state visit another state wherein they also hold nationality. Under traditional international law, a state can extend no diplomatic protection to its nationals when in the jurisdiction of a state of nationality.[10] This lack of international sanction may not deter a national from calling for state protection or diminish a state's felt obligation to extend protection in certain circumstances. There is then a legitimate concern that plural nationality can become a source of conflict between states over claims of individuals who hold nationality in both states, but these sources of conflict are manageable. Through the 1906 Convention on the Status of Naturalized Citizens, for example, several states in the Western Hemisphere adopted rules to regulate the nationality effects of those naturalized citizens who returned to their country of origin. Under this convention, naturalized persons who resume permanent residence in the state of their original nationality and who do not intend to return to the country in

9. 37 I.L.M. 44 (1998). As of this date, seventeen states have signed this treaty, but only Austria, Moldavia, and Slovakia have ratified it.

10. Art. 4 of The Hague convention (discussed above) stipulates: "A State may not afford diplomatic protection to one of its nationals against a State whose nationality such person also possesses."

which they were naturalized are considered to have renounced their naturalized nationality.[11]

Where states have been parties to cases involving dual nationals, international tribunals have increasingly relied on a general rule that has come to be known as the doctrine of dominant (or effective) nationality. In the *Nottebohm* case, the International Court of Justice explained the basis for this doctrine (*Liechtenstein v. Guatemala,* International Court of Justice, 1955, I.C.J. Rep. 4, pp. 4–65). The case involved Liechtenstein's attempt on behalf of one of its naturalized citizens to assert a claim against Guatemala, which argued that the person concerned was not a genuine Liechtenstein national because he had had little substantive contact with Liechtenstein.[12] The court found:

> International arbitrators have decided in the same way numerous cases of dual nationality, where the question arose with regard to the exercise of protection. They have given their preference to the real and effective nationality, that which accorded with the facts, that based on stronger factual ties between the person concerned and one of the States whose nationality is involved. Different factors are taken into consideration, and their importance will vary from one case to the next: the habitual residence of the individual concerned is an important factor, but there are other factors such as the centre of his interests, his family ties, his participation in public life, attachment shown by him for a given country and inculcated in his children, etc.
>
> Similarly, the courts of third States, when they have before them an individual whom two other States hold to be their national, seek to resolve the conflict by having recourse to international criteria and their prevailing tendency is to prefer the real and effective nationality. . . . National laws reflect this tendency when, *inter alia,* they make naturalization dependent on conditions indicating the existence of a link, which may vary in their purpose or in their nature but which are essentially concerned with this idea.

11. A provision in U.S. law based on this principle was invalidated by the U.S. Supreme Court in 1964 on the ground that it unconstitutionally discriminated between naturalized and native-born citizens (*Schneider v. Rusk,* 377 U.S. 163 [1964]). This convention, however, is still in force (Donner, 1994, 43).

12. The court explicitly refused to consider "whether international law imposes any limitations on [a State's] freedom of decision" with respect to determining its own rules of nationality and naturalization. The dispute turned on the question of whether a sovereign state had the right to extend diplomatic protection to a person who had been formally naturalized against another sovereign state in which the person resided.

The same tendency prevails in the writings of publicists and in practice. (p. 22)

The rule of effective nationality applied in *Nottebohm* diverges from The Hague
convention's rule that barred diplomatic protection against another state if the
individual also carried its nationality. But the two rules are not necessarily irreconcilable. The effective nationality principle may be applied to those cases
where the links of the dual national with the states in question are unequal (as
determined by such criteria as habitual residence). Where no clear dominance
of nationality is discernible, The Hague convention rule may still govern.

The *Mergé* case has reinforced the precedent established in *Nottebohm*. Here
a national of the United States who had acquired Italian nationality through
marriage sought compensation from the Italian government for wartime losses.
The dual nationality of the individual was not disputed. In considering the rules
governing diplomatic protection under The Hague convention and the doctrine
of effective nationality, the tribunal found that "no irreconcilable opposition
between the two principles exists; in fact, to the contrary . . . they complement
each other reciprocally."[13] Relying (in part) on *Nottebohm,* the tribunal concluded that a state is entitled to extend its protection in claims on behalf of its
nationals whenever this nationality is effective.[14] The tribunal determined that
the United States nationality was not predominant under the facts of this case,
because (among other reasons) the individual had not held habitual residence
in the United States for many years. Absent a showing of effective nationality,
the tribunal applied The Hague convention rule and denied admissibility of the
compensation claim.

In both these two leading cases then, the application of the effective nationality principle limited claims asserted by individuals against states of which

13. In delineating this complementary relationship, the court explained: "The principle, based
on the sovereign equality of States, which excludes diplomatic protection in the case of dual
nationality, must yield before the principle of effective nationality whenever such nationality is
that of the claiming state. But it must not yield when such predominance is not proved because
the first of these two principles is generally recognized and may constitute a criterion of practical
application for the elimination of any possible uncertainty" (14 UN Rep. Int'l Arb. Awards 236).
The validity of effective nationality as a principle of international customary law is supported by
widespread practice. Citing *Nottebohm* (among others), the Iran–United States tribunal concluded:
"The principle of effective nationality has long been applied to resolve conflicts of nationality in
international arbitration" (Decision in Case A/18 concerning the Question of Jurisdiction over
Claims of Persons with Dual Nationality [April 6], 23 *International Legal Materials* 489 [1984]).

14. The tribunal explained: "In order to establish the prevalence of the United States nationality in individual cases, habitual residence can be one of the criteria of evaluation, but not the
only one. The conduct of the individual in his economic, social, political, civic, and family life, as
well as the closer and more effective bond with one of the two States must also be considered."

they were citizens, but the practice of international tribunals suggests that dual nationality does not pose any insurmountable problems. The development of the doctrine of effective nationality illustrates how issues of dual nationality can be managed on a practical basis.

Part III: Distinguishing State Regimes for Managing Plural Nationality

In this section, we group dual nationality regimes into three general categories of *open, tolerant,* and *restrictive.* (We have identified no liberal democracy that fully bars dual nationality.) In the category of *open regimes,* we include Canada, France, Russia, and the United Kingdom. Each of these states follows some form of the jus soli principle that gives rise to dual nationality at birth for children born on their territories to noncitizens; none requires subsequent election of one nationality. Each state also permits its citizens to naturalize elsewhere without forfeiting citizenship, and none requires that naturalizing citizens renounce prior citizenships or demonstrate expatriation.

We see *tolerant regimes* in Australia, Germany, Israel, Mexico, South Africa, and the United States. These jus soli states permit dual nationality at birth, and each has some but not all the characteristics of open regimes. Thus, the United States permits citizens who naturalize elsewhere to retain U.S. citizenship, but it requires that persons naturalizing in the U.S. renounce prior citizenships.[15] Mexico, following a recent amendment to its constitution, and Germany now have similar rules. Israel requires persons who naturalize to renounce prior citizenships; Jews who obtain citizenship under the Law of Return may keep their native citizenship. Australia and South Africa exhibit the converse: citizens naturalizing elsewhere lose their native citizenship, but persons naturalizing in Australia and South Africa face no renunciation requirement. Mexico also has an election requirement for persons who acquire dual nationality at birth; Australia and the United States do not. In the early decades of the twentieth century, the United States took away the citizenship of a woman

15. Although the loyalty oath that naturalized U.S. citizens are required to swear presumes the exclusivity of state allegiance, the United States government recognizes the de facto status of plural nationality as a practical matter. Thus, e.g., the U.S. State Department has included a statement in U.S. passports that recognizes: "A person is considered a dual national when he owes allegiance to more than one country at the same time. A claim to allegiance to be based on facts of birth, marriage, parentage, or naturalization. A dual national may, while in the jurisdiction of the other country which considers that person its national, be subject to all its laws, including being conscripted for military service."

who married a foreigner and denationalized naturalized citizens who resettled in their countries of origin. Those laws are no longer on the books.[16]

Austria and Japan are examples of states with *restrictive regimes*. Both states follow jus sanguinis principles and limit possibilities for dual nationality. Austria requires that persons seeking naturalization demonstrate that they have expatriated themselves from their countries of origin. Japan makes renunciation a requirement for naturalization and requires that persons who attain dual nationality at birth elect a single nationality before reaching the age of twenty-two.

A priori, one can imagine factors that might account for a state's policies on dual nationality. Whether a state is a country of immigration or emigration might be significant. Countries of immigration that need to forge a common bond between new and old members may be less tolerant of new citizens retaining prior loyalties; countries of emigration may be willing to permit their nationals to retain citizenship when they naturalize elsewhere as a way to maintain ties with their diaspora. To some extent, this hypothesis holds true: the United States, a classic country of immigration, requires that naturalizing citizens renounce prior allegiances; and the Dominican Republic, a classic sending country to the United States, amended its law a decade ago to permit dual nationality for citizens who naturalize in another country. But there is much counterevidence as well: neither Australia nor Canada requires renunciation by naturalizing citizens; and the United States does not treat naturalization elsewhere as a ground for loss of U.S. citizenship.

Another relevant factor might be the newness of the state. That is, newly formed states interested in attracting and retaining members may adopt open policies toward dual nationality. Israel and Russia fit this model. New states, however, may feel the need to instill a single loyalty to get the state off to a strong start.

Policies toward dual nationality may also be a function of whether the state has a strong or weak conception of itself, either in ethnic or civic terms. Thus, Austria and Japan—both jus sanguinis states with strong ethnic identities—have restrictive dual nationality regimes. (The dual nationality rules are coordinated with laws in each state that make naturalization somewhat difficult.) Canada may be the best example at the other end of the spectrum. But, again, there are powerful counterexamples. Israel and France are states with strong national identities, yet both are open to dual nationality.

Ultimately, the search for any grand theory here may falter on the fact that histories and cultures peculiar to each state may have a significant effect on

16. The former repealed in legislation starting in 1922; the latter held unconstitutional in *Schneider v. Rusk*.

citizenship policies. For example, the strong protection of citizenship in the United States is difficult to understand without recognizing the history of slavery and race discrimination that denied citizenship to black Americans for almost a century (Aleinikoff, 1998, 8). Canadian citizenship policy is a product of a colonial past and a multinational present. Citizenship rules in the Baltic states are saturated with the experience of Soviet domination and the continued presence of hundreds of thousands of ethnic Russians. Mexico's new rules are more tolerant toward dual nationality and have everything to do with its immigration relationship with the United States.

The inability to derive an overarching theory can be understood in two ways. On the one hand, it may mean that the search for a workable set of international norms is likely to founder on the shoals of the particularity of state experiences and goals. On the other hand, it may indicate that the search for a more coherent system will not have to overcome a well-entrenched and logically structured reigning paradigm.

A convergence among states in tolerating, if not embracing, dual citizenship as a legitimate status seems to be growing. After long resisting dual nationality as a legitimate status, Germany's new jus soli provision may indicate that even the most hard-line states on this issue are succumbing to the reality of an increasing world population of dual nationals. Mexico's 1997 amendment of its nationality law, which permits Mexicans by birth to acquire second nationalities without forfeiting Mexican nationality, demonstrates how the issue can be managed in a balanced fashion. Since virtually all states give citizenship to the children of their nationals born abroad, the practice of jus soli by many states means that the incidence of dual nationality will increase. The practice of states of allowing naturalization elsewhere with no loss of native citizenship will further increase this incidence. Both of these factors are closely related to international migration. The first seeks to avoid having second- and third-generation immigrants in a receiving country who are noncitizens; the second reflects the interests of countries of emigration that seek to maintain influence over or protect the rights of their nationals beyond state borders.

Through international cooperation, states might drastically reduce the incidence of plural nationality by agreeing on an enforceable set of uniform standards by which nationality is acquired and lost. The prospect of any such agreement is highly doubtful, because the perceived domestic interests of states differ widely in defining their respective nationality policies.

Part IV: Problems (Real and Imagined) Associated with Dual Nationality

Theoretical arguments can be made that dual nationality is a potential time bomb in a world of nation-states or, to use a different metaphor, that dual citizens are walking contradictions. The argument runs as follows. For reasons of administrative order and international peace, a regime of nation-states needs to know where individuals belong. Belonging means membership or citizenship. The fundamental rule of the international regime is that states should look after their own, and only their own. To do more is to interfere in the affairs of other states. Persons with no state affiliations (those who are stateless or refugees) are a troubling anomaly. Who is charged, states may ask, with accepting their presence or undertaking their protection and assistance? To answer that no one is, is to admit the existence of persons outside the state system. To avoid such anomalies and to bring such persons back within the regime of states we have international conventions on the protection of refugees and on promoting the reduction of statelessness.

So, too, persons with two or more state memberships might be seen as causing headaches for states. Which state has the right to demand the citizen's allegiance? Which has the duty to protect the citizen? Suppose different states give conflicting orders. Which is the dual citizen bound to obey? Assume that X is a citizen of states A and B. May (or should) state A intervene on X's behalf if it believes that X is being mistreated by state B, or would such intervention violate the sovereignty of state B to deal with its citizens as it sees fit (subject, of course, to international human rights obligations)? The solution to these problems, adopted in the early decades of the past century, was an international regime dedicated to ensuring at least one, but no more than one, citizenship for all.[17]

Now, at the beginning of a new century, we are witnessing a significant increase in dual nationality. There are literally millions—indeed, tens of millions—of persons who live in one state and are citizens of that state, but who are also subject to the call of another state of which they are also citizens. Either we have a radically altered conception of the singularity of the state-citizen relationship, or we have a large number of accidents waiting to happen. So the argument might run.

Yet, to a remarkable extent dual nationality has not occasioned a noticeable increase in world tensions. The fact that many Israelis are dual nationals is not a cause of the tension in the Middle East; that 25 percent of Australians have more than one nationality has not produced a hot or cold war in Asia. The Mexican constitutional amendment sparked a few media reports and editorials, but not (at least not yet) a congressional hearing, a plank in a political party platform, or a démarche from the U.S. Department of State. Military service for dual nationals—an issue with enough significance to produce a multilateral European convention in 1930—is not even on today's radar screen.

17. See Spiro (1997). The rules had a gender twist: to avoid dual nationality, a woman whose spouse was a citizen of a different state was deemed to take her spouse's citizenship during the pendency of the marriage.

Still, it is unlikely that the significant increase in dual nationality will pass by wholly unnoticed in the days ahead. We can identify several possible points of tension that may arise in the future: (1) voting by dual nationals, (2) office holding by dual nationals, (3) the "unfair advantage" of dual nationality, and (4) the (in)divisibility of loyalty and community building. We should stress at the outset that although we find these controversies of intellectual interest, we do not believe that, in the scheme of things, they will represent the major flash points between states. Economics, environmental issues, nuclear proliferation, religious fundamentalism, and (closer to home) migration, seem to present far more significant challenges for states.

Voting

Voting by dual nationals raises two separate concerns. First, if the country in which the dual citizen is not residing permits absentee voting, then he or she is entitled to vote in two sets of national elections. Second, it is sometimes supposed that a dual national (particularly one who has been naturalized in the current country of residence) may vote the interests of his or her other country (Spiro, 1997, 1412–85; Schuck, 1998). There is much less to these problems than meets the eye.

As to dual voting, it is hard to see exactly what the nature of the objection is here. Suppose Juan Smith is a citizen of the United States and the Dominican Republic, living in New York. Suppose also that he flies to Santo Domingo on election day to cast a ballot in the Dominican elections, returning to New York the next day. It is arguable that Smith's interest in Dominican elections may take away from the time he can spend thinking about U.S. political issues. Perhaps a more important argument against double voting is, as David Martin (1998, 19) has argued, that "[f]ocusing political activity in the place where you live encourages a deeper engagement in the political process—perhaps even civic virtue—and also helps develop affective citizenship and a sense of solidarity." Finally, double voting allows persons a vote in a polity in which they are not living and therefore they do not have to deal with the consequences of the electoral outcome. These objections appear to be more symbolic than real (as Martin acknowledges; 1998, 21). It is equally likely that those persons who double vote are more politically engaged in both polities than is the usual citizen. Indeed, there is evidence that dual U.S-Dominican citizens who take an active interest in Dominican politics also are politically active in the United States (Graham, 1996). Accordingly, this does not appear to be a zero-sum game. If, under ideas as old as Aristotle, we believe that participation in politics is a primary goal of citizenship, then it is not clear on what basis we should condemn such conduct.

It is true that double nationality allows people to avoid the consequences of their votes. Yet this is really an objection to the very idea of dual citizenship, which always endows the dual national with the ability to "flee" to another state if circumstances turn sour in his or her current country of residence (the phrase "sunshine patriot" springs to mind). It is plausible that this option may produce less of a community spirit than would be possessed by a mononational, who must deal with the bad times as well as the good, but it seems that dual voting is a minor part of this broader problem (which we address below).

Another objection to dual voting might be that the dual citizen has an extra benefit not afforded a person with only one citizenship: he or she can seek to attain his or her interests by casting ballots in two separate polities. This inequality seems far down the list of the world's inequities and certainly below the claim that those with money and resources may exert far more influence in elections than those without do.

The second major concern about dual nationality and voting is that a dual citizen might be likely to reflect the interests of one state when voting in the elections of the other. Although under some circumstances this might be so, we have no empirical evidence for it either way. It is far more likely that voting is an intensely local affair, reflecting perceived costs and benefits for the voter (and perhaps groups with which he or she is affiliated) in the immediate context. There is also little reason to suppose that dual nationals vote "the national interest" of either country any more than mononationals do. Furthermore, if there is a "marching order" problem, having a requirement that dual nationals become mononational, shedding the citizenship of the state where they do not reside, does not solve it. A citizen of Ecuador who at naturalization in the United States forswears all prior allegiances does not at that moment give up all psychological or cultural attachments to Ecuador. If he or she were inclined to vote Ecuadorian interests before naturalization, it is far from clear why he or she would not be so inclined after naturalization. So too, a mononational may have a significant interest in the affairs of a foreign state whether or not he or she is a citizen (some U.S. citizens of Irish descent and American Jews are examples). In short, the problem of divided loyalty reflected in the franchise is not peculiar to dual nationals. Rather it appears to be the price a society pays for accepting immigration.

Office Holding

In the past few years, several naturalized U.S. citizens have returned to their native lands in eastern European states to assume high government posts. Under these circumstances, it may begin to make sense to talk about a possible conflict of loyalties (Schuck, Martin, and Aleinikoff, 1986). Interestingly, however, the domestic politics of the home state usually produces a denouement, leading each of these officials to announce his intention to renounce U.S. citizenship. In cases where officeholders are open about their dual national status, both states are put on notice about potential conflicts of interest and may act accordingly to minimize the possible risks. If dual nationals are permitted to occupy influential positions in large multinational corporations with business enterprises in the same states of which they are nationals, it seems unclear why they should be prohibited from doing likewise in most areas of government service.

Unfair Advantage over Noncitizens (The Exit Option)

Robert Frost (1979), in "The Death of the Hired Hand," defined home as "the place where, when you go there, [t]hey have to take you in." In this sense, dual nationals have two homes because, under international law, states must permit their nationals ingress to state territory, and dual nationals are likely to possess two passports to facilitate interstate travel. A dual national, then, has an exit option that mononationals do not. When times are tough in one state, the dual citizen can move to the other state. Not only might this be said to give dual citizens an unfair advantage over mononationals, but it might also cause the dual national to take less interest in contributing to the solution of problems in his or her current state of residence.

Holding nationality in another state doubtless facilitates relocation, but so do wealth, business and professional contacts, family ties in the location, and many other factors. A second nationality should be viewed as just one potential advantage that individuals may enjoy to which differences in personal circumstances inevitably give rise. No one has brought forward any evidence to show that the exit option weakens the commitment dual nationals feel toward their state of residence (in comparison to otherwise similarly situated persons, except, perhaps, in such situations as the transfer of sovereignty over Hong Kong from the United Kingdom to China). An individual's perceived interest in contributing to his or her local community will always be shaped as much, if not more, by the concrete stakes he or she has in that community as by any formal right to relocate that may be exercised in the future.

The (In)divisibility of Loyalty

We might be correct about everything we have said so far and still be accused of not getting to the heart of the matter. The issue, some might argue, is not material or electoral but symbolic. In a world divided between competitive and mutually exclusive nation-states, we need ultimately to know which side everyone is on. The domestic laws of Western-style democracies prohibit bigamy, not for economic reasons, but because of our belief that certain relationships, to be true and successful, cannot be plural. Many argue that citizenship is one such relationship, based on such a consideration as the following: Nation-states are increasingly fragile entities, under attack from both supra- and subnational forces. To maintain their efficacy they need members willing to contribute to, and perhaps even sacrifice for, a common good. That kind of commitment can be watered down and rendered weak if it is not made exclusive. Just as persons do not belong to two religions or two political parties, so too it is sensible to affirm loyalty to a single state. The power of this line of argument need not appeal only to strong nationalists who see in the state the embodiment of a national identity or ideology.

Communitarians who seek to promote national policies by addressing, for example, deep inequalities in a state may find such programs achievable only if persons and groups are fully committed to the welfare of all those within the state's territory. Again, such a commitment may require the kind of identification with a polity that is not indivisible.

From these perspectives, dual nationality is not so much a problem between states as it is one within a state. It might be seen as sapping the national commitment that states need and have a right to demand of their citizens. The problem with this argument, however, is that it is probably false, at least at current levels of dual nationality. Whatever decline we are witnessing in civic commitment and pride, no one has made the case that dual nationality is the cause. Rather, it appears to be a problem with the institution of citizenship itself, caused perhaps by various late-twentieth-century phenomena. Indeed, persons who attain dual nationality through naturalization in the United States have shown a fair level of commitment, a level not required of the native-born (who may feel a psychological alienation or at least take citizenship for granted). Those who are dual citizens at birth might feel the tug of two nationalities, but they are considerably more likely to feel committed, at whatever level, to the place of their birth and continued residence. Does the existence of a second citizenship undermine the first to the point of endangering the state? If the danger rises to that level, the polity suffers from a disease that probably afflicts all citizens, not just dual nationals.

At the most extreme, some worry that dual nationals might form a potentially dangerous fifth column committed to subverting the domestic politics of their country of residence. Alternatively, might country X use the presence of its nationals in country Y as a pretext for intervention? It is difficult to find historical examples to support such fears. It is comparatively easy, however, to point to examples of national minorities with no legal affiliation to an outside power who worked for the cause of that power. One such classic example is the German minority in Czechoslovakia during the 1930s. That minority had no formal affiliation with Germany. They had been part of the Austro-Hungarian Empire and not the German Empire. Hitler never claimed that they had any legal status as dual nationals of the Reich or proposed such a status as a pretext for intervention. The German minority in Czechoslovakia may have understood themselves to be German as a matter of ancestry and culture, but not because of any shared legal affiliation with the citizens of the Reich.

The Acquisition of Nationality for Commerce or Convenience

The Caribbean islands of Dominica, Grenada, and Saint Kitts–Nevis offer second passports for investments ranging from $50,000 to $250,000 without requiring any enduring residential or familial ties. The selling of nationality unquestionably cheapens its value as a form of allegiance. No one knows how frequently this practice occurs, however, and its long-term consequences are unclear. If evidence emerges that these consequences are becoming a serious problem, then concerned states will always have the option of discouraging the practice by diplomatic means. These examples may be extreme, but they may also point to an emerging trend of individuals being able to purchase or otherwise acquire second and third nationalities without substantial connection to the state conferring nationality. Such acquisition may occur in less extreme ways. Under some versions of jus sanguinis rules, children are able to inherit the nationality of their parents even when neither generation has established or preserved a concrete relationship with the state in question. The emerging consensus in international law reflected in the *Nottebohm* case suggests that a substantial connection should tie the individual to the state of which he or she is a national. Nationality should not become a commodity that individuals can purchase to further their business or personal interests. However, no clear means is now available to prevent or discourage states like Dominica from selling nationality as a commodity.

*   *   *

Dual nationality is a product of the movement and settlement of people across state boundaries. In a world of nation-states, members of states who are located beyond state borders may cause complications in interstate relations. Legal nationality in two states might make things more complicated. The problems of dual nationality, however real, are hardly likely to subvert international order fundamentally. Indeed, if the movement of peoples across state borders presents problems, the fact that some of those persons might have two nationalities appears to add surprisingly little to interstate relations. Why might this be so?

First, like politics, the practice of citizenship tends to be local. That is, most citizens are most concerned about events immediately before them, such as schools, local crime, traffic, drug problems, the cost of housing, and the availability of day care. On these issues it matters little whether a Mexican American has one or two nationalities or even whether he or she votes in elections in both the United States and Mexico.

Second, it is difficult to identify situations around the world where tensions approaching hostility exist between nations with significant numbers of shared dual nationals. Australia and China are not on the verge of war, nor are the United States and Mexico, or Israel and the United States. It may well run just the other way: increasing ties between the populations of such paired states may create greater opportunities for peaceful interaction.

Third, the number of dual nationals is dwarfed by the number of cross-border migrants and refugees. Conceding, for the sake of argument, that such "out-of-state" persons create tensions and complications on the world scene, the relatively small number of dual nationals is hardly likely to be noticed. Put another way, states will be concerned about the treatment of their nationals residing in other states, whether those nationals have the citizenship of the other state or not.

Fourth, dual nationality appears to be more an individual than a group phenomenon. Most persons acquire dual nationality as an accident of birth, being born in one state to a parent or parents who are citizens of another state. The nationality passed on by parents may have little real meaning to the dual national, other than giving him or her a sense of ethnicity or a romantic tie to a distant homeland. To be sure, those emotions can be mobilized at times, but so can the ethnic ties of a person with just one citizenship. Generally, however, lives are lived locally, and one's second nationality is more an aspect of identity than practice. Perhaps the recent Mexican constitutional amendment can be viewed as the exception that proves the rule. The amendment might be seen, in part, as an attempt to assert a group-based dual nationality. One of its aims was to remove a disincentive to naturalization in the United States so that more Mexicans would be naturalized and thereby obtain political rights in the United States that could be used to protect their interests. As we noted earlier, however, at this point no evidence exists that the amendment has had an impact on Mexican naturalization rates. Indeed, surprisingly few Mexicans naturalized in the United States have returned to Mexican consulates in the United States to reclaim Mexican nationality. Thus, even here the concerns about dual nationality, at least for now, appear to be more symbolic and theoretical than real.

Conclusion: Prospects and Proposals

It is perhaps curious that no international regime exists to define and regulate citizenship. One might suppose that a system of nation-states would require firm, agreed-upon rules as to who belongs where. These decisions have been left, under international law, largely to the states themselves. The Universal Declaration of Human Rights may declare that "[e]veryone has a right to a nationality" (Art. 15[1]), but international law does not pervasively regulate how citizenship may be acquired or lost or how the issue of multiple citizenships should be resolved. This is not to suggest that, were the international community to derive a set of rules or standards on dual nationality, such norms would seek to limit or prevent multiple citizenships. It does mean that the current sets of arrangements are largely the result of the (uncoordinated) decisions of individual states. These rules for local citizenship are usually grounded in particular historical narratives about the state and in such perceived current needs as recent decisions by states to permit citizens to retain nationality despite naturalization elsewhere. There is little reason to expect that such policies would yield a coherent whole at the world level. There is good reason to believe that the goals of various states will not be compatible. Sending states may adopt policies that create tensions for receiving states (witness the reaction in the United States to Mexico's recent constitutional amendment). States with descent-based concepts of citizenship may embrace norms that conflict with the norms of jus soli states. Economists might say that the world system does little to internalize the externalities of state citizenship norms.

That being said, we do see an increasing toleration—if not yet an embrace—of dual nationality among liberal democracies around the globe. Again, this is not the result of a coordination of state policies. Instead, much of the new tolerance may simply be a local accommodation to a world in which conflicting state citizenship rules and significant immigration flows are producing higher levels of dual nationality. It is significant, however, that in a time when nation-states are reportedly under siege from subnational, supranational, and transnational forces, states have not circled the wagons by adopting more restrictive citizenship policies than currently exist.

We have suggested that the limited state reaction to dual nationality can be explained primarily by the paucity of actual adverse consequences. The theoretical and symbolic objections we have canvassed here seem not, at least not yet, to have materialized.

The future? We are not prepared to make a firm prediction, but we see little cause for serious concern. In all likelihood, dual nationality will continue to increase owing to high levels of immigration, changes in state policies, and the continuation of both jus sanguinis and jus soli citizenship norms. In some states at some point, there will be backlashes against dual nationality. Nationalistic groups will condemn plural citizenship as undermining state strength and identity. Yet, the rise and apparent decline of Le Pen in France and Pauline Hanson in Australia may indicate that the majority of the populations in these states see no necessary conflict between dual nationality and loyalty. One can add to these the fairly remarkable proposals from the new Schroeder government in Germany that introduce elements of jus soli and permit dual citizenship. Although legally enacted in restricted form, they represent an important shift in traditional German thinking on the issues. All told, we can see a world that remains relatively tolerant of dual nationality.

If it is believed that increasing levels of dual nationality may contribute to interstate or intrastate tensions, then various proposals might be entertained. David Martin (1998) has made several suggestions that are worthy of consideration, including the adoption of norms that permit dual nationals to vote only in the state in which they are residing, that require dual nationals who assume policy-level government positions to relinquish other nationalities, and that limit the indefinite continuation of nationality for future generations outside a state if a family has lost a genuine link with the state. Whether one agrees with these proposals or not, it is apparent that they tinker at the margins.[18] They also reflect an emerging international consensus that the goal is no longer to reduce plural nationality as an end in itself, but to manage it as an inevitable feature of an increasingly interconnected and mobile world.

Works Cited

Aleinikoff, T. Alexander. 1998. *Between Principles and Politics: The Direction of U.S. Citizenship Policy*. Washington, D.C.: Brookings Institution.

Brownlie, Ian. 1992. *Basic Documents on Human Rights*. 3rd ed. Oxford: Clarendon Press.

Brubaker, Rogers. 1992. *Citizenship and Nationhood in France and Germany*. Cambridge: Harvard University Press.

Clarke, James, Elsbeth van Dam, and Liz Gooster. 1998. "New Europeans: Naturalisation and Citizenship in Europe." *Citizenship Studies* 2(1): 43–67

Donner, Ruth. 1994. *The Regulation of Nationality in International Law*. 2nd ed. Irvington on the Hudson, N.Y.: Transnational Publishers.

Frost, Robert. 1979. "The Death of the Hired Man." In Edward Connery Lathem (ed.), *The Poetry of Robert Frost*. New York: Henry Holt.

18. Other scholars are equally tolerant of dual nationality. See Schuck (1998) and Spiro (1997).

Goldstein, Eugene, and Victoria Piazza. 1996. "Naturalization, Dual Citizenship and Retention of Foreign Citizenship: A Survey." *Interpretative Releases* 73(16) (April 22): 517.

Graham, Pamela M. 1996. "Re-Imagining the Nation and Defining the District: The Simultaneous Political Incorporation of Dominican Transnational Migrants." Ph.D. diss., University of North Carolina, Chapel Hill. Unpublished.

Martin, David. 1998. *New Rules on Dual Nationality for a Democratizing Globe: Between Rejection and Embrace*. Prepared for the CEPIC/FSNP International Conference on Nationality Law, Immigration, and Integration in Europe and the U.S.A., Paris, June 25–27.

Plender, Richard (ed.). 1997. *Basic Documents*. Boston: Martinus Nijhoff Publishers.

Schuck, Peter H. 1998. *Citizens, Strangers, and In-Betweens*. Boulder, Colo.: Westview Press.

Schuck, Peter H., D. Martin, and T. A. Aleinikoff. 1986. "Theories of Loss of Citizenship." *Michigan Law Review* 84: 1471–503.

Spiro, Peter. 1997. "Dual Nationality and the Meaning of Citizenship." 46 *Emory Law Journal* 1412.

Weis, P. 1979. *Nationality and Statelessness in International Law*. Germantown, Md.: Sitjhoff and Noordhoff.

CHAPTER FOUR

Relational Nationality:
On Gender and Nationality
in International Law

KAREN KNOP

SINCE THE European Convention on Reduction of Cases of Multiple Nationality and Military Obligations in Cases of Multiple Nationality (the "European
Convention on the Reduction of Multiple Nationality") (Council of Europe,
1963) was opened for signature in 1963—so the introduction to the new European Convention on Nationality (Council of Europe, 1997a) begins—"there
has been a growing recognition that numerous problems concerning nationality, in particular multiple nationality, have not been sufficiently considered by
the 1963 Convention" (Council of Europe, 1997b, 21). Among the problems
that led the new convention to modify the old convention's principle of avoiding multiple nationality was the problem of how to respect the principle of
gender equality in regulating the growing number of marriages between spouses
of different nationalities (Council of Europe, 1997b, 23–24).

   This perspective, both on gender equality and on multiple nationality, is at
odds with the scholarly literature on nationality. Few international legal schol-

   In this chapter, I draw on my work as rapporteur on women's equality and nationality in
international law for the International Law Association Committee on Feminism and International Law, 1998. The views expressed are mine alone and should not be attributed to the committee. I am grateful to Gillian Hadfield, Mayo Moran, and Ayelet Shachar for helping me to
think through some of the ideas in this chapter. I should also like to thank Sara Hossain of Interights,
London, and Alison Symington for their invaluable assistance in obtaining information on the
litigation of women's nationality issues in South Asia, and Alessandra Prioreschi for her translation of a key judgment of the Italian Constitutional Court.

ars in the West still write about gender equality as a problem in the law of nationality, and the few who do, write about it as a problem mainly for women in non-Western states (see Women's Human Rights Resources). And, multiple nationality is now being presented by scholars as desirable as well as possible or necessary.[1]

Quite apart from the European Convention on Nationality, we might quarrel with each of these scholarly assumptions. Although the 1979 United Nations Convention on the Elimination of All Forms of Discrimination against Women (the "Women's Convention") (UNTS, 1979) and other international human rights treaties (Council of Europe, 1950; Organization of African Unity, 1981; UNTS, 1966; UNTS, 1969) guarantee equality for women, there are both Western and non-Western states with nationality laws that discriminate explicitly on the basis of gender (see, e.g., Equality Now, 1999, 10–14). Even in Western states that have revised their law to remove gender-based distinctions, domestic litigation continues to uncover residual problems of discrimination. In Canada, for example, revisions to the Citizenship Act in 1977 enabled all Canadian citizens, no longer just Canadian fathers and Canadian unmarried mothers, to pass citizenship to their children born abroad. In 1997, the Supreme Court of Canada ruled unconstitutional the difference that remained under the act between the automatic entitlement to citizenship upon registration for children born abroad before 1977 to a Canadian father or a Canadian unmarried mother, and the stricter application process, including security and criminal record checks that could result in the denial of citizenship, required of children born abroad before 1977 to a Canadian mother married to a non-Canadian (Canadian Supreme Court, 1997). More recently, the United States Supreme Court upheld a provision of the U.S. Immigration and Nationality Act that makes it harder for American fathers than for American mothers to pass citizenship to their children born abroad. Where a child is born abroad to an American mother and a foreigner who are not married to each other, U.S. citizenship passes virtually automatically to the child. If the American parent is the father instead of the mother, the act not only requires him to prove his parental relationship to the child, a relationship assumed for the mother, but to meet a deadline for establishing a formal legal relationship with the child and to agree to support the child financially until she reaches the age of eighteen (U.S., 1998) (for commentary, see Pillard and Aleinikoff, 1998). A lower court has since ruled this statutory distinction unconstitutional, reading the Supreme Court's decision as based on nonjusticiability and a majority of the justices as finding that the pro-

1. Proponents of multiple nationality include Franck (1996) and Spiro (1997), with such others as Aleinikoff and Klusmeyer (see chap. 3) and Martin (1999) offering more qualified support.

vision relied impermissibly on stereotypes about the different parenting roles of men and women (U.S., 1999). Outside the West, cases challenging much broader gender-based distinctions in nationality law are currently before the courts in Bangladesh, Nepal, and Pakistan.[2]

Even if nationality laws worldwide no longer formally discriminated between men and women, concerns about discrimination in their application would remain, especially as increasing numbers of women work abroad owing to the economic pressures of globalization or seek refuge abroad from civil war or other emergencies. For instance, the UN Special Rapporteur on Violence against Women has documented that for the Polish women who are part of a recent wave of women trafficked from central and eastern Europe into western Europe to work in the sex trade (UN, Commission on Human Rights, 1997, ¶¶ 6, 44–45), nationality is not a means to diplomatic assistance because often their passports are taken away by the pimp or brothel owner and they are unable to prove their nationality (¶¶ 23, 66, 105; see also Caldwell, Galster, and Steinzor, 1997).[3] Thai women who work abroad are another example of the gendered problems of nationality in practice. According to one Thailand-based nongovernmental organization, many of these women are unregistered in Thailand and have no identity papers to document their nationality. Among the difficulties they face on their return to Thailand is that without proof of nationality, their children born abroad have ambiguous or no nationality (Development and Education Programme for Daughters and Communities, 1997).[4]

The scholarly assumption that multiple nationality is increasingly the norm and, indeed, a desirable norm is no less open to question than the assumption that problems of gender equality are a thing of the past. Authors who herald the trend toward multiple nationality cite few non-Western states that allow more than one nationality (e.g., Alcinikoff and Klusmeyer, see chap. 3; Franck, 1996, 378–82; Spiro, 1997, 1457–58, and 1999, 623, n.129, and 624, n.136). Relatedly, many critics of multiple nationality would resist the liberal cosmopolitan vision associated with it, whereby each individual is free to compose his own

2. This update (as of March 10, 2000) was provided by Sara Hossain and Alison Symington through Interights, London.

3. The UN Secretary General has since recommended that any barriers for trafficked women to return to their countries, with or without passports or identification documents, be eliminated (UN Secretary General, 1998, ¶ 34). Similar problems are encountered by women in the "maid trade": the temporary legal migration of unaccompanied women from less developed Asian states to western Asia (the Middle East) or to prosperous eastern Asian states (e.g., Hong Kong and Singapore) to take positions as live-in domestic servants (see Fitzpatrick and Kelly, 1998, 79–80, on seizure of passports by employers).

4. On statelessness caused by the inability to establish one's nationality, see, generally, UNHCR, 1997.

identity from membership in different states, communities, and associations from the nation to the Internet (Franck, 1996).

However, my aim in this chapter is not to examine gender equality and multiple nationality separately. It is to use the history of the European Convention on Nationality to show a link between the two, a link that I propose should lead us to reconceive not only equality and nationality, but nationalism as well. Although the European Convention on Nationality is formally neutral on multiple nationality, the Council of Europe developments that preceded and are partly codified in the convention connect the realization of gender equality in the European law of nationality with the choice of dual nationality for all members of a family where the husband and wife originally have different nationalities. From the perspective of equality, this need for dual nationality illustrates why the simple absence of legal distinctions between men and women is insufficient. From the perspective of nationality, gender equality makes a case for dual nationality in mixed marriages, which contains a view of identity different from the liberal cosmopolitan one.

The emergence of dual nationality as a European solution to the problem of gender equality in the law of nationality thus sheds light both on the shape that equality might take and on the potential justifications for dual nationality. But beyond this mutual illumination, the web of relationships reflected and created by such a solution may be contrasted with the linear bond between individual and state that structures our conception of nationality and, as well, our conception of the sentiment to which nationality is intended to correspond. What this contrast suggests to me—if not necessarily to the drafters of the European Convention on Nationality—is that the dimension missing from analyses of equality and nationality, and even nationalism itself, has been the relational. Accordingly, in the chapter, I seek to show the limitations of the familiar perspective and' to begin to address them through the development of a new perspective that I call *relational nationality*.

The idea of relational nationality draws on relational feminism,[5] in particular, its attention to the moral significance of relationships that exist in the domain between the self and others in general. Whereas moral theory has traditionally been concerned with the poles of the egoistic individual and the universal "all individuals," relational feminists have examined the neglected middle region of family relations, friendship, group ties, and neighborhood involvement, especially from women's points of view. Virginia Held (1993) has written of this intermediate realm:

5. Although I apply certain insights of relational feminism to problems of gender and nationality, I do not necessarily analyze these problems in the same way as relational feminists have (cf. Nedelsky, 1997, 33).

In the domain of particular others, the self is already constituted to an important degree by relations with others, and these relations may be much more salient and significant than the interests of any individual self in isolation. The "others" in the picture, however, are not the "all others," or "everyone," of traditional moral theory. . . . They are, characteristically, actual flesh-and-blood other human beings for whom we have actual feelings and with whom we have real ties. (pp. 57–58; see also Benhabib, 1992)

Part one of the chapter argues similarly that nationality and nationalism have been understood in the individualistic and abstractly universalistic terms of liberalism and standard moral theory and draws attention to the concrete relationships that go unnoticed on this understanding. The power of the individualistic perspective is such that, as Patrick Weil (see chapter 1) notes, many writers on nationality overlook marriage as one of the common legal bases for naturalization. This focus on the isolated individual is even more remarkable if we consider, for instance, that family-sponsored immigration is by far the most frequent type of immigration to the United States (Aleinikoff, Martin, and Motomura, 1998, 284–89, 294–95).

Seen relationally, the history and significance of nationality begin to look different. Part two shows that the law of nationality has historically situated and protected individuals in the context of traditional family relationships. The importance of this historical protection was overshadowed, however, by its patriarchal form: the principle of dependent nationality, which made a wife's nationality depend on her husband's. As part three traces, the movement for equality concentrated initially on the blatant discrimination of giving men, but not women, the right to choose their nationality; and, once this right was won and a woman's nationality could therefore differ from her husband's, on discrimination involving her husband's and children's acquisition of her nationality. Yet the reformist goal of identical treatment, by itself, is sufficient neither to achieve meaningful equality nor to safeguard family relationships. The relational function of nationality must be ensured in a nondiscriminatory form, or some substitute must be found. The developments that led to the European Convention on Nationality are unique in recognizing this need for a common nationality or equivalent protection in the case of families whose members have different nationalities.

A relational perspective not only clarifies the equality justification for allowing dual nationality in the case of mixed marriages, it aids in evaluating the objections. The main objection to dual nationality in general has long been the citizen of convenience whose loyalty lies elsewhere, the nonnationalist national.

Its opponents fear that dual nationality will weaken the correspondence between nationality and attachment to the nation-state. Increasingly, however, these fears have been dismissed as old-fashioned or overblown. But this general debate assumes that an individual's loyalty to a nation-state is directly to the polity at large. Part four suggests, by example, that nationalism may also be mediated by relationships with particular individuals, such as parents, spouses, lovers, and children, who belong to that nation-state. As a result, the sociology of dual nationalism may require a more complex analysis and may actually prove to be different in the case of mixed marriages.

I   Relational Nationality

This chapter's premise that nationality and nationalism are not now thought of as relational may seem strange. After all, nationality, as the International Court of Justice (1955) wrote in the *Nottebohm* case, is

> a legal bond having as its basis a social fact of attachment, a genuine connection of existence, interests and sentiments, together with the existence of reciprocal rights and duties. It may be said to constitute the juridical expression of the fact that the individual upon whom it is conferred . . . is in fact more closely connected with the population of the State conferring nationality than with that of any other State. (p. 23)

While it is true that nationality may rest on the strength of an individual's personal and professional relationships with others in his state of nationality, the concept is traditionally understood as the legal bond of that individual alone with the state. Whatever network of relationships substantiates his nationality and establishes the genuineness of his connection to the state where that is challenged, as in *Nottebohm,* international legal thinking on nationality generally treats the individual atomistically and his nationality independent of the nationality of others. In this, the conception of nationality resembles the abstract individualism underlying some versions of liberal political theory, which considers individual human beings to be social atoms, abstracted from their social contexts.[6]

---

6. Feminists have begun to examine the ways in which women's relationship to the state, expressed by nationality, was historically conceived of as inferior to that of men. Jean Elshtain (1995), for example, shows that in the political tradition of Sparta and Rome, of Machiavellian city-states and autonomous republics on the Rousseauian model, women were lesser civic beings because civic virtue was military virtue. For a contemporary example, see Shachar (1999, 258–64). Elshtain's work, however, problematizes the idea of allegiance and not the atomistic, presocial self it supposes.

While nationalism, like nationality, is based on social relationships, it too is not relational. In *Imagined Communities,* Benedict Anderson (1991) argues that a nation is a community that individuals imagine between themselves and a finite number of other individuals whom they need not know personally, where that community may come to be imagined through various historical and cultural processes. What I mean when I say that nationalism is not relational is that it involves ties to general rather than particular others. These ties are not with all others, as they would be in an internationalist utopia; they are abstracted within the state or nation. But nationalism does not differentiate between ties such as family and friendship and ties of a purely imagined kind. In ignoring the particularities of relationships and the possibility that different relationships might play different roles in forming an individual's national identity, nationalism also shares something with abstract individualism, namely, its disregard for the role of the particularities of relationships and community in constituting the very nature and identity of individuals.

Against the atomistic and generalized view of the self taken by abstract individualism, many feminists have asserted a concept of the social or relational self (e.g., Baier, 1995; Friedman, 1990; Held, 1993; Keller, 1986; Nedelsky, 1989). This reconception of the self fundamentally acknowledges that the particularities of relationships play a part in constituting both the meaning of individual lives and self-identity. For such feminists, it follows that the moral and legal ideals based on the prevailing view of a disembedded and disembodied self must also be rethought. Jennifer Nedelsky (1989), for example, argues that the notion of autonomy should not be seen as a state of independence to be protected from relationships. Instead, autonomy should be understood as a capacity that is developed through relationships and encompasses interdependence. What actually enables people to be autonomous, Nedelsky maintains, is relationships of support and guidance—with parents, teachers, friends, loved ones (p. 12; see also Nedelsky, 1991).

The foundational importance of relationships suggests that they must be protected and fostered by morality and law, including, potentially, the law of nationality. Relational feminism is not alone in providing support for the idea that nationality should involve the protection of relationships. Liberalism might well recognize the centrality of relationships to the individual. Indeed, some versions of liberalism describe the role of relationships in forming the individual (e.g., Green, 1986), a role that communitarians clearly identify and value (e.g., MacIntyre, 1984; Sandel, 1998). However, the view of the self developed by relational feminists is the most fruitful for analyzing both nationality and nationalism. The experience of women grounds relational feminism not only in the underlying reality of our embeddedness in relations with others, but also in the oppressive social forms these relations can take. Relational feminism therefore tends to be more attentive than liberalism or communitarianism to the importance of power in relationships (Held, 1993, 58–59, 188–91; Okin, 1989; Friedman, 1990). This is particularly relevant in my discussion of nationalism, as I speculate that an individual's relationships with family of a different nation have an effect on her own sense of national identity and that the effect may be partially determined by the structures of power within those relationships. It is therefore in light of relational feminism that this chapter begins to retheorize nationality and nationalism.

II Rethinking History

Until World War I, the nationality laws of virtually all countries made a married woman's nationality dependent on her husband's nationality (UN, 1962, 3). The first of Virginia Woolf's (1993) three clarion phrases in her 1938 political work, *Three Guineas*—"as a woman, I have no country. As a woman I want no country. As a woman my country is the whole world" (p. 234)—is a bitter allusion to British laws of the day that deprived a woman of British nationality on her marriage to a foreigner. This principle of dependent nationality, also called the principle of the unity of nationality of spouses, rested on the conviction that the members of a family should have the same nationality and on the patriarchal notion that the husband should determine that nationality (see Inter-American Court of Human Rights, 1984, 174; UN, 1962, 3).

On the principle of dependent nationality (see generally UN, 1963, 8), a woman who married a foreign national lost her own nationality and acquired that of her husband simply by virtue of marriage. If her husband's nationality changed or was lost during the marriage, her nationality altered accordingly. Particularly galling to women was the situation where a woman after marriage continued to live in her own country but was deprived of the civil, political, economic, and social rights that depended upon nationality. For feminists of the time, this situation reproduced the second-class citizenship of all women in society (Miller, 1992, 193).

A woman who was abandoned or widowed did not have the right to return to her own country, since that right is a function of nationality. If she were able to reenter, she would find herself without the rights attached to nationality. Dependent nationality, moreover, could render a woman stateless upon divorce. In many cases, women became stateless without even being aware of it.

After World War I, women's organizations campaigned actively for changes to the domestic laws on nationality and for an international treaty that would guarantee women's equality with men in matters of nationality.[7] In 1931, Chrystal Macmillan, a leading figure in this campaign, wrote:

> Under the present law a man can never have his . . . nationality taken from him unless he voluntarily naturalises in another country or is disloyal, and a woman should receive the same treatment. She, despite her sex, is a human being, and should have the rights enjoyed by male human beings. Marriage should not be a reason for penalising a woman by treating her as a minor and refusing her the status of an adult. Nationality and allegiance are matters of too great importance to be imposed upon or taken away from any adult citizen without consent. It is an indignity to a woman to assume that an outside force shall determine to what country her loyalty is to be directed. (p. 7; see also Macmillan, 1925, 143–44)

In the next part of this chapter, I trace international law's attempts to deal initially with the issues of statelessness and dual nationality raised by the principle of dependent nationality, and later with the issues of equality. The point that I want to make here is that if we look back on the principle of dependent nationality from a relational perspective, we can see that opposition to its inequality and patriarchal premise has obscured the value of its premise that the members of a family should have the same nationality, this value being that the unity of the family was legally secured by a common nationality.

Because international law requires a state to admit its nationals and to allow them to reside within its territory (see, generally, Weis, 1979, 45–61; Sohn and Buergenthal, 1992, 39–47, 85–88), a common nationality guarantees that the members of a family can live together within the state of nationality (the right to enter) and can continue to do so (the right not to be expelled). Within the state, a common citizenship promotes the material well-being of the family.[8] Theories of citizenship have more often focused on citizenship as the possession of full political rights, but citizenship also carries important economic and social benefits. As the UN Committee on the Elimination of Discrimination against Women (CEDAW, 1992), which monitors the implementation of the

---

7. It should be noted that not all international women's organizations were like-minded. See Hudson (1933, 118) and Makarov (1937, 155, n.4) on the International Union of Catholic Women's Organizations.

8. Although the terms *nationality* and *citizenship* are often used interchangeably, in many legal systems, including international law, they technically refer to different aspects of membership in a state. Thus, in western Europe, nationality corresponds to membership in a state vis-à-vis other states, whereas citizenship is associated with full membership within the state. This is not true in central and eastern Europe, where many states use the term *citizenship* to refer to the international aspect (Council of Europe, 1997b, 3).

Women's Convention, emphasizes: "Nationality is critical to full participation in society. . . . Without status as nationals or citizens, women are deprived of the right to vote or to stand for public office and may be denied access to public benefits and a choice of residence" (¶ 6). A family's ability to support itself through private means may depend on whether all its members have the right to freedom of movement and whether its adult members have the right to work. Access to public benefits, including education, health care, and social security, may also depend on citizenship.

Thus, while the principle of dependent nationality for married women historically reinforced the patriarchal family, it also constitutes a tradition of protecting and fostering the relationships between husband and wife and parent and child through the attribution of a common nationality. It is this tradition that I argue should be maintained, but reinterpreted relationally.[9]

In the European context, the right to respect for private and family life in Article 8 of the European Convention for the Protection of Human Rights and Fundamental Freedoms (the "European Convention on Human Rights") (Council of Europe, 1950) is an example of such a reinterpretation.[10] As commentators have noted (Opsahl, 1973, 183–85; Harris, O'Boyle, and Warbrick, 1995, 312–17), the original emphasis on the father's family life in the *travaux préparatoires,* or drafting history, of the European Convention on Human Rights has not been maintained in the interpretation given to Article 8 by the European Court of Human Rights. For a majority of the drafting committee, the importance of the right to respect for private and family life derived from the belief that "the father of a family cannot be an independent citizen, cannot feel free within his own country, if he is menaced in his own home and if, every day, the State steals from his soul, or the conscience of his children" (quoted in Opsahl, 1973, 184). In contrast, not only has the European Court of Human Rights extended family life beyond legally formalized relationships (see Harris, O'Boyle, and Warbrick, 1995, 312–17; Liddy, 1998), some judges have interpreted family life as part of a private life that involves the establishment and development of

9. Compare Held's (1993) discussion of the postpatriarchal family as a possible model for society (chap. 10).
10. Art. 8 of the convention reads:
  1. Everyone has the right to respect for his private and family life, his home and his correspondence.
  2. There shall be no interference by a public authority with the exercise of this right except such as is in accordance with the law and is necessary in a democratic society in the interests of national security, public safety or the economic well-being of the country, for the prevention of disorder or crime, for the protection of health or morals, or for the protection of the rights and freedoms of others.

"relationships with other human beings, especially in the emotional field, for the development and fulfillment of one's own personality" (Dictum of the European Commission of Human Rights, adopted by Judge Martens in European Court of Human Rights, 1992, 38). In *Beldjoudi v. France* (European Court of Human Rights, 1992), a case concerning the deportation of an Algerian citizen from France, Judge Martens wrote:

> Read as a whole, [Article 8] apparently guarantees immunity of an *inner circle* in which one may live one's own, one's *private,* life as one chooses. This "inner circle" concept presupposes an "outside world" which, logically, is not encompassed within the concept of private life. Upon further consideration, however, this "inner circle" concept appears too restrictive. "Family life" already enlarges the circle, but there are relatives with whom one has no family life *strictu sensu.* Yet the relationship with such persons, for instance one's parents, undoubtedly falls within the sphere which has to be respected under Article 8. The same may be said with regard to one's relationships with lovers and friends. (pp. 37–38)

In a subsequent deportation case (European Court of Human Rights, 1995), Judge Morenilla speaks of the applicant's "essential social environment, his emotional and 'social circle,' including his family" (p. 31); and Judge Wildhaber of "the whole social fabric which is important to the applicant, and the family is only a part of the entire context, albeit an essential one" (p. 32). This conception of private life thus not only enlarges the sphere of relationships protected under Article 8, it understands these relationships as worthy of protection in part because they are fundamental to a person's life and, further, fundamental to that person's ability to realize her full potential.

The development of Article 8 of the European Convention on Human Rights by the European Court of Human Rights thus shows signs of a shift in the court's understanding of the importance of relationships to the individual. This change from a patriarchal rationale for the legal protection of relationships to a relational one offers a concrete example of how we might rehabilitate nationality's historical function of securing the unity of the family.

III Equality Enters

While the principle that the nationality of the wife follows that of the husband governed the nationality of married women in the vast majority of domestic legal systems at the turn of the twentieth century, it was not a principle of international law. International law did not begin to regulate the issue until the 1930s, by which time the principle had already slowly and in piecemeal fashion begun to change.

The result of this process of gradual state-by-state reform was that the nationality laws of states ranged from those that were still based on the principle of dependent nationality for married women to those that had adopted the principle of independent nationality and covered a variety of intermediate options. As a result of conflicts between these different nationality laws, women at the time of marriage or divorce were increasingly likely to become either stateless[11] or dual nationals. If a woman from a state that automatically deprived her of her nationality on marriage (based on some form of dependent nationality) married a man from a state that did not automatically grant her nationality on marriage (based on some form of independent nationality), then she became stateless. Conversely, if marriage, under the nationality laws of her state, had no effect on her nationality (independent nationality), and marriage, under the laws of her husband's state, gave her his nationality (dependent nationality), then she became a dual national.

International law was initially more receptive to the reform of women's nationality as a problem of statelessness and dual nationality caused by conflicts between the nationality laws of different states than as a problem of gender equality. Women and others who supported the principle of independent nationality for married women were active at the 1930 Hague Codification Conference (Makarov, 1937, 149–50), but the resulting Convention on Certain Questions relating to the Conflict of Nationality Laws addressed women's nationality only insofar as it was necessary to reduce statelessness and dual nationality (League of Nations Treaty Series, 1930). The convention's philosophy of nationality, and implicitly of nationalism, is clearly articulated in its preamble.

> Being convinced that it is in the general interest of the international community to secure that all its members should recognize that every person should have a nationality and should have one nationality only;
>
> Recognizing accordingly that the ideal towards which the efforts of humanity should be directed in this domain is the abolition of all cases both of statelessness and of double nationality.

The aim of the 1963 European Convention on the Reduction of Multiple Nationality, a forerunner of the new European Convention on Nationality, is

11. Statelessness was also caused by other types of conflicts between nationality laws. For a series of examples, see International Law Association (1924, 26–28). For an overview of the contemporary causes of statelessness, see Batchelor (1995).

similarly to eliminate dual nationality. Accordingly, where a woman is entitled to retain her original nationality on marriage and she chooses to acquire her husband's nationality as well, the 1963 convention requires her to renounce one of the two nationalities (Council of Europe, 1963, Art. 1[1]).[12]

Distinct from its general antipathy to statelessness and dual nationality, international law, and particularly international human rights law, gradually came to deal with women's nationality as an issue of equality. Although generally lumped together, the issues of equality produced by the principle of dependent nationality divide into three *generations*. The first generation may be defined as the issue of a married woman's right to an independent nationality. The second generation of issues involves the inequalities that come to the fore once a married woman has a nationality independent of, and hence potentially different from, her husband's nationality. The main examples of these inequalities concern a woman's ability to pass nationality to her children and the acquisition of nationality for a foreign husband. Traditionally, the husband's nationality determined the nationality of the children of the marriage, as well as the nationality of the wife. But whereas the wife's nationality followed from the principle of dependent nationality, the children's nationality was based on the principle of jus sanguinis. On the principle of jus sanguinis, which still governs much of nationality law, nationality is traced through descent or origin rather than determined by birth in the state's territory, as it is under the rival principle of jus soli. Since dependent nationality and jus sanguinis were separate principles, reforms that gave a woman the right to keep her own nationality on marriage did not in and of themselves modify jus sanguinis such that she too could pass her nationality to her children. The other major inequality that emerged from the elimination of dependent nationality involved a foreign spouse's acquisition of nationality by naturalization. The potential for husband and wife to have different nationalities meant that where the family lived in one spouse's state of nationality, the other spouse would lack the security of that nationality. On the assumption that a wife would live in her husband's state, a foreign wife's automatic acquisition of her husband's nationality was sometimes replaced with a special procedure for her to acquire his nationality by naturalization or to acquire residency status in his state (UN, 1963, 15–18),[13]

12. An annex to the convention originally made it possible for states to reserve the right to allow dual nationality for *wives* under certain circumstances (Council of Europe, 1963, Annex ¶¶ 2, 4), but a protocol later withdrew this possibility (Council of Europe, 1977, Art. 4) in light of "the trend of law concerning the nationality of married women" (preamble). (See Killerby, 1998, 27–28.)

13. Although the case law has involved both naturalization and residency status, the focus here is on naturalization.

but no such procedure was provided for a foreign husband. While this and other second-generation issues of equality are most prominent in the contemporary case law on nationality and immigration, their successes may be compromised in ways that raise a third generation of issues.

A relational approach to nationality highlights a further distinction between these three generations of equality issues. Whereas the first generation was concerned with the equality of women as individuals and their equal right to choose their nationality, the second involved discrimination in the protection of women's relationships with family members. Did nationality law treat a mother's relationship to her children in the same way as a father's, and was a wife's relationship to her foreign husband equated to a husband's relationship to his foreign wife? These issues are not about equal respect for the will of the individual as much as equal recognition of her connectedness to others. As will be seen, however, the legal strategies developed for the second generation of equality issues do not attend to the tensions between protection of the mother-child relationship through reform of jus sanguinis and protection of the wife-husband relationship through reform of naturalization. Only a third generation of reforms, exemplified by the developments leading to the new European Convention on Nationality, pursues equality in the full context of the individual's relationships of care, nurture, and support.

The 1957 Convention on the Nationality of Married Women (UNTS, 1957) is representative of the first generation of equality-seeking reforms to the principles of nationality in international law.[14] The convention establishes the principle of the independent nationality of married women, providing that a woman's nationality is not automatically affected by her marriage to or divorce from a foreign national nor by his change of nationality during the marriage (Arts. 1–2). At the same time, it provides that the foreign wife, but not the foreign husband, of a national may choose to acquire that nationality "through specially privileged naturalization procedures" (Art. 3; for the drafting history of Art. 3, see UN, 1962, 40–44).

The 1979 Women's Convention (UNTS, 1979) goes beyond entrenching the first-generation equality principle of independent nationality for married women. Whereas the Convention on the Nationality of Married Women is silent on the nationality of children, the Women's Convention grants women and men equal rights in this regard (Art. 9). As well, it is generally assumed that the Women's Convention requires the same naturalization procedures for both wives and husbands, and CEDAW may indicate (1992, ¶¶ 13, 18) also for de facto

---

14. The first of this generation of reforms was the Montevideo Convention on the Nationality of Women in 1933 (Conference of American States, 1933).

partners. This interpretation of equality is consistent with the case law under the International Covenant on Civil and Political Rights, the American Convention on Human Rights, and the European Convention on Human Rights. Decisions under each of these international human rights treaties have found special treatment for foreign wives discriminatory (UN Human Rights Committee, 1981; Inter-American Court of Human Rights, 1984; European Court of Human Rights, 1985). But while a state must provide such treatment to foreign wives and foreign husbands equally if it provides it to either, the state is under no obligation to provide special treatment in the first place. Legal challenges may therefore not result in the extension of special treatment to foreign husbands, but in its withdrawal altogether. In response to *Abdulaziz, Cabales, and Balkandali v. United Kingdom* (European Court of Human Rights, 1985), a case challenging British immigration rules as discriminatory under the European Convention on Human Rights, the British government changed the immigration rules so that it became as hard for foreign wives to join their husbands settled in Britain as it already was for foreign husbands to join their wives (Mullen, 1988, 159–60).

The Convention on the Nationality of Married Women and the Women's Convention represent the progression of equality-based reforms to nationality law. From a relational perspective, however, they demonstrate how ridding nationality law of its patriarchal foundation may have come at some cost to the security of the family. Once the members of a family can have different nationalities, there is the risk that the family may be divided by discrimination, in particular as regards residence permits, work permits, foreign travel, and, in the case of separation, the right to see the children regularly (Council of Europe, 1994, 5). The first generation of equality reforms to nationality law, exemplified by the Convention on the Nationality of Married Women, granted women equality as individuals but also sought to restore the protection for family relationships this destroyed. The Convention on the Nationality of Married Women thus coupled the hard-won principle of independent nationality for married women with specialized nationalization procedures for foreign wives. While this constituted an attempt to reestablish a common nationality for the family, it was one that discriminated against women.

The Women's Convention and other second-generation reforms to nationality law extended equality beyond a woman's choice of nationality to her right to pass nationality to her children and to the acquisition of her nationality by her foreign spouse. Although these reforms protected men's and women's family relationships equally, there was no version that resolved the tension between equality and the protection of family relationships as a whole.

While the argument for a woman's right to pass her nationality to her children is based on equality—a man has this right—its importance is also relational. Such cases as *Malkani v. Secretary of the Ministry of Home Affairs of Bangladesh* (Bangladesh Supreme Court, 1997a) and *Unity Dow v. Attorney General of Botswana* (Botswana High Court, 1991; Botswana Court of Appeal, 1992) demonstrate the psychological, physical, and material relevance of a common nationality for the mother-child relationship. The High Court Division of the Bangladesh Supreme Court in *Malkani* upheld a law that prevents Bangladeshi women from passing their citizenship to children born from a marriage to a foreign husband.[15] In a case comment, Lubna Mariam (n.d.) describes the emotional and cultural dissonance that results.

> Mothers may croon Bangla ghoom pardani lullabies at their child's cradle, guide them through their first Bangla rhymes, enjoin them to love Sonar Bangla; mothers may even send their sons and daughters to lay [down] their lives for Bangladesh, if need be; but mothers, in Bangladesh, cannot give their children the right to call themselves Bangladeshis.

A mother's ability to give her nationality to her children may also be crucial to the physical security of their relationships with her and to their material welfare. Children born outside marriage or of an unknown or stateless father may otherwise be stateless, a problem that potentially affects, among others, single mothers and lesbian couples. While children of a marriage have the father's nationality and are therefore not stateless, the mother's inability to pass on her nationality to the children may nevertheless cause problems of residency, mobility, and access to state benefits. In *Unity Dow,* for example, both the Botswana High Court and the Court of Appeal used the Women's Convention, the African Charter on Human and Peoples' Rights, and other international instruments to find that a law allowing only a father or an unmarried mother to pass Botswana citizenship to his or her children born in Botswana was unconstitutional on the ground of sex discrimination.[16] The applicant, Unity Dow, was a citizen of Botswana married to a U.S. citizen. Although she was born in Botswana, she and her husband lived in Botswana, and their children were born and were

15. On Bangladesh nationality law generally, see Goonesekere (1997, 90–92, 95) and Islam (1990).

16. *Unity Dow* also challenged an identical provision of the law regarding the citizenship of children born outside Botswana and a provision for application for naturalization by a woman married to a Botswana man that had no counterpart for the naturalization of a man married to a Botswana woman. The high court did not rule on the latter provision. Although the high court did declare the former ultra vires, the court of appeal deleted that part of the high court's declaration owing to the lack of locus standi.

growing up in Botswana, Unity Dow, as a woman, was unable to pass Botswana citizenship to her children. Had the children instead been born in Botswana to a Botswana father and a non-Botswana mother, they would have been Botswana citizens. Without citizenship, Unity Dow's children could remain in Botswana as legal aliens only if they formed part of their father's residency permit, which Botswana granted for no more than two years at a time. Since the children would have to travel on their father's passport, Unity Dow would not be entitled to return to Botswana with her children in the absence of their father. While she was jointly responsible with her husband for the education of their children, her children, as noncitizens, did not qualify for financial assistance for a university education.

On separation or divorce, a common nationality becomes even more critical for the protection of the mother-child relationship. A court-appointed amicus curiae in the *Malkani* case argued that denying Bangladeshi citizenship to the children of a Bangladeshi mother and foreign father might effectively deny the mother's preferential rights of custody of children of tender years because the children would not be assured the visas and visa renewals necessary for them, as noncitizens, to reside with her in Bangladesh (Bangladesh Supreme Court, 1997b, p. 2, ¶ 3[c]). Ruth Donner (1994, 300, n.37) points to the possibility for "legal kidnapping" in the situation where divorced parents have different nationalities and the mother has custody of the child in her state of nationality. If the child has only the father's nationality, then the mother's state of nationality has no standing to intervene diplomatically where the child is concerned. Thus, if the father abuses his visitation rights by taking the child back to his state of nationality, the mother's state cannot exercise its right of diplomatic protection to recover the child.[17]

While recognizing that a mother's equal right to pass her nationality to her children thus protects important aspects of her relationship with them, it compromises international law's traditional conviction that "every person should have a nationality and should have one nationality only." It has always been possible for children to be born dual nationals—for example, where one nationality is acquired by birth in the state's territory and the other by descent from the father—but international law regarded this as an unavoidable by-product of differences in domestic nationality laws. Granting men and women equal

---

17. It should be noted that, traditionally, dual nationality for the child would not solve this problem because the one state of nationality could not intervene where the other's treatment of the dual national was concerned. Donner (1994, 200) argues, however, that the newer Iran–United States Claims Tribunal jurisprudence would permit the mother's state of nationality to intercede with the father's state of nationality in the case where the dual national child's connections are solely to the mother's state.

rights to pass nationality to their children is tantamount, however, to recognizing children of mixed marriages as a category of potential dual nationals. In this sense, equality has made inroads into the avoidance of multiple nationality. In a 1983 case, the Italian Constitutional Court found unconstitutional a 1912 law providing that the child of a male Italian citizen was an Italian citizen by birth but making no such provision for the child of a female Italian citizen. It concluded that the need to avoid dual nationality was not a valid reason to ignore the articles of the constitution on equality before the law without distinction as to sex and on the moral and legal equality of spouses. According to the court, the need to realize the constitutional principle of equality as regards the acquisition of citizenship by birth must take precedence, despite the serious inconveniences caused by dual nationality. Difficulties arising from children's dual citizenship could be minimized by legislation (Italian Constitutional Court, 1983). In *Unity Dow,* where a similar law was at issue, Judge President Amissah wrote:

> Such a child may continue with this dual citizenship for the rest of his or her life. But those states which want to avoid dual nationality would then require the child to opt for the citizenship which he or she wishes to continue with upon attaining majority. The device for eliminating dual citizenship does not, therefore, appear to me to lie in legislation which discriminates between the sexes of the parents. (Botswana Court of Appeal, 1992, 644)

Thus, the second-generation reform of granting women the same rights as men with respect to their children's nationality, when considered in isolation, achieved both equality and the protection of the parent-child relationship. In comparison, the other major reform of requiring the same naturalization procedures for foreign wives and husbands, even in isolation, did not necessarily result in greater protection for the spousal relationship. As with the *Abdulaziz, Cabales, and Balkandali* case, states might equalize downward by eliminating the specialized naturalization procedures that existed for foreign wives.

However, even if states were obliged to equalize naturalization procedures for foreign spouses upward or—farther reaching—to facilitate or guarantee a spouse's acquisition of nationality more generally, the result would not reconcile equality with the protection of family relationships as a whole unless states also recognized dual nationality, and this is the limitation of the second generation of equality reforms to nationality law. Without dual nationality, the foreign spouse can take advantage of a fast-track naturalization procedure only by giving up his or her own nationality. Depending on the security, entitlements, and benefits which that state attaches to nationality, this may be the only feasible option. In effect, the foreign spouse has no choice but to sacrifice his or her own nationality for the sake of the family. But more important from the perspective of equality is that the foreign spouse can no longer pass his or her own nationality to the children. Protecting the spousal relationship through naturalization therefore undermines the equality of the parents unless the rights extended to nonnationals by the state make not naturalizing a realistic choice or that state recognizes dual nationality.

It is this reasoning that ultimately led the Council of Europe to a third generation of equality reforms that carves out the spouses of different nationalities, as well as their children, as permissible exceptions to the traditional principle of avoiding dual nationality. Early resolutions by the Council of Europe were limited to maximizing the protection for family relationships within the second generation of equality reforms. Resolution (77)13 of its Committee of Ministers (Council of Europe, 1977b) recommends that governments grant their nationality at birth to children born in wedlock if one of the parents is a national or, alternatively, provide for such children up to the age of twenty-two to acquire that nationality. Resolution (77)12 (Council of Europe, 1977a) equalizes up the treatment of foreign spouses by recommending not only that states eliminate distinctions between foreign husbands and foreign wives as regards the acquisition of nationality, but that they take steps so that foreign spouses of their nationals may acquire their nationality on more favorable conditions than those generally required of other aliens. Underlying both resolutions, however, is the continuing ideal of a single nationality. Recognizing that the application of the principle of equality would lead to a greater number of children with dual nationality, Resolution (77)13 anticipates that these children would be made to choose one nationality or the other when they reach the age of twenty-two. Similarly, the explanatory report to Resolution (77)12 presents the resolution as a strategic second-best, "the most desirable and theoretically ideal solution" being to give a married couple the right to choose the nationality of either husband or wife (Council of Europe, 1995a, 9–10).

With the adoption of Recommendation 1081 by its Parliamentary Assembly in 1988, the Council of Europe embarked on a third generation of reforms, premised on the acknowledgement that the principle of equality might also require a relaxation of the principle of the avoidance of multiple nationality. Recommendation 1081 reads in part:

4. Reaffirming the principle of equality of the spouses before the law;

5. Considering that, in view of the gravity of the economic and social problems affecting spouses in mixed marriages, that is to say marriages

where the spouses have a different European nationality, it is desirable that each of such spouses may have the right to acquire the nationality of the other without losing his or her own nationality of origin;

6. Considering that the children born from mixed marriages should also be entitled to acquire and keep the nationality of both of their parents; . . .

8. Considering that it is only in exceptional cases that the fact that a person has several nationalities may render difficult the application of other Council of Europe conventions and that this can hardly be considered an argument against the multiple nationality principle. (Council of Europe, Parliamentary Assembly, 1988)

Several years later, a protocol was concluded amending the 1963 European Convention on the Reduction of Multiple Nationality to the same effect (the "Second Protocol") (Council of Europe, 1993). Recommendation 1081 and the Second Protocol thus establish the right to dual nationality for spouses of different nationalities and their children as a justifiable departure from the convention's central principle of the avoidance of multiple nationality. Although neither goes so far as to require states to allow dual nationality for families of mixed nationality, both offer reasons for states to do so. Recommendation 1081 emphasizes the reconciliation of gender equality with socioeconomic security for family relationships, whereas the Second Protocol stresses the encouragement of unity of nationality per se in families (Council of Europe, 1993, preamble; 1994).

In comparison, the 1997 European Convention on Nationality downgrades, rather than merely relaxes, the principle of the avoidance of multiple nationality. The principle is nowhere among the convention's general principles (Council of Europe, 1997a, chap. 2), and Article 15 confirms that the convention is neutral on multiple nationality.[18] Unlike Recommendation 1081 and the Second Protocol, however, the European Convention on Nationality is silent on the desirability of allowing dual nationality. The only exception is that states party to the convention must respect dual nationality ex lege where a spouse or child has acquired two nationalities automatically (Council of Europe, 1997a, Art. 14). By not identifying families of mixed nationality in general as a distinctly persuasive case for dual nationality, the convention resists the logic of the third generation of equality reforms begun by Recommendation 1081 and the Second Protocol.

18. As such, the European Convention on Nationality technically does not modify the obligations of states party to the earlier European Convention on the Reduction of Multiple Nationality (Council of Europe, 1997a, Art. 26).

Nevertheless, by promoting the acquisition of nationality by spouses and children of nationals and by dropping the opposition to multiple nationality of the earlier international conventions on nationality, the European Convention on Nationality creates the possibility that equality not be achieved at the expense of family life. Because a family is able to have dual nationality, it has unity of nationality, with the security that provides, without sacrificing the nationality of one spouse or the other. In the first place, Article 6(1)(a) provides that a state party shall grant its nationality at birth to children born to a national within the state, and Article 6(4) that a state party shall "facilitate in its internal law the acquisition of its nationality" for spouses of its nationals and those children of its nationals who are not already nationals by birth. The examples of facilitation given in the explanatory report to the convention include a reduction of the length of required residence, less stringent language requirements, an easier procedure, and lower procedural fees (Council of Europe, 1997b, 35). In the second place, Article 15 specifies that the convention does not limit a state's right to determine that its nationality can coexist with another nationality, which would include the state's right to allow dual nationality for both spouses of mixed marriages and their children.

Indeed, in light of the equality and family-based justifications contained in Recommendation 1081 and the Second Protocol, we may even read the European Convention on Nationality's hierarchy of norms as implicitly requiring dual nationality for families of mixed nationality. It is clear from the preamble that, unlike earlier international conventions on nationality, the convention does not treat statelessness and dual nationality as twin evils. Instead, it bases nationality law on the principles of the avoidance of statelessness and equality, reducing dual nationality to a problem of coordination. The preamble recites:

Desiring to promote the progressive development of legal principles concerning nationality, as well as their adoption in internal law and desiring to avoid, as far as possible, cases of statelessness;

Desiring to avoid discrimination in matters relating to nationality;

Aware of the right to respect for family life as contained in Article 8 of the Convention for the Protection of Human Rights and Fundamental Freedoms; . . .

Agreeing on the desirability of finding appropriate solutions to consequences of multiple nationality and in particular as regards the rights and duties of multiple nationals.

The principle of independent nationality of married women is among the basic principles in Article 4 of the convention, and, more generally, Article 5(1) provides:

The rules of a State Party on nationality shall not contain distinctions or include any practice which amounts to discrimination on the grounds of sex, religion, race, colour or national or ethnic origin.[19]

It is striking, moreover, that the explanatory report to the European Convention on Nationality matter-of-factly presents the principle of equality as requiring states to allow dual nationality for spouses of mixed marriages and their children (Council of Europe, 1997b, 23–24, 44).

This part of the chapter has tracked actual developments in international law to demonstrate that Recommendation 1081, the Second Protocol, and the European Convention on Nationality represent the first efforts to achieve gender equality in nationality law without sacrificing the protections that nationality has historically afforded family relationships. If we interpret this traditional protection relationally, rather than patriarchally, as I suggested in part two, then the significance of the Council of Europe developments is not limited by their emphasis on marriage. Rather, their importance lies in the recognition that equality in nationality law must respect some set of relationships of care and that dual nationality is one way to accomplish this. We might imagine that the specific relationships to be safeguarded should be determined by the societies concerned. In the European context, these might include nontraditional families, such as de facto relationships and same-sex partnerships, and the non-Western marriage customs of immigrant communities, such as arranged marriages.[20]

---

19. Feminist critiques of consent and reasonableness as based on a male norm may suggest two additional arguments under the convention for mandatory dual nationality in the case of mixed marriage. First, Art. 7 allows a state to withdraw its nationality from an individual only in a limited number of cases, including the case of an individual who has "voluntarily" acquired another nationality (Art. 7[1][a]). The need to help provide for one's family or to secure access to one's children that leads one spouse to naturalize in the other's state is arguably not voluntary when seen in this context. A similar argument might be made concerning Art. 7(1)(e). Second, Art. 16 refers to a renunciation or loss of another nationality that cannot "reasonably" be required. Feminists have sought to show that what counts as reasonable also reflects the experiences of men. (See, e.g., Réaume, 1996, 278–91.)

20. As a matter of positive law, the reference in the preamble of the European Convention on Nationality to the right to respect for family life as contained in Art. 8 of the European Convention on Human Rights might be read as incorporating the past or even future development of the concept of family by the European Court of Human Rights. However, the use of the term *spouse* in the operative provisions of the European Convention on Nationality can be interpreted as restricting the convention's benefits to legally married couples, even though the term is undefined. Similarly, the deletion from the European Convention on Nationality's preamble of a reference to Art. 14 of the European Convention on Human Rights (on nondiscrimination) (Council of Europe, 1996) and the drafters' insistence on fully enumerating the prohibited grounds of discrimination in Art. 5 of the European Convention on Nationality (Council of Europe Parliamen-

IV Nationalism

If allowing dual nationality for spouses of mixed nationality and their children is a way to do justice both to equality and to the relational role of nationality, what does it do to the correspondence between the legal concept of nationality and the sociological attachment of nationalism? In traditional international law, the ideal was that every individual would have a nationality, but one nationality only. An individual's nationality would therefore be the legal expression of his feeling of belonging to a state. Where a family can have dual nationality, as under the new European Convention on Nationality, how should we conceive of their national identity? Those who believe that nationalism is born and bred might argue that a spouse with dual nationality will have a "genuine" nationality (namely, his or her original nationality) and a "nationality of convenience" (the nationality of his or her spouse). This picture is painted more generally by opponents of dual nationality, who fear a Fifth Column within the state: a group of citizens whose allegiance lies elsewhere and who are therefore ready to work against the state from within.[21] The argument would then be that for spouses with different nationalities and their children, equality has changed the concept of nationality from a reflection of the individual's public loyalty to the state to an instrument for protecting private relationships. In this part of the chapter, I suggest that a relational perspective on nationality and nationalism allows us to see public loyalty and private relationships as connected; in particular, that an individual's relationships with particular others— parents, siblings, spouses, children—help to constitute her loyalties to her own state and theirs.

We may wonder why historically the principle of dependent nationality for married women did not raise the issue of disloyalty. After all, a wife's involuntary change of nationality did not necessarily change her feelings of nationalism. Indeed, it was precisely the inability of law to command the heart that united feminists and xenophobes against the principle of dependent national-

---

tary Assembly, 1997, 10) make it harder to argue by analogy. Notably, sexual orientation, unlike sex, is not listed in Art. 5. While the UN Human Rights Committee has interpreted sex discrimination in the International Covenant on Civil and Political Rights as including sexual orientation (UN Human Rights Committee, 1994, ¶ 8.7), the European Court of Human Rights recently confirmed that sexual orientation is prohibited as a nonenumerated ground of discrimination under Art. 14 of the European Convention on Human Rights (European Court of Human Rights, 1999, ¶ 28), which would exclude it from Art. 5. In any event, the interpretive strategy for incorporating same-sex couples into the European Convention on Nationality must take account of the debate over whether gay and lesbian relationships should have to conform to the concept of family to be recognized by the law. See, e.g., Cossman (1994); Freeman (1994).

21. See, e.g., Spiro (1997), tracing the varying intensity of this fear over time.

ity. Defenders of dependent nationality, however, assumed away the problem of disloyalty, either through the wife's duty of obedience to the pater familias or through her indirect consent to his nationality. Under the institution of the pater familias, a wife was bound to obey her husband and therefore to obey the state that he obeyed (Makarov, 1937, 166). Alternatively, the United States Supreme Court held in *Mackenzie v. Hare* (U.S., 1915) that in consenting to marry a foreigner a woman also consented to his nationality. As Anne McClintock (1995, 358) observed: "For women, citizenship in the nation was mediated by the marriage relation within the family."

While these fictions of indirect obedience and indirect consent to the husband's state were objectionable in their patriarchy and implausible as descriptions of women's loyalty, there may have been a grain of truth to them. What seems true is that our feelings for a state may be created by our feelings for particular members of that state.[22] In a recent United States Supreme Court decision on nationality, Justice Stephen Breyer speaks of "the bonds of loyalty that connect family with Nation" (U.S., 1998).[23] Loyalty to our state of birth is bound up with our love for our parents and siblings, who are part of that state; it is possible that loyalty to a spouse's state is affected by our love for him or her or by our love for our children, who have ties to that state. If this is true, then an analysis of the ways in which a family with dual nationality experiences nationalism must go beyond an analysis of dual nationals generally.

Some commentators on dual nationality have sought to dispose generally of the objection that dual nationality creates a group of citizens who will be actively disloyal to the state or simply not identify strongly enough with the state to make the civic sacrifices required of them.[24] Alexander Aleinikoff and Douglas Klusmeyer (see chap. 3) argue essentially that this objection is misplaced. Since feelings of nationalism are not created or destroyed by a change in nationality alone, requiring an individual to renounce his previous nationality in order to become a national will not necessarily make him more committed to his new state than allowing him to retain his previous nationality. Disloyalty or lack of identification with the state are not problems of nationality.

22. Although I do not pursue it in this chapter, the converse may also be true, namely, that feelings for others are associated with the state they symbolize. In particular, women are identified with their nation or state, as colonialism and, more recently, the mass rape of women in ethnic conflicts have tragically shown. See, e.g., Déjeux (1989, pt. 1); McClintock (1995, chap. 10).

23. In *Miller,* the promotion of a foreign-born child's early ties to American relatives is associated with the promotion of the child's ties to the United States (U.S., 1998, pp. 1433–34, 1439–41, 1461–63).

24. See commentators cited in n.1.

Moreover, the concern that dual nationals may be disloyal is fueled by the assumption that individuals have only one real loyalty; that where an individual has dual nationality, one nationality corresponds to a genuine nationalism and the other to nothing. If one nationality is real and substantial, and the other merely formal and instrumental, then the risk of disloyalty or indifference to the latter state of nationality seems significant. But if this assumption about loyalty is too simple, then dual nationality may not be just a shell game where nationalism is hidden under one of the two nationalities. And the risk of disloyalty will also be different. The citizenship literature has shown that loyalties are potentially multiple, variable, and interactive.[25] Individuals may have loyalty to more than one state, and each loyalty may wax or wane over time. Nor is it necessarily true that nationalisms are always stronger or weaker versions of one another. Scholars of federations and, more recently, the European Union have argued that an individual's attachment to different orders of government may not be comparable (see, e.g., Bauböck, 1997; Weiler, 1998). Her attachment to Europe, for instance, may reflect a belief in its civic virtues, while her attachment to her own state may be rooted in the emotions of culture and history. On this hypothesis, the liberal nationalism of Europe is capable of tempering the Romantic nationalism of the nation-state.

What the general sociological discussion neglects, however, is the possibility that the national identity of a family with dual nationalities (or different nationalities or originally different nationalities, since nationality does not command nationalism) may be particularly complex because it is also relational. In the 1930 novel *Mrs. Fischer's War,* by Henrietta Leslie, Janet Fischer is an Englishwoman married to a German who has lived in England since before their marriage without bothering to become naturalized. While the couple are on holiday in Germany, World War I breaks out and awakens in Janet's husband, Carl, long-forgotten feelings for the country of his childhood. Without telling Janet, Carl disappears and volunteers to fight for Germany. The story of the novel is the story of Mrs. Fischer's experience in London during the war as an enemy national by marriage. Not only must she officially register[26] as such and obtain permission to move outside London, but her daily life becomes a series of social snubs, polite rejections, and outright ostracism. Janet eventually receives word from Carl, only to find that their son, John, has enlisted in the British army and is being sent to the front.

25. In this volume, see the discussion by Linda Bosniak in chap. 8, *Denationalizing Citizenship.*

26. Under the British Aliens Restriction Act, the names of twelve thousand women who were aliens by marriage were entered into an official register (Hiley, 1986, 646).

When Janet tells John that his father has become a German soldier, he hotly rejects her plea to think of Carl "like he is."

> "Fancy choosing Germany, with all its beastliness, instead of England. You'd think only a beast would do that, and he . . . he didn't seem like a beast. He seemed like . . ."
> "Like he is," Janet said gently.
> "My God, you still believe in him? I don't know how you can. I couldn't, oh, I couldn't!"
> Janet was stricken with pity for the boy.
> "You can," she said. "Think of him, shut your eyes and think of him."
> John shook his head.
> "It's no use." (Leslie, 1930, 175–76)

Whereas John can now think of Carl only as the enemy, Janet clings to her memory of Carl as an individual. John's response to his parentage is the recoil of nationalism.

> "You see, I argue it this way. One can't belong to two countries, any more than one can have two mothers or two fathers. In peace time, it doesn't matter; one doesn't have to think about these things; one hasn't got to choose, but in war time one has—and I choose England."
> "I see," said Janet. There might be a flaw in the child's reasoning. If there were, from his point of view, she couldn't find it. (Leslie, 1930, 126)

Janet represents the opposite, if unarticulated, response: the internationalist prediction that marriage between people of different nationalities will diminish nationalism (see Knop, 1999, 386–88). Her love for Carl survives the war, and she is ultimately reunited with him and estranged from John. Ironically, one of the many poignant rejections Janet suffers is from a group of women pacifists, who are afraid that her German nationality will taint their case.[27]

In *Mrs. Fischer's War,* Janet Fischer and her son represent conflicting views of how marriages of mixed nationality influence the identity of the spouses and their children. Janet conceives of herself and Carl as individuals for whom nations do not matter, whereas John assimilates his father to the enemy nation.

---

27. In real life, the executive of the Women's International League, part of the women's peace movement that developed during the war, decided to exclude British-born wives of aliens for fear of controversy (Mitchell, 1966, 286).

This opposition suggests the difficulty of predicting how national identities will be constituted by mixed marriages. As Albert Memmi writes:

> The mixed marriage, which seems an ideal place of synthesis and harmony, of reciprocal opening and generosity, most often turns out to be a dangerous cross-roads, open to all winds and favourable to all collisions. The mixed couple, instead of being a model oasis, a neutral zone between countries that tear each other apart, often transforms itself into a jousting court where the whole world charges in. (Memmi, in Déjeux, 1989, 168; author's translation)

But Henrietta Leslie's rather melodramatic novel also makes one wonder whether there is something gendered about the difference between Janet's and John's reactions to Carl's German nationalism. In France, there is growing attention to the problem of French-Maghrébin[28] children, "couscous pommes frites" in French slang, abducted by the father who decides to leave France and return to his native country. Historian Martine Muller profiles how having a child strengthens the Maghreb father's feeling of alienation from French society and his longing to regain his own.

> The Maghreb father aspires, over the course of the years, to rediscover his country. Does he not live in a state of frustration? In his wife, the mother of his children, he finds no trace of the image of his own mother; his children are progressively formed by the rules of their mother's country; he feels alone. The desire to find himself at home again takes hold of him so strongly that one day he leaves— and takes his children. (Muller, 1987, jacket; author's translation)

This example suggests not only that nationalism is shaped by family relationships, but also that the structures of power within those relationships may help determine that shape. Forms of gender oppression may interact with forms of oppression of immigrants[29] to produce the Maghreb father's identification with his homeland that Muller portrays as intensified by the existence of a child.[30] In the context of families of mixed or dual nationality created by shared

28. The states of the Maghreb are Algeria, Tunisia, and Morocco.

29. In American legal literature, the narratives of immigrant women are increasingly being used to problematize the law. See, e.g., Hernández-Truyol (1997); Lewis (1997).

30. According to Muller the abduction of French-Maghrébin children occurs mainly among working-class couples where the husband is a worker and the wife usually holds a slightly higher position. Muller (1987, 197–98) views this gap as contributing to the husband's desire to return to his country, where he can enjoy greater social and economic importance.

immigration, Greta Gilbertson and Audrey Singer's (1999) work on naturalization among Dominican immigrants in New York City offers a rich case study of such interaction. Gilbertson and Singer record how the experience of Dominican women who return regularly to the Dominican Republic differs from that of Dominican men who intend to return permanently. The men are partially motivated by a belief that in the Dominican Republic they can regain some of the gender status and privilege that they felt they lost in the United States (Gilbertson and Singer, 1999, 16). Paradoxically, the women experience their life in the Dominican Republic as giving them greater independence and equality than their life in the United States, where they live with their grown children and are responsible for most of the housework and care of their grandchildren (pp. 13–14). Paul Johnston's research (see chapter 9, this volume) on the emergence of transnational citizenship among Mexican immigrants in California is another important contribution to our understanding of how family and gender influence the ways that individuals inhabit their national identities and, as in Gilbertson and Singer's case study, decide whether to become dual nationals by naturalizing in the United States. Johnston finds that in California, Mexican immigrant women in particular associate their Mexican citizenship with their family's roots and their acquisition of U.S. citizenship with their children's future and have played a key role in the drive to naturalize.

In this part of the chapter I have argued that because the rules on nationality in international law correspond to assumptions about the nature of nationalism, a relational analysis should extend to nationalism as well as nationality. In particular, I have suggested why concerns about loyalty that often underlie resistance to dual nationality generally should be analyzed differently in the context of extending dual nationality to families of mixed nationality. While the examples in this part do not go so far as to develop a relational approach to nationalism, they show why such an approach might be helpful.

Conclusion

In his study of access to citizenship in twenty-five countries in chapter 1 of this volume,[31] Patrick Weil shows that every country that had a provision for the automatic acquisition of citizenship through marriage has repealed the provision within the past forty years. In seven of the countries, there is no specific

---

31. The countries are Australia, Austria, Belgium, Canada, Denmark, Estonia, Finland, France, Germany, Greece, Ireland, Israel, Italy, Latvia, Lithuania, Luxembourg, Mexico, Netherlands, Portugal, Russia, Spain, South Africa, Sweden, United Kingdom, and the United States.

provision that facilitates the acquisition of citizenship by a foreign spouse. In others, the waiting period before a foreign spouse can apply, although shorter than the ordinary waiting period, has been lengthened. Weil attributes the repeal of the automatic nature and timely consideration of citizenship to, among other things, the goal of ensuring equal treatment of men and women. These changes aimed at equality in states' nationality laws together with the prohibition on dual nationality that Weil's study indicates still exists in a number of states, invite comparison with recent Council of Europe developments, most notably, the 1997 European Convention on Nationality, that require states to facilitate naturalization for spouses and children of nationals and permit them not to condition this naturalization on the renunciation of another nationality. This comparison highlights the inadequacy both of the standard treatment of equality in the field of nationality law, which has centered on identical treatment for men and women, and of the growing literature on dual nationality, which is inattentive to equality as a justification for dual nationality. In linking gender equality with the acceptance of dual nationality for all members of a family where the husband and wife originally have different nationalities, moreover, the background to the European Convention on Nationality suggests that our analyses of equality and nationality and even our underlying analysis of nationalism are fundamentally limited by a view of the self as atomistic and general, rather than relational and particular.

My claim in this chapter has thus been that a relational understanding of the recent European provisions on gender and nationality is both possible and preferable. But this is not to say that it is the only or even the most probable one. The European Convention on Nationality can instead be understood nonrelationally as the reconciliation of gender equality with the traditional European notion of the legal unity of the family. Indeed, the explanatory memorandum to an earlier resolution on the nationality of spouses of different nationalities reads in this vein: "The concept of the family as a single unit, however much it may now be founded on the independence and freedom of both spouses, nevertheless remains basic to the view taken by European peoples of the marriage tie" (Council of Europe, 1995a, 8; see, generally, Girard, 1994). And the centrality of marriage in the convention is also consistent with a simple updating of the pater familias.

In contrast, the idea of relational nationality looks to the importance of a relationship for the individual and not to the formality, or even necessarily the analogy, of marriage. While the chapter has not detailed how to determine which relationships should be recognized through the attribution of nationality, the shift in perspective from the traditional European family to the relationships central to the individual's way of being in the world may prove fruitful for this discussion. Relationality neither presses a common nationality on all family relationships, as the nonrelational "unity of the family" might,[32] nor does it exclude from consideration all relationships that do not conform to the notion of family. Moreover, the idea of relational nationality, like the idea of relational feminism (see Nedelsky, 1997, 10–11), seems promising beyond Europe because the relationships to be protected through nationality are to be determined within a particular culture and because this determination, as in European human rights law, should be an inclusive process.

At the same time, dual nationality is one possible solution to the problem of equality and nationality reached in one possible context. While nationality is the traditional legal protection for family relationships in international law and remains the strongest protection, a combination of international human rights already affords many of the same protections and thus provides a functional alternative (see Killerby, 1998, 32–34; and, more generally, Soysal, 1994). The International Law Commission's (ILC) draft articles on the nationality of natural persons in relation to the succession of states provides, for example, that where the acquisition or loss of nationality in relation to the succession of states would impair the unity of a family, states must take "all appropriate measures to allow that family to remain together or to be reunited" (UN ILC, 1999, Art. 12). The ILC's commentary explains that this need not entail a common nationality, let alone dual nationality, for the family. For states firmly opposed to dual nationality, this functional alternative may be the only or—depending on the reasons for the state's resistance—the better one.

This chapter has, above all, proposed a new starting point for thinking about nationality. The European Convention on Nationality and the ILC's draft articles, two of the most recent international law initiatives on nationality, begin similarly with the need for the law of nationality to take account of both the legitimate interests of states and those of individuals. The chapter has sought to show that before considering what balance nationality law should strike between these two sets of interests, and even what these interests are, we need to problematize the view that nationality takes of the individual herself.

Works Cited and Bibliography

Aleinikoff, Thomas Alexander, David A. Martin, and Hiroshi Motomura. 1998. *Immigration and Citizenship: Process and Policy*. 4th ed. St. Paul, Minn.: West.
Anderson, Benedict. 1991. *Imagined Communities: Reflections on the Origin and Spread of Nationalism*. Rev. ed. London: Verso.

32. This point about pressure was made to me by Rainer Bauböck.

Baier, Annette C. 1995. *Moral Prejudices: Essays on Ethics*. Cambridge, Mass.: Harvard University Press.

Bangladesh Supreme Court. 1997a. *Malkani v. Secretary of the Ministry of Home Affairs of Bangladesh*. Writ Petition no. 3192 of 1992. High Court Division, Dhaka, Sept. 1. (Uncertified copy on file with author.)

———. 1997b. Written submission of Dr. Kamal Hossain as amicus curiae. Uncertified copy on file with author.

Batchelor, Carol A. 1995. "UNHCR and Issues Related to Nationality." *Refugee Survey Quarterly* 14(3): 91–112.

Bauböck, Rainer. 1997. "Citizenship and National Identities in the European Union." Jean Monnet Working Paper 4/97. Harvard Law School. <http://www.law.harvard.edu/programs/JeanMonnet/papers/97/97-04-.html>

Benhabib, Seyla. 1992. "The Generalized and the Concrete Other: The Kohlberg-Gilligan Controversy and Moral Theory." In *Situating the Self: Gender, Community and Postmodernism in Contemporary Ethics*, pp. 148–77. New York: Routledge.

Botswana Court of Appeal. 1992. *Attorney-General of Botswana v. Unity Dow*. Law Reports of the Commonwealth (Constitutional and Administrative Law), vol. 1992, p. 623.

Botswana High Court. 1991. *Unity Dow v. Attorney-General of Botswana*. Law Reports of the Commonwealth (Constitutional and Administrative Law), vol. 1991, p. 574.

Caldwell, Gillian, Steven Galster, and Nadia Steinzor. 1997. *Crime and Servitude: An Exposé of the Traffic in Women for Prostitution from the Newly Independent States*. Global Survival Network. <http://www.globalsurvival.net/femaletrade/9711russia.html>

Canadian Supreme Court. 1997. *Benner v. Canada (Secretary of State)*. Supreme Court Reports, vol. 1997, no. 1, p. 358.

Conference of American States. 1933. "Montevideo Convention on the Nationality of Women." Dec. 26. *American Journal of International Law* (suppl.) 28:61 (1934).

Cossman, Brenda. 1994. "Family Inside/Out." *University of Toronto Law Journal* 44: 1–39.

Council of Europe. 1950. "Convention for the Protection of Human Rights and Fundamental Freedoms." Nov. 4. ETS no. 5.

———. 1963. "Convention on Reduction of Cases of Multiple Nationality and Military Obligations in Cases of Multiple Nationality." May 6. ETS no. 43.

———. 1977. "Protocol Amending the Convention on the Reduction of Cases of Multiple Nationality and Military Obligations in Cases of Multiple Nationality." Nov. 24. ETS no. 95.

———. 1993. "Second Protocol Amending the Convention on Reduction of Cases of Multiple Nationality and Military Obligations in Cases of Multiple Nationality." Feb. 2. ETS no. 149.

———. 1994. "Second Protocol: Explanatory Report." In *The Reduction of Cases of Multiple Nationality and Military Obligations in Cases of Multiple Nationality: Explanatory Report, Second Protocol Amending the Convention Opened for Signature on 2 February 1993*, pp. 3–7. ISBN 92-871-2402-7. Strasbourg: Council of Europe Press.

———. 1995a. "Resolution (77)12: Explanatory Memorandum." In *Nationality of Spouses of Different Nationalities and Nationality of Children Born in Wedlock.*

Resolutions (77)12 and (77)13 Adopted by the Committee of Ministers of the Council of Europe on 27 May 1977 and Explanatory Memorandum, pp. 7–11. ISBN 92-871-0523-5. Strasbourg: Council of Europe Press.

———. 1995b. "Resolution (77)13: Explanatory Memorandum." In *Nationality of Spouses of Different Nationalities and Nationality of Children Born in Wedlock. Resolutions (77)12 and (77)13 Adopted by the Committee of Ministers of the Council of Europe on 27 May 1977 and Explanatory Memorandum*, pp. 15–20. ISBN 92-871-0523-5. Strasbourg: Council of Europe Press.

———. 1996. "Draft European Convention on Nationality." In Council of Europe Parliamentary Assembly. *Request for an Opinion from the Committee of Ministers to the Assembly on the Draft European Convention on Nationality*. Doc. 7665.

———. 1997a. "European Convention on Nationality." Nov. 6. ETS no. 166.

———. 1997b. "European Convention on Nationality: Explanatory Report." In *European Convention on Nationality and Explanatory Report*, pp. 21–57. ISBN 92-871-3470-7. Strasbourg: Council of Europe Publishing.

Council of Europe. Committee of Ministers. 1977a. "Resolution (77)12 on the Nationality of Spouses of Different Nationalities." May 27. In Council of Europe, *Council of Europe Achievements in the Field of Law: Nationality*, p. 22. Doc. DIR/JUR(98)1. Strasbourg: Council of Europe (1998).

———. 1977b. "Resolution (77)13 on the Nationality of Children Born in Wedlock." May 27. In Council of Europe, *Council of Europe Achievements in the Field of Law: Nationality*, p. 23. Doc. DIR/JUR(98)1. Strasbourg: Council of Europe (1998).

Council of Europe. Parliamentary Assembly. 1988. "Recommendation 1081 (1988) on Problems of Nationality in Mixed Marriages." June 30. In *Council of Europe Achievements in the Field of Law: Nationality*, pp. 76–77. Doc. DIR/JUR(98)1. Strasbourg: Council of Europe (1998).

———. 1997. *Report Giving an Opinion on the Draft European Convention on Nationality*. Doc. 7718.

Déjeux, Jean. 1989. *Image de l'Étrangère: Unions mixtes franco-maghrébines*. Paris: La Boîte à Documents.

Development and Education Programme for Daughters and Communities. 1997. "Nationality Problems Add to Child Exploitation in Thailand." *Connect* 1(6) (Feb.–Mar.): 6–7.

Donner, Ruth. 1994. *The Regulation of Nationality in International Law*. 2d ed. Irvington-on-Hudson, N.Y.: Transnational Publishers.

Elshtain, Jean Bethke. 1995. *Women and War*. Chicago: University of Chicago Press.

Equality Now. 1999. "Words and Deeds. Holding Governments Accountable in the Beijing + 5 Review Process." *Women's Action* 16(1). <http://www.equalitynow.org/action_eng_16_1.html>

European Court of Human Rights. 1985. *Abdulaziz, Cabales and Balkandali v. United Kingdom. Publications of the European Court of Human Rights, Series A: Judgments and Decisions*, no. 94.

———. 1992. *Beldjoudi v. France. Publications of the European Court of Human Rights, Series A: Judgments and Decisions*, no. 234-A.

———. 1995. *Nasri v. France. Publications of the European Court of Human Rights, Series A: Judgments and Decisions*, no. 320-B.

———. 1999. *Salgueiro da Silva Mouta v. Portugal* (Dec. 21).

Fitzpatrick, Joan, and Katrina R. Kelly. 1998. "Gendered Aspects of Migration: Law and the Female Migrant." *Hastings International and Comparative Law Review* 22:47–112.

Franck, Thomas M. 1996. "Clan and Superclan: Loyalty, Identity, and Community in Law and Practice." *American Journal of International Law* 90:359–83.

Freeman, Jody. 1994. "Defining Family in *Mossop v. DSS*: The Challenge of Anti-essentialism and Interactive Discrimination for Human Rights Litigation." *University of Toronto Law Journal* 44:41–96.

Friedman, Marilyn. 1990. "Feminism and Modern Friendship: Dislocating the Community." In Cass R. Sunstein (ed.), *Feminism and Political Theory,* pp. 143–58. Chicago: University of Chicago Press.

Gilbertson, Greta, and Audrey Singer. 1999. "Naturalization under Changing Conditions of Membership: Dominican Immigrants in New York City." Paper presented at the conference "Citizenship: Comparisons and Perspectives," cosponsored by the International Migration Policy Program, Carnegie Endowment for International Peace, and the Fundação Luso-Americana para o Desenvolvimento, Lisbon, Portugal, June 4.

Girard, Philip. 1994. "Why Canada Has No Family Policy: Lessons from France and Italy." *Osgoode Hall Law Journal* 32:579–611.

Goonesekere, Savitri W. E. 1997. "Nationality and Women's Human Rights: The Asia/Pacific Experience." In Andrew Byrnes, Jane Connors, and Lum Bik (eds.), *Advancing the Human Rights of Women: Using International Human Rights Standards in Domestic Litigation,* pp. 86–100. Papers and Statements from the Asia/South Pacific Regional Judicial Colloquium, Hong Kong, May 20–22, 1996. London: Commonwealth Secretariat.

Green, T. H. 1986. "Prolegomena to Ethics: Selections." In Paul Harris and John Morrow (eds.), *Lectures on the Principles of Political Obligations and Other Writings,* pp. 250–301. Cambridge: Cambridge University Press.

Harris, D. J., M. O'Boyle, and C. Warbrick. 1995. *Law of the European Convention on Human Rights.* London: Butterworths.

Held, Virginia. 1993. *Feminist Morality: Transforming Culture, Society, and Politics.* Chicago: University of Chicago Press.

Hernández-Truyol, Berta Esperanza. 1997. "Borders (En)gendered: Normativities, Latinas, and a LatCrit Paradigm." *New York University Law Review* 72:882–927.

Hiley, Nicholas. 1986. "Counter-Espionage and Security in Great Britain during the First World War." *English Historical Review* 101:635–70.

Hudson, Manley O. 1933. "The Hague Convention of 1930 and the Nationality of Women." *American Journal of International Law* 27:117–22.

Inter-American Court of Human Rights. 1984. *Amendments to the Naturalization Provisions of the Constitution of Costa Rica.* Advisory Opinion. *Human Rights Law Journal* 5:161.

International Court of Justice. 1955. *Nottebohm Case (Liechtenstein v. Guatemala).* Judgment. I.C.J. Reports, vol. 1955, p. 4.

International Law Association. 1924. *Thirty-Third Conference Report.*

———. Committee on Feminism and International Law. 1998. *Preliminary Report on Women's Equality and Nationality in International Law.* In International Law Association, *Sixty-Eighth Conference Report,* pp. 278–316.

Islam, M. Rafiqul. 1990. "The Nationality Law and Practice of Bangladesh." In Ko Swan Sik (ed.), *Nationality and International Law in Asian Perspective,* pp. 1–25. Dordrecht: Martinus Nijhoff.

Italian Constitutional Court. 1983. Judgment no. 30 (Jan. 28). *Raccolta ufficiale delle sentenze e ordinanze della corte costituzionale,* vol. 62. (Unofficial translation provided by Alessandra Prioreschi.)

Keller, Catherine. 1986. *From a Broken Web: Separation, Sexism, and Self.* Boston: Beacon Press.

Killerby, Margaret. 1998. "Steps Taken by the Council of Europe to Promote the Modernization of the Nationality Laws of European States." In Síofra O'Leary and Teija Tilikaninen (eds.), *Citizenship and Nationality Status in the New Europe,* pp. 21–37. London: Institute for Public Policy Research/Sweet and Maxwell.

Knop, Karen. 1999. "The Making of Difference in International Law: Interpretation, Identity and Participation in the Discourse of Self-Determination." Unpublished S.J.D. diss., University of Toronto.

League of Nations. Treaty Series. 1930. "Convention on Certain Questions relating to the Conflict of Nationality Laws." April 12. *Treaties and International Engagements Registered with the Secretariat of the League of Nations.* Vol. 179, no. 4137, p. 89 (1937–38).

Leslie, Henrietta. 1930. *Mrs. Fischer's War.* London: Jarrolds.

Lewis, Hope. 1997. "Lionheart Gals Facing the Dragon: The Human Rights of Inter/national Black Women in the United States." *Oregon Law Review* 76:567–632.

Liddy, Jane. 1998. "Current Topic: The Concept of Family Life under the ECHR." *European Human Rights Law Review,* 1998 (1): 15–25.

McClintock, Anne. 1995. *Imperial Leather: Race, Gender, and Sexuality in the Colonial Context.* New York: Routledge.

MacIntyre, Alasdair. 1984. *After Virtue.* 2nd ed. Notre Dame, Ind.: University of Notre Dame Press.

Macmillan, Chrystal. 1925. "Nationality of Women: Present Tendencies." *Journal of Comparative Legislation and International Law* (3rd series) 7:142–54.

———. 1931. *The Nationality of Married Women.* London: Nationality of Married Women Pass the Bill Committee.

Makarov, Alexandre Nikolaevitch. 1937. "La Nationalité de la Femme Mariée." *Recueil des Cours. Académie de Droit International* 60: 115–241.

Mariam, Lubna. n.d. "Whither Equal Rights?" Unpublished.

Martin, David A. 1999. "New Rules on Dual Nationality for a Democratizing Globe: Between Rejection and Embrace." *Georgetown Immigration Law Journal* 14:1–34.

Miller, Carol Ann. 1992. "Lobbying the League: Women's International Organizations and the League of Nations." University of Oxford. Unpublished Ph.D. diss.

Mitchell, David. 1966. *Women on the Warpath: The Story of the Women of the First World War.* London: Jonathan Cape.

Mullen, Tom. 1988. "Nationality and Immigration." In Sheila McLean and Noreen Burrows (eds.), *The Legal Relevance of Gender: Some Aspects of Sex-Based Discrimination,* pp. 146–69. Atlantic Highlands, N.J.: Humanities Press International.

Muller, Martine. 1987. *Couscous pommes frites: Le couple franco-maghrébin d'hier à aujourd'hui.* Paris: Éditions Ramsay.

Nedelsky, Jennifer. 1989. "Reconceiving Autonomy: Sources, Thoughts and Possibilities." *Yale Journal of Law and Feminism* 1:7–36.

———. 1991. "Law, Boundaries, and the Bounded Self." In Robert Post (ed.), *Law and the Order of Culture,* pp. 162–89. Berkeley: University of California Press.

———. 1997. "A Relational Approach to Citizenship." Paper prepared for Gender and Citizenship Conference, Beirut, Lebanon, March 19–23. (Edited version forthcoming as "Citizenship and Relational Feminism," in Ronald Beiner and Wayne Norman [eds.], *Canadian Political Philosophy at the Turn of the Century: Exemplary Essays.* Toronto: Oxford University Press.)

Okin, Susan Moller. 1989. *Justice, Gender, and the Family.* Basic Books.

Opsahl, Torkel. 1973. "The Convention and the Right to Respect for Family Life Particularly as Regards the Unity of the Family and the Protection of the Rights of Parents and Guardians in the Education of Children." In Arthur Henry Robertson (ed.), *Privacy and Human Rights,* pp. 182–254. Manchester: Manchester University Press.

Organization of African Unity. 1981. "African Charter on Human and Peoples' Rights (Banjul Charter)." June 27. *International Legal Materials* 21:58 (1982).

Pillard, Cornelia T. L., and T. Alexander Aleinikoff. 1998. "Skeptical Scrutiny of Plenary Power: Judicial and Executive Branch Decision Making in *Miller v. Albright.*" *Supreme Court Review* 1998:1–70.

Réaume, Denise G. 1996. "What's Distinctive about Feminist Analysis of Law? A Conceptual Analysis of Women's Exclusion from Law." *Legal Theory* 2:265–99.

Sandel, Michael. 1998. *Liberalism and the Limits of Justice.* 2d ed. Cambridge: Cambridge University Press.

Shachar, Ayelet. 1999. "Whose Republic? Citizenship and Membership in the Israeli Polity." *Georgetown Immigration Law Journal* 13:233–72.

Sohn, Louis B., and Thomas Buergenthal (eds.). 1992. *The Movement of Persons across Borders.* Studies in Transnational Legal Policy, no. 23. Washington, D.C.: American Society of International Law.

Soysal, Yasemin Nuhoğlu. 1994. *Limits of Citizenship: Migrants and Postnational Membership in Europe.* Chicago: University of Chicago Press.

Spiro, Peter J. 1997. "Dual Nationality and the Meaning of Citizenship." *Emory Law Journal* 46:1411–85.

———. 1999. "The Citizenship Dilemma." *Stanford Law Review* 51:597–639.

United Nations. 1962. *Convention on the Nationality of Married Women: Historical Background and Commentary.* UN Doc. E/CN.6/389, UN Sales no. 62.IV.3.

United Nations. 1963. *Nationality of Married Women.* UN Doc. E/CN.6/254/Rev. 1, UN Sales no. 64.IV.1.

United Nations. Commission on Human Rights. 1997. *Report of the Special Rapporteur on Violence against Women, Its Causes and Consequences, Ms. Radhika Coomaraswamy. 1996. Addendum: Report on the Mission of the Special Rapporteur to Poland on the Issue of Trafficking and Forced Prostitution of Women* (May 24 to June 1). UN Doc. E/CN.4/1997/47/Add.1.

United Nations. Committee on the Elimination of Discrimination against Women (CEDAW). 1992. "General Recommendation 21 (Thirteenth Session) on Equality in Marriage and Family Relations." In *Compilation of General Comments and General*

Recommendations Adopted by Human Rights Treaty Bodies. UN Doc. HRI/GEN/1/
Rev.1, p. 90 (1994). <gopher://gopher.un.org:70/00/ga/cedaw/HRI-G1R1.EN> <http:
//www1.umn.edu/humanrts/gencomm/generl21.htm>
United Nations. High Commissioner for Refugees (UNHCR). 1997. Executive Com-
mittee of the High Commissioner's Programme. Note on UNHCR and Statelessness
Activities. EC/47/SC/CRP.31.
United Nations. Human Rights Committee. 1981. *Aumeeruddy-Cziffra v. Mauritius.*
Communication no. 35/1978. UN Doc. CCPR/C/OP/1, p. 67 (1984). <http://
www1.umn.edu/humanrts/undocs/html/35_1978.htm>
———. 1994. *Toonen v. Australia.* Communication no. 488/1992. UN Doc. CCPR/C/
50/D/488/1992 (1994). <http://www1.umn.edu/humanrts/undocs/html/vws488.htm>
United Nations. International Law Commission (ILC). 1999. Draft Articles on Nationality of Natural Persons in Relation to the Succession of States. In Report of the
International Law Commission, chap. 4. <http://www.un.org/law/ilc/reports/1999/
english/chap4.htm#E_1>
United Nations. Secretary General. 1998. *Report of the Secretary General: Trafficking
in Women and Girls.* UN Doc. A/53/409.
United Nations. Treaty Series (UNTS). 1957. "Convention on the Nationality of Married Women." Feb. 20. *Treaties and International Agreements Registered or Filed
and Recorded with the Secretariat of the United Nations*, vol. 309, no. 4468, p. 65
(1958).
United Nations. Treaty Series (UNTS). 1966. "International Covenant on Civil and
Political Rights." Dec. 19. *Treaties and International Agreements Registered or Filed
and Recorded with the Secretariat of the United Nations,* vol. 999, no. 14668, p. 171
(1976).
United Nations. Treaty Series (UNTS). 1969. "American Convention on Human Rights."
Nov. 22. *Treaties and International Agreements Registered or Filed and Recorded
with the Secretariat of the United Nations,* vol. 1144, no. 17955, p. 123 (1979).
United Nations. Treaty Series (UNTS). 1979. "Convention on the Elimination of All
Forms of Discrimination against Women." Dec. 18. *Treaties and International Agree-
ments Registered or Filed and Recorded with the Secretariat of the United Nations,*
vol. 1249, no. 20378, p. 13 (1981).
United States. 1915. *MacKenzie v. Hare,* 239 U.S. 299.
———. 1998. *Miller v. Albright,* 118 S. Ct. 1428.
———. 1999. *United States v. Ahumada-Aguilar,* 189 F. 3d 1121 (9th Cir.).
Weiler, Joseph. 1998. "To Be a European Citizen: Eros and Civilization." University of
Toronto Faculty of Law Legal Theory Workshop paper 1997–98 (7).
Weis, Paul. 1979. *Nationality and Statelessness in International Law.* 2nd ed. Alphen
aan den Rijn; Germantown, Md.: Sijthoff and Noordhoff.
Women's Human Rights Resources. Bora Laskin Law Library. University of Toronto.
"Nationality and Citizenship": Articles. <http://www.law-lib.utoronto.ca/Diana/
nation/articles.htm> (at March 11, 2000).
Woolf, Virginia. 1993. *Three Guineas.* In Michèle Barrett (ed.), *A Room of One's Own
and Three Guineas,* pp. 115–365. London: Penguin.

PART TWO

Locations of Citizenship

CHAPTER FIVE

Citizenship and Federalism

VICKI C. JACKSON

THERE HAS BEEN an enormous growth in the scholarship on citizenship, which has frequently given more attention to the meaning of citizenship and to policy issues that are closely linked to immigration policies than to questions about the constitutional structures involved in deciding citizenship questions (for notable exceptions, see Spiro, 1994; Skerry, 1995; Schuck, 1998a; Schuck, 2000). In this chapter I identify certain structural aspects of federal polities' approaches to citizenship and then explore the possible bearing of federal forms of citizenship on contemporary debates over "dual" or multiple nationalities. I proceed from the premise that citizenship, as a formal status, *matters* in defining the legally enforceable parameters of rights and obligations that exist between governments and persons subject to their jurisdiction.[1] In addition, national citizenship can be expected for a long while to continue to play a dominant role in defining the rights and duties between governments and people. On these assumptions, I describe in part one how federal structures may affect the

I thank Alexander Aleinikoff, Douglas Klusmeyer, Peter Schuck, and Robert Taylor, as well as Kim Forde-Mazrui and the other participants of the University of Virginia Law School's Comparative Constitutional Law Workshop, November 6–7, 1999, for helpful comments on earlier drafts.

1. Discussing the meaning or utility of citizenship could be a way of talking about the relative decline of the traditional nation-state as an important organizing feature of human political geography. Should we understand citizenship as referring to a discrete set of rights and duties, or more as a concept about membership and affiliation? Should it also be understood as the mechanism

definition and implementation of citizenship. In part two I draw out some implications of the federal experience with citizenship for current debates over dual or multinational citizenship.

To begin with, I suggest that federal nations provide one set of positive structural models for the construction of multinational citizenships. First, federal nations reveal that new affiliative identities can be created without destroying the old ones: one can be a citizen of Texas and the United States at the same time, and, perhaps as well, a citizen of Mexico and the United States. Second, federal nations often have "nested," or overlapping, concepts of citizenships that are legally workable provided that there is a "conflicts" rule designating which citizenship, in which level of government, is controlling for what purposes. The experience of federal nations thus supports the further development of international norms or treaties that establish conventional rules of primary (or dominant) citizenship to resolve potential conflicts of laws and loyalties that will increase along with increasing numbers of people who experience themselves as multinational and who seek multinational citizenships.[2]

Next, I argue that although a classic defense of Western constitutions is that they perform a "settlement" or "precommitment" function, there may be some benefits to uncertainty in constitutional design. Citizenship can be seen as a place of contest and, in a federal nation, the presence of multiple forums for contesting who belongs, who does not, and what difference citizenship makes

---

for societal regeneration? For the assertion of the scope of sovereignty in the international community? Questions of citizenship and federalism might invite us to look at the entire spectrum of relations between governments and individuals (or even corporate entities that in some polities are treated for some purposes as "citizens") in areas of civil, political, economic, social, and group rights, and examine whether and how federal constitutional structures affect those relationships: one could ask, e.g., what are the permissible degrees of variation in the relationships of governments under a federal umbrella and of persons subject to their jurisdiction with respect to these rights (or correlative duties). For helpful discussion of "modes of citizenship talk," see Schuck (1998a, 176–78); see also ch. 8 of this volume: Linda Bosniak, "Denationalizing Citizenship." Within the limits of this chapter, I propose neither to explore generally the meaning of citizenship nor to identify a theory of citizenship in federal nations. Instead, I assume that for some still-important purposes (though perhaps a declining number), citizenship matters—enough for governments to care about who is a citizen of what entity. For an interesting challenge to the claim that national sovereignties are losing power to control migration, see Freeman (1998) (arguing, inter alia, that the EU's development of a policy on migrants has been designed to enhance, rather than supplant, traditional state efforts to bar unwanted immigrants).

2. In a federal nation like the United States, a simple priority rule—demands of national law trump demands of subnational law—in effect prioritizes most areas of potential conflict between state and federal loyalties. In many federal nations, subnational citizenship is linked to or nested within rights of national citizenship, a feature that would be lacking in multinational citizenship situations. Yet this distinction means only that developing conventional rules of primary citizenship for different purposes is more complex in the multinational setting than in the federal nation setting, not that it is undoable.

may be a positive feature.[3] Subnational and national governments in federal systems provide alternative forums for the assertion of competing claims about citizenship that, given the multiple understandings of citizenship in both its expressive and more functional capacities, may benefit from such alternative forums. Yet, there are risks in devolving substantive lawmaking authority to subnational units, risks that arise from tensions between the idea of citizenship as an expressive affiliation and citizenship as a form of political equality.

Thus, while part of my argument is that international and national legal regimes can (and may have to) accommodate multiple nationalities, I caution against abandoning too rapidly the traditional links between political rights and some version of exclusive nationality. Multiple citizenships have a potential to undermine the capacity of the concept of citizenship to generate intrapolity equalities. Multiple citizenships may also increase the possibility of destabilizing ethnonationalisms. Yet multiple citizenships may have compensating advantages in acknowledging and facilitating felt affiliations and in promoting universal, transnational, and inclusive senses of equality. The rise of devolutionary federalisms at the same time as supranational legal regimes might suggest that any attempt to hold on to a model of exclusive nationality or even to a concept of primary citizenship will fail as not adequately providing expression for the more fluid complexity of citizenship affiliations in this new century.[4] But that does not mean that this is to be sought after or accelerated through a premature abandonment of national citizenship as a constitutive feature of public law. The federal form provides a useful set of models for a gradual process of developing new legal regimes in which multiple citizenships are accommodated but not necessarily encouraged.

I. History and Structure of Federal Citizenship

Citizenship as a concept has evolved from a limited idea in classical Athenian terms to an expansive, multifaceted modern notion. If the citizen of Athens was a particularly privileged male member of a small city-state, after the French and U.S. revolutions the citizen became (at least in theory) the political actor of the modern nation-state. In the United States, citizenship as the "birth-

---

3. Moreover, others argue, devolving enforcement of national immigration and naturalization policy to subnational units that are particular sites of immigration may have benefits in increasing the effectiveness of implementation (Schuck and Williams, 1999).

4. See Hobsbawn (1996, 1065) (arguing that increases in economic and other forms of migrations will continue so as to prevent any nation with open borders from remaining monoethnic or monolinguistic, other than by "ruthless exclusion" or the creation of "apartheid societies") as quoted and excerpted in Gewirtz and Cogan, 1999.

right" of the entire nation did not become functionally well established until after World War II, though the legal basis for the concept was laid down in the Fourteenth Amendment in 1868.[5] In the post–World War II period, the concept of citizenship expanded—more nations in the world have citizens, rather than subjects, and the idea of what are the rights of citizenship has expanded along with our conception of what governments should do for their citizens. The 1950 essay of T. H. Marshall (1992) is still widely cited for its description of the move from civil to political to social citizenship as a way of capturing the expansion of relationships that have come to be seen as the rights of all citizens, or as duties owed by governments to their citizens.

The development of international human rights law, like the development in the United States of the equal protection and due process rights of *persons* under the Fourteenth Amendment, has in recent years expanded the requirements for government in dealing with persons *regardless* of nationality or citizenship. As the rights of "persons" vis-à-vis governments (and other persons) have expanded, the significance of whether one is a citizen has in some respects correspondingly declined. This can be viewed as an expansion of the concept of citizenship (if rights holding is seen as a form of citizenship), as a contraction of its importance (if most significant rights accrue based on personhood and the growth of universalism in legal norms that constrain government conduct), or both.

Like citizenship, federalism in its modern form—that is, as an agreed relationship in the same territory between different levels of governments that contemplates direct relations between the national government and the people of the subnational governments as well as between the governments themselves—dates to the revolutionary period of the late eighteenth century. It is widely spoken of as an innovation of the U.S. Constitution of 1787. The U.S. system of federalism has generated the idea of multiple, tiered, or nested citizenships.[6] Justice Anthony M. Kennedy, in his concurrence in *U.S. Term Limits v. Thornton* (514 U.S. 779, 838 [1995]) wrote that the 1787 Constitution "split the atom of sovereignty," and in so doing, made possible the idea of coexisting multiple citizenships in which the citizens of states were also citizens of the United States.

Leading scholars of citizenship in the United States agree that the primacy of federal citizenship was not fully worked out until after the Civil War (see, e.g., Kettmer, 1978). What the Fourteenth Amendment provides, at least in

5. The Fourteenth Amendment was intended in part to provide a firm constitutional foundation for the 1866 Civil Rights Act, which had also provided for birthright citizenship. See, generally, Schuck and Smith (1985, 74–75).

6. See Neuman (1994, 270) (describing U.S. federalism as creating "dual citizenship in nested polities").

theory, is a model of primary citizenship in which a person can hold multiple citizenships, but one is understood to be primary.[7] Under the Fourteenth Amendment, federal (i.e., national) citizenship became primary. States lost any claim to have the power to deny state citizenship to a resident of the state who held national citizenship.[8] It is this model of primary citizenship that constitutes a possible contribution of federal systems to the evolving debate over dual and multiple nationalities.

Note, however, that the U.S. Supreme Court's decision in *The Slaughterhouse Cases* (83 U.S. [16 Wall. 3] 36 [1873]), subverted the potential of the Fourteenth Amendment to fully establish the primacy of national citizenship in defining people's rights in the United States and thus, somewhat ironically, state citizenship (or residence) became a more important engine for elaborating equality than federal citizenship for many years.[9] This course of the treatment in the United States of national and state citizenship (or residency) cautions against ready assumptions that trends toward more universal understandings of human rights and toward the diminishing significance of citizenship can necessarily be expected to move in a straight line toward more progressive national and international communities.[10]

So perhaps it is also appropriate to conceive of federalism as providing structures for contesting visions of citizenship over time, as well as for a positive model of the possibility of multiple but compatible citizenships.[11] In the United States, the supremacy clause and the *Erie* principle provide the constitutional

7. See Tushnet (1996b) (arguing that even the language of the Amendment identifies national citizenship as primary).

8. For a representative expression, see *MacKenzie v. Hare,* 165 Cal. 776, 779, 134 P. 713, 714 (Supreme Court of California, 1913) ("The status of persons as citizens or aliens, respectively, is controlled entirely by the Constitution of the United States and the Acts of Congress passed in pursuance thereof").

9. Cf., e.g., *Strauder v. West Virginia,* 100 U.S. 303 (1879) (holding that a state law limiting jury service to "white male persons" who are citizens of the state denied to the black criminal defendant rights guaranteed by the Fourteenth Amendment) with *Fong Yue Ting v. United States,* 149 U.S. 698, 728 (1893) (upholding federal law that, inter alia, required testimony from "white" persons to substantiate alien's entitlement to labor certificate); *Korematsu v. United States,* 323 U.S. 214 (1944) (upholding federal racial and alienage classifications of Japanese American citizens). Not until 1954 did the Court assert that standards similar to those applicable to the states constrained the federal government's authority to discriminate based on race. See *Bolling v. Sharpe,* 347 U.S. 497 (1954).

10. This concern is not based solely on the U.S. experience. See Chesterman and Galligan, 1997 (121–55) (arguing that the Australian states became more authoritarian from 1901 to the 1930s in dealing with the Aborigines).

11. In *Saenz v. Roe,* 119 S. Ct. 1518 (1999), the Court invalidated both a California law requiring that welfare levels for California citizens who migrated from other states be set at a level no higher than the benefits in the prior state of residence for the first year of residency in California and a federal statute that had authorized states to so provide. The Court insisted that

guideposts that structure this contest, the first establishing the supremacy of
federal law, the second asserting the primacy of the states in determining the
content of state law (see U.S. Const., Art. 6; *Erie R.R. v. Tompkins, 304 U.S. 64
[1938]).*[12] Struggles over the availability and meaning of citizenship in the United
States take place over the boundary line between federal and state law and over
the content of federal law. If one were to expand this model of federalism to
provide "structures for contesting" citizenship at the international level, one
might conceive of international law as needing to supply the legal norms of
hierarchy that, in the United States, are supplied by the principles of the supremacy clause and the *Erie* doctrine.[13]

---

the national citizenship clause of § 1 of the Fourteenth Amendment "expressly equates citizenship with residence" (p. 1528) and reaffirmed the assertion in *Zobel v. Williams,* 457 U.S. 55, 69
(1982), that "[t]hat Clause does not provide for, and does not allow for, levels of citizenship
based on length of residence." The Court in *Saenz* went on to state: "It is equally clear that the
Clause does not tolerate a hierarchy of 45 subclasses of similarly situated citizens based on the
location of their prior residence" (119 S. Ct. at 1528). *Saenz's* implications for federal power to
authorize states to discriminate against aliens are uncertain. *Saenz* is clear in rejecting the claim
that Congress could authorize the states to violate the Fourteenth Amendment (albeit not in the
context of aliens or immigrants): "Congress has no affirmative power to authorize the States to
violate the Fourteenth Amendment and is implicitly prohibited from passing legislation that pur-
ports to validate any such violation." 119 S. Ct at 1529. Whether Congress can authorize states to
discriminate against aliens, then, may depend on whether earlier decisions holding various state
discriminations against aliens unconstitutional (see, e.g., *Sugarman v. Dougall,* 413 U.S. 634
[1973]), and *Nyquist v. Mauclet,* 432 U.S. 1 [1977]), are now understood to rest, not on the
Fourteenth Amendment, but on a theory of national preemption. Insisting on Congress's broad
power to distinguish between aliens and citizens and between classes of aliens, *Mathews v. Diaz,*
426 U.S. 71 (1976), upheld the constitutionality of a federal law that barred aliens present in the
United States for less than five years from Medicare eligibility. But since *Diaz,* the Court has
interpreted the Fifth Amendment due process clause to impose limitations on Congress's power
to use race as a classification virtually identical to those imposed on the states by the Fourteenth
Amendment's equal protection clause. *Adarand v. Pena,* 515 U.S. 200 (1995). If states are prohibited by the Fourteenth Amendment, rather than by the preemptive effect of national policy,
from most discrimination against aliens, would the federal government also be so constrained?
Despite the logic of the question, it seems unlikely that this Court would reach such a result given
the strength of the "plenary power" doctrine.
    12. The supremacy clause of Art. 6 establishes a clear hierarchy of laws, in which first the
Constitution, and then federal statutes and treaties, constitute the law of the land. Federal statutes must be consistent with the Constitution. State and local laws must be consistent with the
Constitution and with valid federal laws and treaties. The extent to which treaties must be
consistent with substantive aspects of the Constitution is subject to some ambiguity, though
recent cases suggest that treaties cannot abrogate the constitutional rights of persons within the
United States or of U.S. citizens with respect to the U.S. government elsewhere. See *Reid v.
Covert,* 354 U.S. 1 (1957). The *Erie* doctrine, conversely, stands for the supremacy of the
states' organs of government in defining the content of those areas of law that are properly and
validly governed by state law.
    13. International law and treaties already seek to play this role through, e.g., the presumption
against statelessness; see, e.g., The Hague Convention concerning Certain Questions relating to

Federal Structures and Defining Citizens

A federal structure is one in which two or more levels of government agree to share governing power over the same territory. In the United States, the federal government shares power with the state governments; in Germany, the national government *(Bund)* shares power with the *Länder* governments; and in Canada, the federal government shares power with the governments of the provinces.

As a formal matter, there are a number of possible relationships between citizenship in the subnational unit and citizenship in the nation; these relationships may be independent or dependent one to the other.[14] Variables include (1) whether the polity has concepts of both national and subnational unit citizenship; (2) which level or levels of government have lawmaking authority with respect to definitions of citizenship; and (3) which level or levels of government have law-enforcing authority. Such authorities may be concurrent or exclusive, and sometimes it is unclear which level has what authority.

Miriam Feldblum (2000) has urged attention to what she describes as the way "in which a state can structure the practice of dual membership" (p. 479). Rather than treat questions of dual or multiple citizenship as either-or propositions, she argues for an analysis of the "components" of citizenship even in a context in which multiple nationalities are recognized. Monar (1998), in an essay on dual citizenship in the European Union (EU), echoes Feldblum's call. Monar argues that the developing concept of a European citizenship "should reflect as much as possible the relative weight of both levels of public authority (the Member States and that of the Union) in the exercise of real powers over citizens" (p. 179).[15] These calls for what I describe as a more functional analy-

---

the Conflict of Nationality Laws, 1930, 179 U.N.T.S. 89, and rules on nationality and military service; see Convention on Reduction of Cases of Multiple Nationality and Military Obligations in Cases of Multiple Nationality, May 6, 1963, 634 U.N.T.S. 222; European Convention on Nationality, Nov. 7, 1997, ETS no. 166.

14. Some constitutions, e.g., that of Austria, specifically contemplate a third level of government (local government), and may define membership in that municipal or "Commune" level of government for purposes of voting. See Aust. Const., Art. 117(2) (defining eligibility to vote in elections to Communal Council as no more limited than eligibility to vote for the Land legislature and providing that certain temporary residents can be excluded from voting). See Flanz (1998a). For simplicity, I do not consider questions relating to "citizenship" or membership at the local government level.

15. Note, too, the recommendations of a Canadian parliamentary committee on citizenship and immigration that those who hold dual citizenship be required, while living in Canada, to accord primacy to their Canadian citizenship and that those becoming naturalized be required to declare that they will accord primacy to Canadian over other citizenships. See Galloway (1999, 216–17) (describing Report of the Canadian Parliamentary Standing Committee on Citizenship and Immigration [1994]).

sis of the components of citizenship and how they may be allocated in multiple nationality situations might be met, in small part, by a consideration of how multiple citizenships in federal states are handled.

National and Subnational Citizenship

For U.S. scholars the notion of nested citizenships that are sustained simultaneously is familiar. Most U.S. citizens are also citizens of a state.[16] In the original Constitution of 1787, it was assumed that there was a national citizenship, since it was made a qualification for elected federal office that the holder be a "citizen of the United States" (U.S. Const., Art. 1, §§ 2, 3; Art. 2, § 1).[17] Article 4 of the original Constitution clearly recognized the concept of state citizenship as well, providing that "[t]he Citizens of each State shall be entitled to all Privileges and Immunities of Citizens in the several States," as did the Article 3 provision for the extension of federal judicial power to "[c]ontroversies . . . between Citizens of Different States" and other heads of jurisdiction referring to the state citizenship of one of the parties. The Fourteenth Amendment, which provided the first constitutional federal citizenship rule, declares that "[a]ll persons born or naturalized in the United States and subject to the jurisdiction thereof, are citizens of the United States and of the State wherein they reside." While this language requires states to recognize as their citizens all U.S. citizens who reside within their borders, it does not exclude the possibility of states extending their citizenship more broadly.[18]

In any event, at a formal level most U.S. citizens hold a form of dual citizenship, that is, in a state and in the United States. Similar provisions are found in the constitution of Austria that provides that "there is one uniform nationality" and that Austrian citizens "with their principal domicile in one Land are their Land citizens."[19] It appears that this constitution, like the Fourteenth Amendment to the U.S. Constitution discussed above, contemplates both national and

16. Note, however, that a U.S. citizen need not be a citizen of any state to retain U.S. citizenship.

17. Note that the original U.S. Constitution referred to the need for a member of Congress to be "a Citizen of the United States" and an "Inhabitant of that State" in which he is chosen (U.S. Const., Art. 1, § 2, 3).

18. Others have noted this possibility as well. See, e.g., Schuck (2000, 223); Spiro (1999, 619 n.111), although I am aware of no state that does so today.

19. See Flanz, 1998a (Art. 6 of the Austrian Constitution provides: "(1) For the Republic of Austria there is one uniform nationality; (2) Nationals who have their principal domicile in one Land are their Land citizens; however, Land laws can provide that nationals, who have their domicile in a Land, but not their principal domicile, are citizens of that Land; (3) The principal domicile of a person is established, where he/she has settled with provable intention . . . that this was to be the central point of relations of life; if the real assumption in an overall professional, economic, and social relations of life is met by several domiciles, then the person has to designate the one to which he/she has the prevailingly closest proximate relationship").

subnational unit citizenships, in which national citizenship is in some sense primary.

In other federal nations with dual national and subnational citizenships, the subnational citizenship may in some respects be primary. In Switzerland, as in the United States, the constitution itself appears to contemplate both subnational and national levels of citizenship. At least until recently, however, national citizenship was largely based on cantonal citizenship: Swiss national citizenship was "acquired and lost as a consequence of the acquisition or loss of . . . [cantonal citizenship,] and this [cantonal citizenship] is again linked to . . . citizenship of a municipality" (de Groot, 1998, 117–19).[20] While Article 4 of the former Swiss Constitution provided that "all Swiss citizens are equal before the law," former Article 43 provided that "[e]very citizen of a Canton is a Swiss citizen" (Flanz, 1982). It was in this capacity that the person took part in federal elections and voted at his or her domicile. This principle evidently continues in Article 37 of the new constitution.[21] Likewise, in Australia, at least for many years, state citizenship was effectively controlling, for example, on eligibility for the national franchise (see Galligan and Chesterman, 1996, 177–78; see

20. In December 1998 the Swiss adopted a new constitution, designed largely to codify principles established under the prior constitution (see Flanz, 1999b). According to Flanz, Art. 8(1) of the new constitution provides, "All humans *[alle menschen, êtres humains, tutti]* are equal before the law," while Art. 37(1) provides, "Any [female or male] person who has the citizenship of a Municipality and of a Canton, has Swiss citizenship." This apparently preserves the primacy of cantonal and local citizenship, making national citizenship logically entailed in cantonal citizenship. The national government's powers over acquisition and loss of citizenship are precisely described: Art. 38(1) declares, "The Confederation regulates the acquisition and the loss of citizenship through descent, marriage and adoption . . . [and] the loss of Swiss citizenship on other grounds, and the reinstatement of citizenship." Art. 38(2) empowers the Confederation to set "minimum requirements for the naturalization of foreigners by the Cantons" (Flanz, 1999b), evidently contemplating that the Cantons will play an important role in administering naturalization and possibly in establishing additional requirements.

21. See n.20. The current constitution, like the old one, also states, "No one can exercise political rights in more than one Canton." See Switz. Const., Art. 39(3) (Flanz, 1999b); Art. 43(3) (Flanz, 1982). Art. 39(2) specifies that "political rights are exercised at the place of domicile," but that the "Confederation and the Cantons may provide exceptions." Under the old constitution, former Art. 43(4) seemed to contemplate that there may be Swiss citizens who are not members of a Canton, even if they are domiciled there. See Flanz (1982) (translating Art. 43[4] to provide that "[t]he established Swiss citizen shall enjoy at his domicile all the rights of the citizens of that canton. . . . However, sharing property belonging in common to local citizens or to corporations and the right to vote in matters exclusively regarding local citizens are excepted unless cantonal legislation should provide otherwise"). Former Art. 44 provided that citizenship can be acquired both through the Confederation's rules or through naturalization in a canton, exercised with permission of the Confederation (see Flanz, 1982), a sharing of power apparently continued under the new constitution, Art. 38 (Flanz, 1999b).

also Zappalà and Castles, 1999).[22] And in the EU, which is a federal entity (if not a federal nation), *supranational* (i.e., EU) citizenship, is a logical corollary of *state* citizenship; citizens of the member nation-states are EU citizens.[23]

As these examples suggest, in many federal nations citizens are accustomed to being citizens of more than one political entity.[24] In some, national citizenship may be derivative of subnational citizenship; in others, notably the United States, national citizenship is primary and state citizenship depends on national citizenship plus residency.

This is not the uniform practice of federal nations. In Canada, for example, neither the 1982 charter nor the Constitution Act, 1867, refers to a concept of provincial citizenship, though the 1867 act does require that senators be inhabitants of the province they represent. Under the charter, some rights are guaranteed to "citizens of Canada," some to "any person," some to "any member of

22. The formal language of the constitution, referring as it does to the Queen's *subjects* who are *resident* in a state, leaves somewhat unclear whether the residents of the different Australian states are "citizens" of that state. See Austr. Const., pt. 5, ch. 5, § 117 ("A subject of the Queen, resident in any State, shall not be subject in any other State to any disability or discrimination which would not be equally applicable to him if he were a subject of the Queen resident in such other State").

23. Under the 1992 Maastricht Treaty nationals of member states are also citizens of the EU. In theory EU citizenship extends to any EU national in any EU country and includes mobility rights (including rights of residence), the right to vote and stand for office in local elections (though this right has been qualified in implementation to respect, e.g., France's constitutional requirement that local mayors be citizens); the right to vote and stand for office in the European Parliament; the right to diplomatic protection in other countries by diplomats of any Member States on the same terms as nationals of that state; and the right to petition EU organs (the Parliament and the Ombudsperson). See Maastricht Treaty of Union of 1992, Arts. 8-8(e); see, generally, Monar, 1998 (concluding that EU citizenship is meaningful since it involves "a combination of rights, duties and possibilities of political participation"). Given relatively limited powers in the EU Parliament and relatively low voting rates in EU parliamentary elections, the full significance of this extension of citizenship remains to be realized in the future.

24. Although at one time citizenship in the German Confederation was determined by the different member states (see Brubaker, 1992, 68–70), this situation changed dramatically over time. In the German Basic Law there is a provision asserting the equality of the civil rights and duties of all Germans in every German state (Art. 33); an assertion of exclusive federal competence over "citizenship in the Federation" (Art. 73[2]), but it seems there is no explicit reference to citizenship within the länder. Brubaker describes efforts by some länder (Bavaria and Baden-Württemberg) to obstruct settlement of non-German migrants by requiring "rotations" of foreign workers (Brubaker, 1992, 172). Bultmann (1998) has discussed naturalization to national citizenship in Germany, rather than to some form of subnational citizenship, though his paper indicates that the länder have some discretion about which of the general naturalization requirements set by federal law they will enforce (see text after n.13, stating that many länder gave up requirement that an alien not be naturalized if this would cause "deviant citizenship within one family"); see also Hailbronner, 1998 (stating that the requirement of giving up dual nationality is part of the administrative regulations developed by federal and länder ministries, and not technically part of the law).

the public" (Charter of Rights and Freedoms, § 20, concerning communication with Parliament), and some to "citizen[s] of Canada [and] permanent resident[s]" (Charter of Rights and Freedoms, § 6, Mobility Rights), but there is no reference to citizenship in a particular province. In India, the supreme court has held that there is only a single, national concept of citizenship.[25] The Indian Constitution refers only to "citizens" of India, with fairly detailed provisions relating to the separation from Pakistan and determinations of citizenship in connection with that difficult transition. So federal structures may provide for dual citizenship in national and subnational entities but need not do so.

Lawmaking Authority over Citizenship and Related Questions

In federal polities with two levels of constitutionally secured governments that do have citizenship at both the subnational and national levels, there are several possibilities for which government has authority to make laws governing citizenship: for example, (1) the national government can make national citizenship laws while the subnational governments make subnational citizenship laws; (2) the national government can make both national and subnational citizenship laws; or (3) the subnational governments can make both national and subnational citizenship laws.[26] Examples of each of these three regimes exist. A brief review illustrates that in defining citizenship at both subnational and national levels, powers may be even more complexly mixed and concurrent—that is, both national and subnational governments may play lawmaking roles.

The United States at different times in its history illustrates aspects of each of the three regimes noted above. Before enactment of the first federal naturalization law in 1790, the states largely determined the standards and procedures for becoming a citizen, both of the state (for purposes of the comity clause in Article 4 of the 1781 Articles of Confederation and the privileges and immunities clause of Article 4 of the 1787 Constitution) and of the nation. From 1790 until the enactment of the Fourteenth Amendment, it is roughly accurate to say that the states made citizenship laws for the states, and the federal government

---

25. See *West Bengal v. India,* A.I.R. (S.C.) 1241, 1255–56, 1259–60 (1963) (holding that state governments have no independent sovereignty but only those powers granted by the federal constitution); *Pradeep Jain v. India,* A.I.R. (S.C.) 1420, 1424 (1984) (educational institutions may not reserve seats for residents of the state in which they are located since residents of all states are Indian citizens); Sastri (1994); see also Basu (1987, 213–14).

26. In theory there is a fourth possibility: the subnational governments could make national citizenship laws while the national government made state citizenship laws. As far as I am aware, this category is an empty set in the real world.

provided by statute for the naturalization of U.S. citizens. (It was not for several decades that it was firmly established that persons could become naturalized U.S. citizens only in accord with the federal naturalization law (see Kettmer, 1978, 249–50; Neuman, 1996, 64–65). During this period, however, while the definition of state citizenship was arguably committed to the separate states of the United States, there was federal responsibility for defining state citizenship as well. For the purposes of some federal rights—notably, access to the federal courts in diversity jurisdiction—a federal standard controlled. This lay at the base of the notorious Dred Scott decision (60 U.S. 393 [1857]), in which the Court held that Congress lacked the power to provide for slaves to become free on entry into free territories and asserted that black people could not be "citizens of a state" for purposes of diversity jurisdiction.[27]

In the United States, the authority of the states to define the criteria for state citizenship was substantially constrained by the Fourteenth Amendment's citizenship clause, providing that any person born in the United States (and subject to the jurisdiction thereof) is a citizen both of the United States and of the state of residence, thus providing an interdependent link between the two statuses. One can conceive of the Fourteenth Amendment, then, as an instance of national law substantively regulating both national and subnational citizenship. With enactment of the Fourteenth Amendment and its requirement that states recognize the state citizenship of any U.S. citizen resident therein, the federal government's requirements for national citizenship in effect determine the citizenship of the state, at least in defining those who must be included among the states' citizenry.[28]

Finally, note that under U.S. law, states have some latitude in determining bona fide residency for purposes of determining state citizenship.[29] To the ex-

27. See *Dred Scott,* 60 U.S. at 405 (distinguishing between "the rights of citizenship which a State may confer within its own limits, and the rights of citizenship as a member of the Union," and asserting that no state could naturalize an alien so as to invest the alien with the "rights and privileges secured to a citizen of a State under the Federal Government, although so far as the State alone was concerned, he would undoubtedly be entitled to the rights of a citizen, and clothed with all the rights and immunities which the Constitution and laws of the State attached to that character").

28. While the states may retain authority to be more expansive in recognizing persons as citizens of the state than is required by the Fourteenth Amendment, it seems clear that the federal government will not be bound to recognize as a national citizen someone who is recognized as a citizen of a state who does not qualify for citizenship under federal law.

29. Note that in the United States state citizenship is considered both a question of federal law, for determining the scope of the "diversity jurisdiction" of the federal courts, and a question essentially of state law (within certain federal parameters) to determine the state's right to impose taxes based on residency. Cf. Wright, Miller, and Cooper (1984, §§ 3611, 3612) (describing adoption of "domicile" as the single place that is a person's true and fixed home, as the intended

tent that this is so, then, one can conceive of the states and the federal government both having some control over definitions of state citizenship.

Looking at other federal polities, we find that the Austrian Constitution appears to provide that even with respect to "State citizenship and the right of domicile," legislative power belongs exclusively to the central government, while specifying that enforcement or execution is the responsibility of the länder (see Aust. Const., Art. 11(1), in Flanz, 1998). If this language means what it appears to, then Austria may be an example of the second category mentioned above—a polity in which the national government has complete lawmaking authority over both national and state citizenship.

Switzerland might be considered in some ways an example of the third possibility, in which the cantons' determination of who is a citizen will help define, at least in part, the makeup of the federal citizenry. As noted earlier, until fairly recently the cantons had substantial lawmaking power over cantonal, and hence national, citizenship. While the confederation had power over immigration and aliens, naturalization was "carried out by the Cantons after the Confederation has granted permission for naturalization," according to Article 44. De Groot (1998) reports that in 1983 the constitution was changed to authorize the central government to legislate aspects of citizenship, including establishing minimum conditions for the cantons to apply for naturalization and also specifying that the cantons can naturalize citizens only with the "permission of the Confederation" (de Groot, 1998, 119; Switz. Const., Art. 44). De Groot concludes by remarking that "the power to naturalize is thus at the cantonal level, but the federation keeps an eye on the whole issue" (de Groot, 1998, 119).

Thus, in Switzerland as in the United States, one might conclude that there has been movement from a situation in which subnational units exercised substantial lawmaking powers not only over qualifications for citizenship in the subnational unit but for national citizenship, to a situation in which the central government controls greater aspects of the process (de Groot, 1998, 117–19). In the European Union, citizenship is at present entirely dependent on national citizenship and the formal law is that each nation determines largely for itself who are its citizens. Yet pressures are emerging in the EU to harmonize national citizenship laws in order to curtail naturalizations of immigrants who would then be entitled to mobility and other rights in the EU (Koslowski, 1998).

---

meaning of state citizenship of a natural person, both in Art. 3 and in the Fourteenth Amendment's reference to "residency") with *Cory v. White,* 457 U.S. 85 (1982) (apparently endorsing the view that there is no federal due process violation in two or more states treating the same person as their domiciliary for purposes of death taxes). Several lower courts have treated a person's place of voting or voter registration as not dispositive in determining citizenship for diversity purposes. See, e.g., *Krasnov v. Dinan,* 465 F. 2d 1298, 1362 (3d Cir. 1972) (collecting cases).

Once one goes beyond formal authority to define citizenship, to consider which level of government defines and enforces the rights and duties of civil, political, or social citizenship, the need to examine the actions of both levels of government in a federal system increases, as is suggested by a brief consideration of India and Russia. Despite its federal character, India (as noted earlier) lacks a formal constitutional concept of state citizenship; under the Indian Constitution there is no state citizenship, but only national Indian citizenship.[30] Yet, it is reported that both the Indian Parliament and the Meghalayan and West Bengali legislatures have enacted laws discriminating in favor of existing or longtime state citizens vis-à-vis other Indians in eligibility for elective state office (in Nagaland), in the right to take up residence without a permit (in Meghalay), and in the availability of employment preferences (in West Bengal) (see Gosselink, 1994, 98–99). While possibly not constitutional, these laws may be regarded as de facto efforts to regulate the content of state citizenship.

In Russia, a 1991 statute set forth the principle of *double citizenship,* which seems at first blush similar to the principle of the U.S. Fourteenth Amendment. According to Ginsburgs (2000, 184), the statute "enunciates the principle according to which citizens of the RSFSR [Russian Soviet Federative Socialist Republic] who permanently reside on the territory of a republic that forms part of the RSFSR are simultaneously considered citizens of that republic." As he describes it, "[w]hat the authors of the federal legislation truly had in mind was that the citizenship of the republics would, in practical terms, function as a passive appendage to federal citizenship. . . . [T]he sole requirement for a citizen of the Russian Federation to incur the citizenship of a republic is the incidental fact of his permanent residence on the territory of the respective republic" (p. 185). Quoting a Russian authority, he suggests that it is the intent of the federal law to invalidate "any other supplementary conditions for acquisition by a citizen of the Federation of the citizenship of a republic besides permanent residence therein" (p. 185). Under the 1993 constitution the federal government has exclusive jurisdiction over citizenship in the Federation. Ginsburgs suggests that the effort to universalize citizenship based on a primarily federal citizenship in Russia is quite contentious in Russia, being seen as an unwarranted intrusion on the sovereignty of the republics (closely tied to ethnonationalism within the republics), at least in Tatarstan and Chechnya. Tatarstan, for example, asserts a right to grant ethnic Tatars in the United States or Turkey citizenship in Tatarstan without compelling them to be citizens of Russia.[31] It

---

30. See *Pradeep Jain v. India,* A.I.R. (S.C.) 1420, 1424–25 (1984) (holding unconstitutional an attempt by a state to reserve seats in universities for state residents on the ground that the constitution recognizes only one form of citizenship, that of India, for all citizens). See also Palande (1956).

also appears that the republics are using their legal authority to issue or withhold *residency* permits to circumvent the universalistic, free-movement-oriented theory of citizenship evinced by the national statute and constitution (Ginsburgs, 186, quoting Avakian). Ginsburgs is doubtful of the authority or will of the federal government in Russia to eliminate the republics' resistance to universal and mobile citizenship (p. 217).[32]

Both the Russian and Indian examples suggest an obvious point: that one should look both to formal mechanisms of lawmaking authority over citizenship and to indirect or informal mechanisms for making (or unmaking) those laws in effect, to understand the relations between federalism and citizenship.

Law-Enforcing Authority over Citizenship, Naturalization, and Related Matters

National governments can have exclusive or concurrent *enforcement* authority, as can subnational governments, and with respect to either or both levels of substantive legal requirements. As I have indicated, it is common for federal nations to possess substantive lawmaking authority over citizenship at the national level. This is the case in Australia, Canada, Germany, India, and the United States.[33] This authority may, however, be exercised concurrently with subnational lawmaking authority (including authority over immigration) and often involves enforcement responsibilities by subnational units. As noted

31. See Ginsburgs, 2000, 187. Although it is unclear from English translations that under the existing laws Tatarstan could do this, the assumption of Ginsburgs' paper seems to be that they cannot.

32. Contrast this with the immediate announcement by states in response to the U.S. Supreme Court's decision in *Saenz v. Roe,* decided May 17, 1999, that they would cease to enforce one-year residency requirements for full welfare benefits. See, e.g., Biskupic (1999) (noting that Maryland Department of Human Resources announced it would immediately cease enforcement of residency requirement).

33. Belgium and Switzerland are more complex and harder to characterize. Switzerland, discussed in text above, appears to be moving to somewhat greater central national control over citizenship. As to Belgium, the Constitution of Belgium (as of 1998) provided in Art. 8 that "Belgian nationality is acquired, retained and withdrawn in accordance with the rules laid down by civil law," and that "[t]he Constitution and the other laws governing political rights determine what conditions apart from nationality are necessary for the exercise of those rights" (see Flanz, 1998b). But under Art. 9, "Naturalization is granted by the federal legislative power" (Flanz, 1998b). (For changes to reflect right of EU citizens without Belgian citizenship to vote, see Flanz, 1999a.) It appears that at the formal level the national government still controls the definition of Belgian citizenship. Given the increasing power, even in foreign affairs, of Belgium's subnational components (the regions and the communities), one might speculate that the presence or absence of formal citizenship in the subnational units bears little relation to the exercise by those units of traditional powers of sovereignty.

above, in the early days of the United States, the states took steps to define citizenship that worked simultaneously to define national citizenship.[34] Although a federal law on naturalization was enacted in 1790,[35] until 1876 the states were primarily responsible for immigration policy and enforcement in the United States, and they had substantial responsibilities for enforcing federal naturalization laws in the state courts.[36]

For another instance of subnational units administering national citizenship law (and in the process of administration, affecting its substantive content) consider Germany, where immigration and citizenship laws are in important respects administered by the länder. (A distinctive feature of German federalism is that the federal government exercises most of the legislative power, while the länder have authority in most areas to carry out the federal laws; this division of lawmaking and law executing is probably the most important division of powers between the federal government and the länder.) One study found significant differences between the German länder in how the provisions pertaining to granting citizenship to foreign residents were administered (see Bultmann, 1998). German citizens must seek permission to remain citizens of Germany if they seek to become a citizen of another nation, and the decisions of whether to permit retention of German citizenship are made by the länder, with real variation in approaches (see Franck, 1996, 381). Another study found striking differences in länder acceptance of dual nationality of those seeking to naturalize (Hagedorn, 1998).[37]

---

34. See Kettmer, 1978, 191–203 (describing activities in different states during early Revolutionary period); p. 209 (concluding that the questions before the American states at that time "rarely required a close examination of the possible distinctions between a general American citizenship and membership in a particular state"); pp. 214–19 (describing post–Declaration of Independence state constitutions defining "citizenship" criteria for aliens); p. 224 (during the period of the Articles of Confederation, "the idea that citizens belonged to a larger national community surfaced frequently, never fully articulated or theoretically explored, but persuasive, almost instinctive, in certain contexts").

35. See Kettmer, 1978, 238–39 (noting that the debate over the 1790 act did not clarify whether Congress's control over naturalization was exclusive of state authority or merely supplemental). For a more recent inquiry into the role of the states in immigration, see Neuman (1996, 19–71).

36. For a description of early state court responsibilities in naturalization under federal statutes, see *Printz v. United States,* 521 U.S. 898, 905–6 (1997). See also Jackson (1997, 2190 n.39) (noting provisions of federal immigration law of 1882 contemplating continued state responsibilities in enforcing federal immigration laws); Jones (1992, 225) (noting that states administered the 1882 federal law until 1891, when immigration was placed "wholly under federal supervision"). For a call to devolve enforcement responsibilities to the states in identifying "criminal aliens" for deportation, see Schuck and Williams (1999).

37. Hagedorn found that discrepancies between the länder could not be explained by differences in the origins of the aliens but rather resulted from more liberal or conservative postures on dual nationality, and possibly, on information dissemination, of the different länder.

In Canada, where only the federal government has jurisdiction over citizenship laws as such, the provinces have concurrent power with the federal government over immigration, which in turn influences the composition of groups likely to seek to become eligible for citizenship (see Canada's Constitution Act, 1867, § 95). Moreover, Canadian law grants the provinces a role in determining levels of immigration and permits administrative agreements with the provinces to facilitate, coordinate, and implement immigration policies and programs (see Young, 1992).[38] Under the Canada-Quebec Accord, the French-speaking province of Quebec has special authority to administer national immigration laws (though not citizenship laws) in Quebec and, in so doing, to give added weight in evaluating applicants for immigration as to their ability to speak French (see Tessier, 1995, 229).[39] In 1986 Quebec established its own Ministry of Immigration and as of 1992 had immigration offices in nine countries (Young, 1992, 6, n.59).[40] Moreover, the 1991 version of the accord, adopted after the failure of Meech Lake, allows Quebec to receive up to 30 percent of all immigrants to Canada (25 percent based on past patterns and an extra 5 percent "to make up for historical shortfalls in attracting newcomers") (Tessier, 1995, 229, n.104). The federal government also agreed to pay a substantial sum to Quebec to compensate it for taking on full responsibility for settlement and integration programs for immigrants in that province (responsibilities that Quebec wanted to take on) (see Young, 1996, 22).[41]

It should be no surprise to today's scholars that the power to enforce is in substantial respects the power to define the substantive content of a general norm. Nor should it be surprising that when enforcement authority is diffused to quasi sovereign subnational entities, and particularly to the extent that a scheme of naturalization involves large elements of discretion, significant differences will emerge among the subnational units. This suggests that the at-

38. Young reported that all provinces except British Columbia, Manitoba, and Ontario have immigration agreements with Canada, the most extensive of which is the Canada-Quebec Accord.

39. Tessier cites Immigration Canada, Canada-Quebec Accord relating to Immigration and Temporary Admission of Aliens, preamble, annex A (14) (Can.-Quebec) (giving primary control to Quebec over immigration of aliens, who must be found to contribute to Quebec's distinct identity).

40. Young notes that in six of the nine countries, the offices were not located in the Canadian embassy, while in three they were; the offices are in Bangkok, Brussels, Buenos Aires, Hong Kong, Lisbon, London, Mexico City, New York, and Paris.

41. According to Young (1996), Quebec is allowed its own point system for independent immigrants, rewarding knowledge of French with up to 15 points, whereas knowledge of English earns only up to 2 points. Quebec's special role in immigration extends to Canada's Immigrant Investor Program as well. See Canada Newswire, 1999 (noting Quebec's agreement to "harmonize its regulations with the new program" while retaining the ability to select its own investors).

tempted classification of lawmaking and law-enforcing authority may draw too sharp and artificial a line through a continuum of legal activities that give meaning and substance to the effective legal norms.

Finally, there is an intermediate position with respect to both lawmaking and law enforcing in which power is not allocated with clarity to one or another level of government but rather is shared through negotiations and consultations. Conceptualized as a model of cooperation, comity, or good faith dealing, it is perhaps embodied in Canada's statutorily authorized practice, discussed above, of negotiations between the federal Ministry of Immigration and the provinces regarding both general levels of immigration and mechanisms for provincial involvement in implementing and enforcing immigration regimes (especially those leading to citizenship).[42]

The broader point of this section is the complexity of analysis—both of lawmaking and enforcement competencies and of formal and informal mechanisms to control citizenship—required to define citizenship in federal polities.

Rights, Obligations, and Participation: Citizens and Persons

Still another element to consider is the actual distribution of benefits, rights, and obligations to citizens and others in federal nations. What, if any, is the role of subnational units in determining what benefits or rights an individual receives if he or she is regarded as a citizen, a citizen of another subnational unit in the same national polity, or as an alien? What difference does being a citizen make to the packages of rights and duties individuals hold with respect to a government in whose territory they reside?[43]

Recent studies find that, without regard to their federal structure, in most European nations rights, duties, and benefits are restricted to national citizens in only limited circumstances;[44] both national and international law and legal institutions treat "persons" rather than "citizens" as the "holders" of most basic

42. Arguably analogous practices exist in Germany concerning the making of treaties by the federal government in areas of concern to the länder. See Rauschning (1989, 135–36); Michelmann (1990) (describing, inter alia, the Lindauer Abkommen establishing consultative body for treaty making in which länder and federal representatives work together). Although the United States does not have the same level of formalized intergovernment consultative mechanisms, in the 1980s and 1990s states with high levels of immigrants were instrumental in pressuring Congress and the Immigration and Naturalization Service (INS) to increase identification and removal of criminal aliens (see Schuck and Williams, 1999).

43. I exclude corporations, though the question of federalism and the treatment of corporate citizenship would be an interesting component of a study of comparative citizenship. The concept of a corporation having "citizenship" may strike some legal systems as peculiar. E.g., in India, corporations cannot be citizens, even though they have Indian nationality (see Agerwal, 1993, 211–21).

44. See Garden (1994) (studying eleven European Union nations). This Green Paper does not consider any distinctions or similarities between federal and nonfederal nations. It does identify

rights as against governments. The most important differences may be in external relations: citizens have rights to reenter their home country and to the protection of their nation-state in the international realm. With respect to internal relations, perhaps the most widespread (though not universal) distinction is in voting rights. Turning now to obligations, we find that the duties imposed on noncitizens (such as to obey the laws generally or to pay taxes) are likely to be similar to those imposed on citizens, although the legal fact of citizenship may afford a basis for a subnational unit (or, in the international sphere, a state) to assert the right to punish a citizen for conduct lawfully committed in another jurisdictional entity. Within federal entities, however, the assertion of such a power to punish is likely to be met with a claim that citizenship in the larger federal entity entails rights of movement inconsistent with recognizing one subnational unit's power to punish for extraterritorial conduct legally permitted in another subnational entity.[45] Although in some nations military service is an obligation only of citizens (and, typically, only of male citizens), in both Australia and the United States, resident aliens have been drafted during periods of conscription.[46]

---

some eighteen "hallmarks" of citizenship, such as the duty to perform military service, the right to vote, freedom of speech, and social welfare rights, and analyzes whether in each of the countries studied citizenship is essential, relevant, or irrelevant to whether a person has a right or duty with respect to the government. Of the eighteen hallmarks studied, only in a few areas was citizenship always essential: voting rights, standing for office, and rights to a passport and diplomatic protection. This work is consistent with others in finding that the saliency of citizenship in describing, functionally, the rights and duties of persons physically present under a government's jurisdiction is limited. It is also consistent with the view that citizenship maintains high saliency in international relations (where it is often referred to as nationality); the authority and willingness of a nation to assert a claim on behalf of or extend protection to a person is, importantly (though not exclusively, given the growth of human rights–based interventions), associated with nationality and citizenship. This in turn supports the view that *membership* in a polity has different meanings depending on whether the perspective is internal or external, and, if internal, from political, civil, or social perspectives.

45. For an argument that states in the United States are constitutionally barred from penalizing their own citizens for travel to another state to engage in conduct lawful in the nonresident state, see Kreimer (1992) (explaining that early-nineteenth-century concepts of citizenship carried the right to travel among different states). Similar issues have arisen in the European Union concerning Ireland's efforts to restrict advertising in Ireland for abortion services outside Ireland and West Germany's attempts to detect (through medical examinations at the border) and punish its female citizens who obtained abortions outside Germany. See Kreimer (1992, 457–58).

46. U.S. law has at least since 1970 required permanent resident aliens to register with the Military Selective Service, see 50 USC § 453(a) (1999); see also 50 USC § 454(a) (allowing permanent resident aliens to be drafted in the event of a call-up). Foreign nationals are exempt from conscription in wars against their own country, and under particular treaties; however, aliens who have sought exemption from military service based on alienage are "permanently ineligible to become a citizen of the United States." See 8 USC § 1426(a) (1999). On Australia's policy, see Rubenstein (1995, 520).

The large picture, then, is of citizenship playing a small role in determining rights, and duties, of persons living in Western federal democracies. Yet there are some areas in which distinctions between citizens and aliens with respect to rights against the government exist in ways that permit or facilitate different approaches among units of a federal nation. I briefly discuss below three areas of potential difference.

Mobility rights. Of the federal nations studied, all guarantee some "mobility rights" to citizens of one subnational unit to travel freely and settle throughout the nation.[47] Free movement of other persons, including aliens and aboriginals not recognized as national citizens, is not as clear. The German Basic Law, for example, guarantees "Germans" a right to move freely about the country, subject to restriction only by law "where a person does not have sufficient livelihood and his or her freedom of movement would be a considerable burden on the community [or in limited other circumstances]" (Basic Law for the Federal Republic of Germany, Art. 11 [official translation] [rev. 1995]). If in Germany it is clear that national citizens have at least a presumptive right of mobility, as the earlier discussion of Russia indicates it is at least theoretically possible that subnational units can thwart national mobility rights through, for example, control of residence permit systems.[48] Canada guarantees mobility rights within the nation not only to its own citizens but to permanent resident aliens, and these mobility rights are more deeply entrenched from legislative change than many other rights.[49]

47. Intra-Australian mobility is guaranteed by the Australian Constitution. Sec. 117 of the constitution provides that a "subject of the Queen, resident in any State, shall not be subject in any other State to any disability or discrimination which would not be equally applicable to him if he were a subject of the Queen resident in such other State." See also Rubenstein (1995). (Although the phrase "subject of the Queen" has apparently come to mean an Australian citizen and not to include persons from the United Kingdom, New Zealand, or Canada [see Lane, 1997, § 57, 809], the difference between Australian citizens and British subjects was not clear as late as 1949, and British citizens in Australia as recently as 1984 could vote in Australia even if they were not Australian citizens [see Zappalà and Castles, 1999, 278–80].) In the United States, the "right to travel" is a right of national citizenship protected by the structure of the Constitution (see *Crandall v. Nevada,* 73 U.S. 35, 48–49 [1868]) and the privileges and immunities clause of the Fourteenth Amendment (see *Saenz v. Roe,* 119 S. Ct. at 1525).

48. In Germany, for example, Art. 75 of the Basic Law provides that the subject of registration of residence is a matter for federal framework legislation. Under German constitutional law, federal framework legislation is required to allow the länder some real discretion in defining the details of the legislative approach. This shared control over registration of residence might be a vehicle to constrain movement (a subject on which I have found nothing in English).

49. See Canadian Charter of Rights and Freedoms, § 6; see also § 33 (authorizing legislature to enact laws "notwithstanding" certain rights but excluding, inter alia, § 6 rights from legislative abrogation).

Freedom of movement is often reinforced by constitutional provisions securing citizens of one subnational unit rights of fair or equal treatment in other subnational units. In the United States, the privileges and immunities clause of Article 4 plays this role. In Germany, Basic Law Article 33(1) assures every German "the same rights and duties of citizenship in every Land" (Currie, 1994, 323). Currie observed, however, that the provision has played little role in constitutional court decisions.[50] Under German equal protection decisions the rights of citizens of one land to benefits within another may be more securely protected than those of citizens of the states of the United States are under the privileges and immunities clause. A university in one German land, for example, is forbidden to discriminate against residents of another (Currie, 1994, 304; cf. *Vlandis v. Kline,* 412 U.S. 441 [1973]), while in the United States, many state universities favor in-state residents in ways that have been upheld (at least in the lower federal courts).

Social welfare rights. A range of practices exists with respect to the validity of minimal residency requirements for social welfare rights when citizens, or legal aliens, move from one subnational unit to another. As noted, the German Basic Law appears to authorize some restriction of movement of German citizens on grounds of the economic burdens movement would place on a community, yet in most respects Germany vigorously protects the rights of citizens of one land to public benefits, such as education, in another.[51] In Canada, Section 6 of the Charter of Rights and Freedoms, which guarantees both citizens and legal aliens the right to move and take up residence and to pursue a livelihood in any province, also specifically authorizes the provinces to provide for "reasonable residency requirements as a qualification for the receipt of publicly provided social services" (Canadian Charter of Rights and Freedoms, § 6[3]).[52]

By contrast, residency requirements for receipt of welfare in the states in the United States have been repeatedly rejected by the Supreme Court, most recently in *Saenz.*[53] Yet in the United States, states are permitted to favor their

50. See Currie (1994, 323 n.331) (noting that Art. 33 was not even mentioned when the German court struck down a preference for local applicants for university admission as a violation of the general equality principle of Art. 3 in conjunction with occupational freedom guarantees of Art. 12).

51. According to one report, "comprehensive federalization of social assistance dates to 1924" in Germany, and as early as 1871 the central government enforced rights to free movement within the nation with respect to local welfare systems. See Leibfried (1979, 176 n.6); Wurzel (1996, 45–46).

52. Under this provision, lower courts have upheld geographical residency requirements for various social services. See, e.g., *Irshad v. Ontario Ministry of Health,* 1999 CRDJ LEXIS 153 (Ont. Ct. Gen. Div. Feb. 4, 1999) (upholding three-month residency requirement).

53. Although states can apparently limit the benefits of free or subsidized tuition at state universities to bona fide state residents (who, in the case of U.S. citizens, are thus state citizens as

own citizens in access to some government benefits or permissions (e.g., tuition for public universities and fees for hunting licenses)[54] by charging higher amounts to citizens from other states. In Germany the länder are not permitted to discriminate against nonresidents in access to universities. The experiences of these countries suggest that while federal nations will preserve internal mobility, they vary in the extent to which internal units are required to share subsidies with out-of-staters or newcomers to the state.

Voting rights and public office or employment. Cross-nationally (as Rosberg, Neuman, and Spiro have shown in the United States), citizenship and voting rights are not necessarily coterminous.[55] Yet, they are closely associated. In Canada, which extends many charter rights to "everyone" or to "all persons," voting rights appear to be limited to citizens (Hogg, 1997, 839).[56] At least one federal nation refrained from establishing clear definitions of national citizenship in order to be able to exclude disfavored minorities from the franchise.[57]

---

well), they cannot exclude legal permanent resident aliens from that benefit if they reside in the state. See *Toll v. Moreno,* 458 U.S. 1 (1982) (holding the state policy unconstitutional as preempted by the constitutional role of the federal government). States cannot deny welfare benefits to recently arrived resident citizens from other states, nor, as a matter of current constitutional law, deny children of illegal immigrants access to free public education. See *Plyler v. Doe,* 457 U.S. 202 (1982); *League of United Latin American Citizens v. Wilson,* 908 F. Supp. 755 (C.D. Cal. 1995), 997 F. Supp. 1244 (C.D. Cal. 1997). Whether states can deny welfare benefits to legal immigrants is unsettled. A federal law authorizing states to do so was tested and upheld in lower court decisions, but the law was then amended to restore certain benefits to legal resident aliens.

54. See *Baldwin v. Fish & Game Commission,* 436 U.S. 371 (1978); see also *Vlandis v. Kline,* 412 U.S. 441, 442 (1973) (noting that many states charged higher tuition to out-of-state residents).

55. Voters in state and federal elections must be citizens, though some localities in the United States have extended the vote to resident aliens. See Rosberg (1977, 1093); Raskin (1993); cf. Neuman (1996, 64–65) (describing alien voting in early days of United States). Although the U.S. Constitution of 1787 imposed citizenship requirements for being elected to national office, it left qualifications for voters in federal elections to be the same as those established for voting for state legislatures. Amendments prohibit states from denying "the right of citizens of the United States to vote" based on race, color, gender, inability to pay a poll tax, or age (for ages eighteen and older). See U.S. Const., amendments 15, 19, 24, and 26.

56. Hogg (1997, 1048) reports that until 1946 there was no clear legal concept of Canadian citizenship (before the 1946 Citizenship Act, effective in 1947, deportation orders against British subjects of Japanese ancestry were issued and upheld by the court). Apart from voting rights, the other rights in the charter that specifically apply to "citizens" are rights to educate children in minority languages (see Charter of Rights and Freedoms, § 23) and mobility rights, which are extended to permanent resident aliens as well.

57. The only reference to citizenship in the Australian Constitution is that citizens of foreign states are disqualified from membership in the Australian Parliament. See Austr. Const., 44(1); see also Rubenstein (1995, 505) (describing unsuccessful effort in Australian Federal Convention to create a "national citizenship above State citizenship" and concluding that "citizenship in Australia is not a constitutional concept"). National and state voting rolls are restricted to citi-

According to Galligan and Chesterman (1997), the framers of the Australian Constitution sought to avoid use of the term or definitions of citizenship in the constitution in part to facilitate states' exclusion of aborigines from voting rights (though some Australian states included them).[58] Conversely, in Germany an effort to allow foreign nationals who had lived legally in Germany for more than five years to vote in municipal elections was resoundingly rejected by the German constitutional court in 1990. Strongly asserting that only citizens could vote, because citizens constituted the people from whom state authority emanates, the court found the extension of the franchise in municipal elections to legal resident aliens inconsistent with the Basic Law's requirements of self-governance:

> According to the Basic Law, the people, from whom state authority emanates . . . comprises German citizens. . . . Membership in this body politic is determined by citizenship. Citizenship is both the legal precondition for the equal status of individuals and the foundation for equal rights and duties; the exercise of legal rights and duties legitimates democratic state authority. . . . "[T]he body politic [i]s the German people." (Foreign Voters I Case [1990], 83 BVerfGE 37, trans. in Kommers [1997, 197–99])[59]

Ironically, the effect of this decision was undone within two years, when the Maastricht Treaty required members of the European Union to permit nationals of other EU members to vote in local elections. German law was accordingly amended to permit EU member state citizens to vote in local elections in Germany (as well as for EU Parliamentary elections) (see Kommers, 1997, 199).

It is not uncommon for nations, including federal nations, to restrict certain forms of high public office or even civil service employment to national citizens. Recently, Australia's High Court held a dual national ineligible to sit in the House of Representatives, a ruling that, because of the massive numbers of

---

zens, and jury service under state legislation is linked to voting thereby limiting jurors to citizens. Public service laws distinguish between citizens and aliens with respect to permanent employment (pp. 508, 514).

58. Chesterman and Gilligan (pp. 79–82) argue that one of the principal reasons why delegates to Australia's constitutional convention in 1898 refused to spell out an Australian citizenship was the desire not to interfere with the rights of Australian states to discriminate against aboriginals. § 41 of the Constitution Act tied the federal franchise to those who were allowed to vote in the states, thus in essence allowing the subnational units to determine "voting citizenship" in the national level. Soon after enactment of the constitution, aboriginals lost the right to vote that had been in effect in a few Australian states that had permitted it, through state-level legislation that prohibited recipients of federal charity from voting.

59. For further discussion, see Neuman (1992).

immigrants in Australia, was feared to disqualify several other sitting members (Rubenstein, 1995, 524). Federal structures, however, permit some subnational units to take different positions on this issue. In some Australian states noncitizens can become permanent civil service members, while in others the permanent civil service is restricted to citizens. In the EU, member states are prohibited from restricting at least some government positions to their own nationals (see *EC Comm. v. Luxembourg,* 1996 ECR I-3207).[60] In the United States, the Constitution prescribes that candidates for federal office must be U.S. citizens, and the Court has implied that Congress would have the power to exclude aliens from the *federal* civil service (U.S. Const., Art. 1, § 2, Art. 2, § 1; *Hampton v. Mow Sun Wong,* 426 U.S. 88 [1976]).[61] States of the United States, however, are more constrained by the federal Constitution in their ability to make distinctions based on alienage: states, for example, are not permitted to exclude aliens from all civil service positions (see *Sugarman v. Dougall,* 413 U.S. 634 [1973]), but only from elective or other important government positions that involve discretionary decision making or policy execution affecting representative self-governance for members of the political community. (See, e.g., *Foley v. Connelie,* 435 U.S. 291 [1978], which upheld a requirement that state police officers be citizens; and *Ambach v. Norwick,* 441 U.S. 68 [1979] [upholding similar requirements for public school teachers].) Other questions of whether state residency rules can be invoked against citizens from other states to exclude them from public contracting are unsettled and currently there is some variation among the states.[62]

60. The European Court of Justice, in interpreting Art. 48 of the EEC Treaty (which provides the principle of free movement of workers who are nationals of other member states but which also states that its provisions do not apply to employment in public service) held that Luxembourg's limitation of large numbers of public positions to its own citizens in transport, health, water, gas, and electrical supply were too "remote from the specific activities of the public service because they do not involve direct or indirect participation in the exercise of powers conferred by public law or duties designed to safeguard the general interests of the State." The court also rejected a nationality limitation for public teachers.

61. The court there invalidated a Civil Service Commission policy that excluded aliens from most jobs, absent a clear statutory directive from Congress. See also *Mathews v. Diaz,* 426 U.S. 67 (1976) (upholding federal law limiting federal medical insurance program to citizens and aliens who had been admitted as permanent residents and had lived for five years in the United States).

62. See *United Bldg. & Constr. Tr. Council v. Camden,* 465 U.S. 208 (1984) (remanding to apply standard for whether residency requirement for public contractors was permissible). See also *Supreme Court of New Hampshire v. Piper,* 470 U.S. 274 (1985) (invalidating residency requirement for lawyers). In Canada, see *Andrews v. Law Society of British Columbia* [1989] 1 S.C.R. 143 (invalidating as a violation of § 15 equality rights a ban on non-Canadian lawyers, as applied to a British permanent resident); *Black v. Law Society of Alberta* [1989] 1 S.C.R. 591 (invalidating as violation of § 6 mobility rights a ban on interprovincial law practices); but cf.

Depending on allocations of authority, then, the federal form of organization provides multiple levels for carrying out debate and decision making over the degree to which the status of citizen differs from that of alien in the allocation of duties and rights. A federal nation can accommodate states that do and do not permit aliens to vote in their local elections, for example, or that do and do not permit aliens to hold public office. In some polities the nature of the requirements for naturalization can vary from one subnational unit to another, and, in several, the severity with which national requirements are enforced varies in the subnational units depending on enforcement priorities and interpretation. Concepts of a single national citizenship exist in the world with some degrees of real variation between subnational units in the functional meaning of this status. In the United States, constitutional case law seems both to require and allow greater integration of legal aliens in state and local communities (as represented by voting and public office holding rights) than in the national community, perhaps reflecting the opportunities federalism provides for independent national courts to constrain illiberal, exclusionary state government action without directly challenging coordinate branches of the national government.

II. Federalism: Insights toward Models of Multiple Nationalities?

The experiences of federal nations illustrate both positive and negative possibilities for a world more tolerant of multiple citizenships. First, ideals of citizenship as equality are in conflict with ideals of citizenship as a form of identity embracing multiple nationalities. Unlike holders of nested citizenships in federal nations, dual (or multiple) nationality citizens who are members of a polity (in which the norm is uninationality) are differently located in relation to their government and their co-citizens. At the most basic level, a dual national has a stronger right of exit, since by definition the dual national has another country that is obligated to receive him or her. Second, however, it is clear that multiple citizenships can peacefully coexist, at least subject to priority rules that prescribe which obligations and rights can be exercised concurrently with respect to all countries of citizenship (e.g., property, or possibly even voting rights) and which can be exercised with respect to only one nationality (e.g., holding public office). Third, multiple citizenships and priority rules are likely to be dynamic, not stable, and federal structures provide models of locations for contests over the meaning and scope of citizenship that may be salutary means of

---

Law Society of Upper Canada v. Skapinker [1984] 1 S.C.R. 357 (holding that § 6[2][b] did not give foreign citizen, resident in a province, the right to work there as an attorney).

managing inevitable conflicts. Finally, in the midst of this dynamism, perhaps the posture of Western liberal democracies should be neither resistant to nor encouraging of multiple nationalities, but should be an intermediate posture: to accommodate and manage the growing reality of multiple nationalities to which increased migration, enhanced norms of gender equality, and globalization of communications and transportation technologies have contributed. I discuss each of these points briefly below.

Citizenship as Equality and Citizenship as Identity

The concept of citizenship is at once in tension with and a part of liberal egalitarian values. It is in tension with these values to the extent that the idea of citizenship functions to exclude or differentiate; citizenship is in some sense meaningful only in contrast to noncitizenship, and thus is in some sense founded upon an essential inequality of status or rights as between citizen and noncitizen. (See Brubaker, 1992, 23, identifying citizenship as performing the important function of closure.) At the same time, citizenship has been an engine of equality, as it is a norm that embodies within it the idea of an essential equality of relationships between all citizens and their state; hence the use of the terms *Citoyen* and *Citoyenne,* in the French Revolution.

Today, it is not clear whether there are any universal rights or duties associated with the status of being a citizen in Western liberal democracies, other than the rights to leave and enter your country freely, to carry a passport, and to receive diplomatic protection from the government of which you are a national (see Legomsky, 1994). Civil rights, social rights, even political rights (such as voting) are at times held or exercised by noncitizens. Voting is the activity most likely to come to mind (in Western liberal democracies) as what it is that citizens can do that others cannot. Yet as Gerald Rosberg and others have pointed out, "historical experience rebuts the argument that the terms 'citizen' and 'voter' are synonymous," noting that aliens had at times enjoyed suffrage while "a great many citizens" did not (Rosberg, 1977, 1093; Raskin, 1993, favoring voting rights for legal aliens in local elections). Yet the sense of many is that "only citizens" should be able to vote, and some have argued that if voting rights were extended to aliens, citizenship would be improperly devalued.

Federalism, too, is in some tension with egalitarian norms; it presupposes that within a national entity there is some range of permissible difference—in law, in how laws are enforced, and in how the people of the subnational units choose to constitute their governments.[63] Federalism generates its own sets of

---

63. In "symmetric" federal systems an equal right to be different is accorded each subnational unit, as in the United States; in "asymmetric" federal systems (as Canada's relationship with

normative debates. Interestingly, some proponents of federalism argue in its favor on grounds that relate, loosely, to some of the functions claimed for the concept of citizenship, that is, of permitting closer concordances between people's senses of identity, of what is important to them, and their geographically salient unit. Opponents of federalism point to the same phenomena, but through a darker glass, emphasizing federalism's potential for magnifying, rather than diminishing, cleavages between peoples that increase rather than decrease prospects for tolerance and peace.

With respect to both federalism and citizenship, debates over how to enhance their value are based on assumptions about why the concept—and here I return to citizenship—is (or is not) a good thing.[64] Answers to this question are contextual. In one hundred years, national citizenship may not be a good thing. Right now, however, it is, first of all, necessary, given the actual existence of nation-states that control movement at borders and in which a system of nationally issued passports is needed to determine movement rights (other than for asylum seekers and refugees in limited circumstances). In addition, citizenship as a status is beneficial in that it offers an alternative concept of meaningful group membership and community to the forces of ethnonationalism and religious fundamentalism. In contrast to ethnonational movements,[65] citizenship can be acquired by those outside of a group defined by descent and thus embraces norms of freedom and choice. Citizenship is preferable in some respects to religion as a source of group meaning and identity when the group in question has the coercive use of state power (through lawmaking and military means),

---

Quebec arguably is or might become) some subnational units have greater autonomy rights than other subnational units. Within asymmetric federal polities, members of the different subnational states may have "nested citizenships" with different meanings, in ways arguably more analogous to a polity in which some of the members hold multiple "parallel" nationalities. References in text to "federal systems" refer to "symmetric" federal systems except where noted.

64. Note the debate over *how* to enhance the value of citizenship in *Lavoie v. Canada*, 31 CRR (2d) 109, 1995 CRR LEXIS 190 (1995). Schuck, testifying as an expert for the Canadian government in support of the constitutionality of Canada's preference for its own citizens in public employment, advanced a vision that one enhances citizenship by making it mean more by carrying more rights than noncitizen status (and possibly harder to get) (p. 135). Carens advanced a contrary vision that one enhances citizenship by making it more accessible (p. 135). The trial court found the discrimination against aliens to violate Canada's constitutional principle of equality of treatment. The court of appeals reversed, relying in part on Schuck's views, concluding that such a distinction between citizens and aliens was permissible. See *Bailey v. Canada* [1999] F.C.A.D.J. 103, 1999 F.C.A.D.J. LEXIS (May 19, 1999).

65. See Martin (1999, 15) (discussing Michael Ignatieff's argument that "civic nationalism" is an "antidote" to ethnic nationalism). I do not mean to imply that ethnonational cultural affiliations are a bad thing for a society. To the contrary, they can be a rich and meaningful source of personal identity. Ethnically based affiliative groups, however, do not permit easy entrance and exit. Such nonconsensual "born to" groupings, when relied on as the basis for constituting government authority in polyethnic nations, can pose real threats to human autonomy and equality and to political tolerance.

because of citizenship's egalitarian orientation and openness to participation by all adults on equal terms and its association with commitments to democratic forms of decision making that allow communities to change their self-definition and notion of the good.[66]

Knowing whether and why citizenship is a good thing provides some guidance in considering models of citizenship in the future. In thinking about how federal experiences might contribute to defining citizenships and allocating rights and duties of citizenships in a more migratory world of overlapping loyalties, goals should include enhancing both equality and freedom, both tolerance and democracy—sets of paired values that can come into conflict with each other, but all of which are necessary for the healthy functioning of stable democracies, respectful of minority and human rights. Any workable system of multiple nationalities that emerges is likely to be conceptually difficult to make fully coherent, because of the competing pulls of these different norms. The hope is that citizenship, in its multiple senses of special affiliation and equal membership, will help maintain a balance between these competing norms.

Federalism and Multiple Citizenships: Tolerating Differences

For these competing perspectives, federal systems offer some intriguing possibilities. They suggest that healthy polities can tolerate some differences in the treatment accorded citizens of different states. Thus, uniformity in approach is not essential, provided that national citizenship plays an overarching role in defining minimal standards of treatment and so long as the domains of national and subnational responsibilities are clearly understood.[67] Federal models also suggest that people are capable of holding multiple citizenships, and that, in the ordinary course of things, those citizenships are not likely to conflict in a highly problematic way. A citizen in New York, for example, may have voted for and approved her Republican governor's policies and voted against and disagreed

66. Cf. La Torre (1998, 446) (arguing that human beings have a fundamental need to belong to a group and that there is a fundamental human right to citizenship); Smith (1997, 480–87) (criticizing cultural pluralist views of citizenship for neglecting the nation-building functions of citizenship and for failing to address how to foster common civic identity and thereby meet "basic political imperatives" driving citizenship laws). Smith goes on to argue for an understanding of citizenship as analogous to political party affiliation, an analogy that I do not think captures the common civic identity he is seeking to formulate. Again, my comment in text is not intended to devalue religious affiliation at all, but rather to argue that citizenship as an affiliation serves affirmative purposes (e.g., of enabling participation in self-governance) that are not served as well by other forms of affiliation.

67. As I suggest later in the chapter, in the multinational setting this observation would favor some form of "primary" citizenship.

with her Democratic president, without having had to abandon her national citizenship. A basic premise of democracy is that citizens are free to disagree with their own governments. In light of this premise, short of war there are few occasions when holding multinational citizenships should be seen as inconsistent with being a citizen in a democratic nation.[68] Federal nations demonstrate that liberal democracies can work even when the possibility of differences is ensured through federalism: people living in federal systems carry multiple citizenships and loyalties that can be successfully and simultaneously managed.

How enthusiastic one should be about encouraging multiple citizenships, and whether the particular kinds of dual citizenships of federal nations offer positive models for a theory and practice that accommodates multiple national citizenships, are harder questions. In the United States the primacy of national citizenship coexists with citizenship in particular states, which may offer certain benefits in terms of government employment, access to contracts with the state governments, social welfare, and education. But in a federal system, all citizens stand in a position of at least formal equality with respect to the national government, even if differences are allowed among the subnational governments. There is no world government comparable to a national government in a federal system (with the possible exception of the supranational government of the EU, which for purposes of this chapter I treat as a quasi federal system itself). Is dual citizenship in a federal system nonetheless relevant to the question of dual or multiple nationalities? Although I argue below that it is, I

---

68. This observation has other implications: first, that democracies should not try per se to discourage multinational citizenships, and second, that the standard for tolerating multiple citizenship might vary depending on the extent to which the alternative citizenships are those of an essentially democratic nation or a nation that does not require ideological consistency from its citizens. As to the first point, I argue later in the chapter for a rather neutral stance by Western democracies toward dual nationality, a stance that focuses more on managing the practical aspects of felt dual nationalities than on attempting either to encourage or discourage the retention or development of such dual nationalities. On the second point, that dual citizenships may work better to the extent that both affiliations are with liberal democratic or tolerant states, this may be right (i.e., there may be a greater potential for conflict with the country of origin of dual nationals from oppressive regimes), but it should not be implemented as policy. First, many would-be citizens may be fleeing illiberal regimes in their home countries for which country, but not regime, the immigrants feel loyalty; to withhold dual nationality from this group may withhold it from those who as a practical matter may be most in need of achieving a new nationality that will protect them. Second, a dual nationality regime that required the United States, or another nation, to develop an official list of nations sufficiently democratic to qualify its nationals for dual nationality would invite foreign policy imbroglios. Cf. Spiro (1997, 1450–51) (discussing whether voting in foreign elections can result in denationalization in United States and arguing that voting in Israeli election "could not have offended underpinnings of exclusivity paradigm" because Israel was an ally).

also take issue with some of the more enthusiastic proponents of relaxing barriers to dual nationalities.

Some cautions. The question of accepting dual or multiple nationalities is a pressing one in many Western democracies.[69] Several scholars in the United States and abroad have argued that views of citizenship as resting on notions of exclusive loyalty are no longer relevant, especially in a post–Cold War era in which the likelihood of Western democracies going to war with each other is remote.[70] Peter Spiro, an enthusiastic U.S. advocate for recognizing dual nationality, argues that, with the diminution of cold war hostilities, the potential costs of dual nationality are lowered. By this, Spiro means that there are fewer

69. France has permitted aliens to naturalize without giving up their other nationality, and dual citizenships are permitted for citizens in New Zealand, Switzerland, the United Kingdom, the United States, and even, to a limited extent, Germany (which, however, has resisted proposals to legitimize dual nationality fully). See Franck (1996, 380); Brubaker (1992, 173). Hailbronner (1998, 5) reported that a 1993 liberalization of German law provided exceptions for some dual nationalities (i.e., an applicant for citizenship need not renounce a preexisting citizenship if the country of origin requires military service before renunciation). Since the 1993 change, 23 percent of German naturalizations were accepted as dual nationalities. Ethnic Germans, moreover, have been allowed to retain their other nationality for some time while acquiring formal German citizenship. See Feldblum (1998, 239); see also Hagedorn (1998) (reporting that since 1991 German law no longer requires that families of naturalization applicants hold the same citizenship). In 1999, Germany adopted a new naturalization law that will permit children born in Germany to (nonethnic German) immigrants, at least one of whom has lived in Germany eight years before the birth, to become German citizens automatically. While this new law represents a substantial departure from German traditions of citizenship by descent, and embraces a limited version of the jus soli, it did not include earlier proposals that would have generally allowed dual citizenship for children of aliens born in Germany. Substantial popular opposition to this proposal forced its removal. Instead, the law allows children until age twenty-three to decide which passport to keep. News reports state that only "in exceptional cases, such as when 'unreasonable conditions' are imposed for giving up a foreign passport, will dual citizenship be permissible" (see Cohen, 1999, A3). Whether those "unreasonable conditions" would include having to perform military service before renunciation or would also embrace possible losses of property rights in the event of renunciation, is unclear.

70. See Spiro (1997); Schuck (1998a, 219, 230–32); see also Carens (1987). As Spiro, Schuck, and others note, in Germany, the United States, and other Western nations there has been in addition to large amounts of migration, an increase in national mixed marriages and their babies—increasing automatic dual citizenship. Although earlier international conventions strongly discouraged dual citizenship (see, e.g., 1930 Hague Convention), the 1997 European Convention on Nationality takes a different stance, requiring states to allow dual nationality in cases where the nationality is automatically acquired by marriage or where renunciation or loss of other nationality "is not possible or cannot reasonably be required." Art. 16. See also Feldblum (1998, 236–37) (noting expansion of dual nationality possibilities, including talks between Germany and Turkey re dual nationality). Although the U.S. oath of citizenship currently requires the renunciation of other allegiances, many naturalized citizens are able to retain multiple nationalities and passports, depending on the practices of their state of origin. See Schuck (1998a, 222; see also Aleinikoff (1997, 26–27) (describing different rules that can result in dual citizenship).

occasions for conflicts in loyalties derived from a presumed lack of independence of a dual national from the interests or even directives of his home country that would have grave consequences for a country naturalizing someone who may commit espionage or treasonous activities. He argues, however, that the likelihood of foreign nations having such leverage is low, and that single U.S. citizenship does not preclude maintenance of affiliations with other nations that drive a person's interests and decisions. From the communitarian viewpoint, Spiro argues that while dual nationalities may not be as powerful as single nationality affiliations, the world is full of multiple forms of affiliation that are often recognized as good in civil society. Spiro acknowledges that his argument may imply that "national citizenship as an institution is less important than it once was," and that "the significance of citizenship in another state is now equivalent to membership in a religious or civic organization," and that it is likely that citizenship in the United States has also moved to this level (Spiro 1997, 1478).

Both this claim, and his further claim that "there is no longer any respect in which holding additional nationality essentially precludes full identification with the community," can be questioned (see Spiro, 1997, 1474).[71] First, it may not be as correct in other nations as in the United States. His argument on the possibility of full citizenship in the United States with dual nationality elsewhere might be understood as limited to the experiences of the United States, which has a history of being both a country of immigration and a country of easy naturalization;[72] a country in which both the federal structure and the separation of powers embody the possibility of divided sovereignty and multiple affiliations; and a country with the power, influence, and connections to participate, both directly as a government and indirectly through the organized actions of its citizens, in the affairs of other countries around the world. In a polity where some of these experiences or powers are lacking, the risks of dual citizenship might be seen as greater than in the United States, and it is thus important to keep in mind whether one is considering dual citizenship for persons residing in the United States or dual citizenship more generally in the world.

Second, Spiro's confidence that the days of military conscription are past, as are the days of armed conflict between Western democracies or their close

---

71. For different questions along lines similar to mine, see Schuck (1998a, 239) ("one can acknowledge the general tendencies that Spiro identifies while still doubting that they will apply in every case and reduce the risks to zero").

72. With some obvious and important exceptions reflecting racist assumptions, e.g., the exclusion of immigrants from China from naturalization procedures until well into the twentieth century.

allies, seems strikingly optimistic in the wake of recent fighting in Europe over Kosovo. Nation-states, especially powerful ones, are still looked to in the world to provide military intervention and this seems likely to continue for the foreseeable future, particularly given weaknesses in international commitments to UN decision making on international use of force issues. While there may be something of a liberal peace, it is likely that Western liberal democracies will continue to fight wars, and calls for reinstating the draft are even now occasionally heard in the United States.[73]

Third, citizenship functions as an instrument for human equality within the polity in ways that affiliations in organizations such as churches or civic clubs are less likely to do. Citizenship implies a right and obligation to participate in self-governance across the enormously wide range of activities that governments engage in, and in particular, powers of coercion based on territorial control that, in democracies, are not widely granted to private organizations. In this sense, citizenship is a concept and an affiliation that is worth promoting, though how this ties in to dual nationality is hotly contested.

The federal analogy. In the debate over dual or multinational citizenships, empirical experience will be important to evaluating normative value. Experiences may vary depending on the country or countries involved in dual or multiple nationality regimes and on the particular distribution of rights and obligations that the status as multiple national brings with it. But the experience of federal nations illuminates this debate.

First, federal nations establish the possibility of persons holding two levels of citizenship simultaneously. Granted, they are *nested* citizenships, in that they are related to one another, in some cases may derive from one another, and function toward each other in a clear hierarchy of legal norms. Note that the proliferation of citizenship questions is related to the federal form; the development of a European citizenship is a nested citizenship, tiered on top of and tied to citizenship in a member state of the European Union.[74] Moreover, as devolu-

---

73. See, e.g., Califano (1999, A23). The need for use of force may not be diminishing, but simply shifting focus from large-scale conflagrations to multiple, smaller wars. The so-called volunteer army is more of a "market-based army," far removed from the idea of military service as a universal (or universal for men) obligation of citizenship.

74. Note the uncertainty among European scholars as to whether EU "citizenship" is "really" a form of citizenship. See, e.g., Hoffman (1998, 158–65) (identifying "criteria of citizenship" under German law, the extent to which EU citizenship differs, and the consequent disagreement over the "legal nature" of EU citizenship). Although there can be no doubt that EU citizenship is at present limited in the scope of its appurtenant rights, it also seems clear that the intended meaning of EU citizenship is precisely to develop that sense of loyalty and alliance to the Union as a whole that the idea of "citizenship" frequently conveys.

tionary federalism wreaks its progress in, for example, the United Kingdom, three-tiered concepts of divisible citizenships may become more significant: a person may be a Scottish citizen, a citizen of the United Kingdom, and a citizen of the EU, all at once.

That the citizenships in federal nations are nested in one direction does distinguish them from dual nationalities, in which the claims to multiple national citizenships exist independently of one another. One cannot be a U.S. citizen living in New York without being a New York citizen; one cannot be a citizen of France and not be a citizen of the EU. One can, however, be a citizen of the United States and not be a citizen of Mexico. This difference, between *nested* federal citizenships and *parallel* multiple nationalities, may be significant in several ways.[75] Most important for present purposes is that such interdependent citizenships as exist at the state and federal levels in the United States, or the nation-state and union level in the EU, come embedded within a legal regime that seeks to accommodate and prioritize the relationships between different levels of law across a spectrum that extends well beyond questions of citizenship and individual rights and duties. Thus, in their daily lives and business, federal citizens experience the laws or enforcement authorities of both levels of government, subject (in the United States) to the hierarchical conflicts-of-laws principle of the supremacy clause. Multinational citizenships typically do not experience this simultaneous regulation in their daily life and do not experience a supremacy clause principle at all unless they are members of nation-states that, through treaty or convention, have agreed on priority rules (typically based on principal residency).

In light of this difference, does the experience of nested multiple citizenships in federal polities have any bearing at all on what has been regarded as the distinct problem of dual or multiple nationalities? While it is true that the priority rules for conflicts between the obligations of state and federal citizenship are established in the U.S. Constitution and are not established for many claims

---

75. E.g., abandoning state-level citizenship in the United States is relatively easy—one simply moves from one state to another (assuming one has the resources to do so). Abandoning U.S. citizenship (short of clear renunciation), by contrast, is very difficult. Existing national and international regimes frequently provide a decision point at which a simple election among nationalities can be made. It may not be as simple, however, to renounce a dual nationality as it is to change the state of one's residence in the United States, and hence one's state citizenship. In this respect, the EU may be closer to the "multinational" situation, since member states retain control over their own definitions of citizenship, and thus, while nationals of one member state can take up residency in another, they cannot, so quickly as a U.S. citizen can switch state residency, switch their member-state nationality. Cf. Neuman (1992, 277) (describing German opposition to alien suffrage on the ground that aliens, unlike citizens, were not "inescapably tied to the fate of the community"). Exit from one subnational citizenship to another is presently far easier than exit from (renunciation) and acquisition of national citizenships.

of dual nationality, this does not mean that such rules could not be developed. And in other respects, multiple citizenships in federal nations speak to concerns of those opposed to expanded recognition of dual nationality citizenships.

Consider some of the principal disadvantages of dual nationality referred to in the literature, including (1) uncertainty in conflicts regimes, (2) effects on diplomatic protection, (3) fiscal effects on the nation offering the more liberal social welfare reforms; and, most importantly, (4) conflicting political loyalties (and possibly destabilizing backlash against dual nationals perceived as disloyal or as unfairly benefiting from dual nationality). Determining whose law governs and who owes protection are complex matters that international law already has begun to address.[76]

The concern over fiscal effects from more liberal social welfare assistance offered by nations that attract immigration raises a problem familiar to federal nations. Federal nations display a range of behaviors in dealing with this problem, some designed to allow economically successful subnational entities to hoard their resources for a time from newcomers.[77] A question to consider is whether increases in dual nationality would be accompanied by increased pressures for such hoarding; if so, however, several federal nations provide models for how to address those possibilities without long-term exclusionary effects.[78]

With respect to the key questions of loyalty and independence, federal systems accommodate these possibilities on a regular basis: federal citizens who vote in state and national elections may have conflicting loyalties about what is best for their own state as compared to the entire country. An implication from federal systems for dual nationality is for the need to develop international

76. For efforts to address conflicts of law issues, see, e.g., the International Court of Justice decision in *Liechtenstein v. Guatemala,* 1955 I.C.J. 4, 4–65 (April 6) (explaining doctrine of "dominant (or effective) nationality"). And on the obligation to extend diplomatic protection, see The Hague Convention concerning Certain Questions relating to the Conflict of Nationality Laws, 1930, 179 U.N.T.S. 89, Art. 4 (providing that one state cannot protect its national when its national is in another state in which he or she also holds nationality).

77. See, e.g., Canada's Charter of Rights and Freedoms, § 6(c) (allowing provinces to impose reasonable residency waiting periods before making social welfare benefits available); *Saenz v. Roe,* 119 S. Ct. at 1533–34 (Rehnquist, C. J., dissenting) (arguing that it is reasonable for states to require newcomers to wait).

78. For a suggestion that liberalization of naturalization (sometimes with possibilities of dual nationality) has been coupled with increased barriers to migration for permanent resettlement in Europe, see Feldblum (1998, 236–37, 242–43) (noting European states' "loosening of citizenship regulations" facilitating naturalizations and dual citizenship coincident with "efforts to tighten and restrict access into the countries"); but cf. Motomura (1999, 1368) (noting that many U.S. states and localities provided "more generous" welfare to aliens than required under federal law provisions permitting discrimination against permanent resident aliens). Both Canada and Germany seem to allow their subnational units to erect residency requirements that permit limited but not long-term hoarding of social welfare resources. See discussion above in this chapter.

legal norms or conventions dealing with questions of hierarchy, or dominance, should conflicts arise in the demands of the multiple citizenships, and of (perhaps standing) mechanisms for resolving them. While there is some precedent for international agreements harmonizing, for example, obligations of military service of dual nationals, there are other areas that need to be resolved.[79] But with the development of such coordinating or hierarchical norms, concerns over voting in two or more countries could well be mitigated.

Voting, loyalty, and democracy. In federal nations with dual citizenships at the national and subnational (state) level, citizens vote in subnational state elections and may vote in favor of candidates for subnational state assembly who, for example, oppose federal interventions in environmental law or favor declaring that their state will not purchase goods from countries that it deems human rights violators. In the elections for national office, that same citizen may or may not vote for candidates for federal office whose positions are as close to this as possible. We do not tend to see the citizen, in these capacities, as having such conflicted loyalties as to raise questions about whether she or he should be allowed to vote. Why, then, might we see someone who is a citizen of Mexico and of the United States having such conflicted loyalties that he or she should not be permitted to vote in the elections of both?[80] While there may be reasons, the mere invocation of loyalty and the possibility of a conflict in goals between nations is not a sufficient answer, since we allow citizens of states whose goals may be in conflict with those of the national political community to vote in elections for both.[81]

79. Several bilateral conventions govern military service for dual nationals. There are also international precedents on the obligations of third countries with respect to dual nationals to the effect that third countries can choose to recognize the dominant nationality as the nationality of a dual citizen for certain purposes. For a discussion of these and other emerging rules of international law (e.g., concerning the relations between two countries of a single person's dual nationality with respect to that person), see generally, Donner (1994, 106–12).

80. Multiple pulls on political loyalty can occur in even more complex contexts. E.g., the Eastern Canadian provinces and the New England States of the United States have had a series of meetings to discuss problems of acid rain, discussions that continued even during periods of inactivity at the national government level. While the participants in those conferences did not have "dual" loyalties in the sense of dual national citizens, they did have perspectives and perhaps even goals that may have differed in part from those of their national governments and that could be advocated and advanced in the setting of these interprovincial discussions. See Feldman and Feldman (1990). This volume contains a number of excellent (though now dated) essays on the activities of subnational entities in federal nations in the area of international relations and foreign affairs.

81. See Rosberg (1977, 1131) (noting, in considering whether aliens' purported lack of loyalty to the United States should disqualify them from voting here, that a Texan living in New York is allowed to vote in New York, even if he remains sentimentally attached to Texas and

The problem of multiple loyalties in the case of nested citizenship may be mitigated by the assumed acceptance by voters of the hierarchy of legal norms that define the relationships of the different levels of government of which the voter is a citizen. That is, a citizen in a state who expresses opposition to particular policies through votes for her representatives will nonetheless recognize that if (contrary to her wishes and votes) the policies are enacted as valid federal law, they trump conflicting state and local law. On this assumption, we can live with a system that allows this citizen and others like her to seek change. In the setting of dual or multiple nationalities of separate sovereigns—that is, unnested, parallel, multiple citizenships—a set of international conventions or norms, establishing priorities, will need to emerge to coordinate possession of these multiple citizenships in the rare cases where rights or obligations otherwise would conflict. But even without such a coordinating international legal order, it is not clear to me that the possibility of conflict in loyalties as they are expressed in voting is sufficiently great at present to strongly support a prohibition on voting by dual nationals in both national polities.[82]

Nor does the argument from democracy necessarily disfavor permitting dual nationals to vote in both of their countries. Martin (1999, 27) has advanced an argument from democratic theory: one person, one vote means that a voter cannot vote in the same election in more than one place. Martin's logic seems correct if one thinks about a single federal nation: it would offend the principle that each person's vote should count the same as another if one person were able, for example, to vote for a representative in the U.S. House of Representatives both in New York and Massachusetts.[83]

---

plans to return). During the Cold War, U.S. law clearly operated on different assumptions, providing for loss of U.S. citizenship for voting in foreign elections. See Spiro (1997, 1443–47) (describing, inter alia, *Perez v. Brownell,* 356 U.S. 44 [1958]). More recently, Martin (1999, 25–31) has advanced a nuanced and thoughtful argument against permitting voting in two nations' elections by dual nationals, to be enforced by rules prohibiting recognition of rapid changes of residence for purposes of establishing eligibility to vote. Martin's proposal—to vote only where you are a resident—is eminently workable, since determining principal residence is a task that courts in federal systems engage in for several purposes (including jurisdiction to adjudicate, jurisdiction to tax, and conflicts of laws more generally). But, as discussed in the text, I am not sure it is necessary.

82. Even in the absence of some coordinating principles of priority, voting rights for dual nationals could in theory be coordinated so that a dual national does not vote in both national elections but is able to vote in local and subnational elections in one polity, and in elections at all levels in the other. Note that in the EU, citizens of member states are permitted to vote in most local elections of member states, although not in their national elections. I assume this is partially to avoid the possibility of head-to-head conflicts of interests in selecting the leadership of two sovereign nations, a conflict unmitigated by any present rule of law that provides a hierarchy between the actions of equally sovereign nations.

83. See also Bauböck (1994, 175) (noting that in a liberal democracy a basic feature of political membership is that the weight given to individual votes in a collective decision should be

This logic, however, has only the most remote bearing on the question of voting in the national elections of two countries, since there is no international body in which countries are essentially represented on the basis of population and to which the one person one vote principle applies. Ironically, were a world or multinational legislative assembly, based on principles of representation proportioned to population, some day to exist, the arguments against permitting dual nationals to vote in the national elections of more than one country might be more compelling.

I am guardedly optimistic that international regimes for establishing priorities for the obligations of dual nations can and will eventually emerge, probably starting out in bilateral agreements, and it seems plausible to think that allowing voting in both countries is unlikely to be harmful to the development of such norms and might even be helpful. Schuck (1998a, 217–47) notes that dual citizenship is becoming both more common and more controversial than ever.[84] Notwithstanding his concerns for the threat of devaluation of U.S citizenship through a diminishment of the differences between citizens and others, Schuck favors legally accommodating the trend toward allowing dual nationality. He argues that the most essential rights associated specifically with citizenship are political in character (the right to vote and to stand for office), and yet he also suggests that these rights could be decoupled from citizenship in settings of dual nationality.[85] The benefits of multiple nationalities, he notes, flow not only to the individuals who hold them, but arguably to both of the nation-states of citizenship, facilitating the dual national's contributions to both polities. Multinational businesses benefit from the added mobility of holders of dual nationalities.[86] Schuck (1998a, 234) argues that "we should conceive of

---

equal). Note that the Swiss Constitution specifically provides that Swiss citizens can exercise their political rights in only one canton. See n.21 above.

84. See Schuck (1998, 217–47) (discussing plural citizenships). He notes that both international marriage and migration are increasing, which will have the effect of creating more dual nationals by birth. In addition to Mexico, Canada, the Dominican Republic, India, and the Philippines confer nationality on children born to their own citizens on U.S. soil; thus, these children are born with dual nationality. Schuck points out that 60 percent of Swiss nationals now live abroad as dual citizens. Aleinikoff (1997, 28) reports in addition that Argentina, Colombia, Costa Rica, France, Israel, Ireland, El Salvador, Panama, and the United Kingdom now permit their citizens to retain nationality even if they are naturalized elsewhere.

85. See Schuck (1998a, 227) (suggesting that Congress could provide that U.S. citizens who subsequently naturalize in other countries may not exercise political rights there). Decoupling citizenship from rights associated with its status—including rights to vote—may help preserve citizenship's capacity to express affiliation while changing its capacity to promote equality among co-citizens.

86. Spiro (1997, 1477) argues that dual nationalities held by American citizens may help spread Western liberal democratic values if they retain the ability to participate in politics in other countries. He suggests that for dual nationals holding office in the United States, a "con-

the national interest of the United States as including those preferences" of dual nationals that might be expressed in domestic elections. That being so, one must also consider that other countries of dual nationals might reach similar conclusions about their national interests—conclusions that can be accommodated by allowing dual nationals to vote in both their parallel nations of citizenship.[87]

Oaths of allegiance and asymmetrical citizenships.   Schuck and other scholars in the field have concentrated on the need to modify the oath of allegiance. Schuck (1998a, 245) argues for a modification so that instead of renouncing all other loyalties the immigrant would have to express something like primary loyalty to the United States. Spiro (1997, 1479–80) argues in theory for eliminating any requirement of renunciation of loyalty elsewhere and for an oath requiring allegiance to the Constitution and government of the United States, but recognizes the advantages of Schuck's proposal.[88] According to Aleinikoff, Lawrence Fuchs also argues for an oath of primary allegiance, as in, "My allegiance is to the United States above any other nation." Aleinikoff (1997, 38–40) favors this idea, arguing that a "primacy, not exclusivity, oath would continue to serve the gate-keeping function . . . [but] would assist immigrants who want to naturalize but are caught between . . . the renunciation requirement" and laws of their home country that adversely affect those who renounce their first citizenships.

Two features about an oath of primary loyalty should be noted. First, it establishes a basic hierarchy of allegiances and norms, in somewhat the way that the supremacy clause of the U.S. Constitution does; consider especially the portion of that clause addressed to state court judges and directing them to treat

---

flicts" rule should preclude office holding only in positions where there are likely to be many situations of apparent conflicts in loyalty (pp. 1480–81). He thus disagrees with Schuck (1999a, 245), who would bar dual nationals from holding high public office in another polity, arguing (correctly, I think) that the risk of conflict is higher in office holding than in the voting context. Note the extent to which both Spiro and Schuck seem prepared to accept the primacy of citizenship in the United States as a baseline in arguing for rules for dual citizenship in the United States that could not be sustained on a reciprocal basis. What I mean by this is that insistence on a primary loyalty oath in a dual citizenship setting is a rule that only one of the countries of citizenship could insist on. In theory, one could swear primary loyalty to only one country. See discussion below on asymmetrical multiple citizenships.

87. I think Schuck would agree with this point as well. See Schuck (1998a, 235) (indicating that voting by U.S. citizens in the elections of other countries is "unproblematic," as long as it does not "embroil the U.S. in unwanted disputes with the other country or involve situations in which the voter subordinates the interests of the United States to those of another country").

88. For a thoughtful analysis of the "renunciation" requirement from various perspectives within liberal, republican, and communitarian traditions, see Neuman (1994, 268–77).

the U.S. Constitution and federal treaties and laws as "supreme," "notwithstanding" anything to the contrary in the state constitutions. Although a hierarchy of allegiances is not entirely the same thing as a hierarchy of legal norms, they are closely related,[89] and the hierarchy of allegiance presumably would play a role in the distribution of other rights and obligations as and between dual citizens and their countries.

Second, an oath of primary loyalty implies a necessarily asymmetrical vision of multiple citizenships. That is, if the idea of an oath of primary loyalty is to establish that, in the event of a conflict, one's primary loyalty is to one country, then the other country cannot (at least in theory) insist on the same oath of primary loyalty to it. Now, regimes might be made technically symmetric insofar as they provided that it is only when citizens from another country seek to naturalize that they must take a primary oath of loyalty. But such an approach may be too narrow to deal with the reality of questions of dual nationality that arise in a world in which there are many children born with dual nationality who may spend parts of their lives connected to both countries and who under current law must elect nationality at adulthood. The person, in this case, is not in some sense "naturalizing" from outside into the polity, but is choosing a primary affiliation. So it is fair to say that an oath of primary loyalty does envision a fundamental asymmetry in the regime of dual nationality.

This is not necessarily to condemn it. One could say that the supremacy clause of the U.S. Constitution is asymmetrical in that it establishes the supremacy of federal law over state law; or in that it does not bind federal officers to uphold valid state law in the way state officers are bound to uphold valid federal law. But the purpose of this supremacy clause, or of comparable clauses in other federal constitutions, was in part to build a working sovereign nation. What is the purpose of allowing dual nationality?

Multigenerational or transitional communities? Some writers appear to view dual nationality as a way of expanding the inclusiveness of the powerful, economically viable states that attract migration, and as primarily improving

---

89. Although some might treat the content of an oath as merely a matter of form, in dealing with citizenship, nationality, and sovereignty matters of form bear heavy symbolic connotations that can have important mobilizing effects politically. Thus, for instance, in the pre–Civil War U.S. south, South Carolina at one point adopted a loyalty oath requiring militia members to swear loyalty first to South Carolina, and then to the Union, a form of oath struck down by a closely divided court in the state. See Kettmer (1978, 265–67) for a detailed discussion. More recently, news articles report demands by some Quebec separatists for a revised loyalty oath for new citizens naturalizing within Quebec. See "Quebec Group Urges Dual Allegiance Oath," *London Free Press,* April 23, 1999, A10 (reporting Guy Bouthillier's argument for pledging allegiance both to Canada and to Quebec).

the transition to citizenship in those nations. This vision is in some ways consistent with recent changes in the citizenship laws of some nations to operate more restrictively on subsequent generations' acquisition of citizenship by descent than previously, for example, in Mexico (see Aleinikoff, 1997, 30–36).[90] Others appear to regard dual nationality as the coming wave of a future world order, in which nation-states decline in importance. On this view, dual nationalities are the wave of a postnational future.[91] So it is important to analyze the citizenship laws of nations to determine whether regimes of multiple nationality are to be understood as persisting into the future, or as largely involving a single transitional generation. If the former, then the need for coordinating legal principles is stronger; if the latter, a more ad hoc approach may suffice, such as Aleinikoff's anticipation of bilateral agreements to provide for allocation of particular rights and duties based on residence or other criterion.[92]

Internal constitutional constraints, however, may prevent the development of "divisible" forms of citizenship, in which a dual national citizen has fewer "rights" in his or her nation than a single national citizen. Such a development, while perhaps necessary to accommodate multinational citizenships, nonetheless contemplates that there will be, for some purposes, "classes" of citizens within the same polity. But recognizing "classes" of citizens is in some tension with citizenship's equality-promoting characteristics in each polity internally. Note, further, that the development of multigenerational dual national communities is far more likely to require the development of some supranational struc-

90. Aleinikoff (1997, 30–36) explains recent changes in Mexican law that permit Mexicans who naturalize elsewhere to remain Mexican nationals (albeit without voting rights in Mexico) but that also preclude transmission of Mexican nationality according to jus sanguinis rules beyond the second generation.

91. On the need not to move too quickly in assuming the disappearance of nation-states as important political organizations, note that even Soysal (1994), whose vision of postnational citizenship in Europe has been so influential, acknowledged that, at least for the present, enforcement of most international human rights norms are dependent on the will of sovereign nation-states (p.144–45).

92. It will be important to clarify whether dual nationalities involve transitional regimes to presumed states of primary or single nationality, or are instead designed to foster a multigenerational, permanently multinational community of dual nationals owing equal allegiances to different sovereigns, entitled to vote in one, perhaps obligated to serve militarily in another. Would Aleinikoff's proposal envision abandoning efforts to define a primary citizenship for all purposes and instead seek to develop rules based on, e.g., the primary place of residence for voting, the primary place of employment for taxes, etc.? Courts are familiar with determining the principal place of residence and, in settings where none can be determined, the Swiss approach—from time to time requiring the citizen to declare a primary domicile—may be an adequate alternative. But note that an alternative approach to a disaggregated distribution of rights associated with citizenship, which uses residence as a point of allocation, would be to take residence as the basis for citizenship itself, an argument being advanced today by some scholars writing in the EU (see, e.g., Garot, 1998; Marín, 1998).

ture for adjudicating and resolving disputes between communities than are transitional communities of dual or multinationals.

Federalism and Dynamic Conceptions of Citizenship

As many scholars of federalism have noted, federal nations can be created in quite different ways. For Lenaerts (1990, 263), devolutionary federalism is distinguished from integrative federalism: in integrative federalism, formerly separate states come together to form a stronger centralized government; in devolutionary federalism, a unitary state devolves power to subnational units. For Ackerman (1997), there is prospective federalism, which is created by the movement from a treaty to a constitution, and devolutionary federalism, which is characterized by movement from a constitution to a treaty. Both models illustrate the possibility for shifting paradigms of primacy of citizenships: in the integrative model, one might see a movement from primary identification with the citizenship of the subnational unit to identification with the national unit (i.e., as from a Virginian first to a U.S. citizen first); and in the latter, one might expect to see a contrary movement, from thinking of oneself, for example, primarily as a Belgian to thinking of oneself primarily as a Walloon.[93]

These different models of federalism suggest the fundamental dynamism of our concepts of both sovereignty and citizenship. After a century of consolidation of national power over immigration and citizenship, Schuck (1998b) has noted the importance of devolutionary trends in redefining conceptions of citizenship, particularly in the United States. Including within the devolutionary model both the return of certain powers to the state governments and the development of private residential enclaves, Schuck (1998b, 213) argues that devolution is "fundamentally transforming the rights and duties of membership in the various layers of American polities."[94] Arguing that "nothing in the nature of immigration policy requires that it be an exclusively national level responsi-

---

93. Schuck (2000) suggests more generally the importance of "originating" conditions that lead to federation as having continued effects on a nation's concept of citizenship.

94. Schuck (1998b, 212) emphasizes the depth and importance of these devolutionary changes, asserting that "the structures supporting national power will be almost impossible to restore once they are dismantled" (absent what he sees as the unlikely convergence of a severe crisis accompanied by renewed confidence in national governance and the willingness of states to yield power). Although to some extent I share his concern about the aggressiveness with which the U.S. Supreme Court has sought to constrain national power and elevate the sovereignty of the states, Schuck may be too pessimistic, ignoring the extent to which systems of regular elections for national representatives permit people to shift powers to the levels of government most responsive to their preferences.

bility," he envisions further devolution of policy-making functions with respect to immigration to the states.[95]

Schuck's emphasis is on the changing nature of responsibility for citizenship-related decisions in the U.S. federal system and on a renaissance of efforts to define the national community more narrowly to exclude aliens from the benefits—especially the social welfare benefits—of membership. Feldblum (1998), too, has noted that along with trends toward "post-national citizenship" (p. 241), there are countervailing trends toward what she calls "neo-national membership"—that is, she observes movements that are designed not only to embrace expanded polities but also to achieve what she calls "new closures." Examples abound. The phrase "Fortress Europe" may capture some of this dualism of expanded notions of citizenship within the EU but exclusion of non-EU members from this expanded notion of citizenship. It can also be seen, for example, in France's tightening of its traditional territorial requirements for citizenship to insist that second-generation immigrant children file formal requests to become French, or in Britain's 1981 limitations on citizenship. Feldblum notes a logical relation between facilitating access to citizenship for those already effectively within a polity and closing off physical access to new immigrants and their accompanying demands in the future for admission to citizenship.

Dynamic understandings of citizenship might imply that subnational citizenship in the United States is simply a remnant of its past forms of evolution.[96] For many in the United States, the sense of affiliation derived from citizenship is more likely to be strongest at the national level. There is, however, evidence of stronger feelings of state affiliation in some parts of the country, and there is a danger in relying on the perceptions of academics, who, because of their

95. Schuck (1998a, 201) speculates that the U.S. courts would uphold federal laws authorizing states to adopt policies discriminating against aliens (including legal permanent resident aliens who have lived and worked in the United States less than ten years) in areas where under current interpretations states are not permitted to discriminate against aliens even though the federal government is. *Saenz v. Roe,* however, reiterates that the federal government cannot authorize states to violate the Fourteenth Amendment; so if states are prohibited from certain discriminations because of the equal protection requirements (rather than from a concern for congressional supremacy in foreign affairs), federal authorization to discriminate would not sustain such state laws (see n.11 above).

96. See Rubin and Feeley (1994) (arguing that "federalism" is a "national neurosis," a psychological remnant of a former time, and that it should never be the basis for interpreting or invalidating a national law). Rubin and Feeley contrast the thin state loyalties in the United States with what they regard as "real" bases for federalism, e.g., in Catalonia in Spain, or in Quebec in Canada. I have argued elsewhere that Rubin and Feeley undervalue the states in U.S. federalism, and that federalism is a useful principle even where subnational entities do not correspond to lines of ethnic or linguistic group cleavages. See Jackson (1997, 2217–23).

professional communities, may be particularly postnational in their orienta-tions in generalizing to the meanings of affiliations to others (see Joppke, 1998, 25–26). As both Schuck and Feldblum's essays suggest, affiliative senses of citizenship can wax and wane, sometimes in different directions at once, and thus it would be a mistake for scholars to assume that the only relevantly im-portant affiliations are national or postnational. That is, the danger of both na-tionalist and "anticentral government" backlashes is a real one. Experience sug-gests that federal systems may be particularly likely to give expression to such backlash in subnational units even if not at the national level.

The role of federal organization and changing conceptions of federal citi-zenship are perhaps relevant to one further "cost" of dual nationalities. As Aleinikoff (1997) notes,[97] insisting on unitary citizenship might "serve as a brake" (p. 30) on transnational developments that undermine the loyalty and commitment needed for the healthy functioning of polyethnic national states. He rejects this as a basis for policy making, apparently for empirical reasons. First, he is skeptical that law can "turn the clock back" (p. 36), that is, reverse feelings of multinational affiliation that people who seek dual citizenship have. Second, he argues, that a rule requiring abandonment of one nationality to ac-quire another works to the unfair detriment of people from states that do not allow expatriation. Aleinikoff may be correct in implying that law cannot so much control realities as capture, contain, and manage newly emerging reali-ties, which, in this context, are that economically successful nations like the United States and Germany have attracted many nationals from other states, some of whom would like to become citizens of the place they reside if they can retain their other nationality as well. To these purposes, the primary loyalty oath may make good, practical sense. But the question of whether dual nation-ality will risk increasing ethnonationalist politics is not a trivial one, particu-larly to the extent that dual nationality is maintained in a more ethnically ho-mogenous nation than the United States. For these reasons, the United States might want to move more cautiously in facilitating dual nationality than some postnationalists might prefer.

A cautious move, albeit one raising questions of asymmetry discussed above, would be toward a primary loyalty oath rather than abandoning requirements of loyalty altogether.[98] Dual nationality on a primary loyalty oath basis is in

97. Peter Schuck's (1998b, 223) work also raises concerns that extending dual nationality would facilitate the development of ethnic-national politics and that "the normative foundation of a post-national citizenship may be so thin and shallow that it can easily be swept away by the tides of tribalism or nationalism."

98. Although an even more cautious move would be to maintain the status quo, in which naturalizing immigrants must renounce all other loyalties, the apparent gap between that require-

tension with the idea that citizenship implies equality of those who hold the status, not only within polities like the U.S and Germany, but in others that would then be expected to tolerate something less than primary loyalty from their dual national citizens. Yet the equality implied by citizenship has always been imperfect and qualified by other commitments and demands on citizens. The history of federalism suggests that it is perfectly feasible to insist on primary loyalty to one of multiple polities in which membership is held. It also suggests, however, the need for a more highly developed legal framework— and structure for conflict resolution—by which to reconcile the many components of rights and duties that citizenship in different polities can entail.[99]

Locating (and Managing) Conflicts about Citizenship: A Greater Responsibility for Subnational Units?

Federal nations offer more complexity on the question of who will make and enforce laws relating to citizenship and immigration than do unitary states. They also provide a welter of complex, often interlocking structures for both conflict resolution and negotiation. Federal structures can both invigorate disagreements that might not otherwise come to a pitch,[100] and provide a mechanism for peaceful management and resolution of differences that might otherwise lead to violence. That federalism provides structures for contest—over substantive rules, the allocation of resources, and membership—does not of itself answer the question for any given polity whether a particular federal structure on balance is a good thing. As an example of how contextualized this question is, let me comment briefly on two proposals to devolve power to U.S. states in this arena.

---

ment and the ability of many naturalized citizens to maintain or reacquire dual citizenship is so large that it suggests that the law needs to be brought more into conformity with the realities arising from the practices of other nations and from the absence of enforcement of the implications of the renunciation requirement. For some of the best arguments in favor of a renunciation requirement, see Neuman (1994) (acknowledging that some justifications rest on contestable empirical assumptions).

99. But note again that the internal constitutions of some federal nations may make it difficult to reconcile dual citizenship regimes, whether based on notions of primary loyalty or on allocations of rights based, e.g., on residency. The question of internal constitutional restraints on the powers of nations to establish bilateral or multilateral regimes for the treatment of dual nationals requires more research, at least for the United States, where the Constitution itself is difficult to change.

100. See, e.g., Murphy (1995) (arguing that Belgium's geographical division along language lines has unnecessarily increased the number of disagreements that are seen as disagreements based on language communities).

Some scholars, notably including Spiro (1994), have argued that the states generally ought to exercise a stronger role in immigration and nationality matters.[101] The "fiscal and political geography" of illegal immigration falls unevenly on border states, and, Spiro argues, federal burden sharing has been inadequate. States ought to be free to adopt laws that may impose burdens on immigrants, particularly illegal immigrants, that do not conflict with federal statutes, he argues, and states should not be constitutionally barred from acting because of the "dormant" effects of the foreign affairs powers of the United States.[102] Greater state controls over immigration are appropriate and, he claims, would not result in interference with the foreign relations of the United States, because the other countries of the world now understand the federal structure of the United States and will not attribute conduct by, say, California, to the rest of the United States. This greater understanding derives in part from the greater visibility that subnational units (including the states of the United States) have on the international scene, through, for example, trade and tourism offices abroad. Foreign retaliation, if it occurs, would be directed only at California, according to Spiro, and thus need not concern the rest of us so much.[103]

Spiro's argument from greater international understanding is, I believe, mistaken. While some countries may have such an understanding, it is by no means clear how widespread it is. Moreover, to the extent that the foreign understanding of U.S. federalism is truly a deep one, it would cut against Spiro's argument. As he later suggests, the federal government would retain power to preempt state rules governing such things as immigrant eligibility for services. If

---

101. For a thoughtful argument against the devolution of authority to the states and in favor of exclusive federal power on immigration, see Motomura (1999); and Motomura (1997, 1587–1601) (arguing that the control of immigration is central to the exclusively national concern of self-definition and linking states' absence of authority to exclude citizens from other states to absence of authority to exclude aliens); Motomura (1994, 214–16) (arguing that requiring states to seek relief through a national process rather than engage in self-help provides beneficial slowness, making fair results more likely).

102. Spiro is particularly critical of such cases as *Zschernig v. Miller,* 389 U.S. 429 (1968), holding unconstitutional a state inheritance law that worked to disadvantage citizens of Eastern Europe, and *Plyler v. Doe,* 457 U.S. 202 (1982), holding invalid a state law excluding the children of illegal immigrants from a free public education. In both these cases, he argued, there was no plausible evidence of federal preemption or conflict with extant federal policy. By contrast, he is more accepting of such cases as *Graham v. Richardson,* 403 U.S. 365 (1971), holding unconstitutional state discrimination against legally admitted aliens, as resting on a plausible notion of preemption, which would not constrain the states' policies toward illegal aliens. See, e.g., *DeCanas v. Bica,* 424 U.S. 351 (1976) (rejecting a broad preemption challenge to state law imposing sanctions against those who employed illegal aliens).

103. Spiro thus argues that the rationale of *Chy Lung v. Freeman,* 92 U.S. 275 (1875), which invalidated a state law authorizing a California official to exclude particular incoming passengers, is irrelevant in today's world.

so, and if this were understood, then the federal government's failure to pre-empt in the face of foreign unhappiness could well focus retaliation on the U.S. government. Indeed, although Spiro's article, written in 1994, notes Mexico's restraint in the face of California's enactment of Proposition 187 and its target-ing of expressions of unhappiness to California, some regard Mexico's subse-quent relaxation of its rules on dual nationality, designed to permit its nationals in the United States to become U.S. citizens while retaining Mexican citizen-ship, as a response to Proposition 187 (see Aleinikoff, 1997, 33).

Finally, the notion that the United States as a government does not have a concern if retaliation is "only" focused on a state is surely in tension with the classic observation of Justice Cardozo in *Baldwin v. G. A. F. Seelig, Inc.* that "the Constitution was framed . . . upon the theory that the peoples of the several states must sink or swim together, and that in the long run prosperity and salva-tion are in union and not division" (294 U.S. 511, 523 [1935]; see also *Edwards v. California,* 314 U.S. 160, 171 [1941]). Even if it were the case (as I believe it is not) that Mexico, in response to Proposition 187, would target only Cali-fornia, a basic premise of U.S. federalism, suggested by Justice Cardozo, is that neither the nation nor the states are allowed to act on a basis that harms that befall one state are of no concern to the rest of the nation.

Other scholars have made narrower arguments for the devolution of author-ity on the states to enforce agreed-on norms embodied in national law. Schuck and Williams (1999), for example, argue that the enforcement of national laws requiring the deportation of criminal aliens would be improved if states were given greater enforcement authority, training, and funding, both because states with large immigrant populations have appropriate incentives to enforce these laws and because they are better situated to do so due to their more substantial initial responsibilities for criminal law enforcement. Since states under this pro-posal would be enforcing an agreed-on national norm, the potential for state conduct creating unanticipated foreign policy difficulties or anti-immigrant backlash is diminished (though not entirely eliminated).

The future of subnational entities, both in citizenship and immigration mat-ters and more generally, is the subject of real controversy. Spiro's observation that the states are playing a greater role in the international sphere, with trade offices and the like, touches on an interesting point: whether the effect of so-called globalization will be to increase or decrease the role of the subnational units. Spiro's suggestion is that globalization entails increased international involvement of the states, as the significance of national borders begins to dis-appear. Others are less sure. Friedman (1994), for example, has argued that globalization of law will result in a reduced arena for state regulation, and that only if people become sufficiently alienated from national and supranational governments will they be likely to turn to state and local government structures as sources of opposition.

It strikes me that they are in some respects both likely to be correct. There may be areas in which subnational units exercise greater involvement on the international arena, trade being one area in which the regions in Belgium, the states in the United States, and the provinces in Canada have all undertaken forays. There are other areas—such as the control of military forces—in which I think it likely that central national authorities would strongly resist efforts by subnational units to acquire power or influence.[104] If existing national governments are likely to retain power to decide whether to commit armed force against other sovereign nations (either singly or in collaboration with multinational or international bodies), allowing "too much" subnational unit influence may pose a problem of inappropriate allocation of power to entities that do not have to bear the ultimate costs of diplomacy or military action to deal with conflicts.

Insofar as the social costs of immigration are concerned, some argue that allocating greater power to subnational units (where they bear greater social welfare costs) would increase efficiencies. Devolution of the responsibility for making and funding welfare policy seems likely to increase the odds of subnational units seeking to exclude poorer immigrants; at the same time, subnational units may have incentives to offer benefits to aliens whose skills or talents are perceived to be economically advantageous, notwithstanding national immigration policy. Subnational units with large concentrations of members of particular ethnic groups will be more likely to sustain further immigration of those groups as a result of political and familial pressures. So the consequences of a devolution of responsibility to subnational units are multifarious in terms of immigration and citizenship, though they could be as hostile to extension of social welfare benefits to poorer migrants as constitutional and international law permit.[105]

104. The trend in the United States, e.g., with respect to state militias, has been the increasingly federal control of militias, notwithstanding constitutional language arguably reserving a greater role to the states. See, e.g., *Perpich v. Dept of Defense*, 496 U.S. 334 (1990). For an interesting discussion of the purposes of the militia and military clauses of the U.S. Constitution, see Amar (1998, 46–59).

105. But cf. Schuck (1998a, 143) (finding that many states did not take advantage of what federal law permits in terms of disfavoring legal aliens but instead filled gaps with their own funds and lobbied for the return of full benefits to permanent legal resident aliens); see also Schuck (2000, 203 n.33). Perhaps there is a rapprochement in U.S. and continental ideas that long-term residency entitles one to be treated increasingly as a full member of society. See Feldblum (1998, 238); see also ch. 2 of this volume: Christian Joppke, "The Evolution of Alien Rights in the United States, Germany, and the European Union."

More generally, one could say that the existence of subnational units offers the possibilities of departures from national policies, *both* in the direction of greater inclusiveness and in the direction of greater exclusiveness.[106] While one might be tempted to predict that a federal structure—holding all else equal—might result in a slightly greater tendency to exclusivity, particularly if decision making is at the subnational level (because of concerns that the costs of new immigration should not fall disproportionately on the single state of entry), this would depend on the economics of particular patterns of migration.

In a provocative article, Skerry (1995) suggests that the federal structure of the United States facilitates the assertion of objections to the federal immigration policy by California and other large states: the issue of immigration-related burdens on the states has "been brought to the fore not *in spite of* but *on account of* the federal system" (p. 84, emphasis in original). As he and others note, the notion that the states have not participated in the practical application of immigration and naturalization policy in the United States is not accurate (Skerry, 1995; Shuck and Williams, 1999). States, he points out, as recently as the 1980s sought to encourage immigration, legal as well as illegal, and to distance themselves and protect their illegal immigrant residents from federal enforcement. To the extent that economically successful states tend to attract larger numbers of illegal immigrants who may impose burdens on local resources, moreover, Skerry suggests that the federal form of government permits those states efficaciously to influence the national government's allocation of expenditures and support. Schuck and Williams (1999), too, have noted the political efforts of states that are the major sites of immigration in forcing the federal government to increase its enforcement efforts against illegal immigrants. These instances may demonstrate the capacity of a federal system to manage conflicts peaceably by providing multiple governmental forums in which to contest responsibilities for immigration control.

Skerry's observation suggests a deeper point: that federal systems, perhaps like multinational systems, offer multiple points for the assertion of competing points of view. These multiple points can function as structures of tolerance, particularly if they are formed not around ethnically homogenous, but around culturally diverse, populations. Even if the subnational units do coincide with socially important differences among groups, a federal structure may provide

106. For an older example of a subnational government departing in a more liberal direction, consider the efforts by the Australian state of Western Australia in the 1940s to extend state citizenship to aborigines. While the regime to qualify was onerous and the conferral of state citizenship did not carry with it Australian citizenship, it was nonetheless a deviation from the even more exclusionary policies of the national government at the time. For a more complete description, see Chesterman and Galligan (1997, 132–33).

better possibilities for the development of tolerance than such other alternatives as secession.[107] At the same time, comparative federalism suggests that the allocation of special citizenship rights on the basis of membership in geographical units that coincide with homogenous ethnic, religious, or linguistic groups offers a dangerous potential for exacerbating and heightening conflict, multiplying reinforcing cleavages between people.[108] This may be particularly likely where a national minority group is in the majority in only one unit.[109] Where federalism is built around geographical units with high levels of ethnic, religious, or linguistic unity in a more diverse nation, multiple citizenships have both benign and dangerous possibilities.[110]

On the normative question of whether policy makers should seek to facilitate, encourage, or discourage multiple citizenship, I am thus of many minds. To some extent the answer would depend on the functional significance of the

107. See Linz (1997). As Linz and others have pointed out, in most subnational units with a dominant majority group that is a minority within the nation, there are persons who are, with respect to the majority in the subunit, themselves minorities. The problem of tolerance for minorities within a minority-majority group is a difficult one. A federal system offers opportunities for the protection of the rights of both minorities through the application of nationwide norms of tolerance and enforcement through national organs of government. While international human rights norms may be coming to serve similar functions, enforcement mechanisms are not as well developed and may carry with them higher symbolic costs of inappropriate "intervention" than do the actions of a central government in a federal system. Tushnet (1996a) makes a different point about federalism and the development of tolerance, arguing that by slowing down the force of economic pressures toward assimilation, a federal structure may allow for the gradual development of crosscutting involvements and allegiances between the people in a subunit and the people of the nation that will lead ultimately toward the kind of consensus needed to sustain liberal constitutionalism.

108. History provides many examples of federal structures (particularly where they are closely aligned with homogenous ethnolinguistic groups) built around existing divisions, and thus increasing the opportunities for conflicts. See, e.g., Murphy (1995, 73–100) (arguing that bipolar division of Belgium has reinforced language-based cleavages instead of providing a basis for the development of crosscutting alliances); Haile (1996) (arguing that Ethiopian Constitution will lead to Ethiopia's demise as a country because it devolves too much power to ethnically based subnational units).

109. See Murphy (1995) (arguing that Belgian federalism would have been advanced had the country been divided into federal units corresponding to the eleven existing provinces rather than with the essentially bipolar division into French and Flemish communities). With more subnational governments in the mix, he argues, the possibility for crosscutting alliances on different issues is greater; with the bipolar form, he suggests, a larger array of issues are seen to coincide with the linguistic division, thereby reinforcing it.

110. In other words, it would be a mistake to think that federal structures are necessarily benign, either for the purpose of defining and contesting evolving membership questions or for other purposes. As Linz (1997) has noted, multinational federal nations are "based on the affirmation of . . . characteristics that are not common, that differentiate and separate people" and argues that democratic federalism may, but will not necessarily, help to manage nationality-based conflict.

allocation of rights and duties relating to citizenship (for some of the reasons discussed by Feldblum). There is a sense in which citizenship serves as a marker of membership, affiliation, and group and individual identity in ways that might be inconsistent with allocations of different rights and duties on a functional basis. Moreover, there may be constitutional constraints in some systems on efforts to disaggregate important rights from the status of citizen (e.g., to vote, to hold office, to own property). So, for example, under the U.S. constitutional regime there may be more flexibility to extend voting rights to permanent resident aliens (as suggested by Hammar's denizenship idea),[111] than to extend dual citizenship (i.e., to naturalizing citizens) subject to treatment different than that accorded citizens by birth (other than as specifically set forth by the constitutional disqualification for office).

Note that federalism as a structure offers both barriers and possibilities, different from those of a unitary state, for integration of new groups to citizenship. The barriers may seem more obvious than the possibilities. To the extent that subnational units want to resist immigration and naturalization favored at the national level, they are more likely to be able to do so when they are recognized as having some sort of sovereign status than otherwise. So far so good. But the importance of the subnational units in a federal polity also offers the opportunity for them to take pro-immigration, pro-naturalization positions that may be inconsistent with federal policy. Geographical concentrations of migrant groups in particular states may influence the politics of that state (even before their members are naturalized and able to vote).[112] In the 1980s, numerous jurisdictions (including in New York and California) had official policies of noncooperation with the INS, as they benefited from influxes of immigrants to perform tasks in growing economies. These possibilities of difference, or organized frameworks for resistance to or deviation from national policy, make the study of federalism so interesting and predictions about its tendencies so difficult.[113]

111. See Hammar (1989, 83–84) (discussing "privileged noncitizens," or denizens, in continental Europe and defining denizens as "foreign citizens who have a secure permanent residence status and who are connected to the state by an extensive array of rights and duties"). Hammar (1989) favors, on democratic grounds, either extending voting and other political rights to denizens, or increasing the rates of denizens' naturalizations (p. 93).

112. Note as a possible example the involvement of the New York senators in extending the vote to Spanish-speaking Puerto Ricans, perhaps because some members of the Puerto Rican community had established voting rights in New York and favored the further extension of voting rights to family and friends. For a description, see *Katzenbach v. Morgan,* 384 U.S. 641 (1966).

113. For discussion, see Bauböck (1994,165) (arguing that within present democracies, local definitions of membership can be more open than national ones are).

Conclusion

Federal systems display some remarkable similarities (both among themselves and in comparison to unitary governments) in their treatment of citizenship. There are also marked differences in the evolution of citizenship as a concept within the polity and in the allocation of enforcement powers in the immigration and naturalization process that may precede acquired citizenships. Successful federal systems suggest that multiple citizenships and multiple political affiliations can coexist in ways that rarely conflict with each other and that, when conflicts arise, they can be resolved through conflicts-of-law rules.

Whether multiple citizenships are to be encouraged or discouraged through legal regimes, however, is a difficult question. In part this is because citizenship has strong social, affiliative components; if people can continue to feel affiliated with two or more countries (in part through modern communications and transportation technology) it is not clear that a legal regime of unitary citizenship will significantly displace that sense of affiliation. Nor is it clear that it should be the goal of law to do so, given the emphasis of Western constitutionalism on individual freedom to shape one's own personality and commitments. Moreover, permanent resident immigrants in nations may have both civil and welfare rights that make denial of political rights over the long haul difficult to sustain in a world that values equality to the extent that many nations do. Citizenship is in some ways an engine of equality within a polity, and in some respects the prospects for equality will be enhanced by recognizing multiple citizenships: in successful federal nations state citizenships have not threatened the development of national senses of citizenship and rights.

Yet recognition of multiple citizenships may not be without cost. While multiple citizenships in federal nations have functioned with success, that success is dependent not only on legal principles of priority but on the ability of both levels of government to offer benefits (resources, symbolic benefits, opportunities for participation) that foster public allegiances; the daily life of nested citizenships may offer greater opportunities for building this kind of connection than do multinational multiple citizenships. Citizenship is a concept worth retaining and building on, for its capacity to foster civic, political identities that can be shared with persons of diverse demographics; yet whether in a particular nation that goal is fostered by encouraging, remaining neutral on, or even discouraging multiple national citizenships may elude generalization. The world has had little experience with large groups of persons sustaining dual nationalities over multiple generations, or functioning genuinely as citizens of more than one nation. This possibility is now upon us. Law should recognize and legitimize dual or multiple nationalities that reflect real attachments—hopefully—under a legal regime that coordinates and provides hierarchical rules for defining primary obligations and loyalties in cases where conflicts arise, perhaps drawing on the experience of federal nations. But otherwise law and legal regimes should proceed with real caution before pursuing changes that affirmatively encourage multiple citizenships.

Works Cited

Ackerman, Bruce. 1997. "The Rise of World Constitutionalism." *Virginia Law Review* 83:771.

Agerwal, D. K. 1993. "India." In *International Encyclopedia of Laws*. Vol. 2, *Constitutional Law,* suppl. 3.

Aleinikoff, T. Alexander. 1997. *Citizenship and Membership: Policy Perspectives.* Washington, D.C.: Carnegie Endowment for International Peace.

Amar, Akhil. 1998. *The Bill of Rights: Creation and Reconstruction.* New Haven, Conn.: Yale University Press.

Basu, Durga Das. 1987. *Comparative Federalism.* New Delhi, India: Prentice-Hall.

Bauböck, Rainier. 1994. *Transnational Citizenship.* Aldershot, England: Edward Elgar.

Biskupic, Joan. 1999. "New Resident Limits on Welfare Rejected." *Washington Post,* May 18.

Brubaker, Rogers. 1992. *Citizenship and Nationhood in France and Germany.* Cambridge, Mass.: Harvard University Press.

Bultmann, Peter F. 1998. *Naturalization Policies in the German Länder.* Paper prepared for International Conference on National Law, Immigration, and Integration in Europe and the USA, Paris, June.

Califano, Joseph A., Jr. 1999. "When There's No Draft." *Washington Post.* Apr. 6, Op-ed.

Canada Newswire. 1999. "Implementation of New Immigrant Investor Program." Canada Newswire, March 24.

Carens, Joseph H. 1987. "Aliens and Citizens: The Case for Open Borders." *Review of Policy* 49:251.

Chesterman, John, and Brian Galligan. 1997. *Citizens without Rights: Aborigines and Australian Citizenship.* Melbourne, Australia: Cambridge University Press.

Cohen, Roger. 1999. "Germany Makes Citizenship Easier for Foreigners to Get." *N.Y. Times,* May 22.

Currie, David P. 1994. *The Constitution of the Federal Republic of Germany.* Chicago: University of Chicago Press.

de Groot, Gerard-René. 1998. "The Relationship between the Nationality Legislation of the Member States of the European Union and European Citizenship." In Massimo La Torre (ed.), *European Citizenship: An Institutional Challenge.* The Hague: Kluwer Law International.

Donner, Ruth. 1994. *The Regulation of Nationality in International Law.* 2nd ed. Irvington-on-Hudson, N.Y.: Transnational Publishers.

Feldblum, Miriam. 1998. "Reconfiguring Citizenship in Western Europe." In Christian Joppke (ed.), *Challenge to the Nation State.* Oxford, U.K.: Oxford University Press.

————. 2000. "Managing Membership: New Trends in Citizenship and Nationality Policy." In T. Alexander Aleinikoff and Douglas Klusmeyer (eds.), *From Migrants to Citizens: Membership in a Changing World*. Washington, D.C.: Carnegie Endowment for International Peace.

Feldman, Elliot J., and Lily Gardner Feldman. 1990. "Canada." In Hans J. Michelmann and Panayotis Soldatos (eds.), *Federalism and International Relations: The Role of Subnational Units*. Oxford, U.K.: Clarendon and Oxford University Press.

Flanz, Gisbert H. 1998a. "Austria." In Gisbert H. Flanz (ed.), *Constitutions of the Countries of the World*. Dobbs Ferry, N.Y.: Oceana Publications.

————. 1998b. "Belgium." In Gisbert H. Flanz (ed.), *Constitutions of the Countries of the World*. Dobbs Ferry, N.Y.: Oceana Publications. Release 98-4 (June).

————. 1999a. "Belgium." In Gisbert H. Flanz (ed.), *Constitutions of the Countries of the World*. Dobbs Ferry, N.Y.: Oceana Publications. Release 99-6 (Sept.)

————. 1999b. "Switzerland." In Gisbert H. Flanz (ed.), *Constitutions of the Countries of the World*. Dobbs Ferry, N.Y.: Oceana Publications. Release 99-7 (Nov.).

————. 1982. "Switzerland." In Gisbert H. Flanz (ed.), *Constitutions of the Countries of the World*. Dobbs Ferry, N.Y.: Oceana Publications.

Franck, Thomas M. 1996. "Clan and Superclan: Loyalty, Identity, and Community in Law and Practice." *American Journal of International Law* 90:359.

Freeman, Gary P. 1998. "The Decline of Sovereignty?" In Christian Joppke (ed.), *Challenge to the Nation State*. Oxford, U.K.: Oxford University Press.

Friedman, Barry. 1994. "Federalism's Future in the Global Village." *Vanderbilt Law Review* 47:1441.

Galligan, Brian, and John Chesterman. 1996. "Citizenship and Its Denial in Our Federal State." In S. Rufus Davis (ed.), *Citizenship in Australia: Democracy, Law, and Society*. Carlton, Victoria, Australia: Constitutional Centenary Foundation.

Galloway, J. Donald. 1999. "The Dilemmas of Canadian Citizenship Law." *Georgetown Immigration Law Journal* 13:201.

Garden, J. P. (ed.). 1994. *Hallmarks of Citizenship: A Green Paper*. London: The Institute.

Garot, Marie-José. 1998. "A New Basis for European Citizenship: Residence?" In Massimo La Torre (ed.), *European Citizenship: An Institutional Challenge*. The Hague: Kluwer Law International.

Gewirtz, Paul, and Jacob Cogan (eds.). 1999. *Global Constitutionalism: Life and Death, Citizenship*. New Haven, Conn.: Yale Law School.

Ginsburgs, George. 2000. "Migration and Admittance to Citizenship in Russia." In T. Alexander Aleinikoff and Douglas Klusmeyer (eds.), *From Migrants to Citizens: Membership in a Changing World*. Washington, D.C.: Carnegie Endowment for International Peace.

Gosselink, Robert G. 1994. "Minority Rights and Ethnic Conflict in Assam, India." *Boston College Third World Law Journal* 14:83.

Hagedorn, Heike. 1998. "Falling Borders: Liberal Trends in German Naturalization Policy." Paper prepared for International Conference on National Law, Immigration, and Integration in Europe and the USA, Paris, June.

Hailbronner, Kay. 1998. "Germany's Citizenship Law under Immigration Pressures." Paper prepared for the International Conference on National Law, Immigration, and Integration in Europe and the USA, Paris, June.

Haile, Minasse. "The New Ethiopian Constitution: Its Impact upon Unity, Human Rights, and Development." *Suffolk Transnational Law Review* 20:1.

Hammar, Tomas. 1989. "State, Nation, and Dual Citizenship." In William Rogers Brubaker (ed.), *Immigration and the Politics of Citizenship in Europe and North America*. Lanham, Md.: University Press of America.

Hobsbawn, Eric. 1996. "Language, Culture, and National Identity." *Social Research* 63:1065.

Hoffman, Rainer. 1998. "German Citizenship Law and European Citizenship: Towards a Special Kind of Dual Nationality?" In Massimo La Torre (ed.), *European Citizenship: An Institutional Challenge*. The Hague: Kluwer Law International.

Hogg, Peter. 1997. *Constitutional Law of Canada*. 4th ed. Scarborough, Ontario: Carswell.

Jackson, Vicki C. 1998. "Federalism and the Uses and Limits of Law: Printz and Principle?" *Harvard Law Review* 111:2180.

Jones, Maldwyn A. 1992. *American Immigration*. 2nd ed. Chicago: University of Chicago Press.

Joppke, Christian. 1998. "Immigration Challenges to the Nation-State." In Christian Joppke (ed.), *Challenge to the Nation State*. Oxford, U.K.: Oxford University Press.

Kettmer, James H. 1978. *The Development of American Citizenship, 1608–1870*. Chapel Hill, N.C.: University of North Carolina Press.

Kommers, Donald P. 1997. *The Constitutional Jurisprudence of the Federal Republic of Germany*. 2nd ed. Durham, N.C.: Duke University Press.

Koslowski, Rey. 1998. "European Union Migration Regimes, Established and Emergent." In Christian Joppke (ed.), *Challenge to the Nation State*. Oxford, U.K.: Oxford University Press.

Kreimer, Seth F. 1992. "The Law of Choice and Choice of Law: Abortion, the Right to Travel, and Extraterritorial Regulation in American Federalism." *New York University Law Review* 67:451.

Lane, P. H. 1997. *Lane's Commentary on the Australian Constitution*. 2nd ed. North Ryde, New South Wales: Law Book Co.

La Torre, Massimo. 1998. "Citizenship, Constitution, and the European Union." In Massimo La Torre (ed.), *European Citizenship: An Institutional Challenge*. The Hague: Kluwer Law International.

Legomsky, Stephen H. 1994. "Why Citizenship?" *Virginia Journal of International Law* 35:279.

Leibfried, Stephan. 1979. "The United States and West German Welfare Systems: A Comparative Analysis." *Cornell International Law Journal* 12:175.

Lenaerts, Koen. 1990. "Constitutionalism and the Many Faces of Federalism." *American Journal of Comparative Law* 38:205.

Linz, Juan. 1997. "Democracy, Multinationalism, and Federalism." Paper presented at International Political Science Association Meeting, Seoul, Korea, Aug. Preliminary draft.

Marín, Ruth Rubio. 1998. "Equal Citizenship and the Difference That Residence Makes." In Massimo La Torre (ed.), *European Citizenship: An Institutional Challenge*. The Hague: Kluwer Law International.

Marshall, T. H. 1950. "Citizenship and Social Class." In T. H. Marshall and T. Bottomore, *Citizenship and Social Class*. London: Pluto Press, 1992 ed.

Martin, David A. 1999. "New Rules on Dual Nationality for a Democratizing Globe: Between Rejection and Embrace." *Georgetown Immigration Law Journal* 14:1.

Michelmann, Hans J. 1990. "The Federal Republic of Germany." In Hans J. Michelmann and Panayotis Soldatos (eds.), *Federalism and International Relations: The Role of Subnational Units*. Oxford, U.K.: Clarendon Press and Oxford University Press.

Monar, Jörg. 1998. "A Dual Citizenship in the Making: The Citizen of the European Union and Its Reform." In Massimo La Torre (ed.), *European Citizenship: An Institutional Challenge*. The Hague: Kluwer Law International.

Motomura, Hiroshi. 1994. "Immigration and Alienage, Federalism, and Proposition 187." *Virginia Journal of International Law* 35:201.

———. 1997. Review Essay, "Whose Immigration Law? Citizens, Aliens, and the Constitution." *Columbia Law Review* 97:1567.

———. 1999. "Federalism, International Human Rights, and Immigration Exceptionalism." *University of Colorado Law Review* 70:1361.

Murphy, Alexander. 1995. "Belgium's Regional Divergence: Along the Road to Federalism." In Graham Smith (ed.), *Federalism: The Multiethnic Challenge*. London: Longman.

Neuman, Gerald L. 1992. "We Are the People: Alien Suffrage in German and American Perspective." *Michigan Journal of International Law* 13:259.

———. 1994. "Justifying U.S. Naturalization Policies." *Virginia Journal of International Law* 35:237.

———. 1996. *Strangers to the Constitution*. Princeton, N.J.: Princeton University Press.

Palande, M. R. 1956. *Introduction to the Indian Constitution*. 6th ed. Bombay: Oxford University Press.

Raskin, Jamin B. 1993. "Legal Aliens, Local Citizens: The Historical, Constitutional, and Theoretical Meaning of Alien Suffrage." *University of Pennsylvania Law Review* 141:1391.

Rauschning, Dietrich. 1989. "The Authorities of the German Länder in Foreign Relations." In *1989 Hague Yearbook of International Law*. Norwell, Mass.: Kluwer Law International.

Rosberg, Gerald M. 1977. "Aliens and Equal Protection: Why Not the Right to Vote?" *Michigan Law Review* 75:1092.

Rubenstein, Kim. 1995. "Citizenship in Australia: Unscrambling Its Meaning." *Melbourne University Law Review* 20:503.

Rubin, Edward L., and Malcolm Feeley. 1994. "Federalism: Some Notes on a National Neurosis." *UCLA Law Review* 41:903.

Sastri, Shivadev. 1994. "Lessons for the European Community from the Indian Experience with Federalism." *Hastings Constitutional Law Quarterly* 17:633.

Schuck, Peter H. 1998a. *Citizens, Strangers, and In-Betweens*. Boulder, Colo.: Westview Press.

———. 1998b. "The Re-evaluation of American Citizenship." In Christian Joppke (ed.), *Challenge to the National State*. Oxford, U.K.: Oxford University Press.

———. 2000. "Citizenship in Federal Systems." *American Journal of Comparative Law* 48:195.

Schuck, Peter H., and Rogers Smith. 1985. *Citizenship without Consent: Illegal Aliens in the American Polity*. New Haven, Conn.: Yale University Press.

Schuck, Peter H., and John Williams. 1999. "Removing Criminal Aliens: The Pitfalls and Promises of Federalism." *Harvard Journal of Law and Public Policy* 22:357.

Skerry, Peter. 1995. "Many Borders to Cross: Is Immigration the Exclusive Responsibility of the Federal Government." *Publius: The Journal of Federalism* 25:71.

Smith, Rogers M. 1997. *Civic Ideals: Conflicting Visions of Citizenship in U.S. History*. New Haven: Yale University Press.

Spiro, Peter J. 1994. "The States and Immigration in an Era of Demi-Sovereignties." *Virginia Journal of International Law* 35:121.

———. 1997. "Dual Nationality and the Meaning of Citizenship." *Emory Law Journal* 46:1441.

———. 1999. "The Citizenship Dilemma." *Stanford Law Review* 51:597.

Soysal, Yasemin Nuhoğlu. 1994. *Limits of Citizenship: Migrants and Postnational Membership in Europe*. Chicago: University of Chicago Press.

Tessier, Kevin. 1995. "Immigration and the Crisis in Federalism: A Comparison of the United States and Canada." *Indiana Journal of Global Legal Studies* 8:211.

Tushnet, Mark. 1996a. "Federalism and Liberalism." *Cardozo Journal of International and Comparative Law* 4:329.

———. 1996b. "What Then Is the American?" *Arizona Law Review* 38:873.

Wright, Charles Alan, Arthur R. Miller, and Edward H. Cooper. 1984. *Federal Practice and Procedure*. Vol. 5. St. Paul, Minn.: West Publishing.

Wurzel, Eckward. 1996. "Germany: The Welfare System." In *OECD Observer* 1202 (Oct.–Nov.).

Young, Margaret. 1992. *Immigration: Constitutional Issues*. Law and Government Division, Research Branch, Library of Parliament. Rev.

———. 1996. *Canada's Immigration Program*. Law and Government Division, Research Branch, Library of Parliament.

Zappalà, Gianni, and Stephen Castles. 1999. "Citizenship and Immigration in Australia." *Georgetown Immigration Law Journal* 13:273.

CHAPTER SIX

Ethnic Marginalization as Statelessness: Lessons from the Great Lakes Region of Africa

FRANCIS M. DENG

IN MY VISITS to countries with serious problems of internal displacement in my continuing dialogues with governments as the representative of the UN Secretary-General on Internally Displaced Persons, I begin by discussing the problem with leaders at the national level. I then move down the ladder of authority, ending with the affected population. I discuss their conditions and specific needs for protection and assistance. I then go back to the leaders at various levels to share what I have learned and to offer recommendations.

In this context, I asked displaced persons in one Latin American country what they wanted me to take back to their national leaders. "Those are not our leaders," responded their spokesman. "To them, we are not citizens, but criminals, and our only crime is that we are poor." It was interesting that he emphasized a class aspect, although the people involved were clearly members of an indigenous ethnic group. It showed the class dimension of the Marxist-inspired guerrilla movements in the country.

In a country of the former Soviet Union, the same question received an almost identical response: "We have no leaders there! Those are not our leaders." The spokeswoman was clearly speaking in ethnopolitical terms. In yet another country, this time in Africa, the prime minister, talking about the civilian population in a conflict zone, reportedly said to a senior representative of a

I am profoundly grateful to Anne-Marit Austbo, who, as my research assistant at the Brookings Institution, contributed substantially to the preparation of this chapter.

UN humanitarian agency, "The food you give to those people is killing my soldiers." Unlike his regard for his soldiers, the prime minister clearly did not regard "those people," whom he identified ethnically with the rebel movement fighting his government, as citizens, as his people.

These examples represent a mild version of marginalization. Oftentimes, sentiments of inclusion and exclusion can be deadly and in extreme cases genocidal as the cases of Rwanda and the former Yugoslavia tragically dramatize. Following the 1994 genocide in Rwanda and its outflow of refugees, ethnic carnage spread into the Congo. By October 1996, the eastern Congo erupted into rampant violence that rapidly spread throughout the Great Lakes region, with ripple effects reaching far beyond. Although the conflict, which today involves at least six neighboring states, has multiple factors at its root, the dispute over the citizenship rights of the Banyarwanda, a group of people of Rwandan origin living in the eastern Congo, is both a contributing factor and a consequence of the crisis. The issues, which affect the entire region, are nationality, ethnicity, and political and economic power. Formally and informally, individuals are being denied the right to citizenship owing to their ethnicity. The denial is a manifestation of a more pervasive and diffused process of discrimination and marginalization in the political, economic, and social processes of the country.

An example of the complexity of the issues is the case of the Banyamulenge (Tutsi) in the Congo. It illustrates the dilemmas of the role of ethnicity in the process of statecraft and nation building in Africa. Many African countries face similar dilemmas at varying levels: definitional issues of the legal meaning of statelessness versus the broader notion of ethnic marginalization; the interplay between ethnicity as an exclusive notion of group identity and citizenship as an inclusive concept of nationhood; and the interconnectedness of the conflicts emanating from ethnic marginalization, which calls for regional cooperation in developing a comprehensive framework of protection and assistance for all those under state sovereignty.

The ways these factors have developed in the Great Lakes region of Africa all indicate that these themes seem to turn (in one way or another) on the problem of boundary making, be it the membership of a race, ethnicity, nation, class, legal category, or state. The Banyamulenge case demonstrates with exceptional clarity the myriad ways such boundaries are constructed; their importance in the allocation of power, position, and resources; and the role of contingent and contextual factors in the definition of any boundary.

The Parameters of Citizenship

Citizenship, used synonymously with nationality, is predicated on elements of ethnic and cultural affiliation. As one specialist on the subject observes,

In the practice of states, nationality is not granted indiscriminately, but generally reflects factors, which in turn indicate an established link between the individual and the state. Evidence of this "link" is found specifically, for example, in place of birth, descent, or strong ties established through residence, among others. (Batchelor, 1998, 157)

The right to citizenship is a means of acquiring status under the law and through that status the right to enjoy many other entitlements of life, such as the right to vote, to own property, to health care, to send one's children to school, to employment, and to travel outside one's country of residence. In the often-quoted words of Chief Justice Earl Warren, "Citizenship is man's basic right, for it is nothing less than the right to have rights" (*Trop v. Dulles,* 1958, quoted in Batchelor, 1998, 159).

But the status of citizenship is more than one of legal determinism. It is often a condition of belonging and being accepted as a member of a nation, characterized by a collective sense of identity through such factors as descent, ethnicity, and culture. In a tribal community or a nation-state, these elements normally converge in homogeneity. The modern state, particularly in Africa, is a construct that has severed tribal, ethnic, and cultural groups and brought together other groups, creating a framework of unity in diversity, often with sharp discrepancies in the shaping and sharing of power, wealth, and other entitlements.

In this respect, the distinction between the exclusivist understanding of ethnicity and the inclusive concept of citizenship is pertinent. On the one hand, it represents an ascriptive concept of ethnicity defined through such means as shared bloodlines, common (inherited) cultural characteristics and practices, and a shared origin of historical descent. On the other hand, it is a *democratic* concept of citizenship based on shared political allegiances, common territorial residence, and collective participation in self-government. The first highlights an ascriptive model of membership; the second emphasizes a consensual or voluntary (and participatory) model of membership. Since nearly every modern state comprises multiple ethnic groups, a state's use of ascriptive membership criteria can be a potent source of division, conflict, and marginalization. By contrast, a democratic model of citizenship offers an important alternative basis (to the ethnic model) of demarcating national membership boundaries that transcend particularistic group identities.

In this chapter I challenge a naturalized account of ethnic membership directly by showing how contingent or circumstantial the self-understandings of ethnic group memberships can be in terms of the common construction of collective identities. In addition, I argue that all practical models of citizenship have fundamental ascriptive dimensions in demarcating boundaries and in determining membership. The institution of citizenship may then offer a potentially broad basis for the civic inclusion of diverse groups within a shared polity. Perceiving this potential, however, should not obscure the strong exclusionary aspects of citizenship or its limitations as a framework for cooperation, cohesion, and the mediation of differences.

In many countries, diversity is accepted as a feature of the modern state that does not significantly affect the enjoyment of the rights of citizenship. In other countries, notably in Africa and in the countries of the former Yugoslavia and the former Soviet Union, diversity was either nominally recognized or it persisted as a state policy or beneath the surface because of the repressive policies of forced unification and uniformity. In these situations, diversities may generate a crisis of national identity reflected in a gap between the way the state is perceived and the way individual groups perceive themselves or are perceived by others. As a matter of policy, the dominant group then either attempts to assimilate the other groups or relegates them to a lower status of citizenship in the enjoyment of their civil, political, economic, social, and cultural rights. In either case, the result is marginalization, which the subordinate group accepts, if its members lack the capacity to resist, or oppose, sometimes through violent means, if they have the capacity to resist. When these contradictions erupt into violent conflict with tragic humanitarian consequences, the tenor of the state's response to the needs of affected populations also reflects the marginalization of the subordinate groups.

The tensions and conflicts between the expectations associated with citizenship and the deprivations of ethnic marginalization cause African states serious dilemmas. If they recognize ethnicity as a reality that should be used in nation building, then they risk encouraging divisiveness and fragmentation. If African countries choose to disregard ethnicity, as they often do, by burying their heads in the sand, serious political repercussions result.

Attitudes on ethnicity and the threat of marginalization leading to the denial of citizenship or the rights associated with it are encouraged by the wide discretion that nationality laws appear to give the state in determining a person's legal status. In international law, statelessness refers to the status of a "person who is not considered as a national by any State under the operation of its law" (1954 Convention relating to the Status of Stateless Persons, Art. 1). This technical definition, it has been argued, precludes full realization of an effective nationality, including the quality and attributes of citizenship (Batchelor, 1995, 232). An individual may hold a nationality in the legal sense but still lack the usual attributes of nationality, including the provision of protection and other basic needs. The crucial question then becomes one of how effective nationality is in granting the rights of citizenship. Often, there is a gap between the technical question of being ascribed a nationality and the enjoyment of all the rights associated with citizenship. It has been observed that "states tend to view the matter in either simple legal terms or with highly charged sentiments of membership based on exclusive notions of race, descent or other qualifying factors" (Batchelor, 1995, 238). Approaching the issue in this broad perspective opens doors to appreciating the multifaceted challenges of forging a commonsense view of nationhood in countries that are characterized by racial, ethnic, cultural, linguistic, religious, and regional diversity.

If citizenship is "nothing less than the right to have rights," stateless people are stripped of the right to have rights. The question is whether the legal definition of statelessness covers the many people for whom this is the reality. This question is of particular relevance to those situations where many people may not be formally deprived of their citizenship, but are so marginalized that it makes little sense to identify them legally as citizens. The situation of the Tutsi in Rwanda during the early 1990s provides an extreme example. One can argue that they were not deprived of the right to have rights—their formal citizenship—but they were certainly denied the rights that flow from citizenship. However, the distinction becomes academic when what is being denied is the fundamental right to life, evidenced by the genocide of 1994. "There is a need to address the issue as a question of protection rather than one simply of recognition under the law as either a national or a non-national" (Batchelor, 1995, 234).

The term *de facto statelessness,* introduced during World War II in response to the situation of German Jews, was intended to provide a status for people who had a nationality on paper, but who lacked effective national protection. When the conventions on the status of refugees and stateless persons were drafted, it was assumed that all de facto stateless persons would fall under the refugee convention and that there would be no need to include them in the Convention on Statelessness. There were two reasons for this. First, there was an underlying assumption that all de facto stateless persons would be outside their habitual country of residence. Second, it was also assumed that de facto statelessness was the result of some act by the individual concerned, such as fleeing the country of nationality because of persecution. Today, it is clear that not all de facto stateless persons are refugees. There are many people who do not enjoy effective protection but for whom both the refugee and statelessness conventions do not apply. They are individuals who have the nationality of the country where they live on paper and have effective ties to those countries but who are marginalized insofar as they cannot be considered to be receiving the rights and responsibilities normally associated with nationality (Batchelor, 1995, 233).

Ethnicity and the Challenge of Nationhood

As noted earlier, concepts of identity based on race, ethnicity, culture, language, religion, and territory or region often overlap with notions of national identity and citizenship. The diversities and disparities in these areas also influence the determination of status in sharing national values, including power, economic resources, and opportunities for social and cultural development. In Africa, descent and the continuation of lineage as a form of genetic and social immortality are the foundation stones of its value system. African traditional religious beliefs are worldly oriented and focus on a form of life in the hereafter that is largely dependent on continuity through the ancestral line as perpetuated by successive generations in the lineage. Closely associated with this genealogically based identity is an attachment to land, often perceived as the resting place of the ancestors whose graves, marked or anonymous, symbolize the group's belonging to a given piece of land or territory. These values explain the inalienability of land in African customary law. A classic dictum attributed to a Nigerian chief holds that "land belongs to a vast family of which many are dead, few are living, and countless members are unborn" (statement to West African Lands Committee, 1912, quoted in Elias, 1956, 162). The sanctity of land as a symbol of identity therefore lies primarily in its embodiment of material, moral, and spiritual values associated with continued ancestral identity and influence. Implicit in this notion of continuity is a sense of group solidarity that delicately balances individual interests with those of the lineage or the community. It is the pride and dignity associated with this sense of belonging that keeps alive the memory of the dead, on which depends the immortality of every individual in the ancestral chain. These concepts are then broadened to encompass tribal or ethnic group identity and, at the most inclusive level, race.

Anthropological literature usually identifies several characteristics as indicators of ethnicity: it is largely self-perpetuating biologically; it shares fundamental cultural values, overtly realized in a unity of cultural forms; it is a matrix of communication and interaction; and it has a membership that identifies itself, and is identified by others, as distinguishable from other categories of the same order (Barth, 1969, 10–11). This definition supports "the traditional proposition that a race [equals] a culture [equals] a language and that a society [equals] a unit which rejects or discriminates against others" (pp. 10–11).

Although these criteria are accepted as objective indicators, scholars generally recognize self-identification with a particular group as the crucial determinant of identity. As Crawford Young (1976, 20) argues, "In the final analysis, identity is a subjective, individual phenomenon; it is shaped through the constantly recurrent question to ego, 'Who am I?' with its inevitable corollary,

'Who is he?' Generalized to the collectivity, these [questions] become 'Who are we?' and 'Who are they?' " Young qualifies the element of subjectivity by noting that "subjective identity itself is affected by the labels applied by others" (p. 43), but as he implies, there is more to the objective factors than their effect on subjectivity:

> Although identity is subjective, multiple, and situationally fluid, it is not infinitely elastic. Cultural properties of the individual do constrain the possible range of choice of social identities. Physical appearance is the more indelible attribute; where skin pigmentation serves to segment communities, only a handful of persons at the color margins may be permitted any choice of identity on racial lines. (Young, 1976, 43–44)

Race, which breeds *racism,* the "stepchild of prejudice," is "based . . . on conspicuous physical differentiation . . . which facilitates the stereotyping process" (p. 49). Ethnicity is often based on verifiable attributes that may include language, territory, political unit, or common value systems. Nelson Kasfir (1990, 365–66) defines ethnicity to encompass "all forms of identity that have at their root the notion of a common ancestor-race as well as 'tribe'" and broadens the concept to include religion and region, which, though quite different from ethnicity, are "sometimes also taken as stereotypical indicators of common ancestry." After observing that individuals usually have multiple identities from which to choose, Kasfir concedes that the choice "depends on the particular situation, not merely on the individual's preference," but he emphasizes that while "objective ethnic characteristics (race, language, culture, place of birth) usually provide the possible limits, subjective perception of either the identifier or the identified—whether objectively accurate or not—may turn out to be decisive for the social situation" (p. 366).[1]

It is widely accepted that the salient element in the national identity of Africa is the "tribe." But as one scholar observed,

> European colonizers not only denied that African tribes were nations, dismissing them as peoples without history, but artificially and mechanically joined several of them into administrative and/or political units. . . .

---

1. Objective indicators can indeed be so nebulous that it is not easy to tell the ethnic identity of an individual or, for that matter, to distinguish between groups. In addressing large audiences in Burundi, I often found myself recognizing some people who looked like typical Tutsi, and, others who looked stereotypically Hutu, and many I could not identify. When I asked some ministers whether they could always tell a Tutsi from a Hutu, the foreign minister's response was, "Yes, but with a margin of error of 35 percent."

[P]eoples of different nations were invested with common citizenship if they were subjects of the same colonial state. It also meant that the same notion could be vivisected across state territories. . . . Therefore, African states cannot be characterized as nation-states of the Western European type. . . . In fact, colonialism thwarted the natural development of state-hood and citizenship in Africa. (Oommen, 1997)

The basic characteristics of the colonial state have been adopted and assimilated by independent African states. The marginalization of indigenous cultures in the political, economic, social, and cultural development of African countries has in most cases set the state apart from the context of its people. While this was to be expected of the colonial state, in most cases, independent African states have tended to be even more oblivious to indigenous cultures than were the colonial masters. Nonetheless, ethnicity continues to assert itself, giving the notion of citizenship a duality that relates to both the inclusive concept of nationhood and the exclusive notions of group identity.

Current discussions about citizenship are focused on how to solve the problem of the inherent tension between these two sets of identification. It has been observed: "Citizenship is intimately linked to the ideas of individual entitlement on the one hand, and of attachment to a particular community on the other" (Kymlick and Norman, quoted in Lehning, 1997, 2). In other words, citizenship has to do with both individual rights and collective identity. *Inherent tension* lies in the paradox that excessive focus on one aspect can undermine the other. The liberal approach to citizenship, which focuses on individual rights, can undercut the effective ties between the national community and the individual. The communitarian approach also has its problems. If the national community is based on one dominant culture, important segments of the society might be excluded. Yet, if the differences between all subgroups are affirmed and promoted, a common national culture might cease to exist (Heilman, 1998, 370).

There is no doubt that Africa's arbitrary borders have contributed to the tension and instability associated with ethnic diversity within the state. Questions have been raised as to whether the problems of the continent are attributable largely to the artificiality of Africa's borders or the mismanagement of ethnic differences. There is an increasing tendency in the Africanist community to play down the significance of ethnic diversity and disparity created by colonial borders. Mahmood Mamdani (1998b) is among the group of scholars who believe that arbitrary borders are not the source of Africa's problems, saying that "all borders are more or less arbitrary" (p. 1). The problem lies in "the way the state is being run" (Mamdani, 1997). While he is of course correct, there is no denying that the problem of ethnic diversity, which the state is called upon to manage, emanates from arbitrary state borders that did not consider ethnic composition. The problem is compounded because the colonial state preserved exclusive notions of identity through tribal and ethnic affiliation, while encouraging a progressive move toward an inclusive sense of nationhood that is inherently in conflict with tribalism and such other factors of exclusion as language, religion, and region.

This duality has been thoroughly analyzed by Mamdani (1996) in his influential study *Citizen and Subject: Contemporary Africa and the Legacy of Late Colonialism*. Mamdani argues that the system of indirect rule established by the colonial powers created two different ideas of citizenship that postcolonial governance has failed to abolish. During colonialism, only the white settlers were granted rights under civil law enforced by the state. Natives were considered to belong to an "ethnic space" governed by customary law, which was enforced by a "native authority."

> Every colony had two legal systems: one modern, the other customary. Customary law was defined in the plural, as the law of the tribe, and not in the singular, as the law for all natives. Thus, there was not one customary law for all natives, but roughly as many sets of customary laws as there were said to be tribes. The genius of British rule in Africa ... was in seeking to civilize Africans as communities, not as individuals. More than anywhere else, there was in the African colonial experience a one-sided opposition between the individual and the group, civil society and community, rights and tradition. (p. 22)

To enforce customary law, tribal leadership was either reconstituted selectively to ensure loyalty or reinvented and imposed where none had existed, as was the case in the so-called acephalous, or stateless, societies.[2] But the power of the native authority was more than one of administering justice by applying customary law. "Not only did the chief have the right to pass rules (bylaws) governing persons under his domain, he also executed all laws and was the administrator in 'his' area, in which he settled all disputes. The authority of the chief thus fused in a single person all moments of power: judicial, legislative, executive, and administrative" (Mamdani, 1996, 23).

These rigid formulations ran against the fluidity of ethnicity as "culturally defined identities, malleable over time and contextual in their meanings"

---

2. In his review of *Citizen and Subject,* Pierre Englebert (1997, 773) draws attention to Mamdani's emphasis on the "uncustomary" nature of native authorities, which contests Goran Hyden's view that the African peasantry is uncaptured.

(Newbury, 1997, 219). According to Elizabeth Colson (1969), whose observations support Mamdani's view that colonialism reinforced and may have even created tribal structures,

> Tribal organizations were created during the colonial period when the desire for orderly administration led administrators to amalgamate formerly independent communities into larger units under officially appointed leaders. Wherever possible, European officials drew political boundaries to coincide with language or cultural boundaries, since they assumed this would provide a natural cohesion and stability to the administrative unit. (p. 29)

Note that the "civil," or modern, legal system was not entirely closed to Africans, for those Africans who were *de-tribalized*—urbanized or otherwise "civilized"—could change their status and be governed by the inclusive laws of the country. Indeed, even after colonialism, when the classification could no longer be based on a racial and cultural stratification, the duality of the legal system persisted. Civic space was de-racialized in the sense that the rights of the individual did not depend on membership in a racial group. Civic citizenship ceased to be exclusive to group membership. While introducing the rule of civil law to all its citizens, however, many African countries left the native authorities in charge of local administration in rural areas. Civic rights continued to be defined as individual rights in the civil and political sphere, while customary rights were defined as group rights, accessed by virtue of belonging to an ethnic group. For poor people, however, ethnic citizenship was far more important than civic citizenship because belonging to an ethnic group gave one a customary right, especially to land.

While Mamdani's analysis focuses on the dichotomy between the indigenous and the nonindigenous, the settlers and original inhabitants, marginalization in postcolonial Africa is a dynamic that characterizes the relations of various indigenous groups in the process of competing for power and other national resources. The contest for state power and wealth becomes a conflict of identities with the objective of capturing the state and excluding others or incorporating them selectively in a stratified political, economic, social, and cultural hierarchy. The response of marginalized groups ranges from an effort to restructure state power, to a demand for decentralization, and, at the opposite extreme, a claim for self-determination that might result in secession, where there is a correlation between ethnic and territorial identification.

Citizenship and Dynamics of the Great Lakes Region

I have pointed to the Banyarwanda in the Congo. For them, the issues of ethnic identity and the extent to which they determine inclusion or exclusion from citizenship are prominent. *Banyarwanda* is a collective term for people of Rwandan origin who started settling in the eastern Congo more than two hundred years ago. The Banyarwanda speak the Rwandan language, Kinyarwanda, and comprise the two traditional castes in Rwandan society, the Tutsi and Hutu. The Banyarwanda are mainly settled in two regions of eastern Congo, North and South Kivu. While the composition of the Banyarwanda in North Kivu is mixed, being composed of both Hutu and Tutsi, the Tutsi predominate in South Kivu.[3] The Banyarwanda in South Kivu are known as Banyamulenge, a term that today refers to the Tutsi living in the Congo.

Rwandan Immigration to the Congo (Zaire)

Rwandan immigration to the Congo can be divided into two different waves, one to North Kivu and the other to South Kivu. Before the massive influx of about 1 million Rwandan refugees in 1994, about half the 3 million people of North Kivu were Banyarwanda. Approximately 80 percent of these were Hutu (Human Rights Watch: Africa, 1997, 8). The first group of Banyarwanda—both Hutu and Tutsi—are estimated to have arrived in North Kivu more than two hundred years ago (Prunier, 1997, 195). According to Gerard Prunier (1996a), they constituted a protectorate west of the main Rwandan kingdom (p. 2, n.1). When the colonial powers drew their borders, the Rwandans living in this area found themselves in the Belgian Congo.

Another influx of Rwandans to the Congo took place between 1937 and 1955. Some eighty thousand Banyarwanda, mostly Hutu, were forced by the Belgians to move from the overpopulated Rwanda-Urundi region to work on colonial plantations in the eastern Congo. Others were encouraged by the colonial power, which gave them land, tools, and other incentives to move (Makombo, 1998, 51). It is estimated that two hundred thousand persons immigrated to Kivu during the colonial period (De Saint Moulin, 1975, 115).

The next wave of immigration consisted of Tutsi who fled massacres in Rwanda in 1959–1963 during the revolution that created a Hutu-dominated state at independence. Many other Banyarwanda also immigrated into the fertile regions of Kivu for economic reasons (Makombo, 1998, 52). Finally, in

3. Hutu clients who had come with their Tutsi patrons were "Tutsified" over the years (Prunier, 1997, 195).

August 1994, a wave of Hutu refugees arrived in North Kivu after the Rwandan Patriotic Front (RPF) won the civil war and ended the genocide in Rwanda.

Immigrants into South Kivu included Banyarwanda Tutsi, often referred to as Banyamulenge. The number of Banyamulenge in the eastern Congo before 1994 is estimated at two hundred thousand to four hundred thousand.[4] The date of the first arrival of Kinyarwanda-speaking people in South Kivu is more disputed than that of Banyarwanda in North Kivu. The question is highly political and central to the citizenship debate; estimates of the date range from the sixteenth to the nineteenth centuries. Banyamulenge advocates argue that their ancestors settled in present-day eastern Congo during the seventeenth century in the hills they have named Mulenge, and from which their name, Banyamulenge, derives (Nzongola-Ntalaja, 1999, 2). Indigenous Congolese groups, as well as the former Zairean government, on the other hand, have claimed that the Banyamulenge did not arrive until the colonial period.[5] According to Mamdani, Mulenge is the name of the area where the Tutsi were first allowed to settle by a local tribe, the Balfuro. In 1924, the colonial power granted the Banyamulenge permission to occupy the high plateau farther south. This is why some claim that the Banyamulenge did not arrive until 1924 (Mamdani, 1997). The United Nations's Special Rapporteur on Human Rights in Zaire has gathered strong evidence that Banyamulenge were settled in Kivu at least by the end of the eighteenth century (ECOSOC, 12, n.6).

It is not just the date of arrival of Banyamulenge that is controversial. The term *Banyamulenge* is contested by Balfuro, who feared that the claim to a place-based identity really masks an immigrant strategy designed to lay claim to local land. "Why else, many ask, would the Banyamulenge seek to distinguish themselves from the Banyarwanda, except to erase their history, the fact that they came from Rwanda?" (Mamdani, 1997).

There are, however, other possible reasons for the Banyamulenge wanting to distance themselves from the Banyarwanda in North Kivu. According to David Newbury (1997, 216), the first Tutsi to settle in South Kivu were not subjects of the royal court, as the Banyarwanda in North Kivu were, but refugees who fled intense competition between diverse political units in Rwanda. Consequently, the Banyamulenge remained separate from the Rwandan state. "Over the years the southern Kivu Tutsi diverged more and more from their truly Rwandese brothers, to the point that they speak a distinct dialect of

---

4. The number seen most frequently is four hundred thousand. However, Prunier (1996a, 3) argues that this is an incorrect number, presented by Banyamulenge advocates, and that the real number is two hundred thousand.

5. Deputy Prime Minister Kamanda wa Kamanda informed the UN Security Council that the Banyamulenge arrived in 1924 (ECOSOC, 12, n.6).

Kinyarwanda, easily recognizable from the standard language" (Prunier, 1996a, 2).

According to Mamdani, the Banyamulenge in South Kivu used to be known simply as *Banyarwanda,* or *Batutsi,* until 1972, when the Tutsi sought to separate themselves from Tutsi in Rwanda because of the Hutu massacre in Burundi (Mamdani, 1997). Since mid-1996, the term *Banyamulenge* has been used widely to refer to ethnic Tutsi in the eastern Congo (Human Rights Watch: Africa, 1997, 8).

Early Sources of Conflict between the Banyarwanda and Indigenous Groups

According to Georges Nzongola-Ntalaja (1999, 2–3), Congolese peoples welcomed the Kinyarwanda-speaking immigrants with open arms "until the numbers of Banyarwanda grew progressively owing to a natural increase and to clandestine immigration in the post-colonial period." The basis of the conflict was laid during the colonial period, however, and is strongly related to the ways that land is distributed in the region.

In Kivu, the power to allocate customary land lies with a Native Authority. Membership in a Native Authority is restricted to the members of an ethnic group, and only ethnic groups classified as indigenous have the right to have a Native Authority. Only one group of Banyarwanda in Kivu—those of the precolonial settlement in North Kivu—was considered indigenous and had its own Native Authority and consequently also its own land. Other Banyarwanda had to pay homage to existing chiefs to get access to land in the areas where they settled. The Native Authority in Kivu comprises hierarchical levels. Those considered nonindigenous usually have a chief of the lowest order from their ranks who must answer to the higher chiefs. In addition to the power to allocate land, these higher chiefs confirm ethnic belonging, issue identity cards, run local markets, and oversee administration.

The system of Native Authorities has been a source of conflict in two ways. First, some Banyarwanda who arrived during colonial rule claimed their own Native Authority, and the Belgians at certain times granted this claim. This situation led to protests among indigenous Congolese groups. Second, when they found themselves unable to gain access to land, the Banyarwanda started to purchase it through the market. This practice conflicted with the customary right to land. While the Banyarwanda considered their land to be private property, the chiefs expected a tribute to be paid from those immigrants using the land without a customary right to it. According to the land laws established by the Belgian colonizers, all "vacant land" belonged to the state, while lands occupied by the native population continued to be governed by customary laws. The problem was that the notion of vacant land was never clearly defined, and, in practice, land that lay fallow was considered vacant, even though it was meant to be used eventually by indigenous cultivators (Meditz and Merrill, 1993, 170). Furthermore, a system of land registration was introduced whereby any land coming under the state's domain ceased to be governed by customary law and was eligible to be granted by the state to individuals and enterprises.

This tension between the Banyarwanda and indigenous groups grew more intense as Rwandan immigration to the region increased. At the time of independence in 1960, the Banyarwanda in some areas had tilled and valorized most of the land and had come to constitute a majority of the population. The end of colonial rule did not solve the problem. The land system of the colonial period, which recognized two ways of acquiring land, remained in force after independence. In North Kivu, the tension resulted in a Kinyarwanda rebellion in 1965. Although the rebellion lasted for only two years, the underlying conflict continued for decades: "As a consequence all Kinyarwanda speakers came to be considered non-indigenous" (Mamdani, 1997).

In South Kivu, tensions between the Banyamulenge and their neighbors became more intense after 1964–1965 (Sebiterko, 1996a), when the Banyamulenge helped the army to crush a rebellion supported by indigenous Congolese groups. There seems to be a general consensus that it was only during and after the 1964–1965 civil war that the tension in South Kivu started between the Banyamulenge and their neighbors (Mamdani, 1997). This event "instilled a deep and lingering resentment against the Banyamulenge within other ethnic groups in the region" (IRIN, 1996, 3). In North Kivu, however, the alliances were reversed; the Banyarwanda sided with the rebels, whose indigenous groups supported the army. Nevertheless, the consequences were the same in the two regions: "The whole thing left deep scars in the local consciousness" (Prunier, 1996a, 2).

Another factor that contributed to resentment toward the Banyarwanda was their relative economic strength. This power, however, was not reflected in local political power, which was restricted to the indigenous population. Tension created by disputes over land, the civil war, and economic envy did not translate into explicit disputes about citizenship until the Banyarwanda began to develop strategies to overcome the problems that the system of Native Authorities had created for them.

Excluded from exercising power locally, [the Banyarwanda] made every effort to be elected at higher provincial and national levels. This in turn provoked a response from amongst the 'indigenous' majority. Afraid that

the Banyarwanda would use national representation to acquire power locally, 'indigenous' Congolese came to oppose citizenship rights for them."
(Mamdani, 1997)

Disputed Citizenship

In 1920, a Congolese roundtable conference was held in Brussels to discuss which indigenous peoples would legitimately inherit an independent Congo. The conference, in which a Congolese delegation participated, concluded that the Banyarwanda should be included among the beneficiaries. No explicit reference was made to nationality, but a resolution was adopted that recognized the right of the Banyarwanda to vote on the same ground as Belgians with metropolitan or Congolese status, provided they could prove ten years' residence in the Congo (Cyubahiro, 1989, 43). According to Nzongola-Ntalaja (1999, 2), the legal distinction between the Banyarwanda and other Congolese "became academic" between 1920 and 1962, when Belgium governed present-day Burundi, the Congo, and Rwanda as a single colonial entity.

In 1959, a legislative decree reaffirmed the 1920 resolution on the Banyarwanda's right to vote on condition of ten years' residency and added they also had the right to run for office (ECOSOC, 6, 18). In 1960, Electoral Law 13 reaffirmed that a person required Congolese status or ten years' residence in the country in order to vote. Most of the Banyarwanda, including those immigrants who arrived during independence, voted in the first municipal elections, and in 1960 the Banyarwanda were broadly represented in almost all the Congo's political institutions.

Just before independence in 1960, a new roundtable was held in Brussels (ECOSOC, 17). According to Mamdani (1997), tension between the Banyarwanda and indigenous groups in North Kivu had rendered the nationality status of the Kinyarwanda-speaking minority so sensitive that the roundtable conference was simply unable to fix the juridical status of the Banyarwanda. "It concluded that the Congolese people themselves should decide on this issue, introducing an element of insecurity in the juridical status of the Kinyarwanda-speaking minority." The 1920 resolution remained in force until 1964, when the Luluabourg Constitution was adopted. Article 6 of the constitution stated that "Congolese citizenship is recognized [for] every person, one of whose parents was or had been a member of one of the tribes established within the territory of the Republic of the Congo in its borders as defined on 18 October 1908."[6]

6. "[E]st attribuee a le date du 30 juin 1960, a toute personne dont un des ascendants est ou a ete membre d'une tribu ou d'une partie de tribu etablie sur le territoire du Congo avant le 18 octobre 1908" (Cyubahiro, 1989, 57).

There is little doubt that Rwandan-speaking Hutu and Tutsi were established within the territory of the Congo before 1908. Robert Garreton, the UN Special Rapporteur on the Human Rights Situation in Zaire, actually defines the Banyarwanda as the "Bahutu and Batutsi who were established in the territory of Congo before that date" (ECOSOC, 17). This definition, however, excludes many Kinyarwanda-speaking Hutu and Tutsi who immigrated later and who are normally referred to as Banyarwanda. Cyubahiro argues that the immigrants who came later "belonged to ethnic groups [Hutu and Tutsi] whose traditional territorial seat was part of the Congo long before 1908," and are therefore Congolese according to the 1964 constitution (Cyubahiro, 1989, 57, my translation).

However, local authorities in North Kivu refused to recognize the Banyarwanda as citizens. In the 1965 local elections, the Banyarwanda were allowed to vote, but the local authorities refused to let them run for office because they were foreigners. In addition, many Banyarwanda who had positions in the local administration during the colonial period were, as of 1960, dismissed and replaced by members of indigenous ethnic groups (Makombo, 1998, 52–53). There are indications, however, that the attitudes of local authorities in North Kivu were not representative of the whole region. When a member of the provincial government in South Kivu contested the nationality of a member who had just been elected on the basis that he was a Tutsi, he did not receive support from the rest of the provincial government (Cyubahiro, 1989, 60).

In 1971, President Mobutu Sésé Seko signed a decree-law that stated, "[A]ll persons of Rwanda-Burundi origins established in the Congo by June 30, 1960, are Zairean from this date" (Cyubahiro, 1989, 63). In 1972, the nationality act required under the constitution promulgated as Law 002, repeated Article 6 of the 1964 constitution, but added that "persons originating from Rwanda-Urundi who had taken up residence in the province of Kivu before January 1, 1950, and had henceforth continued to reside in Zaire until the entry into force of the law acquired Zairean nationality as of June 30, 1960" (ECOSOC, 17).

These laws have been criticized for collectively granting citizenship to the Banyarwanda. President Mobutu allegedly passed the decree-law after receiving strong pressure from his chief of staff, Bisengimana Rwema, himself of Rwandan descent (ECOSOC, 17). According to the UN Special Rapporteur,

If the Decree-Law granted "collective recognition" of nationality, it was only to those who, like Bisengimana, were not Congolese, i.e., to those who did not meet the requirements of previous laws, not to those who were already Congolese? [The 1972 Law] is consistent with those of the colonial period and those first adopted after independence in that it refers to a period of ten years of residence in Zairean territory, and at the most it can be argued that under its provisions Zairean nationality is "collectively" taken away from—not granted to—persons of Rwandan origin who arrived in Zaire between 1 January and 30 June 1950. Those transplanted before that date were already Zairean.

It becomes clear that the Banyarwanda were granted citizenship implicitly through the electoral laws passed right after independence, and not by the 1964 constitution. The constitution does not refer to a condition of ten years' residency in the country.

Cyubahiro offers another interpretation. As I have noted, he argues that the 1964 constitution itself granted citizenship to the Kinyarwanda-speaking Hutu and Tutsi who immigrated during colonial rule. According to him, the new nationality laws are nothing but clarifications of the Luluabourg Constitution. To support his view, he quotes a statement made by the legislative council that voted the law into effect: "This law thus defines in the best conditions possible who is Zairean and thereby ends the intrigues and speculations which have existed in this area since our independence" (Cyubahiro, 1989, 64). Cyubahiro does not, however, explain why the new law contains a condition of ten years' residency, while the constitution has no such provision.

The 1972 law was an attempt to dispel a growing sense of insecurity among the Banyarwanda, who were experiencing increased hostility from indigenous groups. This increased hostility was caused by the massive influx of refugees from Burundi after the 1972 Hutu massacre. The effect of the 1972 decree, however, was counterproductive, since the Hutu among the Kinyarwanda-speaking minority joined the indigenous majority in their demands that the Tutsi in Kivu be sent back to Rwanda (Mamdani, 1997).

In 1981, Mobutu agreed to sign a new law on nationality that had been passed by his one-party parliament and that invalidated the 1971 decree (Makombo, 1998, 55). The new law was adopted and voted on in a context of pressure resulting from the fact that in North Kivu indigenous groups became a minority and feared marginalization (ECOSOC, 19). According to the new law, only persons who could demonstrate an ancestral connection to the population residing in the territory in 1885 then-demarcated as the Congo would qualify to be citizens of the Congo (p. 19).

The 1981 law clearly deprived those Banyarwanda who were not descendants of pre-1885 settlers of their right to citizenship, whether one argues that this was granted to them in 1964, 1972, or by the electoral laws before independence. In practice, however, one can also argue that the descendants of precolonial settlers were deprived of their citizenship:

> Not only did the 1981 Act disqualify those tens of thousands of Banyarwanda and Burundi who came into Zaire at the request of the Belgian authorities, along with Tutsi elements that fled the Rwanda Revolution; even more exasperating was the absurdity of a piece of legislation that made it virtually impossible for anyone to comply with the provisions given that (a) the boundaries of Zaire in 1885 had yet to be fixed, and (b) proof of a pre-1885 ancestry is impossible to establish in juridical terms. (Lemarchand, 1997, 14, n.16)

The National Sovereignty Conference in 1991 and 1992 agreed that the matter of citizenship of the Banyarwanda should be settled in order to prevent statelessness. However, the result was a confirmation of the 1981 law, and the problem has not been resolved (Amnesty International Report, 1996, 3).

In a letter to the UN Security Council dated October 23, 1996, the Zairean government wrote that it did not consider that the Banyarwanda in general and the Banyamulenge in particular belonged to a Zairean ethnic group. They were therefore not entitled to Zairean citizenship unless they were to acquire such nationality through naturalization procedures (Makombo, 1998, 54).

The Violent Reaction to Marginalization

The 1981 law was not supported by any specific administrative measures of enforcement. "Identity cards of Banyarwanda were not revoked and political leaders who feared the number of votes represented by Kinyarwanda-speakers in coming elections inflamed indigenous Zaireans' resentment towards the Banyarwanda" (Makombo, 1998, 56). By the time of the 1985 provincial assembly elections, the authorities in Kivu had reacted in the same way as they had in 1965. Kinyarwanda-speakers were allowed to vote but not to run for office. The Banyarwanda responded by smashing ballot boxes, with the result that no government assemblies were elected in North and South Kivu (Mamdani, 1997).

When, in 1990, many Tutsi in Kivu crossed the border into Uganda to join the Rwandese Patriotic Front, the Mobutu regime authorized an on-the-ground verification of those among the Banyarwanda who had families that had come there before 1885 and of those that had arrived later. Violence ensued, causing many deaths (Makombo, 1998, 53). The effect of the verification mission was increased cross-border movement of young Congolese Tutsi. This again gave credibility to the notion spread by some indigenous organizations that the Congolese Tutsi were really Rwandans, not just culturally, but also in their political allegiances.

In 1993, clashes took place between Banyarwanda peasants and indigenous groups in North Kivu, causing three thousand deaths and displacing another three hundred thousand. The clashes resulted from a land conflict that had originally started as a class conflict among the Kinyarwanda-speaking Hutu and then turned into an ethnic conflict between Kinyarwanda-speaking Hutu and indigenous groups over whether the former should have the right to their own Native Authority.

While this conflict was going on, two million refugees streamed from Rwanda into Kivu. The arrival of the refugees had two effects: first, "The anti-Rwandan feeling . . . was increased" (ECOSOC, 22). According to the UN Special Rapporteur, the conclusion of an investigation of the impact of the refugees conducted by the Zairean government "reveals an 'ethnic cleansing' spirit, since it is stated that Rwanda has been attempting to acquire Zairean territory and to supplant its indigenous population" (ECOSOC, 20). In fact, Zaireans claimed that the crisis was orchestrated by the Tutsi as part of a plan to create a Hima empire in central Africa, "Hima" being the umbrella term for the original "royal" ethnic group with which the Tutsi are associated in popular perception (Craven, 1996). Second, Hutu refugees belonging to the Interhamwe soon started to commit violence against Banyarwanda Tutsi. The result was that collective identities quickly sorted themselves into rival communities. "[T]he Banyarwanda frame of reference quickly dissolved into a rigid Hutu–Tutsi dichotomy . . . driving Hutu and Tutsi irrespective of other distinctions, into opposing camps" (Lemarchand, 1997, 6). The Zairean local authorities, on their part, increased the tension through "xenophobic appeals, while the ill-disciplined and unpaid Zairean soldiers became implicated in arms trafficking and offered their services as mercenaries to the rich Hutus to fight the Tutsi as well as their indigenous Zairean countrymen" (Makombo, 1998, 53). Because of the atrocities, several thousand Tutsi from North Kivu left to find refuge in Rwanda (Lemarchand, 1997, 4). In Rwanda these Tutsi are considered foreign refugees; the Rwandan authorities have affirmed them to be Zairean and not Rwandan (Medecins Sans Frontiers [Doctors without Borders], 1996, 5).

In South Kivu, the citizenship problem was less heated until the 1994 refugees arrived. Only then did the local administration begin to appropriate Tutsi property in the valley, openly supported by members of the Parliament (Mamdani, 1997). On April 28, 1995, the High Council of the Transitional Parliament passed a resolution, ostensibly aimed at preventing Rwandan and Burundian refugees from acquiring Zairean nationality. A report by the UN

Integrated Regional Information Network (IRIN, 1996) that comments on this resolution states, "The most surprising aspect of the resolution was that it treated the Banyamulenge as recent refugees" (p. 4). The resolution included a list of people to be arrested and expelled; the cancellation of any sale or transfer of assets that benefited "immigrants who have acquired Zairean nationality fraudulently"; the replacement of existing governors and commanders with new officials; and the banning of Tutsi from all administrative and other posts (p. 4).

Finally, in September 1996, the South Kivu former deputy governor stated in a radio broadcast that if the Banyamulenge did not leave Zaire within a week, they would be interned in camps and exterminated (Makombo, 1998, 53). The response of the Banyamulenge was to join forces with the support of neighboring countries to launch a rebellion in late 1996. This rebellion, backed by the governments of Rwanda and Uganda, ultimately led to the overthrow of the Mobutu government by Laurent Kabila, who renamed the country the Democratic Republic of the Congo.

Toward a Comprehensive Framework of Protection

How much the Congolese laws relating to citizenship were casually altered to discriminate, marginalize, and even persecute Rwandans generally and Tutsi particularly and the way this generated a violent conflict that has threatened the disintegration of the Congolese state are specific to context. Taken together, however, they exemplify a crisis in nation building that is evident at various levels throughout the African continent. Further, how far conflict in the Congo has engulfed neighboring countries in the region underscores the interconnectedness of ethnic-identity crises across what are arbitrary state borders. This interconnectedness calls for a normative framework that postulates sovereignty as a concept of responsibility for all those falling under the jurisdiction of the state and without discrimination on the basis of race, ethnicity, religion, or place of origin.

Increasing ethnic discrimination must also be seen in the context of the influx of refugees from Rwanda, both in the early 1960s and in 1994. It was the arrival of Hutu refugees after the 1994 genocide, and particularly of members of the Interhamwe, that pitted the Hutu and the Tutsi in Kivu against each other and eventually led to the expulsion of the Banyamulenge. Analyses of the crisis in the Congo normally treat the existing nationality dispute in Kivu and the spillover from Rwanda as separate factors. The sources of the two phenomena essentially are connected to ethnic marginalization and to political exclusion.

The 1994 genocide was planned by a Hutu elite as a means of preventing the implementation of the 1993 Arusha Peace Accord that would have led to the return of Tutsi populations that had been forced into exile in Uganda following the 1959–1963 massacres (Chege, 1996/97, 33). The Arusha Peace Accord was preceded by a civil war when the Rwandan Patriotic Front launched an insurgency in northern Rwanda in October 1990. Ironically, it was the oppression of Tutsi exiles by the Ugandan government under Milton Obote that led Tutsi youth to join the National Resistance Army (NRA) led by Yoweri Museveni. As many as four thousand of the sixteen thousand NRA guerillas who marched into Kampala in January 1986 are said to have been Banyarwanda. The Banyarwanda problem became a major question in Uganda as individuals of Rwandese origin occupied prominent state positions under the NRA. The question of land became a major public issue when Banyarwanda squatters confronted Baganda ranchers in the late 1980s. The squatters claimed the land and used their majority status in the country to press their claim as a democratic demand. Ranchers questioned their status as a nonindigenous group, which therefore did not have customary land rights. The land question was translated into a nationality question, focusing national attention on the prominent position of individuals of Rwandese origin in the hierarchy of the NRA and the state. All this triggered a political crisis.

The impetus behind the decision of the Rwanda Patriotic Front to cross the border from Uganda into Rwanda in 1990 was not so much the political crisis in Rwanda as it was a reaction to the Tutsi crisis in Uganda (Mamdani, 1998b). Museveni's regime paid the Tutsi back by supporting the RPF to seize power from the Hutu-dominated government in Rwanda. The border crisis pitting the Hutu refugees in Zaire against the new Tutsi rulers in their home country eventually led to a subregional assault on the Mobutu regime, triggering its downfall. The logic of subregional dynamics led to the subsequent involvement of Angola and the Republic of the Congo, which, although not ethnically based, signified the emerging regional security consciousness and interest in the affairs of neighbors.

The experience of the Rwandans in general and the Tutsi in particular in the Great Lakes region underscores the increasing realization that because of the artificiality of state borders, Africa's political and economic problems, challenges, and prospects are interconnected and should be approached regionally. Domestic crises uproot masses of people, displacing them internally before turning them into refugees, which may result in the destabilization of an entire region. States therefore see it as being in their national interest to be involved in the domestic affairs of their regional neighbors and to find solutions to reinforce regional peace and security. Salim Ahmed Salim, the secretary-general of the Organization of African Unity, has called on African countries to reinforce international standards with African traditional values, and to see themselves as their brothers' keepers. Salim challenged Africans to reconceptualize sovereignty to harmonize with regional solidarity, working collectively and collaboratively to put domestic and regional houses in order for the common good (Council of Ministers, 1992, 12, quoted in Deng, 1996, 15).

The core of the African crisis today, however, is not so much the artificiality of borders as the conditions of pluralism they create and the failure of governments to manage ethnic diversity constructively. The challenge, then, is not so much to question the validity of state borders as it is to address the issue of managing diversity in an equitable sharing of power and national resources to foster national consensus.

It is worth recalling that twentieth-century European history abounds with examples that illustrate the limitations and failures of the supposedly inclusive institution of citizenship to provide an effective basis for the accommodation of ethnic differences within a regional state system. Conversely, the comparative success of the European Union suggests the need to look for solutions beyond membership constructs that are too closely tied to nation-state models, and to seek broader federal (or confederal) institutional structures that provide a multitiered framework for accommodation and representation across regions.

Any assessment of the European Union's "success," however, in such an endeavor must consider three facts. The first concerns how the forcible population transfers that occurred before, during, and after World War II and the genocidal policies pursued during the war simplified the ethnic map of Europe and dramatically reduced the problem of accommodating national minorities within the nation-state framework. The second concerns the difficult challenge of grafting representative functions onto a supranational body such as the European Union. Although the EU has been successful in establishing a transnational economic market across a regional system of states, it remains unclear whether it will provide an adequate institutional framework for the effective exercise of transnational citizenship. Third, the EU has done little to protect or extend the rights of non-EU member-state aliens or to promote their integration therein.

The example of the EU suggests that such regional models are subject to their own distinct limitations, just as is any model of democratic citizenship. This leaves the question of the limitations of regional models of protection applied to the Great Lakes region or of any particular citizenship model in the Congo.

A regional awakening to the common threat of internal conflict in the Great Lakes region and in other regions of Africa remains nascent, but the dangers of the shared threat are being realized, especially since the demographic makeup of the regions cross state borders. Examples of collective responses to this threat have been the actions taken by the Economic Community of West African States (ECOWAS) in Liberia, the Southern Africa Development Community (SADC) in several southern African countries, and the Inter-Governmental Authority for Development (IGAD) in the Sudan and Somalia. What is significant about these regional interventions is not that they are desirable in themselves, but rather that they are signs of the interconnectedness of the crises across state borders and of the need to develop standards of responsible sovereignty and a collective response to noncompliance with stipulated norms.

The regional approach is a double-edged sword. Countries are motivated because they know more about local conditions than outsiders do and because their interests are vested ones. Likewise, because they can hardly be considered impartial, the manner and outcome of their involvement can be a problem. Yet, they do signify a concern for things beyond the state and underscore the need for more inclusive normative and operational arrangements.

The first line of action needed is to develop a policy framework that would oblige states to treat their citizens with dignity by ensuring their physical protection and enjoyment of democratic values, respecting fundamental rights and freedoms, and providing reasonable standards of social and economic welfare. These are what a citizen needs to feel a sense of belonging and loyalty to their nation. Although these norms should stipulate a special responsibility for the protection of minorities, the conditions in Africa, where virtually every ethnic group is a minority in a multiplicity of ethnicities, demand inclusiveness based on a national consensus. Thinking of marginalization as a form of statelessness, while not creating a legal status, draws attention to the gross inequities, discrimination, and lack of protection for many people that call for effective remedies.

This domestic situation necessitates the second line of action: the creation of strong subregional arrangements for security and development cooperation. The foundations for these arrangements have already been laid by ECOWAS, IGAD, and SADC, but they need to be strengthened. The support the international community has given to the peacemaking and peacekeeping activities of these organizations, though limited, suggests a much greater role for subregional organizations in promoting regional peace, security, stability, and development.

Given the lack of capacity of these subregional organizations, especially in terms of material resources, it is pragmatic to focus on the role of the pivotal states in the regions and provide them with support to enhance their capacity for regional responsibilities. Donor countries and the international community in general can assist financially and technically.

As a third line of action, precisely because minimum conditions for peace and tranquility would be expected to result from the postulated arrangements, states are likely to be more receptive to opening their borders to those who, for whatever reasons, find themselves compelled or obliged to leave their countries of origin. Julius Nyerere of Tanzania, who was mandated by both the United Nations and the Organization of African Unity to mediate in the Burundi conflict, envisaged such a line of action when he concluded that the problem was primarily one of the overconcentration of population within too small a territory and advocated opening the borders of neighboring countries to allow for free migration and residence in the region. Although current immigration policies indicate contrary trends, it should be possible to adopt an approach that would reconcile the maintaining of state borders with making them permeable enough to permit those driven by circumstances to move across them.

Correlated with this as a fourth line of action is the need to make the requirements of residency and citizenship liberal (including the acceptance of dual or multiple citizenships) to reflect what is reality for Africa: the multiplicity of identities within pluralistic states and even more complex regional configurations. There will, of course, be a fear that liberal residency and nationality laws might be abused and become unmanageable, but this danger can be minimized by a code-of-conduct agreement that would foster the discharge of the responsibilities of sovereignty to ensure respect for fundamental human rights, civil liberties, and the general welfare of citizens. Nevertheless, the threat of a massive exodus is itself a challenge for governments to create conditions that encourage their citizens to remain at home and be involved in nation building.

Finally, nation building has internal and external dimensions. The internal dimension requires an inclusive framework to involve all groups within the state, some of which have been sidestepped, excluded, or marginalized. The external dimension should begin with regional cooperation and a rethinking of borders, not to question their legitimacy, but rather to make them responsive to regional dynamics. Ultimately, what Africa needs is a comprehensive policy framework, stipulating principles of state responsibility and accountability, with enforcement mechanisms as a basis for addressing realistically the continent's problems at national and regional levels and in partnership with the international community.

Works Cited

Amnesty International Report. 1996. "Lawlessness and Insecurity in North and South-Kivu." AFR 62/14/96. Nov.

Annan, Kofi. 1996. "The Peacekeeping Prescription." In Kevin M. Cahill (ed.), *Preventive Diplomacy*. New York: Basic Books.

Barth, Frederick (ed.). 1969. *Ethnic Groups and Boundaries: The Social Organization of Culture Difference*. Boston: Little, Brown.

Batchelor, Carol A. 1995. "Stateless Persons: Gaps in International Protection." *International Journal of Refugee Law* 7(2): 231–59.

———. 1998. "Statelessness and the Problem of Resolving Nationality Status." *International Journal of Refugee Law* 10(½): 156–83.

Chazan, Naomi, et al. 1988. *Politics and Society in Contemporary Africa*. Boulder, Colo.: Lynne Rienner.

Chege, Michael. 1996/1997. "Africa's Murderous Professors." *The National Interest* (winter 1996/97): 32–40.

Cohen, Roberta, and Francis Deng (eds.). 1998. *The Forsaken People: Case Studies of the Internally Displaced*. Washington, D.C.: Brookings Institution Press.

Colson, Elizabeth. 1969. "African Society at the Time of the Scramble." In Peter Duignan and Lewis Gann (eds.), *Colonialism in Africa, 1870–1960*. Vol. 1. Cambridge: Cambridge University Press.

Council of Ministers. 1992. *Report of the Secretary-General on Conflicts in Africa: Proposals for an OAU Mechanism for Conflict Prevention and Resolution*. CM/1710 (L.VI). Addis Ababa: Organization of African Unity. Quoted in Deng, 1996.

Craven, Colette. 1996. "Zairean catastrophe could reshape a continent." *The Irish Times* (online). Nov. 1.

Cyubahiro, Ngirabatware. 1989. *Heritage Colonial, Histoire des Ethnies frontiales du Zaire: Le cas des Hutu et des Tutsi du Kivu*. Kinshasa: Depot legal no. 093/89, 2e trimestre, June 27.

Deng, Francis M., et al. 1996. *Sovereignty as Responsibility: Conflict Resolution in Africa*. Washington, D.C.: Brookings Institution Press.

De Saint Moulin, L. 1975. "Mouvements récents de population dans la zone de peuplement dense de l'est du Kivu." In *Etude d'Histoire africaine*. No. 7, special issue: L'Afrique des Grands Lacs. Kinshasa: Presses Universitaires du Zaire.

Economic and Social Council (ECOSOC). 1997. "Report on the Situation of Human Rights in Zaire." Prepared by the Special Rapporteur, Mr. Roberto Garretón, in accordance with Commission resolution 1996/77. January 28. Fifty-third session, Commission on Human Rights, item 10 of the provisional agenda: Question of the Violation of Human Rights and Fundamental Freedoms in Any Part of the World, with Particular Reference to Colonial and Other Independent Countries and Territories. E/CN.4/1997/6.

Elias, T. Olawale. 1956. *The Nature of African Customary Law*. Manchester: Manchester University Press.

Englebert, Pierre. 1997. "The Contemporary African State: Neither African nor State." *Third World Quarterly* 18(4): 767–75.

Heilman, Bruce. 1998. "Who Are the Indigenous Tanzanians? Competing Conceptions of Tanzanian Citizenship in the Business Community." *Africa Today* 45(3–4): 369–88.

Human Rights Watch/Africa. 1997. "What Kabila Is Hiding." Vol. 9, no. 5 (A). Oct.

Integrated Regional Information Network (IRIN). 1996. "The Conflict in South Kivu, Zaire and Its Regional Dimensions." Briefing. Oct. 7.

Kasfir, Nelson. 1990. "Peacemaking and Social Cleavages in Sudan." In Joseph V. Montville (ed.), *Conflict and Peacemaking in Multiethnic Societies*, pp. 363–87. Lexington, Mass.: D. C. Heath.

Lehning, Percy B. 1997. "European Citizenship: Towards European Identity and Beyond?" Paper presented for panel "Political Identity as a Global Concept." Research Committee on Political Philosophy, World Congress, Aug. 17–19.

Lemarchand, Rene. 1997. "Patterns of State Collapse and Reconstruction in Central
    Africa: Reflections on the Crisis in the Great Lakes." *African Studies Quarterly* 1(3).
    <http://web.africa.ufl.edu/asq/>
Makombo, Angele N. 1998. "Civil Conflict in the Great Lakes Region: The Issue of
    Nationality of the Banyarwanda in the Democratic Republic of the Congo." *African
    Yearbook of International Law*.
Mamdani, Mahmood. 1996. *Citizen and Subject: Contemporary Africa and the Legacy
    of Late Colonialism*. Princeton, N.J.: Princeton University Press.
———. 1997. Report of the CODESRIA Mission to the Democratic Republic of Congo.
    Sept.
———. 1998a. "When Does a Settler Become a Native?" *Electronic Mail and Guard-
    ian*. May 26.
———. 1998b. "Why Foreign Invaders Can't Help Congo." *Electronic Mail and Guard-
    ian*. Nov. 1.
Medecins Sans Frontiers [Doctors without Borders]. 1996. "Ethnic Cleansing Rears Its
    Head in Zaire." Nov.
Meditz, Sandra, and Tim Merrill (eds.). 1993. *Zaire*. Federal Research Division, Li-
    brary of Congress.
Mkandawire, Thandika. 1997. "Shifting Commitments and National Cohesion in Afri-
    can Countries." Copenhagen: Center for Development Research. Unpublished
    manuscript.
Mutua, Makau wa. 1996. "The Ideology of Human Rights." *Virginia Journal of Inter-
    national Law* 36 (spring): 589–657.
Newbury, David. 1997. "Irredentist Rwanda: Ethnic and Territorial Frontiers in Central
    Africa." *Africa Today* 44(2): 211–22.
Nzongola-Ntalaja, Georges. 1999. "Anatomy and History of the Zaire-Congo Crisis."
    USAfrica (online), Feb. 18.
Oommen, T. K. 1997. "Introduction: Conceptualizing the Linkage between Citizen-
    ship and National Identity." In T. K. Oommen (ed.), *Citizenship and National
    Identity: From Colonialism to Globalism,* pp. 13–51. Thousand Oaks, Calif.: Sage
    Publications.
Prunier, Gerard. 1996a. "The North Kivu Crisis." Paper part of the CDR Writenet
    Programme. Oct. 18.
———. 1996b. "The South Kivu Crisis." Paper part of the CDR Writenet Programme.
———. 1997. "The Great Lakes Crisis." *Current History* 96(610): 225–28.
Rothchild, Donald. 1997. *Managing Ethnic Conflict in Africa*. Washington, D.C.:
    Brookings Institution Press.
Sebiterko, Rukundwa. 1996a. "The Aftermath of the Genocide in Rwanda." *Africanews*
    (online). June. <www.peacelink.it/afrinews.html>
———. 1996b. "The Banyamulenge of South Kivu Still Persecuted." *Africanews*
    (online). Sept. <www.peacelink.it/afrinews.html>
Woodward, Peter. 1990. *Sudan, 1898–1989: The Unstable State*. Boulder, Colo.: Lynne
    Rienner.
Young, Crawford. 1976. *The Politics of Cultural Pluralism*. Madison: University of
    Wisconsin Press.

CHAPTER SEVEN

City-States
and Citizenship

RICHARD T. FORD

DESPITE THE WEALTH of literature on globalization and national fragmentation, few observers have considered the possibility that the two phenomena are linked. This chapter analyzes the phenomena of globalization and subnational disintegration as linked trends. These links are indicative of a significant reorientation of the nation-state and its role as an organizing framework in society. As this role changes, fundamental institutions, such as citizenship, which have been embedded in this framework, are also changing. Globalization is having a profound transformative effect on nearly all aspects of domestic and international life, but these effects vary widely in their pace, scope, and intensity. They are especially pronounced in major urban centers. The growing importance of these centers as focal points for international commerce and as magnets for immigration (from increasingly diverse foreign sources) has earned them the label of *global cities*. Because these global cities experience the complex effects of globalization in exaggerated form, they offer an especially rich vantage point from which to explore the interplay between trends toward subnational disintegration on the one hand and those toward internationalization in economic, demographic, cultural, technological, and legal spheres on the other.

Given their international affiliations, it should not surprise us that global cities often have policy priorities that are at odds with those of the nation-state of which they are a part. These conflicts profoundly affect the meaning of *membership* in the national community. The civic culture of global cities will provide important insights into the nature of the transformation of national civic life and citizenship at the beginning of the millennium.

A characteristic of modernity is the close identification of citizenship with the nation-state. A nation is defined by its territory and its citizens and the status of citizen generally refers to a relationship with a specific nation. One might use the term *citizen* in other contexts, but only as a metaphor: a globetrotting cosmopolitan may consider herself a citizen of the world, while a local politician may refer to the "citizens of Gotham City." These uses, however, while evocative, are formally inaccurate. Cities, states, provinces, and territories have residents, property owners, or domiciliaries; corporations and communes have stakeholders; the global village has its cosmopolitans and its humanists who dream of a day beyond territorial divisions. But only nations have citizens.

It has not, of course, always been so. Ancient Athens (not Greece, as we, citizens of a national consciousness, often carelessly say) had citizens, as did Rome. In these republics the ideals of democracy coexisted with the formal exclusion of many people from their benefits (see Weber, 1958, 199–200). Citizenship referred to a status that was linked to an institution, the imperial center, rather than to a territory (ibid., 199–203). The European city-states of the Renaissance replaced the Greco-Roman political status of citizenship with the political title of burgher, noble, or lord and with the economic-political organizations of the guilds (ibid., 1958, 135–37).

In the past, economic changes have given birth to new political forms: the city-states of the Renaissance gave way to mercantile metropoles and colonies, which in turn gave way to a modern political system of national sovereigns. It is conceivable that our present political institutions are in a similar state of crisis or at least transition. Today we live in an era of globalization. The global economy transcends national economies; global alliances supersede purely national politics; cosmopolitan affinities challenge the exclusive loyalties of patriotism. At the same time, we have a multiplication of informal "nationalisms" that fragment the formal nation-state. Of course, we have economies of scale, but we also have niche marketing that targets small but intense pools of demand. We have the global village, but we also have identity politics that fractures the nation along the dimensions of race and ethnicity, religion, place, and styles of living.

Nationalism and, indirectly, national citizenship, are under attack, not from one, but from two opposite vectors: one toward multinational and global affiliations that transcend the nation-state, and one toward subnational, regional, and local affiliations that fracture the nation-state. These global and local affiliations are both formal and informal, political and economic, hardheaded and strategic, and irrational and romantic. They are defined by geography, ethnicity, religion, culture, and by the vectors of rapid transportation and the media of communication.

These changes will affect the nature of citizenship as they transform its modern foundation, the territorial nation-state. The contemporary bookend forces of globalization and intranational fragmentation threaten to undermine the historical power of nation-states worldwide and threaten to transform it in at least three distinct senses.

—Globalization threatens the ability of nation-states to make and enforce meaningful laws and policy. In one sense, globalization undermines the ability of nations to act *as nations*. In other words, it undermines the ability of the citizens of a nation to act collectively. International trade provides the classic example of this problem. No national economy can thrive in isolation from the currents of international trade. International competition undermines national priorities by undercutting national industries and eroding national wages, working conditions, and environmental protections. At the same time, of course, international competition benefits consumers by providing better and more plentiful consumer goods at reduced costs. Yet national policies that protect domestic industries and favor particular industries of national importance have explicitly sought to trade off lower consumer prices in favor of higher wages and better working conditions. International competition and the imposition of free trade shift the decision about this trade-off from the state to individual consumers. From one perspective, this shift simply empowers the individual over the state. From another perspective, however, it empowers the individual as consumer over the individual as citizen. It emphasizes the power of the purse over the power of the ballot. In this sense, free trade undermines the meaning of citizenship by making the formal rights of citizenship less significant.

—Globalization complicates the cultural identity of the nation-state. The legal anthropologist Sir Henry Maine ([1864] 1986, 100–1) notes that the nation-state had its origins in tribe sovereignty, or the sovereignty of a ruler over a people who have ethnic or cultural solidarity. This idea of the nation-as-a-people has been supplemented by the idea of the territorial nation state,[1] the sovereignty of a ruler over a territory. To borrow an example from Maine, the king of the Franks (a people) became the king of France (a territory). The notion of a nation as a people, however, continues to animate national identity,

---

1. Maine is best understood as referring to the "idea" of tribe sovereignty, not its reality. Of course, that national identity has been tied to the idea of the nation-as-a-people does not mean that the nation was or is, in fact, ethnically or culturally homogenous.

both in terms of national folklore and ideology and in formal legal terms in the doctrine of national citizenship. Citizenship establishes the nation as a people both by excluding some individuals (noncitizens) present on national soil and by including some who are not present. So it is that contemporary nationalism requires both the nation as a people and the nation as a territory. Indeed, nationalism assumes an identity between the two: the land of a nation belongs to its people, and the people belong to the soil of the land. In the myth of King Arthur, the land and the sovereign are one; in the ideology of U.S. democracy, "this land was *made for* you and me." Yet globalization disturbs this relation between people and land by introducing to the national landscape large numbers of long-term residents who are ethnically and culturally diverse. Although polyethnicity has always been a feature of nation-states, national ideology can accommodate such diversity, as long as it remains relatively static, by redescribing distinctive subnational groups as organic parts of a national whole (see Ford, 1999, 843, 864). Conspicuous and widespread immigration, however, undermines this typical nationalist redescription. And while relatively small numbers of such individuals can be accommodated by traditional nationalist ideology as exceptions (such as resident aliens and expatriates), a large number undermines the identity of the nation-state and the institution of citizenship by disrupting the tie between a people and their territory.

Identity politics undermines the nation-state from within by fragmenting the idea of "a people." As even long-standing citizens begin to identify themselves more as members of ethnic groups than as members of a nation-state, citizenship becomes a strictly formal status rather than an identity with cultural meaning and ethical weight. Of course, citizenship can accommodate identity politics as an exception, such as in the case of the black power movement of the 1960s and 1970s in the United States. The question for today's world is whether citizenship can accommodate identity politics as the rule. For instance, in the contemporary United States, racial and ethnic difference, gender, sexual orientation or preference, and cultural heritage or affinity all assert themselves as identities that potentially supersede national loyalties and call for "extraordinary" legal protection that, as the number of protected identities multiply, may well become the norm.

"Globalization" and the Structure of Government

The distribution of political power is generally conceived of as opposing centralization in favor of decentralization. Historically, the formation of nation-states is understood to involve the centralization of power in the hands of a national government. This historical process has subsumed previously autonomous regional and national structures of rule under a single sovereign. Thus, formally, regional and local governments are subdivisions of the nation-states of which they are a part.

"Internationalization" seems the logical next phase of this historical trend. Just as regional and local political institutions, languages, cultures, and affiliations have been subsumed under national governments, so too nations are being subsumed under international organizations. The internationalist dream culminates in a single world government, a global economy, a cosmopolitan culture. Technological advances in communication and transportation make the global village a reality. International human rights and a universally valid technocratic expertise replace local tyrannies and backward customs. An efficient market in goods replaces local protectionism and corrupt favoritism and spreads the benefits of capitalism worldwide. An aesthetically refined and technologically advanced international style of architecture replaces crude local idiom in design, planning, and construction. The franc and deutsche mark yield to the euro, anticipating a common coin of the international realm. Esperanto (or is it English?) becomes a global lingua franca.

The graphic model is one of concentric circles with similar institutions at different scales. The global subsumes the continental, which in turn subsumes the national, which encompasses the regional, which contains the local. At each level is government, an economy and, to some extent, a culture, but the institutions at the smaller levels are not only physically subsumed under those at the higher levels, they are also morally, formally, and pragmatically subordinate. If the national economy requires the free movement of goods, local protectionism must yield. If the European economy requires the free movement of individuals, national controls in immigration must yield. Similarly, if the global economy requires the free movement of goods, national protectionism is inconsistent with the General Agreement on Tariffs and Trade (GATT).[2]

This internationalism is characterized, not only by the creation of multinational institutions, but also by the dramatic expansion of their authority at the *expense of traditional nation-states.* Instead of political organizations regulating the economy, as with a traditional monetary policy, the economy drives public policy. Even international institutions that are designed to accomplish only limited goals may expand to assume larger responsibilities. The European

---

2. The careful reader will already have some objections. The pound, for instance, did not yield to the euro: Great Britain has so far refused to join the European monetary union. National protectionism survives GATT. The treaty exempts many protected industries and even regulations that are inconsistent with GATT are not preempted but rather sanctioned, indicating a recognition that the nation-state remains sovereign. The internationalist, however, will respond that this is only evidence that the inevitable process of globalization is not yet complete.

Union, for example, was originally designed to accomplish only economic integration, while leaving the realms of political decision making and cultural formation to the nation-states.[3] Still, many commentators have predicted that economic integration will inevitably require the integration of other governmental functions. In others words, it will prove impossible to sever the economic from the cultural and political realms (Roht-Arriaza, 1997, 413). Indeed, more recent negotiations have expanded the power of the European Union to include political and social rights.[4]

Governmental arrangements like the European Union have therefore taken on functions that have not only long been within the authority of the nation-state but that have traditionally *defined* the nation-state, such as the issuance of currency, the control of immigration, the regulation of the economy, and in some cases even the administration of civil and criminal justice.

Contemporary trade agreements between nations, such as the North American Free Trade Agreement (NAFTA) and the General Agreement on Tariffs and Trade, while not as dramatic an institutional arrangement as the European Union, still effectively create multinational institutions that regulate much more than trade, including labor laws, environmental standards, and intellectual property rules. The important point here is that these agreements are not simply "moments in time," contracts between discrete arm's-length bargainers. They establish institutional arrangements that enforce the agreement. At some level, these institutions assume the traditional function of the nation-state in the areas over which they have authority.

There is also growing recognition among scholars and political commentators that revitalized localism and regionalism have accompanied the growth of international organizations. While economic, cultural, and political relations are becoming increasingly interdependent—increasingly global—they are also becoming more fractured, more particularistic, more place-based, and more local than before. European governments have created regional governments or strengthened long-moribund provisions for regional autonomy and "federalist" structures of government.[5] In the United States, after several decades of a consistent federalization of political power, there has been a rebirth of local

3. 1986 EC Treaty Art. 3b: "The community shall take action, in accordance with the principle of subsidiarity, only if and insofar as the objectives of the proposed action cannot be sufficiently achieved by the member state."

4. See 1992 Treaty on European Union, expanding the political rights of EU citizens, including the right of nonnationals to vote in local and European elections in the country of residence.

5. See, generally, the Scotland Act 1998; the Government of Wales Act 1998; see also Putnam (1993, 2–26), describing the devolution of political power in Italy since the 1970s; Kelly (1999, 209); Roht-Arriaza (1997, 413).

autonomy, home rule, and a decentralization of authority. Ancient values of community and place have replaced modern priorities of uniformity, coordination, and economy of scale.

Much of this decentralization can be seen as the penultimate move on the way to a dismantling of governmental power in general, a way station on the road to Robert Nozick's (1974, 25, 26–27) night watchman state. There is something else afoot, however, something else that explains the support for a decentralization of power, a support that threatens and promises to bypass the states altogether as county and municipal governments seek additional authority, as neighborhood organizations grow in strength, and as private associations begin to assume some of the abandoned functions of the state.

Likewise, cultural affinities fracture national identity even as they aspire to recognition as separate "nations." In the United States there is of course the venerable black nationalism, the Nation of Islam, Aztlan (the nation of *La Rasa Cosmica*),[6] and Queer Nation (a homosexual political group). Consider also the now-infamous Montana Freemen and the Republic of Texas, both groups that claimed independence from the federal government of the United States, setting up independent courts to enforce autonomous laws and promising armed resistance to any agent of the national government that sought to enforce its laws. Meanwhile, ethnic nationalism in Europe is on the rise, in the Basque separatist movement, in Corsican nationalism, and in the Northern Italian bid for autonomy. Great Britain, stripped of its global empire, has now granted limited autonomy to Scotland and Wales, suggesting that Tom Nairn's predicted "breakup of Britain" may be at least partially realized (see Nairn, 1977; Sullivan, 1999).

The Global City

Simultaneous and seemingly opposite trends toward globalism and localism may at first blush appear to be a paradox. Instead, however, the two trends are complementary and mutually reinforcing. The combination of multinational governmental and cultural affiliations and the expansion of local affiliations, both formal and informal, call into question, or at least complicate, the traditional opposition between the global and the local. The important point is that international affiliations—whether legally formalized (the European Union, NAFTA), economic (multinational corporations), or cultural (pan-ethnic and diasporic communities and religions)—are accompanied and supplemented by

6. *La Rasa Cosmica* is an evocative description of Latin Americans, the race that is a marriage of races (indigenous and Caucasian.)

local affiliations. They are tied to place, but they are also linked to other localities in a way that transcends both geographical continuity and formal jurisdictional boundaries.

The Global Dynamic

The dynamic of globalization is well known and has been the subject of countless scholarly works. What follows is a necessarily brief summary of its vast literature. Globalization is driven by technological innovations that reduce or eliminate the significance of spatial distances, such as increasingly rapid modes of transportation for goods and individuals and rapid or virtually instantaneous communication. These innovations have resulted in what geographer David Harvey (1989) calls *time-space compression* (pp. 240–42, 265, 350–52). The result of this time-space compression is that national economies are now thoroughly a part of a global economy that not only produces a worldwide distribution of goods and services, but also a worldwide distribution of labor. The latter reflects, but also exaggerates and distorts, the previous distribution of labor under the national "Fordist" industrial economies of the wealthy capitalist democracies. The global economy's labor force consists of a growing, highly compensated class of information analysts and producers working in the FIRE industries (finance, insurance, and real estate), high technology, cultural production, the facilitating professions, and a much more numerous class of low-wage laborers in the service and manufacturing sectors. These latter, the laborers, struggle with reduced wages, little or no job security, and part time, seasonal, and "flex time" employment.

The postindustrial, global economy has produced a division of labor that increasingly ignores the older distinctions between North and South or first and third worlds, as well as national borders. Instead, an informationally and technologically savvy elite has emerged in many third world countries, while the unskilled and unlucky in the United States and western Europe find themselves involuntarily conscripted into a latter day "reserve army of the underemployed." This of course is not to say that the poor or underemployed of the first-world nations are as badly off as are their counterparts in the third world. Yet citizenship in a first-world nation-state is no longer the guarantee of material privilege that it once seemed to be.

Global Cities and Uneven Development

Globalization has not affected national economies, demographics or built landscapes smoothly or evenly. Instead, its effects are concentrated within major urban centers, what Saskia Sassen has called global cities. These global cities display the effects of globalization in exaggerated form. They have especially large concentrations of immigrants, forming ethnically and linguistically distinct communities. Further, they are characterized by a pronounced bifurcation of income, split between a cosmopolitan elite that regularly jets off to trade and socialize with their counterparts in other global cities—Hong Kong, London, Los Angeles, Milan, New York, Paris, Singapore, Tokyo[7]—and a disadvantaged group of disinherited natives and recent immigrants with family and cultural ties to South and Central America, South East Asia, Africa, and the Caribbean. Thus, a growing share of the residents of global cities, in both the privileged and underprivileged classes, have strong economic and cultural ties to foreign nations.

These global cities are part of a new type of international community that is paradoxically both intensely place-specific and completely decentered and without geographical boundaries. Rather than centers of regions, "spheres of influence," or "cores" opposed to the periphery, these global cities are better understood as points in a worldwide network or grid, connected by high-speed trains, superhighways, transcontinental flights, satellite communications, Ethernet connections, and international courier services.

At the same time, major cities are cultural and political bases for ethnic subgroups and minorities that are too small to gain significant power at the national level. In the United States such groups include African Americans in the northeastern cities of New York, Newark, Philadelphia, and Chicago and the Southern cities of Washington, D.C., Baltimore, and Atlanta; Hispanic Americans in the Southwest and Miami; and Asian Americans in Los Angeles, New York, San Francisco, and Seattle. They also include such religious minorities as Muslims in western Europe, Jews in Europe and the United States, minority Christians sects (such as the Mormons and the evangelical denominations in the United States), and expatriate, immigrant, and exiled communities from such politically volatile nations as Cuba, Ethiopia, Somalia, the Congo, the Balkans, and the former Soviet states. Immigration has literally produced a third world within the metropole: for example, Los Angeles, California, now has the largest Spanish-speaking population in the world outside Mexico City, and the largest Korean-speaking population outside Seoul. The new global-

7. The recently launched travel and design periodical *Wallpaper* serves as an internationalist manual for this class of individuals. It is explicitly urban, elite, and international (the editors refused to publish a separate U.S. edition, even after the magazine's purchase by Time-Warner, and the magazine regularly uses a variety of national currencies: pounds for one item, dollars for another, Swiss francs for a third, yen for a fourth).

local identity is obscure: both an elite cosmopolitanism and an inclusive, chaotic multiculturalism.

Cities, Citizenship, and Law

The global city has the potential to alter the link between application of the law and national territory in at least three ways.

—In theory, nation-states are the fundamental political units from which law emanates. Although many nations are divided into subterritories with some power to make and enforce law within their borders, the national government generally retains authority to control the processes by which the subterritories make law and to vacate or preempt local laws when in the national interest. The residents of global cities, however, have cultural and economic ties to the global village that can be as strong as their ties to their national capitals. Global cities have metropolitan economies that depend on relations with other global cities as much as on trade within the national economy. Given their international affiliations, it should not surprise us that global cities often have policy priorities that are at odds with those of the nation-state of which they are a part. At times, the global and local concerns of a major city can drive federal policy: for instance, no one doubts that the decision of the U.S. Congress to penalize companies doing business with Cuba was driven by the Cuban-American exile community in Miami, Florida. Here the concern is both global and local. It is specific to Miami but can be understood only in relation to the international ties that link Miami and Cuba.

More often, however, the national and regional governments impede the goals of these global cities. While the federal government of the United States, for example, has advanced a series of punitive anti-immigrant measures, the city of San Francisco, with its large immigrant population, recently considered extending the franchise to noncitizen residents (see Raskin, 1993, 1391).[8] Now San Francisco is considering mandating foreign-language translators at public meetings to serve the city's large Spanish-, Mandarin-, and Cantonese-speaking communities. The city's attempts to intensify its international ties, however, have been consistently thwarted by federal initiatives that cut public services to immigrants and state laws that prohibit extension of the local franchise to noncitizens.

A global city whose interests are at odds with the nation-state in which it is located may attempt to use its "centrality" in the global networks of commerce,

8. Arguing that noncitizen local residents should be allowed to exercise the franchise in local elections.

travel, and communication to set policy that is outside and beyond its formal political and territorial authority. The age-old tension between centralized authority and local autonomy thus takes on new meaning in the context of global cities. Traditionally, the decentralization of power was thought to provide local governments with autonomy in a range of narrow "local affairs": land use regulation, traffic control, the punishment of petty crimes, and infractions (see, e.g., McBain, 1916, 673).[9] Increasingly, however, global cities strain against the narrow confines of their formal power in an attempt to set broader public and economic policy, in the manner of medieval city-states. Global cities, in response to global economic pressures and cultural affiliations that manifest themselves in locally specific ways, attempt to act independently of the larger jurisdictions of which they are a part.

In 1998, for example, the city of San Francisco passed an ordinance that prohibited city departments from contracting with businesses that did not provide employee benefits to domestic partners on an equal basis with spouses (San Francisco Admin. Code § 12B.1[b]). Although to the casual observer the ordinance was similar to the type of conditions American cities regularly impose on public contracts, it was in fact distinct. The ordinance was an attempt to use San Francisco's position as a crucial hub in international trade, travel, and commerce to affect a larger number of businesses on a global scale. The ordinance did not limit the requirement to employees who worked in San Francisco or on city projects. Instead a company had to provide domestic-partner benefits to all its employees as a matter of company policy. A consortium of airlines challenged the ordinance when the city applied the requirement to leases at the airport and threatened to refuse the renewal of United Airlines' lease unless it provided the benefits. The airlines argued that the city ordinance was preempted by the federal law governing employee benefits (namely, ERISA) and air traffic, that it was an unconstitutional burden on commerce, and that it constituted an extraterritorial exercise of jurisdiction (see *Air Transport Assoc. of America v. City and County of San Francisco* [n.d. Cal. 1998]). The city countered that it was acting in its proprietary capacity (the ordinance simply placed a condition on a contract; the airlines were free to reject the contract if the condition was unacceptable), and it therefore was not limited by federal preemption, con-

9. See, e.g., McBain (1916, 673), "By common understanding such general subjects as . . . domestic relations, wills and administration, mortgagees, trusts, contracts, real and personal property insurance, banking corporations and many others have never been regarded . . . as appropriate subjects of local control"; Dillon (1911, 448–55), "a municipal corporation can exercise the following powers and no others: first, those granted in express words; second, those necessarily or fairly implied in or incident to the power expressly granted; third, those essential to the accomplishment of the declared objects—not simply convenient but indispensable."

stitutional restrictions on state action, or its jurisdictional boundaries. Although the city claimed victory in the press, the federal district court found that much of the ordinance was preempted by ERISA, and it enjoined the city from enforcing the most important provisions of the contract.

Here the city is engaged in ideological policy making that could potentially disrupt a node in the global transportation network. The desire to appease a gay-friendly local majority led the San Francisco Board of Supervisors to disregard the national (and international) interest in a smoothly functioning air transportation system. The airlines noted that they could be subject to conflicting laws in different jurisdictions. A city with a right-wing government might refuse to lease airport space to any airline that *did* provide domestic partners benefits.[10]

From a traditional local government perspective, the city's ordinance was outrageously overreaching. Because the city happens to control an airport, it was able to leverage its way into nationwide policy. Still, in one sense, San Francisco was acting reasonably from the perspective of its position in the global network. Most of the things that affect its citizens are not limited to the city's forty or so square miles. To be sure, the city wanted to exercise extraterritorial jurisdiction, just as any other institution whose fate is so profoundly affected by international commerce would try to influence that commerce. The city was thinking globally and acting locally in a shrewd tactical sense.

—Nation-states enforce their laws within their territorial borders and for the most part anyone—citizen and noncitizen alike—is subject to the laws of the nation in which they are physically present. Nations may also govern their citizens even while they are abroad, bringing them to justice for offenses committed on foreign soil. Thus, a principle of citizenship and sovereignty is that each nation makes its own laws to regulate its territory and everyone physically present within that territory (regardless of their citizenship) and their citizens (regardless of their location). Individuals are not, however, generally subject to the laws of foreign nations for actions committed at home, even when those actions are criminal under the laws of the foreign nation.

---

10. A similar argument has been made in the context of race. Until 1963 the U.S. Supreme Court struck down state laws that either prohibited or required racial segregation when applied to multistate businesses on the ground that an inconsistent law might be applied in another state, thereby impeding interstate commerce. The Court reversed the decision in *Colorado Anti-discrimination Commission v. Continental Airlines*. The Court rejected the claim of the airlines that a state antidiscrimination statute violated the Commerce Clause as applied to the airline, but only because the development of the constitutional law made it clear that any conflicting prodiscriminatory statutes were invalid, and therefore no conflict could in fact arise. Because no similar constitutional protection prohibits anti-gay statutes, the logic of the earlier commerce cases arguably applies. An actual conflict with another state law may invalidate a pro-gay statute that applies to multistate businesses.

Because global cities are particularly affected by actions that occur on foreign soil and are taken by foreign citizens, they have a strong incentive to attempt to control these actions and a greater moral justification for so doing. Further, because globalization places these cities in especially pivotal positions, a global city, acting alone or in conjunction with its national government, may be able to use its position in the global economy to extend national jurisdiction beyond these traditional limits.

In 1995 U.S. citizen Gary Lauck was arrested in Copenhagen on the strength of an international arrest warrant held by the German government. Lauck's crime was the distribution of Nazi symbols, propaganda, and anti-Semitic literature, all illegal in Germany (Fisher and Coll, 1995). From his home in Lincoln, Nebraska, Lauck operated an international organization that made and distributed the literature worldwide and most likely facilitated its distribution within Germany. Lauck himself did not enter German territory to distribute the materials, and he may not even have solicited sales there. At trial his lawyer argued that German residents initiated the transactions by requesting the materials (Fisher and Coll, 1995).

Aware that the German authorities were monitoring his activities, Lauck scrupulously avoided German soil. He did attend a neo-Nazi rally in Denmark, where such activity is protected. While in Denmark, Lauck was arrested by Danish authorities and extradited to Germany. He was eventually convicted under German law for anti-Semitic hate speech, the possession and distribution of Nazi symbols, and for propagating the "Auschwitz lie" (Fisher and Coll, 1995).

Lauck's plight may garner little sympathy from all but the most adamant of free-speech absolutists. It does, however, raise important questions about the nature of national sovereignty, citizenship, and territorial jurisdiction in a globally connected and culturally diverse national milieu. German authorities were struggling to control the dissemination of Nazi propaganda in Germany, as they are unquestionably entitled to do under any accepted theory of national sovereignty. In today's interconnected world, however, they had to control the activities of a U.S. citizen in the United States. They used the legal means at their disposal and seized the opportunity (and Mr. Lauck) through their arrangements with Denmark. In a sense, the Germans fought fire with fire. Since Lauck took advantage of global networks to distribute Nazi literature in Germany while avoiding punishment under German law, German authorities likewise took advantage of global networks to secure Lauck's arrest on foreign soil.

Let us hypothesize a somewhat more extreme case. Suppose Lauck ran a neo-Nazi web site from Nebraska. The site would clearly violate German law if run in Germany. Because the web is worldwide, the site is seen in Germany and develops a small following there. The site is published only in English. Lauck travels internationally but avoids countries where his web site is illegal. On one foreign trip his plane is diverted owing to bad weather and forced to land in Hamburg. The plane is kept on the tarmac for four hours. Meanwhile German authorities are notified by antidefamation groups in the United States that Lauck is on German soil. The authorities delay the flight's departure, arrest Lauck, and try him under German law.

Suppose Lauck beats the rap in Germany. Rather than release him, the German authorities extradite him to Israel, where he is tried under Israeli law, convicted, and sentenced. If Germany does not have an extradition treaty with Israel, they make an exception and extradite him anyway. If they cannot make an exception under German law, they apologize for detaining him and offer to send him home to the United State with the apologies and compliments of the German people. Then they arrange for him to be sent home by way of Tel Aviv and inform the Israelis that he is on his way.

Alternatively, suppose that after Lauck serves his sentence in Germany (or after he is acquitted) he is extradited seriatim to every country where his web site may be illegal under domestic law. He will face trial and serve sentences if convicted under each nation's law, and then he will be sent to the next country for another trial.

Although the Lauck case formally involved only national governments, it implicates global cities in several ways. Lauck's tactics most directly centered on global cities and the critical masses they provide: Lauck was apprehended near Amsterdam, a city that could attract a sufficient number of extremists to stage a white supremacist rally. Lauck relied on information and delivery networks that employ global cities as their hubs. He used not only the Internet, but also shipping and delivery to distribute his noxious products to the consumers of hate worldwide (see Fisher and Coll, 1995). Because global networks of communication and commerce made Lauck's American activities relevant to Germany, that country not only had an incentive to intervene, but also a "right" to do so despite Lauck's scrupulous avoidance of German soil.

Finally, a global air traffic network with hubs in various global cities makes Lauck's international network of hate possible, but also makes it more likely that he will inadvertently wind up on the soil of a nation where his activities are not protected. In my hypothetical example, the same networks that enable Lauck to spread hate worldwide from Nebraska eventually enable the German government to apprehend him.

It may seem illegitimate to capitalize on formal territorial jurisdiction in an airport that is simply a hub in a global network. (Suppose a Muslim theocratic government used such a tactic to apprehend Salman Rushdie and prosecute his publication of *The Satanic Verses*.) After all, in a sense, the "fugitive" never entered the nation or consented to be subject to its laws. Simply changing planes in an airport generally requires no visas or passport checks, and planes are regularly rerouted because of weather without the knowledge or consent of passengers. Such jurisdictional tactics, however, can become a source of national sovereignty in a world dominated by the commerce of global cities. As nation-states are affected by activities that occur outside their territorial jurisdiction, they may compensate by tactically leveraging their jurisdiction over global cities to control activities throughout the global network.

—Even in democratic nations, premised on a reciprocal relation between the franchise and subordination to the law, only citizens are empowered to change or affect those laws. The restriction of the franchise to citizens is a universally accepted limit of democracy, occasionally relaxed (such as in the EC's provision for extension of the franchise to resident noncitizens who are nationals of another EC member state for local elections) but never eliminated. The citizenry are the people who, along with national territory, define the nation-state.

The citizen is therefore the fundamental lawmaker in a democratic society. All power is thought to flow from the citizen, upward to the elected representatives and legislative and executive bodies. This, at least, is the theory of popular sovereignty.

The reality, of course, is a dizzying variety of levels of government, electoral systems, checks and balances, separations of political power, party politics, interest-group lobbying, and graft and corruption. Yet even in its complex and fallen, real-world state, lawmaking is generally still believed to be the exclusive province of nationals and their representatives. National politics may not conform to the image of a seamless and unified national democratic populism, but the factions are at least domestic factions, the parties are national parties, and the graft is paid in national currency by homegrown bribers. Otto von Bismarck is rumored to have warned: If you like law or sausages do not look at how they are made. He never thought to ask *where* they are made. And while the global market in foodstuffs means that the pedigree of one's bratwurst may be questionable, most citizens still think that at least their laws are made at home.

Indeed, law has historically been one of the defining artifacts of a national culture. Nations developed specific legal systems that grew from and responded to national conditions and cultural mores. The common law of England, for example, was believed to define the nation as an institutional and cultural body politic. The common law was the product of the experiences, struggles, and beliefs of the English people, and it distinguished England from the European continent with its predominantly Roman code–based legal system (see Blomley, 1994, 74).

Today, however, there is a growing international market in laws, not simply legal services, but actual laws—statutes, codes, and constitutions—made to order by international legal consultants and law firms for the upwardly mobile developing nation or the sovereign under pressure from the International Monetary Fund (IMF) (Sassen, 1991). If a nation is having trouble attracting foreign capital owing to insufficiently rigorous protections for private property, there are consultants who can amend the civil code in ways that will signal stability to nervous investors. If the courts are unreliable, arbitration firms will provide an internationally esteemed alternate system of dispute resolution (see Dezalay and Garth, 1996). This market in "bespoke law" inverts the traditional relation between cities and nation-states and undermines the close identification of lawmaking and citizenship. The legal service tailors of the global cities can now write the laws of nations.

We should expect that the influence of legal consultants will produce substantively different laws from those that would result from more traditional national political processes. Legal consultants will emphasize (and construct) the norms of international business in the process of consulting on the production of statutory law and in arbitrating disputes. The explicit goal of legal consultants and international commercial arbitration is to make justice standard and universal, "attacking a local and fragmented justice, and promoting a more universal business justice" (see Dezalay and Garth, 1996, 13). In this context, law as a symbol of national identity, lawmaking as the performance of citizenship, and the administration of justice as a central and exclusive activity of the nation-state are all at least partially displaced. Alongside the institutions of the state and of the citizen is a professional lawmaking apparatus tailored to the needs of business and located, not in the grand palaces and stone halls of national capitols, but in the glass and steel canyons of global cities.

The Devolution of Power and the Restructuring of Citizenship

Citizenship has its origins in ancient republican city-states. Many political theorists have argued that the normative political philosophy of civic republicanism that originated in these ancient city-states holds the key to revitalizing modern democracy and citizenship. Yet these theorists have also worried that the values of civic republicanism may not reside easily in the conceptual and territorial expanses of the nation-state. The city, with its small and more circumscribed public life and a set of experiences and concerns common to all, may be the most nourishing environment for civic virtue and meaningful political participation. If so, the reemergence of the global city as a meaningful territorial and economic location may have potentially salutary consequences for citizenship.

Global cities will not displace nation-states, but rather exist within them in a formal and territorial sense, and perhaps, with them as players in the global economy. Thus, while the revitalization of citizenship within global cities will necessarily compete for attention with national patriotism and citizenship, it need not come at the expense of national citizenship. Yet perhaps some of the prestige and influence that nation-states lose can be redirected away from extranational capitalist oligarchies and technocratic multinational institutions toward democratically organized cities.

Contemporary Devolution: Federalism and Regionalism

The devolution of power can be a mechanism for empowering distinctive subgroups within a national political system (Ford, 1997, 1365, 1366–71). This is, of course, not the only purpose of devolution: decentralization of power can also promote technical efficiency by allowing a more effective collection of information and a more precise tailoring of policies to specific local circumstances. Most semi-autonomous cities and regional governments serve both functions simultaneously: they balance the demands of national policy priorities with the imperatives of local politics.

Many self-identified national minorities push for "self-determination": either full-blown secession or a partial devolution of power within a federal system (Ford, 1999, 843, 913–20). These claims are almost always cast in terms of cultural or ethnic difference, although many are undoubtedly motivated by economics as well (see, e.g., Kelly, 1999, 225–31). These ethnic minorities may be relatively recent immigrants, historically subordinated minorities (e.g., African Americans, European Muslims, and Jews) or indigenous groups that were subsumed by a central national government (such as the Basques in Spain and France, the Corsicans in France, or the Scots and Welsh in Great Britain). They may be geographically concentrated in historically distinctive regions or clustered in the neighborhoods of major cities.

The self-determination strategies of these groups vary accordingly. Regionally based groups argue for strong regional government or nationalist secession, while urban minorities push for local "home rule," neighborhood autonomy, or secession and the creation of smaller semi-autonomous local governments.

These self-determination struggles are, in many cases, generations-old. They have, however, reemerged with renewed force in recent years (Kelly, 1999).

Although they may seem to be unrelated and even a countervailing force to globalization, many such autonomy movements are deeply intertwined with the forces of globalization. Global cultural and economic ties can empower subnational regions at the expense of the national capital, and the forces of globalization may disturb long-standing political and social compromises, leading to renewed conflict. Regional autonomy movements may be articulated exclusively in terms of ethnicity and culture, but economics often plays an important role as well. The Italian Northern League, for instance, is clearly driven by the disparity between the economically successful North and the less economically dynamic but politically empowered South (Bohlen, 1996). Similarly, the Spanish Basque region is an economic engine for the nation (Kelly, 1999, 228–29).

In both the Italian and Basque cases, important international economic and cultural networks bypass the national capital and center in major cities. Design, fashion, and industry have made Milan a global city with a diverse economy, reducing the importance of Rome in northern Italian life. The Basque regional government is actively promoting Bilbao as an international cultural center, pouring billions of pesetas into infrastructure, scholarly pursuits, and such cultural institutions as the celebrated Guggenheim Museum.

European subnational regions have, somewhat ironically, sought the greater protection of local autonomy through supranational organizations, such as the European Union. The Basque government has lobbied the EU directly over the objections of Madrid. Similarly, the English county of Kent lobbied Brussels out of frustration with the British government's management of the Eurostar "Chunnel" train that had surfaced in Kent (see Darian-Smith, 1995).

The important point here is that regional and ethnic autonomy movements are not articulated in a locally homogenous manner or in a pristine vacuum. Despite claims of historical pedigree and cultural autonomy, these local regional struggles are partially the product of the contemporary globalization of the economy and culture (Ford, 1999, 906–22). Like global cities (and indeed often centered in global cities), they are a manifestation of globalization.

The City as a Supplemental Site of Citizenship

One of my themes of this chapter has been that globalization and subnational fragmentation both threaten the integrity of the nation-state and therefore of citizenship. Citizenship is an institution based on membership and loyalty that transcend ethnic, religious, racial solidarity, and economic self-interest. It requires a location that is sufficiently cosmopolitan to cut across parochialism, yet sufficiently limited to cultivate identity and inspire esprit de corps. The nation-state has traditionally been that location.

Still, national citizenship suffers from well-chronicled deficiencies. National governments are large, bureaucratic, and remote from the daily lives of individuals. National citizenship therefore struggles to provide the sense of immediacy and belonging that can inspire loyalty and the sacrifices necessary for the common good.

Meanwhile, regional and local government, while smaller and closer to the problems of everyday life than national governments, are (especially in today's complex and interconnected world) generally too weak politically to affect the issues that are most important to their residents (see Castells, 1983, 318–31). Although globalization also entails a reassertion of what is local, their new localism is very different from that of even the recent past. The devolution of power to governmental institutions that are formally identical to eighteenth-century towns and industrial-era cities cannot adequately respond to the conditions of today's global economy. Similarly, territorial provincialism in the form of ethnically homogenous regional government is a bad approach to modern group pluralism in a world characterized by global cosmopolitanism.

Yet a reformed and empowered city government could provide another focus for citizenship. Ancient city-states were the birthplaces of formal citizenship and the civic ideals that animate it. Medieval cities served as havens from the oppression of feudalism (*stadt luft macht frei:* the city air makes free) (see Sennett, 1994, 151). Modern cities have been the source of civic idealism and demotic community, the "being together of strangers" described by political philosopher Iris Marion Young (1990, 237).

In many ways the devolution of power to cities could serve the purposes of regional devolution while avoiding its pitfalls. Because cities often are the centers of regional and ethnic communities, a decentralization of power to cities would accommodate the autonomy of ethnic groups. City-level devolution, however, could avoid the fostering of an ethnic factionalism that leads to secessionist tendencies. Power would be devolved to reflect distinctive cultural and economic interests, but it would not reinforce potentially volatile ethnic divisions. Urban-level devolution would be more likely to provide political empowerment to ethnically, racially, and religiously diverse entities, thereby promoting an urban citizenship based on shared experiences, struggles, and civic institutions rather than an ethnic separatist ideology. Because even those cities that serve as centers of ethnic community politics are generally diverse environments where tolerance is a necessary part of life, urban citizenship would make politics of insularity less feasible and less attractive. Politicians would have to appeal to a broad cross section of groups to achieve meaningful political power.

Urban citizenship would not replace national citizenship, but rather supplement it. The city would become a place of stronger political affiliation and political power, reflecting the importance of the contemporary global village and the real virtues of decentralization of power. It would not necessarily compete with the nation. Rather, cities would be members of a federal republic. City-states would work, negotiate, and at times struggle with one another and with centralized federal governments. They would of necessity at times act against the wishes of the federal government, but they would bolster national citizenship by introducing the habits of democracy at a level that is manageable and at the same time relevant.

Scale as the Axis of Reform, or: "Honey, I Shrunk the State"

Most proposals to alter the jurisdictional distribution of political power are greeted with a well-deserved skepticism. Those who defend the centralization of power often find it difficult to reject a call for ever greater centralization on their own terms: the arguments for regional over local control of some governmental service (economies of scale, control of economic externalities, superior coordination, inclusion, egalitarianism) apply as well to state over regional administration and with even greater force to a nationwide scheme. Can a new world order be far behind? At the same time, those who argue for devolution (citing freedom of choice, elimination of wasteful bureaucracies, and experimentation) are hard-pressed to escape the logical conclusion of their arguments: privatization, the ultimate devolution to the jurisdiction of the private estate and a political community of one.

Yet a lack of innovation is not a result of widespread satisfaction with contemporary jurisdictions and the governmental institutions they define. To the contrary, citizens attempt to alter jurisdictional boundaries through the annexation of additional territory, consolidation with neighboring jurisdictions, and (most often) secession from larger jurisdictions. Scholars, politicians, and grassroots political movements challenge the present scale of jurisdictions. Some advocate regional government over local fragmentation; others extol the virtues of "community autonomy" and the devolution of political power to states, localities, and even to vaguely defined neighborhoods.

The usual attempts at jurisdictional reform fail because they examine only one element of the jurisdiction: scale. This results in one of two barren approaches. In the first it is tacitly assumed that the jurisdiction must remain, more or less as we receive it today: a territorially defined domain in which a single governmental authority exercises control, generally without regard to the specifics of the territory. It is assumed that the template of government must be the territorial jurisdiction. It is unquestioned that the territory must be contiguous and relatively compact, and it goes without saying that membership in the jurisdiction is established by domicile and subjugation to its authority accomplished by physical presence.[11]

This taken as given, the only avenue of reform open is a tinkering with scale. If local government is subject to collective-action problems, clannishness, insularity, or poor administration, then we will replace it with a regional government structured in more or less the same way: an enlarged copy of the problematic entity, a monster version: "Honey, I Blew up the City." If federal administration is plagued by inefficiency, special-interest politics, bureaucracy, and inertia, then we will "devolve" the same bundle of powers to state governments, created in the image of the federal government we have condemned, and therefore inevitably characterized by smaller versions of the same problems and pint-sized budgets to deal with those problems: "Honey, I Shrunk the State."[12]

Proposals

Multinationalism and a regional devolution of power are inadequate responses to the challenges that confront late-twentieth-century nation-states. Traditional scale-based reforms of the polity are unsatisfying because they do not respond to the changes in economic and sociocultural life that give rise to the need for reform in the first place. Globalization does not simply enlarge the sphere of economic and political relations. It unmoors such relations from smooth and contiguous geographical spheres of any shape and size. Rather than spheres of influence, we have networks and nodal points. Similarly, contemporary ethnic and cultural fragmentation does not always fall into neat regional divisions, and contemporary economic divisions do not create easily mapped regional

11. If pressed, one might admit that some jurisdictions do not conform to these specifications, but such entities are aberrations, anomalous and embarrassing.

12. A related error consists of failing to recognize the institutional specifics of a given jurisdictional structure: thus, the federal government is assumed to be cumbersome and inefficient because of its size and its public nature, without reference to the layers of procedural safeguards designed to reduce the scope of individual discretion (and therefore also individual initiative); the requirements of public access to official documents and meetings designed to increase accountability (but which also encourage mediocrity and timidity over boldness of action, ambiguity, and hedging over precision and directness in communication); the archaic senatorial filibuster (until recently); and the absence of an executive line-item veto. Yet we find that state and local governments that labor under similar impediments are similarly cumbersome and bureaucratic, as are similarly encumbered private corporations.

economies. Rather, groups can cluster unevenly, and economic interconnection may jump from city to city, ignoring national and regional borders. Jurisdictional reform must respond to these realities if it is to foster renewed and meaningful citizenship. I advance the following proposals with this in mind. None of these proposals would be appropriate in every circumstance. I advance them only to suggest that new types of reform are possible.

Allow localities to influence international affairs as an incidence to local autonomy.   To some extent, this proposal is simply an extension of the home rule autonomy that many American cities already enjoy and of the potential to intervene directly in continental political affairs that many European regions enjoy. Most commentators see the ability of localities to make policy decisions with international implications as a threat to be quashed. For instance, when American states and municipalities passed local ordinances and state laws that effectively made divestment and a boycott of Myanmar a condition of all contracts with the government, many attacked the ordinances as an inappropriate intervention into foreign affairs. The United States Supreme Court recently struck down such a Massachusetts "Burma law." Since local governments are formally subdivisions of states by long-established constitutional doctrine, this decision will also invalidate similar local laws.

By contrast, my proposal would allow localities to make such "foreign affairs" interventions, both by directly lobbying at the level of international organizations and by such financial interventions as setting conditions in public contracts and leases.

Even such limited local power will undoubtedly affect the ability of national governments to conduct foreign affairs, especially in matters of trade. In a world in which so much of what is global is also local, however, local intervention in foreign affairs is a necessary consequence of meaningful local government. Moreover, local power can act as a useful check on the policies of national governments. Local politics, as Alexis de Tocqueville opined, is a laboratory for democracy. In the context of globalization, this laboratory can provide an incubator for grassroots political movements in which citizens can understand the connection between their local concerns and global affairs. The result will be not only to forestall or prevent foreign policy that does not have the informed support of the rank and file citizenry, but also to foster a more meaningful democratic consensus for those foreign policies that are adopted.

Establish nondomiciliary voting in the localities.   One may object that expanding the power of localities to influence foreign policy inappropriately empowers the residents of global cities over the residents of smaller or less centrally positioned cities, while the international affairs in question may be equally important to both groups. A similar problem already infects local politics. Often even strictly local affairs of a major city affect nonresidents who are excluded from the local franchise. Scholars of local government have developed proposals to deal with this problem, and these proposals would address issues of foreign affairs as well.

Here is one of many possible solutions: Local elections could be open to all members of a metropolitan region, or even to all citizens of a state, rather than be limited based on residence. All local elections would be held on the same day, and voters would receive a number of votes equal to the number of open seats, which they could cast in any election they wished (see Frug, 1993, 253, 324–25, 329–30).[13] In this way, voters would effectively draw their own jurisdictional boundaries, decide which local governments were most important to them, and allocate their votes accordingly.

> They [could] define their interests differently in different elections. . . . People are unlikely to vote in a jurisdiction they do not care about, but there are a host of possible motives for voting. . . . [T]he voting system might . . . mimic . . . proportional representation by allowing someone to cast all [of her] votes in one locality. (Frug, 1993)

Allow foreign nationals to obtain local citizenship. The European Union already provides that foreign nationals who are citizens of member states may vote and stand for office in the local election of their place of *residence* (so for instance, an Italian citizen living in Paris could vote in Parisian local elections, although she would not be allowed to vote in Parisian national elections). This sensible compromise recognizes the importance of both national citizenship and a type of local citizenship based on the immediate concerns of day-to-day life and the potentially long-term commitment to a "foreign" locale. The proposal is simply to extend this idea to other contexts. Foreign nationals could be allowed to vote in U.S. local elections with only statutory reforms in many jurisdictions and with state constitutional reform in others. Nothing in the U.S.

---

13. The use of cumulative voting is not an untried proposal. Not only do many corporations use such a scheme as a mechanism to protect minority shareholders, see *Robert C. Clark, Corporate Law* § 9.1.3, 361–66 (1986); *William M. Fletcher, Fletcher Cyclopedia of the Law of Private Corporations,* vol. 5, § 2048, nn.10–11 (rev. perm. ed. 1987), noting state constitutional and statutory provisions requiring cumulative voting in shareholder election, but some intralocal elections (for multimember boards) are also conducted in this manner (see Buckley, 1994, reporting a federal district court's decision to require cumulative voting in the election of county commissioners as an alternative to creating a majority black district). Frug's innovation is to propose that citizens would vote in jurisdictions in which they do not reside.

Constitution prohibits it. Such reform could be contingent on reciprocal agreements to allow American residents to vote in foreign local elections, or they could be implemented unilaterally as a matter of an enlarged conception of local political community.

Conclusion

The idea of the global city-state is an attempt to decenter the nation-state as the primary geographical and political unit of analysis in the study of international law and in what is loosely called globalization. Because of changes in the technologies and patterns of economic development, trade, and migration, major cities are crucial nodal points in international relations. This *spatial* position makes such cities much more significant than even their large populations would suggest. At the same time, cities are intensely local and located. They are homes to individuals, they have local cultures, and they are the repositories of intense symbolic meaning and emotional loyalty as unique places. The impact of globalization therefore need not be homogenization, transparency, and a global monoculture in which such institutions as citizenship are irrelevant. Instead, it can be a mutation of such political affiliations: the creation of a local citizenship that is at once national and global.

My analysis is, of course, not global in its implications. Its primary focus has been the United States and Europe, and although the analysis may apply in certain other contexts, it will not travel well to many others. Moreover, I mean to describe only an emergent phenomenon and a potential (I believe, hopeful) implication of that phenomenon. I do not mean to assert a new "dominant paradigm" or universal structure. Most important, the analysis of what I somewhat playfully call global city-states is not meant to suggest that the nation-state is irrelevant or has been superseded. Much less does it entail "centering" the global city, simply replacing one privileged jurisdiction site with another. Instead, the idea of city-states and the decentering of the nation-state it implies simply allows other jurisdictional arrangements and potential political affiliations to come into view. The trope of the global city-state is important, not because it describes a new hegemony, but because it allows us to escape cemented notions of what law and policy can and should be in order to respond to a rapidly changing global village.

Works Cited

Blomley, Nicholas. 1994. *Law, Space, and the Geographies of Power*. New York: Guilford Press.

Bohlen, Celestine. 1996. "Italy's Secessionist Party Exploits a Growing Army of Malcontents." *New York Times*. June 11, A; p. 1, col. 5.

Buckley, Stephen. 1994. "Unusual Ruling in Rights Case." *Washington Post*. Apr. 6, A1.

Castells, Manuel. 1983. *The City and the Grassroots*. Berkeley: University of California Press.

Darian-Smith, Eve. 1995. "Rabies Rides the Fast Train: Transnational Interactions in Post-Colonial Times." *Law and Critique* 6(1): 75.

Dezalay, Yves, and Bryant G. Garth. 1996. *Dealing in Virtue*. Chicago: University of Chicago Press.

Dillon, John. 1911. *Municipal Corporations*. Vol. 1. Boston: Little, Brown

Fisher, Marc, and Steve Coll. 1995. "U.S. Extremists Are Active in Global Network of Hate." *International Herald Tribune*, May 12.

Ford, Richard T. 1997. "Geography and Sovereignty." *Stanford Law Review* 49.

———. 1999. "Law's Territory." *Michigan Law Review* 97.

Frug, Gerald. 1993. "Decentering Decentralization." *University of Chicago Law Review* 60.

Harvey, David. 1989. *The Conditions of Postmodernity*. Oxford: Blackwell.

Kelly, Michael. 1999. "Political Downsizing: The Reemergence of Self Determination." *Drake Law Review* 47.

Maine, Sir Henry. [1864] 1986. *Ancient Law*. Tucson: University of Arizona Press.

McBain, Howard. 1916. *The Law and Practice of Home Rule*. New York: Columbia University Press.

Nairn, Thomas. 1977. *The Break Up of Britain*. London: Atlantic Highlands Humanities Press.

Nozick, Robert. 1974. *Anarchy, State, and Utopia*. New York: Basic Books.

Putnam, Robert. 1993. *Making Democracy Work*. Princeton, N.J.: Princeton University Press.

Raskin, Jamin. 1993. "Legal Aliens, Local Citizens." *University of Pennsylvania Law Review* 141.

Roht-Arriaza, Naomi. 1997. "The Committee on Regions and the Role of Regional Governments in the European Union." *Hasting International and Comparative Law Review* 20.

Sassen, Saskia. 1991. *The Global City*. Princeton: Princeton University Press.

———. 1995. *Losing Ground*. New York: Columbia University Press.

Sennett, Richard. 1994. *Flesh and Stone*. New York: W. W. Norton.

Sullivan, Andrew. 1999. "The End of Britain." *New York Times Magazine*, Feb. 21, Sect. 6, p. 38.

Weber, Max. 1958. *The City*. New York: Free Press.

Young, Iris Marion. 1990. *Justice and the Politics of Difference*. Princeton: Princeton University Press.

PART THREE

Redefining Citizenship:
Concepts and Practices

CHAPTER EIGHT

Denationalizing Citizenship

LINDA BOSNIAK

MOST TALK ABOUT citizenship has concerned two questions: Who is entitled to enjoy citizenship, and what does citizenship entail for its holders? The debate has focused, in other words, on defining the class of citizenship's subjects and on elaborating the meaning of citizenship in substantive terms. And there is certainly a great deal to say about these matters. Yet most analysts have tended to ignore another set of questions that are fundamental to citizenship. These are questions concerning citizenship's location—that is, questions about where citizenship takes place and where it *should* take place. The reason these questions have largely been disregarded is that citizenship has been conventionally assumed to be a national enterprise; it has been assumed to be an institution or a set of social practices situated squarely and necessarily within the political community of the nation-state (e.g., Wiener, 1998, 27).[1] Given this assumption, there has not seemed to be much of anything to talk about.

In the past few years, however, this national presumption in the citizenship literature has come under increasing challenge. Scholars from various disci-

This chapter is an abbreviated version of the article "Citizenship Denationalized," *Indiana Journal of Global Legal Studies* 7(2) (2000): 447–510.

1. Weiner (1998): "Most scholars who have studied citizenship . . . would—notwithstanding their differences in choice of conceptual or historical approach—agree that to talk about citizenship always involves a notion of stateness." Of course, citizenship has not always been regarded as a project of the modern nation-state. In fact, the concept has its origins in the classical Greek city-state. For a history of the concept of citizenship, see Heater (1990, 211–19); see also Walzer (1989).

plines have begun to argue that citizenship is, in fact, taking increasingly nonnational forms, and political activists have likewise articulated and promoted conceptions of citizenship that locate it beyond the state. The common theme in this emerging discourse is that exclusively nation-centered understandings of citizenship are unduly parochial in this period of intensive globalization. Citizenship is said to be increasingly denationalized, with new forms of citizenship that exceed the nation developing to replace the old.[2]

These new forms of citizenship have been described by their exponents in a variety of terms. Some have spoken of the emergence of *transnational citizenship,* others, of the development of *global citizenship.* Within the university community, we hear a great deal as well about the advent of *postnational* forms of citizenship, a term most closely associated with sociologist Yasemin Soysal (1994, 1997).

These are formulations that have been summarily dismissed by conventional political thought, which treats the nation-state as the natural and inevitable site of citizenship and views the notion of citizenship outside the context of a state as simply incoherent and, perhaps, affirmatively dangerous as well.[3]

But *is* citizenship, in fact, an inherently national project? Certainly, citizenship has a history that long precedes the development of the nation-state.[4] Nevertheless, today it is undeniably a part of our political common sense to think of citizenship in national terms. Still, does this mean that citizenship cannot possibly take anything *other* than a national form in the current period, that it has not done so already, or that it should never do so? These are the questions I address in this chapter.

I am ultimately sympathetic to the view that citizenship need not be conceived of in a way that confines it to the nation-state. Significantly, I do not consider the location question a purely empirical one (although it is partly that). Any debate over the merits of the idea of denationalized citizenship is a debate about the meaning of citizenship in the first instance. To assume that the question can be settled categorically or empirically is to assume that citizenship's meaning is fixed. In fact, it is anything but fixed. Citizenship is one of those

2. For a sampling of this emerging literature, see Soysal (1997, 509, 512); Spiro (1999, 597); Vogel and Moran (1991, various articles); Held (1991); Falk (1993); Bauböck (1994); and Torres (1998).

3. For the classic denunciation of the notion of world citizenship, see Arendt (1968, 81–94, 89) ("A world citizen, living under the tyranny of a world empire, and speaking and thinking in a kind of glorified Esperanto, would be no less a monster than a hermaphrodite.") More recently, Himmelfarb (1996, 72, 74) criticized Martha Nussbaum's (1996) cosmopolitan argument on behalf of "world citizenship," by asserting that the term *citizenship* has "little meaning except in the context of a state."

4. See note 1, p. 237.

core political concepts whose conventional meaning has been subject to constant struggle and renegotiation (e.g., Shklar, 1991, 1).[5] Much of what is struggled *over* are questions of how far the term properly extends, in what circumstances it is appropriately employed, and who is entitled to claim it.[6]

Thus, to ask whether the concept can extend so far as to include transnational or postnational practices and institutions is to ask, in part, what we understand citizenship to mean in our collective lives. It is also to ask what we believe citizenship *ought to* mean. I suggest, in fact, that any struggle over the scope of the application of the term is, in part, a normative struggle, a political struggle— a struggle over the visions of collective life that we want to embrace and enact.

I

But I begin this chapter by investigating the claim of denationalization as an empirical claim, since those are the terms over which much of the debate over postnational citizenship is actually conducted. Most of the literature on postnational and transnational citizenship is written in a descriptive mode by social scientists who portray themselves as disinterestedly describing the changing state of the world; their claim is that citizenship is being reconfigured in postnational terms as a matter of fact. This claim is advanced against the backdrop of the conventional view, which holds that citizenship has been, and remains, inherently national in character.

In response, how are we to assess denationalization as an empirical claim? Is citizenship, in fact, becoming increasingly denationalized? Not surprisingly, we cannot answer this question simply by going out into the world and observing the current condition of citizenship in order to test the claim. Instead, first we have to determine what it is we want to observe. To do this, we have to

---

5. Shklar (1991): "There is no notion more central in politics than citizenship, [yet] none more variable in history or contested in theory." See also Balibar (1988, 723) ("[H]istory still shows that this concept has no definition that is fixed for all time. It has always been at stake in struggles and the object of transformations"). The confusion is not merely a contemporary one; see Aristotle (1946, 93) ("The nature of citizenship . . . is a question which is often disputed; there is no general agreement on a single definition").

6. Citizenship is a classic example of what William Connolly describes as an "essentially contested concept." Connolly (1993) writes: "When [a concept] is appraisive in that the state of affairs it describes is a valued achievement, when the practice described is internally complex in that its characterization involves reference to several dimensions, and when the agreed and contested rules of application are relatively open, enabling parties to interpret even those shared rules differently as new and unforeseen situations arise, then the concept in question is an 'essentially contested concept.' Such concepts 'essentially involve endless disputes about their proper uses on the part of their users'" (his emphases), quoting Gallie (1955–1956).

define our terms. There is, first, the question of what is meant by *denationalization*. The various articulations of the denationalization idea—postnational citizenship, transnational citizenship, and global citizenship—are not necessarily interchangeable, and none of them is defined in any clear way in the emerging literature.

Broadly speaking, most analysts who employ these terms appear to be referring not so much to an alleged collapse of the nation-state system as to a moment in time when national forms of public life have simply lost their assumed authority and predominance. For present purposes, I approach the denationalization concept in this way: I read it as an idea that expresses the claim that the nation-state is becoming decentered as the locus of our collective institutional and affiliative lives. Nonetheless, there remains a real lack of clarity in the literature on the precise meaning of the various terms used to express the denationalization position, and this is something that requires attention by its exponents.

Beyond the concept of denationalization, we are faced with the more formidable problem of figuring out what we are talking about when we use the language of *citizenship*. Citizenship is not a unitary concept, and conventional understandings of the term are multiple and disputed. Most commentators concur that citizenship designates community membership of some kind,[7] but the term has an enormously broad range of uses, not all of which are compatible. The concept is used to refer to modes of governance and participation, rights and duties, identities, and commitments and legal statuses. As political theorist Judith Shklar (1991, 1) remarked in a book on U.S. citizenship several years ago, "There is no notion more central in politics than citizenship, [yet] none more variable in history, or contested in theory."

In response to this conceptual disarray, several theorists of citizenship have proposed organizing schemas to help make sense of the citizenship debates. Their formulations vary, but many of them distinguish broadly between several understandings of citizenship, which I will reduce to four.[8] *Citizenship*, first, is commonly used in a legal sense to designate the formal status of membership in

7. See, e.g., Walzer (1989, 211); Barbalet (1988, 20); Held (1991, 20) (citizenship entails "membership, membership of the community in which one lives one's life").

8. See, e.g., Kymlicka and Norman (1994, 352) (distinguishing between three approaches to citizenship, which they call citizenship-as-rights, citizenship-as-activity, and citizenship-as-identity, and contrasting all these with "immigration and naturalization policy," by which they seem to mean citizenship as legal status and which they choose not to address); Carens (1996–1997, 111) (distinguishing between the legal, psychological, and political dimensions of citizenship); Heater (1990) (distinguishing between "the feeling of citizenship," "political citizenship" and "the status of citizenship"). For other efforts toward conceptual organization, see Kratochwil (1994, 485) (distinguishing between citizenship as status and citizenship as belonging); Vogel and Moran (1991, xii) (examining what they call the territorial, temporal, social, political, and behavioral frontiers of citizenship).

a political community. In the sociological tradition of T. H. Marshall (1949), the term is employed to refer to the individual's possession and enjoyment of fundamental rights in society. In the civic republican tradition, *citizenship* names a state of active engagement in the life of a polity. Finally, in psychological or cultural terms, the term *citizenship* is invoked to refer to an experience of identity and solidarity that a person maintains in collective or public life.

For some commentators, these different understandings reflect distinct " dimensions" of a single phenomenon (e.g., Carens, 1996–1997).[9] But other commentators seem to regard these categories as designating sometimes-incommensurable discourses about citizenship. The largely liberal tradition of citizenship-as-rights and the largely republican tradition of citizenship-as-political-activity, in particular, might be said to be highly incompatible in some readings (e.g., Kymlicka and Norman, 1994).

Because the concept of citizenship is subject to various, sometimes irreconcilable, understandings (or senses, in linguistic terms), no single empirical answer is available to the question of whether citizenship has begun to take a postnational form. The meaning of the claim will vary depending on the dimension, or discourse, of citizenship at issue, and the plausibility of the claims will presumably vary as well.

My position, briefly, is that a reasonable case can be made that all the various practices and experiences that we conventionally associate with citizenship do, in some respects, exceed the boundaries and jurisdiction of the territorial nation-state. But there *are* differences in the power and persuasiveness of the claim across the various discourses or dimensions. The denationalization claim is probably least plausible when we speak of citizenship as a legal status. With the exception of the European Union, formal citizenship status remains largely tied to the national state (or to plural states, in the case of dual or multiple citizenships). Even in Europe, where citizenship status *is* arguably being denationalized to some extent,[10] Union citizenship remains subordinate to European national citizenships in important ways. Among other things, possession of Union citizenship still depends upon possession of citizenship status in a mem-

9. See also Conover (1995, 133, 134) (citizenship "encompasses a variety of elements, some legal, some psychological, and some behavioral").

10. See Treaty of European Union (TEU) (1991, ratified 1993), Art. B (stating an objective of the European Union is "to strengthen the protection of the rights and interests of the nationals of its Member States through the introduction of a citizenship of the Union"); Treaty Establishing the European Community (EC Treaty), Art. 8 (amended 1993) ("(1) Citizenship of the Union is hereby established. Every person holding the nationality of a Member State shall be a citizen of the Union. (2) Citizens of the Union shall enjoy the rights conferred by this Treaty and shall be subject to the duties imposed thereby"). According to Soysal (1994, 148), "'European citizenship' clearly embodies postnational membership in its most elaborate legal form."

ber state,[11] and states remain empowered to determine who will be accorded their citizenship or nationality.[12]

The postnationality claim is somewhat more convincing when citizenship is understood as the enjoyment of certain rights. The claim seems plausible here because the various rights associated with citizenship in this tradition are, in fact, no longer guaranteed exclusively at the nation-state level.[13] The international human rights regimes that have taken shape in the post–World War II period are designed to implement standards for the treatment of individuals by states. These standards, which encompass civil, political, social, and cultural rights, serve as an alternative source of rights, one that transcends the jurisdiction of individual nation-states.

Of course, there are real limits to the international human rights system, and people still face serious constraints in enforcing their rights. But it remains true that the rights commonly associated with citizenship are no longer entirely constrained by nation-state boundaries, and it therefore seems reasonable to describe this development as an incipient form of postnational citizenship. This citizenship may be more symbolic than real, but this is often true for citizenship rights within nation-states as well.

The claim that citizenship is becoming postnational is more convincing still when citizenship is approached as a form of political activity. Increasing numbers of people are engaged in democratic political practices across national boundaries in the form of transnational social movements, including those of environmentalists, feminists, human rights workers, and trade unions.[14] Some will no doubt argue that such activity, however transnational, cannot be de-

11. EC Treaty, Art. 8(1) ("Every person holding the nationality of a Member State shall be a citizen of the Union").

12. Under international law, states are ordinarily regarded as having sovereign authority to determine who will be accorded citizenship or nationality. See, e.g., *Liechtenstein v. Guatemala* (Second Phase) ("In re *Nottebohm*") (1955) I.C.J. 4, p. 20 ("It is for Liechtenstein, as it is for every sovereign State, to settle by its own legislation the rules relating to the acquisition of its nationality, and to confer that nationality by naturalization granted by its own organs in accordance with that legislation").

13. Some scholars have recently begun to characterize the rights guaranteed under the international human rights regime as representing a burgeoning form of citizenship-beyond-the-nation. Soysal (1997, 512), e.g., contends that the postwar era has witnessed a "breakdown of the link between the national community and rights," giving rise to the development of a new "postnational form of citizenship." Political theorist Rainer Bauböck (1994) has similarly asserted that "human rights are the cornerstone as well as the most extended application of a transnational conception of citizenship." Bauböck also writes, however, that the "[s]tronger enforcement of human rights by international agencies should not be seen as a move toward 'global citizenship' but it could be characterized as the quest for a 'polity of polities'" (p. 248).

14. For a comprehensive study of this phenomenon, see Keck and Sikkink (1998) (describing such movements as "transnational value-based advocacy networks"). See also Magnusson, 1994;

scribed in the language of citizenship, since citizenship can be meaningfully practiced only within a distinct institutional context: that of the political community, by which is meant a formal, organized, territorially based community with some degree of sovereign self-governance.[15] In response, however, one can draw on rich, antistatist conceptions of the political—conceptions that urge the recognition of citizenship and its practices in the economy, the workplace, the neighborhood, professional associations, and even in the family. In this understanding, citizenship is practiced in the realm of civil society and not merely the state, often by way of the "new social movements."[16]

The idea of postnational citizenship takes this approach one step further by looking at political practices in the domain of what some have called global civil society.[17] There seems to be no a priori reason that such activity cannot be described in the language of citizenship. Furthermore, transnational political activity arguably fulfills the normative criteria of republican and participatory democratic conceptions of citizenship well. It is robust and engaged and reflects a "commitment to the common good and active participation in public affairs" (Dagger, 1997, 99). The difference is simply that the notions of common good, as well as the public domain involved, are drawn more expansively than they usually are within the tradition.

With respect to citizenship in its identity and solidarity modes, anthropologists and others have recently made it clear that people maintain crucial identities and commitments that transcend or traverse national boundaries. This includes not merely the identifications and solidarities that may develop among members of transnational social movements, but also the experiences of migrants who live in various diasporic and other cross-national communities.[18]

Drainville, 1995; Lynch, 1998, 149; Wapner, 1995, 311, Spiro, 1994, 45; and Brecher, 1994, 81–118. Note that while much of the focus in the above sources is on the increasing transnationalization of progressive social movements, many right-wing movements can be described in these terms as well. See, e.g., Lynch (1998, 150).

15. See, e.g., Kukathas (1996, 80, 88) (arguing that a political community, as distinct from other forms of community, "has a territorial base," and that "the most significant institution of a political community is its government").

16. See, e.g., Pateman (1970, 45–102); Dahl (1989, 324–32); and Pateman (1989). This is a pluralist conception of politics and of citizenship, one that rejects confining "the definition of political action to formal interactions between citizens and the state" (Jones, 1998, 233) and holds that citizenship is "rooted in groups and communities within which people actually live" (Nisbet, 1975, 286–87).

17. See, e.g., Wapner (1995, 311, 312–13) ("Global civil society as such is that slice of associational life which exists above the individual and below the state, but also across national boundaries").

18. There is a growing empirical literature in anthropology and sociology on such communities. See, e.g., Basch, Glick Schiller, and Szanton Blanc (1994); Smith (1998, 196–240); Portes (1996, 74); and Soysal (1997, 519–21).

This overview offers only a cursory treatment of the various questions implicated here, and there remains much room for empirical debate. But the broader methodological point I want to make is that citizenship does not have an essential nature or objective meaning. The term is used to represent a variety of institutions and social and political practices in ways that are sometimes at odds with one another. To determine whether citizenship is indeed becoming denationalized, as some scholars and activists claim, we ought to determine whether the practices and institutions standardly designated by the term exceed the bounds of the nation-state. By this measure, the denationalization claim seems entirely plausible, although, as I have said, it varies in its power and persuasiveness according to the discourse of citizenship at issue.

II

The approach suggested here differs markedly from that taken by most citizenship scholars. In the first place, most scholars of citizenship do not even acknowledge that there are several, sometimes competing, citizenship discourses at play in our discussions. Beyond this, many are likely to adopt the following position: even if it is true that the statuses and rights, politics and identities, and solidarities of membership are becoming transnationalized in various ways, these developments do not signal the postnationalization of citizenship so much as the citizenship's *displacement or decline* in the face of other forms of collective organization and affiliation, as yet unnamed. The sociologist David Jacobson (1996), for example, has argued that the rise of international human rights law represents a "devaluation" or displacement of citizenship; in so doing, he is assuming citizenship to be a national institution by nature and by definition.[19]

But scholars and activists who employ the concepts of postnational, transitional, and global citizenship are not willing to cede the concept of citizenship to the domain of the national. They want to take the term beyond its presumed national location. In effect, they are arguing that (in Quentin Skinner's [1989,

---

19. Some analysts concur with the exponents of post- or transnational citizenship that the norms of universal personhood associated with the international human rights regime have become increasingly important in organizing national and international public life, but they argue that this development reflects a *decline or devaluation* of citizenship—rather than a form of post- or transnational citizenship. See, e.g., Jacobson (1996); Sassen (1996, 89) ("Human rights override . . . distinctions [of nationality] and hence can be seen as potentially contesting state sovereignty and devaluing citizenship"). In this approach, citizenship is an intrinsically national enterprise, and the increasing salience of personhood norms represents *not* a novel species of citizenship, but a loss of the possibility of citizenship altogether.

15] terms) "the ordinary criteria for applying [the] term are present in a wider range of circumstances than has commonly been allowed."

So here the disagreement is no longer an empirical one, but has become linguistic and conceptual. The dispute turns on differences over citizenship's proper range of reference. Specifically, the debate concerns the question of whether, when the social practices and institutions ordinarily designated by the term begin to take nonnational forms, they can still be characterized as citizenship. Disputes over the proper range of reference of an important political term are common, as linguistic theorists make clear (see, generally, Ball, Farr, and Hanson, 1989). These disputes, however, are settled conventionally. Once again, there is no impartial way of determining how a key political term should be used, or how far it can extend.

The question we need to ask, however, is why it should *matter* whether the word citizenship can extend to designate nonnational or transnational phenomena. Why do people argue over this? What is at stake? Certainly, everyone wants to get the facts and categories right, but there is also more at issue. This is because citizenship is not merely a word that describes the world. It is also a powerful term of appraisal, one that performs an enormous legitimizing function.[20] To characterize a set of social practices in the language of citizenship is to honor them with recognition as politically and socially consequential, as centrally constitutive and defining of our collective lives. To refuse them the designation is to deny them such recognition.

In this respect, the designation of nonnational social and political arrangements in the language of citizenship is not just an act of empirical labeling. It is a political act; it is a claim that conveys at least some criticism of the prevailing assumption that citizenship is necessarily a national project. And it conveys, by implication, some approval of, or aspiration toward, plural and denationalized membership forms. This means, in turn, that any effort to assess the postnational citizenship claim has to contend with its normative content; it has to ask whether citizenship beyond the nation is something desirable.

Thus, the question: *Is* citizenship beyond the nation something worth aspiring to? The answer to the desirability question, it seems to me, is that it depends. It is easy enough to argue that in some circumstances a decoupling of citizenship from the nation-state will support principles of social justice and democratic equality (however precisely these are defined). From the perspective of a person concerned with ensuring the protection of human rights, for example, it is indisputably a good thing that those rights traditionally associ-

20. See Bosniak (1998, 29); see also Fraser and Gordon (1994, 90) (describing *citizenship* as "a weighty, monumental, humanist word" that has "no pejorative uses").

ated with citizenship are increasingly being guaranteed at the international level because, very simply, it means that more people are likely to enjoy more human rights protection more of the time than under an exclusively national rights regime.

However, the fact that there are good normative arguments on behalf of citizenship-beyond-the-nation should not lead to an indiscriminate celebration of things postnational.[21] It is easy to find examples of postnational and transnational developments that might be described in the language of citizenship that many people committed to democratic and egalitarian values would not support. For instance, Richard Falk (1993, 43–44) describes the denationalized fellowship that links many members of the transnational corporate and managerial classes as a form of denationalized citizenship for the elite.[22] This description is obviously not the emancipatory image of transnational citizenship that many exponents have in mind. Citizenship extending beyond the nation, in other words, is not going to be desirable or dangerous per se. Postnational citizenship takes many forms (just as citizenship does) and can sometimes support and sometimes undermine democratic and egalitarian values.

If we are not going to engage in sweeping celebrations or condemnations of postnational citizenship, how should we approach the normative questions that the concept implicitly raises? Advocates of postnational and transnational citizenship *themselves* do not have much to say about the normative questions, because they usually purport to describe rather than prescribe the state of citizenship.

But for those of us who *are* trying to engage with these questions, the idea of postnational or transnational citizenship is potentially useful. It is useful not so much as an affirmative vision of what a denationalized world might look like, but as a critical trope that enables us to challenge the prevailing conviction in normative political thought that citizenship is rightfully and appropriately a national enterprise. The idea of postnational citizenship, in other words, serves as a useful vehicle for critically interrogating normative nationalism.

Although in theory the nationalist premise can be challenged in relation to all dimensions of citizenship, my focus in the normative discussion is on citizenship as collective identity and solidarity. Focusing on this aspect of citizen-

21. There is a strain of thought in cultural studies that has tended in this direction. Appadural's (1996) essay "Postnational Patriotism" is a prominent example (see ch. 6, "Patriotism and Its Futures").

22. Falk describes as one form of citizenship the unification of the world "around a common business and financial elite, [one] that shares interests and experiences [and] comes to have more in common within its membership than it does within the more rooted, ethnically distinct members of its own particular civil society; the result seems to be a denationalized global elite that is, at the same time, virtually without any sense of global civic responsibility."

ship makes sense because of its constitutive relationship with citizenship in its other aspects. Citizenship as status, as rights, and as political activity are all fundamentally grounded in experiences of collective identification with and attachment to others. All evoke an emotional response from their participants. Further, it is only in this context that political and legal theorists have explicitly and systematically addressed the question of where citizenship should be located. There is, consequently, a literature to respond to on the subject.

Historically, the issue of the proper location of citizenship commitments and identities has been addressed in the context of the perennial debate between supporters of cosmopolitanism and patriotism.[23] There is more recent work on the subject, one strand of which has been developed by so-called liberal nationalists who have been concerned with defending the continued centrality of national affiliations and solidarities in an era of intensive globalization.[24] Analysts, including David Miller (1995), David Hollinger (1995), and Richard Rorty (1998), recognize the enormous pull that both subnational and transnational connections have on people's affiliative experiences these days. They even make a point of recognizing the value of these attachments. Yet they deny that sub- and transnational commitments have to any great extent displaced national ones as a matter of fact. Moreover, they argue that national commitments *must* not be displaced; they contend that national identities and solidarities need to remain primary. Liberalism itself depends on it, they maintain; as Miller (1995, 187) has written, "the welfare state—and indeed, programs to protect minority rights—have always been *national* projects, justified on the basis that members of a community must protect one another and guarantee one another equal respect."

Many liberal nationalists argue as well that not only is nationalism necessary for liberal democratic outcomes, but it is intrinsically desirable because the nation-state is the only large-scale contemporary institutional setting in which people may develop the sense of "common good" or a "shared fate" that is so vital to collective human flourishing (Taylor, 1989, 170).[25]

23. While this debate is wide-ranging and includes a variety of positions on both sides, it is centrally defined by a controversy over the relative merits of ethical universalism and particularism.

24. The phrase seems to have originated with Tamir (1993). Many others have since made use of the term. See, e.g., Lind (1995); Hollinger (1995); and Miller (1995). The liberal nationalist literature is diverse, but broadly contains two principal strands. The first is concerned with questions of national self-determination; the second focuses on questions of national identity and transnational ethics. It is mainly the latter stream of scholarship that is of interest here. For a selection of commentary on this latter aspect of liberal nationalism, see, e.g., Lichtenberg (1996–1997, 53); and Levinson (1995).

25. Taylor (1989): "[T]he bond of solidarity with my compatriots in a functioning republic is based on a sense of shared fate, where the sharing itself is of value. This is what gives this

Exponents of postnational citizenship for the most part have not engaged these questions, so we do not know exactly what a postnational response to liberal nationalism might look like. However, it seems to me that the liberal nationalist position requires a response. Here, I can outline only preliminarily what such a response might look like.

The place to begin is with the fact that nationalism is deeply exclusionary, however liberal it may purport to be. The very act of normatively privileging identification with and solidarity toward fellow nationals presumes the existence of a class of nonnational others who are necessarily excluded from the domain of normative concern. Some outsiders are located outside the national territory; some reside within it, as aliens or foreigners. In either case, the question arises as to why the people with whom we happen to share formal nation-state membership and territory should be the objects of our identification and solidarity more than others with whom we are joined through other affiliative ties.

Nationalism's fundamentally exclusionary character points, at one level, to a contradiction at the heart of liberal nationalism itself. Liberal theory, in all its forms, stands for a universal regard for persons, while nationalism denotes a special attachment to particular other persons. The resulting tension between universalism and particularism has led some observers to suggest that the very notion of liberal nationalism is an oxymoron (Levinson, 1995).

Beyond this problem of internal coherence is a substantive ethical problem: why should national ties matter more than others? Why should "compatriots take priority" (Shue, 1980, 131–32)? Liberal cosmopolitans have argued for years that nationality should be treated as a "morally irrelevant" feature in distinguishing persons (e.g., Nussbaum, 1996, 133). I am sympathetic to this view but more inclined to emphasize the need for solidarity with the marginalized and subordinated and to focus on the exclusionary and unjust effects that nationalism can have on them.

Thus, for example, while many liberal nationalists argue that primary solidarity among members of a national community is necessary for the redistributive policies that liberals and progressives often support in advanced capitalist countries, I am inclined to consider as well the interests of those who are excluded from these redistributions and to consider how the resources to be distributed are amassed in those countries to begin with.

---

bond its special importance, what makes my ties with these people and to this enterprise peculiarly binding."

These considerations form the least developed part of this chapter. I am committed in the long term to continuing to work to develop an affirmative case for a kind of postnational ethics—one that goes beyond liberal cosmopolitanism. Part of this ethics, it seems to me, is a commitment to the pluralization of identities, solidarities, and membership forms. A commitment to pluralization in this context would treat national affiliations as one type of affiliation among many.

This pluralist understanding of affiliations and identities is one that many theorists are beginning to urge with increasing frequency (e.g., Robbins, 1998, 3; Sen, 1996, 116). One of the challenges, in my view, is to begin to make sense of the relation between the pluralization impulse and the antisubordination impulse. There are versions of each that might easily be at cross-purposes.

There is, further, the problem of determining how such commitments might be institutionalized. Although a few theorists have recently sketched an image of citizenship that is decoupled from the nation-state, none offers much in the way of a blueprint.[26] The difficulties involved in giving flesh to these nascent visions are not surprising; they reflect the broader challenges we face in reimagining our political lives in a world marked by ever-deepening processes of globalization.

Ultimately, the question I am asking here is whether the concept of citizenship can help to bridge the gap. Perhaps it can. But it is also possible that the idea of citizenship is so closely tied to the hegemony of nation-centered thinking that it will resist redefinition in denationalized terms. In that case, an alternative rhetorical strategy would be to argue not that citizenship is moving beyond the nation-state, but that we are moving *beyond citizenship* altogether. There might be good reasons for taking a postcitizenship stance. For now, however, the idea of citizenship is sufficiently flexible and open and resonant to make its refashioning worth the fight.

If any lesson can be drawn from the foregoing discussion, it is this: citizenship is as much an idea as it is a set of institutions and social practices. Paying attention to how we think about citizenship can cast new and useful light on the institutions and practices that the term is conventionally used to designate. Evolving conceptions of the idea both reflect and help to shape the political and social worlds we inhabit. All our efforts to redescribe citizenship matter deeply; there is a great deal at stake.

26. Sandel (1996, 345, 347) advances a vision of "a multiplicity of communities and political bodies—some more, some less extensive than nations—among which sovereignty is diffused" and where "citizenship [is] formed across multiple sites of civic engagement." David Elkins (1995, 38–39) has proposed "unbundling" citizenship from nations, states, and territories.

Works Cited

Appadural, Arjun. 1996. *Modernity at Large: Cultural Dimensions of Globalization.* Minneapolis: University of Minnesota Press.

Arendt, Hannah. 1968. *Men in Dark Times.* New York: Harcourt, Brace and World.

Balibar, Etienne. 1988. "Propositions on Citizenship." *Ethics* 98.

Ball, Terrence, James Farr, and Russell L. Hanson (eds.). 1989. *Political Innovation and Conceptual Change.* Cambridge: Cambridge University Press.

Barbalet, J. M. 1988. *Citizenship.* Minneapolis: University of Minnesota Press.

Basch, Linda, Nina Glick Schiller, and Cristina Szanton Blanc. 1994. *Nations Unbound: Transnational Projects, Postcolonial Predicaments, and Deterritorialized Nation-States.* Toronto: University of Toronto Press.

Bauböck, Rainer. 1994. *Transnational Citizenship: Membership and Rights in International Migration.* Aldershot, England: Edward Elgar.

Bosniak, Linda. 1998. "The Citizenship of Aliens." *Social Text* 56.

Brecher, Jeremy, and Tim Costello. 1994. *Global Village or Global Pillage.* Boston: South End Press.

Carens, Joseph. 1996–1997. "Dimensions of Citizenship and National Identity in Canada." *Philosophical Forum* 28.

Connolly, William E. 1993. *The Terms of Political Discourse.* Princeton, N.J.: Princeton University Press.

Conover, Pamela Johnston. 1995. "Citizen Identities and Conceptions of the Self." *Journal of Political Philosophy* 3.

Dagger, Richard. 1997. *Civic Virtues: Rights, Citizenship, and Republican Liberalism.* New York: Oxford University Press.

Dahl, Robert. 1989. *Democracy and Its Critics.* New Haven, Conn.: Yale University Press.

Drainville, Andre. 1995. "Left Internationalism and the Politics of Resistance in the New World Order." In M. P. Smith and J. Borocz (eds.), *A New World Order: Global Transformation in the Late Twentieth Century.* Westport, Conn.: Greenwood Press.

Elkins, David J. 1995. *Beyond Sovereignty: Territory and Political Economy in the Twenty-First Century.* Toronto: University of Toronto Press.

Falk, Richard. 1993. "The Making of Global Citizenship." In Jeremy Brecher, John Brown Childs, and Jill Cutler (eds.), *Global Visions.* Boston: Beacon Press.

Fraser, Nancy, and Linda Gordon. 1994. "Civil Citizenship against Social Citizenship? On the Ideology of Contract-versus-Charity." In *The Condition of Citizenship* 90.

Gallie, W. B. 1955–1956. "Essentially Contested Concepts." In *Proceedings of the Aristotelian Society* 56. London: Williams and Norgate.

Heater, Derek. 1990. "Citizenship: The Civic Ideal in World History." *Politics and Education.* London: Longman.

Held, David. 1991. "Between State and Civil Society: Citizenship." In Geoff Andrews (ed.), *Citizenship.* London: Lawrence and Wishart.

Himmelfarb, Gertrude. 1996. "The Illusions of Cosmopolitanism." In Joshua Cohen (ed.), *For Love of Country: Debating the Limits of Patriotism.* Boston: Beacon Press.

Hollinger, David. 1995. *Postethnic America.* New York: Basic Books.

Jacobson, David. 1996. *Rights across Borders: Immigration and the Decline of Citizenship.* Baltimore: Johns Hopkins University Press.

Jones, Kathleen B. 1998. "Citizenship in a Woman-Friendly Polity." In Gershon Shafir (ed.), *The Citizenship Debates*. Minneapolis: University of Minnesota Press.

Kratochwil, Friedrich. 1994. "Citizenship: On the Border of Order." *Alternatives* 19.

Keck, Margaret E., and Kathryn Sikkink. 1998. *Activists beyond Borders: Advocacy Networks in International Politics*. Ithaca, N.Y.: Cornell University Press.

Kukathas, Chandran. 1996. "Liberalism, Communitarianism, and Political Community." *Social Philosophy and Policy* 13.

Kymlicka, Will, and Wayne Norman. 1994. "Return of the Citizen: A Survey of Recent Work on Citizenship Theory." *Ethics* 104.

Levinson, Sanford. 1995. "Is Liberal Nationalism an Oxymoron? An Essay for Judith Shklar." *Ethics* 105 (April): 626–45.

Lichtenberg, Judith. 1996–1997. "How Liberal Can Nationalism Be?" *Philosophical Forum* 28.

Lind, Michael. 1995. *The Next American Nation: The New Nationalism and the Fourth American Revolution*. New York: Free Press.

Lynch, Cecilia. 1998. "Social Movements and the Problem of Globalization." *Alternatives* 23.

Magnusson, Warren. 1994. *The Search for Political Space*. Toronto: University of Toronto Press.

Marshall, T. H. 1949. *Citizenship and Social Class*. Cambridge: Cambridge University Press.

Miller, David. 1995. *On Nationality*. Oxford: Oxford University Press.

Nisbet, Robert. 1975. *The Twilight of Authority*. New York: Oxford University Press.

Nussbaum, Martha. 1996. "Patriotism and Cosmopolitanism." In Joshua Cohen (ed.), *For Love of Country: Debating the Limits of Patriotism*. Boston: Beacon Press.

Pateman, Carole. 1970. *Participation and Democratic Theory*. Cambridge: Cambridge University Press.

———. 1989. *The Disorder of Women*. Stanford: Stanford University Press.

Portes, Alejandro. 1996. "Global Villagers: The Rise of Transnational Communities." *American Prospect*. March–April.

Robbins, Bruce. 1998. "Introduction, Part I: Actually Existing Cosmopolitanism." In *Cosmopolitics*. Minneapolis: University of Minnesota Press.

Rorty, Richard. 1998. *Achieving Our Country: Leftist Thought in Twentieth Century America*. Cambridge, Mass.: Harvard University Press.

Sandel, Michael. 1996. *Democracy's Discontent*. Cambridge, Mass.: Harvard University Press.

Sassen, Saskia. 1996. *Losing Control? Sovereignty in an Age of Globalization*. New York: Columbia University Press.

Sen, Amartya. 1996. "Humanity and Citizenship." In Joshua Cohen (ed.), *For Love of Country: Debating the Limits of Patriotism*. Boston: Beacon Press.

Shue, Henry. 1980. *Basic Rights: Subsistence, Affluence, and U.S. Foreign Policy*. Princeton, N.J.: Princeton University Press.

Shklar, Judith. 1991. *American Citizenship*. Cambridge, Mass.: Harvard University Press.

Skinner, Quentin. 1989. "Language and Political Change." In Terrence Ball, James Farr, and Russell L. Hanson (eds.), *Political Innovation and Conceptual Change*. Cambridge: Cambridge University Press.

Smith, Robert C. 1998. "Transnational Localities: Community, Technology, and the Politics of Membership within the Context of Mexico and U.S. Migration." In Michael Peter Smith and Luis Eduardo Guarnizo (eds.), *Transnationalism from Below*. New Brunswick: Transaction Publishers.

Soysal, Yasemin Nuhoğlu. 1994. *Limits of Citizenship: Migrants and Postnational Citizenship in Europe*. Chicago: University of Chicago Press.

———. 1997. "Changing Parameters of Citizenship and Claims-Making: Organized Islam in European Public Spheres." *Theory and Society* 26.

Spiro, Peter. 1994. "New Global Communities: Nongovernmental Organizations in International Decision-Making Institutions." *Washington Quarterly* 18.

———. 1999. "The Citizenship Dilemma." *Stanford Law Review* 51.

Tamir, Yael. 1993. *Liberal Nationalism*. Princeton, N.J.: Princeton University Press.

Taylor, Charles. 1989. "Cross-Purposes: The Liberal-Communitarian Debate." In Nancy Rosenblum (ed.), *Liberalism and the Moral Life*. Cambridge, Mass.: Harvard University Press.

Torres, Maria de los Angeles. 1998. "Transnational Political and Cultural Identities: Crossing Theoretical Borders." In Frank Bonilla et al. (eds.), *Borderless Borders: U.S. Latinos, Latin Americans, and the Paradox of Interdependence*. Philadelphia: Temple University Press.

Vogel, Ursula, and Michael Moran (eds.). 1991. *The Frontiers of Citizenship*. London: Sage.

Walzer, Michael. 1989. "Citizenship." In Terrence Ball, James Farr, and Russell L. Hanson (eds.), *Political Innovation and Conceptual Change*. Cambridge: Cambridge University Press.

Wapner, Paul. 1995. "Politics beyond the State: Environmental Activism and World Civic Politics." *World Politics* 47.

Wiener, Antje. 1998. *"European" Citizenship Practice: Building Institutions of a Non-State*. Boulder, Colo.: Westview Press.

CHAPTER NINE

The Emergence of Transnational Citizenship among Mexican Immigrants in California

PAUL JOHNSTON

THE LATE 1990s were years of paradox for immigrants to the United States, years of expanded membership in a more exclusionary society. On the one hand, the new nativist movement launched in 1994 produced a barrage of policy changes that limited the rights of noncitizens. On the other hand, as "settlement" became "citizenship," unprecedented numbers of legal permanent residents made their way into and through the naturalization process. The huge scale of today's expansion of the formal boundaries of citizenship is only one expression, moreover, of a broader and more complex shift in collective identity and increasing membership in public life by first-generation immigrants to the United States.

These two trends are not sustainable. Much remains at issue in this unfinished struggle over the boundaries and terms of citizenship. At this writing, in 2000, the tension between a more inclusive polity and a diminished democracy is still building and is likely to lead to new social movement activity and to new policy changes, with unanticipated consequences. It is clear, however, that the late 1990s witnessed the naturalization of more immigrants to the United States than ever in history, proportionately more than at any time since World War II, and certainly, the greatest expansion in participation in citizenship since the civil rights era. Thanks to "family unity" criteria in U.S. immigration law, the rate of naturalization will continue to be high in the coming decade.

This investigation is grounded in participant observation in the tumultuous history described here.

Where are these new citizens coming from? Since the mid-1970s, many have come from Asian countries; as late as 1987, fully half. But by 1996 this proportion had declined to 25 percent, while the proportion of those coming from countries immediately to the south of the United States—Mexico, Central America, and the Caribbean—had grown from 23 percent to 43 percent. Although Mexican immigrants had long been among those least likely to become naturalized (Liang, 1994; Portes and Rumbaut, 1996), beginning in 1994, more new citizens have come from Mexico than any other single country. By 1996, 20 percent were of Mexican origin, a proportion that probably increased in 1997. In 1996, 70 percent of these new citizens of Mexican origin lived in California (INS, 1998), where their presence triggered the anti-immigrant movement of the mid-1990s. Accordingly, my focus is on the emergence of U.S. citizenship by Mexican immigrants in California.

I begin by asking what citizenship development means. I offer in response a notion of citizenship as our participation in public life, not just in the active sense of self-conscious public action, but in the everyday sense of lives pervasively shaped by a great array of public institutions. I turn then to the origins of the new culture of citizenship among Mexican immigrants in California, in the farm workers movement. I proceed to the amnesty experience, through which nearly two million Mexicans moved from the outlaw status of unauthorized immigrant to that of second-class citizen or legal permanent resident. Next, I review the Mexican experience of response to the anti-immigrant backlash that ensued in the 1990s. After briefly considering the consequences for labor relations of the new anti-immigrant political environment, I describe the naturalization movement of the mid- to late 1990s. I watch that surge of public engagement as it enters other institutions, including education and the electoral arena. I conclude with a description and discussion of the new array of institutions for the "production of citizenship," themselves produced by this history.

I show that the struggle of Mexican immigrants in California for citizenship is intimately related to and rooted in the long and continuing struggle for labor rights of Mexican immigrants. Labor markets draw migrants across borders; employment relations stimulate their demands for basic rights; labor movements produce their main political-organizational resources. Immigrant workers' labor movements disclose and challenge what is routinely obscured: those political arrangements that define the terms of participation and indeed constitute the very participants in capitalist employment relations. When they converge in this context, immigrant rights movements and labor movements display a kinship that joins them in a single family of what might be termed *citizenship movements* (Johnston, 2001).

In addition, I show that family relationships are part of this fabric of U.S.-Mexican transnational citizenship development. Although enduring family ties sustain and even strengthen cross-border ties and *Mexicano* identities, family formation—and especially, the aspirations of immigrants for their children's future—cements a settlement process that unfolds into citizenship. Because border-spanning family relationships are the criteria of eligibility for immigration and citizenship, they have become formal elements of an increasingly transnational immigration and naturalization policy domain.

Although industrial relations and family relations are important factors shaping the citizenship experience, the central pattern unfolding here is citizenship development. Citizenship development refers not only to changes in the behavior and identities of individuals, but also to changes in the character of institutions; not only to institutions specifically organized around immigration and naturalization, but also to the array of public institutions that define the terms of membership in, and exclusion from, our increasingly transnational society.[1]

Citizenship as Participation in Public Institutions

What does it mean, then, to speak of citizenship development among Mexican immigrants in California? At least in part, the expression *citizen development* must refer to the explosion of applications for naturalization in the mid- to late 1990s. Does it also refer to more than this?

Before naturalization, the legal permanent resident already enjoys certain rights and responsibilities. What those rights and responsibilities *are* is a focus point of struggle. In recent decades, however, they have included basic civil, educational, labor, and social welfare rights and also a responsibility to pay taxes, register for military service, and send the family's children to school. Even the undocumented immigrant shares in each of these rights and responsibilities, although these matters too are points of struggle. Yet these have long been considered important elements of citizenship for students of political processes.

The Mexican immigrant is also a citizen, of course, of Mexico, who upon becoming a U.S. citizen retains Mexican nationality. And today not only is the nature of U.S.-Mexican dual citizenship a focal point of struggle, the political culture of Mexico itself is in flux, possibly democratic upheaval. Here, too, naturalization appears to be part of a larger and longer process.

---

1. *Citizenship development* can also refer to a mode of practice or a kind of organizing that aims to evoke and support citizenship.

Moreover, the same constituencies currently involved in the naturalization process have long been engaged in other kinds of individual and collective activities that look much like citizenship behavior. Examples are the United Farm Workers' forays into electoral politics, starting in the 1970s, and, more recently, the Service Employees International Union's Justice for Janitors campaign dating from the mid-1980s, focusing as it did on mobilizations and coalitions calculated to exercise political power. In this writer's experience, Mexican citizens frequently play leading roles in political campaigns, community organizing, school-based migrant parent involvement groups, and in the day-to-day work of assisting immigrants of various statuses in learning and exercising their rights. If this is not citizenship, then what is it?

All these examples suggest that it is useful to grasp the naturalization process as part of a larger and longer process of *expanded involvement in evolving public institutions*. There is a certain openness to the notion of "the citizen" defined and shaped by and responding to involvement in a public order.[2] Rather than define citizenship as associated with a particular kind of public institution—with a liberal, republican, or social democratic public order, for example, or with the nation-state as an exclusive political community—this view allows us to grasp citizenship as a status that can vary just as public institutions vary, across populations and over time. It reframes the conventional liberal, republican, and social democratic notions of citizenship, grasping them less as normative agendas than as empirical phenomena, each anchored in particular kinds of public institutions or in struggles to establish or extend them. It also offers a way to understand the possibility of a variety of forms of transnational citizenship. This last possibility is particularly important as states embrace more than one nationality, as public institutions cross national borders, and as populations participate in more than one public. The struggle over the boundaries and terms of citizenship in California—not only for Mexican immigrants, but more generally in the public life of that state—has given rise, I shall show, to several kinds of transnational citizenry. Specifically, these "border-crossing" groups include the citizenries of multiple nationalities within a single state, citizenries of single nations that straddle state borders, and citizenries that simultaneously belong to more than one national polity.

---

2. Alternate views grasp citizenship as a power relation (Tarrow,1994; Tilly, 1996), a self-legitimizing cultural logic (Meyer, 1980; Soysal, 1994), or as voluntary activity rooted in a third sector, distinct from the state (Cohen, 1982; Walzer, 1995). Still others—Marxists, some feminists, most economists—dismiss citizenship as an illusion, because "the public interest" always cloaks some class, gender, or other private interest. They miss the point. It does not matter whether the public interest is real; it matters only whether our movements and our institutions operate as though it were.

The historical sketch that follows concludes that these developments may permit us to build a more expansive citizenship in California over the coming decade. Our success in such an effort offers no promise of success in the far more difficult circumstances facing other multiethnic societies (including Mexico). Our failure in these favorable conditions, however, will certainly have sobering implications for the planet.

The Early Emergence of Citizenship in Immigrant Worker Movements

In late July 1970, after five years of strikes and a global boycott, much of the table-grape industry in California finally agreed to sign union contracts with the United Farm Workers (UFW) union led by Cesar Chavez. In the same week, corporations growing lettuce and tomatoes and other produce on the central coast of California entered into an agreement with the Teamsters Union to represent more than eight thousand farm workers. Their aim: to head off an impending UFW organizing drive. Neither the employers nor the Teamsters, however, had consulted with the workers of the Salinas River valley.[3]

Two days later, at 6:00 in the morning, three small bands of about twenty-five UFW supporters set out to march through Gilroy and Hollister to the north, through Watsonville and Castroville to the west, and through King City, Greenfield, and a string of other rural towns to the south, all converging on the central city of Salinas, California. For each of three days, more and more small groups of farm workers appeared along the routes of these marches. Unlike the U.S. citizens of Mexican descent and the longtime legal immigrants from the Philippines who worked in the grape fields, most of these workers were recent arrivals from Mexico, drawn into California's agricultural labor market after the termination of the *bracero* guest-worker program five years earlier. Many lacked legal work permits. Typically they stood silently in the sun, watching the column of marchers pass, often driving ahead to stand and watch again. Quietly, then, they entered the ranks. After a time, first one, then another, accepted the red flag with the black eagle offered them by other marchers. Gradually, their steps took on the buoyancy of the energized file. Gradually, they joined in the chant of "¡Cesar Si, Teamsters No!"

The image of the Virgin of Guadeloupe led each column, and hundreds of red-and-black banners fluttered along the line. The largest march, coming from the south, carried other icons as well. These included a huge cross wrapped in

---

3. This account draws on my experience as a UFW organizer in the 1970 strike movement I describe here.

barbed wire, marked with the names of a dozen labor camps, and carried by five men. And just behind the image of the Virgin, mounted on poles on the shoulders of four men and flanked by two others carrying large U.S. and Mexican flags, was a huge ballot box with one word painted on each side: "¡Vote!"

On Sunday, as they converged in the city of Salinas at the center of the valley, the number of marchers swelled to thousands. At Salinas they were met by thousands more, and on that day they voted by acclamation to launch one of the largest and strongest agricultural worker strikes in U.S. history: the general strike of farm workers in the agricultural industries centered in the Salinas valley. The strike followed the harvest as it moved across the state during the fall and winter months, through the Coachella valley to the south, and then to the Imperial valley on the Mexican border. The strikers made one single demand: the right to vote for their own union representatives.

The activity of the citizenship movement had already surfaced much earlier among Mexicanos in California, most notably in the Community Service Organizations built by Fred Ross and the young Cesar Chavez and Dolores Huerta in the 1950s. The modern farm workers movement began earlier as well, mostly with U.S. citizens in California's great Central Valley. That mid-summer week in the Salinas valley, however, was the first great explosion of a still-unfolding working-class citizenship movement in a new generation of unauthorized Mexican immigrants drawn from their rural communities of origin by employment opportunities in the agricultural labor market. Over the next several decades this force erupted up and down the state and increasingly elsewhere in the United States as well, not only in strikes, but also in a series of electoral campaigns that produced new labor relation laws and a new layer of Latino elected officials. These mobilizations blended the participation of new immigrants with native-born Latino leaders and others with long-established identities as U.S. citizens. As in other times and places, however, the culture of citizenship first emerged and took root in these migrants as a claim to fairness in employment.[4]

This new culture of citizenship followed these workers over the next quarter century out of the fields and into other industries. Beginning in the mid-1970s, for example, union democracy movements surfaced among the Mexicanos and Chicanos, overwhelmingly former farm workers, who had moved into most of the unionized jobs in the food-processing and building-maintenance industries. They typically demanded more assertive and more accountable leadership and Spanish translations of contracts and at union meetings.[5] Ironically, in fact, one such movement fifteen years later led to the election of a slate of Mexicano and

4. See, e.g., Marshall (1950); Hobsbawm (1968); Thompson (1974); Montgomery (1993); Foweraker and Landman (1997).

5. It is significant that the early janitors' movement and the union democracy movement in the Teamsters' cannery unions surfaced at the same time and were centered in the same place that

Chicano rank-and-file reformers. They were supported both by the reform group Teamsters for a Democratic Union and by the UFW—in the union that was the target of that 1970 strike—the Teamsters' own giant Salinas-centered farm and food-processing-industry union, Local 890.

Over these decades, the Mexican immigrant workers movement grew in strength not only among the newly "legal" immigrant workers, but also among undocumented immigrants, empowered by a porous border and lax enforcement of the laws that prohibited their employment (Delgado, 1993; Milkman and Wong, 1999). Elsewhere in the United States, other farm worker labor movements also gained ground. After years of decline, the UFW itself began to experience organizing success again in the early 1990s, and a series of immigrant worker movements surfaced in a wide variety of other industries as well. Best-known of the new movements was the Service Employees International Union's Justice for Janitors campaign, which began in the late 1980s and succeeded in many cities in reorganizing an industry whose union membership had virtually collapsed after the mid-1970s (Johnston, 1994; Milkman and Wong, 1999).

Entering into Public Bureaucracy

In the late 1980s these new labor movements of immigrant workers accelerated, during and after the enactment of the Immigration Reform and Control Act, which regularized the status of 2.7 million formerly undocumented immigrants across the United States. That law strengthened immigrant worker movements by increasing job security, extending access to unemployment and other public resources, and generally encouraging workers to assume and assert rights. It also led nearly two million immigrants of Mexican origin to assemble their documentation, complete application packets, and attend interviews with the Immigration and Naturalization Service (INS). Most eventually acquired legal permanent resident (LPR) status in the United States.

The amnesty process, moreover, was a citizenship experience of a new type. More than a simple change in status, it began to shape individuals in new ways by focusing their attention on eligibility criteria for immigration and naturalization for themselves and their family members. It began to construct, or mold, them, in other words, as persons able to exercise eligibility rights in a public bureaucracy. Through familial criteria of eligibility for immigration, moreover,

---

produced the new organizational culture of Silicon Valley, along with meaningful patterns of innovation in public employee unionism (e.g., public service unionism and comparable worth), vocational training (e.g., the Center for Employment and Training), and public administration. Elsewhere, I attribute this broad pattern of innovation to the recomposition of that region by waves of *in-migration* from elsewhere in the United States and the world (Johnston, 1994, 100–101).

it activated an awareness of eligibility and a general orientation toward U.S. public bureaucracy that extended to millions of family members far into Mexico.

Still, deep divisions lay between unauthorized immigrants, on the one hand, and the INS bureaucracy, on the other. Until the late 1980s, as outsiders to citizenship, the population was neither client nor constituent. Rather, it was the target of INS enforcement. Largely rural in origin and with little formal education, moreover, most immigrants were not well prepared to present themselves to a ponderous and impersonal bureaucracy, much less to one historically committed to hunting down and deporting unauthorized immigrants. Language barriers and pervasive patterns of racial inequality compounded the challenge of implementing the amnesty program.

It was not surprising, however, that many labor unions moved to help their members take advantage of the amnesty opportunity. Joining them, and serving the broader constituency of unorganized workers and their families, were Latino community-based schools, churches, social service agencies, and advocacy groups. Recognizing that organizations rooted in immigrant communities could usefully participate in easing the mistrust of undocumented residents, the INS licensed hundreds of organizations and special projects in other immigrant-community-based organizations as "Qualified Designated Entities." These organizations screened eligible applicants, helping them to assemble documentation, and accepted applications for forwarding to the INS for processing. At the same time, public adult education programs and other less formal schools responded to the increased demand for classes in English and preparation for the simple test in U.S. history and government required of amnesty applicants.

The amnesty process also produced the beginnings, then, of a new kind of organizational infrastructure in the policy domain of immigration and naturalization. Many of these projects folded after the amnesty ended in 1989. Yet they left behind new models for INS behavior, new capabilities of the applicants themselves, and new local and national networks of expertise and support in individuals, activist groups, and organizations for Mexican immigrant incorporation in this developing public policy arena. In sum, the amnesty episode changed the Mexican-oriented immigration policy domain from being an apparatus focused on the exclusion of aliens to one able to cross racialized boundaries of language and national difference to treat Mexicans not only as "targets" but also as clients and constituents.

Family Formation and Citizenship Development

The most important network of support for naturalization, however, was and remains the increasingly transnational Mexican family. Although first-generation immigrants remained rooted in their communities of origin, the birth of U.S. citizen children with the opportunity to acquire an education in U.S. public schools produced an intense new motivation, especially among women, to settle and stay in the United States. These roots grew and developed in the 1970s and 1980s, as young women followed the early male Mexican pioneers north to the United States (Honagneu-Sotelo, 1994). At the same time that the formation of families in U.S. communities gave Mexican immigrants local roots, however, the extended family still served as a bridge across the border. Family relationships produced a settlement process that also sustained and sometimes, as U.S.-born Chicanos married Mexican immigrants, strengthened cross-border identities and relationships.

In addition, the family itself increasingly became an element of the transnational immigration policy, as an unintended consequence of eligibility criteria that emphasized family relationships as the basis for immigration. Ironically, in adopting family relationship as the main criterion for immigration in the 1965 Immigration Act, the U.S. government intended to reinforce the white, or European-origin, composition of the U.S. population after the elimination of country quotas that had favored those origins. Instead, first Indochinese refugees and then Mexican, Caribbean, and Central American immigrants dominated the flow of migrants to the United States over the next several decades, and their family members were the principal beneficiaries of the new policy.

In particular, because family formation for unauthorized immigrants produced children who were U.S. citizens, immigration enforcement increasingly implied the deportation of the parents of U.S. citizens, persons who would eventually be entitled to legal immigration and U.S. citizenship themselves. The Immigration Reform and Control Act (IRCA) of 1986 responded to this dilemma and simultaneously broadened the bridge of transnational family relationships, further extending eligibility for immigration to the millions of spouses, siblings, children, and parents of the new legal permanent residents incorporated through amnesty provisions of that law. Thus invested with legal significance and increasingly central to immigration policy, family relationships became avenues of transnational citizenship as they extended eligibility for immigration and naturalization across the border.

Toward a New Apartheid?

As the growth of Mexican and other immigrant populations in California began to transform the complexion and to diversify the culture of the state, a white backlash ensued. By 1994, politicians had discovered that attacks on Mexican immigrants could function as a new fulcrum for rightward political alignment in U.S. politics. The anti-immigrant agenda served, they found, to mobilize white support for "centrist" Democrats and for Republicans in a manner similar to the familiar "race card" in U.S. politics.

The new anti-immigrant campaign was launched by Democratic Senator Dianne Feinstein of California in early 1994 in a television campaign that deployed the powerful image of dark figures scurrying across the landscape to invade the state of California. Republican governor Pete Wilson followed Feinstein's lead with an endorsement of Proposition 187, which targeted undocumented families for identification and deportation through schools and health services and was overwhelmingly passed by California voters in November 1994. By August 1996, the anti-immigrant crusade captured Washington, D.C., as Democratic president Bill Clinton signed new welfare and immigration laws produced by Republican majorities in the House and Senate.

Although participants in the anti-immigrant crusade pressed for intensified border enforcement and the reduction or elimination of the flow of immigrants from nonwhite countries, their energies also focused on limiting existing access by legal residents to social, civil, educational, and cultural rights. Although the anti-immigrant crusade began with Proposition 187 by reinforcing the exclusion of "illegal" aliens, it quickly unfolded to include the reduction or elimination of many social welfare rights for all noncitizens, restrictions on due process rights for refugees, and challenges to the educational and language rights of immigrants. The regressive citizenship asserted by this nativist movement was not limited to formal immigration and naturalization, then, but also included the various dimensions of societal membership I have stressed here.

Some of the provisions of these new laws were stymied by legal challenges or moderated by legislative change. Yet each new policy, each implementation step, and even each proposed or merely rumored new change sent shock waves through immigrant communities across the United States over the next several years. During the period from August 1996 through mid-1997, for example, all low-income legal immigrants faced an approaching cutoff from virtually all means-tested public benefits unless and until they made it through the citizenship process.[6] Then, effective January 1998, Congress rescinded provisions of the old immigration law that had permitted the undocumented family members of U.S. citizens and legal residents with valid applications for immigration to live in the United States with their family members during the five-year or longer wait for INS processing. In addition, throughout the period the INS

6. Though rescinded in part by mid-1997, these exclusions produced a year of panic among low-income legal permanent residents who were elderly, disabled, or very poor single mothers. Their rescission applied, moreover, only to those already in the United States in August 1996. Within a decade, then, as the new cohort of immigrants grows, this new exclusionary social service regime will be fully in effect again.

steadily intensified border enforcement and sharply increased the rate of deportation. Other legislation, legal rulings, and administrative decisions in the same period restricted immigrant and refugee due process rights, limited access by young immigrants to higher education, and strengthened the ability of employers to identify and terminate undocumented workers. In California in 1998, voters passed related propositions that outlawed affirmative action and banned bilingual education.

Reeling from this barrage of policy setbacks, immigrant communities were increasingly filled with fears about what would come next. Republican proposals to repeal the provisions of the Fourteenth Amendment to the U.S. Constitution that extend U.S. citizenship to all children born in the United States, for example, produced intense anxiety for Mexican immigrant parents, many of whom feared that the measure would be retroactive.

These measures failed to halt the flow of undocumented workers to the United States, from Mexico as well as from the traumatized Central American communities to the south. Instead, they quickly consolidated a deep divide in the social structure of the state, based on differences in citizenship status.

Undocumented immigrants constituted between 30 and 40 percent of the agricultural workforce in the late 1980s (Mines and Martin, 1986), dropping to about 10 percent owing to the 1989 and 1990 implementation of the amnesty provisions of IRCA (Commission on Agricultural Workers, 1992). Less than a decade later, however, the number of agricultural workers willing to acknowledge their undocumented status in the Department of Labor's National Agricultural Worker Survey had risen to 43 percent (Rosenberg, 1998). Actual numbers, both in rural and in low-wage urban workforces, were probably much higher. At this writing, the economies of whole regions in California are heavily dependent on the labor of "illegal" workers, in industries ranging from strawberry farming on the central coast to garment manufacturing in Los Angeles. The growth of this population, its increasingly criminalized and vulnerable status, and its impoverished, furtive, marginalized way of life under the new anti-immigrant policy regime has created circumstances that might fairly be described as a new apartheid in California.

In the 1990s, increased border enforcement increased the physical difficulty, and doubled the dollar cost (from $200–500 to $1,000), of crossing and recrossing the border. Another direct consequence of this exclusionary trend in immigration policy has been an increase in border deaths. By blocking the most accessible routes, the INS directed the stream of migration into more difficult and dangerous regions. In particular, INS's Operation Gatekeeper on the California-Mexico border pushed the flow of migration away from the border region and into the rugged inland mountains and arid desert of the Imperial valley. As a result, more and more immigrants met death by dehydration, hypothermia, drowning, or other causes related to border crossing. In California alone, 354 border deaths were reported between 1995 and 1998, including 145 in 1998. The latter figure represents a 63 percent increase over the previous year (Centro de Apoyo al Migrante, 1998).

Perversely, moreover, it is likely that an unintended consequence of intensified border enforcement was an increased rate of settlement and family formation among unauthorized immigrants. According to many informed participants, by increasing the risk associated with border crossing, intensified border enforcement reduced the rate of return to Mexico of immigrants (particularly women) who had originally intended to return to their community of origin after a period of working in the United States. More hazardous border crossings also produced an increased reliance on professional smugglers, or "coyotes." Increasing INS and Social Security Administration scrutiny of employer practices also produced increased reliance on labor contractors by employers seeking to distance themselves from their undocumented workforce. As a result, advocates of border rights call the new immigration law the "coyote's full-employment law," while union organizers refer to it as the "labor contractor's full-employment law."

Toward a New Transnational Labor Regime?

Not coincidentally, the accelerating labor movement of immigrant workers stalled after the passage of Proposition 187. To be sure, labor union experience and commitment and grassroots involvement in immigrant worker organization increased over this period. Latino labor union leadership continued to emerge in various cities, most notably in Los Angeles. This has produced new possibilities for political coalitions between labor, Latino, and other neighborhood interests that, to the extent that they can assemble policy agendas, may well unfold into new urban governing coalitions with far-reaching implications for U.S. politics. In spite of a strong demand for labor in low-wage labor markets, however, the climate of general hostility toward immigrants and the growing vulnerability of undocumented workers to employer reprisals has left them much less likely to organize.

Thus, the late 1990s saw little progress and notable failures in immigrant worker organizing campaigns, including high-profile efforts by the United Farm Workers and the Teamsters in California's strawberry fields and in Washington's apple industry.[7] Both of these industries depend heavily on undocumented la-

---

7. Home health care workers were the major exception; organizing success on that front reflects the radically different labor relations environment of their public or quasi public workplace (Johnston, 1994).

bor. In other industries, moreover, even the presence of a small proportion of undocumented workers presented major new challenges to organizers. In particular, the Social Security Administration began in 1998 to notify employers of invalid employee social security numbers, handing them a new resource for disrupting an organizing campaign. Frequently, the union's inability to provide any protection for this vulnerable group undermines the confidence of the larger workforce.

More ominous still is that in 1998 the INS field-tested a new strategy of regionally and industrially targeted employer audits. In March 1999, the INS announced that in the future it would rely on this method instead of the less-effective, more labor-intensive, and scarcely implemented practice of workplace raids and employer sanctions (*New York Times,* 1999). If implemented without effective opposition, this agenda is likely to be an effective tool for purging entire workforces. Presumably, it will be implemented on a highly selective basis, since the result would be gaping labor shortages and a strong upward pressure on wages.

This "industrial audit" strategy may be rendered more widely useful, however, through a complementary initiative: Republican legislation to make the currently temporary and limited guest-worker programs permanent, remove the cap on the number of guest workers, expand it from agriculture to the food processing industry, make it easier for employers to qualify for the program, and prohibit families from accompanying the guest worker. In effect, the measure would reenact the bracero program. In the face of strong Democratic and labor opposition, that measure passed in the House and failed in the Senate in 1998. In March 1999, however, Clinton's secretary of labor met with her Mexican counterpart and discussed the possible enactment of such a system. At this writing the stage is set, then, for the imposition of a new transnational labor regime in low-wage labor markets in the United States, which more effectively and selectively excludes undocumented immigrants while selectively inserting an expanded guest-worker workforce into the lowest rung of the labor market.

The adoption and full implementation of this dual agenda ("industrial audits" and more indentured guest workers) is likely to be a focus of struggle. It is by no means ensured. In particular, both the U.S. and Mexican labor movements are likely to resist the new guest-worker legislation. Even were it to be fully implemented, moreover, unintended consequences are likely to surface again. By politicizing and regulating secondary labor markets and by creating explicit institutional bridges between related public institutions in the United States and Mexico, this policy direction may well create the context for workable transnational unionism.

The Naturalization Movement

Yet another unintended consequence of the new assault on immigrant rights, however, was a sharp acceleration in the gradual turn of Latino immigrants toward participation in U.S. public institutions, mainly reflected, to date, in the growth of applications for U.S. citizenship. Naturalization was already on the rise in the 1980s, as figure 9-1 suggests, owing mainly to the influence of Asian immigrants, who (more affluent, better educated, and farther removed from their homelands) have a particularly high propensity to naturalize. In 1994, however, Mexican nationals were for the first time the largest group of naturalized new citizens. Figure 9-2 shows the naturalization trend for immigrants of Mexican origin. The number of new citizens doubled in 1994, increased still more in 1995, and then exploded in 1996 to more than eight times the number only three years earlier.

How can this explosion of formal naturalization among Mexican immigrants be explained? On the one hand, the surge in naturalization reflects the passage of five years, since most participants in the amnesty program became legal permanent residents in 1989 and 1990, rendering them eligible to apply for citizenship in late 1994 and 1995. On the other hand, only 22 percent of the more than one million new citizens in 1996 obtained their legal residency under the amnesty program. Even for Mexican immigrants, fewer than half were amnesty applicants, and 40 percent had been legal residents for more than thirteen years, already eligible to apply for citizenship for at least eight years (INS, 1998). Moreover, amnesty applicants themselves naturalized in numbers that far exceeded INS projections.

To a degree, the explosion in applications for naturalization in 1997 reflects the passage of welfare laws excluding even long-term legal permanent residents from eligibility for social services. Yet, again, most were *not* directly affected by changes in welfare eligibility. Of those who applied from August 1996 to December 1998, in one rural sample of ten thousand examined by this writer, only 12 percent reported receiving any public assistance. At the period of peak anxiety (from January 1, 1997, to August 1, 1997), only 18 percent reported receiving any public assistance. The largest single category of reported public assistance was for public health assistance (10 percent).

The timing of these trends is misleading, moreover, because it is partially a product of the uneven pattern of delays in application processing by the Immigration and Naturalization Service. More accurate than the number of *new citizens* as a measure of the timing of the naturalization movement is the annual volume of *applications*. As figure 9-3 shows, the acceleration in applications for naturalization actually began in the early 1990s and took its most dramatic jump in 1995, immediately after the passage of Proposition 187 in California,

Figure 9-1.   *Naturalized Immigrants, 1907–1998, and Backlog, 11/30/97*

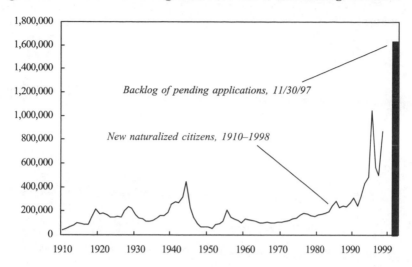

and long before the passage of exclusionary welfare and immigration laws in late 1996. Figure 9-3 also shows that in 1998 the volume of new applicants declined by half from its all-time high in 1997, although it still remained significantly above the years before 1995.[8]

If the recent embrace of U.S. citizenship by Mexican immigrants was more than the product of increased eligibility due to the amnesty program of the late 1980s, and if the motivation cannot be reduced to maintaining eligibility for social welfare, then how are we to understand the decision to naturalize? Although I refrain from offering a model of the decision-making process here, I draw attention to three suggestive observations: the evocation of public interest, the coincidence of self-interest and broader identities, and child-centered decision making.

First, applicants widely cite as a motivating factor an increased interest in and desire to vote on public policy. This interest appears to have been evoked largely but not exclusively by the appearance on the ballot of measures affecting the status of immigrants or their immediate family members.[9] Ernestina, a

8. Figure 9-3 also shows the large backlog in unprocessed applications as of November 30, 1997, suggesting that despite the decline in volume of applications in 1998, the volume of new citizens will continue to be high for the next several years.

9. This process of "evoking" citizenship is familiar to this writer, who in a past life had considerable experience organizing union membership in "open shop" situations. I found that one of the most effective methods for inducing people to join the union was to organize a decision-making process—a steward election, a survey on possible work-rule changes, and so on—in which only members could vote.

Figure 9-2.   *New U.S. Citizens, Mexican Origin, 1990–1996*

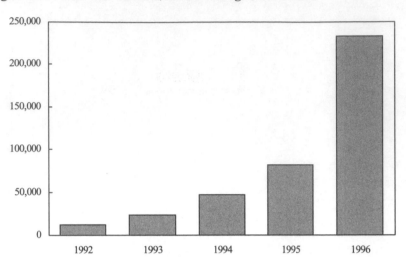

fifty-nine-year-old woman with thirty-nine years of employment in tomato-processing plants, describes, for example, her reaction in 1996 to Republican proposals to curtail social security benefits:

> I am Mexican and I will always be Mexican because the friends of my childhood are there and because that is where I went to school. But Proposition 187 woke me up; but it's not only Proposition 187. I looked at my check stub, and I said to myself, I have been paying for social security all of these years and now they're going to take it away and I can't even vote on it? I have to vote!

Second, it is a mistake to counterpose "real citizenship" against self-interested decision making. Rather, individuals offer multiple accounts for their decisions and usually align their private and public interests. Teresa, a very low-income mother of five, expressed an interest in becoming a U.S. citizen until she learned that the application fee had increased to $225. "I don't want to apply anyway," she said. "I am a *Mexicano*." One month later, Teresa joined a grass-roots group composed of low-income immigrants who were using their applications as test cases to advocate for the right to low-income fee waivers. "I'm not just doing it for myself," she said. "I'm doing it for everyone."

Third, while many applicants were ambivalent about their decision to acquire U.S. citizenship, they were also almost universally preoccupied with the

Figure 9-3.   *Applicants and New Citizens per Year, 1990–1998, and Backlog 1997–1999*

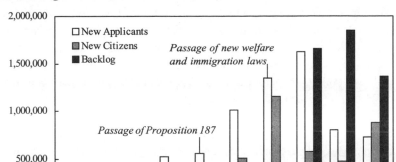

status and future of their children. From extensive interviews with applicants, a picture is emerging of a decision process in which individuals, especially women, weigh multiple competing reasons and ultimately decide to naturalize because they conclude it will be best for their children. Ana, the mother of four U.S.-born children, worked for years as a volunteer and then as a staffer in a community organization helping hundreds of others to apply for U.S. citizenship, but preserving her own exclusively Mexican identity. She finally changed her mind in response to a rumor that proposals to end birthright citizenship would be retroactive. Significantly, in our sample of Mexican-born applicants in the Salinas valley region, 83 percent were the parents of U.S.-born citizen children (34 percent had Mexican citizen children).

Women played a key and growing role in this expansion of citizenship for Mexican immigrants. Although more men than women were naturalized in earlier periods, female applicants outnumbered male applicants by the late 1990s, and unmarried female applicants sharply outnumbered unmarried males. In the sample mentioned earlier, for example, most applicants were women (54 percent). This reverses an earlier trend. A baseline survey in the same community in 1995 showed that 21 percent of Mexican-born men had become citizens, while only 10 percent of Mexican-born women had done so. It is also significant that male applicants were much more likely to be married (83 percent) than were female (57 percent), while unmarried applicants were much more likely to be female (74 percent) than male (26 percent). This pattern suggests a strong role for women in the decision for citizenship, and it supports the interpretation I offered earlier of a child-centered decision-making process.

In families, work groups, and other social networks, moreover, women typically took the initiative and provided much of the support for decision making, application, problem solving, and other preparations for naturalization. A female family member frequently completed her own application packet. She then persuaded other family members to apply and helped them to complete their own applications. Women assembled small family groups of eligible applicants and brought them to locations where application assistance was available. Women were also a strong majority of the volunteers in community mobilizations in support of the naturalization process.

Family relationships also helped to drive the naturalization process because of the link between citizenship status and the immigration rights of family members. Under U.S. immigration law, country quotas still limit the immigration by family members of legal permanent residents (requiring a wait of five years or longer, depending on the family relationship and country of origin) but do not apply to the family members of U.S. citizens. By becoming U.S. citizens, then, LPRs could accelerate the flow of their own family members across the immigration bridge.

The Long March into Public Institutions

The citizenship movement of the recent generation of Mexican immigrants did not disappear when the volume of new applicants declined in mid-1997. Rather, that decline reflects the simple fact that a person normally applies for naturalization only once and so the moment of application is only one milestone on this cohort's long march into the institutions of public life. This march began, I have suggested, in immigrant worker movements such as the great Salinas strike of 1970. It left its mark on labor laws and other industrial relations institutions and overflowed into electoral politics.

Increasingly in more recent years, moreover, other public institutions are also confronted with the broader citizenship movement. Criminal justice, social welfare, and educational and political institutions all confront an increasingly differentiated set of challenges. Most are unprepared, since they were shaped by relations either with a more homogenous white population or by the white–black racial divide. Welfare reform agendas, for example, framed by a debate over multigenerational welfare dependency in urban centers, have proved radically unresponsive to the childcare, housing, and nutritional needs of poor Mexicanos, who are likely to underuse public assistance. In addition, the realities of cross-border labor markets force law enforcement agencies and local prison systems to turn a blind eye to the growing reliance of many industries across the country on undocumented labor, in effect, becoming conspirators in the evasion of immigration enforcement. In communities with a large Spanish-speaking membership, most police officers are unable to communicate with a large proportion of those they are sworn to protect and serve, and so they are limited in their ability to understand a resident's request for assistance and to elicit information.

Educational institutions, however, have become particular epicenters in the crisis and upheaval in public institutions that face an increasingly differentiated public. They have long been essential institutions for both the qualification of workers and the construction of citizenries. Now, in the informational age, educational institutions are ever more central to the chances individuals have in life and to community development. By the 1970s, schools had already become terrains of racial conflicts over integration and affirmative action in much the same way, and for many of the same reasons they became so in conflicts over the status of immigrants in the 1990s. It is not surprising, then, that educational institutions oriented to the old national configuration are also key barriers to incorporation by Mexican immigrants and their children. In the meantime, educational strategies that respond to this increasingly differentiated polity are key avenues to expanded citizenship.

It was no coincidence that a surge of interest in adult education swept immigrant communities beginning in the mid-1990s. Understandably, a growth in applications for U.S. citizenship was associated with a sharp increase in enrollment in those adult education classes that related directly to naturalization: citizenship classes, up 100 percent in 1996–1997 over the previous year, and English as a second language, up 62 percent. This increase, however, also spilled over to other subjects: Elementary Basic Skills (up 104 percent), High School Basic Skills (up 56 percent), Vocational Education (up 47 percent), and Programs for Older Adults (up 83 percent) (California Department of Education, 2000).[10] Unfortunately, in a new form of "creaming," familiar to students of public services (Lipsky, 1980; Pressman and Wildavsky, 1973), those applicants who are most likely to fail their citizenship exams are systemically excluded from many of the citizenship classes of adult education programs because they lack minimal competency in English, which is a prerequisite.

The focus of Mexican immigrant interest in education, however, is on their children's educational opportunities. In 1998, the appearance of a measure banning bilingual education on the California ballot drew the attention of many immigrant parents, including new citizens and applicants for citizenship. Record numbers of these typically uninvolved parents attended informational meet-

10. I am currently exploring this apparent spillover effect through systematic follow-up interviews with a sample of applicants.

ings at school sites across the state, where they discussed and debated the implications of the proposed policy for their children's education. In the months before the election, participants observed an evolution over time of the "common wisdom" in this discourse. It began with support for the measure based on an appreciation of the importance of learning English, which reflected a new determination to do so by aspiring citizens. It progressed to an affirmation of the importance of maintaining fluency in Spanish and to the Mexican culture. In effect, in 1998 the citizenship movement of Mexican immigrants began to surface in local schools.

Finally, the citizenship movement began to appear in the rate of voter participation as the increasing centrality of immigrant rights in the electoral arena drove expanded Latino voter turnout. As I show in figure 9-4, this trend became evident as early as 1996 and expanded in 1998.

Increased Latino voter turnout helped to produce widely noted Latino victories in statewide races and less-noted but perhaps even more significant electoral success in local school board and city council elections across the state. In part, this was a result of an increased propensity to vote by young Latinos who were newly eligible to vote and by longtime citizens who had not bothered to vote in the years before the passage of Proposition 187. By 1996, however, in a sharp departure from past trends and from voting patterns in other constituencies, newly naturalized Latino citizens were voting at a higher rate than had their native-born Latino counterparts, comparable to that of the eligible population of voters as a whole (U.S. Bureau of the Census, 1998).[11]

By November 1998, moreover, the INS had yet to process most of the backlog accumulated during the peak in the wave of applications for citizenship or those submitted after the passage of new welfare and immigration laws in late 1996. Much of the wave of new citizens did not come "on line" as eligible voters, then, until the year 1999. Now, in the year 2000, California's population of eligible voters, who typically produce between 9 and 10 million actual votes in major statewide elections, has expanded by between 750,000 and 1 million first-generation Mexican immigrants, along with the growing propensity to vote by native-born Chicanos and longtime immigrant citizens. This development has already changed the constellation of power and possibilities for change at local, regional, and state levels. These changes have only begun to unfold. In particular, rural areas that have long been Republican strongholds and reliable bases for exclusionary agendas have begun to see the growth of new Latino power and the beginning of political upheaval.

11. According to the U.S. Census Bureau, 42 percent of native-born Latinos voted in 1996, compared with 53 percent of naturalized Latinos and 54 percent of eligible voters as a whole.

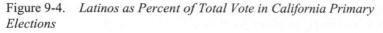

Figure 9-4.   *Latinos as Percent of Total Vote in California Primary*
Elections

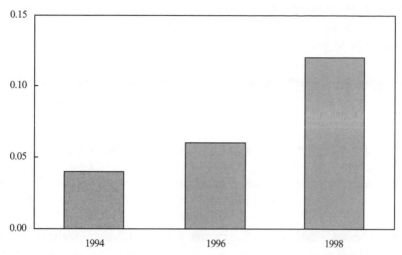

Increased Latino voter participation is likely to strengthen the hand of progressives in urban areas as well. To be sure, Latino constituencies are themselves heterogeneous, and an array of social, cultural, and political gulfs divide Latinos from African-Americans, other immigrant communities, environmentalists, non-Latino labor, and other potential allies. To the extent, however, that coalitional strategies are able to bridge these gaps, the near future may well witness the emergence of a new urban-rural coalition around an unabashedly progressive and inclusive agenda and so change the direction of history in California.

Toward the Production of Citizenship

Taken together, this rapid pattern of change in the immigration policy, in the social and educational policy related to immigrants, in the demand for naturalization, and in the volume of voter participation has triggered a further round of organizational development similar to that described in my discussion of the amnesty program earlier here. Organizations involved in the amnesty-era mobilization of support for immigration intensified their support for naturalization, and some new organizations emerged as well. In 1996, the INS resurrected its amnesty-era practice of relying on nonprofit immigrant community-based organizations, this time to screen and otherwise assist applicants for U.S. citizenship.

After August 1996, two new players entered the naturalization policy domain: state and local governments and grant-making foundations.[12] Their interest was triggered by the passage of social welfare legislation. State and local governments were motivated to act because the exclusion of legal permanent residents from federally funded means-tested social welfare programs would have had adverse impacts on their budgets by shifting health care costs and increasing participation in other state and local social welfare programs. In response, to varying extents, they began to encourage and sometimes actively to assist immigrants in the preparation of applications for citizenship.

Philanthropic organizations, meanwhile, had already assumed much control over programs in the nonprofit sector through control of the economy of taxpayer-subsidized grants. Their interest in naturalization was stimulated by the exclusionary provisions of new welfare laws. In particular, financier Georg Soros's endowment of the Lazarus Fund in 1996 infused $50 million into application assistance, which in turn attracted the interest of other major foundations to this and related areas of immigrant assistance. As a result, tentatively at least, naturalization assistance became established as a new item on the menu of local community services by the late 1990s. Although Soros's one-shot infusion of cash was exhausted by the end of the decade, these services now enjoy such support by state and local policy elites that they may sustain themselves, in many areas, through other funding streams from local community foundations, miscellaneous community service funding, and state budgets.

Also by the late 1990s, philanthropic planning had become strongly committed to an amorphous agenda of "civic participation," appealing in principle to both conservative and progressive policy elites. Late in the decade some foundations began to recognize a relation between the civic participation agenda and support for immigrant incorporation that went beyond naturalization assistance, to promote the exercise of civil, social, educational, economic, political, and cultural rights in immigrant communities.

As a result, by the end of the decade the new ensemble of immigrant-related public and quasi public organizations, which emerged during the earlier amnesty program, now began to assume a stable institutional form. In the course of implementing laws and policies that granted some eligibility rights to resident noncitizens, an immigration complex emerged no longer limited to the exclusion of aliens and the servicing of citizens. Now it also included systems of client services, constituent advocacy, and participation for resident noncitizens. Even more than before, this system continued to enforce the exclusion of

12. Some smaller and more progressive foundations became involved earlier on in response to Proposition 187.

ineligible noncitizens, but now far more than before, its menu of products included the production of citizenship itself.

"What kind of citizenship?" however, remains at best a contested issue. Most often, for the cluster of social service and other community organizations involved, "the production of citizenship" means the processing of passive clients. Nonetheless, the author's observations also suggest that the continuing emergence of U.S. citizenship for Mexican immigrants offers an opportunity for citizenship support work that taps the social movement potential of Mexican immigrants through popular education and other organizing methods (Johnston, 1999).

Conclusion

Three main ideas have informed my historical sketch here. First, potentially at least, labor relations are a crucible of citizenship. This perspective departs from conventional industrial relations theory that stresses exchange relations and market principles. The core idea here is that even where industrial relations appear to follow a nonpolitical market logic, they do so according to basic assumptions, underwritten by public law, about the rights and resources of the parties to the employment contract. These parameters of labor market behavior may be taken for granted some or most of the time, but in conditions of crisis—most commonly, when they are systematically violated—they become starkly visible as the focus of labor conflict. Then labor becomes a social movement, basic patterns of citizenship become the focus of struggle, and political and organizational processes become more important than labor market relationships in labor-management relations. In this sense the labor movement itself can be grasped as a citizenship movement (Johnston, 2001). In this case, I suggest, the continuing stream of immigrants who lack basic rights into low-wage labor markets in the United States is likely to provide continuing fuel for the emergence of a militant and politically oriented industrial unionism.

Second, I have suggested that the family is an integral component of emerging transnational polities, both as a criterion of eligibility for immigration and citizenship and as a living network of relations that extend both across borders and into local communities. Through public policies that rely on family relationships and birthplace as criteria of eligibility for immigration and citizenship, foreign national family members not resident in the United States acquire certain eligibility rights, while in the United States birthright citizenship irrevocably anchors undocumented parents to the U.S. society and polity. Moreover, though the development of transnational families, enduring family relations across borders sustain national identities that cross country borders, while family formation drives a settlement process that unfolds, especially with the birth of children, into citizenship. To be precise, two overlapping transnational societies emerge as a result: on the one hand, we have national communities that span country borders, and on the other hand, we have countries that encompass multiple nationalities.[13]

Third and most central to my interest here, I have relied on a notion of citizenship as membership in public institutions to explore the emergence of citizenship among Mexican immigrants in California in their encounter with industrial relations, immigration and naturalization, education, social welfare, and other public institutions. This encounter between U.S. public institutions and a cohort of first-generation immigrants enduringly tied to their homeland has consequences, I suggest, comparable in some respects to that between "national" public institutions and African Americans here in the United States and indigenous peoples here and elsewhere when they have asserted their own citizenship rights (Marx, 1995). Yet it also projects citizenship rights outward, so to speak, pointing implicitly to a transnational public order. Unless these fragile webs of transnational citizenship are shredded by a reversion to a homogeneous national citizenship—which can occur only at the not-inconceivable price of regression from democracy itself—that order is likely to continue developing.

Works Cited

California Department of Education. 2000. <www.cde.ca.gov/demographics/reports/statewide/adultyrs.htm>

Centro de Apoyo al Migrante. 1998. *Situacion general de los Trabajadores Migratorios en la frontera de California y Baja California*. Tijuana, Mexico.

Cohen, Jean L. 1982. *Class and Civil Society: The Limits of Marxian Critical Theory*. Amherst: University of Massachusetts Press.

Commission on Agricultural Workers. 1992. *Report of the Commission on Agricultural Workers*. Washington, D.C.

Delgado, Hector L. 1993. *New Immigrants, Old Unions*. Philadelphia: Temple University Press.

Foweraker, Joe, and Todd Landman. 1997. *Citizenship Rights and Social Movements: A Comparative and Statistical Analysis*. Oxford: Oxford University Press.

Hobsbawm, E. J. 1968. *Labouring Men: Studies in the History of Labour*. London: Weidenfeld and Nicolson.

Honagneu-Sotelo, Pierrette. 1994. *Gendered Transitions: Mexican Experiences of Immigration*. Berkeley: University of California Press.

Immigration and Naturalization Service (INS). 1998. *1996 Yearbook*. Washington, D.C.

13. It remains to be seen whether newly established rights for U.S.-Mexican dual nationality will add the force of formal status to these cross-border connections.

Johnston, Paul. 1994. *Success while Others Fail: Social Movement Unionism and the Public Workplace*. Ithaca: Cornell University Industrial and Labor Relations Press.

——. 1999. "Citizenship Work." Citizenship Project. <www.newcitizen.org>

——. 2001. "Organize for What? The Resurgence of Labor as Citizenship Movement." In Harry Katz and Lowell Turner (eds.), *Strategies for Union Renewal*. Ithaca, N.Y.: Cornell University Press. Available at <www.newcitizen.org>

Liang, Zai. 1994. "Social Contact, Social Capital, and the Naturalization Process: Evidence from Six Immigrant Groups." *Social Science Research* 23:407–37.

Lipsky, Michael. 1980. *Street-level Bureaucracy: Dilemmas of the Individual in Public Services*. New York: Russell Sage Foundation.

Marshall, T. H. 1950. *Citizenship and Social Class and Other Essays*. Cambridge: Cambridge University Press.

Marx, Anthony W. 1996. "Contested Citizenship: The Dynamics of Racial Identity and Social Movements." In Charles Tilly (ed.), *Citizenship, Identity, and Social History*. Cambridge: Cambridge University Press.

Meyer, John. 1980. "The World Polity and the Authority of the Nation-State." In A. Bergesen (ed.), *Studies of the Modern World System*. New York: Academic Press.

Mines, Richard, and Philip Martin. 1986. *A Profile of California Farmworkers*. Berkeley: University of California Division of Agricultural and Natural Resources. Giannini Information Series, no. 86-2.

Mink, Gwendolyn. 1986. *Old Labor and New Immigrants in American Political Development: Union, Party, and State, 1875–1920*. Ithaca, N.Y.: Cornell University Press.

Milkman, Ruth, and Kent Wong (eds.). 1999. *Immigrants and Union Organizing*. Ithaca, N.Y.: Cornell University Press.

Montgomery, David. 1993. *Citizen Worker: The Experience of Workers in the United States with Democracy and the Free Market during the Nineteenth Century*. New York: Cambridge University Press.

New York Times. 1999. "INS's Latest Tack: Firing of Undocumented Workers." In *San Jose Mercury News*. April 2, p. 4.

Portes, Alejandro, and Rubén Rumbaut. 1996. *Immigrant America: A Portrait*. 2nd ed. Berkeley: University of California Press.

Pressman, Jeffrey, and Aaron Wildavsky. 1973. *Implementation*. Berkeley: University of California Press.

Rosenberg, Howard. 1998. *Who Works on California Farms?* Oakland: University of California Division of Agriculture and Natural Resources.

Soysal, Yasemin Nuhoğlu. 1994. *Limits of Citizenship: Migrants and Postnational Membership in Europe*. Chicago: University of Chicago Press.

Tarrow, Sidney. 1994. *Power in Movement: Social Movements, Collective Action, and Politics*. Cambridge: Cambridge University Press

Thompson, E. P. 1974. *The Making of the English Working Class*. Hammondsworth: Penguin Books.

Tilly, Charles (ed.). 1996. "Citizenship, Identity, and Social History." Introduction to *Citizenship, Identity, and Social History*. Cambridge: Cambridge University Press.

U.S. Bureau of the Census. 1998. *Voting and Registration in the Election of 1996*. Washington, D.C. Special report.

Walzer, Michael. 1995. "The Civil Society Argument." In Ronald Beiner (ed.), *Theorizing Citizenship*. Albany: State University of New York Press.

CHAPTER TEN

Immigrant and Minority Representations of Citizenship in Quebec

MICHELINE LABELLE
DANIEL SALÉE

IN THE PAST DECADE, most Western societies have looked for institutional and political ways to renew their views of citizenship (Labelle and Salée, 1999; Pickus, 1997; Schuck, 1996; Weil, 1997). This renewal has taken shape mainly through immigration policies that increasingly emphasize the development of control mechanisms to regulate immigrant entry (Brochmann, 1998; Hollifield, 1997; Weil, 1998). This is part of a sociopolitical and ideological vision that focuses on issues of security and acts as "a moralizing discourse, articulated around the idea of anomie and the loss of values" (Bigot, 1998, 13, authors' translation).

As the illegal fringe of international immigration is often perceived and presented as a significant threat to the health and security of citizens of existing states, several member countries of the Organization for Economic Cooperation and Development (OECD) are now committed to policies designed to enhance and strengthen their control over immigration. The guiding logic behind this policy overhaul is based upon a two-pronged strategy that focuses on the interstate harmonization of immigration laws and entry procedures and relies on measures to restrict access to citizenship (see Hreblay, 1994; Papademetriou and Hamilton, 1995; Martiniello and Rea, 1997), whether acquired by naturalization or by filiation (SOPEMI, 1995). Clearly, the laws and policies that structure international immigration and access to citizenship are being reelaborated from new political and normative bases.

The pressures of globalization and transnationalism compound the problem as new migratory flows transform social fabrics and diasporic longings stretch beyond national boundaries, raising concerns about the future of the nation-state. Like most other Western societies today, Canada is grappling with particularistic agendas based on issues of identity, individual rights, and compensation for past injustices that have come to take center stage in the political process. As they express minority voices long kept silent, they force serious reconsideration of dominant social practices and patterns of power, and by extension, they question age-old institutional formulas largely unchallenged. Conversely, those who feel aggressively interpellated and undermined by these agendas also feel that the integrity of the political community and social cohesion is threatened.

To cope with this new, emerging environment, the Canadian state has in the past decade modified its immigration policies and revised the parameters that have traditionally defined citizenship. In the hope of defusing Quebec's sovereignist claims, strengthening social cohesion, consolidating political unity, and bringing about a renewed sense of loyalty to the Canadian nationality—particularly among immigrants—policies have been proposed to tighten the requirements for Canadian citizenship.

For its part, Quebec is driven by a will to independent statehood. It is also wrestling with the social and political imperatives of citizenship. Although its attempts to emerge as a sovereign state have been denied by the Canadian state, Quebec imposes itself as a virtual state within the Canadian state and aspires to develop its own concept of citizenship based on a distinct vision of the Quebec political community. Like the Canadian state, the Quebec state is working toward the emergence of a socially entrenched sense of belonging, a universally accepted political language, and a common civic framework to unite all those residing on the Quebec territory.

Although the policies of the Quebec state are motivated by political aims significantly different from those pursued by the Canadian state, they also seek to consolidate the unity of the political community. Consequently, immigrant and minority groups in Quebec are often made to choose between competing visions of citizenship and belonging, a situation that many among them find perplexing and that complicates the politics of intercultural relations in Quebec. To shed light on this situation, we conducted a series of qualitative interviews in multiethnic Montreal neighborhoods to explore how state intentions toward citizenship are perceived by community activists from ethnic and racialized minorities in Quebec.[1]

1. We use the words *racialized* and *racialization* in the same way that Michael Omi and Howard Winant (1986, 64) use them. As they explain: "We employ the term *racialization* to signify the extension of racial meaning to a previously racially unclassified relationship, social practice or group. Racialization is an ideological process, an historically specific one. Racial

Montreal offers interesting and highly relevant features for a study of this kind. Almost nine in ten immigrants living in Quebec reside in Montreal, and the ethnic origin of more than one-third of the Montreal population is neither French nor Anglo-Celt. Politically, Montreal is also Canada's center stage for debates over issues of belonging and membership that underscore the citizenship question. Indeed, competition between Canada and Quebec for the civic allegiance and loyalty of citizens is more salient than anywhere else in the country.

In this chapter, we present an overview of current Canadian and Quebec discourses on citizenship and compare these with the visions of citizenship that emerged from our interviews.

The Challenges to Citizenship in Canada and Quebec

The Canadian State and Citizenship

Following the failure of the Meech Lake constitutional accord in 1990, the Canadian government launched a massive process of public consultation over the institutional and civic renewal of Canada. Several task forces, working groups, town hall meetings, and parliamentary committees discussed the future of Canada as a political community. This operation led to a new constitutional accord (the Charlottetown Accord), which was defeated in a 1992 national referendum. During those years of heightened public debate, the Canadian state engaged in a thorough reflection on the terms and constitutive parameters of "Canadianness" and on the means that would best facilitate the integration of immigrants and ethnocultural minorities into mainstream Canadian society. Various departments and bureaucratic agencies were summoned to the task of reconstructing the national unity discourse.[2] The propositions made by official

ideology is constructed from pre-existing conceptual (or, if one prefers, discursive) elements and emerges from the struggles of competing political projects and ideas seeking to articulate similar elements differently."

2. Citizenship and Immigration Canada, Canadian Heritage, and the Privy Council Office have been at the forefront of this process. Over the past decade, standing committees of the House of Commons and Senate have looked into the matter and proposed recommendations. Among them are the Standing Committee of the House of Commons on Citizenship and Immigration and the Standing Committee of the Senate on Social Affairs, Science and Technology. In 1996, the Clerk of the Privy Council launched the "Policy Research Initiative" (PRI). This broad and encompassing undertaking, which involves thirty federal departments and agencies as well as research partners in the academic and policy analysis communities, has been put forward to retool the policy capacity of the federal government. Initiated in the wake of the political trauma caused by the results of the 1995 Quebec referendum on sovereignty (Quebecers came extremely close to opting for sovereignty from Canada), the PRI aims at taking stock of the social, political, and economic situation of Canada, and developing policy orientations that would guarantee greater

stakeholders did not always converge. As the Canadian political community was particularly strained by competing national allegiances vying for attention (Aboriginal people and Quebecers),[3] they expressed different positions and nuances of opinions as to the best possible way of ensuring national unity and social cohesion. The interface between multiculturalism and citizenship was at the center of discussions. In the end the notion of citizenship emerged as a pivotal concept. It is interesting that while most government documents refer to the idea of citizenship in its broadest sociopolitical sense, in their actual treatment of it issues related to immigration stand out. Conceptually, the Canadian state's understanding of citizenship is largely determined by the question of immigrant integration (Labelle and Salée, 1999; Abu-Laban, 1998).

In 1994 the Honorable Sergio Marchi, then minister of Citizenship and Immigration, requested the Standing Committee of the House of Commons on Citizenship and Immigration to review the 1977 version of the Canadian Citizenship Act in order to "modernize" the legislation. The minister's aim was unequivocal: in his mind and that of his government, it was important that immigrants be well integrated into Canadian society, that they understand what being Canadian really means, and that they learn to appreciate and adopt the core values and principles that define Canadian society; hence, a new citizenship law would foster greater appreciation of the benefits of Canadian citizenship on the part of immigrants (Canada, Citizenship and Immigration Canada, 1994a, 17).

Clearly, the issue of citizenship arises essentially in response to the challenges immigration seems to pose to the integrity of the Canadian social fabric. While still open to immigration, the Canadian state is concerned that as "resources once plentiful are now dear" (ibid., viii–ix), it may put a stress on Canada's ability to integrate newcomers viably and equitably. Hence, in recent years, immigration targets have been reduced (from roughly 250,000 new entrants annually in the early 1990s to around 200,000 currently). But more significant is the federal government's insistence on welcoming mainly financially independent immigrants and, as the case may be, genuine refugees and asylum seekers. Notable also is the government's emphasis on "responsible" immigrants and its concerns over the perverse effects induced by the globaliza-

---

social cohesion, a more solidly entrenched sense of belonging and attachment to Canada among its population, and a stronger position for the country in the global economy.

3. The Canadian state contributed actively to the politicization of citizenship. The 1992 proposals for constitutional reform, for example, put on a par the affirmation of Canadian identity and citizenship in the Constitution with the symbolic recognition of the distinct character of Quebec and with governmental autonomy for Native peoples. See Canada, Privy Council Office (1991, 5–13). For an analysis of this context, see Rocher and Salée (1993); Salée (1995).

tion of migrations (criminal activities being imported through certain immigrant connections, for example).

In the end, in its attempt to redefine the parameters of Canadian citizenship, the Canadian state is firmly establishing its intention to increase its control over the quality, volume, and sources of migration flows to Canada. The thrust behind recent legislative measures and regulations on immigration is to ensure that immigrants become fully integrated Canadian *citizens*.[4] There can be no doubt of the nature of the engagement expected of them. In the words of a Privy Council document, citizenship is first posed as "an emotional tie, a sense of shared values, and commitment to our country. Our shared Canadian citizenship provides a focus for unity that encompasses its parts, and brings our people together" (Canada, Privy Council, 1991, 1). As the members of the Standing Committee of the House of Commons on Citizenship and Immigration (1994, 5) wrote in their report, "Diversity is one of Canada's enormous strengths, but the importance of the whole must be emphasized. We must be a choir not a cacophony."

Immigration is part and parcel of Canada's national and historical makeup, but it has become clear that to minimize the impact of recent migratory movements, globalization, and attendant social fragmentation, the Canadian state needs to foster immigration that will readily enhance social cohesion and conform to the established, normative parameters of Canadian society. Unsurprisingly, the state discourse on citizenship essentially remains addressed to immigrants and to ethnocultural minorities whose integration in the Canadian mainstream may be regarded as problematic by the state and the general population. The state's message to immigrants and minorities is loud and clear: the acquisition of Canadian citizenship is a "great privilege" (Canada, Citizenship and Immigration Canada, 1994b, 25). Once bestowed upon anyone it should command unconditional allegiance to Canada, its norms, values, and priorities (Canada, House of Commons, Standing Committee on Citizenship and Immigration, 1994, 15).

---

4. The new orientations on immigration are based upon the following principles: accountability and transparency (principles and policies must be clearly set out in legislation); supporting family reunification in keeping with two new social realities (family life outside marriage and same-sex couples); upholding Canada's humanitarian tradition while supporting greater effectiveness in decision making; balancing privileges and responsibilities (i.e., greater responsibilities for sponsors, actions against people who fail to meet their obligations under the law or abuse of the refugee determination process); enriching the country's human resources (Canada's selection system for independent immigrant applicants needs a sharper focus on flexible and transferable skills); promoting public safety as international crime becomes more pervasive and sophisticated; fairness, effectiveness, and integrity of the system. (Canada, Citizenship and Immigration Canada, 1998c, 10–11).

In the eyes of the Canadian state, Canadian citizenship is not a given. Although it admittedly opens access to an attractive array of rights, the benefits of Canadian citizenship entail obligations and responsibilities. This is more than a simple rhetorical urging. In the wake of the restructuring of the Canadian welfare state, more emphasis than ever is put on individual responsibility as a criterion of sound civic-mindedness. As the state gradually reduces its involvement (in social programs), citizens are expected to assume responsibility in occupying the space left vacant by public powers.

The emphasis on responsibility conveys in no uncertain terms that Canadian citizenship must be deserved and comes with moral and political requirements. As a 1996 information brochure distributed by Citizenship and Immigration Canada reminds Canadians (and in particular new Canadians), being a good Canadian citizen implies "being loyal towards Canada; being loyal towards the Queen of Canada and her representatives; obeying Canadian laws; respecting the rights of others; respecting private and public property; taking care of the Canadian heritage; upholding the ideals of Canada," and, of course, subscribing to the values of democracy, compassion, and tolerance that the Canadian state holds to be fundamental.

By insisting on linking citizenship, individual responsibility, and partnership with the Canadian state, the government's discourse hints obliquely that some immigrants may be tempted to abuse Canadian citizenship and that that situation must be prevented.[5] Immigrants are accountable to society and to state institutions. The onus is on them to demonstrate that they deserve to be incorporated into the Canadian political community. Explains one government document: "Integration . . . is about finding a place in Canadian society, about a sense of belonging, and about assuming the rights and responsibilities of being Canadian. It is about being able to take part—free of barriers—in Canadian life" (Canada, Employment and Immigration Canada, 1990, 14). It is the duty of immigrants and members of ethnic minorities to adapt to the existing cultural and institutional norms, not the reverse.

---

5. The report of the Standing Committee on Citizenship and Immigration is replete with explicit references to the notion of abuse committed by certain categories of the population, whether they be of immigrant origin or members of minority groups. It recommends that the criteria of residence be reformulated to meet the requirement of "Canadianization" which is put "in peril" by women who come to Canada to give birth so that their babies can have Canadian citizenship; or similarly the absence of real affinities with the country in the case of people who inherit this status while always living abroad. (See Canada, House of Commons, Standing Committee on Citizenship and Immigration, 1994, 11). In the newly proposed law on citizenship, which was tabled on November 25, 1999 (Bill C-16) and is currently being debated by Parliament at this writing, the state limits the transmissibility of the second generation in the case of children born abroad to Canadian parents. (See Canada, Citizenship and Immigration Canada, 1999, 22).

The discourse of the Canadian state on citizenship is ideologically rooted in the nonnegotiable expectation that immigrants and ethnic minorities will bind their sense of loyalty and allegiance to the Canadian state, first and foremost. As Quebec and Aboriginal nationalisms seem to threaten the structural integrity of the Canadian state and the unity of the Canadian political community, the federal government feels compelled to counteract their influence by establishing once and for all the primacy of Canadian citizenship.[6] The emphasis on loyalty, allegiance, and responsibility is in fact meant to "reflect the true value of Canadian citizenship" (Citizenship and Immigration Canada, 1998a). Immigrants may be allowed to carry dual citizenship,[7] but to the Canadian state there should be no question as to where their primary loyalty should lie: Canadian citizenship is an invaluable good and should be treated as such by those upon whom it has been bestowed.

The expectation repeatedly expressed in recent years by the Canadian state that immigrants give primacy of loyalty and attachment to Canada is perplexing in light of Canada's policy of multiculturalism, which since 1971 has determined the state's attitude toward immigrants and its general approach to ethnocultural plurality. As defenders and supporters of that policy often point out (see Kymlicka, 1998), it is premised on the prospect of immigrants and ethnocultural minorities preserving, celebrating, and developing their original identity. "Hyphenated" identities, they argue, are at the core of multiculturalism in Canada and are indeed made legitimate through the funding of ethnic groups and ethnic cultural activities by the state. The legalization of dual citizenship is further proof of the legitimacy and acceptability of multiple civic allegiances in the Canadian context.

The fact is that since Canada's policy of multiculturalism was implemented in the early 1970s, there has always been at the heart of the state's own concep-

---

6. The citizenship oath contained in the proposed legislation on Canadian citizenship is telling in this regard: "From this day forward, I pledge my loyalty and allegiance to Canada and her Majesty Elizabeth the second, Queen of Canada. I promise to respect our country's rights and freedom, to defend our democratic values, to faithfully observe our laws and fulfil my duties and obligations as Canadian citizen" (Canada, Citizenship and Immigration Canada, 1998a, 9). In the eyes of the minister responsible for citizenship and immigration, this formulation responds both to the propositions of the Standing Committee on Citizenship and Immigration which, since 1994, was pushing for the inclusion of loyalty toward Canada and the respect of its laws in the pledge and to the "wishes" expressed by Canadians to have a pledge "which reflects contemporary values and which expresses clearly loyalty towards Canada" (Canada, Citizenship and Immigration Canada, 1998a).

7. Canada recognized dual citizenship in 1977. Recent findings of Statistics Canada demonstrate that one immigrant out of five (some 17 percent) had dual citizenship, which, incidentally, constitutes about 3 percent of the total Canadian population. Eighty-three percent of admissible immigrants obtained their status as Canadian citizens in 1996 (Statistics Canada, 1997).

tion of Canadianness a tension between its stated will to acknowledge ethnocultural diversity as a central feature of Canadian society and its growing concern over the seemingly wavering unity and social cohesion of the country. As a recognition of diversity often translates into particularistic claims for greater administrative, jurisdictional, or, more simply, symbolic autonomy, the integrity of the state and the cohesiveness of society are tested, sometimes painfully. Reconciling the sovereignty of the individual—which the policy of multiculturalism and an array of individual rights–oriented mechanisms protect—and the state imperatives of collective unity and cohesion often proves complicated in the reality of everyday politics.

Through most of the 1970s and part of the 1980s, an unconstrained multiculturalism was favored. By the late 1980s, however, the changing nature and shifting sources of immigration combined with the pressures of Quebec nationalism and Aboriginal claims concerned many who felt that multiculturalism might fragment rather than unify the Canadian political community. The 1988 review of the Multiculturalism Act reflected this concern as it took pain to emphasize the commonalities of all Canadians (shared values, shared purpose, solidarity) over the constitutive diversity of Canadian society. Yet in spite of a refurbishing of the Multiculturalism Act, the concern did not abate. A 1996 report of the Department of Canadian Heritage evaluating multiculturalism programs conceded that large segments of the Canadian public were ambivalent about multiculturalism. Their ambivalence, noted the report, "is attributable, at least in part, to their perception that multiculturalism has the potential for threatening social cohesion by encouraging the retention of ethnocultural identification." This observation prompted the authors of the report to conclude that "Canadians have not fully accepted Canada's unique status as a 'multinational' and 'poly-ethnic' state" (p. 68).

The changes in policy content toward multiculturalism and citizenship in recent years have thus emerged largely in response to the public's and officials' admonitions that people interested in taking up Canadian citizenship must understand that "loyalty to Canada must be given pride of place" (Canada, House of Commons, Standing Committee on Citizenship and Immigration, 1994, 5). In this spirit, the renewal of multiculturalism focuses on a three-pronged approach that clearly emphasizes citizenship values: *Canadian identity*—people of all backgrounds should "feel a sense of belonging and attachment to Canada"—*civic participation*—they must be "active citizens," concerned with "shaping the future of their communities and their country"—and *social justice*—they must be involved in "building a society that ensures fair and equitable treatment and that respects the dignity of and accommodates people of all origins" (Canada, Canadian Heritage, 1997).

In the nearly thirty years between the first multiculturalism policy and the process of policy renewal currently under way, the Canadian state has progressively moved to resolve the perennial tension between multiculturalism and citizenship in favor of the latter, at least for now. While state rhetoric continues to insist on the advantages and benefits of diversity, Canadian policy makers can hardly conceal their wish that identities of all types be subsumed into a global, more encompassing, and generalized Canadian civic identity. Few among them, if any, would openly call for the abandonment of the policy of multiculturalism, although the current concern over social cohesion has many yearning for an unequivocally unified vision of the Canadian political community in which immigrants and new Canadians would unquestioningly endorse and rally around Canada's existing, and historically determined, value system and sense of self. The Canadian state may not demand of immigrants strict adherence to its defining socio-institutional parameters as imperatively as other countries are wont to do. Still, the immigrant integration it now favors is clearly meant to pave the way for an unambiguous, unitary citizenship.

Citizenship and the Quebec State

Quebec citizenship does not exist in the legal sense, as Quebec is not yet constituted as a sovereign political entity. Because of the nationalist strivings of the past three decades and Quebec's own insistence on being acknowledged as a distinct political or national entity within the Canadian federation, most Quebecers today have a clear, Quebec-based sense of identity and community. Since the early 1960s, the Quebec jurisdiction has operated in many ways as a de facto state that constantly calls upon the residents of the territory upon which it is allowed to legislate to embrace Quebec as their primary home of civic attachment. The state-building process that has led, among other things, to the secularization of most institutions; the recognition of French as the official language of public transactions; various legislation for the protection of minority cultures and languages; and direct administrative involvement in immigrant selection and integration have, together, contributed to the construction of a readily identifiable, distinctly Québécois, collective civic consciousness. As a result, most Quebecers, especially within the French-speaking majority, are and feel unquestionably Québécois.[8]

8. The term Québécois (Quebecer) is politically charged and therefore somewhat problematic. In principle, everyone living and residing in Quebec is Quebecer. That is indeed the state definition of the term. In practice, in everyday use, however, many people make a distinction between those who are Francophone Québécois and those who are Anglophone Quebecer. The former is usually thought to include anyone whose mother tongue is French, was socialized in

To large segments of ethnocultural minorities, though, things are not as clear. While some do willingly proclaim their civic Québécois identity, most will insist on being identified as Canadian first and generally resist the prospect of Quebec's sovereignty. The distance that separates them from the mainstream of Quebec society is a source of tension with the Francophone majority. These tensions inevitably bring to the fore the question of their sense of belonging, inclusion, or incorporation into Quebec society. Citizenship, then, to the extent that it is intimately associated with belonging, has indeed become a central issue in Quebec.

Over the past decade, in an effort to foster intercultural coexistence and instill all Quebecers, regardless of their origin, with a sense of being Québécois— in the civic understanding of the term—the Quebec state has developed and clarified its position on issues of belonging to Quebec society. In 1990 the document *Policy Statement on Immigration and Integration of 1990: Let's Build Quebec Together* was proposed by the Liberal government as the mainstay of the official discourse on immigration and integration. This statement presents Quebec as a distinct society. The notion of a distinct society implies that "a clear affirmation of the French-speaking community and institutions as the pivot for the integration of newcomers is essential if the enduring reality of the French Fact is to be assured in Quebec" (Québec, Ministère des Communautés culturelles

---

French, and uses French as their first language at home. In this sense, people of Haitian origin or from former French, African, or Asian colonies, most (but not necessarily all) Sephardic Jews, and people of British descent who with time and community intercourse have been "incorporated" into the Francophone community are considered part of that category. Similarly, the expression *Anglophone Quebecer* encompasses anyone whose mother tongue is English, who was socialized in English, and who primarily speaks English at home. This includes people of British descent, East Indian, West Indian, Asian, or African origin, most (but not necessarily all) Ashkenazi Jews, and people of French descent or of any other European origin who with time and community intercourse have been incorporated into Quebec's Anglophone community. This distinction is controversial though. While the usage of *Anglophone Quebecer* is unproblematic in terms of whom it does and does not include, the usage of the expression *Francophone Quebecer* is not. It is generally accepted that an Anglophone Quebecer is essentially an English speaker: being an Anglo in Quebec has first and foremost a linguistic connotation, not an ethnic one. Being a Francophone, on the other hand, does not carry the same descriptive connotation: in common parlance, to the linguistic marker is often implicitly added an ethnic marker. In other words, the expression *Francophone Quebecer*, which is regularly used interchangeably with *Québécois*, is used to identify native Quebecers whose mother tongue is French and who are descendants of the inhabitants who peopled New France before the British Conquest of 1760. Demographically, they represent 82 percent of the total Quebec population. The French term *Québécois* is regularly used by large segments of the population to identify that particular ethnolinguistic group. In this sense, *Francophone Quebecer* and *Québécois* are loaded with an ethnicized charge that *Anglophone Quebecer* does not have. This situation irritates sovereignists and other Quebec nationalists who claim that their nationalism and "Quebecness" transcend the narrow ethnic image for which their political foes are all too bent on castigating them.

et de l'Immigration du Québec, 1990, 16). It further suggests an integration plan for immigrants and "cultural communities" based on an idea of a moral contract as the foundation upon which Quebecers of all origins can together build Quebec's future. This implies that newcomers to Quebec should fully assume their responsibilities in the development of the host society and live by the tenets of a "common public culture," that is, of shared values and universally agreed upon rights and sociopolitical practices.

The moral contract is a citizenship pact that rests on three central parameters of social interaction and intercommunity relations to which anyone living in Quebec should adhere: Quebec is "a society in which French is the common language of public life"; it is "a democratic society where everyone is expected and encouraged both to participate and contribute to public debate"; it is also "a pluralist society that is open to multiple influences within the limits imposed by a respect for fundamental democratic values and a need for intergroup exchanges" (Québec, Ministère des Communautés culturelles et de l'Immigration du Québec, 1990, 15). That is, it is a society that offers a peaceful resolution of conflicts; a guarantee of collective and individual rights and liberties provided by law (to the point of adapting institutional practices to suit individual and cultural specificities); antidiscriminatory legislation, gender equality, secularism of the state, and equal and universal access to health and social services.

The Quebec state's willingness to transcend the historical ethnolinguistic marker of Quebec society is genuine, but, as the *Conseil des relations interculturelles du Québec* has noted, though its approach is meant to elicit immigrant endorsement of the founding principles of Quebec society and uphold the necessity to adapt institutions, it is often received with perplexity (Québec, *Conseil des relations interculturelles,* 1997a, 8; authors' translation).[9] The lack of information on the intended goals of the approach, the gap between principles and reality, the absence of concrete policies in line with principles, and the uneasy application of those policies that exist are most commonly cited as the major stumbling blocks, accounting for the reticence of immigrants and non-Francophone minorities.

Since the election of the Parti Québécois in 1994, the general orientation of this discourse has been reassessed. Though Quebec's policy about immigration and the management of cultural diversity is still very much in progress, the idea of a Quebec-based citizenship is now firmly rooted in public discourse. In 1996 a new department, the *Ministère des Relations avec les citoyens et de l'Immigration,* was created to replace the old *Ministère des Communautés*

9. Council for Intercultural Relations: a governmental advisory body dealing with issues pertaining to immigration and integration.

culturelles et de l'Immigration. This constituted not only a structural change, but also a shift in emphasis as the government clearly indicated its willingness to deal with citizens first and not necessarily only with representatives of ethnocultural communities. The underlying message was unequivocal: everyone living in Quebec is a Quebecer first, and it is as Quebecers first that the state will interact with them, within a common civic framework, applicable to all without distinction. By focusing on the relation of the state to its citizens, the government downplayed ethnocultural differences and stressed rather the formal equality of every citizen in the eyes of the state.

*   *   *

Contemporary state practices and discourses about citizenship in Canada, whether expressed by the federal or Quebec government, can be summed up in one key objective: bring immigrants to develop a genuine sense of belonging to the society that welcomes them. Although some members of immigrant communities are prepared to make this objective their own unreservedly, our study reveals infinitely more nuanced and complex critical positions about the vision of citizenship expounded by the Canadian and Quebec states.

We conducted forty thorough one-on-one interviews and held a focus group with Montreal-based, immigrant community activists involved in promoting immigrant integration in Quebec society. Three main sets of considerations guided our approach. First, we asked them how they spontaneously identify themselves, inviting them to justify their choice of identity, particularly when they did not identify themselves as Canadian or Quebecer only. State discourse, whether federal or Quebec-based, insists on the importance of developing a Canadian or Quebec-based civic identity before any other. The legitimacy of that identity must be paramount in the minds of both those who declare it as such and the interlocutors who will eventually have to recognize it. Our questions about identity were intended, therefore, to appraise both the nature of the imagined identity of our respondents and the impact of government discourses upon them.

Second, we asked our respondents to discuss their views of Canadian citizenship. We wanted to know what it meant for them (which values, norms, principles, duties, and obligations they associate with it) and what the nature of their personal feelings was toward it. We also probed their views on dual citizenship, the current conditions for the acquisition of Canadian citizenship, and issues of belonging. Our questions regularly related to social, economic, and cultural integration. Our goal was to determine to what extent the state valorization of Canadian citizenship was shared by the interviewees.

Finally, in light of the importance of the repeated and significant attempts of the Quebec state to offer immigrants an alternative citizenship (through access to independent statehood), we believed it was necessary to question our respondents about this dimension of political life in Quebec. We sought to learn whether the Quebec discourse on citizenship appealed to them and what they thought Quebec citizenship would "look like" if Quebec were to become a sovereign state.

Identification, Identities, and Citizenship

Barely 10 percent of our respondents spontaneously identified themselves, without hesitation, as Canadian or "Québécois," that is, without recourse to an identity other than that determined by the general civic framework of Canada or Quebec. Five percent identified themselves only with the national identity or citizenship of their country of origin. The remainder of our sample group (85 percent) readily hyphenated their identity, using two or more national, civic, and even ethnocultural referents. Of this group, close to half (44 percent) referred to their country or cultural place of origin first, before associating it with *Québécois* or Canadian (i.e., Italo-Canadian; *Péruvien-Québécois*). Twenty-nine percent identified themselves as Quebecer first (e.g., Quebecer of Haitian origin), and 24 percent as Canadian first (e.g., Canadian of Ghanaian origin).

Two observations stand out: (1) the almost general tendency of our interviewees to adopt dual or multiple civic identities, which in most cases, reflected their reluctance to accept both the Canadian and Quebec state's penchant for a uniform civic identity, and (2) the relative importance of Quebec-based identity (associated or not with another identity) over Canadian identity. We examine these in turn.

The dual or multiple character of identities

It would be premature to conclude from the multiple identity options of our sample that the state's attempts at subsuming individual identities into a unitary civic framework and at channeling people's allegiance to the advantage of Canadian citizenship have failed. Several studies in the United States show that the persistence of multiple identities after several generations in no way weakens the attachment of citizens to their adopted country (Alba, 1990; Rumbault, 1997; Waters, 1990). In nearly two out of three cases in our study, Canada or Quebec was mentioned as the first label of self-identification, and by and large, many respondents expressed a strong willingness to be considered inherent members of the host society and its political community. Be that as it may, for most of the people we interviewed civic identification with Canada or Quebec was not automatic or easy. Many raised serious concerns over prevailing government notions of citizenship, in particular the idea of citizenship that implies the uncontested primacy of the host country.

Several factors may explain their concerns. First is the strength of transnational bonds, often maintained through remittances to family members or friends living in the country of origin, various practices of international cooperation, and continued solidarity with the motherland, or more simply for purely emotional reasons. For several respondents, the pervasiveness of a self-imposed sense of obligation toward countries of origin seems to legitimate the use of hyphenated or multiple civic identities. As one woman of Italian descent put it: "I am a Quebecer of Italian origin. I can't simply say that I am a Quebecer. I am a Quebecer because I was born in Quebec, but the link with Italy remains, and I feel I must acknowledge it"[10] [translated from French]. Similarly, for a woman of Haitian origin whose roots are indelible: "I feel I belong to Quebec, the country I have chosen to live in. I am a Quebecer; Canada does not mean much to me. But by birth, skin color, language, and culture I am and will always be Haitian" [translated from French]. These are typical declarations that say a great deal about the importance of roots and therefore about the emotional bond (symbolic or real) with a preimmigration culture or past that has little or nothing in common with Canada or Quebec, and that ultimately inhibits the unquestioned endorsement of Canadian or Quebec citizenship currently prevailing in public discourse.

Second, the classificatory discourse of the state also plays a role. The tendency of both the federal and Quebec states to impose ethnocultural and sometimes racial categories for administrative purposes often operates with deeply rooted social stereotypes about ethnic minorities and gives individuals a sense of self marked by difference and social boundaries. As a result, immigrants often feel compelled to adopt a designated identity:[11] Time and again respon-

10. Depending on the preferred language of the interviewees some of our interviews were conducted in French, others in English. For convenience, we have translated in English all the quotes drawn from French interviews. For accuracy, we mention if it is a translation at the end of the quotes.

11. The term *designated identity* is used to describe the tendency of the host society to label the "other" according to distinct and different physical traits. For example, the Canadian state uses its bureaucratic and census-driven "visible minorities" to refer to "persons, other than Aboriginal peoples, who are non-Caucasian in race or non-white in color" and includes in that group Chinese, South Asians, Blacks, Arabs and West Asians, Filipinos, Southeast Asians, Latin Americans, Japanese, Koreans, Pacific Islanders, and Lebanese. With this official definition, the Canadian state points out the difference of the individuals who happen to be part of that group. The same thing could be said of the Quebec state's use of the term "cultural communities." Although such terms are primarily meant as administrative categories for redistributive purposes, they nev-

dents told us: "We are constantly reminded of our ethnic origin, of our difference." One respondent who insisted on identifying herself as "just Bangladeshi" further explained: "I know I am a Canadian citizen, but even if I say I'm Canadian, [people] want to know about my origins, my color, my language, my religion." In one case, the respondent's reluctance to be identified as Canadian or Quebecer was unequivocal and without appeal: "I most likely identify with Guayanese. I don't consider myself a Quebecer, and I have some resentment towards Canada."

The multiculturalist perspective that pervades public discourse has a distinct influence in bringing about this kind of attitude. It may boast respect for individual difference and tolerance, but its urgings are often understood as an invitation to celebrate subjective singularity. As a result, essentialist and stereotypical visions of some immigrant communities or minorities tend to dominate the way they are dealt with by the state as well as how they present themselves or vie for power in the public arena. Still, though most of our respondents readily used the classificatory discourse of the state and its attendant ethnoracial lexicon (ethnicity, race, cultural communities, visible minorities), they are torn between two positions on this question. Some, for instrumental and practical reasons, are at ease with this discourse, which they see as unavoidable to guide and inform the state's redistributive action. One man who endorses this position told us:

It is a label, a very crude way of putting a person in a box. It does not disturb me because you need that information. With that information you could have a lot of social programs. It gives you a general indication of what's happening within different communities, but it doesn't give you an accurate representation of the way that community feels and thinks and perceives. As imperfect as it may be, for statistical and research purposes [ethnic or racial categorization] it is useful.

This feeling is shared by another respondent, who noted:

We are all Canadian, or Quebecer, for the census. And it doesn't matter exactly where you were born or who your parents are. By including the question [of ethnicity in the census] you can get important information about your community. Without it, try to get something out of the

---

ertheless pin individuals into implicitly stereotypical status which brings out their "otherness." In a way then designated identity is a result of the gaze the host or "mainstream" society brings to bear on immigrants and minorities in general.

government: they're going to ask you what exactly is your population, what exactly are your numbers in this, what is your status for this, what is your status for that, and if you can't produce that information they don't even look at you. So it's a necessary evil. At times [it's a] damned-if-you-do-damned-if-you-don't sort of thing.

Others are adamant in their rejection of any form of ethnic categorization or classification other than a civic one. In their view, ethnic categorization constitutes a major obstacle to the development of a sense of belonging to the host society since it fosters symbolic exclusion, discrimination, and preconceived notions about immigrants and minorities that die hard. It creates difference and social boundaries that divide society rather than stimulate social cohesion. As several respondents clearly put it:

That is exactly why it is difficult for most of us to feel genuinely like Quebecers. We are constantly reminded of our origin, our difference. When we are asked, "Where are you from?" it implies that we can't possibly be from here in the mind of the interlocutor. [translated from French]

I don't like it. I am a citizen like everybody else. I am black. So? That's my skin color. We shouldn't be identified with labels. I find that offensive, and it only creates more prejudices. [translated from French]

It's so silly. It's an insult to me as a human being. All of a sudden someone wants to put you into a little box that they can understand. . . . You think you know me but you don't. You just created a stereotype, and in the past stereotypes have been bad.

Opponents of ethnic categorization are found in two broad groups. One group comprises recent immigrants whose integration is still uneasy and who have experienced authoritarian political regimes or civil unrest. Canadian citizenship is important to them. They see it as a way out of the distressing life they left behind in their countries of origin. Being reminded that they are different or that they come from somewhere else is tantamount to questioning the new civic status they acquired in Canada. The other group is made up of long-standing immigrants and the second-generation youth of immigrant origin who are well integrated in society. For that very reason ethnic categorization, administrative or otherwise, is offensive to them. It implies that regardless of how well they have integrated into the host society, they are perceived as "others," not quite part of that society.

The third factor that accounts for the reticence of most of our respondents to claim Canada or Quebec as their only anchor of civic identity has to do with

their experience of racial discrimination and their perception of their own exclusion, whether real or symbolic. A third of our respondents felt that members
from racialized minorities are treated as second-class citizens both by the majority and by other immigrants of European origin. Discrimination in employment and housing is of particular concern to them. This situation, they argue,
creates adversarial positions that unavoidably hinder the emergence of a feeling of belonging to Canada or Quebec. On this score, their understanding of
reality is clear.

> We're like second-class citizens. When we look for a job, because of our
> accent, we are immediately rejected. We are discriminated against on the
> basis of our language and our nationality. [translated from French]
>
> How can you not feel like a second-class person when you consider
> the way people treat you and the remarks they make if you're not white?
> How are you not supposed to feel second class when you get a door
> slammed in your face because "Hey! We don't rent houses to whoever"
> or whatever. . . . [It is all based on] skin color, money access. If you are a
> minority group and you don't have it, then you are screwed over.

Others are more nuanced or more prudent than these respondents. They are
reluctant to express the notion of second-class citizenship but admit the existence of racism and xenophobia.

> To say that we are second-class citizens is a bit strong. We are perhaps
> more like "citizens on the fringe." The problem is that there is much ado
> about integration, while in fact, we are not really integrated. [translated
> from French]
>
> I don't think that we are considered second-class citizens. We are not
> in a country where racism is really obvious. It does exist, no doubt; it is
> even underhanded at times and in some places. But in this country, people
> are more xenophobic than racist. The difficulties that some may encoun-
> ter really depend on the individual, on his efforts and on his ability to
> face adversity. There are no real obstacles. [translated from French]

The respondents who prefer not to invoke the reality of social marginalization
or exclusion to explain the weakness of the feeling of belonging by certain
immigrant groups dwell rather on the personal dispositions of people. Those
who feel excluded, they argue, will be unable to develop a strong sense of
belonging. Although it is not really expressed clearly, in the end, the will to

belong and the experience of everyday life, they hint, are what determines an individual's civic identification with Canada.

The Relative Salience of the Quebec-based Identity

As might have been expected, the attitude of several respondents toward Quebec-based identity is determined by a negative attitude toward Quebec sovereignty. Civic allegiance entails allegiance to Canada first and foremost. Among minorities, the political project of Quebec sovereignists conjures up images of sociopolitical instability, exclusion, and a fear of the unknown.

> I identify with the country, Canada, first. I am not interested in the politics of the division of the country.

> I would say I'm Canadian. I used to say *Québécois*, but I wouldn't say that now because I've gotten the message that *Québécois* do not perceive me as Québécois.

> [Immigrants] believe that Canada protects [them] against something. They are afraid they might be destabilized. They are afraid they might lose the few things they have. They fear they will be mistreated. [translated from French]

Be that as it may, as we have already noted the greater number of our respondents more readily used the term *Québécois* rather than Canadian (hyphenated or not) when asked about their civic identity. This is in line with what other recent studies have shown: regardless of their cultural or linguistic origin, Quebec residents generally consider Quebec their primary locus of civic affiliation and identity (Kalin, 1995; Kalin and Berry, 1995). The Canadian civic identity and the attachment to Canada are less strong, less emphasized in Quebec than in the rest of the country. Some of our respondents were adamant about their identity as Quebecers:

> I never say I am Canadian, except for administrative reason, at customs, when it is necessary for technical reasons. My personal allegiance is Québécois of Indonesian origin [translated from French]

> I say that I am Québécois. If people insist, I say that I am Moroccan. In Morocco, I fought French; it symbolized colonialism. Here I will fight English when it colonizes French, destroys the French language and identity. [translated from French]

> Most people feel that they are Quebecers. But being a Quebecer does not necessarily mean "old stock" Quebecer. Someone of Italian origin is

as much a Quebecer as anyone else. If things were understood this way, we would have fewer problems. [translated from French]

These responses suggest that for certain immigrant groups and ethnic minorities, Quebec has become a pole of self-identification that is at least as legitimate as Canada. The increasingly civic, as opposed to ethnic, character of Quebec nationalism in the past fifteen years largely explains this evolution.

This said, many seemed torn in their allegiance. The constant political competition between the Quebec and Canadian states has made it difficult for people to choose between them. As their loyalty as citizens is being solicited from all sides, their sense of belonging oscillates. It is often stuck in the middle, which ultimately prevents them from opting clearly for one civic identity or another. As the following two quotes illustrate, they are definitely at ease in Quebec, but the more formal, structured environment that Canada appears to offer as a full-fledged country seems to have a comforting if indefinite appeal.

I say that I am Quebecer-Canadian of Egyptian origin because I have lived here longer than I did in Egypt. My life is here. I have come to Quebec because life here fits my convictions in cultural and religious terms and also from the point of view of the general mentality that prevails. Of all the provinces in Canada, Quebec is the one that suits me best culturally, linguistically, and from a lifestyle point of view. I feel good here. Still, I have also visited the other provinces, and I feel attached to the beautiful country that is Canada. [translated from French]

We are Canadian. In which province? Quebec. I have immigrated to Canada. I want Canada to be united. However, I would not want to live in the English community; they are cold people. Quebecers have Latin blood; they are warm people. That's why I feel good here. But we have to try harder at becoming a more united family, learn about each other, [and] respect our customs. [translated from French]

In a way, this tendency to equivocate about one's civic identity reflects a strategy of prudence, the desire not to offend anyone, and to "cover all angles." On several occasions our respondents admitted that the way they identify themselves depends on who wants to know and on the circumstances in which they are asked. As one man of Peruvian origin told us:

It is all a matter of context. If, for example, we are discussing Quebec's national question, I will say that I am Quebecer. On the other hand, if the discussion has no political implications, I will say that I am, more broadly, Peruvian-Canadian. Deep down, I am Latino-American, Peruvian, Canadian, and then Quebecer. [translated from French]

Or as another of Chinese descent observed:

My father will tell you that he is a Quebecer. Like all Asians, he is basically being polite. But Canada first made an impression on him when he arrived here and that remains strong. [translated from French]

A few respondents refused to define their identity according to the terms seemingly imposed by Quebec's particular political context. One woman, for example, somewhat impatient at our probing on identity issues, gruffly declared: "I am a human being. That's all!" thus clearly underscoring both how inappropriate and superficial identity and labeling are to her, and how unimportant these questions are in the grand scheme of things. Another type of answer from those seeking to avoid sliding into the trap of Quebec's binary politics is simply to say, "I am a Montrealer." This reveals the emergence of a new political identity associated with Montreal's cosmopolitanism and constitutive heterogeneity held as positive, in contrast to the narrow provincialism associated with the sovereignist vote and the rest of Quebec outside Montreal. One respondent commented:

In my experience, the minorities who are Francophone say they feel *Québécois*, but those [who] are Anglophone will feel Canadian first, then Quebecer. It's a linguistic cleavage. But things are changing. They will say Montrealer, they won't say Quebecer, because they feel that Montreal has a distinct character vis-à-vis the rest of Quebec. . . . It's a way to demarcate themselves from the rest of the province. Since the [1995] referendum, the Montrealer thing has become very strong.

This analysis is corroborated by another respondent, who is unequivocal about his Montreal identity:

My first answer is Montrealer. I identify very closely with the city. It's a place that suits me very well. I have lived here for a long time, and I know everyone. Montreal is home. When people discuss Quebec, Canada, or even North America, I don't really get off on all that. [translated from French]

Issues of belonging and civic self-identification are telling indicators of the sense of attachment immigrants to Canada have toward the country. Clearly, it is much more variegated and diffuse than current state discourses and injunctions about citizenship would have us believe. This is not to say that loyalty of immigrants to Canada (or Quebec, as the case may be) is poor or wanting, but the sense of belonging that emanates from immigrant communities and ethnocultural minorities is at odds with the "pride of place" that state officials would like to see them give Canada. Of course, self-identification does not necessarily reveal the view that individuals have of the nature of a country's citizenship.[12] For this reason we thought it essential to probe further into the sense immigrants have of Canadian citizenship proper, how they understand it, and what it means to them.

Immigrant Views on Canadian Citizenship

By and large the perception our respondents have of Canadian citizenship corresponds to the diffuse sentiment of belonging we described above. Noticeable again is the gap between their understanding of Canadian citizenship and what the state expects immigrants and ethnocultural minorities to make of it. We asked our respondents what, in their view, Canadian citizenship entails. We also discussed their position on dual citizenship and the current conditions for acquiring Canadian citizenship.

Canadian Citizenship as Instrument

The majority of respondents had a positive, but passive and somewhat theoretical, view of Canadian citizenship. Human rights and certain specific values generally associated with Canada in public discourse (such as tolerance, pacifism, and social justice) held an important place in their appreciation of it. "Canada is a country of many cultures, of tolerance. Canadian citizenship implies being accepted in a tolerant society, where universal, fundamental human rights are respected" is the almost cliché formulation that would often come up spontaneously in conversation. Yet it is the instrumental qualities of Canadian citizenship that seemed to elicit the most enthusiasm: the quality of life Canada has to offer, geographical mobility, and the ease with which one can travel with a Canadian passport. "When you have Canadian citizenship," many told us, "It

---

12. Liberal politicians and proponents of multiculturalism (Kymlicka) would argue, for example, that the tendency to hyphenate one's identity or claim multiple national or ethnocultural identities, as many of our respondents do, is characteristic of the Canadian identity and is a fundamental feature of "Canadianness."

is easier to travel abroad. You are accepted all over the world." Barely a quarter of our respondents readily associated Canadian citizenship with a sense of belonging. In general, the notion of Canadian citizenship seemed abstract to many. Several respondents had a problem elaborating on the theme, even when probed further. Some even acknowledged that Canadian citizenship is devoid of any particular meaning for them, that it does not bring out any particular sentiment. As one person told us: "Belonging to Canada? This kind of question has never really been a concern of mine."

In fact, only a minority of the respondents (fewer than two out of ten) spontaneously subscribed to the active, responsible citizenship that the Canadian state wishes to see emerge. They talked about responsibilities and obligations toward Canada and the general political community; they felt they have a duty to participate and be a full-fledged partner in the further development of the country.

Dual Citizenship

The issue of dual citizenship illustrates further the instrumentalist nature of Canadian citizenship and the gap that separates the state's and the immigrant's understanding of it.

Dual citizenship in Canada has been permitted since 1977. During the 1995 referendum on Quebec sovereignty, however, this principle was seriously questioned by federalist advocates in their hope to deter Quebecers from voting in favor of sovereignty. They hinted that if Quebec were to become sovereign, it would be impossible to hold both a Canadian and a Quebec passport. Quebecers voted against sovereignty, and the issue became academic, but, as we have seen, the very real threat of sovereignty prompted the federal government to encourage new Canadians to make Canada their primary, unequivocal site of civic allegiance. Indeed, as the Report of the Standing Committee of the House of Commons on Citizenship and Immigration (Canada, Senate, 1994, 15) attests, dual citizenship constitutes, in the mind of many in power, an obstacle to the healthy development of Canadian citizenship. There is also genuine concern in some circles that Canadian citizenship may be nothing more to immigrants than a citizenship of convenience, a useful commodity to have in times of hardship.

Although a small minority of our respondents agreed with this general vision and affirmed the importance of making a symbolic break with their country of origin, the vast majority did not. They felt that dual citizenship did not necessarily hinder individuals from developing an authentic sense of belonging to Canadian society. They believed it possible to have multiple allegiances but stressed that it is pointless to ask people to renounce the feelings they hold for their countries of origin.

I have dual citizenship. I would not be able to get rid of one to the benefit of the other. One cannot force someone to feel Canadian. We continue to like our country of origin, so many things link us to it. Still, we can also feel something special for Canada. [translated from French]

[Dual citizenship] is in no way an obstacle to a sentiment of belonging to Canadian society. If you transplant a tree, it will just make new roots somewhere else and keep growing, giving perhaps nicer blooms and nicer fruits. It's the same thing. [translated from French]

At heart, I will always be a citizen of Haiti even if on paper I am no longer one. By becoming a Canadian citizen I lost my rights and privileges in Haiti. But I still think that one can be a good Canadian citizen and a good Haitian citizen. [translated from French]

[Dual citizenship] is not a problem inasmuch as both citizenships are not antithetical. Take, for example, Canadian and Iranian citizenships. In that case, the social principles that inform them are different. In Iran, men dominate women, and in Canada men and women are equal. As long as the two citizenships are not opposed, there is no problem. [translated from French]

Some added that globalization contributes to the development of a multiplicity of allegiances, and there is little anybody can do about it:

Our world changes so much. Is expecting people to be attached to only one country realistic? Our vision of citizenship is a bit obsolete. To force people to become a permanent fixture in one place is to nail us down. [translated from French]

In fact, three-quarters of our respondents went as far as to say that people who hold dual citizenship should be allowed to retain certain rights in their country of origin (such as a pension, freedom of movement, the right to return to one's country of origin without a visa).[13] Many felt that dual citizenship is a form of protection should antagonistic relations between their country of origin and the host country develop. As one respondent observed:

During the war between the United States and Japan, fingers were pointed at Japanese-American citizens. They were no longer seen as American citizens. You may see yourself as a citizen, but when problems emerge, people don't let you forget your origins. That aspect must not be neglected. [translated from French]

13. On the theme of the transnational links and practices of immigrants, see Labelle and Midy (1999).

They stopped short, however, of calling for maintaining the right to vote in their country of origin, although opinions were divided on this question. Still, most of our respondents felt a strong sense of duty toward their country of origin. They mentioned their obligation to support their extended families still living in the motherland, such as support in times of natural disaster or indirect support to economic development through nongovernmental organizations.

Finally, although nearly half our respondents shared the misgivings of some state officials about Canada being used as a citizenship of convenience, they did not necessarily think that the situation warrants greater restrictions on access to Canadian citizenship.

Acquiring Canadian Citizenship

Public debates about citizenship almost always include discussions over the terms and conditions of acquiring Canadian citizenship. Currently, three years of actual presence in Canada as a permanent resident is the minimum requirement for eligibility for citizenship. In recent years, however, many have argued that this is insufficient and that the residency requirement should be lengthened. The government did not credit this argument but did make the conditions of naturalization somewhat stricter. The minister of citizenship and immigration, for example, has more discretionary powers to grant or revoke citizenship than before, and the law is more insistent now on the duties and obligations of citizens, implying that a failure to fulfill them properly may jeopardize one's citizenship status.

We asked our respondents whether restricting the acquisition of citizenship was in order at this juncture. Forty percent agreed that acquiring Canadian citizenship should be made more difficult than it is. Some argued that Canadian citizenship is too easy to obtain. If anyone and everyone were accepted, citizenship would lose its significance and symbolic value. A better knowledge of the French language, a longer period of residence, and a better selection of international immigrants were generally mentioned as the elements on which tighter controls should be exercised.

The rest of the respondents, a majority, did not believe that the abuses concerning passports and citizenship constituted sufficient reason to review the criteria for citizenship acquisition. In fact, with many respondents we sensed substantial unease over the discussions on the current reform of the Citizenship Act. One respondent commented:

> The young Asian businessmen who have been immigrating to Canada in the past two decades have kept their links abroad, and they travel frequently outside Canada. For them, territorial belonging to Canada may not be as strong. This does not mean that they do not abide by Canada's

mores and social ideals. In this sense, it is hypocritical to expect that those who aspire to be Canadian citizens develop a strong territorial belonging to Canada. They are told, in a way, that they cannot reap the fruits of globalization, while people born here are encouraged to hustle on international markets. The notion of residence is somewhat vague and unrealistic in the age of globalization. [translated from French]

For some, the attempt to reformulate the conditions for acquiring citizenship was but an unjustifiable political strategy, influenced by the Reform Party (a national, right-wing, and leading opposition party in Ottawa, now known as the Canadian Alliance), a self-protective reaction against some of the problems that immigration poses. One respondent offered:

> Any time the Reform Party makes the least bit of noise there is a public government announcement: "Okay. We are going to change the mode of citizenship!" Now all of a sudden there is talk about if you are born in this country, you cannot be a citizen if your parents are not a Canadian citizen. . . . When they do those things, the people they have in mind are visible minority groups, and those are the people the Reform Party hates.

Although the theoretical nature and contents of Canadian citizenship are perceived favorably by most, its concrete application is problematic in the eyes of some. In fact, the people to whom we talked objected to being told what kind of emotional involvement is required of them to be considered by the state as full citizens. By and large, immigrants who come to Canada are satisfied with the kind of social accommodation the state and society provide. Yet they resent their integration being premised on their according unconditional primacy to a particular vision of the country and to a particular understanding of belonging that they cannot or will not fully share. Their reluctance is not vis-à-vis Canadian citizenship as such, but rather toward the implicit expectations of the state. Their attitude toward Quebec and eventual Quebec citizenship is, as we will now see, similar.

Immigrant Perspectives on Quebec Citizenship

Dealing with the Policy Orientations of the Quebec State

As we noted in the first part of this chapter, since the early 1980s the Quebec state has worked at imparting a feeling of belonging to the Quebec culture and society to immigrants and ethnocultural minorities, to making them share in a "common public culture."

Nearly 90 percent of our respondents thought it possible in principle to build a consensus on the constitutive components of this common public culture as the state sees it (French as the common language in the public arena, democratic values, the equality of men and women, pluralism, fundamental individual rights, secularism, social solidarity, the sharing of a common heritage, and the recognition of the historic rights of the Anglophone minority and First Nations of Quebec). Yet many expressed reservations as to their application. As one person said: "This is all nice and reassuring, but it is essentially theoretical." Consensus, they often argued, is attainable, but only under certain conditions. Little emphasis should be put on the sharing of a collective heritage, for minorities cannot reasonably be expected to identify with a history in which they had little or no part. Attitudes and practices on the linguistic front must show great flexibility, and institutional arrangements must be made to accommodate cultural differences when necessary.

Despite initial optimism as to the potential for consensus, our respondents were generally more prudent about the possibility of building a common framework of civic ideals and values with the French language and the Quebec heritage as pivotal elements. To many, the emphasis on language and a so-called common heritage reflects nothing but the will of the French-speaking majority to have its culture dominate public life in Quebec. What follows are typical reactions.

> Common public culture, all you want. Maybe 60 percent of that framework is acceptable. But several elements are problematic, such as equality between men and women, a common heritage. You can teach all you like in our schools. That is not what will generate a warm sense of belonging to the people and history of Quebec. [translated from French]

> It's incredible, they are still fixated on 1760 [the year of the conquest of the French by the British]. In 1837–38 [a pivotal year in the history of Quebec: the French Canadians against the British Crown were defeated], my ancestors were not there. They were trying to come out of slavery (in Haiti). If being a Quebecer means we have to impregnate ourselves with all that history, we will never be Quebecers. Even the two founding nations [of Canada] don't even have the same view of the country's history. Canadian history is glorious for the English Canadians, and for French-speaking Quebecers, it is repressive and an obstacle to development. There is no common heritage. [translated from French]

The will to establish "French as the common language" is interpreted by some members of minorities as a desire to impose the language of the majority, as an attempt to make English disappear.

People equate [the] French language with ethnicity, and as long as people equate the French with ethnicity then you will never get anywhere. French language has to be equated with the language of our society, of a civic society. . . . It is seen as one ethnic group imposing their language on me. Who are they to force me to speak their language? Nobody can force me to do anything. I am an individual, I am free. I have choice, so there is a clash.

A majority of respondents shared, in principle at least, the government's discourse on citizenship. This was especially true of immigrants who come from French-speaking countries or who are immersed in a Francophone cultural environment. Meanwhile, for a minority of respondents, all from the Anglophone community, the new emphasis of the Quebec government on civic relations risks losing the recognition of the minorities and failing to respond to their needs, especially in a context of budgetary problems.

Clearly, the language issue and Quebec's national question were sensitive points for at least half our respondents, who felt they explained some of the tension between minorities and the French-speaking majority. As long as they remain unresolved, most believed that strong feelings of belonging to Quebec society would be hard-won. This said, we noted, as did several respondents, feelings of belonging vary significantly according to specific groups (French-speaking versus English-speaking minorities), people's mastery of French, the length of residence in Quebec, and the level of incorporation of Quebec's social and cultural parameters.

Citizenship and Political Sovereignty

If Quebec were to become independent, what kind of citizenship would be put in place? This question obviously refers to a hypothetical situation, but the answer would also give us a sense of how immigrants and minorities view Quebec's current aspirations to develop a citizenship of its own as well as an idea of the kind of society they anticipate in an independent Quebec.

In a sovereign Quebec, who will a Quebec citizen be? The views of our respondents were close to the official discourse of the current government. They seemed to espouse the civic and territorial views the government has held over the past few years: anyone who is a Canadian citizen residing on the Quebec territory at the time of independence will automatically be considered a Quebec citizen (Québec, Assemblée Nationale, 1995, 13–15). For our respondents, therefore, to be a Quebec citizen is to pay one's taxes, to vote on Quebec's laws, and to reside in the territory of Quebec. Some added the duty to take an active part in public affairs.

To pay one's taxes, and be a resident for three out of five years. That's all. [translated from French]

It's a question of territory. People who currently live here should be recognized as full-fledged citizens of the new state, regardless of their political opinion or whether or not they are "old stock" Quebecers. [translated from French]

There should be nothing more than what is presently. Quebecers are all those who live in Quebec at the time of independence. [translated from French]

"When in Rome . . ." as the old saying goes. Similarly a Quebecer should be anyone who loves Quebec and who has its betterment at heart. [translated from French]

What principles or values should form the basis of Quebec citizenship? In general, the persons interviewed imagined Quebec citizenship as a close copy of Canadian citizenship adapted to Quebec. They invoked already existing principles: a democratic Quebec, in which the Quebec Charter of Human Rights protects freedoms, prohibits discrimination, and fosters openness to pluralism. As one respondent insisted: "A sovereign Quebec should continue to abide by the same fundamental principles. The only things that should change are [things] of an administrative nature" [translated from French].

Some hoped that Quebec would review the Canadian Constitutions of 1867 or 1982. They proposed the recognition of three "founding peoples" (Francophones, Anglophones, and natives) ("Quebec should do all the things that Canada did not do"); a republican form of government ("holding on to this Queen thing, that is a very ethnic thing"); the secularization of institutions; the official recognition of the legitimacy of having more than one allegiance; a more concrete application of openness to difference; and the possibility of re-thinking heritage by taking into account the diversity that makes up the Québécois people. Others insisted on specific values, such as social democracy and social justice.

I sincerely hope that it will be a democratic society, fair and equitable, which will protect the weakest and most vulnerable among us, a partici-patory society, somewhat decentralized, where citizens can be party to the decision-making process. [translated from French]

Nearly half the respondents proposed modifications to the conditions of ac-quisition of Quebec citizenship in the event of sovereignty. The major proposal concerned the French language. In a sovereign Quebec, the knowledge of French should be an essential condition in the acquisition of citizenship. This was mentioned as often by people from the Anglophone community as it was by those from the Francophone community.

The other proposed modifications suggested stricter conditions for the acquisition of Quebec citizenship, such as lengthening the residency requirement to five years, more selective immigration, cracking down on abuses of the health care system by immigrants. One respondent went so far as to suggest refusing access to those who hold fundamentalist religious views or who would be considered unwilling to subscribe to Quebec's basic sociocultural values. Finally, a few respondents hoped that one would be offered a choice between Quebec and Canadian citizenships or be allowed to hold two or three nationalities. This was invoked mostly in reaction to the possible loss of Canadian citizenship in the context of a sovereign Quebec.

In a way, we were surprised to see how willingly our respondents entertained the hypothetical idea of a sovereign Quebec. By and large, when faced with the possibility of Quebec citizenship, their attitude was the same as it was for Canadian citizenship. It was not the constitutive principles or the nature of citizenship that were a problem for them. Rather it was that the state was seen as engineering and imposing a particular vision, one that entails expectations of sociopolitical attitudes and behaviors at odds with their understanding of the society in which they have chosen to live.

Concluding Remarks

State discourses on citizenship have occupied a significant place in the Canadian public debates of the past decade. Our main goal in this chapter has been to take stock of the reaction of immigrants and ethnocultural minorities who live in Quebec to these discourses. Our interviews with people directly targeted by the state show that there exists a gap between how the state envisions immigrant integration—particularly when it comes to unreservedly endorsing Canada's (or Quebec's) core values—and the terms by which immigrants and members of ethnocultural minorities understand their incorporation into Canadian and Quebec society. Although nothing in their responses points to fundamental or irreconcilable differences, it is clear that immigrants and members of ethnocultural minorities are not always prepared to abide blindly by state injunctions on issues of belonging and the sociopolitical ideals that the state holds dear. By and large, our interviewees want nothing more than to feel that they are an integral part of Canadian and/or Quebec society, but on terms that they would contribute to develop, not according to preestablished state notions of citizenship.

We have concentrated on mapping the shape and extent of the discursive divide between immigrants and the state in Canada and Quebec. Explaining the reasons for this divide would require a fuller account than what space allows. We can, however, offer broad outlines of the factors that seem to contribute most to the perplexity and reservations often expressed by our respondents.

State Categorization of Race and Ethnicity

It bears repeating that the institutionalization of essentialist categories to identify members of immigrant groups and ethnocultural minorities often seems to mitigate any enthusiasm they might have for Canadian (or Quebec) citizenship. The Canadian government's notion of "visible minorities" and Quebec's "cultural communities" may have bureaucratic and statistical usefulness. They may even seem unavoidable in any politics of resistance against racism and discrimination. The fact is, they are not neutral, innocent notions. First, they create the illusory impression that minority groups are homogeneous. They essentialize and even lock in their status and identity in the social imagination (Kobayashi, 1993). More significant, however, it creates a boundary between "old stock" Canadians and "ethnics." In this and other fieldwork, a large proportion of the people interviewed objected to the use of ethnoracial terms to identify them. They note its exclusionary effect and insist that it produces an ideology of difference. When do we become Canadian? they would ask. When do we cease to be mere immigrants? To what extent will this state categorization affect the identity and social mobility of new generations born in Canada? Such questions express a genuine concern as immigrants and ethnocultural minorities seem faced with unabashed, though sometimes symbolic, marginalization and perpetual *immigrisation* (Martiniello, 1993). As a result, within certain groups the emergence of a considerably adversarial attitude toward a sentiment of belonging to Canada or Quebec is inevitable.

Economic Exclusion, Racial Discrimination, and the Underrepresentation of Racialized Minorities in the Public Sphere

Actual discrimination, economic exclusion, and poor public representation deter racialized minorities from accepting state discourse. The present study and our previous fieldwork makes clear to us that the major obstacle to the development of a citizenship that conforms to the ideals of the Canadian or Quebec state—that is, a citizenship that implies a feeling of belonging to the nation—is predominantly a result of the differential modes of incorporation (segmented assimilation) and systematic discrimination, of which many Canadians belonging to racialized groups in particular are victims.

As we saw, many respondents stressed that racialized minorities are second-class citizens in Canadian and Quebec society. Others did not want to be so categorical in their responses, but they nevertheless recognized that the racialized minorities often face serious situations of socioeconomic and symbolic exclusion. The feeling of marginalization was therefore strongly shared by many in our sample, even if the assessments as to the intensity of the problem varied.

Unemployment among racialized minorities is the highest. In Quebec, while they represent 6 percent of the Quebec population and 12 percent of the Montreal area population (1996 census), the unemployment rate of racialized minorities reaches 22 percent. In contrast, the unemployment rate of the immigrant population is about 16 percent, and the rate of the population as a whole is 11 percent. Racialized minorities also experience poverty on a larger scale since their personal income is 15 percent lower than that of the average Canadian's income. In spite of affirmative action programs and a commitment to increase the recruitment of racialized minorities in public services, goals have not been met. The proportion of minorities in the Quebec public civil service hovers between 2 and 4 percent; it is at 3 percent in federal institutions. Symbolic racism comes also from European minorities versus racialized minorities. In our interviews, for example, comments on devalued citizenship and abuses generally came from citizens of European background against blacks, Arabs, and so on.

Resistance to Traditional Ideas of Citizenship and Transnational Orientations

The idea of a distinct identity, rights, and duties that are exclusively attached to Canadian citizenship does not take into account the transnational aspects linked to citizenship in everyday life. In several cases, the new belonging, the new identity, and the new allegiance demanded of them could not replace their initial identity and the belonging and allegiance they still felt toward their country of origin. This is especially true in the emerging circumstances prompted by the imperatives of international market exchanges as immigrants appear more as useful partners in the international capacity of the host country than they do as eventual compatriots.

The variability of transnational practices and identities may come from the economic and political situation in the country of origin. They may also come from immigration and integration policies of the host country, the extent of openness of civil society, the job market structure, and the community structure. Indeed, the transnational practices and identities of immigrants and their descendants might be expressions of defensive positions against a subordinate status in the host society and a form of defiance against the normative integration ideologies of the host society. At the same time, these practices are aimed at supporting the material reconstruction (and democratization) of the country of origin, and at encouraging the return to the "homeland." They are fueled by the insecurity and dequalifying of professionals, cadres, and university graduates whenever social mobility is no longer assured.

Last, among the factors accounting for the transnational practices of migrants is the self-directed work by intellectuals of immigrant origin, which fuels expression in the defense and promotion of a migrant identity, the critical reconsideration of racial categories, demands on behalf of and participation in the invention of a culture in flux, the redefinition and resymbolization of political belonging and citizenship, and mobilization toward the democratization of the country of origin (Labelle and Midy, 1999). Other factors that explain the apparent distance of immigrants from current state models of citizenship involve the social and political particularities of the Quebec context.

The Hegemonic Influence of the Federal Policy of Multiculturalism

Quebec policies on the integration of immigrants and members of ethnocultural communities are suspect in many quarters and are ignored and even rejected. For some leaders in those communities, integration to a common public culture was and is still interpreted as a phase of a disguised assimilationist policy. The first phase was the 1977 Language Act, which made French the official language of Quebec, and the next phase is under way as the latest government orientations insist on developing a full-fledged Quebec citizenship. The latter is often perceived as an attempt to downplay Quebec's cultural diversity and defuse aspirations of Canadian national unity.

Detractors of the Quebec policy of immigrant and minority integration contrast it with the federal government policy of multiculturalism, which is readily associated, at least at the official level, with tolerance, bilingualism, pluralism, and a respect for human rights. On this front, then, the federal government is in a favorable position to exercise real power and influence. It has the capacity to grant financial aid to ethnic organizations and institutions; it has political alliances with ethnic lobbies that support federalism; and it can conduct bilingual publicity campaigns on national unity. In fact, the federal government has sole responsibility for services relating to citizenship. There is no restriction on its actions toward the promotion of multiculturalism. Therefore, the federal government's view of citizenship is more likely to gain credence. In contrast, while the federal policy of multiculturalism contributes to the ethnicization of French-speaking Quebecers,[14] the legitimacy of their claim for a distinct but universal and inclusive Quebec citizenship is not strong among immigrants and members of ethnocultural minorities. The Quebec state seems to stand out as the state of a Francophone majority, and French-speaking Quebecers as one ethnocultural group among others, a status that in the mind of immigrants and members of ethnocultural minorities is far from sufficient to impose a Quebec-based citizenship.

The Status of French as the Common Public Language of Quebec

The federal policy of multiculturalism has a corollary: a policy of bilingualism in federal institutions. Canada's bilingual status is often seen as a great gesture of social accommodation. Thus, in the minds of many, there should be no reason for Quebec to "impose" French as the official language when they live in a supposedly bilingual country. The fact is, the attraction of French among certain immigrants and members of ethnocultural minorities remains minimal. It was believed a decade or so ago that making French the main and official language for public transactions in Quebec was a compromise that would ensure linguistic peace and create new relations of power. In reality, immigrants and members of ethnocultural minorities are divided in their allegiance to French or English. Although French has made considerable progress among immigrants, English continues to be a pivotal language in public and private communication in Quebec, and a powerful instrument of socialization for immigrants, even for those of French-speaking origin. The linguistic split within the various communities of immigrants in Quebec influences their position relative to the political status of Quebec and, by extension, to any claim to independent citizenship Quebec may make.

Attitudes toward Quebec Nationalism and Sovereignty

Historically, the resistance of the immigrant, ethnic, and racialized population to the idea of a sovereign Quebec has been significant. There are, however, active sovereignist segments in immigrant communities. Immigrants who endorsed the sovereignist project invoke various reasons for doing so: solidarity

14. Typical of this is the recent proposition by Sheila Copps, Minister of Canadian Heritage, that June 24 be recognized as the day of all French Canadians throughout Canada. June 24 has been celebrated in Quebec for many years now as a national holiday for all who live in Quebec, regardless of ethnic origin.

with the majority of Quebecers of French-Canadian background; recognition of the national character of Quebec; the economic or political rationality of the project; a need for structural changes; and an analogy with struggles for national or anti-imperialist liberation in their countries of origin.

Rejection of Quebec sovereignty is connected to other factors, such as a concern for the economic consequences of sovereignty; an attachment to Canada (which is seen as the true host society); worries that social upheaval will follow; a distrust of the Quebec state, seen as tentacular and intrusive; and the low esteem in which nationalistic movements are held. Many also argue that sovereignist claims are unfounded, given the mildness of national oppression compared with that of the countries of origin of some immigrants; or that nationalism is obsolete and transnational ties and identities are more important. A fairly successful anti-Quebec campaign in the national, local, and ethnic media at the time of the 1995 referendum—accusations of racism and ethnic cleansing by the Quebec government and sovereignists—combined with a vocal partitionist movement have also contributed to the distancing of immigrants and members of ethnocultural minorities from the Quebec state and its project of a distinct Quebec citizenship. Finally, Jacques Parizeau, the premier and leader of the sovereignist forces at the time of the 1995 referendum, on learning that he had been defeated, blamed money and some ethnic votes. His unfortunate words left a scar that many feel has not yet healed. Though denounced later by other sovereignist leaders, Parizeau fueled resentment and in many ways aggravated antisovereignist sentiments among immigrant and ethnocultural minorities, who feel excluded from the sovereignist project and, by extension, from Quebec society.

The cultural and national diversity that today characterizes Canada and Quebec raises complex and difficult challenges. Caught between a desire not to alienate the immigrant segment of the population and the will not to dilute their socio-institutional heritage, which predates recent immigration and gives society its current outlook, the Canadian and Quebec governments have turned to strategies that sometimes border on social engineering. Using a discourse that appears to be motivated by openness, tolerance, and generosity, the hope is to convince immigrants and ethnic minorities to adhere unequivocally to the parameters that currently define Canadian (or Quebec) society and institutions. This approach is dubious, irritates many of the groups and individuals it addresses, and provokes ill will among them. It is as though the state were trying too hard, leaving people with the impression that, in the end, it offers nothing more than a discourse unsupported by concrete action.

Appendix: Research Methodology

We gathered data during fieldwork in 1996 and 1997. We conducted forty interviews with community activists who are from diverse ethnic or racialized minorities in the region of Montreal. These respondents were chosen based on their involvement in diverse community organizations, public institutions, or political parties.

Our study was conducted in two distinct urban Montreal districts: the Francophone-dominated neighborhoods of Rivière-des-Prairies and Montréal-Nord in northeast Montreal and the predominantly Anglophone neighborhoods of Notre-Dame-de-Grâce and Côte-des-Neiges, in west Montreal. These neighborhoods are veritable social microcosms with important challenges with regard to the management of diversity.

The important criteria of these environments were the populations associated with minority groups, cultural heterogeneity, and their relative linguistic polarization. In 1991, 75 percent of the population of Rivière-des-Prairies, for example, declared itself to be mother-tongue French; 4.79 percent were mother-tongue English; and 20.4 percent spoke nonofficial languages. In the case of Notre-Dame-de-Grâce, 31.6 percent declared themselves to be mother-tongue French; 37.4 percent were mother-tongue English; and 30.8 percent spoke nonofficial languages. In both areas, the diversity of the minority groups is still considerable. Côte-des-Neiges in particular is considered the most multiethnic neighborhood in Canada. Finally, its associations with ethnic or racial identities are numerous.

Our respondents were selected from three sectors of community activities in Montreal: the health and social services network in the neighborhoods (the *Centres locaux de services communautaires,* where studies showed a strong presence of ethnic minorities, from clients to administrative council members); multisectoral groupings, such as the *Tables de concertation de quartier* (neighborhood planning boards) and the *Conseils communautaires* (community councils), where the representatives of community groups and public institutions (the *Ministère des Relations avec les citoyens et de l'Immigration,* school boards, police services, municipalities, etc.), meet on community issues; and respondents active in politics at the municipal and provincial levels. All were active citizens and members of their communities.

Our sample comprised an equal number of men and women, and the average age was forty. Twenty-four people had university degrees; 5 respondents were born in Canada, from Haitian, Barbadian, Honduran, Italian, and French origins; 10 from North Africa and the Middle East (Egypt, Morocco, Algeria, and Lebanon); 7 from the Caribbean (Dominican Republic, Haiti, St. Vincent, and Guyana), 6 from Latin America (Argentina, Chile, Colombia, Mexico, and Peru); 4 from Asia (Hong Kong, Indonesia, Laos, and Vietnam); 4 from Africa (Cameroon, Ethiopia, Ghana, and Rwanda); and 4 from Europe (Britain, Belgium, Italy, and the former USSR).

Five important religious groups were represented: Buddhists, Catholics, Christians, Jews, and Muslims. Some respondents claimed not to practice any religion. The vast majority of respondents—thirty-six of forty—were Canadian citizens, and a third of the respondents had two or three citizenships.

Works Cited and Bibliography

Abu-Laban. 1998. "Welcome/Stay Out: The Contradiction of Canadian Integration and Immigration Policies at the Millennium." *Canadian Ethnic Studies* 30(3): 190–211.

Alba, R. 1990. *Ethnic Identity: The Transformation of White America.* New Haven, Conn.: Yale University Press.

Bigot, Didier. 1998. "Sécurité et immigration: Vers une gouvernementalité par l'inquiétude?" *Cultures et Conflits* 31–32:13–38.

Brochmann, Grete. 1998. "Controlling Immigration in Europe: Nation-State Dilemmas in an International Context." In Hans Van Amersfoot and Jeroen Doomernik (eds.), *International Migration: Processes and Interventions,* pp. 22–41. Amsterdam: Institute for Migration and Ethnic Studies.

Canada. Canadian Heritage. 1996. *Strategic Evaluation of the Multiculturalism Programs.* Ottawa.

———. 1997. *Multiculturalism Program: The Context for Renewal.* Ottawa: Canadian Heritage.

Canada. Citizenship and Immigration Canada. 1994a. *Into the Twenty-First Century: A Strategy for Immigration and Citizenship.* Ottawa: Minister of Supplies and Services Canada.

———. 1994b. *A Broader Vision: Immigration and Citizenship Plan, 1995–2000. Annual Report to Parliament.* Ottawa: Minister of Supplies and Services Canada.

———. 1995. *Growing Together: A Backgrounder on Immigration and Citizenship.* Ottawa: Minister of Supplies and Services Canada.

———. 1998a. *News Release 98-59.* Ottawa: Citizenship and Immigration Canada.

———. 1998b. *News Release 98-64.* Ottawa: Citizenship and Immigration Canada.

———. 1998c. *Building on a Strong Foundation for the Twenty-First Century: New Directions for Immigration and Refugee Policy and Legislation.* Ottawa: Minister of Public Works and Government Services Canada.

———. 1999. *Citizenship of Canada Act: Clause by Clause Analysis.* Ottawa: Minister of Public Works and Government Services Canada.

Canada. Employment and Immigration Canada. 1990. *Annual Report to Parliament: Immigration Plan for 1991–1995.* Ottawa: Minister of Supplies and Services Canada.

Canada. House of Commons. Standing Committee on Citizenship and Immigration. 1994. *Canadian Citizenship: A Sense of Belonging.* Report. Ottawa: Queen's Printer.

Canada. Privy Council Office. 1991. *Shaping Canada's Future Together: Proposals.* Ottawa: Minister of Supplies and Services Canada.

Canada. Senate. Standing Senate Committee on Social Affairs, Science, and Technology. 1993. *Canadian Citizenship: Sharing the Responsibility.* Ottawa: Senate of Canada, Standing Senate Committee on Social Affairs, Science, and Technology.

Carnegie Endowment for International Peace. 1998. *Conference on Comparative Citizenship. Report.* June 4–7, Airlie Center, Warrenton, Va.

Hollifield, James. 1997. *L'immigration et l'état-nation à la recherche d'un modèle national.* Paris: Presses universitaires de France.

Hreblay, Vendelin. 1994. *La libre circulation des personnes: Les Accords de Schengen.* Paris: Presses universitaires de France.

Kalin, Rudolf. 1995. "Ethnic and Citizenship Attitudes in Canada: Analyses of a 1991 National Survey." *Nationalism and Ethnic Politics* 1(3): 26–44.

Kalin, Rudolf, and J. W. Berry. 1995. "Ethnic and Civic Self-identity in Canada: Analyses of 1974 and 1991 National Surveys." *Canadian Ethnic Studies* 27(2): 1–15.

Kobayashi, Audrey. 1993. "Représentation de l'ethnicité: Statistextes politiques." In *Les défis que pose la mesure de l'origine ethnique: science, politique et réalité.* Ottawa and Washington: Statistics Canada and the U.S. Bureau of the Census.

Kymlicka, Will. 1998. *Finding Our Way.* Toronto: Oxford University Press.

Labelle, Micheline, and Joseph J. Lévy. 1995. *Ethnicité et enjeux sociaux: Le Québec vu par les leaders de groupes ethnoculturels.* Montreal: Liber.

Labelle, Micheline, and Daniel Salée. 1999. "La citoyenneté en question: L'État canadien face à l'immigration et à la pluriethnicité." *Sociologie et société* 31(2) (fall): 125–44.

Labelle, Micheline, and Franklin Midy. 1999. "Re-reading Citizenship and the Transnational Practices of Immigrants." *Journal of Ethnic and Migration Studies* 25(2): 213–32.

Martiniello, Marco. 1993. *Leadership et pouvoir dans les communautés d'origine immigrée.* Paris: CIEMI/L'Harmattan.

Martiniello, Marco, and Andrea Rea. 1997. "Construction européenne et politique d'immigration." In Marie-Thérèse Coenen and Rosine Lewin (eds.), *La Belgique et ses immigrés. Les politiques manquées,* pp. 121–43. Brussels: De Boeck Université.

Omi, Michael, and Howard Winant. 1986. *Racial Formation in the United States.* New York: Routledge and Kegan Paul.

Papademetriou, Demetrios G., and Kimberly A. Hamilton. 1995. *Managing Uncertainty: Regulating Immigration Flows in Advanced Industrial Countries.* Washington, D.C.: Carnegie Endowment for International Peace, International Migration Policy Program.

Pickus, Noah M. J. 1997. *Becoming American/America Becoming.* Final Report. Duke University Workshop on Immigration and Citizenship.

Québec. Conseil des Relations interculturelles. 1997a. *Un Québec pour tous ses citoyens: Les défis actuels d'une démocratie pluraliste: Avis présenté au ministre des relations avec les citoyens et de l'Immigration.* Montreal.

———. Québec. 1997b. *A Québec for All Its Citizens: The Current Challenges of a Pluralist Democracy.* Montreal. Abridged.

Québec. Ministère des Communautés culturelles et de l'Immigration du Québec. 1990. *Let's Build Québec Together: A Policy Statement on Immigration and Integration.* Quebec: Direction générale des politiques et programmes, Direction des communications.

————. 1993. "Déclaration ministérielle sur la culture publique commune." *Culture publique commune et accommodement raisonnable: Documents de référence.* Montreal: Direction des politiques et programmes de relations interculturelles.

Québec. Ministère des Relations avec les citoyens et de l'Immigration. 1996. *Le contrat moral. Québec: Ministère des Relations avec les citoyens et de l'Immigration.*

Québec. National Assembly. 1995. *Bill 1: An Act respecting the Future of Québec, including the Declaration of Sovereignty.* Québec: Éditeur officiel.

Rocher, François, and Daniel Salée. 1993. "Démocratie et réforme constitutionnelle: Discours et pratique." *International Journal of Canadian Studies* 7:167–87.

Rumbault, R. G. 1997. "Paradoxes and Orthodoxies of Assimilation." *Sociological Perspectives* 40(3): 483–511.

Salée, Daniel. 1995. "Espace public, identité et nation au Québec: Mythes et méprises du discours souverainiste." *Cahiers de recherche sociologique* 25:125–53.

Schuck, Peter. 1996. *The Re-evaluation of American Citizenship.* Badia Fiesolana: European University Institute. EUI Working Paper of the Robert Schumann Centre, no. 96-26.

SOPEMI. 1995. *Tendances des migrations internationales: Rapport annuel 1995.* Paris: OCDE, Système d'observation permanente des migrations.

Statistics Canada. 1997. "Recensement 1996: Immigration et citoyenneté." *Le Quotidien,* 4 Nov.

Waters, Mary. 1990. *Ethnic Options: Choosing Identities in America.* Berkeley: University of California Press.

Weil, Patrick. 1997. *Mission d'études des législations de la nationalité et de l'immigration: Des conditions d'application du principe du droit du sol pour l'attribution de la nationalité française. Pour une politique de l'immigration juste et efficace. Rapport au Premier ministre.* Paris: La Documentation française.

————. 1998. *The Transformation of Immigration Policies: Immigration Control and Nationality Laws in Europe: A Comparative Approach.* Badia Fiesolana: European University Institute. EUI Working Paper of the European Forum, no. 98-5.

PART FOUR

Concluding Reflections

Cultural Citizenship, Minority Rights, and Self-Government

RAINER BAUBÖCK

WHEN MARSHALL (1965) analyzed the evolution of citizenship in England, he identified three components that he called civil, political, and social citizenship and that were associated with the institutions of the judicial system, parliamentary democracy, and the welfare state. Had he forgotten about cultural citizenship? Is there a need for supplementing the traditional conception of liberal citizenship with cultural minority rights? A growing number of liberal intellectuals seem to say no. After two decades when multiculturalism was very much the zeitgeist, a certain fatigue and impatience have set in. In the United States, affirmative action and bilingual education programs have been rolled back in the voting booths and in the courts. Prominent intellectuals have accused multiculturalism of "disuniting America" (Schlesinger, 1992) and of fostering a "culture of complaint" (Hughes, 1993) and "culture wars," which have wracked American society and have distracted the liberal Left from its egalitarian goals (Gitlin, 1995). Some rehabilitate the melting pot for a "next American nation" (Lind, 1995), while others advocate a "postethnic America" in which cultural affiliations are no longer based on descent but on revocable consent (Hollinger,

A version of this chapter was presented at the Internationale Vereinigung für Rechts und Sozialphilosophie World Congress, "Philosophy of Law and Social Philosophy," Pace University, New York City, June 24–30, 1999. I extend special thanks to Joseph Carens for his extensive and helpful comments on the first draft. For the section "Linguistic Diversity and Unequal Recognition," I have borrowed extensively from a forthcoming article on religious and linguistic education for immigrant minorities (Bauböck, n.d.).

1995). We find similar critiques of multiculturalism in Canada, where the concept was first introduced as public policy in 1971 (Bissoondath, 1994; Gwyn, 1995), and in Australia and western Europe.

These critiques illustrate a shift from the liberal discourse of rights toward a new emphasis on integration. Yet this juxtaposition of rights and integration is misleading. The language of rights, and even of conflicts about rights, is part of what integrates liberal democracies. It is both morally wrong and politically naïve to think that appealing to a shared civic identity is sufficient to integrate marginalized groups whose grievances have been brushed aside. Iris Young's (1990) proposition that citizenship has to be group-differentiated in response to discrimination and oppression is still convincing in this regard. What critics fear is that cultural minority rights will instrumentalize public policies for maintaining contested cultural traditions and practices while immunizing internally oppressive communities from interference. It is not at all difficult to gather anecdotal evidence that lends credence to these accusations. But the case against multiculturalism rests upon a whole series of gross generalizations that are facilitated by the ambiguities of the concept itself.

There is an underlying theme that justifies retaining the concept. Paraphrasing John Rawls, I identify this theme as a fact of cultural pluralism,[1] namely, the persistence and salience of internal cultural distinctions in contemporary societies that are marked by religion, language, ethnic origin, racial category, or different ways of life. Accepting this fact is an important starting point for normative analysis. It excludes approaches that hold that these differences can eventually be overcome by assimilation or can be neutralized by separating groups. This starting point, however, is merely the acknowledgment of a problem and does not necessarily indicate how to resolve it. Recognizing it as a problem is necessary to get beyond the naïveté of celebratory multiculturalism, which dominated much of the early manifestations before the 1990s and rested on the belief that affirming the value of diversity is already a solution to identity conflicts. Once we shed that idea, there is no single normative principle of multiculturalism that can tell us how to respond to demands for cultural rights. What we have to do to make sense of these claims is to disaggregate them and then consider how established principles of liberal democracy and equal citizenship might apply to them or be amended.

---

1. Rawls's "fact of pluralism" (1993) refers to the diversity of comprehensive worldviews and moral and religious doctrines. Some of the most intractable conflicts in contemporary societies, however, emerge between groups that endorse rather similar "conceptions of the good" (Rawls) but distinguish themselves with cultural markers of identity. Of these conflicts, national ones over claims to self-government tend to be the most violent.

I propose to disaggregate along three axes: first, by distinguishing various cultural practices and the claims they foster; second, by looking at categories of minorities that are differently positioned in their relation to the political community; and, third, by considering how general principles may have to be modified according to the context in which they are applied. The cultural practices that I discuss are those associated with religion and language. I argue that liberal principles of religious toleration or neutrality are not sufficient to respond to the demands of linguistic minorities. Liberal states cannot avoid establishing one or a few languages and they have a duty to provide a shared public culture. Whether we regard linguistic minorities as disadvantaged and entitled to compensatory recognition depends on our concept of the social functions of language. Language is more than a means of communication. Every language carries a specific identity value and marks political boundaries. The latter of these three functions distinguishes between the claims of immigrant and national minorities. In section three, I consider whether making this distinction is morally and politically justified. My conclusion is that the right to establish a language of public life derives from claims to territorial self-government. This fact explains the need for a third disaggregation of cultural rights by examining the contexts of particular projects or historical traditions of nation building. I point to the need for normative theories of legitimate and illegitimate ways of nation building. There are, of course, many more relevant practices, categories, and contexts to be considered, but the picture that emerges from a few is sufficiently complex to destroy any idea of multiculturalism as a single phenomenon or principle that is either to be endorsed or rejected.

Cultural Citizenship

A Marshallian Approach

How should we then answer the initial question? Is there a cultural component of citizenship? Two contrasting responses will not do: a first one asserts that there is no need to go beyond the Marshallian framework, because all reasonable cultural claims can be satisfied within it; a second one adds a distinct national-cultural dimension to democratic citizenship. The Marshallian approach is blind to the cultural nonneutrality of liberal states; the liberal nationalist approach acknowledges and justifies it but fails to grasp fully its implications for minority citizenship.

I first consider the proposition that one can exhaustively classify all cultural rights as civil, political, or social and that whatever normative principles apply to the distribution of these rights should also settle all cultural claims. If this were the case, there would be no need to add a separate cultural dimension to Marshall's rights-based conception of citizenship. Let me sketch an attractive argument along these lines before exposing its deficiencies. In this view, the rights of cultural minorities are primarily covered by the civil element of citizenship. The free exercise of religion or the free use of a minority language in private communication is guaranteed through the liberties of free speech, association, and assembly. These rights, however, are strictly culture-blind. In liberal democracies they are regarded as universal human rights that do not depend on any particular classification of the beneficiaries as members of a cultural community or even as nationals of a state.[2] The political element of citizenship circumscribes the cultural privileges of national majorities. It applies to legislative decisions that give official status to a certain language, that subsidize theaters and museums through tax money, and that celebrate historical and religious events by making them public holidays. These decisions are collective ones: every citizen has an equal right to participate or to be represented in them, but they bind also those who oppose them. In a liberal democracy, however, the scope of legitimate majority rule is constrained by constitutional safeguards for individual liberties. Finally, the social rights of citizenship specify the fundamental duty of the state in regard to culture. All children have the right to a public education taught in a common national language. Primary socialization in the family reproduces cultural differences attached to class, gender, region, or ethnic identity, but secondary socialization in school creates equal opportunities by providing all children with a shared cultural knowledge.

Such a Marshallian framework for cultural rights does not merely identify basic liberties and entitlements. It also reflects the differentiation of categories of beneficiaries in contemporary democracies. Negative cultural liberties are strictly universal; public education is an entitlement for all residents and their children, but political participation rights are a privilege of citizenship and generate legitimate benefits for majorities. Legal provisions for cultural minorities that transcend this framework may then be regarded as a result of pragmatic accommodation rather than as being grounded in moral rights. Yet this does not capture at all the nature of minority demands, which use the language of civil, political, and social citizenship to challenge the initial distribution of rights and benefits as unfair and press for special exemptions, symbolic recognition, and material support. The charge that modern nation-states are not culturally neutral but tend to privilege dominant majorities cannot be easily dismissed by a normative theory of citizenship. Moreover, Marshall's vision of "function-

---

2. Western democracies that still restrict such liberties for foreign residents are in this respect illiberal.

ally differentiated" citizenship presupposes a unitary democracy. It cannot account for the territorial differentiation of citizenship in federal states that are composite polities combining self-rule with shared rule (Elazar, 1987). In some federations, constituent units have a strong national identity of their own and use their rights of self-government to promote their own languages and cultural traditions. Parity of reasoning suggests again that it is difficult to deny the legitimacy of such claims, which simply mirror the cultural prerogatives enjoyed by majorities in unitary nation-states.

A Liberal Nationalist Approach

The liberal-nationalist approach wants to make an explicit element of citizenship what Marshall tacitly assumed: that integrating a class-ridden society through equal citizenship presupposes a prior sense of national community with specific cultural attributes. In this perspective, the willingness to share the burdens and benefits of political cooperation results from a prior national identity that makes citizens see themselves as part of a transgenerational community. In contrast with earlier ethnoracial views of the origins of nations, contemporary liberal nationalists acknowledge the insights of "constructivist" accounts of nationhood.[3] These emphasize the role of the modern state and economy in bringing about the common culture, which is then retrospectively associated with the historic origins of the nation. The evolution of citizenship is thus closely connected to the promotion of national public cultures and identities. From this perspective it makes sense to add to Marshall's triad a distinctive fourth component that consists of the collective identity and rights—but also, the obligations and daily practices—that tie individuals to particular national communities.

The history of national conflicts has also shaped the internal structure of contemporary polities. Nearly all nation-states have their own ethnic or indigenous minorities that have never been fully incorporated into a mainstream national identity. As I have already pointed out, a small number of contemporary states are multinational federations, which formally break down their citizenship into constituent national components. In some cases their national identity links minorities to a foreign state which they regard as their national homeland and to which they turn as an external protector of their rights. Illib-

3. Contemporary liberal nationalists include, among others: Raz and Margalit (1990), Tamir (1993), Miller (1995), Philpott (1995), MacCormick (1996), and Moore (1997). Among the most influential constructivist or modernist theories of nationalism are those of Gellner (1983), Anderson (1983), Hobsbawm (1990), and Smith (1987).

eral nationalist ideologies make internal and external citizenship rights a prerogative of members of the dominant national community and demand that
minorities either assimilate or be excluded. In contrast, liberal nationalist approaches defend universal, inclusive, and pluralistic conceptions of citizenship.
They affirm everyone's right to a national identity and allow for a differentiation of citizenship along those lines.

The problem with many of these theories is that they associate cultural identities too closely with national ones. National communities share the achieved
status of, or the aspiration for, self-government. To be, or to become, self-
governing, a community must be organized territorially and must develop a
standardized cultural repertoire.[4] Internally, this repertoire consists of symbols
for a common origin and destiny and of a written language that serves as a
general medium of communication; externally it provides markers of the boundaries that identify the group vis-à-vis others. These two features of territoriality
and cultural standardization make national-cultural identities building blocks
for constructing the basic units of political community.

National identities are embedded in a public culture shared throughout a
political community. Other cultural identities are more like dividing lines within
civil society. They undermine the very image of a homogeneous political community that is supported by national-cultural identities. Culture in this broader
sense encompasses all the various practices and symbols through which people
collectively organize their lives and try to make sense of the world (Geertz,
1973). Communal identities built around shared practices and beliefs subdi-
vide national communities and cut across them in many different ways. It is
therefore misleading to think of national cultures as "societal" (Kymlicka, 1995,
76) or "encompassing" (Margalit and Raz, 1994) in the sense that they contain
all these other practices and beliefs as internal components or options.[5] Liberal
nationalists generally understand the encompassing quality of a national culture as that of a thin roof that leaves a lot of space for cultural diversity under-
neath in civil society.

This division of spheres, however, still ignores the fact that for some deeply
held beliefs and cherished practices a dominant national culture, a free market
economy, and a liberal democracy are hostile environments. Religious identities are often more encompassing than national ones are in that they stretch

4. National communities in exile or diaspora still define themselves territorially by referring
to a historical homeland, where they want to become self-governing.

5. Waldron (1992, 1996), Buchanan (1998), Carens (2000, chap. 3). In times of crisis and
mobilization, a national culture may crowd out or invade other cultural practices and acquire a
simultaneously political, religious, and racial character. Such a truly encompassing national identity
undermines liberal citizenship and is of course not what liberal nationalists have in mind.

over many countries and linguistic identities and frequently cut across national borders to link a group to an external homeland. National identities are therefore not generally superordinate, either in terms of range or in terms of importance. Religious, linguistic, and ethnic identities are *constrained* by national identities rather than *contained* in them. These constraints are sources of serious political and legal conflicts. Postulating a shared national identity as a precondition of a liberal concept of citizenship is not helpful for understanding such claims and will further downgrade them.

Cultural citizenship is indeed a missing element in Marshall's account and more generally in liberal political theory. A political theory of multiculturalism should not be construed as being apart from or opposed to liberal democratic citizenship, but ought to be grounded in the same considerations about the kind of rights and institutional arrangements that are necessary to make individuals full and equal members of a well-integrated political community. But taking culture into account is not an easy task. The specific disadvantages that make some culturally defined minorities unequal citizens are not covered in Marshall's class-based account of citizenship. Nor is it sufficient to add a national dimension to the three dimensions he identified.

Linguistic Diversity and Unequal Recognition

As John Rawls has emphasized, the historical origin of political liberalism is the Reformation and its aftermath (Rawls, 1993, p. xxiv). It has eventually led to a new form of religious toleration grounded in the separation of church and state and the freedom of individual conscience and collective religious practice. Can we model the rights of linguistic minorities on the principles of religious toleration and neutrality? The analogy certainly supports a right to use a minority language, not merely in domestic, but also in public contexts. Members of a linguistic minority must be free to associate and promote their language, for example, by establishing their own press and audiovisual media or by conducting their business in their own language. If religious toleration implies a right to private religious schools, the same must be true for linguistic groups. It is still slightly inappropriate to call this a principle of linguistic toleration. Cultural nationalists who value linguistic homogeneity may grudgingly tolerate a minority language, but from a liberal perspective there is no conflict of values. There are illiberal religious practices and beliefs that may have to be tolerated in a liberal society, but there are no illiberal languages. A liberal state should thus be neutral rather than tolerant toward the diversity of languages spoken by its citizens in their daily lives. Freedom of speech not only protects the content of speech, but also the choice of language.

Article 27 of the 1966 International Covenant on Civil and Political Rights covers these liberties for both religious and linguistic minorities: "In those States in which ethnic, religious or linguistic minorities exist, persons belonging to such minorities shall not be denied the right, in community with the other members of their group, to enjoy their own culture, to profess and practice their own religion, or to use their own language." One difficulty with this is, of course, to determine which groups qualify as minorities. Some states have simply denied, against all evidence, the existence of native linguistic minorities in their territories, and many more would disagree that immigrant groups could fall under this heading.[6] Still, the rights implied in this article are primarily negative liberties that impose on governments only duties of noninterference rather than of recognition or assistance. Denying any such rights to immigrant groups would therefore entail explicit discrimination that singles them out by way of special prohibitions. This is clearly unjustifiable in a liberal democracy.[7]

The analogy between religious and linguistic freedom is, however, limited. Liberal states guarantee the free exercise of religion and embrace a norm of neutrality, even if they achieve it only imperfectly. Yet how could they ever endorse an ideal of neutrality with regard to the languages of public life?[8] In pre-modern states the legitimation of political authority was generally justified in religious terms. A demand for religious neutrality would then have seemed either absurd or radically subversive. In modernity, much the same seems to be true for the intimate link between political legitimation and policies of linguistic homogenization.

Gellner's (1983) theory of nationalism is obviously relevant here. For him, it is the industrial division of labor that generates a need for standardized languages. The theory has been often criticized as being functionalist, that is, as explaining a contingent social development by a postulated systemic need for a certain outcome. This lack of explanatory power can be overcome by adding the powerful agency of the modern state to the structural requirements of the

6. The 1995 Council of Europe's Framework Convention for the Protection of National Minorities, which otherwise signals substantial progress for minority rights in international law, has the same basic flaw. It leaves it to each signatory state to specify whether there are minority groups in its territory that are protected under the convention.

7. The general comment on Article 27 issued by the UN High Commissioner for Human Rights in 1994 specifies that "the individuals designed to be protected need not be citizens of the State party," or even permanent residents. "Thus migrant workers or even visitors in a State party constituting such minorities are entitled not to be denied the exercise of those rights" (UNHCR, 1994, 2).

8. "It is quite possible for a state not to have an established church. But the state cannot help but give at least partial establishment to a culture when it decides which language is to be used in public schooling, or in the provision of state services" (Kymlicka, 1995, 111).

economy. For the rapidly expanding state bureaucracy, a standardized language became not only a requirement for internal communication, but also an instrument of social control over the general population. Finally, representative democracy adds a third and normative reason to the requirements of the industrial economy and of the bureaucratic state. Democratic elections and political decisions presuppose that citizens understand the issues of a nationwide political agenda and are able to form opinions in a public discourse on candidates and programs.

None of these three reasons requires a completely monolingual citizenry, but all three demand that each language of public life must exist in a standardized form and must be taught in schools and studied in universities. The number of such official languages will necessarily be limited.[9] A modern liberal democracy can be *pluralistic* by giving official status to several linguistic communities and by assisting smaller and dispersed ones, but it cannot possibly be *neutral*. Even if it does not formally adopt an official state language, it will nevertheless de facto establish it through its public institutions (Kymlicka, 1995, 111–12).

Modern languages are not merely means of communication and markers of regional or ethnic identities in civil society, they are also instruments for the political organization of society. They are public goods whose production and reproduction demand a large-scale investment of public resources. A strictly neutral state that left this task to markets or to the forces of self-organization in civil society would not be a democracy as we understand it today. It would resemble a minimal state (Nozick, 1974) reduced to a territorial monopoly of violence.[10]

What normative conclusions we draw from this fact depends on how we assess the value of a particular language for individuals and groups. I consider three approaches that highlight different values: language as a means of com-

9. This problem is particularly acute within the European Union (EU) (Kraus, 1998). There are now eleven official languages, and over the next decade the number might increase dramatically with eastern enlargement of the Union. Different from international organizations like the United Nations or the Council of Europe, the EU cannot easily agree on limiting the number of official languages. A neutral solution is to reestablish Latin or to introduce Esperanto as an internal language of communication in the institutions of the Union, but this would be like replacing Sundays with Wednesdays for the sake of religious neutrality (Carens, 1997b, 818). Such neutrality would make no language community better off than before and would create a further obstacle for supranational democracy by culturally disconnecting the political institutions from the mass of citizens. English may increasingly become the European lingua franca, but the multinational character of the European Union is emphasized by giving official status to all national languages.

10. The most obvious reason why the attitude of liberal states toward linguistic diversity is fundamentally different from their attitude toward religious toleration is their monopoly in school education.

munication, as an aspect of personal identity, and as a political boundary marker. These views should be seen as complementing one another. Taken together, they enable us to distinguish universal from particular language rights.

A Thin Theory of Language

One possible answer to the fact of linguistic establishment suggests that there is nothing wrong with it. Ought implies can. If states cannot be neutral, they do not have to treat all languages equally. They must only respect the negative liberties of linguistic minorities but need not provide them with public recognition or resources for protecting and promoting their own languages. I call this the liberal assimilationist argument. Its first claim is that religion and language are not merely different in their historical importance for political legitimation, but are also different in their moral status. For liberals religious toleration and the separation of church and state are ultimately grounded in a respect for the moral integrity of individuals. Using political power to impose a faith violates the moral autonomy of individuals to form and revise their own conceptions of the good. It is this liberal norm that does not seem to apply to linguistic diversity. People pray in various languages, but they do not believe in a language. Languages enable us to communicate about facts, emotions, and ideas, including various religious and moral beliefs. In contrast with the holy languages of religious scripts or oral traditions among ethnoreligious groups, modern national languages, which are taught in public schools, seem to be entirely free of religious significance and can be used to express utterly different world views. By imposing a certain language of instruction in public education, the state does not appear to violate the moral autonomy of parents or their children who have been raised in a different language.

A second difference between language and religion reinforces this argument. The number of languages in which individuals can be simultaneously competent is limited by their cognitive capacities, while the number of religions they can simultaneously profess is limited by the doctrinal content of these religions. Human beings are as capable of combining various religious ideas into a syncretic system of beliefs as they are of speaking more than one language. The monotheistic world religions, however, condemn the worshipping of other gods. Some of their traditions severely sanction apostasy and conversion to another religion. In contrast, learning a second or third language does not normally lead to a loss of identity or of status in one's original language community. A requirement to adopt a common national language, then, need not imply that all citizens become monolingual by completely abandoning the use of any other than the national idiom.

Minority languages may still become extinct over the course of a few generations when those languages do not enjoy official status and are not taught in public schools. However, if the only linguistic right that states ought to protect is the liberty to use a language in communicating with other members of the same group, then such assimilation can be seen as entirely voluntary. One might even claim that teaching a minority language as part of a compulsory education is discriminatory for those minorities. Like affirmative action it singles them out for special treatment, which may in itself reinforce majority prejudice and social segregation. Unlike affirmative action it offers them something that is of no advantage to their social status and mobility in the wider society.

All the arguments I have listed rely on what Joseph Carens (1994, 172) has called a thin theory of language. Such a theory regards language merely as a medium for communicating messages between human beings. The communicative value of competence in a certain language increases with the number of people with whom it allows a person to exchange messages, with the amount of stored information it gives access to, and with the complexity of messages that can be expressed in that language. The more widely used a language is and the richer its vocabulary, the higher is its communicative value. From this perspective we might rank all languages by assigning a higher value to written languages than those that exist only as oral vernaculars and by giving the highest value to the major world languages.[11]

If the task of public education were simply to provide future citizens with skills that give them the widest range of possible opportunities, then languages should be primarily chosen by their communicative value. Making the teaching of isolated minority languages like Welsh or Euskera obligatory throughout a region should not be considered a right but rather a burden since it deprives children of the opportunity to learn other languages with a higher communicative value than their own. For the same reason, it would be wrong to divert scarce resources to programs that offer to the children of immigrants

11. This is of course a simplistic argument. A critic might point out that the communicative value of a language for an individual depends on how likely he or she is to establish contact with other speakers of that language and how important such contact is for his or her goals. A native speaker of a small minority language in a rural community may find that she needs English only when she has to communicate with an occasional tourist who is visiting her village. Because competency in a language is itself a powerful factor, however, shaping the pattern of future contacts, we cannot establish first the pattern of contacts an individual is likely to make during her lifetime and then assess the communicative value that learning a certain language might have for her. If our village dweller had learned English early on, she might enjoy much better employment opportunities elsewhere. This is a self-reinforcing mechanism of language distribution that accelerates with the spread of communication technology and with the rate and distance of geographical mobility. The effect is an ever-increasing communicative value of globally dominant languages over merely regional or local ones.

the choice of learning their parents' native languages in school. This theory supports linguistic assimilation into the larger language pools. The argument does not defend a majority privilege, but instead a presumptive interest of minorities themselves.

A Thick Theory of Languages

Several objections can be raised against this view. First, one can doubt the idea that languages are morally neutral media. Although modern languages are not strictly tied to religious worldviews, they nevertheless mark cultural and political forms of membership, which may require respect in their own right. The theory of language underlying the assimilationist argument is therefore too thin (Carens, 1994, 172). It ignores the significant differences between the primary acquisition of a mother tongue in the family and secondary linguistic socialization. A "thick" theory emphasizes the identity value of language, which has individual and collective dimensions. For individuals, the language they have grown up with retains a special emotional and cognitive significance. It determines not only their opportunities, but also shapes a cultural habitus and their way of interpreting the world. The acquisition of a mother tongue makes an individual a member of a language community whose own collective identity depends on maintaining the use of the language among its members. At this collective level, language maintenance allows groups to achieve a continuity of high cultural and folk traditions across generations. The idea that people somehow "belong" to their original language community is reinforced by the observation that after adolescence most people can no longer learn to speak a foreign language without an accent. Our first language is not so different after all from a native religion that we have grown up with. Both can eventually be abandoned, but they will remain a part of what shaped our selves.

Thick theories provide a normative justification for a politics of language recognition. Learning a second or third language increases an individual's opportunities. Yet being deprived of an environment where that individual can use her first language and can relate to the cultural traditions of that language community may lead to a loss of self-esteem, that is, of an individual's relation to herself as a recognized member of a social group in whose achievements she can take pride (Honneth, 1992, 208). For children of national majorities, the transition from oral capabilities in their mother tongue to learning a standard form of the dominant language is relatively smooth. For the children of minority groups it may be an experience of a devaluation of and estrangement from their family background. The loss of a mother tongue owing to compulsory school education will also hurt adult immigrants who find it more difficult to communicate with their children or grandchildren or who depend on them for communication with the authorities of their host country. If speaking a minority language also carries a social stigma and diminishes social and economic opportunities as well as self-respect, then one should remove the stigma rather than press people into abandoning their language. Protecting minority languages may thus be a matter of justice and not merely of utility.

Although these are reasonable arguments, I do not fully subscribe to the thick theory, mainly because it does not allow a distinction between immigrant minorities and other minorities. It is simply an empirical fact that most immigrant groups in Western democracies assimilate into the language of their host country over the course of several generations without being recognizably hampered in their psychological development. Although the process of transition may be difficult and in some respects painful, it does not justify diminishing opportunities for immigrant minorities by giving primacy to the preservation of their mother tongues over the task of learning a national language. What the argument does support is supplementary teaching of "heritage languages" as well as bilingual education programs that smooth the transition and use the implicit grammatical knowledge acquired by first linguistic socialization for learning the national language as a second one. This should be considered as a relevant interest and a prudent policy in immigration societies, although not necessarily as a matter of justice and fundamental rights.

To make a stronger case for linguistic conservation policies the thick theory would have to be applied at the collective rather than the individual level. One might say that even if individual members of minorities have an interest in assimilating, such an interest exists only because the given social context deprives them of opportunities to retain their native language. Their community as a whole may then have a collective interest in changing the context through language maintenance programs that reduce the assimilation pressure. This is a perfectly liberal argument insofar as it is concerned only with eliminating the impact of structural disadvantage on individual choices. It must then stop short of condemning assimilation when it is voluntarily chosen under fair conditions and does not warrant state intervention in order to preserve a language that has already been abandoned by its native speakers.

Other arguments about the value of the collective identity of endangered minority languages are more difficult to accept. Some invoke a collective obligation toward one's culture of origin. Even if we grant that such obligations can be strongly felt by the members of a cultural community, it is nonetheless not legitimate for the state to enforce those obligations. Internal enforcement within the community will often result from a special interest of professional élites such as teachers, journalists, artists, and political or religious leaders. In the absence of democratic accountability within minority communities, there is a real danger that language maintenance programs may not represent a truly collective interest of these groups.

Another argument defends linguistic diversity as a collective interest of the wider society and even of humankind. A greater diversity of languages may enrich the public culture of a society or improve communication with neighboring countries. The extinction of minor languages reduces the cultural wealth of the human experience and is in that sense certainly a loss for humankind. Such reasons, however, do not always support language maintenance policies in a particular context. On the one hand, small and isolated linguistic minorities will not improve their countries' communication with neighboring societies. On the other hand, the assimilation of linguistic diasporas of immigrant or transborder minorities whose original languages remain firmly established in their national homelands reduces regional diversity but does not contribute to global language extinction.

From a normative perspective, there is a more important objection to such arguments. Policies of language conservation should be rejected if they are merely based on the "external preferences" of those who are not minority members themselves.[12] The external value of linguistic diversity should be counted only when it coincides with a group's collective interest in maintaining its language (Bauböck, 1999).

A Political Theory of Language

There is another reason for rejecting liberal assimilationism. Languages do not merely transport cultural knowledge; they also mark collective political identities. I call this the political theory of language. If the thin and thick theories emphasize the *pragmatic* and *expressive* aspects of communication, the political theory stresses the *strategic* use of languages in staking claims to collective self-government. National and ethnic identities are in most cases connected to membership in a language group. Often, a demand to recognize the language of a minority group by having it taught in the public schools comes from the group's broader demand for recognition as a distinct political community and building block of a larger federated polity. In officially multilingual countries like Belgium, Canada, Spain, Switzerland, and the United Kingdom, there are several language communities, each of which claims political powers that enable it to establish its idiom as dominant in the schools and public life of

---

12. See Dworkin (1977, chap. 9; 1981) on the illegitimacy of a utilitarian calculus that includes external preferences.

its provinces. What justification is there for this demand? In many of these
countries the members of the smaller language communities are generally bilingual and understand the language of the majority. Would it not serve their
integration in the wider polity if they had to use that language in courts and in
communication with political authorities? Apart from a few exceptions, these
languages are also not immediately threatened with extinction.[13]

For these minority groups, political self-government is not primarily a means
to protect their languages or to facilitate communication, but the other way
around. They want to preserve the regional language boundary in order to maintain their claims to self-government within a federation. If a national linguistic
minority were to become a minority in its own province through intermarriage,
the immigration of other groups,[14] or the emigration of its own members, this
demographic shift would undermine its power to claim regional autonomy and
special representation at the federal level. In liberal democratic federations,
provinces have no right to restrict intermarriage or internal migration and generally no competence to control immigration from abroad. Yet they may preserve their status by making their language dominant in public life. As long as
they respect the rights of linguistic and other minorities living in their territory,
there is no fundamental liberal objection to granting them the same powers that
dominant national majorities enjoy in unitary states and officially monolingual
federations.

Language rights of this kind derive from self-government, which has an
intrinsic value from a liberal democratic perspective. There is no good reason
why the right to self-government should be confined to states that are currently
independent. To be self-governing, a political community must extend across
several generations, live in a bounded territory, and share a public culture. The
desire for self-government by national minorities can be met within multinational federations or by adopting special arrangements for autonomy. In composite polities of this sort, citizenship is not only functionally differentiated,
but also territorially. Citizens are simultaneously members of a constituent unit
and of the larger federation.

Democratic self-government implies legitimate powers to establish languages
of public life. The choice of these languages is tied to particular nation-build-

---

13. Welsh in the United Kingdom and Rhaeto-Romanic in Switzerland would probably have
become extinct had they not been supported by public policies. This is less obvious for such
larger regional languages as Catalan and altogether wrong for Quebec. What is at stake in Quebec
is of course not the survival of the French language per se, but of a French language community
in North America.

14. This is why in Quebec the children of immigrants must go to schools where French is the
language of instruction.

ing projects and is not dictated by either the thin or the thick theory of language. States support languages not merely for the convenience of communication. They do not have to make English a national language even when it is the most widely spoken second language and the de facto lingua franca. The choice of Hebrew as the official language of Israel or Irish as the second official language of the Irish Republic demonstrates that state languages need not even be widely spoken as first languages by the original population. The justification of such language establishment cannot be assessed by the criterion of communicative value or personal identity value. We need to examine the legitimacy of claims to self-government and the underlying nation-building project.

What this argument does, is limit the strongest language rights to those groups that can also claim territorial self-government. This is not to say that they must all establish their particular languages. First, self-governing minorities have a right, but certainly not a duty, to do so. Some national minorities are not identified by a particular language, but by a religious or political tradition. If the primary task were to preserve the diversity of languages, then presumably Scottish nationalists should attempt to establish their own version of Gaelic. In contrast with Wales, however, Scotland's history and legal institutions are so clearly distinct from England's that the near extinction of the Gaelic language has not dissolved a perception of national difference. Second, indigenous groups that enjoy territorial autonomy may have both the right and the desire to establish their languages but will often be unable to do so simply because there are too many separate languages and because most groups are too small to be supported by a fully developed educational system.[15]

Although the most extensive language rights derive from territorial self-government, this does not mean that non-self-governing minorities cannot also enjoy some of those rights. In Canada, both Anglophones in Quebec and Francophone communities in other provinces can send their children to public schools where their own language is the medium of instruction. This arrangement expresses the idea that Canada is not merely a federation of provinces, one of which is a distinct nation, but that it is also a bilingual federation that guarantees its language communities certain rights that are not strictly territorial. Yet this nonterritorial bilingualism could hardly have been sustained over

15. For Canada, see Carens (2000, chap. 3). In other countries, such as Indonesia, Papua New Guinea, and some African states, the number of native languages is so great that only a few can serve meaningfully as official regional languages. In these contexts nation building requires promoting a common lingua franca throughout the territory. Native languages need not become extinct as long as local cultural traditions remain alive, but the strategy of "nationalizing" them in order to preserve them cannot be successful for all.

time without the strong territorial self-government enjoyed by Quebec as a Francophone province.

Another objection is that for immigrant minorities, too, their languages of origin may have political value. At least for the first and second generations a native language is a marker for a distinct community with particular interests. Media, schools, and businesses that use these languages may serve as rallying points to mobilize people around those interests. Using a minority language for purposes of identification and mobilization in this way, however, still aims at "renegotiating the terms of integration" into the wider society rather than at political autonomy (Kymlicka, 1998a, ch. 3).

Combining the Three Theories

The three theories of language that I have discussed are not strictly incompatible. If we see them as complementary we cannot place the entire burden of justification for language rights on a single theory. The thin conception applies to all individual human beings and grounds a general principle of linguistic toleration, that is, a basic right to the free use of minority idioms in private life and in civil society. In addition, it creates a moral obligation to teach immigrants and their children the languages of their countries of residence in order to facilitate their integration as future citizens. Finally, the communicative value of various languages suggests that governments should increase opportunities for all citizens by teaching them foreign languages. Since failing to do so would not violate anyone's liberties or claims to equal respect, this last point is good policy rather than a moral obligation. The thick theory of language applies also to all individuals, but it identifies them as members of distinct groups, and it is not equally strong for all those groups. For nearly everyone, her or his mother tongue has special importance. However, for dispersed and immigrant minorities, competence in the language of the surrounding society is even more important for their future opportunities. A liberal interpretation of the thick theory must therefore allow for voluntary assimilation. Governments may have to improve the conditions under which this shift takes place. Such policies should include the promotion of transitional bilingualism for first and second generations. This is, however, insufficient to establish a more general obligation to maintain linguistic diversity. Finally, the political theory of language applies only to some groups but not to others. Not all linguistic minorities have the capacity or desire to exercise territorial self-government, and not all can reasonably claim to be constituent historical parts of the larger political community. If immigrant groups were to raise such demands, or if their demands were misinterpreted in this way, it would merely serve as a pretext for reinforcing their unequal status and segregation.

This account is skeptical toward the assertion of a fundamental human right "to learn the mother tongue, including at least basic education through the medium of the mother tongue" (Phillipson et al., 1995, 2), especially if this is interpreted as a right "to have it developed in formal schooling through being taught through the medium of it" and is seen to be "inherent in everyone, even those who leave their community of origin and migrate or flee to another country or community" (p. 12). Denying this does not imply that immigrants can only claim a right to use their original languages in domestic life and in their own associations, media, and private educational institutions. The dichotomy between, on the one hand, human rights to the free use of a language and, on the other hand, group rights of self-governing national minorities to establish their language as the dominant one in public life does not exhaust the full range of rights. We should think of these as the endpoints of a continuum. Bilingual education in public schools falls between the two poles, and there are good reasons for promoting it for immigrant minorities. Immigrant groups exposed to the pressures of language assimilation can expect their native languages to receive public support to ease their integration into the wider society while permitting them to retain social ties to their countries and cultures of origins. Yet the right to establish a language as an official one belongs to the constituent groups of the polity. Making this distinction limits the dangers of proliferating demands that would overstrain public resources and of societal fragmentation based on language differences that would impede democratic deliberation in a shared public sphere.

Immigrants and National Minorities

Making this distinction between various minorities at first glance appears morally arbitrary. Why should one group enjoy the strong power of self-government, which permits it to establish its national culture while immigrants are denied that privilege? Is this not a differentiation of cultural citizenship that denies equal respect by relying on the dubious criteria of descent and national origin? If we accept Kymlicka's basic claim that a secure belonging to a cultural community is a primary social good and a precondition for individual autonomy, then it would seem that migrants are even more disadvantaged than are national minorities. Kymlicka (1989, ch. 9) argues that minorities have to invest more resources to maintain their cultural structure than do national majorities for whom it is provided as a public good. Yet immigrants face even more obstacles to maintain or re-create their culture of origin than do territorially concentrated national and indigenous minorities. The former might therefore deserve more protection than do the latter (Tempelman, 1999, 28). The hierarchy of minority rights assigned to immigrant and national minorities respectively is plainly rejected by Parekh (1997, 62), while other authors want to see it as a continuum rather than as a dichotomy (Carens, 1997a, 43–45; Young, 1997). In this section I consider six reasons that might support the validity of the distinction. I argue that we should reject two of these reasons while modifying and combining the others and present them in ascending order of plausibility.

Waiving Protection through Emigration

Kymlicka's (1995) main argument is that all individuals have an equal right to cultural protection but can waive this right by leaving the country where their culture is established as a public one.[16] This move seems inconsistent with his theory that denies the relevance of choice between different cultural affiliations and emphasizes instead the inclusive nature of the national cultures into which we are born. It is also not obvious that individuals ought to be free to waive their rights to primary goods.[17] Apart from these problems at the level of theory, the argument also has counterintuitive implications. An obvious objection, of which Kymlicka (1995, 98–99) is aware, is that refugees and those who immigrate with their parents at an early age or who are born in the host country have not voluntarily left the country where their culture is fully protected and ought therefore to enjoy the same cultural rights of self-government as national minorities. Finally, as Bhikhu Parekh (1997, 62) has pointed out, "[J]ust as immigrants come voluntarily, the receiving country admits them voluntarily." Immigrants are under a moral obligation to waive some of their cultural rights only if the receiving society is under no duty to grant them those rights. We thus need a prior reason why immigrants cannot claim the same rights as do national minorities.

Waiving Protection through Voluntary Assimilation

It is somewhat more plausible to see immigrants as waiving some cultural rights *after* settlement in the receiving society. This second argument assumes

16. "People should be able to live and work in their own culture. But like any other right, this right can be waived, and immigration is one way of waiving one's right. In deciding to uproot themselves, immigrants voluntarily relinquish some of the rights that go along with their original national membership" (p. 96).

17. See J. S. Mill's (1972, 171–72) argument against the right to sell one's liberty by voluntarily becoming a slave.

that both groups have the same rights, but that immigrants choose, for whatever reason, not to claim full cultural autonomy. The difference is then merely one of empirical patterns of voluntary integration but has no moral foundation. In the first argument, the morally unconstrained choice is whether or not to immigrate, but that choice entails a moral obligation to renounce certain cultural rights. According to the second reason, the receiving society is obliged to offer immigrants all available cultural rights, but immigrants are free to choose which of those they want to activate. Of course, this would imply that a group of immigrants that wishes to segregate from the surrounding society and to establish a separate public culture ought to be free to do so.

No Fundamental Interest in Cultural Protection

A third argument builds on needs and interests. In Joseph Raz's (1986) theory, the moral force of rights does not derive from choices but from interests. X has a right if "an aspect of X's well-being (his interests) is a sufficient reason for holding some other person(s) to be under a duty" (p. 166). We might then say that, in contrast with national minorities, immigrants generally do not have a fundamental interest in re-creating their culture of origin as a public culture in the receiving society, or, if they do have such an interest, that it is not sufficiently strong to create a duty for the state to establish their culture.

Three objections exist against such an argument. First, its validity depends on how we determine the interests of immigrants. If we consider their actual choices as revealing their true interests, we are back to the previous argument. If we think (as Raz does) that persons may be wrong about their interests, there is a danger of paternalism. Who are we to tell immigrants that a certain kind of cultural integration is in their best interests? Second, interests may be shaped by a morally unfair bargaining position. Immigrants will have a strong interest in learning the language of the host country if doing so is the price of equal opportunities. The question is then whether the initial situation of diminished opportunities for native speakers of immigrant languages is not itself unfair.[18] Third, if we think that it is not inherently unfair to tie equal opportunities to cultural integration, then we must ask why national minorities should not also have an overriding interest in integration in the dominant national culture. Although I agree that immigrant and national minorities have different interests in cultural preservation, I must still show why they are different and that immi-

---

18. Carens points out that the renunciation of language claims by immigrants may be a case of what Jon Elster has called adaptive preference formation: "People don't ask for and even say they don't want what they know they cannot have" (Carens, 2000, chap. 3).

grants are not unfairly prevented from developing the same cultural interests that national minorities are allowed to develop.

Scarcity of Resources for Dispersed Groups

The fourth argument concerns the feasibility of allocating the same rights to both types of minorities. This argument is also compatible with the view that immigrant and national minorities may have the same moral claims to cultural protection. While the second argument regards the translation of those claims into positive rights as emerging from the individual and collective choices of the bearers of those rights, we must now consider whether such a spontaneous distribution of rights is constrained by scarce resources.

As Cass Sunstein and Stephen Holmes (1999) have recently reminded us, rights are not cost-free. This is true for all rights, but there is an important difference between negative liberties, which require general enforcement mechanisms against illegitimate interference, and positive entitlements that allocate public funds directly to specific persons or groups to enable them to enjoy the right. The difference is not primarily one of costs (a libertarian state with few provisions for public education and welfare may have to spend a lot more on police and prisons), but concerns the demands of justice.

A liberal state ought to guarantee the same negative liberties of free religious exercise and free use of a language for immigrants as it does for native citizens, even if that implies substantial costs, such as are involved in enforcing effective antidiscrimination legislation. Yet the state need not guarantee for all groups equal opportunities to preserve their religion or culture, unless the circumstances that create unequal opportunities have to be changed as a matter of justice. Immigrants may then often be disadvantaged merely because they reside territorially dispersed throughout the country. Groups of immigrants who live isolated from their ethnic communities have the same rights, but they will have fewer opportunities to practice their religion or speak their language of origin. Where scarce resources are needed to provide specific groups with "enabling rights," cost efficiency and trade-offs with other public policy goals become important considerations. Assigning teachers and school hours to minority language education means diverting limited money and time from other important public purposes. Such an allocation needs to be justified in terms of cost-benefit efficiency. It is obvious that territory cannot be infinitely subdivided to satisfy the interests of all minorities to have their language established as a public one. At the end of the process all would have the same rights, but there would not remain any public space within which any language would be hegemonic.

This argument is perfectly reasonable, but it is merely contingently related to the distinction between immigrants and native minorities. On the one hand, certain immigrant minorities live in sufficiently dense urban and regional concentrations. Should southern Florida be made an autonomous territory so that the Cuban community might fully establish its language and culture there? There are, on the other hand, historical native minorities, such as Eastern European Jews and Sinti and Roma before the Holocaust, who cannot muster regional majorities because they are either territorially dispersed or not sedentary. Should they be treated as immigrants?

Special Obligations toward National Minorities

What the pragmatic feasibility argument omits is the historical dimension of minority rights. The fifth argument, which is also suggested by Kymlicka (1995, 10–13), answers this objection. It puts a positive weight into the scalepan of national minority claims that tips the balance in their favor. National minorities have been self-governing and were either voluntarily or coercively incorporated into the larger state. If incorporation is voluntary, it leads to a multinational federation in which each constituent part secures for itself the necessary rights to preserve its own culture. If it is coercive, as in the case of nearly all indigenous groups, the minority has a right to have its powers of self-government restored or, if that is no longer possible, it has a right to at least some compensatory protection for its culture. In contrast, a receiving country has no special historical obligations toward immigrants who have come voluntarily or as refugees.[19] It may, however, have obligations of this kind to the descendants of slaves whose forebears were also coercively "incorporated" or to immigrants from former colonies. The cultural rights of immigrants would then be constrained not only by conditions of feasibility, but also by the absence of special obligations.

It is awkward, however, to derive strong cultural minority rights exclusively from special historical obligations. First, we have to explain why agreements concluded long ago under different circumstances should still be honored to-

19. As we have seen, Kymlicka's argument that immigrants have implicitly waived their cultural rights does not apply to refugees. However, if we derive cultural rights from state responsibilities rather than from immigrant choices, this distinction is less salient. Refugees have not waived any rights to cultural protection, but if the receiving country has not been implicated in depriving them of those rights in their home countries, its obligations to offer substitutive cultural rights are not necessarily different from those toward voluntary immigrants. If a receiving country has been implicated in creating the refugee movement, it may indeed incur stronger obligations to enable the refugees, if they so wish, to return to their homelands and to retain their cultures and languages in preparation for return.

day and why injustices committed long ago should continue to give rise to claims for restitution. Second, if we go back far enough in history, the distinction between native and immigrant minorities becomes increasingly blurred. In the end we are all descendants of immigrants, and at some point nearly all groups have been coercively incorporated into another state territory. Third, even if we could establish a clear lineage and the moral relevance of historical agreements and injustices, there would remain a nagging doubt about why the prior occupancy of a territory by a group should give it exclusive rights to self-government. We live in a world where Locke's (1956) proviso for legitimate first acquisitions that "there is enough and as good left in common for others" (p. 15) can no longer be satisfied. Why should newcomers have weaker cultural rights than members of territorially self-governing groups?

Conditions for Self-Government

The sixth argument takes a step back by asking the question, why should immigrants not form self-governing minorities in the first place? If certain cultural rights derive from claims to self-government, then the justification for differential treatment must focus on the legitimate conditions for exercising self-government. In liberal democracies territorial self-government has four characteristics: it is territorially inclusive, it is historically continuous, it provides a shared public culture, and it is federally disaggregated in multinational societies. Let me briefly explain each of these characteristics and how they apply to immigrants and national minorities.

First, in a liberal democratic perspective, self-government rights cannot be the exclusive prerogative of culturally defined communities. If government is exercised territorially by issuing laws that are binding for all residents, then it is prima facie the whole resident population of the territory that enjoys the right to govern itself by choosing its rulers or institutions of government. At this level, the argument cannot distinguish between natives and newcomers. Its practical implication is that after a short period, resident immigrants must be treated as citizens or be given the right to become citizens through naturalization.

Second, self-government is a historical project. All polities are imagined as being transgenerational communities. They build upon a common past and are oriented to a common future. Newcomers must accept that the political institutions, which are in place when they arrive, have been formed by the particular historical experiences of previous generations and can be changed only incrementally to reflect their own specific interests. Immigrants cannot change the past of their new society, but the society can and ought to change the narratives of its own past to include the histories of immigrants, and it ought to give immigrants a voice in determining the future of the polity (Bauböck, 1998).

Third, territorial self-government implies a right as well as a duty to provide a common public culture that serves as a medium and background for public education, political deliberation, and economic and social mobility. Such a public culture will be associated with a particular majority tradition, but it must be accessible and open for change to reflect the experiences of all groups in the self-governing polity, including recent immigrants.

Fourth, self-government is a collective right of distinct political communities that need not coincide with the whole population and with the territorial borders of an independent state. Most present borders are the result of wars and oppression directed against rival claims to territory. There is no good reason for considering the claims of victorious nations as more legitimate than those of vanquished national minorities. It is also impossible to grant every group that has aspirations for territorial self-government an independent state. The obvious solution to this dilemma is the devolution of political power by granting territorial autonomy to historical communities having a constant desire and capacity to be self-governing. In some cases this leads to a special status for minorities within a polity that embraces a mononational conception of itself. The status of Puerto Rico or of Indian peoples in the United States is an example for such arrangements (Kymlicka, 1998b, 77). Other states are organized as multinational federations so that the polity itself is regarded as a composite of constituent national communities.[20] In such federations national minorities enjoy a collective right of self-government within their territory and an individual right to participate as equal citizens in the self-government of their national entity and of the larger state. Once immigrants are admitted as citizens, they have the same rights of participation, but they have no collective right to establish self-governing territories where their culture dominates the public sphere.

The reason for this is the territorial nature of self-government. If we lived in a world where political communities were organized merely on a membership basis with no reference to territorial residence, immigrants would have exactly the same cultural rights as all other groups. Such a deterritorialized system of political communities ought to be unattractive for liberals regardless of whether membership is ascriptive or freely chosen. Its effect would be that people who

---

20. In many cases (such as in Canada and Spain), these federations are asymmetrical in the sense that only national minorities see them as composed of distinct nations, whereas majorities associate their national identity with the state as a whole and regard the territorial division of power as one among equal provinces.

meet in streets, neighborhoods, or at work no longer share a citizenship that commits them to a common public good. To maintain power, political groups would have constantly to police the boundaries of their membership, enforcing uniformity within those boundaries. The territorial bases of political power allow for inclusive citizenship shared between groups having different identities and interests. Nonterritorial forms of voluntary association and minority rights can flourish only against a background of a territorially defined domain for the rule of law and democratic representation.

Given the territorial structure of self-government, immigrants who import rights of self-government into a "receiving society" would be invaders. This is what colonial settlers did in the Americas, Australia, South Africa, and New Zealand. For just that reason Immanuel Kant (1984) restricted the right of free movement as the core of a future cosmopolitan citizenship to the right to visit other countries rather than to settle there. Maybe Kant was too conservative in this respect. I can imagine a future world in which free movement between states includes the right to settle and thus becomes like internal migration within liberal states. Still, even such open borders would certainly not imply a general claim by immigrant groups to separate territories in order to become self-governing.

This denial nonetheless allows for exceptions. Although they are under no obligation to do so, receiving states may cede parts of their territories to an immigrant group; they may invite a group to form a territorially cohesive community within the state; or they may grant such a group a nonterritorial cultural autonomy that allows it to remain separate from the wider society. Groups of immigrant descent may also acquire self-government rights when they have in fact become national minorities by occupying over a long time a separate territory and maintaining a distinct culture. The history of colonialism is marked by many different population movements, ranging from European settlers to Asian indentured laborers and African slaves. In several colonies immigrants brought there as indentured workers were segregated from both white colonialists and the indigenous population and have retained their distinct cultural identities and urban concentrations.[21] In postcolonial contexts, however, such groups have more often fought to gain equal citizenship and protection for their economic activities than demanded to be treated as self-governing national minorities. A transformation of immigrant groups into national minorities is even less likely

---

21. A special case that raises interesting problems for democratic theory is Fiji, where the descendants of indentured Indian workers have formed a majority that outnumbers the indigenous population. Carens (1992, 2000, chap. 9) defends the Fiji Indians' right to equal citizenship, but he also defends public efforts to preserve the indigenous Fijian culture.

to occur if the state is liberal-democratic. These societies offer immigrants citizenship rather than a piece of their territory.[22] The inclusion of immigrants as citizens stimulates economic and social mobility and undermines the kind of persistent territorial and cultural segregation that might eventually produce a consolidated national minority.

Conclusions

In liberal societies immigration does not give rise to self-government rights and to those cultural minority rights that derive from self-government. This argument generalizes the "political theory" of language that I have outlined here. It is compatible with three of the other reasons for distinguishing the claims of immigrant and national minorities—namely, arguments of interest, feasibility, and historical claims. Moreover, the self-government argument helps to answer the puzzling questions that the other arguments have left open. It provides a reason why the interests and historical claims of immigrants and national minorities are different, and it effectively resolves the problem of the feasibility argument, which fails to distinguish clearly between the two categories.

A focus on self-government prepares the ground for a contextual normative analysis of multicultural claims. This is the third axis of disaggregation I have suggested at the beginning of this chapter. Territorial self-government in liberal states gives, on the one hand, a dominant regional or statewide majority the legitimate power to shape the public culture of the society but commits, on the other hand, this majority to respond to internal cultural diversity by transforming its own culture and accommodating minorities. Some projects of nation building deny such commitments and lead to illiberal forms of establishing a dominant culture. It should be possible to develop a normative critique of national self-government on these grounds. A list of the many national policies that prima facie violate the constraints on self-government that I have advocated would include among others the way that Israel defines itself as a Jewish state and discriminates against its Arab citizens; the restrictions on immigrants' access to English schools in Quebec; the preferential treatment of ethnic Ger-

---

22. Walzer (1983, 46–48) suggests that, faced with the claims of needy migrants, a country with abundant unpopulated land could choose either to yield territory in order to preserve its ethnic homogeneity or to preserve its claim to the land but to welcome such immigrants as future citizens. I agree that this might be a permissible choice under the assumptions of this rather hypothetical example. I also think that liberal democracies will always choose the second option because a liberal conception of citizenship cannot be "diluted" by ethnic heterogeneity.

man immigrants over Turkish ones in Germany; the French refusal to recognize any ethnic minorities; and the denial of bilingual schools and topographical inscriptions for Austria's regional linguistic minorities.

It would be futile, however, to assess these policies without attention to historical context. It is a contradiction in terms to think that universal principles apply to self-governing communities everywhere in the same way and determine completely the range of permissible policies and acceptable arrangements. If this were true, such communities would no longer be able to govern themselves but would instead have to be governed by a global authority that enforces uniform principles of liberalism all over the world.

The normative distinction between immigrant and national minority claims, for which a theory of liberal self-government provides the best argument, should not be misinterpreted as a strict dichotomy. Many groups fall somewhere between the two endpoints, and, accordingly, their claims are mixed. There are old linguistic minorities such as Danes and Sorbs in Germany and Slovenes and Croats in Austria who do not aspire to self-government, because they cannot muster a majority in any subdivision of the territory. There are dispersed groups of self-governing national or indigenous minorities such as Francophone Canadians outside Quebec and the off-reservation members of Indian tribes. There are ethnoreligious sects like the Amish and Hutterites who do not want self-government but demand wide-ranging exemptions in order to preserve their ways of life. There are ethnic communities such as Mexican Americans in the U.S. southwest who were originally coercively incorporated but whose distinctiveness today is primarily maintained through immigration. All these groups and their claims fall somewhere on a continuum, but to describe that continuum it is necessary to identify its endpoints. This is how the distinction between immigrant and national minorities should be interpreted.

There is not yet a fully satisfying answer to the question of how societies that are deeply divided along religious, linguistic, racial, ethnic, and national lines can remain integrated as democratic polities. Many different answers seem to have worked at different times in different places. Political theory should be willing to learn from experience. Where minority rights succeed in integrating historically oppressed and alienated groups into a common citizenship but deviate from liberal norms of neutrality or equal treatment, it may be that the norms need to be corrected rather than the institutions.

Works Cited

Anderson, Benedict. 1983. *Imagined Communities: Reflections on the Origins and Spread of Nationalism*. London: Verso Editions and New Left Books.

Bauböck, Rainer. 1998. "Sharing History and Future? Time Horizons of Democratic Membership in an Age of Migration." *Constellations* 4(3) (Jan.): 320–45.

———. 1999. "Liberal Justifications for Ethnic Group Rights." In Christian Joppke and Steven Lukes (eds.), *Multicultural Questions*. Oxford: Oxford University Press.

———. n.d. "Cultural Minority Rights in Public Education: Religious and Language Instruction for Immigrant Communities in Western Europe." In Anthony Messina (ed.), *West European Immigration and Immigrant Policy in the New Century: A Continuing Quandary for States and Societies*. Westport, Conn.: Greenwood Press.

Bissoondath, Neil. 1994. *Selling Illusions: The Cult of Multiculturalism in Canada*. Toronto: Penguin.

Buchanan, Allen. 1998. "What's So Special about Nations?" *Canadian Journal of Philosophy* (suppl.) 22:283–309.

Carens, Joseph H. 1992. Democracy and Respect for Difference: The Case of Fiji." *University of Michigan Journal of Law Reform* 25(3,4): 547–631.

———. 1994. "Cultural Adaptation and Integration: Is Québec a Model for Europe?" In Rainer Bauböck (ed.), *From Aliens to Citizens. Redefining the Status of Immigrants in Europe*. Aldershot: Avebury.

———. 1997a. "Liberalism and Culture." *Constellations* 4(1): 35–47.

———. 1997b. "Two Conceptions of Fairness: A Response to Veit Bader." *Political Theory* 25(6) (Dec.): 814–20.

———. 2000. *Culture, Citizenship, and Community: A Contextual Exploration of Justice as Evenhandedness*. Oxford: Oxford University Press.

Dworkin, Ronald. 1977. *Taking Rights Seriously*. Cambridge, Mass.: Harvard University Press.

———. 1981. "What is Equality?" Part 1, "Equality of Welfare." Part 2, "Equality of Resources." *Philosophy and Public Affairs* 3, 4.

Elazar, Daniel J. 1987. *Exploring Federalism*. Tuscaloosa: University of Alabama Press.

Geertz, Clifford. 1973. *The Interpretation of Cultures*. New York: Basic Books.

Gellner, Ernest. 1983. *Nations and Nationalism*. Oxford: Blackwell.

Gitlin, Todd. 1995. *The Twilight of Common Dreams: Why America Is Wracked by Culture Wars*. New York: Henry Holt.

Gwyn, Richard. 1995. *Nationalism without Walls: The Unbearable Lightness of Being Canadian*. Toronto: MacClelland and Stewart.

Hobsbawm, Eric. 1990. *Nations and Nationalism since 1780: Programme, Myth, Reality*. Cambridge: Cambridge University Press.

Hollinger, David. 1995. *Postethnic America: Beyond Multiculturalism*. New York: Basic Books.

Honneth, Axel. 1994. *Kampf um Anerkennung: Zur moralischen Grammatik sozialer Konflikte*. Frankfurt a.M.: Suhrkamp.

Hughes, Robert. 1993. *Culture of Complaint: The Fraying of America*. New York: Oxford University Press.

Kant, Immanuel. 1984. *Zum Ewigen Frieden*. Stuttgart: Reclam Universal-Bibliothek.

Kraus, Peter. 1998. "Kultureller Pluralismus und politische Integration: Die Sprachenfrage in der Europäischen Union." *Österreichische Zeitschrift für Politikwissenschaft* 27(4): 443–58.

Kymlicka, Will. 1989. *Liberalism, Community, and Culture*. Oxford: Clarendon Press.

————. 1995. *Multicultural Citizenship: A Liberal Theory of Minority Rights.* Oxford: Oxford University Press.

————. 1998a. *Finding Our Way: Rethinking Ethnocultural Relations in Canada.* Toronto: Oxford University Press.

————. 1998b. "American Multiculturalism in the International Arena." *Dissent* (fall):73–79.

Lind, Michael. 1995. *The Next American Nation: The New Nationalism and the Fourth American Revolution.* New York: Simon & Schuster.

Locke, John. 1956. "The Second Treatise of Government." In J. W. Gough (ed.), *The Second Treatise of Government and a Letter Concerning Toleration.* New York: Macmillan.

MacCormick, Neil. 1996. "Liberalism, Nationalism, and the Post-Sovereign State." *Political Studies* 44:553–67.

Margalit, Avishai, and Raz, Joseph. 1994. "National Self-Determination." In Raz, Joseph, *Ethics in the Public Domain. Essays in the Morality of Law and Politics,* pp. 125–45. Oxford: Clarendon Press.

Marshall, T. H. 1965. "Citizenship and Social Class." In *Class, Citizenship, and Social Development: Essays by T. H. Marshall.* New York: Asnchor Books.

Mill, John Stuart. 1972. "On Liberty." In *Utilitarianism, On Liberty and Considerations on Representative Government,* pp. 69–185. London: Everyman's Library.

Miller, David. 1995. *On Nationality.* Oxford: Oxford University Press.

Moore, Margaret. 1997. "On National Self-Determination." *Political Studies* 45: 900–913.

Nozick, Robert. 1974. *Anarchy, State, and Utopia.* Oxford: Basil Blackwell.

Parekh, Bhikhu. 1997. "Dilemmas of a Multicultural Theory of Citizenship." *Constellations* 4(1): 54–62.

Phillipson, Robert, Mart Rannut, and Tove Skutnabb-Kangas. 1995. Introduction to Robert Phillipson and Tove Skutnabb-Kangas (eds.), *Linguistic Human Rights: Overcoming Linguistic Discrimination.* Berlin: Mouton de Gruyter.

Philpott, Daniel. 1995. "In Defense of Self-Determination." *Ethics* 105:352–85.

Rawls, John. 1971. *A Theory of Justice.* Cambridge, Mass.: Harvard University Press.

————. 1993. *Political Liberalism.* New York: Columbia University Press.

Raz, Joseph. 1986. *The Morality of Freedom.* Oxford: Clarendon Press.

Schlesinger, Arthur M., Jr. 1992. *The Disuniting of America.* New York: Norton.

Smith, Anthony D. 1987. *The Ethnic Origins of Nations.* Oxford: Blackwell.

Sunstein, Cass, and Stephen Holmes. 1999. *The Cost of Rights: Why Liberty Depends on Taxes.* New York: Norton.

Tamir, Yael. 1993. *Liberal Nationalism.* Princeton: Princeton University Press.

Tempelman, Sasja. 1999. "Constructions of Cultural Identity: Multiculturalism and Exclusion." *Political Studies* 47(1): 17–31.

UNHCR (United Nations High Commissioner for Refugees). 1994. *General Comment 23: The Rights of Minorities (Article 27).* <www.unhcr.ch/tbs/doc.nsf.html>

Waldron, Jeremy. 1992. "Minority Cultures and the Cosmopolitan Alternative." *University of Michigan Law Reform* 25:751–93.

————. 1996. "Multiculturalism and Melange." In Robert K. Fullinwider (ed.), *Public Education in a Multicultural Society*, pp. 90–118. Cambridge: Cambridge University Press.

Walzer, Michael. 1983. *Spheres of Justice: A Defense of Pluralism and Equality*. New York: Basic Books.

Young, Iris Marion. 1990. *Justice and the Politics of Difference*. Princeton: Princeton University Press.

————. 1997. "A Multicultural Continuum: A Critique of Will Kymlicka's Ethnic-Nation Dichotomy." *Constellations* 4(1): 48–53.

CHAPTER TWELVE

Integration Policy and Integration Research in Europe: A Review and Critique

ADRIAN FAVELL

DESPITE THE QUANTITY of research on postwar immigration in Europe, there are in fact no fully satisfactory examples of cross-national comparative research on the integration of immigrants, able to span the different experiences and national conceptualizations of such complex processes of social change in European countries. Why is this? How can research on this question be developed? Drawing on my research and experience in four western European coun-

This chapter is a shortened version of a sixty-page report presented to the Carnegie Comparative Citizenship Project in 1999. The longer version will be available as a working paper. My argument owes a great deal to the many informal conversations I have had with friends and colleagues on the subject, and their own views of the academic research field in which we work. In particular I would like to acknowledge discussions with Karen Phalet (Utrecht), Virginie Guiraudon (CNRS, Lille), Cristiano Codagnone (Milan), Patrick Simon (INED, Paris), Michaèl Bommes (Osnabrück), Marc Swyngedouw, Dirk Jacobs, and Hassan Bousetta (Katholieke Universiteit Brussel), Marco Martiniello (Liège), and Ruba Salih, Bruno Riccio, and Ralph Grillo at the Sussex Centre for Migration Research, who have helped me to piece together different parts of the argument presented here. The revised version benefited greatly from discussions with colleagues at the original Carnegie meeting in Lisbon in June 1999, a meeting of "hard core" survey-based social mobility researchers at the European Science Foundation/European Consortium for Sociological Research conference, September 1999, at Obernai: "Migration and Ethnic Relations in Europe," organized by Hartmut Esser; and, in the same week, a much more qualitative, anthropological conference of the ESRC Transnational Communities program, organized at Sussex. I am also grateful for an invitation to discuss the work in progress at the Ethnobarometer conference at Castel Gandolfo, Rome, June 1999, and to Michèle Lamont, Will Kymlicka, Rainer Bauböck, Pnina Werbner, Thomas Faist, Stephen Castles, Yngve Lithman, Tariq Modood, Michael Banton, and the editors for their suggestions and early sight of new or unpublished research.

tries—Belgium, France, Britain, and the Netherlands—with additional reference to Austria, Germany, and Scandinavia, I review current European integration research. My aim is not simply to synthesize studies of integration strategies in these different countries, with a view to pinpointing best practices, since
a conventional policy report might do this. Rather, I seek to discuss the relation
between academic knowledge and policy constructions in this field to show
how nearly all current thinking on integration (and such associated concepts as
assimilation, incorporation, and inclusion) in Europe is bound up within a reproduction of nation-state-centered and nation-society-centered reasoning. Such
forms of reasoning increasingly fail to represent the evolving relation between
new migrants or ethnic minorities and their host societies.

To break with these restrictions, we need to conceive of doing research that
reduces the nation-state or nation-society to one of several potential structuring
variables that explain the actions of immigrants and minorities and their interaction with existing European populations. After looking at the deep theoretical
features of thinking on integration and at how a cross-national and transatlantic
research agenda has developed on the subject, I show how the (sometimes hidden) framing of the integration paradigm can be seen equally in commissioned
research on immigration politics and policy in Europe and in current national
survey- and census-based studies on the behavior, identities, and social mobility
of immigrant populations. I also attempt to put into practice a thoroughly reflexive approach to sociological work in this area, paying close attention to political
and social contexts and the material conditions of production that have caused
certain types of research and policy intervention to be made.[1]

Integration in Theory and Practice

There is no shortage of comparative and national research on integration
policies in western Europe. The most straightforward overview would be one
that synthesizes various findings and produces a checklist of the policies of
various countries and an evaluation of their relative effectiveness. Issues of
immigration and integration, however, are formulated in distinct, context-
specific ways across Europe. We might learn as much if not more about the
range of integration strategies and policy thinking in Europe by examining in
each case why the work was produced and under what conditions particular
framings of the question have become dominant.

---

1. My approach is influenced by the idea of reflexive sociology developed by Pierre Bourdieu
and expounded by Loic Wacquant (see Bourdieu and Wacquant, 1992 and 1999, on Anglo-
American approaches to race and multiculturalism).

Our starting point is the image of individual bounded nation-states in Europe, each facing more or less similar questions about the integration of ethnic minorities and immigrants who mostly arrived as a result of postwar immigration. At different stages in this long migration-settlement process, each country has been faced with implementing a series of provisions, policies, and social interventions that together might constitute an integration policy. These may include:
—basic legal and social protection
—formal naturalization and citizenship (or residence-based) rights
—antidiscrimination laws
—positive action toward equal opportunities
—corporatist and associational structures for immigrant and ethnic organizations
—redistribution of targeted socioeconomic funds for minorities in deprived areas
—policy on public housing
—policy on law and order
—agreements with foreign countries about military service
—multicultural education policy
—special sections within political parties
—policies and laws on tolerating cultural practices
—cultural funding for ethnic associations and religious organizations
—language and cultural courses in host society's culture[2]
What should be asked first is how and why this disparate range of state policies, laws, local initiatives, and societal dispositions—which could be implemented by many agencies at many levels—comes to be thought of as a single nation-state's overall strategy or policy of *integration*. Who or what is integrating whom and with what? This is by no means an obvious question, unless we consider, as many social scientists do, *the state* and *a society* as the unproblematic, unchallenged backdrops to these debates and processes. When political actors and policy intellectuals talk about integration, they are inevitably thinking about integration into one, single, indivisible (national) state, and one, simple, unitary (national) society. But it is precisely the assumptions behind these terms that need to be examined. Political language is performative: to invoke these conceptions is to attempt to *create* the phenomenon of which they are speaking.

What assumptions does the concept *integration* contain? To talk of integration is to envisage a policy that is distinct from immigration policy per se—

2. See Kymlicka (1995, 37–38); Soysal (1994, 79–82); Guiraudon (1997, 25); Vertovec (1997, 61–62).

such things as border control or rights of entry and abode. It accepts some idea of permanent settlement and deals with and tries to distinguish a later stage in a coherent societal process: the consequences of immigration. It is also a term that partially builds its success on swallowing up other similar, but more precise, partial, or politically unfashionable terms for the same type of process: such terms as *assimilation, absorption, acculturation, accommodation, incorporation, inclusion, participation, cohesion, enfranchisement,* or *toleration.* With a few exceptions, integration policies and provisions are interventions taken to be almost exclusively the province of a nation-state or of more local agencies of the state. The institutions of the European Union (EU), for example—which is involved in many other substantive areas of policy in Europe and which builds its own dynamics around a different use of the same term—is almost wholly excluded in the current treaties from any of the types of integration intervention I have listed here.

By the end of the 1980s in most western European countries a dominant discourse on integration had emerged as an overarching framework for the various types of policies and practices toward immigrants and minorities being experimented with by actors and agencies in all sectors of society.[3] This emergence as the widest possible conceptual consensus invariably followed a period in which older assimilationist ideas vied with the post-1960s' inheritance of ideas about cultural differences and the antiracist struggle, and in which integration became a comfortable, sensible position for the center trying to distinguish itself from xenophobic nationalism on the one hand, and radical antisystem discourses on the other. On one level, the success of a term like this can be said to be superficial, like jargon that is picked up as default language when other arguments become unfashionable or distorted by political usage. Integration, however, has thus far appeared impervious to these problems. Even among academics it is rarely problematized or examined when it is used as a conceptual shorthand. Its effectiveness seems to lie in the fact that it best fits the unde-

---

3. Britain has essentially worked within an *integration* framework since the then–Home Office minister Roy Jenkins's famous speech of 1966 (see Favell, 1998a, 104ff). For reasons of political distinction, many antiracist commentators rejected the term from the 1970s onward, and the term is still seen by some as having a vaguely "incorrect" air about it. It remains, however, widely used in political discussions and is enjoying an academic comeback. French policy intellectuals constructed a conceptual consensus on *intégration* in the mid- to late 1990s, charting it as a consensus term, although it is still sometimes used interchangeably with *assimilation* and *insertion.* The Dutch similarly converged on it in the 1990s as a reaction against excessive cultural differentialism in their original "pillars-based" approach. Belgians on both sides of the country refer to the term as the natural goal of social policies, although they may differ in the details of its application, according to which of the French or "Anglo" influences is uppermost. Elsewhere, in Germany, Austria, Scandinavia, Switzerland, Italy, and Spain, the word is currently widely used.

fined, progressive-minded conceptual space gestured to when academics talk about the (counterfactual) goal of successful interethnic relations or a less dysfunctional multicultural or multiracial society. In this respect, its polar opposite is so obviously bad as to almost force us to accept integration as a necessity. *Disintegration* is one of the most chilling descriptive terms about society (as it is for persons), evoking a disaster striking at an almost molecular level (an imperative that is not felt with quite the same force with *incohesion, disenfranchisement*, or *intolerance*, for example). Crucially, too, in relation to such terms as *assimilation, integration* sounds like a complex, two-way or multiple process to evoke change that is somehow mutual and organic.

Integration also works well as a popular public concept because of its allusion to more long-standing theories and ideas about the nature of modern society. One area where the sociological thinking of the twentieth century has had a deep effect on the self-consciousness of how Western society thinks about itself as a collectivity (with collective *agency*) is in the almost essential link that *society* and *societal integration* are taken to have. The discipline of sociology as a mode of reflection about the world has emerged from the construction of society as a unified, functioning whole as its overall *object* of inquiry. This link, and hence the raison d'être of the discipline, is driven by a fear of the logical alternative: the Hobbesian subconsciousness of a societal breakdown and the war of all against all.[4] The inheritance of Durkheimianism can here be pointed out, filtered in the United States through the systematizing work of Talcott Parsons (1937) as the core representative U.S. social theorist of the twentieth century. Even where conflict is seen to be a fundamental part of Western society, it is accepted as an almost logical truism, that underlying this, there has to be a level of integration, or else. In other words, behind social competition and the organic division of labor, class, social distinction, and so on, the thinking goes, there has to be some kind of value integration somewhere, probably on a normative moral level as Parsons imagined it, but at least embedded in political, economic, or legal structures common to all.[5] The alter-

4. It is significant that the nightmare scenario of the sociological "subconscious" should be the anarchic, individualistic one (this reflects the dominantly Americanized nature of our thinking about society without integration) rather than other states of nature, whether dystopian (the Freudian primordialism behind civilization), or utopian (the Lockean spontaneous community or the Rousseauian and Marxist sense of man in nature before alienation, for example).

5. Older sociological discussions on integration theories versus conflict/power theories of society are still the essential intellectual backdrop for these discussions. For debates about Parsons and the Hobbesian dilemma, including contributions by Lockwood, Rex, and Giddens, see Worsley (1970); see also Haferkamp and Smelser's (1992), and Alexander's (1987), discussion of Rex. Only German sociology on migration continues to reflect these absolutely fundamental questions; without it, a lot of the discussions on integration are hopelessly superficial. My own understanding of the question owes most to the teaching of Pizzorno: see, e.g., 1991.

native is anomie and dysfunctional social forms. These symptoms of break-down, of societal failure, then become the prime empirical material of sociolo-gists, who are thus ultimately driven by a reconstructive urge to provide the useful knowledge by which these fundamental social problems can be answered (in policy). Through some such logic, the commonsense public theory, that integration is at some level a precondition of any society, converges with the other most pervasive public theory of our times: that of legal or political consti-tutionalism.[6] Crucially, they are both hierarchical visions: state-centered and bounded, in which society is able to act upon itself through the agency of gov-ernment and policy making. The idea that society might function without such methods of intervention—without integration of some kind—is not easily broached, just as it is not easy to imagine political life without a state. To do so would be to counterpoise integration, not with conflict and disintegration, but with something much harder to grasp: the disengagement and the decoupling of distinct social systems in or across societies that are somehow able to coexist but that do not necessarily conflict because they do not always interact. For obvious reasons to do with their roles in the maintenance and reproduction of the state, and with the state-society relation they depend on, this is not some-thing a politician or Supreme Court judge is ever likely to talk about.

It is perhaps not surprising that state actors have to speak positively about the possibility and goal of societal integration, but it is interesting that academ-ics in the 1980s and 1990s also adopted the same kind of discourse and under-lying logic, offering a similar state-centric (re-)constructive attitude toward fun-damental social thought, which reimagines social unity or cohesion out of di-versity and conflict. In reading the citizenship and multicultural theorists of the present day, we need constant reminding that they are not speaking from the same social location as the politicians, judges, and bureaucrats who actually make decisions and implement policies. Given their officially autonomous sta-tus in liberal democracy as free-thinking intellectuals, there is no reason why they should have to worry about getting involved in heteronomous, pseudopolicy

6. Of which the most influential public theory is that of Rawls, 1971, 1993, and followers: see Mulhall and Swift (1992) and Kymlicka (1989) for applications to questions of integration/citi-zenship. What is most significant is that the great German inheritor of the social theoretical tradi-tion, Habermas, has now himself converged with the Rawlsian normative paradigm: see Habermas (1995, 1996); Rawls (1995). His constitutional patriotism is the epitome of the Left–liberal col-lapsing of social theory and sociology into normative political philosophy characteristic of so much current reflection on the subject. Symptoms of the normative urge for usefulness that drives most studies are the fact that many of the most significant commentators actually come from a philosophical background (i.e., Kymlicka, Bauböck, or Modood) and that in the current climate, many of the best empirical commentators, such as Stephen Castles, invariably frame their work in normative terms and in concerns over citizenship or democracy (i.e., Castles and Davidson, 2000). See my discussion of the transatlantic field of multicultural citizenship (Favell, 1999).

prescriptions about the building of a better society, instead, say, of engaging in a critique of the fundamental blind spots and self-delusions of those who actually do have this power. Once upon a time, when Marxists roamed the Earth, the academic's vocation was taken to be critical, to refuse hegemony, and to denounce power. In ethnic, racial, and migration studies, they tried to show how the world system was built on colonialism and racial exploitation; how the political economy of western Europe generated exploitative immigration to the continent; how race relations policies masked internal colonialism; how multicultural citizenship subordinates and tames difference with a Western bureaucratic state logic. These days, those who are most successful are far more likely to be chasing after ethnic relations policy consultancies, writing minority rights constitutions for obscure African states, compiling Organization for Economic Cooperation and Development (OECD) reports on world migration, or offering advice about the Balkans to politicians on CNN. One by one, prominent academic voices have been incorporated into the wider, state-sponsored production of practical knowledge. Those who are less successful in the real world of politics and policy making, meanwhile, ally their radical, critical stance with activist identity politics and social movement campaigns (and the urban style alternative publishing market that thrives on it), a cooption equally destructive of academic autonomy and authority.[7]

The institutionalization of this academic field has produced a genuinely constructive turn toward the object of social thought: a multiracial or multicultural society, and to the practical problems it can be seen to have. Academics have

7. The evolving field of British ethnic and racial studies is a case in point here that is worth exploring. Earlier studies were inspired by one of two things. The first came out of an activist antiracist tradition, mediated through a critical Marxist or Marxist-Weberian sociological perspective. It began as a critical current, which over time increasingly became coopted into official policy circles and semi-autonomous research institutes keen to use academic work in the development of British race relations, creating in the process a "canon" of policy-relevant sociological research. The influence of John Rex (i.e., 1967, 1970) was paramount, and the evolution of the field can be traced through the numerous people who followed his work (or, indeed, worked with him), only to then build their own distinctive positions through criticism and the rejection of it (i.e., Malcolm Cross, Harry Goulbourne, Robert Miles, Tariq Modood, Robert Moore, John Solomos, John Stone, Sally Tomlinson, John Wrench, Steve Vertovec). Other influential early constructions of the empirical subject were seen in the work of Michael Banton, director of the first officially funded research center at Bristol, which afterward moved to Aston and then to Warwick (see also Banton, 1955, 1967); the Institute of Race Relations' seminal report, *Colour and Citizenship* (Rose, 1969); and the anthropological collection of studies on different ethnic groups in Britain, *Between Two Cultures* (Watson, 1977). As historical milestones, these studies are striking in showing how the construction of data and concepts of the migration and settlement of postwar immigrants to Britain in the early period resemble much of the work now being done elsewhere in Europe (see Solomos and Back, 1996, which is a useful guide to the evolution of British work on race and racism from this point on, offering an intelligent defense of why British work evolved in this way, as well as an internal guide to a field symptomatically limited to

reconceived their role as offering a counterfactual metadiscourse on policy making for the good of society, one that mirrors the more inclusive and supportive attitude of the state toward including ideas from these origins in the policy process. Intellectuals themselves have thus increasingly engaged in imagining a progressive (future) reality, rather than in unmasking the corruption and lies of the present, with a performative discourse about integration that seeks to theorize social possibility rather than offer a denunciatory counterdiscourse (about power, domination, exploitation, etc.). Such a role is also a self-styled interpretative role, reconstructing history as a movement toward

---

British-centric notions and debates). A second current of work, which almost had a separate but much more international life to it, was that based on Marxist political economy, epitomized by Castles and Kosack's (1973) unsurpassed early comparative study of migrant workers in Europe. Although a major breakthrough in the formulation of international questions, the work had probably more impact outside Britain than in Britain and outside the subfield of race relations and was an approach left behind to some extent by its authors at a later stage. The cultural turn of the early 1980s revealed a "new racism" and gave rise to a new generation of critical works using cultural studies approaches that attacked the canon mentioned above but did not break out of its British-centric limitations. Central to this were the Centre for Contemporary Cultural Studies (1982), Paul Gilroy (1987), and, above all, Stuart Hall (1992), the godfather of the movement. The rise of cultural studies—alongside the new and highly politicized gender- and identity-based studies of race and ethnicity—has fragmented and all but destroyed the original sociological foundations of the field in Britain (although Rex continues to be a key figure in countries with strong sociological traditions, such as Germany). The story of the rise and fall of the Centre for Research in Ethnic Relations (CRER) at Warwick—which split along exactly these lines—crystallizes this intellectual genesis. The center was initially headed by Rex and nurtured many of the leading figures mentioned above. However, caught between its growing policy-oriented role and the increasing radicalization of cultural studies approaches, the center fell apart in the mid-1990s. The center has tried to find a new research identity through "Europeanizing" itself on the new comparative (and EU-funded) wave—as so many other research centers have done—but is a now a shadow of its former importance. Cultural studies approaches, meanwhile, thrive everywhere in Britain, with little or no connection to other current European or North American work in the field. These approaches are, of course, useless for policy purposes, but they have become an extremely strong form of academic production because of their fashionable ability to cross over outside academia into the urban lifestyle markets. English-language publishing houses such as Routledge and Sage have thus had a dramatic effect in the redefining and hollowing out of sociology as a discipline, as it dilutes further into cultural, media, communications, gender, and identity studies. This process is exacerbated by the increasingly market-oriented dynamics of university teaching, which forces syllabi to compete for students with fashionable subjects that focus on the students' own identity concerns and lifestyle preferences. Self-styled marginal and radical approaches have thus, ironically, in the current British professorial generation, become the complacent mainstream. As academics are increasingly forced to compete for policy research money as part of international research networks, it is likely that the cultural studies approach will fade again, in proportion to the growing demand for credible comparative work—in a more "conventional" social scientific style—on the subject. In this sense, work will have to return to reconsidering some of the discarded ways of the past and may in fact prove to be a case of "back to the future." This is the reverse of what British academics on the subject like to think—that it is the rest of Europe that is behind in its understanding of race-ethnic relations.

something better, in which a progressive intellectual position in aligned with progressive political currents in the society.[8]

My point here is not to glorify the good old days of Marxism. Rather it is to emphasize the shifting role of the intellectual in relation to the social power of intellectual work in the nation-state context and to suggest how that has both disciplined and constrained their output, as a necessary condition perhaps for producing more engaged and socially meaningful work for others. As a system of thought, the progressive integration *paradigm*—of trying to imagine how Western societies will deal with their ethnic dilemmas and achieve social cohesion under conditions of cultural diversity and conflict—has forced a pragmatic discipline on thinking that has to also follow the logic of the mainstream integration discourse.[9] This normatively engaged mode of thinking about the problem of multicultural society has thus become the ubiquitous, apparently unavoidable, medium of progressive, constructive social thinking everywhere in the 1980s and 1990s: the idea of *citizenship*.[10]

The key challenge of this mode of thinking—in practical terms that make it meaningful as a policy contribution—is to try to reconcile this rectifying impulse with recognition that there are always going to be de facto inequalities in society. The academic thus must engage in conceiving of a just *equality of opportunity* that allows for special provisions and protection for the disadvantaged but does not threaten the underlying need for common principles and rules that apply to all.[11] When linked to questions about integration or

8. The return of T. H. Marshall (1950) to everyone's theoretical agenda after the post-1989 collapse of the Marxist paradigm (which pushed the Left to look around for a new one), is emblematic of this "progressive, but constructive" turn among scholars. No matter how false his theory can be shown to be, or how limited it is to British history (see Mann, 1988), it nevertheless offers a richly performative theoretical framework that continues to inspire positive-minded academics trying to reconcile the normative and the historical and explanatory, and work with a rights and citizenship idiom (see Bulmer and Rees, 1996). The intellectual trajectory of a certain Anthony Giddens is indicative on this point: from post-Marxist critical social theorist to court intellectual and Marshallian apologist of the "third way."

9. The cue again comes from earlier developments in the United States. See, e.g., the work of Glazer (1983) as an indication of how research and policy concerns about integration have come to shadow one another so closely, in this case, in the work of one of the United States' leading experts on race and immigration.

10. Key defining contributions include Turner (1993), Kymlicka and Norman (1994), and Habermas (1992); see articles collected in van Steenburgen (1994) and Beiner (1998). What is more sinister, perhaps, is how closely these academic concerns shadow the fashion of the 1980s and 1990s in Britain, France, the Netherlands, and elsewhere of talking about citizenship in public policy debates. This coopted use of the idiom surely collapses a great deal of the critical distance needed to question why "citizenship," and why "now"?

11. Hence the basic liberal conundrum of the postwar period, whether we think of Marshall, Dahrendorf (1988), or Rawls: how to reconcile de facto inequality and the persistence of dramatic social distinctions—and the threat of destructive social conflict over this—with the idea of a

multiculturalism, the idea of citizenship thus gestures toward tolerance and the recognition of difference, openness to diversity, and even positive action or cultural rights for minorities.

The apparent inevitability of the idiom of citizenship is not surprising once social thought goes beyond Marxist critique and repositions itself to offer practical interventions in the construction of a multicultural society. What is sometimes less honestly recognized in all this, however, is that you cannot have citizenship without the social and state structures that make its various components realistic and meaningful: in historical terms, the nation-state.[12] Many thinkers in this field have begun to conceive of political and social entities beyond the nation-state. Invariably, however, this involves projecting the features of the nation-state onto a supranational construction. On this point, the recent outbreak of reflection about citizenship projected to a European level, or reconceived as postnational citizenship, seems a misguided and mistaken reading of the European project.[13] At the same time, it is far from clear that in the 1990s the nation-state exists in anything like the ideal form that Ernest Renan or T. H. Marshall imagined, except perhaps in the conceptions of those powerful social actors most embedded in the political forms that gave it its shape and power. The reproduction of ideas of integration and citizenship in academic discourse, for all their progressive veneer, thus may be just reproducing a certain vision of a unitary modern nation-state or nation-society that corresponds closely to what those who speak from a powerful position in society most want to hear, but *not* how these societies really function.[14]

---

classless, just, welfare-state-based society. The Rawlsian form of "solution" has been the triumphant default theoretical position of the current period: full citizenship with equal rights plus equality of opportunity, but individual freedom and any unequal distribution that remains compatible with these conditions (Rawls, 1971). As a legitimizing philosophy it continues to hold firm in postwar Western societies—thanks usually to a strong dose of nationalism and "solidarity" and continued economic growth. In his later work, Rawls (1993) then went on to apply the same method to the reconciliation of cultural pluralism with liberal principles of freedom and equality. Lukes (1985) offers a sympathetic but acute analysis of the seismic paradigm shift—and new moral engagement—that intellectuals have taken in leaving behind Marx for contemporary liberal political theory.

12. On this point, the historical work of Mann (1988, 1993) seems most pertinent: in showing how the recent modern nation-state has emerged to prominence and its necessary presence in any meaningful thinking about citizenship.

13. Normative European Union studies are often characterized by this projection of the EU as being in a state of becoming, in which citizenship and other nation-state functions can be redefined at a supranational level. See Meehan (1993), Weiler (1998), and Wicner (1997) for some of the most influential formulations.

14. A similar discussion of the misleading consequences of the "common sense" in migration research—which is archetypally founded on an unexamined conception of integration and an idea of sociology as dedicated to rectifying inequality—is to be found in Bommes (1998), a

Emergence of a Cross-National Comparative Field

Talking about society as a collectivity naturally leads observers to talk about the particularities of their own societies: of projecting its distinctive nature, its mode of evolution, its future development. As thinkers in the phenomenological tradition would readily point out, all talk about who "we" are depends in part on a simultaneous definition of "others," those whose differences enable us to see who we really are. We need to perceive and judge other societies in order to define our own. The urge to comparativism is, therefore, almost an epistemological necessity in all practical social thought, but it too is distorted by partiality and unequal relations of power.

This is a second important consideration in understanding current thinking on integration. For in looking at how constructive thinking on integration and citizenship has emerged in the 1980s and 1990s, the other key dimension has been the return of a North American perspective on the European situation. This dimension has always been more or less present in European thinking about itself. In an era of postwar reconstruction and the Cold War, Europeans bought into Americanization in a big way, eyeing its version of market-based universalism, personal freedom, and the paradigmatic idea of the immigrant nation or melting pot as possible solutions to its own social future. These ideas have also always been distorted by asymmetrical power relations across the Atlantic, and by Europeans' desire to define a different version of liberal democracy and the liberal market for itself. The EU emerged from this impulse as much as any other. European nations have always had a love-hate relation to outside American cultural influence, and none more so than the French. From the other side, Europe has always been seen as both the motherland of authentic cultures and the hotbed of archaic nationalisms and histories. Behind this, the United States has taken the same developmentalist attitude to Europe that it has to every other part of the globe.

In thinking about race, ethnicity, multiculturalism, or citizenship, the stock of American vocabulary has almost always been adopted uncritically by Europeans trying to understand themselves in American (and lately Canadian) terms. As I argue throughout, this has not always been the most appropriate choice of social scientific language for the study of European cases. Europeans, in fact, should be measuring their *distance* from countries that are built on immigration and from their very different social systems, not their similarities. The British, in particular, are particularly self-deluding in this sense. They often see their

---

brilliant sketch of the intellectual parameters of current research, which mainly discusses the most important work going on in Germany.

society as being closer to North America than to Europe, that place just across the sea. This in turn is reinforced by the use of the completely meaningless adjective *Anglo-Saxon* on the continent to lump English-language societies together as one type of society.

In other ways, the dominant intellectual influence of North America is abundantly clear. The very emergence of a policy-oriented sociological discipline, driven by the practical idea that the primary role of sociologists is to study, chart, and offer remedies to social inequality, owes much to the pioneering work of the Chicago school and its modeling of the social integration process in urban contexts.[15] America has thus provided Europe with its whole model of immigrant integration, ethnic studies, and race relations, and latterly the nightmare vision of ethnic and social breakdown on a scale unimagined in European cities.[16] Again, these approximations have not always been appropriate. Until the 1960s, the term *integration* in the United States was used not to talk about immigrants in American society, but the classic "American dilemma" about the United States' native black minority population. Integration was promoted as the opposite of the official black-and-white segregation practiced before the civil rights movement in many parts of the United States. It was used in sociological studies supporting the desegregation of restaurants, swimming pools, theaters, and (especially) public schools. This usage went out of favor as antiracist discourses in the United States changed.

Integration, however, has now made a comeback in the context of the new immigration of the 1980s and 1990s, as new questions of cultural accommodation and assimilation (concerning Asian and Hispanic groups, for example) have emerged at center stage. The confusion in referencing these American-inspired terms and studies in Europe lies in the fact that immigrants in Europe are usually *also* disadvantaged racial minorities. Both American literatures, therefore, have inspired European work.[17] More generally, in the Cold War

15. A story told in Bulmer's (1984) work on the Chicago school. See also Ballis-Lal (1990).

16. Classic texts by Burgess and by Park are still the building blocks of urban ethnography and urban cultural studies. It was the Chicago school characterization of migrant newcomers in northern cities, assimilating by a step-by-step process of contact-conflict-accommodation-change, that provided scholars everywhere with the problem of ethnic conflict leading to integration (or disintegration), and its ideal-type teleology. The connection with Parsonian forms of thinking about society and norms is made clear in Glazer (1976), to which Parsons contributes, alongside Gordon (1964), whose work offered the definitive sociological model of societal assimilation in the American context. This awareness of the underlying assimilatory motion of American society is currently being revived in new work by Alba et al. (1997).

17. Glazer (1999) makes the case for regarding the United States as an exceptional case. Joppke (1999), meanwhile, does a good job of relating the United States to Europe, as part of a skillful asymmetrical comparison of the United States, Germany, and Britain. In a central theoretical reference used on both sides of the Atlantic, Kymlicka (1995) also explores the conceptual

period Europe has been taught to view itself along scales of comparative civic culture and democracy defined by the United States that specify the ideal components of rights and democracy.[18] What has been interesting in recent years is how North Americans have begun to reverse this trend and have looked instead to western Europe as a source of civic value and political and social virtue, often as a reaction to the perceived social breakdown of the United States and the progress of a damaging individualism in American life.[19] There has thus been a revival in looking at Europe comparatively, as though there were something to learn there.

What Europeanist Americans find, typically, is the one thing the United States has been said to be rolling back in recent years: resilient state-institutional structures and "thick" democratic cultures of civic participation and belonging. Of course, bringing the state back *in* and rediscovering institutions have been two of the great intellectual fads of the past decade or so. Behind this movement, there has been a constructive ambition: not *only* to understand what it is that makes democracy work but, further, to ask what it is that makes multicultural citizenship work. Again, the institutional focus signals the crucial element as being the rooted, bounded, and shared context of "good" pluralist politics: the nation-state finding coherent democratic solutions to its integration dilemmas, with immigrants and minorities in Europe the main focusing issue. The evolving debate has thus concerned how nation-states have dealt with citizenship and integration problems for immigrants and ethnic minorities, seeking to distinguish between generically different national approaches and states of development across Europe. It has then sought to offer prescriptive suggestions about the potential treatment of immigrants vis-à-vis what might be conceived of as the full complement of citizenship rights in a revamped Marshallian scheme.

Although there are European exceptions—which in the early 1980s took their cue from the growing realization that Western states had wrongly as-

---

differences between indigenous or national minorities and ethnically diverse immigrant populations, drawing important normative conclusions for citizenship from the distinction.

18. E.g., in the classic "civic culture" literature of the 1950s and 1960s, in which the United States as an ideal type is compared with other European and non-European examples of democracies (i.e., Almond and Verba, 1963).

19. I discuss the underlying origins of concerns expressed by, e.g., Bellah et al. (1985), Schlesinger (1992), and Putnam (1993), linking them to the reemergent transatlantic citizenship research agenda (Favell, 1998b) . A slightly different aspect of the new Europhilia among American Europeanists is the wave of interest in European Union studies. This is also an institutionalist movement in significant respects, but it draws strength from the obvious attraction of American academics to the EU as a cosmopolitan, postnational project, something doubtful in the actual workings and dynamics of the EU.

sumed that earlier immigrant workers would ultimately return home[20]—the true source of this comparative perspective has been through the work of North American–based scholars able to stand outside nationally bounded European self-perceptions and interests. These innovations aside, the European scene at a national level has often remained dominated by narrowly national perspectives that follow predominantly local political debates. These perspectives persist despite growing external and cross-national influences.

The first and most obvious step was the formulation of cross-national European comparisons of "models": institutionalized state practices, rooted in nationally distinct historical cultures or idioms.[21] This in itself takes its cue from the older civic culture–type literature, which focused on identifying the national cultural bases of democratic political behavior. The opening up of this perspective has been crucial in forcing nationally located points of view to encounter other works grounded in autonomous academic disciplines, such as history, political science, geography, and sociology. In other words, it has given the field both interdisciplinary width and historical depth. For once, comparative method, coupled with sensitivity toward the problems of interpretative comparativism, could be seen to ground cross-national understandings of national differences. This was quite a change from the perspectival influences of national policy contexts and self-comparisons.

Arguably, the result has been the creation of a genuine cross-national comparative research program with scientifically productive internal theoretical debates and an evolving common frame of reference. All scholars working within it, both North American and European, have been aware of that frame of reference. Although its central paradigmatic idea of nation-states and changing citizenship has been fought over and challenged, the basic paradigm and terms of reference have remained.[22] As such, the work we have seen flowering in this area has been richly strengthened by cross-Atlantic exchanges, conferences, and affiliations. Many of the scholars are Europeans who have been educated in North America, have been strongly influenced by North American education at some point, or are American Europhiles, highly active in such associations as the Council for European Studies and with the many exchange programs connected with leading Europeanist centers in the United States and Canada.

20. The two pioneering European works in this respect are Hammar's early work (1985) and Castles et al. (1984).

21. On this, see the pioneering work of Brubaker (1992) and the original collection of scholars he put together (1989). The involvement of Hammar (1990) was also crucial.

22. Joppke (1998) offers the best overview of this research program.

Some of the initial value judgments of the "models" approach might be considered a little superficial.[23] The important thing, however, has been to inspire an evolving set of intellectual responses to an initially limited conceptual framework. Thus the intellectual starting point of generic historical or cultural models has been challenged by more contemporary, political science–grounded explanations of party politics and policy making.[24] Local-level focused studies have been able to point out discrepancies between national rhetoric and local practice.[25] The institutionalist slant has led to more complex studies of mobilization, participation, and contestation of these state frameworks.[26] Further, the idea of models was extended by classifying national differences by typologies of incorporation regimes.[27] In more recent years, a crossover has been made with other studies of welfare state regimes, exploring complex indices of rights

23. E.g., the now tediously well-trodden distinction between "civic" France and "ethnic" Germany. The citizenship models approach can be found everywhere, above all in the edited collections that divide the subject by national case studies within a common comparative framework. For an archetypal collection, see Baldwin-Edwards and Schain (1994). Typical works that try to elaborate on the models theme are Castles (1995) and Bryant (1997), and the approach—needless to say—has been popular among French scholars who defend the French *modèle,* see, e.g., Schnapper (1992) and Todd (1994). When the discussion is comparative in this context, it often breaks down into fruitless polemical standoffs. In the context of trying to synthesize an ideal model of European citizenship, large public funds have also been invested in comparative projects compiling information on national models of citizenship: see Preuß (1995), research similar to another project (with impressive international network and backers) being headed by Richard Bellamy at Reading ("European Citizenship and the Social and Political Integration of the European Union"; <http://www.rdg.ac.uk/AcaDepts/lp/PolIR>). This also produced another series of reports on national models of citizenship, naturalization, and nationhood in its first stages. Carnegie's comparative citizenship project compiled a similar overview of citizenship practices in Western societies and elsewhere in its first stage. There has thus been rather a lot of duplication of effort in many of these large-scale descriptive projects all this, without mentioning the rafts of master of arts and doctoral dissertations that have been launched by the citizenship models' starting point.

24. See, e.g., Freeman (1995), Guiraudon (1997, 1998), Feldblum (1999), Favell (1997), and Joppke (1999). This latest study, which sits at the end of a decade of such work, illustrates an emerging problem in this public policy–focused scholarship: that it can be done entirely through the discussion of secondary political debates and attendant scholarship; and that debate about immigration, citizenship, and integration issues can occur with little focus on the behavior of immigrant groups themselves, actual migration patterns, or theories of migration. By way of contrast, see the comparative policy framework set up from a bottom-up perspective (using migration patterns, postindustrial transformation, and urban theory as starting points) by migration scholars Carmon (1996), Marcuse (1996), and Weiner (1996), in Carmon (1996).

25. Good examples are the arguments put forward by Lapeyronnie (1992) and Schain (1999).

26. Ireland's 1994 comparison of cities in France and Switzerland was a major breakthrough. See also Bousetta (1997, 1999) and work under the UNESCO Management of Social Transformations program (MOST), headed amongst others by Vertovec (1999). See their web site <www.unesco.org/most>; see also Kastoryano (1997).

27. In its most well-known formulation by Soysal (1994).

and incorporation along a variety of scales.[28] Finally, Europeans have responded with the development of more thoroughly self-reflexive studies about how policy knowledge and constructions have been produced, tracing the accumulation of the institutional effects of these constructions, which often overlap and flow into the construction of public perceptions of the subject.[29]

Throughout, the interaction with the ever-stronger political-philosophical reflection on citizenship and multiculturalism has developed, often leading to a strong overt or covert normative flavor to otherwise comparative social scientific projects. Again, the North American—and in particular Canadian—influence has been paramount.[30] As might be expected, these transatlantic concerns have self-confidently translated themselves from what has been a successful emerging academic subfield into direct policy and public intellectual work for many of the scholars involved.

Commissioned Studies on Integration Policy

Although it may ultimately be a matter for the history of ideas to chart the underlying intellectual reasons why a growing number of scholars have been asking these constructive integration and citizenship questions in the 1980s and 1990s, the material and contextual reasons for such interests having been generated in cross-national comparative research are fairly clear.

Although less central to party politics and government agendas than are issues of macroeconomic policy, the future of the welfare state, or of regional development and devolution (for example), ethnic minority and immigrant integration—

28. Janoski and Glennie (1995) looked at the extension of naturalization rights in this light, followed by Janoski's monumental synthesis of citizenship rights and incorporation indices (1998), which builds on Esping-Anderson (1990).

29. See, e.g., the work of Alund and Schierup (1991), Martiniello (1992), Rath (1991), Favell, (1998a), Blommaert and Verschueren (1998), and Castles (2000). The "paradoxes of multiculturalism" these authors identify are linked to the fact that in each case the society incorrectly assumes it can seize itself from above as a collectivity and change itself through new hierarchical structures (policy, law, etc.) alone. This "minorization" (as Rath calls it), where it occurs, typically also has significant perverse effects; e.g., institutionalizing policies also enables the policy sector to be seized by other policy actors for their own social power struggles: hence, there is the pervasive and distorting presence of go-between advocates and coopted ethnic minority leaders in the "representation" of minority or migrant interests.

30. The massive readership of Kymlicka's work (1995) is of course the most dramatic instance of this. In addition, the work of Taylor (1992) has been read widely outside philosophical circles. See the collection of articles in Bciner (1998) for the state of the art with a Canadian slant. Kymlicka is exceptional among the leading philosophical voices in translating his work into genuinely policy-directed applications, going on to do reports on integration for the Canadian government (1998), and also reflecting on the applications to minority rights questions elsewhere, such as eastern Europe (2000).

and the multicultural questions surrounding it—have risen significantly on the political agenda everywhere in the past twenty-five years. In parallel to the evolving philosophical and sociological debates about citizenship, the question has come to be seen as an essential element of policy thinking about the future of liberal democracy and the distinctive possibilities of freedom and equality it may offer beyond mononational conceptions of the nation. The treatment and accommodation of minorities and strangers are seen to be something that liberal democracy, of all the systems of political organization, does best. Indeed, it is widely assumed to be a defining trait of liberal democracy.[31]

National governments themselves have thus generated a public research agenda around these questions, as well as direct policy and political debates. This has led to media activity and the involvement of other actors in the policy process. And, of course, it has sponsored the involvement and cooption of prominent academic scholars who are willing to cross the line and take on the role of public intellectual in one of the various channels of policy thinking. In a parallel learning curve to that achieved by academics who have broadened their intellectual resources by looking comparatively across nations, European states have themselves developed a desire for cross-national self-comparison *within* Europe. In and of itself this does not necessarily produce fair-minded, nonperspectival thinking by public figures. At the early stages of developing public knowledge on the subject, this urge to make comparisons is often a self-justificatory reflex. It is driven by an instinct to defend the culturally distinct national ways of doing things that seeks to improve itself by pointing to negative contrasts in foreign countries as part of the study. Many examples of such argumentation can be found in leading countries with the most developed immigration and integration policies, often with a goal along the way to affirm the link between those policies and a particular national idea of citizenship or idea of democracy.[32]

31. It is by no means certain that this is true. The most genuinely "multicultural" societies (in terms of cultural exchange and conflict not structured uniquely by a dominant nation-state) have historically been within nondemocratic "empires" (see discussion in Brubaker, 1995, and Grillo, 1998). This follows from any power-based conceptualization of multicultural relations of exchange (which I also work with) once it is detached from the normative nation-state-society integration framework of other studies. Another consequence is to push most conventional normative liberal democrats back to a straightforward defense of the (in fact) assimiliatory nation-state as the grounding for liberal philosophies of justice, equality, or "cultural pluralism": a sample of such "honest" forms of liberalism are Miller (1995), Goulbourne (1991), Crowley (1998), Hansen (1998), and Weil (1996).

32. Countless examples of negative comments about the approaches of other countries or flattering self-comparisons could be found in official British, French, Dutch, or Scandinavian policy statements and formulations. This is much less the case in countries that, for various reasons, are more self-questioning or angst-ridden about their own national "philosophies of integra-

The widening scope of policy thinking that encourages such cross-national initiatives also leads to new contacts with foreign counterparts that expand the national legal, political, and bureaucratic policy community. As one can readily tell from the rapid international involvements of the Blair government in Britain, one of the big benefits of election to power is the opportunity to engage in cross-national networking and synergy building that would simply not be possible when one is not in power. In addition, it can be hoped that the parties might remove national blinkers and engage in cross-national *policy learning* while they are fraternizing. The famous example here, of course, is the "liberal hour" in 1960s' race relations thinking in Britain, and the Wilson administration's courting of the American civil rights movement in order to import ideas and moral justifications into Britain's proposed race relations legislation.[33]

To engage in such an import of foreign ideas can prove to be not only practical but also a clear strategy to divert responsibility for the justification of ideas away from the smaller country's national political traditions and discourses. The weak position of exchange between European nations and the United States has in fact enabled European governments to pursue potentially unpopular legislation under the cover of unequal superpower relations, in which they attempt a *self-assimilation* of national particularities to the outside, "universal" moral and political model of North American *civilization*.[34] The unequal transnational relations of power dictate that any common transatlantic agenda will ultimately remain a peculiar one, despite the growth in comparative knowledge of this kind. The asymmetric power relations distort an equal exchange of ideas, and Europeans are often likely to end up uncomfortably trying to implement American ideas and conceptualizations that do not necessarily fit the immigration and integration issues most salient in the European context.[35]

---

tion," such as Germany, Belgium, and Italy. Intellectuals in these countries are also often spectacularly critical and damning about their own country's policy shortcomings on immigration and integration. In Italy and Belgium, intellectual despair is almost a national sport.

33. See work by Bleich (1998) and Hansen (2000). The theoretical paradigm for thinking about the role of ideas in policy making was developed by Peter Hall (1993), who has been involved as a supervisor in several recent contributions to the comparative immigration politics field.

34. I discuss the pathologies associated with Britain's self-assimilation of its race relations paradigm with America's (Favell, 1998a, 121–24).

35. The Carnegie Endowment, the Ford Foundation, the Marshall Fund, and others have all become involved in funding large cross-Atlantic research projects on immigration, citizenship, and ethnic relations in recent years, and there has never before been such a level of transatlantic policy consultation on the subject. The collection of Cornelius et al. (1994) is a typical example of the products of these initiatives. A good example of the asymmetry involved is the Metropolis Project, funded copiously by the Canadian government on one side but with scant resources on the European side. What is troubling are the slightly warped reasons why academics get involved in such activities, which are financially rewarding but do not entail real influence on the policy

An arguably more equitable venue for the cross-national exchange of ideas in European policy thinking has emerged under the sponsorship of the European Union. Bilateral relations between states in the EU are so heavily institutionalized as a competition between equals that it precludes states projecting themselves into a weaker "learning" role. This giving up of "sovereignty" (as the learning or policy-justification process is constructed in public discussion), however, may be accepted if part of a wider pan-European cooperative effort. The common history and similarity of European societies should dictate that they have much more to learn from one another than from such a different society as the United States.

The central difficulty in relation to advancing cooperative research on immigrant integration lies in the European Union's officially having little competence or jurisdiction over those state policies that make up the domain of integration policy. This is not surprising given that nearly all these kinds of policies are traditionally linked to nation-building operations. Opportunities for cross-national thinking have therefore more easily arisen in much less progressive areas in the strongly emerging security agenda on cooperative, but restrictive, immigration policy in the EU, in the security-building "compensatory measures" for dealing with the side effects of building a free movement zone in Europe.

There has therefore been a great deal of cooperative policy thinking between home affairs officials and expert consultants on such issues such as clan-

---

process and can only be a diversion from pure academic research. On the other side, it is unclear how and where their involvement can get translated, say, into Canadian city urban policy, even allowing for the fact that something might be learned from, for example, looking descriptively at Dutch social policies or British race relations jurisprudence (which is not clear). In recent times Canadian civil servants have been trying to control the output of the Metropolis Project more strictly, but this then decreases the side benefits for other research that academics themselves may get from involvement in such projects. Another excellent example of an equally distorted, transatlantic learning process is the fascination many left-wing American social scientists have for Swedish and Dutch social and welfare policies, such as the regulation of sex work. This might be called the Amsterdam phenomenon: being attracted by something "liberal"—that is in fact unrepresentative of the way these highly controlled, conservative societies function as social systems—and using it as a "social policy other" in order to derive normative conclusions for one's own society. The phenomenon also often works in reverse: Europeans using America as a negative dystopian "other." A good example has been the follow-up research on the Modood report (discussed below), the best recent research project on immigrant social mobility in Britain. Instead of pursuing the much-needed but difficult path of cross-national European comparison, the authors have instead opted to compare the findings with those of the United States. It is hard to see how this work will avoid the usual asymmetrical distortions that render such comparisons hugely problematic. As might be expected, the first media reports of this ambitious new project (*The Guardian,* Aug. 4, 1999) immediately saw the Brits claiming how successful some ethnic minorities in Britain are when compared with the black American population, despite the blatant inappropriateness of the analogy.

destine immigration, trafficking in persons (an analogy with drug trafficking), the treatment of asylum seekers, and the uncovering of underground transnational criminal networks. Yet despite its official lack of competence on immigrant and minority integration questions, parts of European institutions have seen the area as one where it can seek to expand its influence, thereby seeking further "integration" of its own (in the EU-building sense of the word). It thus follows the classic tactic of seeking to coopt academics into its policy circles as a way for directorate generals (DGs, the main administrative units of the European Commission) to attempt to accrue new supranational powers in areas where immigrant integration issues can be said to fall: the typical ones being social policy, regional policy, culture and communications, and education and training. This in turn has generated many lines of new research for academics, who have been able to profit from them.

The Targeted Social Economic Research (TSER) program and the European Year against Racism (1997) are two examples of large policy programs that have had important benefits for academics working on issues in this area.[36] This new range of publicly funded integration research has found itself able to seek EU funding that is building a rather different learning process in cross-national policy and policy community in this area than are national groupings. The ultimate aim of the EU in getting involved in a promotional role is, of course, self-legitimization, which is why so much of the thinking in this area has been linked with bolstering the idea of democracy and "European citizenship." The enormous growth in research networks and research institutes de-

---

36. The TSER project ended up funding an impressive array of projects (either as full cross-national projects or funded international networks) that emerged from an intense bidding war between rival European academic networks. These included such subjects as police cooperation and immigration control (headed by Didier Bigo), immigrants and the informal economy (Robert Kloosterman, Jim Rath), migrants in cities (Malcolm Cross), models of European citizenship (Richard Bellamy), and comparative integration policies (Friedrich Heckmann). This latter, a large project located at the University of Bamberg (<http://www.uni-bamberg.de/efms>) is symptomatic of some of the limitations of this predominantly descriptive and documentary network-based research. Its findings are still very much located in the mainstream comparative models approach, something determined by the fact that successful networks have to be made up of well-known national representatives (in this case, for example, Dominique Schnapper for France and Rinus Penninx for the Netherlands) who are likely to have the most conventional national viewpoints (because the best-known figures are policy academics). The fact that the evaluation and selection of projects are also made by similarly established nation-by-nation figures tends to reinforce these limitations. The brief spurt of EU funding for these subjects may, however, be drying up. The new Framework V has dramatically pulled back from funding further work on immigration, integration, or exclusion questions—perhaps reflecting the specific aim of national governments to stop or gain control over discretionary spending by the commission on research and funding of NGOs—in policy sectors where there are no clear competencies at the EU level.

pendent on EU funding has been remarkable. It is a dependency that has only grown as national public funding for research has become more problematic.

The nature of this work is clearly cooptive and self-reproducing. However self-critical one is of one's relation with the EU, working within its integration agenda will inevitably draw scholars into a pro-European integration stance that seeks to diminish exclusive national-level control over these issues (although the logic of every network being made up of national representatives mitigates this tendency somewhat). Yet the benefits of this new cross-national thinking in not automatically reproducing national policy perspectives should be clear.

An additional dimension linked to this is the involvement of professional nongovernmental organizations (NGOs) in this quasi academic-commissioned work.[37] Its necessarily schematic packaging and content means that such work does not contribute much to critical knowledge about integration policies, but it can be an excellent source of descriptive facts and policy practice across national cases. What we invariably learn from such work is that there are clearly distinct national models of justifying and implementing integration strategies and that these frameworks render the idea of policy transferability to other national cases problematic. One thing this research has sustained, however, is the perception that European nation-states are converging on similar policies and problems.[38] This observation can in turn be used to sustain claims for improving rights for minorities and nonnationals across Europe by campaigners at the European level.

37. The prolific output of the Migration Policy Group (MPG), a tiny but influential NGO in Brussels, is a case in point. For two major examples of the projects that they have mounted on citizenship and integration questions, see MPG (1996) and the Vermeulen report (1997) in collaboration with the Institute for Migration and Ethnic Studies, Amsterdam. The first was a massive synthesis of roundtable discussions conducted with policy makers in five western European countries and a further handful of eastern European countries; the second, a five-nation survey of the different integration strategies and policies being used for integration policies, language, schooling, and cultural organization (in France, Britain, Belgium, Germany, and the Netherlands).

38. The MPG report (1996) offers evidence of and normative arguments for convergence (as does the Heckmann project discussed above). What is less clear is whether this convergence comes about through policy learning, isomorphism, or simply a "garbage can" choice of policy. Hansen and Weil (2000) have been putting together a massive comparison of apparent convergence in naturalization or citizenship practices across Western states under the benevolent funding of the German Marshall Fund. But what explains this convergence? We should be suspicious of arguments that suggest it is pulled by some rational "good," as well as of the functionalist consequences of allowing comparative research to be pulled by the teleological idea of harmonization, that has always been a driving rationale for the reproduction of European integration processes. See also Lapeyronnie's (1993) arguments about de facto policy convergence in Britain and France.

A slightly different inspiration and sponsor of cross-national research has been the Council of Europe in Strasbourg, which has wide interests in promoting pan-European relations and security.[39] Much of this work has explicitly sought to link integration policy research on the position of migrants and minorities across West and East, with an interest in guaranteeing human rights and standards of minority rights in the new democratizing societies of the East under the auspices of Organization for Security and Cooperation in Europe (OSCE) conventions. This thinking represents a slightly different form of internationalization, one that posits the conformity of nations to international law as the driving external force of policy progression rather than the discovery of common, convergent western European standards (which is the case with EU-funded research).

There has, however, been a growing interest in EU circles in the connections the Council of Europe makes between integration and minority rights as they relate to EU enlargement accession and the fact that eastern European candidates are being forced to accept minority rights and citizenship guarantees as part of the Agenda 2000 package. These include the Schengen *acquis,* a large and detailed body of rules that make it easier for people to move freely within the Schengen area. The East has thus become the new policy terrain for making multicultural citizenship work. The coercive way the European international community has in imposing its norms clearly suggests that more is at stake than the rights of minorities in the countries concerned. After all, Britain and France went out of their way to refuse explicitly any association of eastern European minority issues with their own internal minority conflicts, despite their problems in Northern Ireland and Corsica.[40]

An interesting consequence of the new European cooperative efforts has been the intellectual struggle over the progressive agenda at the European level: whether it should follow the British antidiscrimination focus or the French ap-

39. The best of its kind is the Bauböck report (1994a) for the Council of Europe, which is able to offer a much more panoramic and detached view than work sponsored by EU institutions. This is an entirely conceptual work that succeeds in opening up migration and integration questions in Europe to the broadest possible schema. In fact, the Council of Europe has sponsored a whole series of recent reports on dimensions of integration within the framework of the European Committee on Migration. The reports cover women and migration (1995), religion (1999), labor markets (1998), and social and political participation (1999). See also the meticulous documentary work of Michael Banton for the Council and the United Nations on minority rights and discrimination issues—which is highly skeptical of the EU—and his regular briefings in *New Community* and *Journal of Ethnic and Minority Studies*. Another international organization now beginning to sponsor research on immigrant integration is the International Labour Organization in Geneva (see Doomernik, 1998, a report that looks at economic data on labor market integration in France, the Netherlands, and Germany).

40. See the caustic account of these developments in Burgess (1999) and Chandler (1999).

proach to citizenship and equality. The British were initially suspicious of the EU's efforts to engage in antidiscrimination issues at the supranational level, arguing that the EU was likely to dilute British standards, which were in any case the best in Europe (an argument reminiscent of Scandinavian arguments about welfare provisions).[41] For many years this led to an almost contemptuous attitude by campaigners and race relation intellectuals in Britain toward the EU's initiatives in this area, but this attitude began to shift during the 1996–1997 Inter-Governmental Conference (IGC) to revise European treaties, when such strongly academic cross-national networks as the Starting Line Group and the Dutch Experts Committee on Immigration began making headway in lobbying on the antidiscrimination possibilities in the upcoming Amsterdam Treaty (e.g., the new Art. 13, which introduces an antiracist clause into antidiscrimination provisions). Their specific legal knowledge was the crucial factor in policy discussions. Blair's coming to power just before the signing of the treaty gave the green light to more concerted efforts in this direction, made more likely by the fact that little progress was being made on the issue of citizenship rights for "third-country nationals" (non-European permanent residents in Europe). The Labour party approving the setting up of the Vienna-based Monitoring Centre on Racism and Xenophobia also encouraged British activists to seek leadership in this field, pushing Anglo-Dutch ideas on antidiscrimination against the French and other conceptions.

The Austrian connection has been important in the development of large-scale surveys comparing the relative standards of integration policies and minority rights provisions. With the Austrian government itself keen to be seen as being involved in progressive efforts in this area (especially while president of the EU), Vienna has become a main center of research in this field, not least because it is the natural geographical base for NGOs (nongovernmental organizations) and IOs (international organizations) working with

---

41. The background to this has been a series of large-scale reports on antidiscrimination provisions and the attempt to rate existing provisions in different countries. The early comparative report by Forbes and Mead (1992) explicitly sets up Britain as the model in Europe, against which other European countries are measured on a declining scale. In more recent years, this message has been conveyed more openly by the Commission for Racial Equality and the Runnymede Trust in Britain, which have been conducting an audit of twenty-five years of race relations in Britain with one eye on selling this experience in a positive way to the rest of Europe. A more nuanced report, drawing on ethnographic work on employment practices and discrimination in the workplace in sixteen countries, is to be found in Wrench (1996). The external influence of ideas of antiracism, however, is having a positive effect on France, which is now beginning seriously to look at the deficiencies of its own legal mechanisms on racism, notably in the more recent reports of the official government Haut Conseil à l'Intégration, while headed by Patrick Weil.

central and eastern European countries, just as businesses have chosen to move east to Berlin.[42]

The creation of the Monitoring Centre points toward the linking of knowledge production on discrimination, racism, and minority rights with the existing machinery for producing such Euro-knowledge as the Eurobarometer surveys.[43] Reminiscent of the huge-scale postwar American civic culture and

42. Of the output has been perhaps the most ambitious comparative integration project of all: the Çinar et al. (1995) project, which puts together an index of legal and policy integration provisions and barriers in seven countries and the EU (see Waldrauch and Hofinger, 1997). This new concentration of legalistic knowledge offers a checklist of types of rights rated on a 0–1 scale, rating each country in terms of separate issues of naturalization laws, family reunification, civil, political, and social rights, and so on, giving each an overall final score of between zero and one. It remains to be seen what comes out of this work, although it is clear that locally it could have some impact on shaming the Austrian government vis-à-vis some of its European partners at a time when anti-immigration is high on the Austrian political agenda. The search for overarching schemes of comparing good practices on a common scale, often only confirms "national" stereotypes and ends up slanted toward more transparently "organized," rights-based, state-dominated societies (Austria does badly; Britain does less well than usual; the Dutch and French do better than the Germans and the Swiss; and the Belgians rate surprisingly well—on paper). Methodologically, the weaknesses of this type of survey are linked to the weaknesses of the Euro-barometer-type surveys discussed below.

43. The existing Euro-barometer surveys already contain questions on attitudes to immigration and race and questions related to citizenship and identity. One of the surveys (Euro-barometer 47.1, 1997) was devoted to these questions, sparking a new round of debate over the data and dubious methods of collection (particularly in Belgium, which apparently had high levels of self-confessed racism). It also launched a thousand research projects based on explaining it. E.g., about a dozen quantitative doctoral research projects are being coordinated on this and related projects by social psychologist Peer Scheepers at Nijmegen. There are limitations in this kind of work, and sometimes absurd conclusions are drawn by constructing such comparative knowledge from ready-made data. More often than not these data reflect what people think about themselves, not what they are. The parody of this is the Dutch declaring themselves almost totally nonracist, while the Belgians declare themselves to be 40 percent racist and then setting out, as some researchers have done, to explain why Belgians are "more" racist than the Dutch. Needless to say, we should be highly suspicious of these figures, which reflect the dramatically different self-perceptions of these two societies, and in particular of the vitriolic rhetoric of the often "racist" Flemish versus Walloon arguments. Another colleague mentioned to me how the Swedish government once commissioned such a survey on the Swedish to prove that Swedish society is not racist (which was "proved" when the survey population duly declared itself to be overwhelmingly nonracist). The self-searching paroxysm of anguish and anger over these results in Belgium is perhaps far preferable to the complacency it inspires in Sweden and the Netherlands. Recently, some French scholars—who because of the fundamental epistemological skepticism that underpins all French social science are often attuned to deeper issues of the social construction of data—have reflected critically on the Euro-barometer project (Brèchon and Cautrès, 1999). Given the overreliance in mainstream research on Euro-barometer from Inglehart (1990) onward, there is a need to put a critical spanner in the works of this cooptive European machine of knowledge production and on the masses of social science work it structures. The Ethnobarometer project (1999) offers the promise of a much-larger-scale comparison of ethnic conflicts and relations across Europe—based on regional reports around a common framework that link up with NGO activities and interventions—if it can overcome formidable methodological, logistical, and fund-

democracy indices that involved managing transitions to democracy, such work attempts to evaluate the relative level of development of European values and consciousness. Typically, it has set up a common European scale that brusquely overrides those arguments based on national distinctiveness and traditions so prevalent among national policy makers when they compare themselves with others in Europe.

While clearly extending the range and repertoire of knowledge about what each country is doing and how each is officially dealing with the problems involved, the results produced by these surveys—that country X is less racist or more tolerant than country Y because country X has better official legal provisions against discrimination and more rights than country Y—can be highly dubious as indicators of integration as such. Predictably, highly state-centered countries, with a high level of coopted academic policy production—such as the Netherlands or Sweden—often rate much higher than do disorganized and intellectually divided countries such as Belgium and Italy. Such figures, however, say nothing about the porousness of a particular national culture or about its propensity to change in relation to minority cultures. In fact, a culture such as the Dutch—which is highly coherent, nationally oriented, and difficult to understand—is in fact resistant to integration and is in some ways a much harder country for foreigners to live in freely (or uncontrolled) than, say, a less well-rated country such as Belgium.

The second problem with these studies and the knowledge they produce is equating integration and interethnic relations with official state structures such as rights, policies, legislation, and so on. Such indicators really measure only the extent to which the state succeeds in defining, controlling, and managing the phenomenon. It says little about whether this control is benevolent or highly dominating in its effects. Here again, intellectuals are involved in legitimizing a view of society to which they should in fact be offering a critique. Knowledge that is reproducing those categories and institutional schema that the state seeks to impose on ethnic relations in society is itself part of the institutional process of enforcing hierarchical state power and jurisdiction on the subject. Intellectual work thus becomes part of the process whereby institutions enforce a coercive and constraining cognitive framing of societal phenomena that perhaps should not fall into the state's domain. It turns complex societal relations and interactions into a categorized object of top-down

ing problems in putting together these surveys. The focus on ethnic conflict is significant, given that it takes the issue away from comparing policies or government discourse. One of the reasons why this work goes further is because it has been based on extensive epistemological reflection and consultation with NGOs and others in the field. See the extremely interesting reflections on this by Codagnone (1998).

"policy," creating bureaucratic norms that can be imposed on social actors on the way to becoming law.

The Dutch way of managing policy problems by funding nearly all academic production in this area—and hence turning academic research into a branch of state-sponsored knowledge construction—is one extreme on a scale that could also envisage a total disconnection between state policy thinking and the work of autonomous intellectuals. Dutch society puts such a central premium on the idea of rationally produced, informed, and structured *beleid* (policy), that nearly all leading social scientists are coopted into the system of producing policy-relevant research for social engineering purposes by numerous ministries and independent research agencies.[44] The result of this academic influence—the wonderfully well-organized schema of rights and provisions for minorities in the country—is both a measure of how seriously the state and government regard policy on integration matters and, inversely, a measure of the scale of pathological effects that such top-down hierarchical structures can have on the social situation itself, if the enormous growth of informal activities among immigrants in the Netherlands is any indication.[45]

The deeper point here is that any discussion of integration that tries to measure it by evaluating the extent of state-institutionalized organization in the country assumes a level of coercive, state-powered pressure on immigrants to conform to this framework. Given the overwhelmingly unilateral direction of social integration pressures imposed by living in a Western social system, positive, fully institutionalized indicators of integration are thus also indicators of the state-organized assimilation pressures on migrant and minority groups to conform to Western norms, which is the opposite of what multiculturalism is often thought to mean.

Survey and Census-Based Work on Integration

My overview of integration research has concentrated on works that approach the matter from the point of view of "policy," that is, of institutionalized legal and political structures in various national contexts in Europe. In a sense,

44. On questions of immigration and integration, a handful of leading academics—with distinct power bases at different universities—have vied for central influence on policy making: among the leading figures are Han Entzinger (Utrecht), Rinus Penninx (Amsterdam), and Justus Veenman (Rotterdam). These are academics who step smoothly in and out of academic and public political roles (they have on occasion been put forward for important political posts in government) and are the first to whom the intelligent press turns when there is a new political development on which to comment.

45. See the superb work by various Dutch scholars on this subject, such as Engbersen (1996), Burgers (1998), Kloosterman, van der Leun, and Rath (1998), and Rath and Kloosterman (1998).

to seek to compare integration strategies along this axis automatically reproduces many of the nation-state-structuring influences that research should try
to control as possible structural factors. Moreover, the role of academics in
structuring their interventions in this way also works to produce the tacit presence of the nation-state as the only meaningful context in which the integration
of immigrants and minorities can be discussed in practical terms. Clearly, such
an approach is one preferred by policy makers, practitioners who explicitly
seek to reproduce and enhance the nation-state in their conceptual construction
of the social problem.

The close identification of scholars with the policy makers' role, however,
is not only a curious misidentification of the role of the academic in producing
independent knowledge on the subject, it also indicates how far the material
conditions of knowledge production and the pressures of the immediate political context influence and distort the basic research program in this field. Yet
the excessive institutional focus of policy and politics-based studies can, on the
face of it, be easily sidestepped. What of the whole other range of integration
research: survey-based studies of integration perceived from the bottom up, as
it were, charting the interaction of ethnic groups with the dominant population,
their social mobility in their new host societies, and the changing perceptions
of immigrants themselves in relation to majority population opinions on the
subject?

Turning, then, to advanced behavioral attitude surveys and to social mobility and social psychological approaches to immigrant integration, what do we
find? A range of ambitious integration surveys are now beginning to emerge
from the empirical expansion of this field, owing largely to the investment of
public funding to address a subject seen to be of rising political and social
concern, and hence the recent technical possibility of doing this work. The
great advantage of survey-based work is that it explicitly seeks to reduce questions about policy frameworks, laws, legislation, and so on, to background variables. Being highly "positivist" in nature, these studies also generally refrain in
their methodologies from taking overtly ideological positions in advance about
what states should be doing from a top-down perspective to achieve policy
goals. This is usually left to an explicitly secondary stage of interpretation,
public framing, and publicity, which may lead to normative conclusions or
engagement in postpublication interventions in the media and public debates. It
is correct, then, to take the self-styled "scientific" credentials of survey-based
work seriously. It is why such work may offer more insights about actual integration processes than do policy- and politics-focused work, which often in the
final analysis has little to say about the immigrants themselves, if rather a lot
about how elites debate and understand the question. This is not to say that the

methodological choices and conceptual assumptions that survey-based studies make reflect any less the material and contextual influences that shape other types of work on the subject.

A significant limitation of survey-based work is that there are virtually no existing examples of genuine cross-national comparative work in the field, and certainly there is no elaborated source of comparable data. There is nothing like the effort of the annual OECD–SOPEMI (Système d'observation permanente des migrations) reports to compile data on migrant flows and stocks in various countries, a report that gathers data from national correspondents in each of the OECD countries.[46] The OECD report does now have a section on integration, but this is by far its weakest part, simply reproducing some of the usual debates about national models or comparative rights frameworks.

Moreover, all data on immigrant (or minority) numbers follow the vastly different conventions in each country about collecting population data. On this basis, integration—if it is so named—can be quantified only in the normatively specific and nationally rooted terms that are set up by the individual national research technologies themselves. This is the basic constraint that limits the construction of survey-based knowledge in the field. The difficulties of collecting meaningful cross-national data will be at the root of the many problems with which scholars must engage.[47] When anyone views the issue at this level, it becomes apparent just how much even the basic elements of comparison—how we categorize the populations themselves—are incommensurable because of the different ways that nation-states gather data on migrants and minorities. Some use censuses, and some do not. Censuses use very different classification schemes, ranging from ethnic self-identification to the parental country of origin and rates of naturalization to registering only those persons classified as nonnationals in the country. Who then or what are we talking about? Ethnic minorities, immigrants, aliens, foreigners, nonnationals, or third-country nationals? Do these groups self-select their identity or are their identities objectively imposed by a family link or by phenotypic category? What of mixed, ambiguous identities and dual nationalities and citizenships?[48]

46. The OECD–SOPEMI reports, detailing the latest trends in international migration (the latest in 1998), are the best we have. These are based on country-by-country reports that are not always strictly compatible. Getting actual comparative data on migration-related phenomena is immensely difficult, and they are not readily convertible from one national context to another, given the intensely political nature of the way data and knowledge are structured and produced.

47. See especially Phalet and Swyngedouw (1998, 1999a, 1999b) on these questions. Their genuinely cross-national approach to survey work on integration may be able to sidestep many of the nationally bounded problems I explore here on these questions.

48. I explore many of these issues about the construction of data and categories in France and Britain (Favell, 1998a). See also the reflections of French INED researcher Simon (1997).

Even an independently constructed survey, if it has to work with official data of any type, will find itself limited to a given external sampling frame that embodies the nation-state structuring influences embedded in the way any state counts, classifies, and controls its population. Nothing whatsoever is agreed on by researchers or state agencies that pursue these questions in the vast numbers of studies on the matter across Europe. These basic difficulties only multiply as the questions move to asking the opinions, feelings, or affiliations of particular populations, or how their behavior, actions, and choices relate to the so-called norms of the majority population.

Of course, survey works of this type are also invariably contextually aware interventions into a domestic policy debate that seek to affirm or transform assumptions about the correct currency of the debate. Because they are highbrow, scientific works, they often carry enormous prestige and weight. In this sense, they are much more significant than are the academic fields of comparative politics and public policy that are often precariously journalistic in their approaches. Crucially, the work also reflects the actual mechanical and material apparatus for conducting this work, something that in some places has recently become possible through the adaptation of national census production, for example, to allow for sensitivity to ethnic minority monitoring and analysis.[49] Again, it cannot be stressed enough how important these material conditions of production are in determining the shape of the final work. They also critically reflect the current social coalition between policy-interested actors who might be interested in the objective and scientific findings of a large-scale survey project. Although survey work is invariably inspired or forced as a progressive reaction to a current perceived social crisis or danger, it is highly significant that they are almost always conducted under such hot and pressing conditions. Recent high-profile studies on Islam and fundamentalism indicate what a dangerous fertile ground this is for sensationalist work.[50] Quality newspapers, in particular, love work of this kind when it produces shocking or anxiety-inducing "facts" from a research project that, by definition, everyday jour-

49. I discuss details of French, British, Dutch, and Belgian data collection below. As well as identifying and counting migrants or ethnic minorities, some census collections incorporate specific samples of subpopulations in other questions. One example is the longitudinal study in Britain, which traces the same small percentage of the population each time in order to trace their social trajectories and physical movements (see Fielding, 1995). Another is the anonymous sample taken in Danish surveys to cross-check for political participation (see Togeby, 1999). In both studies cited, these special data were used to analyze the behavior of the specific immigrant population.

50. The well-known example from Germany is the study by Heitmeyer et al. (1997), which asked young Turkish adolescents provocative questions about their attitudes toward Islam, as "proof" that their difficult social circumstances were leading them toward dangerously militant forms of fundamentalism.

nalism is unable to mount.[51] Yet as with policy and public funding elsewhere, scholars often enter into a Faustian pact when they sign up to do such research work with heteronomous production and publication conditions attached.

The inevitable transatlantic influence on research on integration policy has also been felt in the shaping of survey-based research in Europe. There has been an almost universal effort by academics in Europe to promote the idea that all European nation-states are now countries of immigration, often in polemical discussion with politicians who claim the opposite. The idea is that North American multiculturalism and its cosmopolitan view of national identity is where European nations (or some pan-European EU construct) should be headed. This idea, however, remains a rhetorical construction, one that can be dubiously substantiated only by the low incoming numbers of migrants into Europe (especially in comparison to North America or Asia) or by the low overall percentage population of non-European descendants in each country in Europe. This is not to say that Europe does not have an integration problem. Quite the contrary, in fact. Integration, not immigration control or naturalization, may indeed be the most important immigration issue, particularly in view of problematic research in this area. From this, the American influence on integration studies breaks down in one of two ways. One, the emphasis on managing race relations and treating integration through antidiscrimination measures, is seen in Britain and in the Netherlands to a lesser extent. The other, the idea of assimilation in countries built on immigration (the idea of the *creuset,* or melting pot), is one that remains strongest in France. The historical reconstruction of the idea of France as a country of immigration was the first big achievement of the new republicans of the 1980s.[52] It is no surprise, then, that the most advanced French thinking on integration resembles the standard sociological works that measure dimensions of assimilation in the United States, which date back to the heyday of U.S. sociology on the subject in the 1960s.[53]

51. Work such as this has been sponsored by such newspapers as *La Monde* in France and *Volkskrant* in the Netherlands. See, e.g., the controversial findings of the report on Islam in the Netherlands by Phalet et al. (2000).

52. The historical work of Noiriel (1988)—with its strong U.S. links (Horowitz and Noiriel, 1992)—was vitally important to this. His long-standing message—of France as a country of immigration that had forgotten this—was then repeated without question as the starting point for all subsequent leading works through Schnapper (1991), Weil (1991), Todd (1994), and Tribalat (1995). It also became the motif of progressive political rhetoric on the subject at the time: e.g., Mitterrand's famous speech of May 1987 of the French being *"un peu romain, un peu germain, un peu juif, un peu italien, un peu espanol et (même peut-être maintenant) un peu arabe."*

53. E.g., the unavoidable reference to Gordon (1964). Gordon's work and its legacy are now being revived in the United States by Alba et al. (1997), and it is to this work that the efforts of Tribalat and others in France should be compared.

The somewhat old-fashioned sound of the idea of assimilation is not at all reflected in the technology of research in France. The massive state-apparatus that the French are able to muster in their official production of knowledge on the subject is breathtaking. The reports of the government-appointed Haut Conseil à l'Intégration (HCI) not only sought to formulate the normative, historical, and political grounding for the new republican philosophy it espoused, they also set in motion a machine of empirical evidence gathering, explicitly constructed to find the data that the public theory had set out to prove.[54]

Since the early 1990s, many types of empirical work have been set up to look at the performance and social mobility of immigrants in education and the labor market.[55] Most quantitative or survey work, however, remains constrained by the basic sampling frame offered by the official national survey statistics of the French statistics office (INSEE). These surveys persist only to generate data (albeit wonderfully elaborate data) on *étrangers* (foreign nonnationals) in France compared with the French population. A basic ideological prohibition on gathering data on the ethnic origin of naturalized French citizens of immigrant origin has reigned in official public circles, concerned that it will undermine the republican fiction that being French is an indivisible, universal political identity, one that should not be linked to any ethnic or cultural classification. Many French children of non-French family origin are thus lost to the social radar as and when they leave their immigrant household.

Thus integration research is limited to charting the social mobility of nonnationals only, or to retracing second and third generations solely through family-origin records. Yet everyone—academics and political actors—continues to make claims about whether integration or assimilation is working. In a sense, then, the existing intellectual machinery for producing scientific knowledge to prove or disprove these claims generated internal contradictions that have necessitated the beginnings of a dramatic shift in the methodology of French integration research in the direction of recognizing an "eth-

54. The first report of the series, *Pour un modèle français de l'intégration,* written under the auspices of Jacqueline Costa-Lascoux (see Haut Conseil à l'Intégration, 1993), constructed a survey that was sent to the town halls of seventy-three communes across France requesting general data on immigrants' integration into the norms of belonging to the nation *(appartenance),* family behavior, social advancement, and social involvement *(sociabilité)* (Favell, 1998a, 72–74). This crude, politically oriented survey provided the impetus for the much more scientific efforts of INED and Tribalat's research group.

55. See, e.g., the continuing work of Louis-André Vallet on immigrants in education and Roxane Silberman on immigrants in the labor market, careful empirical work that steers clear of the usual republican polemics and has been developed with an eye on comparative European social mobility research.

nic-but-French" classification of hitherto unrecognized populations in France in terms other than "nonnational" origin.[56]

This was the background to the controversies surrounding the report by Michèle Tribalat and associates (1995, 1996), a major empirical survey of the assimilation of immigrants in France that represents the state of the art in modern French integration research (Tribalat, 1995; Tribalat et al., 1996). For the first time in an officially funded work, a rigorously constructed survey (from official INSEE data) comprised a sample and a series of questions that probed the ethnic proximity of immigrants in France *and* naturalized French persons of immigrant origin to the norms of behavior of *français de souche* (French of nonimmigrant stock). Asking formerly taboo questions about ethnic national origin and linguistic and cultural affiliation, the report came up with an unprecedented panorama of the diversity of France's immigrant population, linked to different migration trajectories, cultural profiles, and political position.

The report, which was put together under the auspices of INED (Institut National d'Etudes Démographiques), thus differed crucially from the regular population surveys done by INSEE or with INSEE's data (Champsaur, 1994). A murky internal bureaucratic struggle about the funding of the report nearly destroyed it at an early stage. A great ideological issue was at stake. As was the case with the enormously important historical public policy study by Patrick Weil of the early 1990s, it took a decisive behind-the-scenes political intervention by the powerful civil servant and president of the HCI, Marceau Long, to ensure that the project was approved. Although this was research still very different from the British way of doing it, a more ethnicity-based study of integration was evidently needed to continue to provide evidence for the grand claims about integration being made everywhere by the ideologues of neorepublicanism among intellectuals, media, and politicians alike.[57] The con-

---

56. This has not yet happened for the national census in France, nor is it ever likely to start looking like the British "ethnic question" or American "race-monitoring forms." Polemics on issues of immigration/integration raged in the run-up to the 2000 national census.

57. The report was greeted with intense polemics in the press about its methodology. It is difficult to reconcile the modesty of the methodological step toward "ethnicity" taken, with the spectacular intensity of its symbolic significance. Across a variety of questions that cover attitudes and behavior on interethnic marriages (a large part of the report), cultural orientation to the homeland, language and the maintenance of traditional cultural practices, housing concentration, intergenerational social mobility and labor market access, and political participation and associational activity, the report charts the socialization of France's immigrants to national norms of the *population de souche* derived from a control group of nonimmigrant-origin French. Its explicit aim, and its empirical result, is to present positive findings about the continued success of these processes in the light of a thus-confirmed public theory and framework of integration, understood as a French national achievement. Such a picture offers no way to gauge how migrant social trajectories might take creative or successful paths that are not convergent with French norms or

troversy is ironic because in other ways, Tribalat's report is as traditional as a French study could be. It offers a break with recent reconstructive formulations by going *back* to the word *assimilation* rather than *integration,* to describe the end point of the social adaptation process in France. The report thus presents integration or assimilation in France as "business as usual," with diversity reported as a minor exception or deviation.[58]

The Tribalat report and its methods have had significant influence on work in other countries. French style work is in this sense a lot closer to the basic methods of survey work being done across Europe than are British methods. A good example is the enormous scale survey project being conducted by Ron Lesthaege (1997) that focuses on the socialization to Western norms of the Moroccan and Turkish population in Belgium (in particular, of women), again

---

its bounded social context. Perhaps most indicative of this is the key exception to the findings of the report that there is one clear ethnic outlier to the generally positive assimilatory progress of ethnic groups in France: the Turkish population in France, which can be consistently shown to perform "worst" (i.e., the least "French") in all the main categories of inquiry. The reaction to Turkish resistance to French social norms and integration is to classify them as a clear case of "integration failure," that this group has failed to be socialized properly and therefore constitutes an objective social problem. Yet it is not at all clear that this group is performing badly according to other types of indicators of integration failure that might be pointed to in Anglo-American studies, such as youth crime and disorder, social deprivation, and poverty. In fact, many of the high-profile public-order problems in France—as seen in films like *La Haine* and in the streets of suburban cities almost weekly—actually have little to do with cultural *intégration* per se as the French conceived it in the early 1990s. These are socioeconomic in origin. The cross-ethnic groups typically involved in these are united by poverty and housing concentration, the misery and exclusion of the *banlieues.* They are, in other words, occurring in groups that are to all intents and purposes well integrated by the Tribalat standards (the same can be said about militant Islamic movements in France). And this leaves the status of the Turkish increasingly anomalous within the French integration scheme. Taken as a group across Europe, it is not at all clear that they can be said to be among the most deprived. The evidence of France thus seems fundamentally distorted by the fact that the behavior and self-organization of the Turkish cannot be described as nation-state-oriented integration (a similar thing might be said about the Chinese in France): the problem lies with the intellectual framework rather than with the group itself.

58. Despite its controversy, then, the report was received by many commentators as proof that good old-fashioned French republican assimilation was still working: arch-republican Emmanuel Todd, for example, made much of its findings about intermarriage in France as opposed to other countries. The mystery remains as to why such ideological work is so powerful in France, given the fairly obvious *décalage* with what happens in reality at local levels. Commentators might cruelly observe how the most prominent Parisian researchers never need set foot in the *banlieues*—all that matters is what happens in the 5th, 6th, and 7th *arrondissements.* However, this perhaps misses the point: that the criterion for competition in this intellectual field is not empirical accuracy, but control of the ideological high ground—something that successful players such as Todd, Taguieff, and Schnapper have well understood. This is rooted in the idealist philosophical tradition in French political thought that all these writers share: it is not what exists that matters, but what you name it (Favell, 1999). Even those who offer a different account of multiculturalism in France (such as Wieviorka, 1996) do so with the similarly theory-first style of work.

with the significant blessing, funding, and technical support of the various Belgian states.[59]

What is noticeable here is not the weaker assumptions about integration or socialization, but the much weaker nation-state policy context for interpreting the findings of this work, which have focused on gender differences and the still-significant integration gap between these ethnic populations and the Belgian population.[60] This offers a potentially very different type of policy context from France, given that no intellectual production in Belgium can comfortably fit in a single policy framework or definition of integration, let alone a single unitary idea about the nation-state into which immigrants might be imagined to integrate.

Integration has always been an area of conflictual positions in Belgium, which habitually imports its more grandiose conceptual vocabulary from the French, but which then faces significant differences in interpretation in the Walloon and Flemish communities (which often look to the Dutch) and more local differentiations at the regional, city, and even commune level. The absence of the nation-state context means that the norms of socialization being identified as the gold standard of immigrant behavior are simply generic Western norms.

In the Belgian context, the critical question is the language used by immigrants in relation to integration. It is vitally important, of course, in the bilingual capital itself, Brussels, where it is thought that immigrants opting to learn French or Flemish might tip the political balance in the city one way or the other. Work on this issue is highly contested in Belgium, which, for reasons of political sensitivity, has not since the 1960s had a census of the languages used in bilingual communes. The enormous recent work undertaken by Swyngedouw, Phalet, and Deschouwer, based on a survey of more than a thousand ethnic minority respondents in Brussels, immediately found public controversy over its findings of illiteracy among immigrants and the apparent dominance of French. Researchers in Belgium are heavily dependent on their location in networks of political patronage and affiliation, which provide major sources of funding. Whatever work is published on such a sensitive subject can spark both immediate and well-publicized debate, but it can also run afoul of what politicians expect for their money.[61] The determining factor in this case, then, was

---

59. Tribalat was, herself, an external adviser for this study.

60. A wealth of interesting work on Belgium is being done by Belgians of both Francophone and Flemish origin: e.g., see recent work by Martiniello (1998), Blommaert and Verschueren (1998), Jacobs (1998), Blaise et al. (1997), and the study by Swyngedouw, Phalet, and Deschouwer (1999).

61. Another recent study by the Swyngedouw group (by Bousetta and Swyngedouw, 1999) found that the granting of votes to nonnational immigrants and resident Europeans in Brussels (who are both assumed to be likely to vote Francophone rather than Flemish) would not in all probability affect political results in the city. One of the Flemish sponsors was not happy with

the reception of the report by Swyngedouw and colleagues, rather than the careful methodology it pursued. Integration is ultimately all about the political struggle over the allegiance of different populations in the city, and whether immigrant groups themselves are able to work the conflictual system to their advantage (see Favell and Martiniello, 1999). At this, the most sophisticated end of the European survey output, there is at least a glimmer of genuinely cross-national comparative work, now that conceptually compatible integration studies are being produced.[62]

Across the water in Britain it comes as no surprise to find integration research significantly out of step with the rest of mainland Europe. At an early stage Britain identified its "race relations" problem with that of the native black population in the United States. The evolution of what might be called multicultural race relations has been shaped ever since by this self-assimilation to a part (but not all) of the U.S. example. Immigration control, on the other hand, is a different matter entirely, and many of Britain's biggest problems today derive from the fact that its thinking deals little with the challenges of new migration and the global refugee crisis of the 1980s and 1990s.[63] Race relations, on the other hand, is widely perceived to be one of the great liberal success stories of the postwar period, and—relative to the perception of ethnic dilemmas in the rest of Europe—one that ministers, activists, and ethnic minor-

---

these results and withdrew support, which then jeopardized the continued funding of various other projects the group had planned.

62. This is one report that may lead to something comparative, at least with the Netherlands, where Phalet and others are conducting similar research on Rotterdam (with some wider promise of extending this to France, Germany, and Britain). The work generates an original view by modeling integration as a social-psychological process, charting without any preconceptions about integration as the end goal, the varied strategies taken by different immigrant groups in relation to the spaces and opportunities they encounter in a variety of local, regional, and transnational contexts. This open-ended approach might be contrasted with another ambitious recent study of integration (in Germany) from a social-psychological perspective, by Nauck et al. (1997), which starts off—as so many integration studies limited by state-centered typologies do—by locating different trajectories within a closed schema of types of integration (in this case, pluralist integration, assimilation, segregation, and marginalization).

63. The key thing about Britain is that (restrictive, culturally closed) immigration control and (liberal, culturally open) race relations/multiculturalism/integration are policy constructions conceived as two separate questions with a different goal and logic (whereas they are one and the same question everywhere else in western Europe). They are, however, interrelated: success with the latter (a more multicultural or multiracial Britain) is always argued to be dependent on success with the former (a tough maintenance of physical borders against migration). Neither Conservative nor Labour governments have deviated from this line of reasoning in more than twenty-five years, and by maintaining an opt-out on Schengen and ever-more restrictive asylum policies, Britain continues to believe it can avoid the migration and free movement tendencies that have simply overrun physical borders and national sovereignty elsewhere in Europe (and the world). See Favell (1998a, 110–22, 202–13) on this island-based British peculiarity.

ity members alike agree to affirm as something the British do best. Not surprisingly, then, there is a strong level of proselytism whenever academics or policy specialists cross the channel to give advice to their mainland European counterparts.

The message is that Britain does it differently, and does indeed have its own state-of-the-art survey on integration: the *Ethnic Minorities in Britain* survey (1997). This report offers a deep contrast in methodology and rhetoric to that of the Tribalat report in France. Reports such as this have been made by the influential Policy Studies Institute (PSI) on a decade-by-decade basis and offer a distinct picture of the official census and survey material produced by either the state, the quasi autonomous nongovernmental organization (QUANGO) the Commission for Racial Equality (CRE)—which regulates the implementation and progress of race relations laws—or clientelist pressure groups such as the Runnymede Trust. This slightly subversive role is underlined by the fact that the latest PSI report was headed by Tariq Modood, who has played a significant role in what may now be considered the breakup of ethnic and racial studies in Britain, partly under the challenge that new ethnic questions have brought to the dominant race relations establishment.[64] The PSI is also notable as one of a battery of new-Left think-tank groups that rose to prominence in the 1990s and that now have a strong presence in the policy circles of the current government. The report therefore offers a distinct perspective on the successes and deficiencies of British multicultural race relations that stands at a distance from current orthodoxies. It is also a highly self-aware work, knowing its place in a long canon of similar national studies and its position in the often-temperamental debates about multiculturalism and antiracism in Britain. The report remains, however, squarely British in its perspective. There is no hint of the research being at all related to, linked with, or aimed at a wider European comparative agenda.[65]

64. See his earlier attacks on the "establishment" in Modood (1992, 1994) based partly on experiences working within the "race relations industry," in which he upset many established dogmas by putting Asians, and then Pakistani and Bangladeshi Muslims, on what had been up until then a black-and-white race relations map. In her sociopsychological work on Brussels and Rotterdam, Karen Phalet notes the possible usefulness of Modood's other work on ethnic identities in Britain (Modood et al., 1994), if it can be adapted elsewhere.

65. The British construction of data on ethnic minorities here dictates a sampling frame—and hence a construction of the integration problem—that follows the British convention of relativizing more or less distinct "ethnic groups" with one another (and, most important, an amorphous majority "white" ethnic group). In the British census and other official data-gathering devices, each individual questioned self-identifies within a given ethnic category, from which wider patterns about groups are generated. In the Modood report, the identification of the sample and the "ethnic" self-categorization questions follow generally the categories created for the latest 1991 census, but also allow cross-checking with declared family origin, some recognition of the problem

This reflects a reluctance to move outside a framework in which Britain as a society remains the one fixed and bounded background within which diversity and difference might be found. As with Tribalat, then, what the Modood report represents is a bid for the national cultural high ground: an argument to preserve the nation by imagining it as universal and inclusive as possible, in which the old nation learns to face the consequences of immigration, but is not forced to acknowledge the consequences of globalization or the breakdown of the nation-state as a dominant mode of social organization. As such, it is a pivotal move in the policy-knowledge struggle in which British academics as others elsewhere have had considerable background influence. The successes of British multicultural race relations have certainly been a powerful example for Europe. Yet when British policy makers turn in that direction on these questions, it is not with a view to build cooperation, but rather to assert a moral hegemony. This represents the reassertion of nation-state primacy over inte-

---

of mixed origin, and distinctions within groups crudely clumped together in the official census. It limits itself only to these, Britain's officially recognized "ethnic minorities." The 1991 census introduced a bizarrely generic postcolonial scheme of self-classification peculiar to Britain: "White, Black-Caribbean, Black-African, Black-Other (please describe), Indian, Pakistani, Bangladeshi, Chinese, Any Other Group (please describe)". American race-monitoring forms are simple when compared to this: "White, Black, Asian, Hispanic, Native." In Britain, the migration history of individuals has thus now become irrelevant, and there is no place for distinguishing many other substantial minority or nonnational groups in Britain. The Modood survey differs primarily in separating the Gujarati "African Asians," who have had a different social trajectory than other Asian groups. Apparently the "ethnic question" is being changed again in 2001, with even more boxes to tick, and some pressure to open the Pandora's box of "whiteness," for example, so that the Irish and Jewish in Britain can be recognized as groups suffering from "racial" *[sic]* discrimination. In Modood, a "disadvantage" is identified by cross-referencing findings with occupational social-class categories that are famous from British sociology of social mobility (i.e., Goldthorpe, 1987). The Modood report explicitly rejects the use of the term *integration,* focusing on representing the diversity of experience, identity, and success of Britain's ethnic minorities and the persistence of disadvantage for some (young Pakistanis and Bangladeshis alongside Afro-Caribbeans) amid the above-average success of certain other highly qualified Asian groups. In a recent article, Werbner (1999) discusses the still-individualistic notion of success that this kind of study of social mobility is limited to identifying. It has to aggregate relative group success from individual paths of mobility, something that may lead to big distinctions between, say, African Asians and Pakistanis. However, as she points out, if success is rethought in anthropological terms as the creation of collective cultural value (and meaning) by groups, it can be argued that Pakistanis are often successful in creating rich community contexts in which the production of individualistic material wealth is negligible, and that those Asians who are materially successful often depend for their success not on individual human capital but on the rich social capital that the ethnic group context produces for them. Moreover, the individualistic conception of success sells short the cultural difference and diversity elsewhere vaunted as the source of ethnic assertiveness. Pnina Werbner is also responding to some stereotyping remarks by Ceri Peach and Roger Ballard about diversity among Britain's ethnic minorities, in which the African Asians are said to be following a "Jewish" path to integration, and the Pakistanis an "Irish" path to social stigmatization and segregation.

gration policies, and of the superiority of the British way over what it sees as an ethnicity-stricken continent, unable to deal either with internal ethnic and national conflicts or with the multicultural difference brought by immigration. This is an understandable posture, born of long-standing self-sufficiency and a defensive attitude to the change that European difference represents. Ironically, it is internal, not external, pressures that may most expose the vulnerability of Britain's multiracial harmony: if the artificial distinctions between race relations in Britain and other forms of identity politics over nationalism and religion fall apart with any future breakup of the British state.

What is perhaps remarkable is that other, smaller European states seem to be following the neonationalist response of Britain and France, taking a similar turn in their thinking about cultural diversity and the changing nature of the nation. The 1990s decade of globalization and the supposed decline of the nation-state have seen both the Scandinavian countries and the Netherlands return to a nation-building idea of integration after previous flirtations with strong state-sponsored versions of cultural pluralism and multiculturalism. In the Netherlands, immigrants find that their access to welfare and rights is conditional on their attending structured tuition in the language and culture of their host country; and that left-wing thinking has shifted markedly to associate the goals of equality and antidiscrimination with a more successful and pro-active integration framework.[66] Unlike Britain and France, however, these small countries have the luxury of being small, cohesive states with strong national identities and minimal regional tensions. They have long mastered (through trade, exchange, and open borders) a dual game of embracing international influences while preserving particularist internal national traditions and customs. The recent Franco-British trade war over beef and farming products, the absurd level of Europhobia in British politics, and the equally absurd anti-McDonald's polemics in France against Americanization, all suggest that neither of these proud, ex-colonial powers in decline have learned any lessons from the Dutch, Danish, or Swedish national examples.

---

66. An example is the impressive integration survey work by Justus Veenman and his team in Rotterdam (1997, 1998) that explicitly links social capital and social mobility research to the persistence of racial discrimination for Dutch ethnic minorities in education and the labor market. It argues for a pro-active national cultural education for immigrants and minorities that will enable them to overcome barriers and prejudice, and against the preexisting multicultural approach in the country. One distinctive feature of Dutch research is that there has been no official population census since the early 1970s. Data and sampling frames (based on national origin) therefore have to be reconstructed either from official police and town hall records of residence or from specific ministry-sponsored official reports on policy, such as the annual *Sociale en Culture Rapport*. This practice has an effect on the numbers game in any discussions of Dutch immigrants and on the unease in particular about unregistered and undocumented migrants in the country.

The Dutch, however, do have something in common with the French and the British on this point. They too are fiercely convinced of the superiority of their national political model and the distinctive policy methods that follow from this. This may be characteristic of the postcolonial condition or of countries that have not had to see themselves on the losing side of twentieth-century wars in Europe. Yet it seems that the shrinking of the generic British, French, and Dutch civilizations into the original national territory in the postwar period has led to the reformulation of a universalist "multiculturalism-in-one-nation" in these countries, built on reworked ideas of integration and nation building.

Nationalizing elites, competing for hegemony over the idea of nation, have used universalist-nationalist discourses to outflank old-fashioned culturally exclusive competitors, refining an international role in the world for these perennial nation-states in decline. At the same time, this openness to internalizing and adapting foreign imported cultures has come with a staunch refusal to see new immigrants as anything other than relocated colonial subjects who import diverse but manageable cultures into the nation-state. Yet could they not equally be the personification of other internationalizing forces deflating the idea of bounded nation-states, such as the global economy or more transnational conceptions of civilization grounded in universal human rights and personhood?[67]

Within this nation-state-sponsored picture, the status and power of immigrants is measured entirely according to social mobility relative to norms of integration into the nation-society or into average national social mobility paths. Yet, it is increasingly normal to think of elites in these countries as becoming more transnational in their roles, influence, and trajectories. Britain and France may be the countries in Europe with the longest immigration experience and the most well-worked ideas of reconciling multicultural diversity with national unity. This does not stop even the most progressive policy intellectuals from espousing nationalizing ideologies that appear increasingly anachronistic in their conceptions of achieving multiculturalism in an international world. It is, therefore, wrong to take France and Britain continually as the ideal type of integration nation, whose example should be followed by less "advanced" na-

---

67. The new literature on transnationalism and postnational citizenship suggests many ways in which thinking might go "beyond the nation-state," but the often-celebratory style of much of this work rarely engages the necessarily structural questions on socialization and the reproduction of social norms that theories of integration raise. On transnationalism, see Basch et al. (1994), Smith and Guarnizo (1998), and Portes (1996); on postnational citizenship, see Soysal (1994) or Bauböck (1994b). Portes, however, the leading figure in the study of transnationalism in the United States, continues to ask vital "integration" questions on residential segregation, education, labor market conditions, and social mobility, amid work that emphasizes the transnational political, economic, and cultural organization of migrants (e.g., 1995, 1997). It is this line of work that needs exploring in the European context (see Cross and Waldinger, 1999).

tions. Instead, they are extreme, dated, and peculiar cases of a tendency unlikely to be feasible anywhere else in Europe.

Directions for Future Research

Comparative research on integration processes and integration policy in Europe is a hugely difficult enterprise. We are far from being even at the stage where the official national data and conceptualizations of the subject are sufficiently compatible for clear cross-national studies to be made.[68] My aim in this chapter has been to clarify why this is so, showing how the nuts and bolts of national and cross-national research must be related systematically back to the political construction of the problem in each country, as well as the material conditions that academics face in working within these frameworks. Although skeptical in tone, my effort has been to clear the way for genuine progress in cross-national comparative research. The question remains of how integration research might be conceived and executed in the future.

I conclude, then, by asking how the subject should be approached as a problem of basic comparative research design. I limit myself here to the comparative study of *political integration,* that is, to research that might compare the levels of participation and representation of migrants and minorities in their host societies, as measured by the rights they are offered, or by their participation in the political system.

First, a precondition for any new research is that solutions to the dilemmas outlined at the preliminary stage must be found. These questions require detailed expert debate by all concerned. We need to determine a common set of categories for identifying migrants or minorities across Europe and thus a suitably corrected set of official data for them. It is clear these categories must be something other than categories of nationality, which render many citizens of ethnic migrant origin invisible. However, the self-attributing racial categories of the British mode of survey work are equally limited. An ethnic classification related to national migrant origin may prove a sensible compromise. We also

---

68. One new hope for integration research in Europe is the new interest being shown in the subject by the European Consortium for Sociological Research, led by John Goldthorpe and Robert Erikson, whose work on Europe and North America remains the central reference in comparative social mobility research (Erikson and Goldthorpe, 1992). Members of this group, such as Hartmut Esser, Walter Müller, and Anthony Heath, are now showing an interest in similar comparative work in Europe on ethnic minorities and migrants. Although their preliminary conference on the subject at Obernai in September 1999 revealed that little thinking had been done about the basic epistemological problems of this work (the subject of this chapter), it is a potentially exciting initiative: not least because it does not primarily involve the usual scholars who have been brought up on national research traditions of race, ethnicity, or migration.

need to specify in advance the relationship that academics doing this research envisage with actual politics and policy making. If the work is excessively context-specific (as is so much that has been done), it will inevitably end up being more strategic and instrumental than scientific.

Stage one of the research proper must be the gathering of existing data. Obviously, this chapter is a step in this direction, which indicates the extent to which most existing studies have to be processed through an interpretative key in order to understand how and why they have been written. In all the countries in question, however, data exist on such things as the numbers and concentration of migrants and minority groups, their social and political organization, their political behavior, and their access to existing political channels.

Stage two must be the determining of what it is we want to compare and explain: our dependent variable. Much normatively directed work conceives this in a vague, indeterminate way. It seeks to compare levels of "citizenship," "democracy," or "civil society" as though it were indeed possible to measure these notions in an open-minded way, that did not already expect certain conditions to be fulfilled before the normative category could be said to be achieved. These concepts are also too often bound to normative ideas about nation building and the progress of national societies. They are too ideologically loaded. On the other hand, narrower studies—such as those that seek to measure the extent of formal rights or the amount of formal legislation that protects migrants and minorities—are too literal, reproducing a highly organized, top-down state perspective in their analyses. The principal measure for political integration should be something in-between, something linked to participation and the mobilization of groups. The important thing will be to stress that it is not just the quantity of participation that needs measuring, but the quality: the extent to which migrant groups actually manage to influence political outcomes (whether it is influence on policy outcome, on agenda setting or issue definition, or on "ethnic" faces in parties or public positions). In other words, we must look for a measure of their relative social power in specific contexts.

Stage three is the measuring of the dependent variable in different national situations, in order to set a cross-national research question and identify the essential possible independent variables (explanatory factors) that might cause a variance in outcomes in different contexts. Almost any stance on measurement will contain a bias toward either disorganized libertarian states (measurements indicating levels of freedom from state control for groups) or highly organized state-centered approaches toward integration (measurements indicating levels of formal protection and policy for groups).

It is here, then, that I suggest an idiosyncratic ploy to make comparison in the European context possible. It is to assume that all the states in Europe of interest are roughly equivalent in the level of integration they enable and, what is more important, not to classify them as better or worse but to compare the ways they frame the question of integration and seek to achieve it in practice. This move is like creating a "G8" of integration nations that, as in the real G8, have different gross domestic products and levels of economic performance, but that within this set of nations are nevertheless considered equals, with an equal status in the select group of developed, industrially advanced states. If, then, we take integration nations as essentially equal members of a select group, within which it is absurd to impose a hierarchy of success on integration, what we are left measuring is not absolute variance, but rather qualitative variance across cases. This means we will not be able discover whether France is "better" than Italy or whether Britain is "better" than Germany in their treatment of immigrants. The exercise may, however, through a series of paired bilateral comparisons, enable us to identify what is comparatively good and bad in a particular country's policies of integration.[69] If we then assume that there is a policy convergence across all these states, it may be possible to synthesize from across the various comparisons a set of best practices.

Stage four moves from this logical design to practical questions of what the unit of comparison will be across nations (i.e., at what level it should take place). Too many studies have compared immigration politics or policies of integration using the general institutional features of national political systems. Although initially productive, this now leads to repetitive research that reproduces national stereotypes and assumptions about the nation-state. It is also often normatively biased in favor of state-centered policy approaches. My suggestion is that the city is a far better unit of comparison, a level for studying political integration that enables both contextual specificity and structural comparisons, allowing for the fact that immigrant integration might be influenced simultaneously by local, national, and transnational factors. From this we can move to the selection of cities and immigrant groups for study. A good deal of descriptive work exists that has generated information and data on the indicators of the independent variables that explain differences across cities. There is no reason why research cannot build on these studies and develop a more extensive range of studies of migrant political integration in European cities.[70]

69. This was in fact the research strategy I used in my study of France and Britain (Favell, 1998a). By refusing to answer the loaded question of which country is better at integration, I was able to contrast the two in such a way as to highlight their relative policy achievements and their distinctive pathological tendencies. The good and the bad are in effect two sides of the same coin.

70. E.g., the UNESCO–MOST program or the various reports produced by the Metropolis Project on migrants in cities (see Hjarnø, 1999). The former program, which involves many of the best European researchers, produced a set of city reports on the participation and representation of migrants in cities, each of which followed a common template specifying indicators (for popu-

I suggest, then, that a simple step-by-step research design process will help to clarify how more effective cross-national comparative research on integration is possible. It may also be possible to envisage such research drawing conclusions on which are the more effective means of political integration of migrants and minorities found in Europe, as well as a sense of the specific problems that nation-state policies have generated in their progressive attempts to build distinctive national philosophies of integration. With such a procedure, it may *even* be possible to envisage the derivation of normative statements or guidelines. It is in this way that social scientific research on integration may be able to redefine an autonomous role for itself in the policy making and politics of integration currently troubling so many European states.

Works Cited

Alba, Richard, and Victor Nee. 1997. "Rethinking Assimilation Theory for a New Era of Immigration." *International Migration Review* 31 (winter): 826–74.

Alexander, Jeffrey. 1987. *Twenty Lectures: Sociological Theory since World War II.* New York: Columbia University Press.

Almond, Gabriel A., and Sidney Verba. 1963. *The Civic Culture: Political Attitudes and Democracy in Five Nations.* Boston: Little, Brown.

Alund, Aleksandra, and Carl-Ulrik Schierup. 1991. *Paradoxes of Multiculturalism.* Aldershot, England: Avebury.

Baldwin-Edwards, Martin, and Martin Schain (eds.). 1994. *The Politics of Immigration in Western Europe.* London: Cass.

Ballis-Lal, Barbara. 1990. *The Romance of Culture in an Urban Civilisation: Robert E. Park on Race and Ethnic Relations in Cities.* London: Routledge.

Banton, Michael. 1955. *The Coloured Quarter.* London: Cape.

———. 1967. *Race Relations.* London: Tavistock.

Basch, Linda, Nina Glick Schiller, and Cristina Szanton-Blanc. 1994. *Nations Unbound: Transnational Projects, Post-Colonial Predicaments, and Deterritorialized Nation-States.* Amsterdam: Gordon and Breach.

Bauböck, Rainer. 1994a. *The Integration of Immigrants.* Strasbourg: Council of Europe.

———. 1994b. *Transnational Citizenship: Membership and Rights in International Migration.* Aldershot, England: Edward Elgar.

Beiner, Ronald (ed.). 1998. *Theorizing Citizenship.* Albany, N.Y.: SUNY Press.

Bellah, Robert, with Richard Madsen, William Sullivan, Ann Swidler, and Steven Tipton. 1985. *Habits of the Heart: Individualism and Commitment in American Life.* Berkeley: University of California Press.

lation numbers, types of political organization, channels of representation, etc.). See their web site: <http://www.unesco.org/most/p97.htm>. Two excellent academic studies that follow the strategy suggested here are by Ireland (1994), on migrants in four localities in France and Switzerland, and by Bousetta (2000) on Moroccans in four cities in three national contexts (Lille, Liège, Antwerp, and Utrecht). See also Body-Gendrot and Martiniello (2000).

Blaise, Pierre, et al. 1997. *La Belgique et ses immigrés*. Brussels: De Boeck University.

Bleich, Erik. 1998. "From International Ideas to Domestic Politics: Educational Multiculturalism in England and France." *Comparative Politics* (Oct.): 81–100.

Blommaert, Jan, and Jef Verschueren. 1998. *Debating Diversity*. London: Routledge.

Body-Gendrot, Sophie, and Marco Martiniello (eds.). 2000. *Minorities in European Cities: The Dynamics of Social Integration and Social Exclusion at the Neighbourhood Level*. London: Macmillan.

Bommes, Michaèl. 1998. "Migration, Nation State, and Welfare State: A Theoretical Challenge for Sociological Migration Research." Paper presented to the European Forum on Migration, European University Institute, Florence, Feb. 16.

Bourdieu, Pierre, and Loic Wacquant. 1992. *An Invitation to Reflexive Sociology*. Cambridge: Polity.

———. 1999. "On the Currency of Imperialist Reason." *Theory, Culture, and Society* 16(1): 44–58.

Bousetta, Hassan. 1997. "Citizenship and Political Participation in France and the Netherlands: Reflections on Two Local Cases." *New Community* 23(2): 215–32.

———. 2000. "Political Dynamics in the City: Citizenship, Ethnic Mobilisation, and Socio-political Participation. Four Case Studies." In Body-Gendrot and Martiniello (eds.), *Minorities in European Cities: The Dynamics of Social Integration and Social Exclusion at the Neighbourhood Level*. London: Macmillan.

Bousetta, Hassan, and Marc Swyngedouw. 1999. "La citoyenneté de l'Union européenne et l'enjeu de Bruxelles: Le droit supranational européen confronté aux réalités d'une société multiethnique et multinationale divisée." Centre de Recherche et d'Information Socio-Politiques (CRISP). *Courrier Hebdomadaire* 1636:43.

Brèchon, Pierre, and Bruno Cautrès (eds.). 1999. *Les enquêtes eurobaromètres*. Paris: L'Harmattan.

Brubaker, Rogers (ed.). 1989. *Immigration and the Politics of Citizenship in Western Europe*. New York: University Press of America.

———. 1992. *Citizenship and Nationhood in France and Germany*. Cambridge: Harvard University Press.

———. 1995. *Nationalism Reframed: Nationhood and the National Question in the New Europe*. Cambridge: Cambridge University Press.

Bryant, Christopher G. A. 1997. "Citizenship, National Identity, and the Accommodation of Difference: Reflections on the German, French, Dutch, and British Cases." *New Community* (23)2: 157–72.

Bulmer, Martin. 1984. *The Chicago School of Sociology: Institutionalization, Diversity, and the Use of Sociological Research*. Chicago: University of Chicago Press.

Bulmer, Martin, and Anthony Rees (eds.). 1996. *Citizenship Today: The Contemporary Relevance of T. H. Marshall*. London: University College London Press.

Burgers, Jack. 1998. "Formal Determinants of Informal Arrangements: Housing and Undocumented Immigrants in Rotterdam." *Journal of Ethnic and Migration Studies* 24(2): 95–312.

Burgess, Adam. 1999. "Critical Reflections on the Return of Minority Rights Regulation to East/West European Affairs." In Karl Cordell (ed.), *Ethnicity and Democratisation in the New Europe*, pp. 49–60. London: Routledge.

Carmon, Naomi (ed.). 1996. *Immigration and Integration in Post-Industrial Societies*. London: Macmillan.

Castles, Stephen. 1995. "How Nation-States Respond to Immigration and Ethnic Diversity." *New Community* 21(3): 293–308.

―――. 2000. "Thirty Years of Research on Migration and Multicultural Societies." In Stephen Castles (ed.), *Ethnicity and Globalization: From Migrant Workers to Transnational Citizens*. London: Sage.

Castles, Stephen, and Alisdair Davidson. 2000. *Citizenship and Migration: Globalization and the Politics of Belonging*. London: Macmillan.

Castles, Stephen, and Godula Kosack. 1973. *Immigrant Workers and Class Structure in Western Europe*. Oxford: Oxford University Press.

Castles, Stephen, et al. 1984. *Here for Good: Western Europe's New Ethnic Minorities*. London: Pluto.

Centre for Contemporary Cultural Studies. 1982. *The Empire Strikes Back*. London: Hutchinson.

Champsaur, Paul (ed.). 1994. *Les étrangers en France: Contours et caractères*. Paris: INSEE.

Chandler, David. 1999. "The OSCE and the Internationalisation of National Minority Rights." In Karl Cordell (ed.), *Ethnicity and Democratisation in the New Europe*, pp. 61–76. London: Routledge.

Çinar, Dilek, Cristoph Hofinger, and Harald Waldrauch. 1995. *Integrations index: Zur rechtlichen Integration von Ausländerinnen in ausgewählten europäischen Ländern*. Political Science Series no. 25. Vienna: Institute for Advanced Study.

Codagnone, Cristiano. 1998. "Monitoring Ethnic Relations in Western and Eastern Europe: Concepts, Indicators, Sources, and Comparative Issues." Ethnobarometer Project Working Paper. <http://www.ethnobarometer.org>

Cornelius, Wayne, Philip Martin, and James Hollifield (eds.). 1994. *Controlling Immigration*. Stanford: Stanford University Press.

Cross, Malcolm, and Roger Waldinger. 1999. "Economic Integration and Labour Market Change: A Review and a Reappraisal." In Jan Hjarnø (ed.), *From Metropolis to Cosmopolis*, pp. 29–93. Esberg: South Jutland University Press.

Crowley, John. 1998. "The National Dimension in T. H. Marshall." *Citizenship Studies* 2(2).

Dahrendorf, Ralf. 1988. *The Modern Social Conflict: An Essay on the Politics of Liberty*. London: Weidenfeld and Nicolson.

Doomernik, Jeroen. 1998. "The Effectiveness of Integration Policies toward Immigrants and Their Descendants in France, Germany, and the Netherlands." *International Migration Papers*, no. 27. Geneva: International Labour Organization.

Engbersen, Godfried. 1996. "The Unknown City." *Berkeley Journal of Sociology* 40: 87–111.

Erikson, Robert, and John H. Goldthorpe. 1992. *The Constant Flux: Class Mobility in Industrial Societies*. Oxford: Clarendon Press.

Esping-Anderson, Gösta. 1990. *Three Worlds of Welfare Capitalism*. Oxford: Polity.

Ethnobarometer Project. 1999. *Ethnic Conflict and Migration in Europe*. First report. Rome: CSS/CEMES.

Favell, Adrian. 1997. "Citizenship and Immigration: Pathologies of a Progressive Philosophy." *New Community* 23(2): 173–95.

―――. 1998a. *Philosophies of Integration: Immigration and the Idea of Citizenship in France and Britain*. London: Macmillan.

————. 1998b. "A Politics That Is Shared, Bounded, and Rooted? Rediscovering Civic Political Culture in Western Europe." *Theory and Society* 27(2): 209–36.

———— (ed.). 1998c. *The European Union: Immigration, Asylum, and Citizenship. Journal of Ethnic and Migration Studies* 24(4)(Oct.) (special ed.): 603–814.

————. 1999. "Comment on Glazer, Schain, and Fassin: How Can We Be European?" In Christian Joppke and Steven Lukes (eds.), *Multicultural Questions,* pp. 242–57. Oxford: Oxford University Press.

Favell, Adrian, and Marco Martiniello. 1999. "Multi-National, Multi-Cultural, and Multi-Levelled Brussels: National and Ethnic Politics in the 'Capital of Europe.'" Economic and Social Research Council (U.K.), Transnational Communities Working Paper Series, WPTC–99–04, April. <http://www.transcomm.ox.ac.uk>

Feldblum, Miriam. 1999. *Reconstructing Citizenship: The Politics of Nationality Reforms and Immigration in Contemporary France.* Albany, N.Y.: SUNY Press.

Fielding, Anthony J. 1995. "Migration and Social Change: A Longitudinal Study of the Social Mobility of 'Immigrants' in England and Wales." *European Journal of Population* 11:107–21.

Forbes, Ian, and Geoffrey Mead. 1992. *Measure for Measure: A Comparative Analysis of Measures to Combat Racial Discrimination in the Member Countries of the European Community.* Sheffield: Employment Dept.

Freeman, Gary. 1995. "Modes of Immigration Politics in Liberal Democratic Societies." *International Migration Review* 29(4): 881–902.

Gilroy, Paul. 1987. *There Ain't No Black in the Union Jack.* London: Hutchinson.

Glazer, Nathan (ed.). 1976. *Ethnicity: Theory and Experience.* Cambridge, Mass.: Bellinger.

————. 1983. *Ethnic Dilemmas 1964–82.* Cambridge: Harvard University Press.

————. 1999. "Multiculturalism and American Exceptionalism." In Christian Joppke and Steven Lukes (eds.), *Multicultural Questions,* pp. 183–198. Oxford: Oxford University Press.

Goldthorpe, John H. 1987. *Social Mobility and Class Structure in Modern Britain.* Oxford: Clarendon.

Gordon, Milton. 1964. *Assimilation in American Life: The Role of Race, Religion, and National Origins.* New York: Oxford University Press.

Goulbourne, Harry. 1991. *Ethnicity and Nationalism in Post-Imperial Britain.* Cambridge: Cambridge University Press.

Grillo, Ralph. 1998. *Pluralism and the Politics of Difference.* Oxford: Oxford University Press.

Guiraudon, Virginie. 1997. *Policy Change behind Gilded Doors: Explaining the Evolution of Aliens' Rights in Contemporary Western Europe.* Ph.D. diss., Harvard University, Dept. of Govt.

————. 1998. "Citizenship Rights for Non-Citizens: France, Germany, and the Netherlands (1974–1994)." In Christian Joppke (ed.), *Challenge to the Nation State: Immigration in Western Europe and the United States.* Oxford: Oxford University Press.

Habermas, Jürgen. 1992. "Citizenship and National Identity: Some Reflections on the Future of Europe." *Praxis International* 12(1): 1–19.

————. 1995. "Reconciliation through the Public Use of Reason: Remarks on John Rawls's *Political Liberalism.*" *Journal of Philosophy* 92(3): 109–31.

————. 1996. *Between Facts and Norms.* Cambridge: Polity.

Haferkamp, Hans, and Neil Smelser (eds.). 1992. *Social Change and Modernity*. Berkeley: University of California Press.

Hall, Peter. 1993. "Policy Paradigms, Social Learning, and the State: The Case of Economic Policy Making in Britain." *Comparative Politics* 25(3): 275–96.

Hall, Stuart. 1992. "New Ethnicities." In James Donald and Ali Rattansi (eds.), *"Race," Culture, and Difference*. London: Sage.

Hammar, Tomas (ed.). 1985. *European Immigration Policy: A Comparative Study*. Cambridge: Cambridge University Press.

———. 1990. *Democracy and the Nation State: Aliens, Denizens and Citizens in a World of International Migration*. Aldershot, England: Avebury.

Hansen, Randall. 1998. "A European Citizenship or a Europe of Citizens?" In Adrian Favell (ed.), *The European Union: Immigration, Asylum, and Citizenship. Journal of Ethnic and Migration Studies* 24(4)(Oct.) (special ed.): 603–814.

———. 2000. *Citizenship and Immigration in Post-War Britain*. D.Phil. diss., Faculty of Social Studies. Oxford: Oxford University Press.

Hansen, Randall, and Patrick Weil (eds.). 2000. *Towards a European Nationality: Citizenship, Immigration, and Nationality Law in the EU*. London: Macmillan.

Haut Conseil à l'Intégration. 1993. *L'intégration à la française*. Paris: La documentation française.

Heitmeyer, Wilhelm, Joachim Müller, and Helmut Schröder. 1997. *Verlockender Fundamentalismus*. Frankfurt a.M.: Suhrkamp.

Hjarnø, Jan (ed.). 1999. *From Metropolis to Cosmopolis*. Esbjerg: South Jutland University Press.

Horowitz, Donald, and Gérard Noiriel (eds.). 1992. *Immigrants in Two Democracies: French and American Experiences*. New York: New York University Press.

Inglehart, Ronald. 1990. *Culture Shift in Advanced Industrial Society*. Princeton: Princeton University Press.

Ireland, Patrick. 1994. *The Policy Challenge of Ethnic Diversity*. Cambridge: Harvard University Press.

Jacobs, Dirk. 1998. *Nieuwkomers in de Politiek: Het parlementaire debat omtrent kiesrecht voor vreemdelingen in Nederland en Belgie (1970–1997)*. Ghent: Academia Press.

Janoski, Thomas. 1998. *Citizenship and Civil Society*. Cambridge: Cambridge University Press.

Janoski, Thomas, and Elisabeth Glennie. 1995. "The Roots of Citizenship: Explaining Naturalisation in Advanced Industrial Societies." In Marco Martiniello (ed.), *Migration, Citizenship, and Ethno-national Identities in the European Union*, pp. 11–39. Aldershot, England: Avebury.

Joppke, Christian (ed.). 1998. *Challenge to the Nation State: Immigration in Western Europe and the United States*. Oxford: Oxford University Press.

———. 1999. *Immigration and the Nation State: The United States, Germany, and Great Britain*. Oxford: Oxford University Press.

Kastoryano, Riva. 1997. *La France, l'Allegmagne et leurs immigrés: Négocier l'identité*. Paris: Armand Colin.

Kloosterman, Robert, Joanne van der Leun, and Jan Rath. 1998. "Across the Border: Immigrants' Economic Opportunities, Social Capital, and Informal Business Activities." *Journal of Ethnic and Migration Studies* 24(2): 249–68.

Kymlicka, Will. 1989. *Liberalism, Community, and Culture*. Oxford: Clarendon.
———. 1995. *Multicultural Citizenship*. Oxford: Oxford University Press.
———. 1998. *Finding Our Way: Rethinking Ethno-Cultural Relations in Canada*. Oxford: Oxford University Press.
———. 2000. "Nation-Building and Minority Rights: Comparing West and East." *Journal of Ethnic and Migration Studies* 26(2): 183–212.
Kymlicka, Will, and Wayne Norman. 1994. "Return of the Citizen: A Survey of Recent Work on Citizenship Theory." *Ethics* 104(2).
Lapeyronnie, Didier (ed.). 1992. *Immigrés en Europe: politiques locales d'intégration*. Paris: La documentation française.
———. 1993. *L'individu et les minorités: La France et la Grande Brétagne face à ses minorités*. Paris: Presses universitaires de France.
Lesthaege, Ron (ed.). 1997. *Diversiteit in sociale verandering: Turkse en Morokkaanse vrouwen in Belgïe*. Brussels: VUB Press.
Lukes, Steven. 1985. *Marxism and Morality*. Oxford: Oxford University Press.
Mann, Michael. 1988. "Ruling Class Strategies, and Citizenship." In *States, Wars, and Capitalism: Studies in Political Sociology,* pp. 188–210. Oxford: Blackwell.
———. 1993. *The Sources of Social Power*. 2 vols. Cambridge: Cambridge University Press.
Marcuse, Peter. 1996. "Of Walls and Immigrant Enclaves." In Naomi Carmon (ed.), *Immigration and Integration in Post-Industrial Societies,* pp. 30–45. London: Macmillan.
Marshall, Thomas H. 1950. *Citizenship and Social Class*. London: Pluto Press.
Martiniello, Marco. 1992. *Leadership et pouvoir dans les communautés d'origine immigrée*. Paris: CIEMI, L'Harmattan.
——— (ed.). 1998. *Multicultural Policies and the State: A Comparison of Two European Societies*. Utrecht: ERCOMER.
Meehan, Elisabeth. 1993. *Citizenship and the European Union*. London: Sage.
Migration Policy Group. 1996. *The Comparative Approaches to Societal Integration Project*. Brussels.
Miller, David. 1995. *On Nationality*. Oxford: Oxford University Press.
Modood, Tariq. 1992. *Not Easy Being British: Colour, Culture, and Citizenship*. London: Runnymede Trust/Trentham.
———. 1994. "Establishment, Multiculturalism, and British Citizenship." *Political Quarterly* 65(1): 53–73.
Modood, Tariq, Sarah Beishon, and Satnam Virdee. 1994. *Changing Ethnic Identities*. London: Policy Studies Institute.
Modood, Tariq, et al. 1997. *Ethnic Minorities in Britain: Diversity and Disadvantage*. London: Policy Studies Institute.
Mulhall, Stephen, and Adam Swift. 1992. *Liberals and Communitarians*. Oxford: Blackwell.
Nanck, Bernhard, and U. Schönpflug (eds.). 1997. *Familien in verschiedenen Kulturen*. Stuttgart: Enke.
Noiriel, Gérard. 1988. *Le creuset français*. Paris: Seuil.
Parsons, Talcott. 1937. *The Structure of Social Action*. New York: Free Press.
Phalet, Karen, Claudia van Lotringen, and Han Entzinger. 2000. *Islam in de multiculturele samenleving: Opvattigen van jongeren in Rotterdam*. Utrecht: ERCOMER.

Phalet, Karen, and Marc Swyngedouw. 1998. "A Comparative Approach to Surveying Minorities: Common Problems and Proper Solutions?" Paper presented to Third International MigCities Conference on Migrants and Minorities in European Cities. Milan, 12–14 November.

———. 1999a. "Integratie ter discussie." In Marc Swyngedouw, Karen Phalet, and Kris Deschouwer (eds.), *Minderheden in Brussel*. Brussels: VUB Press.

———. 1999b. "Values, Acculturation, and Mobility Strategies: A Comparative Study of Turkish and Moroccan Immigrants in Brussels." Paper presented to European Consortium for Sociological Research Conference, "Migration and Ethnic Relations," Strasbourg, Sept. 23–28.

Pizzorno, Alessandro. 1991. "On the Individualistic Theory of Social Order." In Pierre Bourdieu and James S. Coleman (eds.), *Social Theory for a Changing Society,* pp. 209–44. Boulder, Colo.: Westview.

Portes, Alejandro (ed.). 1995. *The Economic Sociology of Immigration*. New York: Russell Sage Foundation.

———. 1996. "Transnational Communities: Their Emergence and Their Significance in the Contemporary World-System." In R. P. Korzeniewicz and W. C. Smith (eds.), *Latin America in the World Economy,* pp. 151–68. Westport, Conn.: Greenwood Press.

———. 1997. "Immigration Theory for a New Century: Some Problems and Opportunities." *International Migration Review* 31(4): 799–825.

Preuß, Ulrich. 1995. "Concepts, Foundations, and Limits of European Citizenship." Bremen: Centre for European Legal Policy.

Putnam, Robert. 1993. *Making Democracy Work: Civic Traditions in Modern Italy*. Princeton, N.J.: Princeton University Press.

Rath, Jan. 1991. *Minorisering: De sociale constructie van "ethnische minderheden."* Amsterdam: SUA.

Rath, Jan, and Robert Kloosterman (eds.). 1998. *Rijp en Groen: Het Zelfstandig Ondernemerschap van Immigranten in Nederland*. Amsterdam: Het Spinhuis.

Rawls, John. 1971. *A Theory of Justice*. Oxford: Oxford University Press.

———. 1993. *Political Liberalism*. New York: Columbia University Press.

———. 1995. "Reply to Habermas." *Journal of Philosophy* 92(3): 132–80.

Rex, John. 1970. *Race Relations in Sociological Theory*. London: Weidenfeld and Nicolson.

Rex, John, and Robert Moore. 1967. *Race, Community, and Conflict: A Study of Sparkbrook*. London: Oxford University Press for the Institute of Race Relations.

Rose, E. J. B., et al. 1969. *Colour and Citizenship: A Report on British Race Relations*. London: Oxford University Press for the Institute of Race Relations.

Schain, Martin. 1999. "Minorities and Immigrant Incorporation in France." In Christian Joppke and Steven Lukes (eds.), *Multicultural Questions,* pp. 199–223. Oxford: Oxford University Press.

Schlesinger, Arthur. 1992. *The Disuniting of America: Reflections on a Multicultural Society*. New York: Norton.

Schnapper, Dominique. 1991. *La France de l'intégration*. Paris: Gallimard.

———. 1992. *L'Europe des immigrés: Essais sur les politiques de l'immigration*. Paris: Bonnin.

Simon, Patrick. 1997. "La statistique des origines: L'ethnicité et la 'race' dans les recensements aux Etats-Unis, Canada, et Grande-Brétagne." *Sociétés Contemporaines* 26:11–44.

Smith, Michael Peter, and Luis Guarnizo (eds.). 1998. *Transnationalism from Below.* New Brunswick, N.J.: Transaction Publishers.

Solomos, John, and Les Back. 1996. *Racism and Society.* London: Macmillan.

SOPEMI (Système d'Observation Permanente des Migrations). 1998. *Trends in International Migration.* Annual report of continuous reporting system on migration. Rome: OECD.

Soysal, Yasemin Nuhoglu. 1994. *Limits of Citizenship: Migrants and Postnational Membership in Europe.* Chicago: University of Chicago Press.

Swyngedouw, Marc, Karen Phalet, and Kris Deschouwer (eds.). 1999. *Minderheden in Brussel.* Brussels: VUB Press.

Taylor, Charles, and Amy Gutmann (eds.). 1992. *Multiculturalism and the "Politics of Recognition."* Princeton, N.J.: University of Princeton Press.

Todd, Emmanuel. 1994. *Le destin des immigrés: Assimilation et ségrégation dans les démocraties occidentales.* Paris: Seuil.

Togeby, Lise. 1999. "Migrants at the Polls: An Analysis of Immigrant and Refugee Participation in Danish Local Elections." *Journal of Ethnic and Migration Studies* 24(4): 665–84.

Tribalat, Michèle. 1995. *Faire France: Une enquête sur les immigrés et leurs enfants.* Paris: La découverte.

Tribalat, Michèle, et al. 1996. *De l'immigration à l'assimilation: Une enquête sur la population étrangère en France.* Paris: INED.

Turner, Bryan (ed.). 1993. *Citizenship and Social Theory.* London: Sage.

van Steenburgen, Bart (ed.). 1994. *The Condition of Citizenship.* London: Sage.

Veenman, Justus. 1997. *Keren de kansen? De tweede generatie allochtonen in Nederland.* Rotterdam: ISEO.

———. 1998. *Buitenspel: Over langdurige werkloosheid onder ethnische minderheden.* Van Gorum: Assen.

Vermeulen, Hans (ed.). 1997. *Immigrant Policy for a Multicultural Society: A Comparative Study of Integration, Language, and Religious Policy in Five Western European Countries.* Brussels: Migration Policy Group/IMES. <http://www.pscw. uva.nl/imes>

Vertovec, Steven. 1997. "Social Cohesion and Tolerance." In *Key Issues for Research and Policy on Migrants in Cities.* Metropolis Discussion Paper. <http:// international.metropolis.net>

———. 1999. "Minority Associations, Networks, and Public Policies: Re-assessing Relationships." *Journal of Ethnic and Migration Studies* 25(1): 21–42.

Waldrauch, Harald, and Christoph Hofinger. 1997. "An Index to Measure the Legal Obstacles to the Integration of Migrants." *New Community* 23(2): 271–86.

Watson, James L. (ed.). 1977. *Between Two Cultures: Migrants and Minorities in Britain.* Oxford: Basil Blackwell.

Weil, Patrick. 1991. *La France et ses étrangers: L'aventure d'une politique de l'immigration.* Paris: Calmann-Lévy.

————. 1996. "Nationalities and Citizenships: The Lessons of the French Experience for Germany and Europe." In David Cesarani and Mary Fulbrook (eds.), *Citizenship, Nationality, and Migration in Europe*, pp. 74–87. London: Routledge.

Weiler, Joseph. 1998. *The Constitution of Europe*. Cambridge: Cambridge University Press.

Weiner, Myron. 1996. "Determinants of Immigrant Integration: An International Comparative Analysis." In Naomi Carmon (ed.), *Immigration and Integration in Post-Industrial Societies,* pp. 46–64. London: Macmillan.

Werbner, Pnina. 1999. "What Colour Success? Distorting Value in Studies of Ethnic Entrepreneurship." *Sociological Review* 47(3): 548–79.

Wiener, Antje. 1997. *European Citizenship Practice: Building Institutions of a Non-State*. Boulder, Colo.: Westview.

Wieviorka, Michel (ed.). 1996. *Une société fragmentée: Le multi-culturalisme en débat*. Paris: La découverte.

Worsley, Peter (ed.). 1970. *Modern Sociology: Introductory Readings*. London: Penguin.

Wrench, John. 1996. *Preventing Racism at the Workplace*. Dublin: European Foundation for the Improvement of Living and Working Conditions.

About the Authors

T. Alexander Aleinikoff, a senior associate with the Carnegie Endowment's International Migration Policy Program, is the director of the Comparative Citizenship Project. He is also a professor of law at the Georgetown University Law Center, where he teaches courses in immigration, constitutional, and refugee law. From 1994 to 1997, he held positions at the U.S. Immigration and Naturalization Service, first as general counsel and then as executive associate commissioner for programs. He has written numerous articles on immigration, citizenship, and refugee law and policy.

Rainer Bauböck is a political scientist at the Austrian Academy of Sciences, Research Unit for Institutional Change and European Integration, and a senior lecturer at the University of Vienna and the University of Innsbruck. His major fields of research are normative political theory and comparative and theoretical research on citizenship, migration, ethnicity, and nationalism. In 1994 he published *Transnational Citizenship: Membership and Rights in International Migration* (Aldershot, U.K.: Edward Elgar).

Linda Bosniak is a professor at Rutgers University School of Law, Camden, New Jersey, where she has taught since 1992. Her research interests include the subjects of immigration, alienage, citizenship, nationalism, and labor under conditions of globalization. She has recently published on these themes in various journals, including the *Northwestern Law Review, Social Text, New York*

University Law Review, International Migration Review, and the *Indiana Journal of Global Legal Studies.*

Francis M. Deng is a senior fellow for the Foreign Policy Studies Program at the Brookings Institution and has served as human rights officer in the United Nations Secretariat and as Sudan's ambassador to Canada, the Scandinavian countries, and the United States. He was also the minister of state for foreign affairs and later Distinguished Fellow of the Rockefeller Brothers Fund and of the U.S. Institute for Peace, and a visiting lecturer at the Yale Law School. In 1992, Ambassador Deng was appointed U.N. Secretary General's Representative on Internally Displaced Persons worldwide. Deng has written or edited more than twenty books in the fields of law, conflict resolution, human rights, anthropology, history, and politics.

Adrian Favell is a lecturer in Geography and Migration Studies at the University of Sussex, UK. He has held postdoctoral positions at the Université catholique de Louvain, CEVIPOF (IEP), Paris, and the University of Utrecht. His work has focused on immigration, citizenship, and nationhood in France, Britain, and Belgium, and on European Union immigration policy. He is the author of *Philosophies of Integration: Immigration and the Idea of Citizenship in France and Britain* (Macmillan and St. Martin's Press, 1998).

Richard T. Ford is a professor of law at Stanford University. He specializes in local government law, housing law and policy, property, civil rights, and race relations. He has written extensively on issues of the legal dimensions of urban geography, city political structures, racial boundaries, and sovereignty. He has published articles in the *Harvard Law Review,* the *Michigan Law Review,* and the *Stanford Law Review* and has lectured widely in universities throughout the United States.

Vicki C. Jackson is a law professor at Georgetown University Law Center, where she has taught courses in constitutional law, comparative constitutional law, the federal courts, gender equality, the U.S. Supreme Court, civil procedure, and related topics. She serves on the executive committee of the International Association of Constitutional Law and has often lectured to foreign jurists on constitutional law issues. She is the co-author of a new course book, *Comparative Constitutional Law* (1999) and of numerous articles on U.S. constitutional law and federalism published in the *Harvard Law Review,* the *Yale Law Journal,* and elsewhere.

Paul Johnston is a sociologist affiliated with the University of California at Santa Cruz. He also serves as the director of the California-based Citizenship Project. Johnston taught at Yale University from 1989 to 1997. His fields of expertise include political, industrial, organizational, and urban sociology and gender, race, and ethnic relations. His writings include *Success while Others Fail: Social Movement Unionism and the Public Workplace* and the work-in-progress, *Citizens of the Future.*

Christian Joppke is professor of sociology at the European University Institute, Florence. His most recent books are *Immigration and the Nation-State* (Oxford University Press, 1999), *Multicultural Questions* (co-edited with Steven Lukes, Oxford University Press, 1999), and *Challenge to the Nation-State* (edited, Oxford University Press, 1998).

Douglas Klusmeyer is an associate with the International Migration Policy Program of the Carnegie Endowment for International Peace, where he coordinates the Comparative Citizenship Project. He has published in such journals as *Daedalus* and the *SAIS Review,* and is the author of *Between Consent and Descent: Conceptions of Democratic Citizenship* and co-editor of *Membership, Migration, and Identity: Dilemmas for Liberal Societies* and *From Migrants to Citizens: Membership in a Changing World.* He received a J.D. and a Ph.D. in modern European history from Stanford University.

Karen Knop is associate professor on the faculty of law, University of Toronto. She is the rapporteur on feminism and international law for the International Law Association (ILA). Professor Knop is the author of ILA's preliminary (1998) and final (2000) reports on women's equality and nationality in international law. Her research and teaching are in the area of public international law. Her book, *Diversity and Self-Determination in International Law,* is forthcoming from Cambridge University Press. She has served on an advisory team of minority rights experts for the High Commissioner on National Minorities of the Organization for Security and Cooperation in Europe in regard to Hungary and Slovakia.

Micheline Labelle is full professor of sociology at the Université du Québec à Montréal, where she currently heads the Center for Research on Immigration, Ethnicity, and Citizenship. Between 1993 and 1996 she held the Concordia–Université du Québec à Montréal Chair in Ethnic Studies. She has published numerous articles on ethnic and racial relations, nation diversity, and citizenship, immigration policies, and issues of integration. She is the author of *Idéologie de couleur et classes sociales en Haïti* (1979, 1987), and co-author of *Histoires d'immigrées: Itinéraires d'ouvrières colombiennes, haïtiennes, grecques et portugaises de Montréal* (1987) and of *Ethnicité et enjeux sociaux: Le Québec vu par les leaders de groupes ethnoculturels* (1995).

Daniel Salée is professor of political science and the principal of the School of Community and Public Affairs at Concordia University in Montreal, Canada. His most recent research has dealt with issues related to identity politics, inter-ethnic relations, nationalism, and citizenship in the context of Canada and Quebec. Publishing in both English and French, his work has appeared in *Ethnic and Racial Studies,* the *International Journal of Canadian Studies, Quebec Studies, Politique et Sociétés,* and *Sociologie et Société.* He is the co-author of *Quebec Politics and Society: Colonialism, Power, and the Transition to Capitalism in the Nineteenth Century* (1992), and *Quebec Democracy: Structures, Processes, and Policies* (1993).

Patrick Weil is director of the Centre d'Étude des Politiques de l'Immigration, de l'Intégration, et de la Citoyenneté (CEPIC) and senior research fellow at the National Center for Scientific Research (University of Paris 1, Sorbonne). Weil's recent publications include *La France et ses Étrangers: L'aventure d'une politique de l'immigration de 1938 à nos jours* (1995); *Rapports au premier ministre: Mission d'étude des législations de la nationalité et de l'immigration* (1997); *Towards a European Nationality: Citizenship, Immigration, and Nationality Law in the EU* (co-editor, 2001).

Index

Acquisition of citizenship, 17–34, 66–
68; marriage, 24; nationality of
origin, 20; naturalization, 22–23;
second-generation immigrants, 26–27
Adoption, 64
Africa, 190–206
Aleinikoff, T. Alexander, 164, 169
Alienage: as suspect classification, 41
Amsterdam Treaty, 38, 54, 371
Anderson, Benedict, 95
Arendt, Hannah, 14
Asylum, right of, 59
Asymmetry, 165, 169
Australia, 146n47, 149–50, 174n;
citizenship, 66; marriage, 24;
nationality of origin, 20;
naturalization, 22; second-generation
immigrants, 26
Austria, 30, 134, 139, 371–72;
citizenship, 66; marriage, 24;
nationality of origin, 20;
naturalization, 22; second-generation
immigrants, 26

Baltic states, 31–32
Bangladesh, 104
Banyamulenge, *see* Banyarwanda
Banyarwanda, 8, 184, 193–203 ;
disputed citizenship, 197–200
Batchelor, Carol A., 184–85, 187
Beldjoudi v. France (European Court of
Human Rights, *1992*), 99
Belgium, 141n33, 175n108, 381–83;
marriage, 24; nationality of origin,
20; naturalization, 22; second-
generation immigrants, 26
Bendix, Reinhard, 58
Botswana, 104–05
Britain, 168, 352n, 355–56n,
383–86; British Empire, 25;
citizenship, 68; Commonwealth
Immigrants Act of *1962*, 25;
Immigration Act of *1971*, 25;
marriage, 24; nationality of origin,
20; naturalization, 23; second-
generation immigrants, 27
Brubaker, Rogers, 4, 18

California, 10, 253–76; anti-immigrant backlash, 261–64; Asian immigration, 254; Mexican immigrants in, 254–76; Proposition *187*, 43–44, 172, 262, 268

Canada, 10–11, 136–37, 143, 146–48, 278–311; bilingualism, 334–35; "Canadianness," 280–81; citizenship, 66, 279, 281–311; dual citizenship, 299–301; gender, 90; immigration, 281–84; marriage, 24; multiculturalism, 285–86, 309–10; nationality of origin, 20; naturalization, 22; second-generation immigrants, 26; *see also* Montreal, Quebec

Chavez, Cesar, 257–58

Chinese Exclusion Case, 39

Cities, global, *see* global cities

Citizen development, 254–57, 270–76

Citizenship, transnational, *see* transnational citizenship

Citizenship movements, 254, 258, 270; educational institutions, 271–72; public bureaucracy, 259–60, 270, 276; voting, 272–73

Colson, Elizabeth, 192

Congo, the, *see* Banyarwanda

Connolly, William, 239n6

Convention concerning Certain Questions relating to the Conflict of Nationality (The Hague, April *12, 1930*), 71–72, 75, 100

Convention on Reduction of Cases of Multiple Nationality and Military Obligations in Cases of Multiple Nationality (*1963*), 72–73

Convention on the Elimination of All Forms of Discrimination Against Women (*1979*), 69, 90, 102–03

Convention on the Nationality of Married Women (*1957*), 65, 69–70, 102

Convention on the Reduction of Statelessness (*1961*), 64–65n, 69

Convention on the Status of Naturalized Citizens (*1906*), 73–74

Council of Europe, 107–09, 117, 370

Council of Europe's Framework Convention for the Protection of National Minorities (*1995*), 326n6

Cultural citizenship, 319–45

De Canas v. Bica, 42

Denationalized citizenship, *see* postnational citizenship

Denmark: citizenship, 66; marriage, 24; nationality of origin, 20; naturalization, 22; second-generation immigrants, 26

Dependent nationality, 96–98, 100–03, 111–12

Dominant nationality, doctrine of, *see* effective nationality

Dominican Republic, 116

Donner, Ruth, 105

Dual nationality, *see* plural/multiple nationality

Effective nationality, doctrine of, 74–76

Elkins v. Moreno, 42

Estonia, 31–32; citizenship, 66; marriage, 24; nationality of origin, 20; naturalization, 22; second-generation immigrants, 26

Ethnic marginalization/conflict, 184–206, 263; early sources in the Congo, 195–97; regional intervention, 205; violent reactions to, 200–02

Eurobarometer, 372–73

"European citizenship," 6–7, 368

European Community Treaty, 48–49, 50, 214n3; Article *48*, 50–51

European Convention on Human Rights, 53–54, 98–99

European Convention on Nationality (*1997*), 73, 89–90, 92–94, 108–10, 117–18

European Court of Justice, 49–50; *Antonissen* case, 50; *Boucherau* case, 51; *Casagrande* case, 52; *Commission v. Belgium* cases, 50; *Hoekstra* case, 50; *Levin* case, 50; *Michael S.* case, 52; *Reina* case, 52

European Union, 6–7, 30, 38, 47–54, 58, 136, 139, 168, 204, 213–14, 241–42, 368–71; association treaties, 53; language, 327n9; migrant workers, 50–52, 56; "privileged" immigrants, 47–48, 49–52; Regulation *1612/68*, 51–52; third-state nationals, 52–54

European Year Against Racism (*1997*), 368

Falk, Richard, 246

Federalism, 127–78, 225–26; and citizenship, 137–41; and multiple citizenships, 154–61; divided loyalties, 161–65; enforcement authority, 141–44; history, 129–33; mobility rights, 146–47; public office, 149–50; social welfare rights, 147–48; structure, 133–37; voting rights, 148–49

Feldblum, Miriam, 133, 168

Fiji, 343n.

Finland: citizenship, 66; marriage, 24; nationality of origin, 20; naturalization, 22; second-generation immigrants, 26

France, 18–20, 28–29, 168, 379–81; citizenship, 67; Maghrebin children, 115; marriage, 24; nationality of origin, 20; naturalization, 22; second-generation immigrants, 26

Frug, Gerald, 231

Gellner, Ernest, 326–27

Gender equality, 6, 89–118

Germany, 18–19, 29, 30–31, 33–34, 37–38, 44–48, 58–60, 136n24, 142, 146–49, 156n69; Alien Law, generally, 44; Alien Law of *1965*, 45; citizenship, 67; *Deutschenrechte*, 45–47; Federal Expellee Law, 44; Foreigner Law of *1990*, 48; guest workers, 45–48, 55–56; *Indian Case*, 46–47; Lauck, Gary, 221–22; marriage, 24; nationality of origin, 20; naturalization, 22; plenary power, absence of, 45; plural nationality, 70–71, 78; *Rechtsschicksal der Unentrinnbarkeit*, 46, 59; second-generation immigrants, 26

Ginsburgs, George, 140–41

Global cities, 8–9, 209–11, 215–32; and devolution of power, 224–28; citizenship for foreign nationals, 232–33; international affairs, 230; nondomiciliary voting, 230–31; supplemental citizenship, 226–28

Global citizenship, see postnational citizenship

Globalization, generally, 216

Graham v. Richardson, 41–42

Greece: marriage, 24; nationality of origin, 20; naturalization, 22; second-generation immigrants, 26

Guiraudon, Virginie, 36, 56

Held, Virginia, 92–93

Herz, John, 37

Identity politics, 212

Immigrants, 41; Britain, 25; California, 253–76; Canada, 281–84; citizenship, 66–68; Israeli Law of Return, 33–34; marriage, 24; nationality of origin, 20; naturalization, 22–23; Quebec, 302–06; second-generation, 26–27; *see also* rights of immigrants

India, 137, 140
Indian Case (Germany, *1978*), 46–47
Industrial audits, 265
Integration, 11, 12–13, 349–91
International Convention on the
  Elimination of All Forms of Racial
  Discrimination (*1966*), 69
International Covenant on Civil and
  Political Rights (*1966*), 326
International Law Commission, 118
Ireland, 28; marriage, 24; nationality of
  origin, 20; naturalization, 22; second-
  generation immigrants, 26
Israel, 33–34; citizenship, 67; Law of
  Return, 33; marriage, 24; nationality
  of origin, 20; naturalization, 22;
  second-generation immigrants, 26
Italy, 226; citizenship, 67; marriage, 24;
  nationality of origin, 20;
  naturalization, 23; second-generation
  immigrants, 26

Jacobson, David, 57, 244
Japan: citizenship, 67
Jus sanguinis, 17, 18–21, 28–30,
  64, 101
Jus soli, 17, 18–19, 21, 28, 64; double,
  28–30

Kant, Immanuel, 343
Kasfir, Nelson, 189
Kymlicka, Will, 337, 340

Labor: Chavez, Cesar, 257–58; Mexican
  immigrant workers in California,
  254–76; guest workers in Germany,
  45–48, 55–56; unions, 257–60, 264–
  65, 275; United Farm Workers,
  257–59
Language, 12, 303–04, 310, 325–36;
  see also Quebec
Latvia, 31–32; citizenship, 67; marriage,
  24; nationality of origin, 20;

naturalization, 23; second-generation
  immigrants, 27
Lauck, Gary, 221–22
Leslie, Henrietta, 113–15
Lithuania, 31–32; citizenship, 67;
  marriage, 24; nationality of origin,
  20; naturalization, 23; second-
  generation immigrants, 27
Location of citizenship, see postnational
  citizenship
Loyalties, divided, *see* plural/multiple
  nationality
Luxembourg: marriage, 24; nationality
  of origin, 20; naturalization, 23;
  second-generation immigrants, 27

Maastricht Treaty, 48, 54, 136n23, 149
Macmillan, Chrystal, 97
Maine, Sir Henry, 211–12
Malkani case (Bangladesh, *1997*),
  104–05
Mamdani, Mahmood, 190–92, 196–97
Marriage, 17, 24, 28, 64, 71, 79n,
  116–17
Marshall, Thomas H., 130, 319; critique
  of, 321–23, 357n8
Martin, David, 80, 87
Mathews v. Diaz, 42, 59
McClintock, Anne, 112
Memmi, Albert, 115
Merge case, 75
Mexico, 172, 254–76; citizenship, 67;
  dual nationality, 78, 85; emigration to
  California, 254; family, 260–61, 275–
  76; immigrants in California, 255–76;
  marriage, 24; nationality of origin,
  20; naturalization, 23, 85; second-
  generation immigrants, 27
Miller, David, 247
Minorities, national, 336–40
Mobility rights, 146–47
Monitoring Center on Racism and
  Xenophobia (Vienna), 371

Montreal, 280–81, 289–90, 297–98, 312–13; *see also* Quebec
Mrs. Fischer's War, 113–15
Muller, Martine, 115
Multiple nationality, *see* plural/multiple nationality
Myanmar, 230

Nationalism, 111–16, 210–11, 326–27; liberal, 247–49, 323–25
Nationality, plural, *see* plural/multiple nationality
Nationality of origin, 20
Nation-state, 210–15, 218–30, 232, 237–38, 249, 351, 362; scale, 228–29; *see also* global cities
Naturalization, 22–23, 64
Nedelsky, Jennifer, 95
Nested citizenship, 158–60, 162
Netherlands, The, 374, 386–87; marriage, 24; nationality of origin, 20; naturalization, 23; second-generation immigrants, 27
Nottebohm case (ICJ, 1955), 74–75, 84, 94

Oaths of allegiance, 164–65, 169–70, 284n6
Oommen, T. K., 189–90
Operation Gatekeeper, 263–64
Orentlicher, Diane, 31
Organization for Security and Cooperation in Europe (*OSCE*), 32

Perpetual allegiance, doctrine of, 70
Personal Responsibility and Work Opportunity Reconciliation (Welfare Reform) Act of *1996*, 44
Plural/multiple nationality, 5, 63, 70–87, 90–94, 100–01, 105–09, 118, 130–37, 151–67, 177; Canada, 299–301; divided loyalties, 5, 80–84, 93–94, 111–13, 161–65; exit option, 82; office holding, 81–82; open state response, 63, 76; restrictive state response, 63, 77; tolerant state response, 63, 76–77; voting, 80–81
Plyler v. Doe, 42–43, 55
Polanyi, Karl, 48–49
Postnational citizenship, 238–49; as an empirical claim, 239–44; definition, 240–44; desirability of, 245–46; displacement of citizenship, 244–48; pluralization of identities, 249
Portugal: citizenship, 68; marriage, 24; nationality of origin, 20; naturalization, 23; second-generation immigrants, 27
Priority, rules of, 7, 151–52
Proposition *187* (California), 43–44, 172, 262, 268
Public office, 149–50

Quebec, 10–11, 143, 278–81, 286–311, 334–35; citizenship, immigrant perspectives on, 302–06; ethnic categorization, 291–95, 307; independence, 279; Montreal, 280–81, 289–90, 297–98, 312–13; minority identity, 290–95; political sovereignty, 304–06, 310–11; *Quebecois* identity, 286–89, 295–98; state policy, 302–04

Raz, Joseph, 338
Relational feminism, 95–99, 118
Relational nationality, 92–118
Residence, 17
Rights of immigrants, 36–60; asylum, 59; educational institutions, 271–72; Proposition *187*, 43–44, 172, 262, 268; public institutions, 259–60, 270, 276; voting, 272–73
Russia/Russian Federation, 33, 140; citizenship, 68; marriage, 24; nationality of origin, 20;

naturalization, 23; second-generation
immigrants, 27
Rwanda, 193–95, 200–03, *see also*
Banyarwanda

Saenz v. Roe, 131–32n
San Francisco, 218–20
Schuck, Peter H., 163–64, 167–68
Schwerdtfeger, Gunther, 46
Second-generation immigrants, 26–27
Sexual orientation, 110–11n
Single European Act of *1987*, 54
Skerry, Peter, 174
Social welfare rights, 147–48
South Africa: citizenship, 68; marriage,
24; nationality of origin, 20;
naturalization, 23; second-generation
immigrants, 27
Soysal, Yasemin, 4, 57, 238
Spain, 226; marriage, 24; nationality of
origin, 20; naturalization, 23; second-
generation immigrants, 27
Spiro, Peter, 156–58, 171–72
Statelessness, 186–87; *de facto*, 187
Subnational citizenship/political units,
128, 134–51, 168–77
Sugarman v. Dougall, 41–42
Sweden: citizenship, 68; marriage, 24;
nationality of origin, 20;
naturalization, 23; second-generation
immigrants, 27
Switzerland, 135, 139

*Takahashi v. Fish and Game
Commission*, 42
Targeted Social Economic Research
(TSER) program, 368
Territorial transfer, 64
Thailand: gender, 91
Transnational citizenship, 9–10, 253 ;
see also denationalized citizenship

Transnational labor regime, 264–65
Treaty of European Union (*1992*),
214n4
Tutsi, *see* Banyarwanda

United Farm Workers, 257–59
United Kingdom, *see* Britain
United States, 28, 37–44, 58–59, 141–
42, 147–48, 150, 217–18, 253–76;
citizenship, 68; deportation, 40, 261;
equal protection, 42–43; expatriation,
70; federal preemption, 42; gender,
90; Fourteenth Amendment, 130–31,
138; Immigration and Naturalization
Act of *1990*, 38–39, 40; labor unions,
257–60, 264–65, 275; marriage, 24;
nationality of origin, 20;
naturalization, 23, 266–70, 273–75;
personhood doctrine, 39–42; plenary
power doctrine, 39–44, 56, 59;
political function, 41; second-
generation immigrants, 27; welfare
reform, 56; *see also* California,
federalism, San Francisco
Unity Dow case (Botswana, *1992*),
104–06
Universal Declaration of Human Rights
(UN General Assembly, *1948*),
65, 86

Voting rights, 148–49, 161–64, 176,
267–68

Walzer, Michael, 344n
Women's International League, 114n

Yick Wo v. Hopkins, 39–40
Young, Crawford, 188–89